MUSHROOMS OF THE MIDWEST

MUSHROOMS OF THE MIDWEST

MICHAEL KUO AND ANDREW S. METHVEN

University of Illinois Press ■ Urbana, Chicago, and Springfield

While every effort has been made to provide accurate information in this book, neither the authors, nor the photographers, nor the University of Illinois Press accepts responsibility for any decision made by anyone on the basis of the text and illustrations herein.

All photos, scans, illustrations, and micrographs are by Michael Kuo unless otherwise credited.

Manufactured in the United States of America
P 5 4 3 2 1
♾ This book is printed on acid-free paper.

Library of Congress Control Number: 2014932849

CONTENTS

MUSHROOMS OF THE MIDWEST

1 INTRODUCTION

An Exciting Time for Amateur Mycology

This is an exciting time for the science of mycology and for amateur mycologists, and we hope this book encourages collectors across the Midwest to participate in the scientific effort to better understand the mushrooms of our region.

Not so long ago, the DNA revolution had not yet penetrated mycology, and mushrooms were understood and identified primarily on the basis of their physical features. The astounding body of work produced by the Midwest's most prolific, most famous mycologist, Alexander H. Smith (1904–86), represents the pinnacle of the morphology-based approach to mushroom taxonomy in North America. Smith was an amazing collector and taxonomist, and his descriptions of fungi serve as an illustrative example of the thoroughness, patience, and dedication required for good taxonomy. Here, for example, is the material cited list for Smith's description of *Lactarius allardii* (see p. 230) in his monograph of the genus *Lactarius*, coauthored with L. R. Hesler:

> Material cited.—*MICHIGAN: Bas 721 (MICH); Hosney 2902 (MICH); Smith, Sep 1951, 35827, 38373, 77951; Weber, 24 Aug 1973, 3903, 3926, 4117, 4155, 4197 (all MICH); NORTH CAROLINA: Coker 160 (type, NCU); Hesler 23478, 30160, 35703; Olexia (TENN 28273); Petersen (TENN 26919); TENNESSEE: Hesler 4992, 17107 (MICH), 20895 (MICH), 21935, 24369, 24855, 30160, 35703 . . . Sharp (TENN 3714, 19220); Smith 9654, 10112, 10328, 10432, 10536; Warise (TENN 8151). (1979, 210)*

This list tells us that Smith and Hesler studied thirty-two collections of *Lactarius allardii* before describing it in a scientific setting and that, over a period of decades, Smith made eight of these collections himself (also, Smith's daughter, Nancy Weber, made five collections, and Hesler made eleven). If we calculate the amount of time involved with collecting and documenting mushrooms (see chapter 2) conservatively at approximately thirty minutes per mushroom, Smith spent about four hours of his life studying fresh *Lactarius allardii* specimens.

But Smith also preserved the collections and studied them later in his laboratory at the University of Michigan, poring over their microscopic details—a process that takes at least as much time, if not more, as working with the freshly picked mushrooms; let us conservatively put Smith's *Lactarius allardii* time sheet at eight hours after the microscope work. Then there was the taxonomic research (studying scientific keys and technical descriptions) and the time spent studying the collections made by others (including the original "type collection" for the species, made by W. C. Coker). All in all, ten hours of work for Smith on *Lactarius allardii* seems like a reasonable estimate. But here's the clincher: *Lactarius allardii*

Alexander H. Smith, *left*; H. H. Burdsall Jr., *right*; photo by Harry Leslie

is one of *over 200* species described in Hesler and Smith's *Lactarius* monograph, and this monograph is one of nearly 200 mycological publications made by Smith in his career.

Contemporary mycological work, however, requires not only substantial field work, microscope work, and taxonomic research but also the work of molecular biologists: DNA extraction, sequencing, and phylogenetic research. The "per-mushroom" time estimate for DNA study is at least equal to the estimate for the kind of work done by Smith, effectively doubling the amount of time required, these days, for taxonomic work on mushrooms. In the Midwest there are about two dozen mycologists doing this work professionally, but there are thousands of mushroom species, a great number of which are poorly understood, undocumented, or unnamed. It should be clear from these numbers that it would take many, many generations of mycologists to arrive at something like a comprehensive "mycoflora of the Midwest" using contemporary taxonomic standards (which might not be very "contemporary" anymore by the time the project was finished).

Enter the amateur mycologists. Amateurs have always been important to mycology, but never has the science needed them more than today. For example, one result of the transition between Smith-style mycology and today's DNA-based mycology is that fewer and fewer mycologists are even trained in field work and documentation, and specimens collected in Smith's generation are getting older, reaching a point at which DNA extraction becomes expensive and difficult, or even impossible, since normal extraction protocols can be less successful when mushrooms are roughly twenty to thirty years old or more. Thus the Midwest's public mycological herbaria (institutions that carefully store specimens for posterity; see p. 14) are in desperate need of well-documented contemporary collections for mycologists to study.

Our friend Ron Kerner is one of several amateur mycologists in the Midwest who has dedicated himself to the science by collecting, documenting, and preserving mushrooms and then frequently depositing them in the Herbarium of the University of Michigan (the same herbarium used by Smith, represented by the acronym MICH in the material cited list quoted above). Ron's website, Indiana Mushrooms (www.indianamushrooms.com), contains pages for over 300 Indiana species he has studied. Another example of midwestern amateurs documenting and preserving collections comes from the Missouri Mycological Society, whose members have preserved collections of nearly 200 Missouri species, accompanied by online records (see www.missourimycologicalsociety.org/vouchers-v1.asp). Additionally, many midwestern amateur mycologists—including several whose fine photographs are featured in this book—make frequent contributions to Mushroom Observer (www.mushroomobserver.org), the wiki-style website devoted to documenting observations and collections of mushrooms. Efforts like these are exactly what mycology needs at the moment—as is evidenced by the recent National Science Foundation grant given to a consortium of mycologists and herbarium administrators to digitize herbarium collection records and collaborate with "[c]itizen mycologists in clubs and nature societies across the country" who "play an important role in documenting macrofungi diversity" (National Science Foundation 2012).

How to Use This Book

This book is not intended to be a comprehensive guide to all the mushrooms of the Midwest; as noted above, such a guide is probably not even possible. Thus it is not a given that any mushroom you find is going to be included in this book or, for that matter, in any other resource. If your mushroom appears to be unidentifiable, however, it may be even more important to collect, document, and preserve it.

Mushroom identification is a painstaking process that begins with careful observation and documentation of the mushroom's features (see chapter 2). While mushrooms can occasionally be identified by comparison to photographs, this is rarely possible; instead, we encourage you to use identification keys—in this book and elsewhere—as your principal identification method. We have provided keys (pp. 22–79) to the 557 mushrooms in the book, and more keys can be found in the bibliography. It must be said, however, that mushroom identification can be difficult, very technical, and sometimes impossible. This is a hard nugget to swallow for those who have used field guides to identify trees or birds, for example, and expect the mushroom world to be equally easy to penetrate. One doesn't need a microscope to identify a North American tree, and plenty of field guides can be found that include more or less all the tree species native to the continent. With mushrooms, however, one does need a microscope much of the time—and no one even knows how many thousands of mushroom species there are on the continent. Still, collecting and documenting mushrooms is rewarding, regardless of whether one is able to quickly pin a name on a collection.

The mushroom descriptions in this book are arranged in alphabetical order by genus and species. We chose this arrangement because contemporary studies have been shifting long-held assumptions about relationships between mushrooms (for example, the polypore *Bondarzewia berkeleyi*, p. 126, is more closely related to *Russula ballouii*, p. 339, than it is to most other polypores), so that a strictly taxonomic arrangement (phylum, class, order, family, genus, species) would not only seem odd to many readers but also probably be subject to change before the book was actually printed. Contemporary studies also make a traditional guidebook arrangement based on physical features like spore print color, the presence of gills or pores, and so on seem antiquated. Thus we opted for the alphabet as our organization principle. However, since genus names are also shifting rapidly these days, we have indexed the mushrooms by genus *and* by species epithet. *Russula ballouii* can therefore be found in the index under *Russula* and under *ballouii*. If you are interested in evolution and want to know how the mushrooms in this book are related, see chapter 6, "The Evolutionary Picture."

Edibility

Edibility is not the focus of this book. While we enjoy foraging for and eating some wild mushrooms (especially morels, chanterelles, black trumpets, and some boletes), we think the mushrooms themselves are infinitely more important and interesting than the question of whether they can safely be passed through the human digestive system. So we have included very few comments about edibility and toxicity in the book. If you are interested in eating wild mushrooms, we recommend *Mushrooms Demystified* (Arora 1986), *100 Edible Mushrooms* (Kuo 2007), and *Edible Wild Mushrooms of Illinois & Surrounding States* (McFarland and Mueller 2009).

Coverage Area

Defining the "Midwest" is not an easy task to begin with, let alone in an attempt to describe organisms in natural ecosystems. The map indicates the coverage area we intend for this book. We wanted to include fairly diverse ecosystems, including the midwestern collection areas we are most familiar with (central

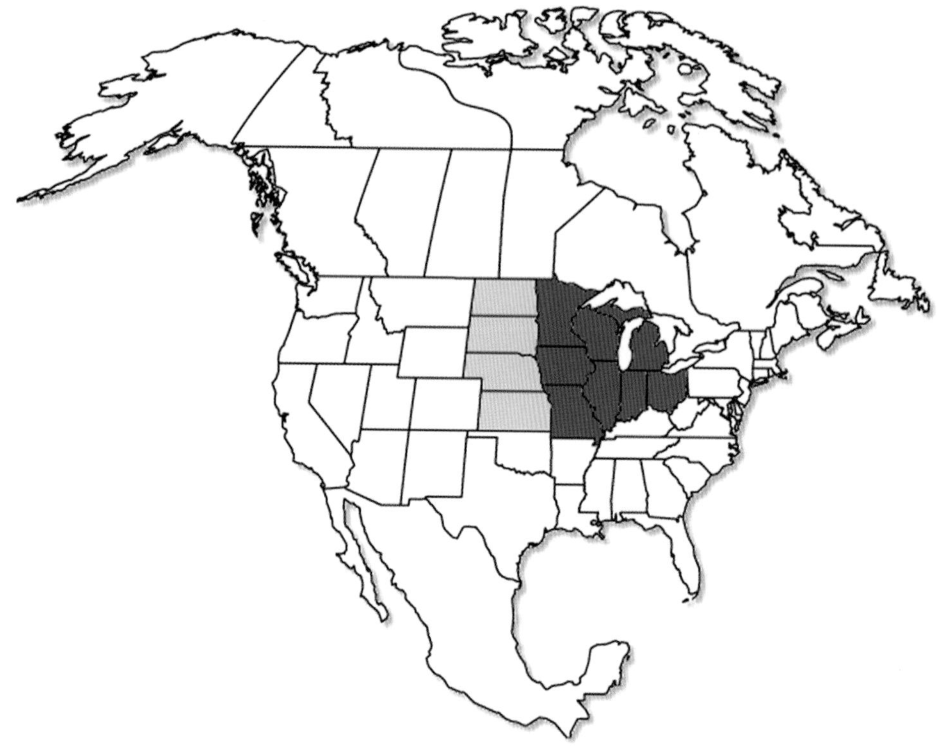

Illinois, southeastern Missouri, and northern Michigan), and we tried to include some areas that are not already represented in contemporary field guides. Thus the coverage area may not correspond precisely with your uncle's definition of the "Midwest," but we hope that if your uncle lives in the area and enjoys mushrooming, he will benefit from the book.

Midwestern Mushroom Clubs

The following list of midwestern mushroom clubs includes those that are affiliated with the North American Mycological Association (NAMA). NAMA is an organization of amateur mycologists originally organized as the People-to-People Committee on Fungi in 1959 with Harry S. Knighton (1915–99) of Portsmouth, Ohio, as the founder and first chairman. Members soon saw the need for an independent organization devoted to amateur mycology and officially launched the NAMA in 1967. The mission of NAMA is to "[p]romote, pursue and advance the science of mycology." More information about NAMA can be found on its website (www.namyco.org).

Illinois
Illinois Mycological Association,
www.illinoismyco.org

Indiana
Hoosier Mushroom Society,
www.hoosiermushrooms.org

Iowa
Prairie States Mushroom Club,
www.iowamushroom.org

Kansas
Kaw Valley Mycological Society,
www.sunflower.com/~pilott29

Michigan
Michigan Mushroom Hunters Club,
michiganmushroomhunters.org

Minnesota
Minnesota Mycological Society,
www.minnesotamushrooms.org

Missouri
Missouri Mycological Society,
momyco.org

Ohio
Ohio Mushroom Society,
www.ohiomushroom.org

Wisconsin
Wisconsin Mycological Society,
www.wisconsinmycologicalsociety.org

The Missouri Mycological Society's annual Morel Madness Foray
photo by Patrick Harvey

Recommended Midwestern Mushrooming Locations

The geography and forests of the Midwest tell a story of glacial advance and retreat, moraines, loess, and erosion by streams and rivers. The result is a fragmented ecosystem of farms, forests, and urban areas. The following list of midwestern mushrooming locations is by no means complete, but these locations represent some of the places we have been fortunate to collect in over the last twenty years—or they are recommendations from our friends and colleagues. Be sure to check park regulations regarding mushroom picking. Enjoy!

ILLINOIS

Fox Ridge State Park

Fox Ridge State Park, located in east-central Illinois, is known locally for its mixed hardwood forests, which cover the ridges and broad, lush valleys amidst the rolling hills along the Embarras River.

Giant City State Park

Nestled in the Shawnee National Forest in southern Illinois, Giant City State Park was named for the unique impressions made by its massive sandstone structures. Eons of geological faulting and folding have molded a landscape that is now clothed in ferns, mosses, and more than 75 species of hardwood trees.

Mississippi Palisades State Park

"Palisade" is the word used to describe the lofty, steep cliffs seen along rivers in the Midwest, and Mississippi Palisades, located in the Driftless Area of northwestern Illinois along the Mississippi River, is certainly worthy of a visit. Wooded ravines of mixed hardwood forests dissect the unglaciated terrain and complement the stands of native pines and paper birch.

INDIANA

Brown County State Park

Indiana's largest state park, Brown County State Park, features a diverse, mixed hardwood forest habitat that encompasses nearly 16,000 acres of rugged hills, ridges, and ravines in central Indiana.

Indiana Dunes State Park

Indiana Dunes State Park is comprised of 2,200 acres of dunes, oak savannas, swamps, bogs, marshes, prairies, rivers, and mixed hardwood forests in northwestern Indiana.

IOWA

Loess Hills State Forest

Loess Hills State Forest, located in west-central Iowa, offers a unique mixture of hardwood forests that feature bur oak, red oak, black walnut, hickories, elms, ashes, cottonwood, and red cedar along with savannas and prairies on loess soils above the Missouri River.

Shimek State Forest

Shimek State Forest, located in southeast Iowa, is one of the largest tracts of contiguous forest in Iowa. The predominant plant communities are oak-hickory forests dominated by black oak, bur oak, and shingle oak along the ridgetops, with bottomland hardwood forests that feature elms, cottonwood, ashes, maples, and black walnut.

MICHIGAN

Highland Recreation Area

The Highland Recreation Area in southern Michigan was one of Dr. Alexander Smith's favorite collecting locales, and a number of new mushroom species were described from this area. Included among the 5,900 acres of forests, marshes, and lakes are all of southern Michigan's principal forest types: cedar, beech-maple, oak-hickory, and mixed hardwoods.

Wilderness State Park

One of our favorite mushroom locations in the world is Wilderness State Park, on the northern edge of the southern peninsula of Michigan. This park features one of the most diverse dune and swale complexes in Michigan, with coniferous forests and mature hardwood forests mixed in with coniferous wetlands.

MINNESOTA

Charles A. Lindbergh State Park

Charles A. Lindbergh State Park, located northwest of St. Paul, is a favorite collecting site of Dr. David McLaughlin at the University of Minnesota. The vegetation is dominated by pine forests with oaks and grassland openings as well as aspen and conifer forests.

Nerstrand Big Woods State Park

Located south of the Twin Cities, Nerstrand Big Woods State Park has rolling hills that are home to a vast oak savanna prairie where maples, hickories, aspens, elms, and ashes shade the land.

Scenic State Park

Scenic State Park in northern Minnesota has an abundance of aspens, paper birch, white pine, Norway pine, jack pine, and mixed hardwood forests along the shores of Coon and Sandwick Lakes.

MISSOURI

Babler Woods State Park

The most notable feature of Babler Woods State Park, located just west of St. Louis, is the maturing old-growth forests of white oak, northern red oak, sugar maple, and black walnut with a well-developed understory of dogwood, redbud, and pawpaw.

Hawn State Park

Hawn State Park in southeastern Missouri features canyon-rimmed valleys with mixed pine-oak forests, which, in places, give way to pure stands of shortleaf pine.

Rock Bridge Memorial State Park

Located near Columbia in central Missouri, Rock Bridge Memorial State Park is well known for its bottomland forests surrounded by hardwood forested hills.

OHIO

Hocking Hills State Park

Hocking Hills State Park in southeastern Ohio features deep gorges where the forests are dominated by eastern hemlock, Canada yew, and yellow and black birch.

Mohican State Park

Mohican State Park in northeastern Ohio features ridgetops with stands of white, red, and black oaks, red maple, and white pine. Beech, ashes, and tulip poplar are found on the slopes of the valleys, with hemlock and yellow birch lining the bottomlands, which contain sycamore, willows, and buckeyes.

WISCONSIN

Devil's Lake State Park

Devil's Lake State Park, located in south-central Wisconsin, is known for its loess soils and mixed conifer-hardwood forests, which surround Devil's Lake.

Perrot State Park

Perrot State Park is found in Wisconsin's Driftless Area at the confluence of the Trempealeau and Mississippi Rivers in west-central Wisconsin. The rivers and wetlands dissect the steep wooded slopes, valleys, and bluff tops that are home to oaks, hackberry, black walnut, and hickories.

Acknowledgments

We are grateful to Joe Ammirati, Rich Baird, Tim Baroni, Melissa Bochte, Brad Bomanz, Ernst Both, Hal Burdsall, Dennis Desjardin, the Edge of Appalachia Preserve (Chris Bedel, Director), Roy Halling, Connie Huber, Karen Hughes, the Illinois Mycological Association, Jay Justice, Ron Kerner, Rick Kerrigan, Patrick Leacock, Ed Lickey, Mary Mattingly, Coleman McCleneghan, Joe McFarland, the Michigan Mushroom Hunters Club, Andy Miller, Drew Minnis, the Missouri Mycological Society, Herb Monoson, John David Moore, Greg Mueller, Mushroom Observer (www.mushroomobserver.org), Cheryl Noll, the Ohio Mushroom Society, Clark Ovrebo, Ron Petersen, Dana Ringuette, Carol Schmudde, John Steinke, Walt Sturgeon, Walt Sundberg, Harry Thiers, Connie Thompson, Jean Toothman, Gordon Tucker, Rod Tulloss, Tom Volk, Arthur Weldon, Ken Wells, C. B. Wolfe, Sue Yocum, and Bob Zordani for help with various aspects of this book.

Thanks to Melissa Bochte, Ken Gilberg, Patrick Harvey, Matthew Johnson, Robert Johnson, Ron Kerner, Rick Kerrigan, Matt Kessler, Martin Livezey, Joe McFarland, Dan Molter, Brenda Nelson, Charya Peou, Noah Siegel, Walt Sturgeon, Carla Wick, and Bob Zordani for the use of photographs. Thanks to Mary M. Hill for diligent copyediting.

2 COLLECTING, DOCUMENTING, AND PRESERVING MUSHROOMS

Equipment

Collecting mushrooms for study does not require much in the way of equipment; a pocket knife, some waxed paper bags, a marker, insect repellent, and a basket will suffice. You will need the pocket knife in order to dig mushrooms up (preserving their underground parts) and to remove some of the tougher species from logs and such. The waxed paper bags are what you will use to store your mushrooms. Several companies make waxed paper sandwich bags; these are the best mushroom holders. If you cannot get waxed paper bags, brown paper sandwich bags are the next-best option. Plastic bags are a bad idea. Mushrooms tend to sweat, especially in hot weather, and you are likely to have a wet mess on your hands if you put them in plastic bags. The marker is for taking notes; although some people use a pen and a notepad, we find that writing directly on the waxed paper bags is a convenient method, especially when it comes to sorting out later which notes correspond to which mushrooms.

Pleurotus pulmonarius (p. 315)

Ecology, Ecology, Ecology!

Mushrooms have evolved along with plants and animals as integral parts of complex ecosystems. It should be obvious that understanding mushrooms, therefore, depends on understanding the whole picture. Recording ecological data when you collect mushrooms is often essential to identifying them later. The checklist on page 9 provides some suggestions for collecting ecological data.

Collection Methods

In order to have much success at all in identifying mushrooms, you will probably need to have *multiple specimens representing all stages of the mushroom's development*. Pick mushrooms in good condition, selecting buttons, medium-sized specimens, and mature mushrooms. Most mushrooms make substantial changes in their appearance during their brief lives, and you will frequently need to know what these changes are in order to identify them. While this "all-stages" rule applies pretty much all the time, it is *especially* important with species of *Russula*, *Cortinarius*, and boletes.

Successful identification of some mushrooms will often depend on whether or not you know what is going on with your mushroom at the base of its stem. Many species of *Amanita* have a characteristic volva enclosing the base of the stem; other mushrooms may have a tap root, like *Xerula furfuracea* (p. 394) and *Polyporus radicatus* (p. 323). So you will need to "dig up" mushrooms—but, as you do, please try not to cause unnecessary damage to the soil or wood they are growing in. Try not to handle the stems of mushrooms—especially small ones—if at all possible, since mushroom stems have very subtle and ephemeral features that can be obliterated with handling. For examples, see the tiny flakes on the upper stem of *Flammulaster erinaceellus* (p. 176), the tiny ring on the stem of the Little Brown *Amanita* (p. 99), and the densely but finely hairy stem surface of *Xeromphalina tenuipes* (p. 393).

Place four or five specimens in the same waxed paper bag, leave the top of the waxed paper bag open or very loosely folded, and place the bag in your basket. Avoid piling things on

Date:
Location:
County & State:
Ecosystem:

GROWTH: ❑ Solitary ❑ Scattered ❑ Gregarious ❑ Clustered

SUBSTRATE for terrestrial mushrooms:
❑ Soil ❑ Moss ❑ Sphagnum ❑ Litter

Litter type if clearly associated:

Apparent mycorrhizal associate (if any):

SUBSTRATE for wood-decomposing mushrooms:
❑ Standing, live ❑ Standing, dead ❑ Stump ❑ Log ❑ Stick
❑ Base of tree ❑ Above ground

❑ Decorticated ❑ Partially decorticated ❑ Bark adnate

Rot type:

Identity of tree (if possible):

Trees within 20 feet:

Further Information:

top of one another. If you are hunting mushrooms on a hot day, be sure to store your basket in a shaded and ventilated place for the car ride home.

As you begin to develop your mushroom identification skills, you will find that some details may need to be checked "in the field" for some mushrooms. Some *Lactarius* species, for example, contain a very scant amount of milk, or "latex." Since you will probably need to know what color the latex is and whether it changes color on exposure to air, you may need to record this information when the mushroom is still very fresh, especially if the mushroom has a long ride in a hot car ahead of it. There are several other examples of mushrooms that may require information to be recorded in the field; experience will help you decide what you need to do immediately and what can wait.

Making Spore Prints

At home you will want to start by making spore prints. While a single mushroom spore can't be seen by the naked eye, a pile of many spores can—and the color of a mushroom's spores, seen en masse, is a crucial identification feature. Obtaining a mushroom's spore print is therefore an essential step in the identification process.

Before going through the nuts and bolts of making a spore print at home, it is worth noting that in nature mushrooms frequently make their own spore prints. If you have ever noticed colored dust covering a leaf or the ground beneath a mushroom's gills or pores, you have probably witnessed this phenomenon. Tightly clustered mushrooms, in fact, frequently leave spore prints on one another, since caps overlap (see p. 298).

In order to make a spore print at home you will need to have a relatively mature mushroom. Buttons, young mushrooms, and mushrooms with some kind of covering over their gills or pores (a partial veil) are not likely to drop spores. Remove the stem from smaller mushrooms and place the cap with gills or pores downward on a piece of paper or glass. For larger mushrooms, slice off a section of the cap and use only the section. Place a cup or glass upside-down on top of your mushroom to keep air currents away.

Making a spore print

While some spore prints can appear within a few hours, it's often best to wait overnight, just to be sure. When you remove the cup and lift the mushroom cap, you should find a "print" like the ones illustrated on page 147. If you have been careful not to move the mushroom while the print was developing, you may find that the spore print reflects the pattern of the mushroom's gills or pores, since the spores fell directly downward. Some collectors advocate using black paper for spore prints, since white prints show up more easily. Then again, brown and black prints don't show up on black paper as well as they do on white paper. We prefer to use glass, which can be held against light and dark backgrounds, rather than paper. In fact, we often use a microscope slide, since we will also be examining spores under the microscope. But if you are not going to be using a microscope, any (safe) piece of glass will suffice.

The *color* of the spore print is what you will compare with descriptions from mushroom guides and keys. Interpreting color can be very subjective, and mycologists have tried several times to "standardize" the interpretations, without much success. But while subtle differences (for example, between "white" and "creamy") may be perplexing, distinguishing a white spore print from a brown one or a pink one is easy enough, and it will help you enormously in identifying a gilled mushroom or a bolete.

For mushrooms such as morels, false morels, saddles, clubs, corals, and cup fungi, a spore print is obtained using a similar method. Place a piece of the cap or spore-bearing surface on the paper or glass with the spore-producing side downward. Polypores are the most difficult mushrooms for obtaining spore prints; often it is nearly impossible, especially with perennial species.

Describing Mushrooms in a Journal

The surest route to success in identification of mushrooms is to keep a journal in which you carefully describe the mushrooms you find *before* you try to identify them with field guides, websites, or technical literature. Describing your finds in a journal is a time-consuming process, but it works best, especially since compromised objectivity is one of the top causes of misidentification. People often read descriptions or look at photos of mushrooms first and then turn to the mushrooms themselves. The result is that the mushroom's details are filtered by preconceptions and the power of suggestion.

You will want to work with your mushroom collections as soon as possible when you get back from the woods. Mushrooms decay fairly quickly, especially in warm weather, and you may be surprised at what you find in your collection bags if you wait too long. Set up spore prints (see above) for each mushroom, sort out your collections, number them somehow so you won't get confused about what corresponds to what, and begin writing descriptions in your journal. You will probably want to start each entry with the collection location and date, together with the ecological information you noted in the woods (see above).

Begin at the top of the mushroom and work downward, recording the details you observe. It is not, of course, imperative that you use this top-to-bottom approach, but since most mushroom guides describe their subjects in this order, comparing your description to other descriptions will be easier if you quell your rebel urges and follow the convention.

It would not be productive for us to try to anticipate here every physical detail you might conceivably need to describe, since mushrooms are so diverse in their physical features. For this reason we generally discourage "checklists" and template pages that prompt would-be mushroom describers feature by feature; in our experience better descriptions result from *not* relying on such tools and, instead, simply becoming familiar with mushrooms and their features.

If you are a beginner, you will probably find that your written descriptions of mushrooms at first are missing some crucial details, and there will be a certain amount of going back and forth between your descriptions, descriptions in mushroom guides, and the mushrooms themselves. However, as you gain experience describing more and more mushrooms, your descriptions will become more complete—and the potential for subjective errors will diminish.

Determining Odor

The odor of a mushroom is often a crucial detail. We recommend taking a piece of the mushroom (or a whole cap, in the case of small mushrooms) and crushing it between your finger and thumb in order to assess the odor. Usually the cap is the best part of the mushroom to test, but occasionally you will discover that some other part of the mushroom should be tested (for example, the stem bases in some *Agaricus* species).

Determining Taste

The taste of a mushroom is also sometimes important—but in this case a healthy dose of caution is in order, since there are some deadly poisonous mushrooms out there. One swallowed bite of *Amanita bisporigera* (p. 89) could contain enough poison to kill you. Do not taste any mushroom you suspect could potentially be poisonous (for example, an *Amanita* or a little brown mushroom). To determine taste, tear off a very small piece of the mushroom's cap (including flesh as well as gills or pores). Put it on the tip of your tongue and hold it in your mouth for a few seconds (perhaps a little longer in the case of *Russula* and *Lactarius* species, since some of their tastes develop slowly). Do not swallow, of course. Then spit the mushroom out and rinse your mouth out thoroughly with water, being careful not to swallow.

Testing Chemical Reactions

How a mushroom's surfaces, flesh, and spores react to the application of certain chemicals can be important information in the identification process. In some cases, nearly identical mushrooms can be easily differentiated by simply applying a drop of common household ammonia to the cap.

It is important to test for chemical reactions on *fresh* mushrooms, preferably within an hour or so of picking them. This is not always possible, unless you are willing to carry chemicals with you when you're collecting. But try to test mushrooms as soon as possible when you get home, remembering that the longer you wait, the less reliable your results may be.

Testing chemicals on *Boletus pallidus* (p. 120)

AMMONIA

Common household ammonia, available in any grocery store, is sometimes used to test chemical reactions, especially with boletes. Place a drop of ammonia on a fresh bolete's cap, stem, sliced flesh, and pore surface. Note any color changes that take place. Some species, like *Boletus illudens* (p. 117), will demonstrate a quick flash of one color (for example, blue green), then settle into another, more permanent color change (for example, grayish). Other species, like *Xanthoconium separans* (p. 392), may demonstrate a single color change.

POTASSIUM HYDROXIDE (KOH)

KOH is an important chemical in mushroom identification. Although it is sometimes difficult to obtain, it can usually be purchased without too much difficulty. Several major online vendors (including Amazon) have it available at the time we're writing this. A fairly strong (5–10 percent) aqueous solution is used to test for color changes on the surfaces of mushrooms; if you have purchased a stronger solution, dilute it with distilled water—but use caution and read the manufacturer's warnings and handling instructions for KOH, since it is a strong base and can damage your skin and eyes. KOH is used in the identification of many mushrooms, including boletes, polypores, and gilled mushrooms. For boletes, place a drop of KOH on the cap, stem, sliced flesh, and pore surface. For polypores, apply the KOH to the flesh and the cap surface. For gilled mushrooms, place a drop on the cap surface. Note any color changes that take place. A change to yellow is sometimes found in species of *Agaricus* and *Amanita*; magenta or olive reactions can help identify species of *Russula* and *Lactarius*; deep red or black reactions can help sort out many gilled mushrooms; black reactions among polypores are crucial separators; and various colors are produced with boletes. Don't forget that a "negative" reaction (no color change) may also be an informative character.

IRON SALTS

A 10 percent aqueous solution of iron salts ($FeSO_4$) is sometimes used to test for color changes. Iron salts are used primarily (but not exclusively) in the identification of boletes and russulas. For boletes, place a drop on the cap, stem, sliced flesh, and pore surface; for russulas, place a drop on the stem surface and the flesh.

Dried specimen of *Xerula megalospora* (p. 395), ready for storage

Preserving Specimens

Mycologists preserve mushrooms by desiccation (drying), and the process is easily replicated at home. (Do not, however, dry mushrooms in your living quarters; some people are allergic to drying mushrooms and can get headaches or even break out in rashes when they are around an operating mushroom dryer.) A commercial food dehydrator (available in most department stores for about $35) will dry specimens effectively.

Dry small- to medium-sized mushrooms whole, if possible. Larger mushrooms may need to be cut into pieces—but you may also be able to rig up a means of lifting your dryer's lid higher (perhaps with some plastic cups) to make space for them. Keep the mushrooms clearly separated in the dryer. When they have been dried, mushrooms often do not look much like they did before drying, so you will want to make sure you know which mushroom is which. The best way to solve this problem is to put a paper label next to each mushroom.

Experience will tell you how long to dry mushrooms; larger specimens, of course, take longer than small ones. The goal is to dry the mushroom so that it is brittle but not cooked. Do not use high heat, if your dryer has adjustable temperatures. Among other reasons, high heat is a bad idea because it can "cook the DNA" of your mushroom, making it impossible for a later researcher to extract information for DNA testing. After you have turned the dryer off, remove the mushrooms and wait at least ten minutes before checking them. Sometimes mushrooms that seemed dry when you took them out of the dryer will soften up in this time period and become flexible; if this happens, dry the mushrooms for a longer time period.

If you also dry edible mushrooms for long-term storage and later consumption, we recommend that you *do not* use the same dehydrator for specimens.

Storing Specimens

We recommend storing your mushrooms in sturdy plastic zip-lock bags. "Real" mycological collections are wrapped in acid-free paper and stored in special cardboard boxes, but the expense of such materials is prohibitive for most of us. Put the mushroom(s) in the plastic bag along with enough of a written record so that you can later figure out what's what, and what corresponds to your journal entries. This may not seem like much of an issue at first, but as your collection grows, you will probably find you need some kind of numbering system in order to make sense out of anything. We write the following on a notecard or piece of paper in each specimen bag:

- Collection number. The most common system (and one that can be sorted out by computers without modifications) is simply to number mushroom collections in ascending order, beginning with "1." Other numbering systems involve the collection date (for example, 09029502 to represent the second mushroom collected on September 2, 1995; 1995.9.2.2 is an alternate form). The mushrooms described in your journal should be labeled with the same numbers as the specimen bags.
- Your identification of the mushroom.
- The location and date of the collection.

Store your collection in a dry location and keep the collections in an air-tight cabinet. Humidity is the biggest enemy for a mushroom collection, so garages and basements tend to be poor locations to store mushrooms.

Midwestern Herbaria

For the past three centuries, scientists have documented the earth's plant and fungal diversity through dried reference specimens maintained in collections known as herbaria. There are approximately 3,400 herbaria in the world today, with approximately 10,000 associated curators and biodiversity specialists. Collectively, the world's herbaria contain an estimated 350 million specimens that document the earth's vegetation for the past 400 years. Index Hebrariorum (online at sweetgum.nybg.org/ih) is a guide to this crucial resource for biodiversity science and conservation.

The following list of midwestern herbaria includes herbaria containing significant numbers of fungal specimens. Please consider contacting one of the curators and donating your collections—along with your photos and journal entries—so that professional and amateur mycologists can study your mushrooms.

ILLINOIS

Field Museum of Natural History
Herbarium
Botany Department
1400 South Lake Shore Drive
Chicago, Illinois 60605–2496
fieldmuseum.org/explore/department/botany/collections

Illinois Natural History Survey
Herbarium
Prairie Research Institute
1816 South Oak Street
Champaign, Illinois 61820
www.inhs.uiuc.edu/animals_plants

Nancy Poole Rich Herbarium
Research Department
Chicago Botanic Garden
1000 Lake Cook Road
Glencoe, Illinois 60022
www.chicagobotanic.org

University of Illinois
Herbarium
Plant Biology Department
1816 South Oak Street
Urbana, Illinois 61820

INDIANA

Ball State University
Herbarium
Biology Department
Muncie, Indiana 47306

Kriebel Herbarium
Purdue University
Department of Botany and Plant Pathology
915 West State Street
West Lafayette, Indiana 47907–2054

IOWA

Ada Hayden Herbarium
Botany Department
Iowa State University
341A Bessey Hall
Ames, Iowa 50011–1020
www.public.iastate.edu/~herbarium

MICHIGAN

Michigan State University
Herbarium
Plant Biology Laboratories
612 Wilson Road, Room 166
East Lansing, Michigan 48824
www.herbarium.msu.edu

University of Michigan
Herbarium
3600 Varsity Drive
Ann Arbor, Michigan 48108–2228
herbarium.lsa.umich.edu

MINNESOTA

University of Minnesota
Herbarium
J. F. Bell Museum of Natural History
1445 Gortner Avenue
St. Paul, Minnesota 55108–1095
www.bellmuseum.umn.edu/ResearchandTeaching/Collections/ScientificCollection/PlantCollection/index.htm

University of Minnesota
Herbarium
Plant Pathology Department
1991 Buford Circle, 495 Borlaug Hall
St. Paul, Minnesota 55108

MISSOURI

College of the Ozarks
Herbarium
Biology Department
P.O. Box 17
Point Lookout, Missouri 65726

OHIO

Miami University
W. S. Turrell Herbarium
Botany Department
MSC 1052
100 Bishop Circle, Room 79
Upham Hall
Oxford, Ohio 45056–1879
herbarium.muohio.edu/herbariummu

Ohio State University
Herbarium
Museum of Biological Diversity
1315 Kinnear Road
Columbus, Ohio 43212–1157
herbarium.osu.edu

University of Cincinnati
Herbarium
Biological Sciences Department
Cincinnati, Ohio 45221–0006

WISCONSIN

U.S. Forest Service, Northern Research Station
Herbarium
Center for Forest Mycology Research
One Gifford Pinchot Drive
Madison, Wisconsin 53726–2398

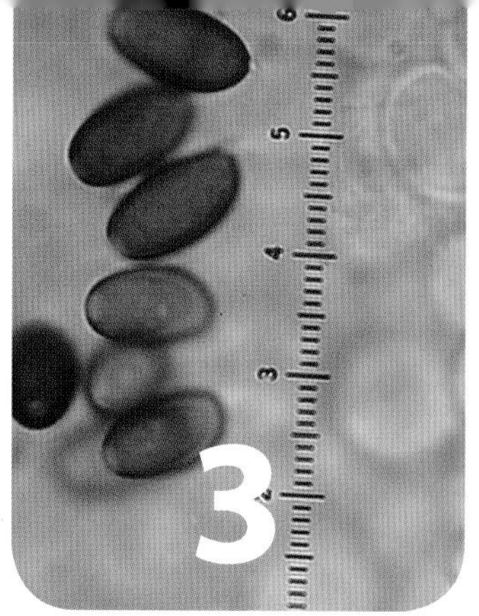

3 USING A MICROSCOPE TO STUDY MUSHROOMS

Microscopic examination of mushrooms is often essential in the identification process. Because field guides often ignore this reality or treat microscope work as an unfortunate and tedious affair, we wanted to break the mold and encourage you to explore mushroom microscopy. It is true that most of the mushrooms in this book can be at least tentatively identified without recourse to microscopic examination, but confident identification of mushrooms usually requires a microscope. Besides, microscope work can be fun and rewarding. Most of the techniques required are not that difficult to learn, and a decent used microscope can often be picked up for under $300. The best part (if you are as obsessed with mushrooms as we are) is that you can spend quality time with your little fungal friends in the off season.

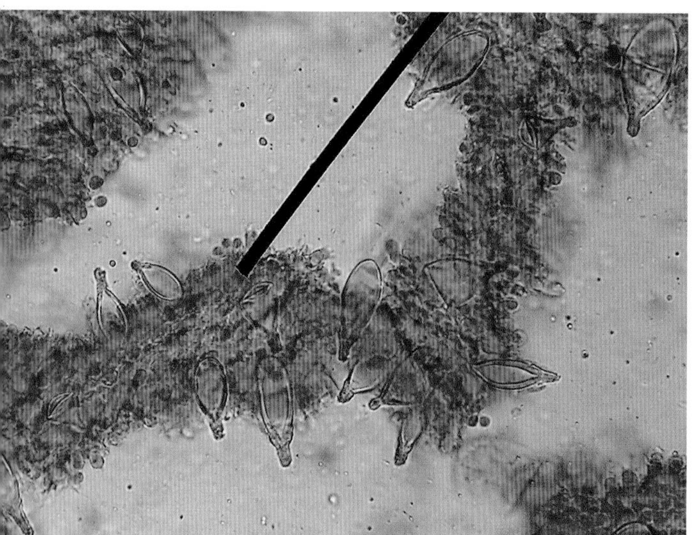

Cystidia of *Hohenbuehelia angustata* (p. 205)

Studying mushrooms with microscopy takes lots of practice, but new frontiers open up at each level. Beginners will find that simply looking at a mushroom's spores is fascinating and helps substantially in the identification process. More advanced microscope skills lead not only to facilitated identification but sometimes to stunning views and gorgeous microstructures.

Equipment

To study mushrooms, you'll need a pretty good microscope. The many microscopes in people's basements and closets—forgotten gifts to twelve-year-olds whose enthusiasm dwindled a few weeks after Christmas—are usually toys, great for looking at hair follicles and the like but usually not powerful enough to help you study mushrooms. Some of the larger microscopic structures of mushrooms can sometimes be seen with these "garage-sale microscopes," however, and if you'd like to whet your appetite, we recommend trying to view the microstructures of morels (pp. 277–80) by slicing a thin section from the surface of a mature morel's pits and using a tap-water mount (equipment required: garage-sale microscope, slide, cover slip, sharp razor blade, tap water, morel).

But if you want to go beyond having a little fun just seeing some of the larger microscopic features of mushrooms, you will need a microscope with an oil immersion lens that is capable of magnifying things about 1,000 times. The eyepiece of the microscope will need to have an ocular micrometer in it so that you can measure things. You will want an electric light source, controls to move the stage (the platform that holds the slide) mechanically, and a fine-focus knob (not just a single, coarse-focus knob).

You could buy a new microscope, of course. However, a used microscope will work perfectly well, assuming it's in good condition. You might want to try shopping for one online, but we suspect that your best bet is to contact someone in one of the life science departments at a local university or community college. Former Biology 101 microscopes are not too hard to get hold of, and they are often dirt cheap in comparison to new equipment.

You will also need some of the obvious microscope equipment—slides, cover slips, extra bulbs, lens paper, and immersion oil—as well as some very sharp razor blades and some chemicals (see at right). Slides and cover slips are available from many sources. If you are an online shopper, try one of the many scientific equipment sites on the Internet. Your experience and preferences will dictate what kinds of slides and cover slips you need. Glass cover slips are wonderful but expensive and easily broken. You will need lens paper to clean your oil immersion lens after each use. If you cannot find lens paper online, try your local camera shop or your optometrist. Immersion oil can be purchased online as well.

Calibrating a Microscope

The little ruler in the eyepiece of your microscope is divided up evenly into units, but those units do not necessarily correspond to anything in particular. Thus you will need to compare the units on your microscope's ruler to the units on a special slide (called a stage micrometer) that has known values on it. Most microscopic mushroom measurements are expressed in "micrometers," also called "microns." One micrometer is equal to 0.001 millimeter; the symbol for a micrometer is µm.

Calibrating your microscope is simply the process of comparing your microscope's units to the predetermined units on a special slide. Borrow the stage micrometer slide, if possible; you won't need to calibrate your microscope more than once. Once you have a conversion basis, you will need to do a little math every time you measure something. For example, if each unit on your yardstick equals 1.07 µm when you're using the highest magnification, something that appears 10 units long to your microscope is actually 10.7 µm (roughly 11 µm) long.

Chemicals, Reagents, and Stains

While a drop of water is occasionally the best way to mount mycological specimens, the features of mushrooms are usually difficult to see without using the stains and/or reagents that mycologists use. The bad news is, these chemicals can be very difficult to obtain (even for mycologists). At a minimum, you will need the chemicals below.

KOH

Potassium hydroxide (KOH) in a 2–3 percent aqueous solution is frequently used as a mounting medium (sometimes in combination with a stain like phloxine; see below). Although it is sometimes difficult to obtain, KOH can usually be purchased without too much difficulty. Several major online vendors (including Amazon) have it available at the time we're writing this. KOH, in a stronger solution, is also used to determine chemical reactions of mushrooms (see pp. 12–13).

PHLOXINE

Phloxine is a red stain that is particularly good for making hyphal (cellular) structures more visible. Ask a local biology teacher for help obtaining phloxine, or purchase it online.

MELZER'S REAGENT

This reagent is often important to mycological microscopy, and it is unfortunately extremely difficult to obtain. It contains water, iodine, and potassium iodide, all of which are fairly easy to acquire, but it also contains chloral hydrate, which is a controlled substance. Thus, you won't be able to buy it online. Virtually your only option is to beg it from a professional mycologist. Offer to pay for it. If she refuses your money, find out what kind of toner cartridge the biology department printer requires and donate one to the office. Even mycologists have difficulty obtaining Melzer's, however, and if the mycologist you know can't afford to provide you with some of her precious supply (or if you cannot find a mycologist), your last resort is to try explaining your situation to your doctor and getting a prescription for chloral hydrate (not likely; it's a date-rape drug) or for Melzer's reagent itself, which a pharmacist could mix according to the formula below if your doctor is willing to write it on a prescription (still not very likely but not unheard of).

Water: 22.0 gm
Chloral hydrate: 20.0 gm
Iodine crystals: 0.5 gm
Potassium iodide (KI): 1.5 gm

Studying Spores

Observing spores is the easiest of the various microscope routines involved in mycology. You will be surprised at how useful it can be in the identification process to know whether a mushroom's spores are smooth, spiny, ridged, pitted, and so on and to know their dimensions.

You want to measure mature spores, since, like other parts of a mushroom, spores are little before they are big. The spore sizes quoted in mushroom guides and in technical mycological literature represent mature spores, which, by definition, have fallen off the mushroom. This means that a spore print (see chapter 2) is the ideal source of your material. Take a clean, dry razor blade and scrape lightly on the spore print, collecting spore dust on the blade's edge. If you have made a spore print on paper, don't scrape too hard; you will be scraping paper particles as well, which will confuse things under the microscope.

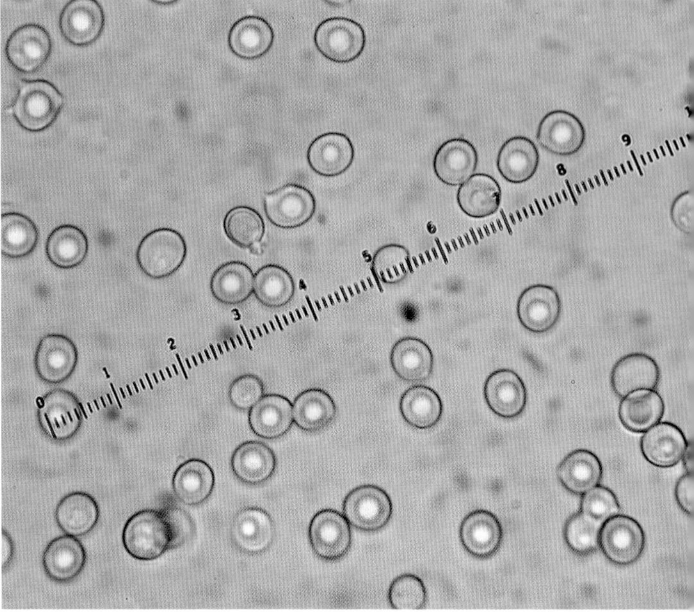

Spores of *Pluteus thomsonii* (p. 320)

Tap the spore dust off the razor blade onto a clean slide. If you are studying a gilled mushroom, place a drop of Melzer's reagent (preferable) or KOH on the spore dust, add a cover slip, and take a moment to note in your journal whether the spores are amyloid, dextrinoid, or inamyloid. Melzer's reagent has iodine in it, and a color reaction may be visible if you hold the slide up to the light. If the spores turn bluish black in Melzer's, they are amyloid; if they turn reddish brown, they are dextrinoid; if there is no noticeable change in color, the spores are inamyloid. In many cases you will need to wait until you are viewing the spores through your microscope before you can see dextrinoid and amyloid reactions, but strong reactions, at least, can often be seen with the naked eye.

Now put the slide on your microscope's stage. Start at low magnification, bringing the spores into focus (they may be *very* tiny), and move progressively through your magnifications, bringing the spores into focus each time. Carefully add a drop of immersion oil to the top of the cover slip before moving to the highest magnification (your oil immersion lens), and then turn the coarse-focus knob very gently and carefully until your spores slide almost into focus. Use the fine-focus knob to make them completely visible. Going from low to high magnification is the only way to first locate the spores and then put them in focus. You probably won't have much luck if you start the process with your oil immersion lens; plus, you may easily break the slide or cover slip by forcing the oil immersion lens too far down.

Sketch and describe the appearance of spores in your journal. You can also use a digital camera to take pictures through your eyepiece—and this works better than you might expect, after a little practice (you will have to experiment with your camera's settings).

If you can't get a spore print out of your mushroom, you may still be able to see spores by taking a single gill and mounting it in a "crush mount" (press on the cover slip with a pencil eraser, gently crushing and stretching out the gill). Under the microscope, search through all of the tissues for spores—but remember that you may be viewing *immature* spores if you find them. If you can't find spores with this method, your mushroom may be simply immature and has not yet developed spores.

Measure spores with the ruler in your eyepiece and convert the values to microns using the conversion multiplier you established when you calibrated your microscope. Be sure your spores are completely in focus before measuring them. Also note that spores with ornamentation can create a little confusion with measurements; it's usually best to measure the width or length of the spore *without* the ornamentation and measure the ornamentation separately. A good practice is to measure the length and width of at least ten spores. Be sure to record the dimensions of the smallest and largest spores you can find, but if these big and little spores seem aberrant, exclude their dimensions from your accounting. You will want to express the dimensions of the spores as two ranges of possibilities, for example, "7–9.5 × 4–5.5 µm," which means that the thinnest spore you found was 4 µm wide, the fattest was 5.5 µm, the shortest was 7 µm, and the longest was 9.5 µm. Tip: only do the math once. Write everything down in terms of your microscope's units, ignoring the fact that your units do not equal microns until you convert the final numbers into the format above.

Creating a Section to Study

In order to study spores from a spore print (see above), you did not have to follow any particularly difficult routines to get what you wanted to examine on the slide ready for viewing. Other microscopic structures, however, require special techniques for creating a "section" you can look at. The difficulty involved results from the fact that you must create a cross section of the mushroom, a cross section so thin that you can look at it under your microscope at magnification of 1000×.

Most of the structures you will want to observe can be seen by creating a cross section of the mushroom's cap, with the gills included. Thus, "sectioning a pileus" is one of the most essential and basic laboratory routines for mycologists. Creating the required cross section can take lots of practice, so you should prepare for disappointing results at first. We will take you through the actual razor-blade-and-mushroom routine in a moment, but first we want to give you the concept involved with sectioning a mushroom's cap, since most sources frustratingly describe the routine without giving you something to visualize and

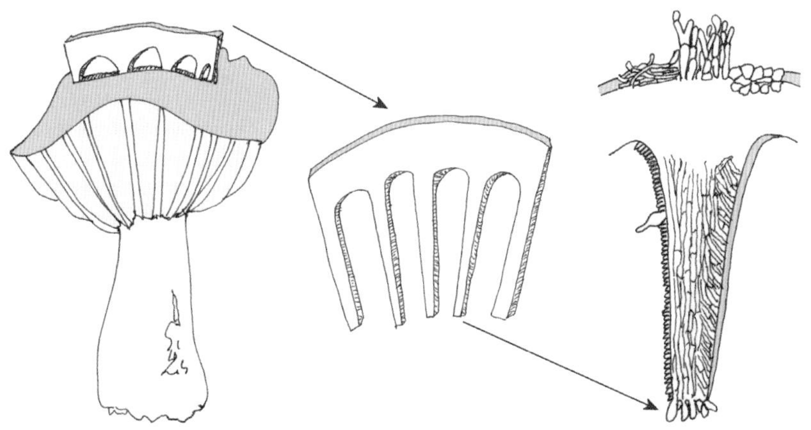

attempt doing with your razor blade. The illustration on page 19 is meant to represent the idea behind sectioning a mushroom cap, but it should not be taken too literally (for example, we have widened the thickness of the section for visual understanding, but your actual section must be paper thin).

The thing in the middle of the illustration represents the section you want to create. On the left is the section in relation to the mushroom and its cap; on the right is a schematized diagram of part of the section under your microscope. You can see that a nice, Roman-aqueduct-reminiscent section would be a pretty nifty thing, allowing you to look at structures on the gills, on the cap surface, and in the flesh of the mushroom, with everything held nicely together so that you can figure out what's what. The bad news is that it took less time to create the illustration than it is likely to take a beginner to actually slice a section like the one depicted. Both of us made many, many clumsy sections and "blood mounts" before getting the hang of it.

Prepare to budget some money for razor blades, because successful sectioning requires very sharp edges. We're talking relatively few uses, and then it's time for a new one. You'll have to search around at your drug store to find the old-fashioned, single-edged blades in the little safety boxes. Avoid double-edged blades; they are flimsy and, more importantly, dangerous, since you don't have a nice, safe edge to handle.

The photos in at left take you through the process of creating a section like the one schematized on page 19. In the illustrations we used a 2 percent KOH mount stained with phloxine.

Working with Dried Specimens

Believe it or not, it is often easier to section a dried mushroom cap than a fresh one—and as we mentioned above, examining dried mushrooms over the winter is a great way to keep your hobby going yearround.

Break off a small piece of the dried specimen's cap and let it soak in 90 percent alcohol for a few minutes. Then transfer your specimen to a distilled-water dish and let it soak until it is soft (usually a few minutes). Don't be surprised if your mushroom piece starts spinning around once it makes contact with the water; something in the alcohol-to-water chemistry often makes this happen.

Next, blot the piece of the cap well with a paper towel, then *roll it up or fold it* so that the gills run lengthwise in your roll-up. With a very sharp razor blade, begin slicing cross sections of the roll-up until you have managed to slice a very thin section. Transfer it to your slide (a dissecting needle or toothpick makes a good tool for this) and add your mounting medium. Your section should begin to magically uncurl itself; help it along a bit, spreading it out so that the gill sections are well separated. Your section should look more or less like the "Roman aqueduct" one creates with fresh material (see above). If your section is large, you may need to trim away parts of the section with the razor blade or dissecting needle to avoid having too much material on the slide.

Additional Resources

Since our goal here is to introduce you to mycological microscopy, we do not want to get too technical; nor do we want to fill up the book with definitions of microscopic terms. In our descriptions of mushrooms in this book we have included more microscopic details than are usually provided in field guides, and we have defined all the technical terms we have used in the glossary at the end of the book. But if you get to a stage in your microscopic studies at which more precise and comprehensive definitions would be useful, we recommend the sources below for further information.

Largent, D. L., D. Johnson, and R. Watling. 1973. *How to identify mushrooms to genus III: Microscopic features.* Eureka: Mad River Press.

Smith, A. H., H. V. Smith, and N. S. Weber. 1979. *How to know the gilled mushrooms.* Dubuque: Wm. C. Brown.

———. 1981. *How to know the non-gilled mushrooms.* Dubuque: Wm. C. Brown.

4 IDENTIFICATION KEYS

A Key to Major Groups of Mushrooms

1) Mushroom with gills or false gills 2
1) Mushroom without gills 6

2) Growing shelf-like on wood; mushroom tough and leathery, corky, or woody (try tearing it in half); gills tough and hard (sometimes slot-like or maze-like) .... Key K, Pored Mushrooms on Wood, p. 62
2) Not completely as above 3

3) Mushroom with false gills (wrinkles or folds that are not plate-like and thus are not easily separable from the mushroom—try removing an entire "gill" with fingers or a knife point) .... Key L, Chanterelles and Trumpets, p. 66
3) Mushroom with true, plate-like gills 4

4) Spore print pink to brownish pink .... Key B, Pink-Spored Gilled Mushrooms, p. 24
4) Spore print not pink to brownish pink 5

5) Spore print white, yellow to orange, lilac, or green .... Key C, Pale-Spored Gilled Mushrooms, First Part, p. 26
5) Spore print brown to purple brown or black .... Key H, Dark-Spored Gilled Mushrooms, First Part, p. 46

6) Mushroom with pores on its underside 7
6) Mushroom without pores 8

7) Mushroom growing on the ground; cap and stem clearly defined; cap usually more or less round in outline.. Key J, Terrestrial Pored Mushrooms, p. 56

7) Mushroom growing on wood, or if on the ground, then usually at the base of a tree trunk; cap and stem clearly defined or not; cap usually fan- to kidney-shaped or irregular (occasionally round) .... Key K, Pored Mushrooms on Wood, p. 62

8) Mushroom with spines or "teeth" either on the underside of a cap, or hanging from a branched structure, or clumped together in an indistinct mass... Key M, Toothed Mushrooms, p. 67

8) Mushroom without spines or teeth... 9

9) Mushroom shaped more or less like a ball (sometimes splitting open with maturity), or a ball raised up on a stem, or a ball set atop a starfish or platter .... Key N, Puffballs and Earthstars, p. 68

9) Mushroom not shaped like a ball..10

10) Mushroom appearing like a tiny bird's nest, complete with "eggs" .... Key R, Miscellaneous Other Mushrooms, p. 77

10) Mushroom not appearing like a bird's nest 11

11) Mushroom shaped like a cup, a saucer, a goblet, a standing rabbit ear, or a bowl, with or without a stem.. Key O, Cup Mushrooms, p. 70

11) Mushroom not shaped as above...12

12) Mushroom developing from a partially buried "egg"; at maturity covered (at least in part) with a brown to olive, malodorous spore slime; most species appearing in lawns and gardens (occasionally in woods) .... Key R, Miscellaneous Other Mushrooms, p. 77

12) Mushroom not developing from an egg; not covered with malodorous slime; habitat varying 13

13) Mushroom with a clearly defined cap and stem 14

13) Mushroom without a clearly defined cap and stem 15

14) Cap shape convex to centrally depressed or vase-shaped; undersurface clearly visible, smooth, wrinkled, or nearly gill-like; rarely fruiting in spring... Key L, Chanterelles and Trumpets, p. 66

14) Cap brain-like, thimble-shaped, irregularly lobed, blocky, or saddle-shaped; undersurface rarely visible; most (but not all) species fruiting in spring.. Key P, Morels, False Morels, and Saddles, p. 73

15) Mushroom shaped like a branched or unbranched club, stick, or cylinder, or shaped roughly like a coral or a head of cauliflower or a rosette .... Key Q, Club and Coral Mushrooms, p. 74

15) Mushroom not shaped as above...................... Key R, Miscellaneous Other Mushrooms, p. 77

B Key to Pink-Spored Gilled Mushrooms

1) Mushroom with a sac-like volva around the base of the stem 2
1) Mushroom without a volva 6

2) Mature cap white, <3.5 cm across; growing terrestrially .... *Volvariella pusilla*, p. 389
2) Mature cap white or not, larger than above; growing terrestrially or on wood 3

3) Growing from stumps, logs, or standing trees; cap whitish to yellowish or brownish, silky .... *Volvariella bombycina*, p. 389
3) Growing elsewhere; cap varying 4

4) Cap white, 5–15 cm across .... *Volvopluteus gloiocephalus*, p. 391
4) Cap gray to brown, size varying 5

5) Growing gregariously or in clusters in woodchips, compost, greenhouses, and other urban settings; cap 5–16 cm across .... *Volvariella volvacea*, p. 390
5) Growing terrestrially in woods (occasionally in urban areas near woody or grassy debris); cap 2–6 cm across .... *Volvariella taylori*, p. 390

6) Mushroom small (cap 1–5 cm); cap and stem brown to reddish brown; growing on the ground; without veils; odor strong, reminiscent of cucumbers or fish; cap, stem, and gills covered with prominent cystidia .... *Macrocystidia cucumis*, p. 267
6) Not completely as above 7

7) Cap dull purple to lilac when fresh, fading to brownish; fresh gills pale lilac; odor fragrant; often growing in piles of organic debris .... *Clitocybe nuda*, p. 142
7) Not completely as above 8

8) Growing on wet logs, usually in creekbeds and spring flood areas; cap dull to bright orange or red, rubbery, usually featuring a distinctive network of raised ridges (see p. 337) .... *Rhodotus palmatus*, p. 337
8) Not completely as above 9

9) Cap brightly colored (green, red, orange, yellow) 10
9) Cap white to tan or brown 17

10) Cap green 11
10) Cap not green 12

11) Odor of anise; stem white .... *Clitocybe odora*, p. 142
11) Odor of mice; stem green .... *Entoloma incanum*, p. 172

12) Stem with a persistent but fragile ring; cap yellow; growing on wood; rare .... *Pluteus mammillatus*, p. 319
12) Stem without a ring; cap variously colored; growing on wood or terrestrially........................ 13

13) Cap orange.. 14
13) Cap yellow 15

14) Growing on the wood of hardwoods; cap convex....................... *Pluteus aurantiorugosus*, p. 315
14) Growing terrestrially or on moss-covered conifer logs; cap conic, with a pointed center........... .... *Entoloma salmoneum*, p. 174

15) Growing terrestrially; cap conic with a pointed center .... *Entoloma murrayi*, p. 173
15) Growing on wood or terrestrially; cap convex to flat.. 16

16) Cap usually bright yellow (occasionally brownish), 1–3 cm across; stem 3–6 cm long; usually growing on deadwood .... *Pluteus chrysophlebius*, p. 316
16) Cap usually dull yellow to brownish yellow, 2–8 cm across; stem 5–12 cm long; growing on terrestrial woody debris or directly from deadwood .... *Pluteus flavofuligineus*, p. 317

17) Cap and stem covered with dark brown granules .... *Pluteus granularis*, p. 318
17) Cap and stem without dark brown granules 18

18) Cap essentially white 19
18) Cap gray to brown.. 21

19) Gills free from the stem; cap with brown scales over the center; growing on wood or terrestrially .... *Pluteus petasatus*, p. 319
19) Gills attached to the stem; cap without scales; growing terrestrially..................................... 20

20) Gills crowded; odor not distinctive; usually growing in clusters .... *Clitocybe subconnexa*, p. 143
20) Gills close or nearly distant; odor mealy; not growing in clusters .... *Clitopilus prunulus*, p. 144

21) Growing on wood 22
21) Growing terrestrially..25

22) Cap brown; stem yellow .... *Pluteus romellii*, p. 320
22) Cap gray to brown; stem not yellow 23

23) Cap gray to brownish gray, small (1–3 cm), prominently lined with cracks and fissures extending from the margin nearly to the center .... *Pluteus longistriatus*, p. 318
23) Cap brown, size varying, not lined 24

24) Cap small (1–4 cm), often with a striking veined pattern over the center .... *Pluteus thomsonii*, p. 320
24) Cap medium-sized to large (3–15 cm), without a veined pattern over the center.. *Pluteus cervinus*, p. 316

25) Mature cap developing distinctive concentric cracks (see illustrations, p. 337); surfaces red with KOH..*Rhodocybe mundula*, p. 337
25) Mature cap not normally developing concentric cracks; surfaces negative with KOH (not tested in one case) 26

26) Cap conical to bell-shaped, brown to tan; appearing in spring............*Entoloma vernum*, p. 174
26) Cap convex to flat, brown to tan or gray; appearing in spring, summer, or fall 27

27) Cap tan to light brown; appearing in late summer and fall .... *Entoloma rhodopolium*, p. 173
27) Cap gray to brownish gray; appearing in spring, summer, or fall.. 28

28) Usually growing near amorphous whitish masses ("aborted" forms) and/or near species of *Armillaria* (see pp. 101–3); summer and fall; clamp connections present..*Entoloma abortivum*, p. 171
28) Not usually growing near aborted forms or species of *Armillaria*; spring, summer, and fall; clamp connections absent ....*Entoloma griseum*, p. 171

C Key to Pale-Spored Gilled Mushrooms, First Part

1) Spore print green; growing on lawns and in meadows; cap whitish with brown scales, 10–30 cm across..*Chlorophyllum molybdites*, p. 135
1) Spore print not green.. 2

2) Mushroom with a universal veil, a slime veil, and/or a partial veil.. 3
2) Mushroom with neither a universal veil, a slime veil, nor a partial veil................................ 24

3) Mushroom with a slime veil (a slimy universal veil that does not leave a volva, patches, or warts); cap sticky when fresh; odor mealy 4
3) Mushroom without a slime veil; cap sticky or not; odor mealy or not.................................. 5

4) Stem dry and shaggy.. *Limacella glioderma*, p. 265
4) Stem sticky and bald.. *Limacella glischra*, p. 265

5) Gills free from the stem at maturity or nearly so 6
5) Gills attached to the stem or running down it at maturity 16

6) With a universal veil that leaves a volva, concentric rings, a rim, or flaky patches at the base of the stem (a few species lack distinct volval remnants on the stem base; the most common and widespread of these have surfaces that bruise reddish); many species with warts or patches (though

some have bald caps); with a ring on the stem, or if lacking a ring, then with a strongly lined cap margin; spores amyloid or inamyloid but never dextrinoid .... *Amanita*; Key E, p. 40

6) Lacking a universal veil that leaves a volva, concentric rings, or flaky patches on the stem base; not blushing reddish to pinkish when bruised, or if blushing reddish, then the cap typically with scales rather than easily removed warts or patches; spores often dextrinoid, never amyloid 7

7) Cap white; scales, if present, essentially white 8
7) Cap more highly colored, or whitish underneath colored scales 9

8) Growing alone or gregariously in grass; stem 5–15 mm thick; cap bald or nearly so .... *Leucoagaricus naucinus*, p. 261
8) Growing in clusters in woodchips and cultivated areas (sometimes in grass); stem 3–6 mm thick; cap covered with mealy granules .... *Leucocoprinus cepistipes*, p. 262

9) Cap at first uniformly pink to brownish orange, becoming pinkish to orangish with a darker center; surfaces not bruising or staining .... *Leucoagaricus rubrotinctus*, p. 261
9) Cap differently colored; surfaces bruising or not 10

10) Mature cap small (2–4 cm) and yellow; often growing near honey locust or black locust trees.. .... *Leucocoprinus flavescens*, p. 262
10) Mature cap small, or larger than above, but not yellow; habitat varying 11

11) Cap whitish under reddish-brown scales; stem surface bruising quickly yellow, then slowly reddish .... *Leucoagaricus americanus*, p. 260
11) Cap and scales variously colored; stem surface bruising faintly brownish, if at all 12

12) Mature cap usually <5 cm across 13
12) Mature cap usually larger than above 14

13) Stem surface bald; odor usually pungent; cap whitish under pinkish to brown scales that are fairly well spaced and sparse except over the center; spores bullet-shaped... .... *Lepiota cristata*, p. 258
13) Stem surface hairy; odor not distinctive; cap yellowish to yellow brown or rusty brown under a dense covering of scales; spores fusiform .... *Lepiota magnispora*, p. 259

14) Stem 5–15 mm thick; ring fairly easily separated to slide up and down the stem; mature cap usually featuring a small central bump .... *Macrolepiota procera*, p. 268
14) Stem 5–30 mm thick; ring not easily separated to slide up and down the stem; mature cap usually lacking a small central bump 15

15) Cap 6–10 cm across, with many small, pointed scales; ring flimsy, often featuring small brown scales on its underside; usually found in woods....................................... *Lepiota aspera*, p. 258
15) Cap 5–20 cm across, with large, coarse scales; ring substantial, without brown scales on its underside; usually found in urban settings .... *Chlorophyllum rhacodes*, p. 136

16) Growing directly from wood 17
16) Growing terrestrially 20

17) Gills running well down the stem; mushroom whitish and fuzzy overall, bruising and discoloring yellowish .... *Pleurotus dryinus*, p. 314
17) Not completely as above 18

18) Cap *and stem* densely covered with reddish-brown to orangish-brown scales; gills attached to the stem by a notch; spores amyloid .... *Leucopholiota decorosa*, p. 264
18) Cap scaly or not; stem not scaly; gills not attached by a notch; spores inamyloid 19

19) Cap often with yellow shades; stem with a persistent membranous ring; stem base often pointed .... *Armillaria mellea*, p. 102
19) Cap usually lacking yellow shades; stem with, at most, a flimsy ring zone; stem base often swollen .... *Armillaria gallica*, p. 101

20) Cap and stem both covered with powdery granules when young 21
20) Cap and stem not covered with powdery granules 22

21) Cap and stem orange to reddish orange .... *Cystodermella cinnabarina*, p. 167
21) Cap and stem brown to reddish brown .... *Cystodermella granulosa*, p. 167

22) Cap tan to pinkish brown, bald or finely hairy but not scaly; gills broadly attached to the stem or running down it .... *Armillaria gallica*, p. 101
22) Cap whitish to brownish, hairy to scaly; gills attached to the stem by a notch 23

23) Growing under oaks and other hardwoods; odor not distinctive; taste bitter or unpleasant .... *Tricholoma caligatum*, p. 376
23) Growing under jack pine; odor spicy, reminiscent of cinnamon; taste similar but not bitter or unpleasant .... *Tricholoma magnivelare*, p. 377

24) Gills very thick, waxy, distantly spaced, yellow, running down the stem; cap red to brown; mushroom appearing from above much like a bolete; spore print yellowish .... *Phylloporus rhodoxanthus*, p. 312
24) Not completely as above 25

25) Fresh, young mushrooms producing a white, colorless, or colored "milk" or juice when injured (best observed by slicing the gills with a knife point or by slicing the mushroom in half); growing terrestrially .... *Lactarius*; Key F, p. 41
25) Mushroom not producing a milk or juice when injured, or if producing milk or juice, then growing on wood 26

26) Flesh white, crumbly, and brittle; stem usually brittle; cap often about as wide as the stem is long, broadly convex to flat or shallowly depressed when mature (never conical); gills not usually waxy; spore print white, creamy, yellow, or orange; spores with amyloid ornamentation .... *Russula*; Key G, p. 45

26) Flesh and stem not usually brittle; cap shape and proportions varying; gills waxy or not; spore print white to creamy; spores with or without amyloid ornamentation 27

27) Gills separable as a layer (see p. 264); cap dry and unpolished, medium-sized to large; odor mealy to foul 28
27) Gills not separable as a layer; cap size and odor varying 29

28) Under conifers; stature often stocky; spores longer than 5.5 µm ....*Leucopaxillus albissimus*, p. 263
28) Under hardwoods; stature not usually stocky; spores <5.5 µm ....*Leucopaxillus laterarius*, p. 264

29) Growing on the ground in leaf litter, in conifer duff, or on cones or nuts ....Key D, Pale-Spored Gilled Mushrooms, Second Part, p. 32
29) Growing on wood 30

30) Cap orange, brownish orange, red, or purplish red 31
30) Cap differently colored 38

31) Stem absent; cap densely hairy; gills orange .... *Phyllotopsis nidulans*, p. 313
31) Stem present; cap hairy, scaly, or bald; gills variously colored 32

32) Cap thick and rubbery, usually developing a conspicuous pattern of ridges and veins, orange to red; usually found on well-decayed, wet wood in streambeds............*Rhodotus palmatus*, p. 337
32) Not completely as above 33

33) On wood of conifers; cap 3–12 cm across, red to purplish red, hairy to scaly; gills yellow .... *Tricholomopsis rutilans*, p. 381
33) On wood of hardwoods or conifers; cap orange to brownish orange, bald; gills variously colored.. 34

34) Stem notably hairy to fuzzy 35
34) Stem bald 36

35) Cap sticky; growing in clusters directly from wood; stem darkening to brown or black from base up ....*Flammulina velutipes*, p. 177
35) Cap dry; growing scattered on and around deadwood; stem not darkening to brown or black.. ....*Xeromphalina tenuipes*, p. 393

36) Mature cap 5–20 cm across; stem 1–2 cm thick .... *Omphalotus illudens*, p. 292
36) Mature cap and stem smaller than above 37

37) Cap convex, sticky when fresh; stem not wiry, also sticky when fresh; gills close or crowded, with edges often darker than faces .... *Mycena leaiana*, p. 286
37) Cap convex with a central depression, dry; stem wiry, dry; gills well spaced, with edges and faces concolorous ....*Xeromphalina campanella*, p. 393

38) Without a stem, or with a rudimentary, lateral stem 39
38) With a well-developed stem 46

39) Cap dark gray to black 40
39) Cap differently colored 41

40) Mature cap 2–10 mm across; gills gray to black .... *Resupinatus alboniger*, p. 334
40) Mature cap 20–50 mm across; gills whitish to dull yellowish .... *Hohenbuehelia atrocoerulea* var. *grisea*, p. 206

41) Gill edges serrated; cap 3–10 cm across; taste bitter .... *Lentinellus ursinus*, p. 256
41) Gill edges not usually serrated; cap variously sized; taste varying 42

42) Gills folded together and "split" lengthwise (see p. 354); flesh leathery and tough .... *Schizophyllum commune*, p. 354
42) Gills not as above; flesh not leathery and tough 43

43) Mature cap 1–3 cm wide, woolly to velvety; taste usually bitter .... *Panellus stipticus*, p. 294
43) Mature cap usually larger than above; taste mild or mealy 44

44) Odor and taste mealy; mature cap to 6 cm across .... *Hohenbuehelia angustata*, p. 205
44) Odor and taste mild; mature cap larger than above 45

45) Appearing primarily in fall, winter, and early spring; cap pale to dark brown; edge of cap not lined .... *Pleurotus ostreatus*, p. 314
45) Appearing primarily in summer and fall; cap whitish to pale tan; edge of cap often lined .... *Pleurotus pulmonarius*, p. 315

46) Gill edges serrated (see p. 256); cap brownish, often with a central depression; taste peppery .... *Lentinellus micheneri*, p. 256
46) Gill edges not normally serrated; cap varying; taste varying 47

47) Cap and stem brown, with a dense layer of hairs; stem tough, 1–2 mm thick; growing on hardwood sticks or woody debris .... *Crinipellis zonata*, p. 165
47) Not completely as above 48

48) Mushrooms medium-sized; growing in clusters on the wood of hardwoods; stem bases narrowed and fused; caps brownish to yellowish; stems whitish above and grayish to brownish below; gills whitish to pinkish, running down the stem .... *Armillaria tabescens*, p. 102
48) Not completely as above 49

49) Usually growing in dense clusters of many mushrooms; cap 5–25 mm across, yellow to orange; gills cross-veined, running down the stem; stem tough; spores amyloid .... *Xeromphalina campanella*, p. 393
49) Not completely as above 50

50) Mushroom mycenoid: fairly small and fragile; stem thin (<5 mm thick), usually hollow and not tough or wiry; cap usually conical or bell-shaped (but occasionally convex or flat); margin or entire cap frequently lined to pleated when moist; many species (but not all) growing in clusters 51
50) Mushroom not mycenoid 58

51) Mushroom with a distinctive odor (crush a cap) 52
51) Distinctive odor lacking 54

52) Odor mealy .... *Mycena inclinata*, p. 285
52) Odor bleach-like 53

53) Cap white to pale gray .... *Mycena niveipes*, p. 288
53) Cap brown .... *Mycena semivestipes*, p. 289

54) Blue shades present on cap and stem, at least when young; growing alone or scattered .... *Mycena subcaerulea*, p. 290
54) Blue shades absent; growing alone, scattered, gregariously, or in clusters 55

55) Fresh stem exuding a red to purple juice when squeezed or sliced .... *Mycena haematopus*, p. 284
55) Fresh stem not exuding red to purple juice 56

56) Cap and stem bright yellow green to green or greenish yellow when fresh .... *Mycena epipterygia* var. *lignicola*, p. 283
56) Cap and stem differently colored 57

57) Cap tiny (usually <1 cm across); mushroom growing on the bark of living trees .... *Mycena corticola*, p. 282
57) Cap 1–6 cm across; growing from well-decayed hardwood logs .... *Mycena galericulata*, p. 283

58) Gills running down the stem (truly decurrent) 59
58) Gills attached to the stem narrowly or broadly, or barely beginning to run down it (adnate, adnexed, sinuate, subdecurrent) 63

59) On wood of conifers in the northern Midwest and Ohio; cap and stem velvety and brown; stem 10–30 mm thick; spore print yellowish .... *Tapinella atrotomentosa*, p. 369
59) Not completely as above 60

60) Cap and stem black to dark grayish brown; cap with a navel-like central depression .... *Arrhenia epichysium*, p. 103
60) Not completely as above 61

61) Cap and stem densely hairy; cap purplish at first, soon fading to brownish; stem often off-center .... *Panus rudis*, p. 296

61) Cap and stem not densely hairy; colors varying; stem central or off-center 62

62) Flesh tough; cap, gills, and stem purplish, becoming brownish .... *Panus conchatus*, p. 295
62) Flesh soft; cap brown, becoming yellow to whitish, gills and stem white to yellow .... *Gerronema strombodes*, p. 183

63) Mature cap >5 cm across 64
63) Mature cap usually <5 cm across 65

64) Usually growing from wounds on standing trees; cap white, becoming buff to pale tan .... *Hypsizygus ulmarius*, p. 219
64) Usually growing on stumps, fallen logs, or buried deadwood; cap brown to gray .... *Megacollybia rodmani*, p. 275

65) On well-decayed wood of conifers; cap and stem yellow to olive yellow; KOH purplish red on cap .... *Callistosporium luteo-olivaceum*, p. 126
65) On wood of hardwoods or conifers; cap and stem differently colored; KOH negative to olive on cap 66

66) Stem black or very dark brown, 1–2 mm thick; cap white 67
66) Stem differently colored, 2–5 mm thick; cap color varying 68

67) Cap widely pleated, with a navel-like central depression; gills usually attached to a collar that encircles the stem .... *Marasmius rotula*, p. 272
67) Cap not pleated, convex; gills beginning to run down the stem .... *Tetrapyrgos nigripes*, p. 370

68) Stem and flesh tough; cap cinnamon brown to pinkish tan; stem velvety, darkening from base upward with age .... *Gymnopus dichrous*, p. 188
68) Flesh soft; cap white to gray; stem bald, not darkening with age 69

69) Usually growing alone, gregariously, or in loose clusters; cap gray to brownish gray .... *Clitocybula lacerata*, p. 144
69) Usually growing in dense clusters; cap grayish brown over the center .... *Clitocybula abundans*, p. 143

D Key to Pale-Spored Gilled Mushrooms, Second Part

1) Mushrooms medium-sized; growing in clusters on the wood of hardwoods; stem bases narrowed and fused; caps brownish to yellowish; stems whitish above and grayish to brownish below; gills whitish to pinkish, running down the stem .... *Armillaria tabescens*, p. 102
1) Not completely as above 2

2) Gills yellowish orange to bright orange, repeatedly forked, running down the stem; cap surface soft to the touch; at least some spores dextrinoid .... *Hygrophoropsis aurantiaca*, p. 215
2) Not completely as above 3

3) Fresh cap green; odor strong, of anise .... *Clitocybe odora*, p. 142
3) Cap not green, or if green, then odor not strongly of anise 4

4) Odor strong, of bleach; cap gray to gray brown or black; under conifers .... *Mycena leptocephala*, p. 286
4) Odor not bleach-like; cap color and habitat varying 5

5) Gills running down the stem (truly decurrent) 6
5) Gills attached to the stem narrowly or broadly, or barely beginning to run down it (adnate, adnexed, sinuate, subdecurrent) 15

6) Cap bright orange 7
6) Cap not bright orange 9

7) Mature cap tiny (<15 mm wide), with a lined margin; growing scattered or gregariously in moss .... *Rickenella fibula*, p. 338
7) Mature cap larger than above, without a lined margin; habitat and growth pattern varying 8

8) Growing in dense clusters near stumps or recently removed trees; mature cap 5–20 cm across .... *Omphalotus illudens*, p. 292
8) Growing alone or gregariously but not in clusters; mature cap 1–3.5 cm across .... *Hygrocybe cantharellus*, p. 210

9) Cap shoehorn-shaped, or rolled into a funnel shape; odor mealy .... *Hohenbuehelia petaloides*, p. 207
9) Cap not normally shaped as above; odor fragrant, sweet, or not distinctive 10

10) Fresh cap convex and pale, dull orange to orangish buff; gills thick, distant or nearly so; odor not distinctive .... *Hygrocybe pratensis*, p. 213
10) Not completely as above 11

11) Cap white to buff 12
11) Cap more highly colored 14

12) Gills distant or nearly so; cap greasy to sticky; stem 2–9 cm long, up to 1 cm thick .... *Hygrocybe virginea*, p. 214
12) Gills close or crowded; cap dry; stem dimensions varying 13

13) Gills crowded; stem to 15 mm thick; stem base with copious mycelium but without rhizomorphs .... *Clitocybe subconnexa*, p. 143
13) Gills close; stem to 7 mm thick; stem base attached to rhizomorphs .... *Clitocybe eccentrica*, p. 141

14) Usually growing under conifers; cap brown; stem often enlarged toward base .... *Ampulloclitocybe clavipes*, p. 101

14) Usually growing under hardwoods; cap pinkish tan; stem usually equal .... *Infundibulicybe gibba*, p. 220

15) Stem with a long, underground taproot; cap convex to flat 16
15) Stem without a taproot, or if with a taproot, then cap conical 17

16) Mature cap large (usually 8–12 cm) and brown; stem usually finely hairy to scaly; spores ellipsoid to ovoid .... *Xerula furfuracea*, p. 394
16) Mature cap smaller (usually <8 cm) and pale brownish to white; stem bald; spores limoniform to amygdaliform .... *Xerula megalospora*, p. 395

17) Cap and stem pink; growing in grass (lawns, meadows, etc.) .... *Calocybe carnea*, p. 127
17) Cap and stem not pink, or if pink, then not growing in grass 18

18) Fresh cap dull to bright yellow 19
18) Fresh cap not yellow 24

19) Growing from shells and nut debris of walnuts and hickories; cap <2 cm across .... *Mycena luteopallens*, p. 287
19) Not growing from shells and nut debris; cap variously sized 20

20) Fresh cap sticky to slimy; gills thick 21
20) Fresh cap dry; gills not thick 22

21) Cap convex to flat, usually bright green when very young and fresh but quickly fading to dull greenish yellow or straw yellow .... *Hygrocybe psittacina*, p. 213
21) Cap bell-shaped to conic, bright yellow .... *Hygrocybe persistens*, p. 212

22) Under conifers; odor usually mealy; stem to 2 cm thick and cap to 12 cm across; cap yellow when young but becoming brownish to yellow brown .... *Tricholoma equestre*, p. 376
22) Under hardwoods; odor not mealy; smaller than above; cap remaining dull to bright yellow 23

23) Found in spring and early summer; stem base attached to pinkish rhizomorphs; cap 1–4 cm across; gills very crowded .... *Gymnopus subsulphureus*, p. 191
23) Found in summer and fall; stem base attached to copious mycelial fuzz, but not rhizomorphs; cap 3–7 cm across; gills close or nearly crowded .... *Marasmius strictipes*, p. 274

24) Fresh cap pink, <2 cm across, pleated; stem wiry, <1 mm thick .... *Marasmius pulcherripes*, p. 272
24) Not completely as above 25

25) Purple shades present on cap and/or gills when mushroom is fresh 26
25) Purple shades absent on cap and gills 30

26) Odor strongly of radish; cap 2–6 cm across; gills thin and whitish .... *Mycena pura*, p. 288
26) Odor not radish-like; cap variously sized; gills varying 27

27) Growing in sand dunes near pine trees; gills purple; cap purplish when young but soon brownish .... *Laccaria trullissata*, p. 229
27) Not growing in sand dunes; gills and cap varying 28

28) Mature cap <4 cm across, usually featuring a central depression, purple fading to lilac buff .... *Laccaria amethystina*, p. 226
28) Mature cap larger than above, convex to flat, variously colored 29

29) Cap purple when young but soon brownish; gills thin, close or crowded, pale lilac fading to buff; odor fragrant .... *Clitocybe nuda*, p. 142
29) Cap pale lilac when young, fading to whitish or brownish; gills thick, distant or nearly so, deep purple; odor not distinctive .... *Laccaria ochropurpurea*, p. 227

30) Odor strong, fishy or reminiscent of cucumbers; cap brown to reddish brown, 1–5 cm across; gills whitish becoming yellowish; KOH olive on cap; surfaces covered with lanceolate cystidia. .... *Macrocystidia cucumis*, p. 267
30) Not completely as above 31

31) Growing in grass (lawns, pastures, etc.), often in fairy rings or arcs; cap pale tan, broadly bell-shaped; gills distant; stem tough .... *Marasmius oreades*, p. 271
31) Not completely as above 32

32) Stem surface densely hairy to velvety or fuzzy 33
32) Stem not densely hairy to velvety or fuzzy, or merely fuzzy at the very base 37

33) Cap and stem densely hairy, tawny brown to golden brown; stem 1–2 mm thick; cap 10–25 mm across .... *Crinipellis zonata*, p. 165
33) Cap bald or finely velvety; stem velvety to fuzzy; colors varying; stem width varying; cap size varying 34

34) Cap sticky when fresh, brownish orange, rubbery; stem 3–5 mm thick, darkening to brown or black from the base upward .... *Flammulina velutipes*, p. 177
34) Cap dry, variously colored, not rubbery; stem not darkening as above, or if darkening, then <3 mm thick 35

35) Stem long and wiry (30–100 mm long and 1–2 mm thick); cap <3 cm across, orange to brownish orange; KOH on cap negative .... *Rhizomarasmius pyrrhocephalus*, p. 335
35) Stem not long and wiry; cap size and color varying; KOH on cap not negative 36

36) Cap 0.5–2 cm across, bald, reddish brown fading quickly to pinkish buff; stem reddish brown, often with spongy lower portion; KOH green to black on surfaces .... *Gymnopus semihirtipes*, p. 190
36) Cap 2–7 cm across, finely velvety, orangish brown to brownish orange; stem colored like the cap, without an enlarged spongy portion; KOH dark reddish brown on cap .... *Xeromphalina tenuipes*, p. 393

37) Stem wiry, 1 mm thick or less; cap pleated, <3 cm across 38
37) Stem not wiry, 2 mm thick or more; cap sometimes lined near the edge but not pleated, size varying 40

38) Growing on petioles of fallen sycamore leaves; cap white to pinkish, usually lacking a navel-like central depression .... *Marasmius felix*, p. 270
38) Growing on leaf litter and woody debris of various hardwoods; cap whitish, pale grayish brown, or orange, with a navel-like central depression 39

39) Cap whitish to pale grayish brown .... *Marasmius capillaris*, p. 269
39) Cap dull to bright orange .... *Marasmius siccus*, p. 273

40) Cap and stem both sticky to slimy; cap 1–3 cm across, at first green but soon fading to greenish yellow or straw yellow .... *Hygrocybe psittacina*, p. 213
40) Not completely as above 41

41) Cap 5–12 cm across, pink to reddish; stem 1.5–3.5 cm thick; stem and gills initially white but soon developing reddish spots and discolorations .... *Hygrophorus russula*, p. 216
41) Not completely as above 42

42) Fresh, young cap bright red to bright orange; gills thick and waxy 43
42) Fresh, young cap differently colored, or if bright red to bright orange, then gills not thick and waxy 46

43) Cap conic 44
43) Cap convex to bell-shaped 45

44) Surfaces bruising and discoloring black with age .... *Hygrocybe conica*, p. 211
44) Surfaces not blackening .... *Hygrocybe cuspidata*, p. 211

45) Cap 2–4 cm across; gills broadly attached to the stem; under hardwoods .... *Hygrocybe miniata*, p. 212
45) Cap 3–15 cm across; gills narrowly attached; under hemlock, other conifers, or hardwoods .... *Hygrocybe punicea*, p. 214

46) Growing in clusters *and* stem 1–2 cm thick 47
46) Growing alone, scattered, or gregariously, or if growing in clusters, then stem <1 cm thick 48

47) Cap white; gills very crowded; usually found in woods .... *Clitocybe subconnexa*, p. 143
47) Cap grayish brown to yellowish brown; gills close; usually found in disturbed ground in urban areas but also found in woods .... *Lyophyllum decastes*, p. 267

48) Cap small (to 2 cm across), conic, brown with a blue or bluish edge when fresh and young; stem 30–80 × 1–2 mm, with blue shades when fresh and young; growing alone or scattered on or around the deadwood of hardwoods .... *Mycena subcaerulea*, p. 290

48) Cap and stem varying, but blue shades absent; habitat varying 49

49) Gills pinkish flesh color, fairly thick; cap and stem orangish brown to brownish orange, reddish brown, or tan 50
49) Not completely as above 55

50) Mature cap <3 cm across; stem <4 mm thick 51
50) Mature cap usually larger than above; stem thicker than above 52

51) Cap usually not strongly lined; spores with spines about 1 µm at the base ....small forms of *Laccaria laccata*, p. 226
51) Cap often strongly lined; spores with spines featuring wide (>1 µm) bases .... *Laccaria ohiensis*, p. 228

52) Growing under hardwoods with no conifers nearby; *not* growing in sphagnum ....*Laccaria laccata*, p. 226
52) Growing under conifers, or growing in sphagnum 53

53) Stem 7–14 cm long; growing in sphagnum, usually with spruces, tamaracks, or alders nearby .. .. *Laccaria longipes*, p. 227
53) Stem shorter than above; usually not growing in sphagnum but, if so, with pines nearby 54

54) Cap usually orangish brown and bald or finely hairy; spores round or nearly so, with spines 1–2 µm long..*Laccaria laccata*, p. 226
54) Cap usually reddish brown and finely hairy to scaly; spores broadly ellipsoid, with spines <1 µm long..*Laccaria proxima*, p. 228

55) Stem exuding a yellow to purple juice when sliced or squeezed; gills yellowish to yellow, with maroon edges; cap to 3 cm across .... *Mycena atkinsoniana*, p. 282
55) Stem not exuding juice; gills not as above; cap size varying... 56

56) Growing in dense clusters on the wood of conifers; cap 1–5 cm across, reddish brown but fading to pinkish buff; stem bald, reddish brown to purplish brown (contrasting starkly with the cap after it has faded) .... *Connopus acervatus*, p. 146
56) Not completely as above 57

57) Cap small (<2.5 cm across) and orange.. 58
57) Cap not both small and orange 59

58) Cap conic to bell-shaped, orange centrally and paler toward the edge; stem whitish to grayish, often with a taproot .... *Mycena leptophylla*, p. 287
58) Cap convex to flat, orange to rusty orange overall; stem whitish above but reddish brown to black below, not forming a taproot .... *Marasmius sullivantii*, p. 274

59) Growing in grass, woodchips, or disturbed ground in urban areas; cap convex becoming flat; stem tough 60

59) Growing in woods; cap and stem varying 62

60) Usually found in woodchips, growing in clusters; cap dark reddish brown, fading to tan; stem often attached to conspicuous rhizomorphs .... *Gymnopus luxurians*, p. 189
60) Usually found in grass or disturbed ground, growing alone or gregariously; cap brown to tan or gray; stem not attached to rhizomorphs 61

61) Cap gray; stem often conspicuously short in comparison to cap width .... *Melanoleuca brevipes*, p. 275
61) Cap brown to tan; stem not as above .... *Melanoleuca melaleuca*, p. 276

62) Cap and stem sticky to slimy when fresh; cap 2–8 cm across, whitish at first but soon becoming brownish to grayish over the center; appearing under hardwoods in fall .... *Hygrophorus occidentalis*, p. 215
62) Not completely as above 63

63) Gills broadly attached to the stem; cap 3–11 cm across, whitish to brownish, with a darker brown center; stem 5–10 cm long and about 1 cm thick .... *Marasmius nigrodiscus*, p. 271
63) Not completely as above 64

64) Cap essentially white overall (perhaps with inconspicuous brownish hairs, reddish-brown spots, or yellowish center) 65
64) Cap more highly colored 71

65) Growing on the blackened remains of other mushrooms; mature cap 1 cm across or smaller........................ *Collybia cookei*, p. 145
65) Not growing on decayed mushrooms; mature cap larger than above 66

66) Stem 1–2 mm thick, darkening to reddish brown or nearly black from the base upward; stem base usually attached to copious whitish mycelium that spreads through leaf litter .... *Marasmius delectans*, p. 270
66) Stem thicker and paler than above; stem base not attached to copious mycelium........................ 67

67) Gills broadly attached to the stem or beginning to run down it 68
67) Gills attached by means of a notch 70

68) Growing on the deadwood or litter of conifers; cap 4–12 cm across, developing cinnamon to rusty spots; gills crowded .... *Rhodocollybia maculata*, p. 336
68) Growing terrestrially under hardwoods or conifers; cap not normally developing rusty spots, size varying; gills not crowded 69

69) Cap 1–7 cm across; gills beginning to run down the stem; stem usually <1 cm thick .... *Hygrocybe virginea*, p. 214
69) Cap 8–20 cm across; gills broadly attached; stem 1–3 cm thick .... *Hygrophorus sordidus*, p. 216

70) Cap overlaid with inconspicuous tan to brownish fibers and scales ....
.... *Tricholoma venenatum*, p. 381
70) Cap basically bald, sometimes developing bluish stains.......... *Tricholoma subresplendens*, p. 380

71) Mushroom tricholomatoid: gills usually attached by means of a notch; cap medium-sized to large, convex, becoming broadly convex, broadly bell-shaped, or flat; stem fleshy, usually 1 cm or more thick at maturity 72
71) Mushroom not tricholomatoid.. 78

72) Gills at first whitish, soon developing many brown to reddish brown spots and discolorations; cap brown to reddish brown .... *Tricholoma pessundatum*, p. 378
72) Gills not developing many reddish-brown spots, or if developing a few, then gills yellow; cap color varying 73

73) Cap yellow to greenish or olive under conspicuous black to blackish fibers; odor mealy ....
.... *Tricholoma sejunctum*, p. 379
73) Not completely as above..74

74) Under conifers.. 75
74) Under hardwoods..76

75) Cap brownish orange to orange; stem distinctively sheathed with orangish scales that terminate in a line near the apex.. *Tricholoma aurantium*, p. 375
75) Cap yellow at first, becoming yellowish brown to brown; stem yellowish to whitish, not sheathed .... *Tricholoma equestre*, p. 376

76) Cap and stem covered with gray hairs or scales .... *Tricholoma squarrulosum*, p. 379
76) Neither cap nor stem covered with gray hairs or scales.. 77

77) Odor strong and unpleasant, reminiscent of coal tar; cap yellowish to greenish, becoming tan to buff .... *Tricholoma odorum*, p. 378
77) Odor mealy; cap reddish brown to yellow brown............................ *Tricholoma fulvum*, p. 377

78) Cap initially reddish brown but soon fading to pinkish tan; stem reddish brown (contrasting starkly with mature cap), often with a spongy base; KOH green to black on cap ....
.... *Gymnopus semihirtipes*, p. 190
78) Not completely as above.. 79

79) Stem 2–3 mm thick, pale at first but soon darkening to reddish brown from the base up; cap 1–3.5 cm across; often growing in clusters of 2–3 mushrooms; usually found under hardwoods
.... *Marasmius cohaerens*, p. 269
79) Stem thicker than above, not darkening; cap usually larger than above; not usually growing in clusters; under hardwoods or conifers 80

80) Found under hardwoods .... *Gymnopus dryophilus*, p. 189
80) Found under conifers 81

81) Mature cap usually broadly convex, greasy; stem enlarged toward the base, up to 1 cm thick; gills close or nearly crowded; some spores dextrinoid .... *Rhodocollybia butyracea*, p. 336
81) Mature cap usually flat, dry; stem equal, up to 7 mm thick; gills crowded; no spores dextrinoid .... *Gymnopus dryophilus*, p. 189

E Key to *Amanita*

1) Stem without a ring........................ 2
1) Stem with a ring........................ 6

2) Cap bright red to orange; stem pale yellow .... *Amanita parcivolvata*, p. 95
2) Cap tawny to brown or gray; stem white 3

3) Cap tawny........................ *Amanita fulva*, p. 93
3) Cap brown to gray........................ 4

4) Cap dusted with mealy powder; volva powdery .... *Amanita farinosa*, p. 92
4) Cap bald or with volval patches; volva sac-like or flimsy 5

5) Volva flimsy; cap brown with prominent grayish patches........................ *Amanita ceciliae*, p. 90
5) Volva durable and sac-like; cap gray to brown, only rarely with a few small patches........................ *Amanita vaginata*, p. 100

6) Stem base enclosed in a prominent sac-like volva........................ 7
6) Volva not sac-like 9

7) Cap white........................ *Amanita bisporigera*, p. 89
7) Cap more highly colored 8

8) Cap bright red to orange or yellow .... *Amanita jacksonii*, p. 94
8) Cap brown .... *Amanita spreta*, p. 99

9) Stem discoloring and staining reddish, at least by maturity........................ 10
9) Stem not staining, or staining brownish........................ 12

10) Cap surface yellow........................ *Amanita flavorubescens*, p. 93
10) Cap surface white to brown, tan, or coppery 11

11) Cap surface white........................ *Amanita salmonescens*, p. 98
11) Cap surface brown, tan, or coppery .... *Amanita rubescens*, p. 97

12) Fresh cap pale green to pale yellow, bald or with a few small patches (but not with numerous warts); bulb at base of stem featuring a gutter or rim on the upper edge........................ *Amanita citrina*, p. 91
12) Fresh cap differently colored, variously adorned; bulb with or without a rim 13

13) Cap red, orange, or bright yellow 14
13) Cap white, brown, tan, grayish, or dull straw yellow 15

14) Stem base not notably enlarged, featuring flakes of fragile yellow volval material .... *Amanita flavoconia*, p. 92
14) Stem base swollen, featuring white, concentric, rim-like bands .... *Amanita muscaria* var. *guessowii*, p. 95

15) Cap brown 16
15) Cap not brown 17

16) Mature cap 4–15 cm across; stem staining brown; stem base often appearing chiseled .... *Amanita brunnescens*, p. 90
16) Mature cap <4 cm across; stem not staining brown; stem base not chiseled .... *Amanita* species, p. 99

17) Stem base with a more or less collar-like rim on the upper edge; cap dull yellow to whitish with a yellowish center (rarely whitish overall) 18
17) Stem base without a collar-like rim; cap white or faintly grayish 19

18) Cap whitish with a yellowish center; margin not lined, or lined faintly for about 1 cm; warts numerous .... *Amanita multisquamosa*, p. 94
18) Cap dull straw yellow; margin prominently lined; warts scattered .... *Amanita russuloides*, p. 98

19) Stem base with prominent, concentric zones of large, sturdy, down-turned scales .... *Amanita cokeri*, p. 91
19) Sturdy, down-turned scales absent on stem base 20

20) Stem base with an abrupt bulb that has a flattened upper side; cap surface not soft and powdery .... *Amanita abrupta*, p. 88
20) Stem base not abruptly bulbous; cap surface soft and powdery 21

21) Growing in grass (lawns, meadows, etc.) .... *Amanita thiersii*, p. 100
21) Growing in woods 22

22) Gills brownish; stem base staining greenish to bluish .... *Amanita pelioma*, p. 96
22) Gills whitish; stem base not staining greenish to bluish .... *Amanita polypyramis*, p. 96

F Key to *Lactarius*

1) Cap color varying from yellowish to orangish or bluish (especially when young), discoloring green and becoming often sordid green overall at maturity; milk scant, yellowish to brownish (but not orange); gills yellowish before discoloring greenish; found under pines .... *Lactarius chelidonium* var. *chelidonioides*, p. 234
1) Without the above combination of characters 2

2) Milk colored as exuded (slice young specimens and check the flesh in the stem apex and near the gills); dark green stains often developing on surfaces........ 3
2) Milk watery, white or whitish as exuded (but sometimes becoming yellow or yellowish after exposure to air); dark green stains rarely developing on surfaces (though cap and stem may be innately colored green, or milk may dry olive to pastel green)........ 6

3) Associated with conifers in the northern Midwest; cap orange; green staining and bruising absent throughout development........ *Lactarius thyinos*, p. 249
3) Range, mycorrhizal associations, and cap colors varying; green stains developing, at least by maturity........ 4

4) Gills and milk blue........ *Lactarius indigo*, p. 240
4) Gills and milk not blue........ 5

5) Fresh cap pinkish to purplish pink; milk purple red........ *Lactarius subpurpureus*, p. 247
5) Fresh cap orange; milk orange........ *Lactarius deliciosus* var. *deterrimus*, p. 236

6) Cap and stem dark green; cap surface magenta with KOH; stem with potholes........ *Lactarius atroviridis*, p. 233
6) Without the above combination of characters........ 7

7) Milk white or creamy as exuded but changing quickly (within 60 seconds) to yellow........ 8
7) Milk watery, white, or creamy as exuded, not changing quickly to yellow (but possibly changing slowly to yellowish or changing to another color)........ 13

8) Associated with birches or aspens; young cap margin bearded or hairy........ 9
8) Associated with oaks and other hardwoods in oak-based forests, or with conifers; young cap margin not hairy........ 10

9) Cap pinkish yellow to pale pinkish orange; stem without potholes........ *Lactarius pubescens* var. *betulae*, p. 243
9) Cap whitish to yellowish, olive buff, or faintly brownish; stem with conspicuous potholes........ *Lactarius scrobiculatus* var. *canadensis*, p. 245

10) Stem with potholes; cap pale yellow to buff........ *Lactarius maculatipes*, p. 242
10) Stem without potholes; cap color varying........ 11

11) Cap and stem white, with a downy, subvelvety feel; gills distant, bruising and discoloring cinnamon to brownish........ *Lactarius subvellereus* var. *subdistans*, p. 248
11) Neither cap nor stem downy or subvelvety; cap not white; gills close, discoloring or not........ 12

12) Cap dull brown to tan, without zones........ *Lactarius imperceptus*, p. 240
12) Cap with zones of pinkish, cinnamon, and reddish shades........ *Lactarius vinaceorufescens*, p. 250

13) Milk staining gills and/or flesh (sometimes only in limited areas) purple to lilac or lavender (sometimes slowly; wait at least an hour before deciding) 14
13) Milk either not staining gills or flesh or staining surfaces pink, red, green, or brown 15

14) Purple to lilac staining pronounced; gills close; cap grayish to yellowish or brownish .... *Lactarius subpalustris*, p. 245
14) Purple to lilac staining weak; gills distant; cap orange to brownish orange .... *Lactarius hygrophoroides*, p. 239

15) Milk turning greenish to green on exposure to air (sometimes slowly) 16
15) Milk not turning green 17

16) Cap at first whitish but soon brownish pink to pinkish brown; gills close or nearly distant .... *Lactarius allardii*, p. 230
16) Cap white; gills very crowded .... *Lactarius glaucescens*, p. 238

17) Gills pinkish to pale pink; associated with aspens, cottonwoods, or willows in the northern Midwest .... *Lactarius controversus*, p. 235
17) Gills not pinkish to pale pink; associations and range varying 18

18) Cap white to buff 19
18) Cap more highly colored 23

19) Gills very crowded; taste very acrid .... *Lactarius piperatus* (see *L. glaucescens*, p. 238)
19) Gills close, distant, or nearly distant; taste acrid or not 20

20) Gills close 21
20) Gills distant or nearly so 22

21) Milk staining tissues brown; odor fishy .... *Lactarius luteolus*, p. 241
21) Milk staining tissues pink or not staining; odor not distinctive .... *Lactarius subvernalis* var. *cokeri*, p. 249

22) Stem to 3.5 cm thick; cap finely velvety, with an even margin; gills nearly distant .... *Lactarius subvellereus* var. *subdistans*, p. 248
22) Stem to 1.5 cm thick; cap bald, developing a scalloped margin; gills very distant .... *Lactarius subplinthogalus*, p. 246

23) Milk white at first, becoming watery with age; cap with zones of reddish brown; KOH on cap olive .... *Lactarius quietus* var. *incanus*, p. 244
23) Milk white or watery; cap not zoned and reddish brown; KOH on cap olive or not 24

24) Cap tan to brown 25
24) Cap differently colored 30

25) Both cap and stem *dark* brown; cap velvety to the touch .... *Lactarius lignyotus*, p. 241
25) Cap and stem tan to medium brown; cap waxy or bald 26

26) Gills distant or nearly so 27
26) Gills close or crowded 28

27) Stem tan to brown; cap margin not usually becoming scalloped; surfaces waxy to the touch..... .... *Lactarius gerardii*, p. 238
27) Stem whitish to tan; cap margin often becoming scalloped; surfaces not waxy to the touch...... .... *Lactarius subplinthogalus*, p. 246

28) Associated with conifers or paper birch in the northern Midwest; odor of mature specimens reminiscent of maple syrup or curry .... *Lactarius aquifluus*, p. 231
28) Associations varying; widely distributed; odor not distinctive 29

29) Surfaces staining pink when sliced .... *Lactarius fumosus*, p. 237
29) Surfaces not staining pink .... *Lactarius imperceptus*, p. 240

30) Cap with zones of buff, orangish, and orange shades; stem with potholes .... *Lactarius psammicola*, p. 243
30) Cap not zoned, variously colored; stem without potholes 31

31) Gills distant; cap orange to brownish orange; milk copious .... *Lactarius hygrophoroides*, p. 239
31) Gills close; cap variously colored; milk copious or not 32

32) Milk staining gills and tissues brown (sometimes slowly); cap color varying......................... 33
32) Milk not staining gills and tissues brown; cap burnt orange to reddish brown or orangish tan.. 35

33) Cap drab cinnamon to drab lilac brown, bald; odor not distinctive .... *Lactarius argillaceifolius*, p. 232
33) Cap orange to brownish orange or brownish red, velvety; odor fishy or not distinctive 34

34) Cap brownish red, with a thin, felt-like covering when young, becoming corrugated with age .... *Lactarius corrugis*, p. 236
34) Cap orange to brownish orange, bald, not becoming corrugated .... *Lactarius volemus*, p. 250

35) Stem tough and pliant, with stiff orange to white hairs at the base.. .... *Lactarius subserifluus*, p. 247
35) Stem not as above 36

36) Cap 2–7 cm, becoming wrinkled with maturity; odor usually not distinctive .... *Lactarius areolatus*, p. 232
36) Cap 1–4 cm, not becoming wrinkled; odor usually reminiscent of maple syrup or curry (especially when old or when dried) .... *Lactarius camphoratus*, p. 233

G Key to *Russula*

1) Mushroom with a distinctive strong odor 2
1) Distinctive strong odor lacking 6

2) Odor shrimp-like or fish-like; iron salts on stem green .... *Russula xerampelina*, p. 351
2) Odor reminiscent of maraschino cherries, almonds, or benzaldehyde, sometimes with a foul component; iron salts on stem not green 3

3) Cap brownish orange to orangish brown; stem becoming yellow to yellow orange with age; KOH on cap surface deep red .... *Russula mutabilis*, p. 345
3) Cap yellowish; stem not becoming yellow orange; KOH on cap not red 4

4) Growing in sand (usually near pines) along the Great Lakes; stem red .... *Russula ventricosipes*, p. 349
4) Growing elsewhere; stem not red 5

5) Cap thin and fragile, with a strongly lined and pimply margin .... *Russula pectinatoides*, p. 345
5) Cap thick and firm, without a lined and pimply margin .... *Russula fragrantissima*, p. 343

6) Surfaces bruising red, then black (sometimes very slowly); cap whitish to grayish or brown .... *Russula densifolia*, p. 341
6) Surfaces not bruising red, then black; cap variously colored 7

7) Gills white, soft, and frequently forked; cap usually mottled purple and green (but sometimes almost completely one or the other color) .... *Russula variata*, p. 349
7) Gills not as above; cap variously colored 8

8) Cap some shade of green 9
8) Cap differently colored 10

9) Cap surface breaking up into mosaic-like patches .... *Russula virescens*, p. 351
9) Cap surface not breaking up into patches .... *Russula aeruginea*, p. 338

10) Cap purple to purplish red; when young with a whitish dusting; stem flushed with purple or pink .... *Russula mariae*, p. 344
10) Without the above combination of features 11

11) Young cap with a layer of yellow, powdery granules; cap brownish to straw-colored .... *Russula pulverulenta*, p. 347
11) Young cap without powdery granules; cap variously colored 12

12) Gills and stem bruising slowly but conspicuously reddish brown; cap nearly white when young, becoming reddish brown with age .... *Russula compacta*, p. 340
12) Gills and stem not bruising conspicuously; cap variously colored 13

13) Cap some shade of yellow or brown 14
13) Cap some shade of red........ 18

14) Cap surface breaking up into mosaic-like patches........ 15
14) Cap surface not breaking up into patches........ 16

15) Patches relatively small; stem colored like the cap .... *Russula ballouii*, p. 339
15) Patches larger; stem white........ *Russula crustosa*, p. 341

16) Cap fairly thin and fragile, with a strongly lined and pimply margin .... *Russula pectinatoides*, p. 345
16) Cap thick and firm, with an unlined or merely faintly lined margin 17

17) Gills relatively thick and distantly spaced; cap with a waxy feel........ *Russula earlei*, p. 342
17) Gills narrow and close or crowded; cap not waxy........ *Russula ballouii*, p. 339

18) Associated with conifers; appearing in fall .... *Russula cessans*, p. 340
18) Associated with hardwoods; appearing in spring, summer, or fall........ 19

19) Flesh extremely fragile and brittle (cap and stem very soon falling apart); stem pink to red; taste strongly acrid (sometimes slowly) .... *Russula tenuiceps*, p. 347
19) Flesh not especially fragile and brittle; stem white or flushed pink; taste mild or somewhat bitter but not strongly acrid........ 20

20) Mature cap thin, usually <5 cm across; stem flushed with pink........ *Russula uncialis*, p. 348
20) Mature cap more substantial, usually >5 cm across; stem white or flushed with pink........ 21

21) Appearing in spring; taste mild; stem discoloring gray with age........ *Russula vinacea*, p. 350
21) Appearing in summer and fall; taste mild or bitter; stem not discoloring gray........ 22

22) Gills and stem turning dirty yellow when dried; cap often somewhat mottled; stem white; taste bitter to unpleasant .... *Russula flavisicans*, p. 343
22) Gills and stem not drying yellow; cap not usually mottled; stem often flushed pink; taste mild .... *Russula pulchra*, p. 346

H Key to Dark-Spored Gilled Mushrooms, First Part

1) Growing on the dung of horses or cows; spore print black; cap margin with small, tooth-like fringes .... *Panaeolus papilionaceus*, p. 294
1) Not normally growing on dung; spore print and cap varying........ 2

2) Growing in grass in lawns, meadows, etc. 3
2) Not normally growing in grass........ 18

3) Gills deliquescing (turning into black "ink"); cap at first egg-shaped, whitish, and scaly .... *Coprinus comatus*, p. 151
3) Gills not deliquescing; cap varying 4

4) Spore print green; mature gills dirty green; cap 10–40 cm across, with whitish to brownish scales .... *Chlorophyllum molybdites*, p. 135
4) Spore print differently colored; cap varying 5

5) Spore print cinnamon or pale to medium brown (not much darker than milk chocolate)....... 6
5) Spore print dark brown (like dark chocolate) to dark purple brown, dark purplish gray, or black 13

6) Cap conical, whitish, 1–3 cm across; stem 1–3 mm thick, fragile; spore print cinnamon .... *Conocybe apala*, p. 147
6) Not completely as above.. 7

7) Mushroom fragile; cap at first sticky and yellow to greenish yellow, fading to tan and becoming lined; stem to 2 mm thick; spore print cinnamon.. *Bolbitius titubans*, p. 108
7) Not completely as above.. 8

8) Margin of fresh cap turning yellow when rubbed; cap 6–20 cm across.. 9
8) Margin of fresh cap not bruising yellow; cap size varying.. 10

9) Flesh in stem base bright yellow; odor unpleasant and phenolic (crush the stem base) .... *Agaricus xanthodermus*, p. 84
9) Flesh in stem base not yellow; odor sweet (like almonds or anise) .... *Agaricus arvensis*, p. 81

10) Cap bald, 1–4 cm across, golden yellow to brownish; KOH on cap reddish .... *Agrocybe pediades*, p. 85
10) Not completely as above.. 11

11) Gills white before turning brown when spores mature; the length of the stem usually at least twice the width of the cap .... *Agrocybe molesta*, p. 85
11) Gills pink before turning brown; the length of the stem usually about equal to the width of the cap 12

12) Cap dull brown, covered with conspicuous appressed brown scales.. .... *Agaricus porphyrocephalus*, p. 83
12) Cap whitish, bald to silky or very finely scaly.. *Agaricus campestris*, p. 81

13) Cap densely hairy (at least when young), 3–12 cm across, yellow brown to orangish brown; gill faces developing a mottled appearance.. *Lacrymaria velutina*, p. 230
13) Cap not hairy, color and size varying; gills becoming mottled or not.. 14

14) Cap becoming conspicuously pleated, small (1–5 cm across); stem 1–3 mm thick.................. 15
14) Cap not becoming pleated, variously sized; stem varying.. 16

15) Cap orangish brown when young, becoming grayish with an orangish brown center; spores ellipsoid; pileipellis with setae.. *Parasola auricoma*, p. 297
15) Cap yellowish brown when young, becoming grayish with a yellowish brown center; spores angular-ovoid; pileipellis without setae .... *Parasola plicatilis*, p. 298

16) Cap 1–3 cm across, often bell-shaped, initially dark brown but fading markedly to tan or buff; stem 1–2 mm thick... *Panaeolus foenisecii*, p. 293
16) Cap usually larger than above, variously shaped, honey yellow to whitish or grayish; stem 3–8 mm thick 17

17) Cap convex to broadly convex; stem not snapping easily; ring fairly persistent, with a grooved upper edge; gills purplish gray to purplish black .... *Stropharia coronilla*, p. 362
17) Cap often (but not always) with a bell-shaped or nearly conical center; stem snapping easily; ring usually disappearing, flimsy; gills grayish to dark brown, without purple shades .... *Psathyrella candolleana*, p. 327

18) Growing on wood or on woodchips, or growing near the bases of stumps or dead trees......... 19
18) Growing terrestrially, not associated with deadwood.. .... Key I, Dark-Spored Gilled Mushrooms, Second Part, p. 52

19) Stem absent or lateral and rudimentary 20
19) Stem well developed and more or less central 21

20) Gills pale orange before the spores mature; cap covered with fine brown hairs or scales .... *Crepidotus crocophyllus*, p. 164
20) Gills whitish before the spores mature; cap essentially bald........... *Crepidotus applanatus*, p. 164

21) Cap and stem brown and velvety; gills running down the stem; cap 4–15 cm across; on wood of conifers... *Tapinella atrotomentosa*, p. 369
21) Not completely as above.. 22

22) Spore print pale brown, cinnamon brown to rusty brown, orange brown, or brown (about the color of milk chocolate)... 23
22) Spore print darker than above, dark brown (about the color of dark chocolate) to purple brown, purplish gray, purple black, or black 39

23) Growing in woodchips in urban settings 24
23) Growing in woods.. 26

24) Odor usually mealy; cap 3–12 cm across, yellowish brown; whitish ring often (but not always) present ....*Agrocybe praecox*, p. 86
24) Odor not distinctive; cap 2–5 cm across, variously colored; ring absent................................25

25) Cap purple, fading to lilac gray .... *Bolbitius reticulatus*, p. 107
25) Cap dull yellow to greenish yellow, fading to grayish or tan .... *Bolbitius titubans*, p. 108

26) Cap sticky when fresh, variously colored and often mottled, but usually with purple and/or olive shades present, adorned with scales that often disappear except along the margin; stem scaly to hairy; KOH greenish yellow on cap .... *Pholiota polychroa*, p. 309
26) Not completely as above 27

27) Cap with small to large scales 28
27) Cap bald or finely silky, perhaps with a few fibrils or veil remnants near the margin when young, but not scaly 32

28) Cap surface yellow and sticky under the scales; cap 3–13 cm across ... *Pholiota limonella*, p. 308
28) Cap surface not yellow, sticky or not; cap size varying 29

29) Cap small (usually <4 cm across), dark brown to rusty brown, granular-scaly; stem also granular-scaly .... *Flammulaster erinaceellus*, p. 176
29) Not completely as above 30

30) On wood of conifers; cap only finely scaly, dark yellowish to tawny or reddish brown .... *Gymnopilus sapineus*, p. 188
30) On wood of hardwoods; cap conspicuously scaly, whitish to pale yellowish under tawny scales 31

31) Taste bitter; spore print rusty brown to orange brown; KOH red on cap surface, black on pigmented scales .... *Gymnopilus fulvosquamulosus*, p. 186
31) Taste not distinctive; spore print cinnamon brown; KOH negative on cap and scales .... *Pholiota squarrosoides*, p. 310

32) Stem with a ring or ring zone 33
32) Stem without a ring or ring zone 36

33) Stem conspicuously scaly; cap tawny to orangish brown, fading markedly to yellowish .... *Pholiota mutabilis*, p. 308
33) Stem bald or finely hairy but not scaly; cap varying 34

34) Usually found in late spring and early summer; cap tan, fading to buff; ring flaring upward before collapsing, developing a rusty brown edge; KOH negative on cap .... *Pholiota veris*, p. 311
34) Found in spring, summer, or fall; cap color varying; ring not as above; KOH red on cap 35

35) Cap 5–10 cm across, yellow to orange yellow; stem yellow, 5–15 mm thick; found in summer and fall .... *Gymnopilus luteus*, p. 187
35) Cap 1–4 cm across, brown to tawny brown; stem whitish, 3–6 mm thick; usually found in early

spring and late fall, but sometimes appearing between late spring and early fall .... *Galerina marginata*, p. 178

36) Cap <5 cm across, purple at first, fading to lilac gray .... *Bolbitius reticulatus*, p. 107
36) Not completely as above 37

37) Cap 1–2.5 cm across, olive to olive brown; cap margin lined; stem with fine white flakes near the apex .... *Simocybe centunculus*, p. 357
37) Cap 2–8 cm across, orange to orange brown or yellow brown; cap margin not lined; stem lacking fine white flakes near apex 38

38) On wood of conifers; when young with an ephemeral, cortina-like partial veil .... *Gymnopilus sapineus*, p. 188
38) On wood of hardwoods or conifers; veil absent .... *Gymnopilus liquiritiae*, p. 186

39) Growing in woodchips in urban settings; cap 1–6 cm across, at first brownish orange, becoming grayish and conspicuously pleated, with a brownish orange center; mature gills black .... *Parasola auricoma*, p. 297
39) Not completely as above 40

40) Growing in dense clusters (often by the hundreds), usually near the bases of stumps; cap <2 cm across, whitish to grayish, becoming grooved .... *Coprinellus disseminatus*, p. 147
40) Not completely as above 41

41) Gills completely or partially deliquescing (collapsing and turning to black "ink") with maturity 42
41) Gills not normally deliquescing 46

42) Mushroom usually arising from a fuzzy mat of orange mycelium; young cap orangish to yellowish, with fine scales .... *Coprinellus domesticus*, p. 148
42) Fuzzy mat of orange mycelium absent; cap varying 43

43) Cap egg-shaped when young, expanding to bell-shaped, with large and conspicuous whitish to tan scales; usually growing from wood above the ground .... *Coprinopsis variegata*, p. 150
43) Cap not as above; usually growing from wood on the ground or near the bases of stumps 44

44) Young cap densely hairy and gray; mature cap 1–4 cm across, bell-shaped to flat, finely hairy or bald; spores 10–14 µm long, ellipsoid .... *Coprinopsis lagopus*, p. 149
44) Young cap bald, silky, or covered with fine granules, color varying; mature cap 3–8 cm across, shape varying; spores <11 µm long 45

45) Young cap covered with fine granules, orangish brown to honey brown .... *Coprinellus micaceus*, p. 148
45) Young cap bald, silky, or finely scaly over the center but without fine granules, gray .... *Coprinopsis atramentaria*, p. 149

46) Cap conspicuously wrinkled and corrugated, reddish brown, 3–10 cm across .... *Psathyrella delineata*, p. 327
46) Cap not corrugated, color and size varying 47

47) Cap sticky when fresh, variously colored and often mottled, but usually with purple and/or olive shades present, adorned with scales that often disappear except along the margin; stem scaly to hairy; KOH greenish yellow on cap .... *Pholiota polychroa*, p. 309
47) Not completely as above 48

48) Usually growing in dense clusters, directly from wood (which may be buried) 49
48) Usually growing scattered to gregariously from woody debris on the ground (including woodchips in urban settings) 51

49) Taste bitter; cap yellow to greenish yellow or sometimes orange; young gills yellow; on wood of conifers .... *Hypholoma fasciculare*, p. 217
49) Taste mild or very slightly bitter; cap color varying; young gills whitish to grayish; on wood of hardwoods or conifers 50

50) On wood of conifers; cap yellow brown to orangish brown or cinnamon .... *Hypholoma capnoides*, p. 217
50) On wood of hardwoods; cap brick red .... *Hypholoma sublateritium*, p. 218

51) Mature stem 2–8 mm thick 52
51) Mature stem 10–30 mm thick 55

52) Cap purple to purplish red, fading markedly to purplish, pinkish, or reddish brown .... *Psathyrella bipellis*, p. 326
52) Cap differently colored 53

53) Young cap honey yellow, fading to pale brownish or whitish; mature cap 3–10 cm across, with a splitting margin; many mushrooms usually present .... *Psathyrella candolleana*, p. 327
53) Young cap yellowish brown to brown, fading to buff or remaining brown; mature cap <5 cm across; margin not often splitting; one to several mushrooms usually present 54

54) Found in spring; stem 3–10 cm long; cap remaining brown; spores <10 µm long; pileipellis without setae .... *Psathyrella pseudovernalis*, p. 328
54) Found in spring or fall; stem 6–19 cm long; cap fading to buff; spores 14–19 µm long; pileipellis with setae .... *Parasola conopilus*, p. 297

55) Cap wine red to reddish brown—or white; growing in woodchips (rarely in woods) .... *Stropharia rugosoannulata*, p. 364
55) Cap yellow to brownish yellow; growing in woods (occasionally in woodchips) 56

56) Cap bald or with tiny, inconspicuous scales; widely distributed .... *Stropharia hardii*, p. 363
56) Cap with conspicuous, innate, hairy scales; northern Midwest .... *Stropharia kauffmanii*, p. 363

Key to Dark-Spored Gilled Mushrooms, Second Part

1) Gills running down, or beginning to run down, the stem 2
1) Gills not running down the stem 4

2) Gills separable as a layer (see p. 299), bruising brown to reddish brown........ *Paxillus involutus*, p. 299
2) Gills neither separable as a layer nor bruising brown to reddish brown 3

3) Under conifers; cap purplish red to reddish brown; spore print dark gray to black; gills running well down the stem........ *Chroogomphus ochraceus*, p. 136
3) Under hardwoods or conifers; cap brown; spore print brown; gills beginning to run down the stem .... *Agrocybe erebia*, p. 84

4) Spore print cinnamon, rusty brown, or pale to medium brown (not darker than milk chocolate) 5
4) Spore print darker than above, dark brown (like dark chocolate) to dark purple brown, dark purplish gray, or black 39

5) Mushroom small (cap 1–5 cm); cap and stem brown to reddish brown; without veils; odor strong, reminiscent of cucumbers or fish; spore print brownish yellow to yellowish brown; cap, stem, and gills covered with prominent cystidia .... *Macrocystidia cucumis*, p. 267
5) Not completely as above 6

6) Gills free from the stem; flesh in base of stem bright yellow and/or surfaces bruising yellow when rubbed repeatedly........ 7
6) Gills attached to the stem; flesh in stem base not bright yellow; surfaces not bruising yellow........ 9

7) Mature cap white .... *Agaricus sylvicola*, p. 83
7) Mature cap brownish, at least over the center 8

8) Stem terminating in a small, abrupt bulb; common below the Great Lakes .... *Agaricus pocillator*, p. 82
8) Stem without a bulb; common from the Great Lakes northward .... *Agaricus placomyces*, p. 82

9) Stem with a persistent, membranous ring; cap convex to flat, 5–15 cm across, dull yellowish to tan, when young with a whitish dusting .... *Cortinarius caperatus*, p. 153
9) Stem without a ring or with a ring zone; cap varying........ 10

10) Cap and stem both orange; under hardwoods; KOH on cap purple to black........ *Cortinarius hesleri*, p. 156
10) Cap not orange; stem orange or not; habitat and KOH reaction varying 11

11) Stem orange, at least over the bottom half; cap purplish, fading quickly to brownish............... .... *Cortinarius rubripes*, p. 159
11) Stem not orange; cap varying 12

12) Cap purple 13
12) Cap not purple (but young cap may be purplish brown) 15

13) Cap 4–12 cm across, densely hairy to scaly; stem at first purple, becoming gray to brownish with age.. *Cortinarius violaceus*, p. 161
13) Cap <5 cm across, bald or finely silky; stem not as above...14

14) Fresh cap and stem dry; cap margin often splitting with age; mature gills dull grayish brown to brown.. *Inocybe lilacina*, p. 223
14) Fresh cap and stem sticky to slimy; cap margin not splitting; mature gills rusty brown .... *Cortinarius iodeoides*, p. 157

15) Cap basically white (but may discolor slightly brownish to yellowish with age) 16
15) Cap more highly colored 18

16) Odor spermatic (crush the flesh); cap initially conic, 1–4 cm across at maturity; cap margin often splitting; spores ellipsoid and smooth .... *Inocybe geophylla*, p. 222
16) Odor spermatic, radish-like, or not distinctive; cap initially conic or convex, larger than above at maturity, with or without a splitting margin; spores not ellipsoid and smooth 17

17) Cap convex to broadly bell-shaped; odor radish-like; spores almond-shaped and verrucose ....*Hebeloma albidulum*, p. 198
17) Cap broadly conic to bell-shaped; odor spermatic; spores nodulose .... *Inocybe fibrosa*, p. 221

18) Young gills dark red; cap yellow brown to cinnamon; KOH on cap purple to black................. ....*Cortinarius semisanguineus*, p. 159
18) Young gills not dark red; cap color and KOH reaction varying 19

19) Cap conspicuously scaly and/or cap conic to bell-shaped (at least when young), with margin splitting at maturity.. 20
19) Cap neither conspicuously scaly nor conic with a splitting mature margin 24

20) Cap *and* stem scaly; scales brownish red; spore print and mature gills rusty brown .... *Cortinarius bolaris*, p. 152
20) Stem bald or silky but not scaly; cap scales if present brown; spore print brown; mature gills brown to brownish 21

21) Cap straw yellow to yellowish or pale yellowish brown, silky; spores ellipsoid and smooth ....*Inocybe rimosa*, p. 224
21) Cap brown to dark brown or purplish brown, scaly or silky; spores varying.......................... 22

22) Cap 3–8 cm across, purplish brown to reddish brown; stem pinkish to purplish, at least over the bottom half; spores ellipsoid and smooth.. *Inocybe adaequata*, p. 220
22) Cap 1.5–4 cm across, brown to dark brown; stem without pink or purple shades; spores varying.. 23

23) Under hardwoods; KOH on cap negative to pinkish; spores globose and spiny ....*Inocybe calospora*, p. 221
23) Under conifers and hardwoods; KOH on cap gray; spores long-ellipsoid to cylindric, smooth.. ....*Inocybe lacera*, p. 222

24) Gills broadly attached to the stem; stem often (but not always) with a fragile ring; odor mealy; cap dry, whitish to yellow brown or brownish; stem base often attached to white rhizomorphs; spore print and mature gills brown ....*Agrocybe praecox*, p. 86
24) Gills usually attached by means of a notch; stem without a ring or with a ring zone; odor varying but not mealy; cap dry or sticky, variously colored; stem base not attached to rhizomorphs; spore print and mature gills brown or rusty brown 25

25) Stem encircled by 2–4 bright orange bands; under paper birch...... *Cortinarius armillatus*, p. 152
25) Stem not as above; under various trees.. 26

26) Gills distant; cap orangish brown, fading markedly to tan, often bell-shaped to conical; stem often with a whitish ring zone; under hardwoods .... *Cortinarius distans*, p. 155
26) Gills close or crowded; cap, stem, and habitat varying 27

27) Gills yellow before the spores mature.. 28
27) Gills not yellow 29

28) Under conifers; stem up to 1 cm thick; fresh cap dry; stem base not enlarged .... *Cortinarius croceus*, p. 155
28) Under hardwoods; stem 1–3 cm thick; fresh cap sticky; stem base usually with a rimmed bulb. ....*Cortinarius olearioides*, p. 158

29) Mature cap distinctively wrinkled and corrugated, dry, orange brown to yellowish brown; odor not distinctive; under hardwoods ....*Cortinarius corrugatus*, p. 154
29) Mature cap not corrugated, dry or sticky, variously colored; odor and habitat varying.......... 30

30) Young gills purple to lilac 31
30) Young gills not purple to lilac 33

31) Stem sheathed from the base with whitish to lilac veil material; odor strong, sweet, and unpleasant; cap dry .... *Cortinarius torvus*, p. 160
31) Stem not sheathed with veil material; odor not distinctive; cap slimy or dry........................ 32

32) Fresh cap and stem slimy; cap bald, tawny brown to yellow brown from the beginning........... ....*Cortinarius collinitus*, p. 153

32) Cap and stem dry; cap hairy to scaly, deep purple at first, maturing to brown .... *Cortinarius violaceus*, p. 161

33) Taste (do not swallow! see p. 12) bitter; cap sticky to slimy when fresh 34
33) Taste radish-like or not distinctive; cap sticky or dry...35

34) Cap yellow to orange yellow; young gills whitish; stem slimy .... *Cortinarius vibratilis*, p. 160
34) Cap grayish olive to olive brown; young gills olive to grayish; stem dry .... *Cortinarius infractus*, p. 156

35) Under conifers; cap and stem slimy when fresh; cap brownish orange, fading to yellowish; odor not distinctive; spore print rusty brown .... *Cortinarius mucosus*, p. 158
35) Under conifers or hardwoods; stem not slimy; cap dry or sticky; cap color varying; odor radish-like or not distinctive; spore print brown 36

36) Growing in clusters; cap and stem covered with small scales; odor not distinctive; stem usually featuring a ring zone.. *Pholiota terrestris*, p. 311
36) Growing scattered to gregariously; cap without scales; stem, if scaly, with large scales; odor usually radish-like; stem with or without a ring zone.. 37

37) Stem 1–3 cm thick, developing more or less concentric bands of white scales that capture spores and become brownish.. *Hebeloma sinapizans*, p. 200
37) Stem 0.5–1.5 cm thick, without bands of scales 38

38) Cortina-like veil absent; cap dirty buff to pale tan; gills when young with droplets of liquid, when mature often with brown spots; under conifers or hardwoods.. *Hebeloma crustuliniforme*, p. 199
38) Cortina-like veil present when young; cap brown to pinkish brown, often 2-toned with a darker center and paler margin; gills not as above; under conifers.. *Hebeloma mesophaeum*, p. 199

39) Cap sticky, reddish orange to brick red or orange, adorned with scattered whitish scales; stem 6–12 cm long and about 1 cm thick, shaggy with white scales below a thin ring....................... *Leratiomyces squamosus* var. *thraustus*, p. 259
39) Cap not sticky, variously colored, bald or scaly; stem variable in size but never shaggy with white scales 40

40) Mature stem 2–8 mm thick...41
40) Mature stem 10–30 mm thick 44

41) Cap purple to purplish red, fading markedly to purplish, pinkish, or reddish brown .... *Psathyrella bipellis*, p. 326
41) Cap differently colored.. 42

42) Young cap honey yellow, fading to pale brownish or whitish; mature cap 3–11 cm across, with a splitting margin; many mushrooms usually present .... *Psathyrella candolleana*, p. 327
42) Young cap yellowish brown to brown, fading to buff or remaining brown; mature cap <5 cm across; margin not often splitting; one to several mushrooms usually present........................ 43

43) Found in spring; stem 3–10 cm long; cap remaining brown; spores <10 µm long; pileipellis without setae .... *Psathyrella pseudovernalis*, p. 328
43) Found in spring or fall; stem 6–19 cm long; cap fading to buff; spores 14–19 µm long; pileipellis with setae .... *Parasola conopilus*, p. 297

44) Cap wine red to reddish brown or white; growing in disturbed ground in urban settings (rarely in woods) .... *Stropharia rugosoannulata*, p. 364
44) Cap yellow to brownish yellow; growing in woods (occasionally in urban settings)................45

45) Cap bald or with tiny, inconspicuous scales; widely distributed .... *Stropharia hardii*, p. 363
45) Cap with conspicuous, innate, hairy scales; northern Midwest .... *Stropharia kauffmanii*, p. 363

J Key to Terrestrial Pored Mushrooms

1) Mushroom a gnarled lumpy mass covered with a whitish pore surface that exudes reddish juice and bruises reddish brown; often engulfing blades of grass and sticks .... *Abortiporus biennis*, p. 80
1) Mushroom not as above 2

2) Flesh tough, often leathery, not readily decaying; pore surface running down the stem; tube layer not easily separable from cap 3
2) Flesh fairly soft, readily decaying; pore surface not running down the stem; tube layer usually separable from cap (with one exception).. 6

3) Blue or green colors present somewhere on mushroom; mushroom sometimes with one to several caps arising from the stem 4
3) Blue or green colors absent; mushroom always with a single cap... 5

4) Mushroom blue when young, becoming brownish with maturity; under hemlock and other conifers.. *Albatrellus caeruleoporus*, p. 87
4) Cap yellow brown, pore surface white; green tints and bruising developing on surfaces with maturity; under hardwoods .... *Albatrellus cristatus*, p. 87

5) Cap 1–3.5 cm across, cinnamon brown to rusty brown, zoned, shiny and silky; stem without a taproot .... *Coltricia cinnamomea*, p. 145
5) Cap 3.5–25 cm across, brown, not zoned, dull; stem with a long, underground taproot.......... .... *Polyporus radicatus*, p. 323

6) Growing under ash trees; stem often eccentric (off-center or somewhat lateral); pores elongated radially; cap dull and brown; veil absent; tube layer not easily separated from cap .... *Gyrodon merulioides*, p. 191
6) Not completely as above 7

7) Spore print blackish; cap woolly and scaly, gray to black; flesh staining slowly red, then black; spores partially to completely reticulate .... *Strobilomyces floccopus*, p. 361
7) Spore print differently colored; cap and flesh varying; spores not reticulate............................. 8

8) Spore print yellow; stem becoming brittle and hollow, at least toward the base, by maturity... 9
8) Spore print not yellow, or if yellow, then stem not becoming brittle and hollow 11

9) Surfaces and flesh bruising blue; cap straw yellow .... *Gyroporus cyanescens*, p. 196
9) Neither flesh nor surfaces bruising blue; cap differently colored..10

10) Cap and stem orangish brown to chestnut color .... *Gyroporus castaneus*, p. 196
10) Cap and stem purplish red ....*Gyroporus purpurinus*, p. 197

11) Partial veil present 12
11) Partial veil absent...19

12) Veil, stem, and pores sulphur yellow; cap reddish; flesh bluing when sliced; under conifers ....*Pulveroboletus ravenelii*, p. 330
12) Not completely as above 13

13) Veil detaching near the base of the stem to form a large, collapsing ring; pore surface bruising brown; under white oaks from the Great Lakes to Kansas; spores globose................................ .... *Paragyrodon sphaerosporus*, p. 296
13) Veil not as above; pore surface not bruising, or bruising faintly; under conifers, variously distributed; spores not globose 14

14) Cap surface dry and prominently scaly to hairy; ring present..15
14) Cap surface sticky to slimy, bald or very finely hairy to finely scaly; ring present or not 16

15) Under tamarack; cap brown; stem becoming hollow in the base............. *Suillus cavipes*, p. 365
15) Under white pine; cap pinkish red to brick red; stem solid .... *Suillus pictus*, p. 368

16) Under white pine; cap and stem mustard yellow, developing reddish to reddish-brown stains; ring usually absent...*Suillus americanus*, p. 364
16) Under various conifers (including white pine); cap and stem variously colored but not developing reddish to reddish-brown stains; ring present...17

17) Cap reddish brown to dark brown; ring when fresh with purple shades; glandular dots present only above the ring...*Suillus luteus*, p. 367
17) Cap orange brown to yellowish brown; ring without purple shades; glandular dots covering entire stem 18

18) Ring thick and baggy; cap orange brown to brown .... *Suillus salmonicolor*, p. 369
18) Ring thin, bracelet-like and somewhat gelatinous; cap yellowish to yellowish brown .... *Suillus intermedius*, p. 366

19) Stem deeply lacerate-reticulate 20
19) Stem reticulate or not, but not deeply lacerate-reticulate 21

20) Cap dry, becoming cracked, cinnamon brown to brown; spores ridged .... *Boletellus russellii*, p. 110
20) Cap sticky, yellow becoming orange brown with a yellow margin; spores pitted .... *Heimioporus betula*, p. 201

21) Stem surface with fine to coarse scabers (tiny tufts of aggregated fibrils); pore surface often (but not always) depressed around the stem at maturity; mature stem usually about twice as long as the width of the cap, or longer 22
21) Stem surface lacking scabers; pore surface rarely depressed around the stem at maturity; mature stem often proportionally shorter than above 30

22) Margin of cap projecting 2–6 mm, becoming torn into segments as the cap expands 23
22) Margin of cap projecting 1 mm or less, or not projecting 24

23) Under conifers; cap brick red; stem usually stained blue to green at the base .... *Leccinum vulpinum*, p. 255
23) Under aspens; cap red-orange; stem base not stained blue to green ...... *Leccinum insigne*, p. 253

24) Cap white or whitish 25
24) Cap more highly colored 26

25) Under paper birch; pileipellis a cutis .... *Leccinum holopus*, p. 253
25) Under oaks; pileipellis a trichoderm .... *Leccinellum albellum*, p. 252

26) Scabers pink; stem base becoming chrome yellow .... *Harrya chromapes*, p. 198
26) Scabers not pink; stem base not becoming chrome yellow 27

27) Sliced flesh staining (sometimes slowly) to reddish, then blackish; cap yellow to brown, often developing a wrinkled or pitted surface .... *Leccinum rugosiceps*, p. 254
27) Sliced flesh not staining, or staining blue; cap variously colored, developing a wrinkled or pitted surface or not 28

28) Pore surface bruising blue; flesh staining blue; often growing near or from well-decayed wood; spores ridged .... *Boletellus chrysenteroides*, p. 108
28) Pore surface not bruising blue; flesh not staining blue, or doing so very faintly; not usually associated with wood; spores smooth 29

29) Fresh cap sticky, orange to reddish orange or brownish orange; KOH cherry red on cap.......... .... *Boletus longicurvipes*, p. 118

29) Fresh cap dry, cinnamon brown to reddish brown or yellow brown; KOH negative to orangish on cap .... *Leccinum subglabripes*, p. 255

30) Spore print pinkish brown or chocolate brown; mature pore surface often with pinkish tints 31
30) Spore print differently colored; mature pore surface rarely with pinkish tints........ 38

31) Stem 0.5–1 cm thick; found primarily under hemlock; cap cinnamon brown; spores pitted .... *Austroboletus gracilis*, p. 106
31) Stem >1 cm thick at maturity; habitat varying; cap variously colored; spores not pitted 32

32) Cap dark brown when young; pore surface becoming brownish with age; flesh and cap margin often staining blue; taste mild........ *Tylopilus sordidus*, p. 385
32) Not completely as above........ 33

33) Cap black or dark gray; pore surface bruising reddish, then brown to black........ *Tylopilus alboater*, p. 382
33) Cap differently colored; pore surface not bruising, or bruising brown without a reddish stage........ 34

34) Cap bright to dull orange; pore surface bruising brown .... *Tylopilus ballouii*, p. 382
34) Cap differently colored; pore surface bruising or not 35

35) Associated primarily with conifers; stem prominently reticulate; taste bitter .... *Tylopilus felleus*, p. 383
35) Associated primarily with hardwoods; stem not reticulate, or finely so at apex; taste mild or bitter 36

36) Taste mild; pore surface bruising quickly brown .... *Tylopilus indecisus*, p. 383
36) Taste bitter; pore surface not bruising, or bruising only faintly 37

37) Cap *and* stem purple to lilac when young; stem not developing olive stains........ *Tylopilus plumbeoviolaceus*, p. 384
37) Cap purplish when young; stem never purple; stem developing olive stains .... *Tylopilus rubrobrunneus*, p. 385

38) Pore surface red, orange, dark brown, maroon, or dull reddish brown 39
38) Pore surface differently colored........ 43

39) Flesh not staining blue when sliced; taste bitter; pore surface dull reddish brown .... *Chalciporus piperatus*, p. 134
39) Flesh staining blue when sliced; taste not bitter; pore surface red, orange, dark brown, or maroon 40

40) Stem reticulate........ 41
40) Stem not reticulate 42

41) Cap bright red and sticky .... *Boletus frostii*, p. 116
41) Cap some shade of brown, dry .... *Boletus luridus*, p. 119

42) Pore surface dark brown to maroon when young, fading to dull reddish; flesh quickly becoming riddled with worm holes and channels; base of stem with whitish mycelium .... *Boletus vermiculosus*, p. 125
42) Pore surface red when young, fading to orange; flesh not becoming riddled as above; base of stem with copious white to yellow or red mycelium .... *Boletus subvelutipes*, p. 124

43) Stem distinctly reticulate, at least near apex 44
43) Stem not reticulate 53

44) Pore surface staining blue; stem reticulate only at apex; cap whitish to pale tan; stem becoming reddish .... *Boletus inedulis*, p. 117
44) Pore surface not staining blue; extent of reticulation varying; cap and stem varying 45

45) Stem yellow overall 46
45) Stem not yellow overall, but possibly developing yellow stains from the base upward 47

46) Stem prominently reticulate; cap yellow to brownish; KOH dark reddish brown on cap .... *Retiboletus ornatipes*, p. 335
46) Stem finely reticulate near the apex; cap brown; KOH negative to yellowish on cap .... *Boletus auripes*, p. 111

47) Cap gray; stem developing yellow stains from the base upward; reticulation usually coarse .... *Retiboletus griseus*, p. 334
47) Cap not gray; stem not normally developing yellow stains; reticulation fine or coarse 48

48) Associated with pines; stem long and slender, with blunt-edged ridges forming a partially reticulate pattern; cap margin often with a projecting sterile portion .... *Boletus projectellus*, p. 121
48) Associated with hardwoods; stem not usually long and slender, lacking blunt-edged ridges; cap margin usually lacking a sterile projection 49

49) Ammonia green, or flashing green, on cap 50
49) Ammonia not green on cap 51

50) Mature pore surface olive yellow; pores angular and large; stem tapering to base, whitish to brownish, with a wide-meshed reticulum over the upper half .... *Boletus illudens*, p. 117
50) Mature pore surface dull yellow; pores small and circular; stem not tapering to base, whitish flushed with liver red, with a fine reticulum .... *Xanthoconium separans*, p. 392

51) Ammonia purple on cap; cap often finely wrinkled .... *Boletus atkinsonii*, p. 110
51) Ammonia not purple on cap; cap wrinkled or not 52

52) Appearing in fall; cap brown to grayish brown, very finely velvety when young .... *Boletus variipes*, p. 124

52) Appearing in summer; cap pale brown, leathery ....*Boletus* cf. *reticulatus*, p. 122

53) Flesh staining blue when sliced, and/or pore surface staining blue 54
53) Flesh not staining blue; pore surface not staining blue 62

54) Cap, pore surface, and stem bright yellow when young, developing reddish and brownish discolorations .... *Boletus pseudosulphureus*, p. 122
54) Not completely as above 55

55) Blue staining faint 56
55) Blue staining well developed... 57

56) Cap pale tan to whitish .... *Boletus pallidus*, p. 120
56) Cap cinnamon brown to reddish brown or yellow brown ....*Leccinum subglabripes*, p. 255

57) Cap reddish brown; stem broadly wrinkled; primarily under hemlock and other conifers......... .... *Boletus badius*, p. 112
57) Not completely as above 58

58) Ammonia flashing blue on cap; tube layer shallow (5–8 mm deep at maturity) .... *Boletus pseudosensibilis*, p. 121
58) Ammonia not flashing blue on cap; tube layer shallow or not 59

59) Cap surface becoming cracked with age.. 60
59) Cap surface not becoming cracked with age 61

60) Cap brown to olive brown; exposed flesh in cracks pinkish to reddish; spores smooth .... *Boletus chrysenteron*, p. 114
60) Cap red to brownish red; exposed flesh in cracks whitish to pinkish; spores ridged.................. .... *Boletellus pseudochrysenteroides*, p. 109

61) Cap 2–4 cm across; tube layer not proportionally shallow .... *Boletus campestris*, p. 114
61) Cap 5–15 cm (or more) across; tuber layer proportionally shallow .... *Boletus bicolor*, p. 113

62) Growing from the earthball *Scleroderma citrinum* (p. 355) .... *Boletus parasiticus*, p. 120
62) Not growing from *Scleroderma citrinum* 63

63) Ammonia green, or flashing green, on cap 64
63) Ammonia not green on cap 67

64) Cap becoming conspicuously corrugated-wrinkled............................... *Boletus hortonii*, p. 116
64) Cap not normally becoming corrugated-wrinkled 65

65) Often growing in small fused clusters; young pore surface bright yellow; pores round; stem usually bulbous, with a small root .... *Boletus innixus*, p. 118
65) Not as above.. 66

66) Pore surface whitish becoming dull yellow to yellowish brown; pores round; stem not notably slender; cap maroon to purplish brown, fading to brown .... *Xanthoconium purpureum*, p. 391
66) Pore surface dull yellow becoming olive; pores angular; stem slender; cap yellowish brown to reddish brown .... *Boletus spadiceus* var. *gracilis*, p. 123

67) Cap pale tan to whitish; pore surface whitish to yellowish, becoming olive .... *Boletus pallidus*, p. 120
67) Cap more highly colored than above; pore surface varying 68

68) Cap slimy to sticky when fresh 69
68) Cap dry to moist when fresh 71

69) Cap yellow, with a conspicuous sterile margin .... *Boletus curtisii*, p. 112
69) Cap not yellow, without a sterile margin 70

70) Young pore surface brown .... *Suillus punctipes*, p. 368
70) Young pore surface whitish to yellowish .... *Suillus granulatus*, p. 366

71) Stem sticky when fresh; pore surface very bright yellow .... *Boletus auriporus*, p. 112
71) Stem dry; pore surface dull yellow to greenish yellow .... *Leccinum subglabripes*, p. 255

K Key to Pored Mushrooms on Wood

1) Mushroom with a distinct stem structure that is centrally or laterally attached 2
1) Mushroom lacking a stem 10

2) Mushroom with many small, round caps arising from a central stem structure .... *Polyporus umbellatus*, p. 324
2) Mushroom with a single cap 3

3) Cap and stem with a varnished appearance 4
3) Cap and stem not varnished 5

4) On wood of hardwoods .... *Ganoderma lucidum*, p. 180
4) On wood of conifers .... *Ganoderma tsugae*, p. 181

5) Pores small (4–8 per mm) 6
5) Pores larger (1–3 per mm) 8

6) Stem tan and velvety; cap whitish to pale brown, velvety .... *Abortiporus biennis*, p. 80
6) Stem black (at least over the lower portion), velvety or not; cap varying 7

7) Cap white to tan or cream .... *Polyporus varius*, p. 324
7) Cap reddish brown to blackish brown .... *Polyporus badius*, p. 322

8) Stem small and laterally attached; cap 1–10 cm across, with reddish-orange scales; pores diamond-shaped to hexagonal .... *Polyporus alveolaris*, p. 321
8) Stem more substantial than above, central or lateral; cap and pores varying 9

9) Cap 1–8 cm across, finely scaly or nearly bald, fringed along the margin with tiny hairs (use a hand lens), round in outline; odorless .... *Polyporus arcularius*, p. 322
9) Cap 5–30 cm across, coarsely scaly, not fringed along the margin, rarely round in outline; odor mealy .... *Polyporus squamosus*, p. 323

10) Mushroom with multiple caps arising from a large, branched framework, or arising in rosettes, or forming shelf-like clusters 11
10) Mushroom with individual caps, not arising from a branched network, nor arising in rosettes; if appearing to form shelf-like clusters, then caps discrete and easily separated from one another 16

11) Mushroom with many caps arising from a large, branched network 12
11) Mushroom with many caps arising in rosettes, or forming shelf-like clusters 13

12) Individual caps 5–20 cm across; pore surface bruising brown to black .... *Meripilus sumstinei*, p. 276
12) Individual caps 2–7 cm across; pore surface not bruising brown to black .... *Grifola frondosa*, p. 185

13) Cap bright yellow to orange overall 14
13) Cap whitish to yellowish or brown overall, though margin and pore surface may be bright yellow or orange 15

14) Pore surface white; growing at the bases of trees .... *Laetiporus cincinnatus*, p. 251
14) Pore surface yellow; growing from wood above ground .... *Laetiporus sulphureus*, p. 252

15) On wood of hardwoods; caps whitish to yellowish; pore surface white, not bruising; KOH yellowish on flesh .... *Bondarzewia berkeleyi*, p. 126
15) On wood of conifers; caps dark brown to reddish brown; pore surface at first bright yellow or orange, later greenish brown, bruising brown; KOH on flesh black .... *Phaeolus schweinitzii*, p. 302

16) Cap 1–10 cm across, scaly and orange; pores diamond-shaped to hexagonal .... *Polyporus alveolaris*, p. 321
16) Cap variously sized, scaly or not, not orange, or if orange, then not scaly, and pores not diamond-shaped to hexagonal; pores varying 17

17) Pores slot-like, radially elongated, maze-like, or nearly gill-like 18
17) Pores round or angular but not as above 21

18) Cap thin, hairy to velvety, often green from algae; flesh with a distinctive black line just beneath the cap surface; pores whitish becoming gray .... *Cerrena unicolor*, p. 134

18) Cap thin or thick, bald to finely hairy, rarely green from algae; flesh lacking a black line; pores varying in color but not becoming gray 19

19) Cap whitish; KOH yellow on flesh; pore surface not bruising........ *Trametes elegans*, p. 370
19) Cap more highly colored, or if whitish, then pore surface bruising; KOH black on flesh; pore surface bruising or not 20

20) Cap faintly to prominently zoned; pores with thin walls; pore surface bruising reddish to red... .... *Daedaleopsis confragosa*, p. 168
20) Cap not zoned; pores with thick walls; pore surface not bruising........ .... *Daedalea quercina*, p. 168

21) Tubes individually discrete (separate along their length; see p. 176); mushroom soft and fleshy; cap red to liver-colored; pore surface bruising reddish brown........ *Fistulina hepatica*, p. 176
21) Tubes fused along their length; mushroom soft or not; cap and pore surface varying 22

22) Tube layer easily separable as a layer when fresh........ 23
22) Tube layer not separable as a layer 24

23) Pore surface reddish brown to orange brown, rubbery; cap margin not forming a rim around the pore surface; cap when present up to 6 cm across, but often fused with other caps; on various hardwoods........ *Gloeoporus dichrous*, p. 184
23) Pore surface white, not rubbery; cap margin forming a wide rim around the pore surface; cap 5–25 cm across, not fused with other caps; on paper birch .... *Piptoporus betulinus*, p. 313

24) Mushroom with violet to purple colors on pore surface and margin when fresh; pores often breaking apart with age and becoming tooth-like .... *Trichaptum biforme*, p. 375
24) Mushroom without violet to purple colors; pores not becoming tooth-like, or if tooth-like, then cap gray and fuzzy 25

25) Flesh whitish, soft, and watery when fresh; odor fragrant; cap whitish to brownish .... *Tyromyces chioneus*, p. 386
25) Flesh variously colored, but not soft and watery; odor and cap varying........ 26

26) Fresh cap margin yellow; cap <15 cm across, lumpy and brown to reddish brown; flesh bright yellow brown to bright orange brown; KOH black on flesh........ *Phellinus gilvus*, p. 305
26) Not completely as above........ 27

27) Mushroom annual, with a single tube layer; flesh often leathery to corky but not usually woody 28
27) Mushroom perennial, with multiple tube layers (one produced each year); flesh woody 36

28) Cap densely hairy to fuzzy, with zones of gray and brown; pores 1–3 per mm, becoming tooth-like with age .... *Trametes villosa*, p. 372
28) Cap bald or finely hairy, variously colored; pores 2–8 per mm, not becoming tooth-like...... 29

29) Cap and pore surface bright orange red to red; KOH on flesh reddish to blackish, on pore surface green .... *Pycnoporus cinnabarinus*, p. 330
29) Not completely as above 30

30) Found in lumpy masses at the bases of hardwoods; cap dull yellow to brown; pore surface bruising brown .... *Inonotus dryadeus*, p. 224
30) Found above ground on sticks or logs; cap and pore surface varying 31

31) Cap bald but wrinkled, with zones of gray, white, and brown; flesh white, yellowish with KOH; pore surface whitish, with 2–4 angular pores per mm, often appearing oddly extended over a lumpy mass between the cap and the substrate .... *Poronidulus conchifer*, p. 325
31) Not completely as above 32

32) Pore surface gray to black; cap whitish to gray or tan, often zoned.... *Bjerkandera adusta*, p. 107
32) Pore surface not gray to black; cap varying 33

33) Cap, flesh, and pore surface dull orangish to cinnamon tan; KOH purple .... *Hapalopilus nidulans*, p. 197
33) Not completely as above 34

34) Cap 5–20 cm across; pore surface bruising brown .... *Ischnoderma resinosum*, p. 225
34) Caps under 8 cm across; pore surface not bruising 35

35) Cap cream colored, faintly zoned or not zoned .... *Trametes pubescens*, p. 371
35) Cap with brown shades, strongly zoned .... *Trametes versicolor*, p. 371

36) On wood of conifers 37
36) On wood of hardwoods 39

37) Cap surface not varnished; pore surface dull yellow; pores large, angular and irregular; KOH black on flesh .... *Porodaedalea pini*, p. 325
37) Cap surface, or at least the margin, varnished; pore surface white becoming brownish with age; pores tiny and circular; KOH reaction varying 38

38) Often with a stubby lateral stem attached; flesh usually corky at maturity (possible to crunch the cap somewhat between thumb and fingers) .... *Ganoderma tsugae*, p. 181
38) Lacking a stem; flesh woody (not possible to crunch the cap as above); on wood of diverse conifers; KOH red on flesh .... *Fomitopsis pinicola*, p. 178

39) Parasitic on standing ash trees; pore surface whitish to brownish, not bruising; KOH black on flesh .... *Perenniporia fraxinophila*, p. 299
39) Not completely as above 40

40) Pore surface brown 41
40) Pore surface white 42

41) On wood of black locust; cap brown to orangish brown; annual tube layers distinct................ ....*Phellinus robiniae*, p. 305
41) On wood of paper birch, beech, and other hardwoods; cap gray brown to gray; annual tube layers indistinct...*Fomes fomentarius*, p. 177

42) Cap brown to gray, surface dull; pore surface bruising brown ....*Ganoderma applanatum*, p. 180
42) Cap variously colored but not gray, surface varnished; pore surface not bruising brown........... .... *Ganoderma lucidum*, p. 180

L Key to Chanterelles and Trumpets

1) Mushroom gray to black; funnel-shaped by maturity.. 2
1) Mushroom not gray to black; funnel-shaped or not... 4

2) Undersurface prominently wrinkled or veined by maturity............... *Craterellus foetidus*, p. 163
2) Undersurface smooth or shallowly wrinkled 3

3) Mature cap wider than 2 cm across.. *Craterellus fallax*, p. 162
3) Mature cap up to 1 cm across... *Craterellus calyculus*, p. 162

4) Cap by maturity developing a perforation in the middle of a central depression 5
4) Cap not developing a perforation 6

5) Cap yellow to orange...*Cantharellus ignicolor*, p. 132
5) Cap brown .... *Craterellus tubaeformis*, p. 163

6) Undersurface smooth or wrinkled 7
6) Undersurface with well-developed false gills 8

7) Cap coarsely scaly, red to orange when fresh .... *Gomphus floccosus*, p. 185
7) Cap not scaly, yellow to orangish yellow when fresh .... *Cantharellus lateritius*, p. 133

8) Cap, gills, and stem cinnabar orange .... *Cantharellus cinnabarinus*, p. 132
8) Cap gills and stem differently colored... 9

9) Mature cap 0.5–2 cm across .... *Cantharellus minor*, p. 133
9) Mature cap larger than above..10

10) Cap brown or brownish, at least in the center, when the mushroom is young.......................... ....*Cantharellus appalachiensis*, p. 131
10) Cap not brown or brownish .... *Cantharellus cibarius*, p. 131

M Key to Toothed Mushrooms

1) Growing on conifer cones; cap 1–3 cm .... *Auriscalpium vulgare*, p. 105
1) Not growing on conifer cones; cap variously sized 2

2) Mushroom small (1–6 cm across), gelatinous and translucent; cap whitish to grayish or brownish in age, spatula-shaped or tongue-shaped; growing on the wood or woody debris of conifers .... *Pseudohydnum gelatinosum*, p. 329
2) Not completely as above 3

3) Growing on wood 4
3) Growing terrestrially 12

4) Cap white to pale tan, with a blackening edge; undersurface bruising black .... *Mycorrhaphium adustum*, p. 291
4) Not completely as above 5

5) Mushroom a patch of tiny orange spines, usually with a folded-over cap edge, but also flattened against the substrate without a fully developed cap (resupinate); on the wood of hardwoods .... *Steccherinum ochraceum*, p. 360
5) Not completely as above 6

6) Mushroom without a distinct cap, consisting of either a clump of hanging spines or a branched structure with spines hanging from the branches 7
6) Cap usually present 8

7) Mature mushroom consisting of one unbranched, clump-like structure of hanging spines .... *Hericium erinaceus*, p. 205
7) Mature mushroom consisting of spines hanging from a multibranched structure .... *Hericium coralloides*, p. 205

8) Undersurface with purple colors when fresh, usually poroid, becoming toothed in old age .... *Trichaptum biforme*, p. 375
8) Undersurface without purple colors 9

9) Cap with concentric zones of texture; undersurface usually poroid, becoming toothed in old age .... *Trametes villosa*, p. 372
9) Cap not zoned; undersurface more clearly toothed than above 10

10) Cap surface matted and hairy; surfaces pink to red with KOH; spines whitish but often darkening to reddish brown with age; hyphae with 1–4 clamp connections at septa .... *Climacodon pulcherrimus*, p. 140
10) Not completely as above 11

11) Spines well spaced, flattened; cap up to about 5 cm across when present, but sometimes absent, or present merely as a folded-over edge .... *Spongipellis pachyodon*, p. 359
11) Spines tightly packed, not flattened; cap always present, 10–30 cm across .... *Climacodon septentrionalis*, p. 141

12) Flesh soft (mushroom easily broken apart) 13
12) Flesh corky or leathery (mushroom not easily broken apart) 14

13) Cap brown to reddish brown, with scales; stem base greenish to bluish or black .... *Sarcodon scabrosus*, p. 352
13) Cap dull orange to orangish tan, without scales; stem base whitish or dull orange .... *Hydnum repandum*, p. 210

14) Growing under conifers 15
14) Growing under hardwoods 16

15) Stem gray to bluish; spore print white; cap whitish to pale gray at first, becoming gray with a whitish to bluish edge .... *Phellodon alboniger*, p. 306
15) Stem orange; spore print brown; cap white with a bluish cast when young, becoming tan to brownish with a blue edge .... *Hydnellum caeruleum*, p. 208

16) Stem becoming swollen and spongy near the base; flesh with a pale, soft upper layer and a darker, corky lower layer; cap slightly rugged, or pitted .... *Hydnellum spongiosipes*, p. 209
16) Stem not swollen and spongy near the base; flesh not layered; cap developing radially arranged ridges or elaborate outgrowths .... *Hydnellum concrescens*, p. 208

N Key to Puffballs and Earthstars

1) Mushroom when sliced open revealing a "mushroom to be" inside 2
1) Mushroom when sliced open consisting only of flesh, powder, or silvery "eggs" 3

2) "Mushroom to be" embedded in brown goo (stinkhorn egg) .... Key R, Miscellaneous Other Mushrooms, p. 77
2) "Mushroom to be" embedded in white flesh (*Amanita* button) .... Key E, *Amanita*, p. 40

3) Mushroom shaped like a ball set atop a starfish or a platter (earthstars) 4
3) Mushroom not shaped as above 6

4) Mushroom 5–10 cm across when mature; arms often cracking so that the spore case seems to sit atop a platter with legs; central perforation fuzzy .... *Geastrum triplex*, p. 183
4) Mushroom 2–5 cm across when mature; arms creating a platter or not; central perforation not fuzzy 5

5) Immature, unopened mushrooms with a reddish to purplish or orangish coating; surfaces bruising pinkish to reddish at maturity; central perforation lined .... *Geastrum morganii*, p. 182
5) Immature mushrooms without a coating; mature surfaces not bruising; central perforation not lined .... *Geastrum saccatum*, p. 182

6) Growing on wood 7
6) Growing terrestrially 9

7) Mushroom black and hard, like a tough glob 2–7 cm across, set in a grayish to black, felt-like covering that remains around the edges at maturity .... *Camarops petersii*, p. 130
7) Mushroom not as above 8

8) Mushroom up to 1 cm across; filled with tiny silvery "eggs"; outer surface powdery to felty, brown to whitish, rupturing irregularly at maturity .... *Nidularia pulvinata*, p. 291
8) Mushroom 1.5–5 cm across; filled at first with soft flesh, then spore dust; outer surface finely spiny to bald, brownish, developing a small apical perforation at maturity .... *Morganella pyriformis*, p. 281

9) Mushroom at first appearing like a gelatinous egg but soon appearing like a reddish ball set atop a shaggy stem surrounded by gelatinous reddish chunks .... *Calostoma cinnabarinum*, p. 128
9) Mushroom not as above 10

10) Odor mealy; mushroom irregular in shape; interior fleshy, white with pink areas; outer surface sometimes bruising pink .... *Entoloma abortivum*, p. 171
10) Odor not mealy; mushroom variously shaped; interior varying but without pink areas; outer surface not bruising pink 11

11) Interior tough and hard before turning to spore dust, whitish at first, but soon dark purplish brown to black; spore dust black 12
11) Interior soft and spongy before turning to spore dust, whitish, becoming olive, brown, purplish, or blackish; spore dust usually not black 16

12) Growing in sand dunes; spore case set atop a stem-like structure 5–10 cm long, consisting of elaborately twisted cords embedded in sand .... *Scleroderma septentrionale*, p. 356
12) Not growing in sand dunes; stem absent or very rudimentary 13

13) Growing in lawns and gardens; spore case 8–13 cm across; outer rind up to 5 mm or more thick, rupturing near the top and often peeling back to create "arms" or "rays" .... *Scleroderma polyrhizum*, p. 356
13) Growing in woods or occasionally in lawns and gardens; spore case variously sized but generally smaller than above; outer rind thick or thin, rupturing but not peeling back as above 14

14) Outer surface bruising pink to red, bald or with a few tiny, inconspicuous scales .... *Scleroderma bovista*, p. 355
14) Outer surface not bruising, covered with small or large scales 15

15) Scales large; rind 2–5 mm thick; spores reticulate .... *Scleroderma citrinum*, p. 355
15) Scales small; rind up to 1 mm thick; spores spiny but not reticulate .... *Scleroderma areolatum*, p. 354

16) Outer surface bruising and maturing to bright yellow or reddish orange; spore case 2–10 cm across; sterile base present; spore powder brown .... *Calvatia rubroflava*, p. 130
16) Outer surface not bruising as above; size varying; sterile base present or absent; spore powder variously colored 17

17) Mushroom baseball-sized or larger at maturity 18
17) Mushroom smaller than a baseball at maturity 21

18) Spore dust and maturing flesh dull purple; sterile base conspicuous .... *Calvatia cyathiformis*, p. 129
18) Spore dust and maturing flesh not purple; sterile base present or not 19

19) Sterile base conspicuous; spore dust yellow brown; underside of spore case usually developing furrows .... *Calvatia craniiformis*, p. 128
19) Sterile base absent or inconspicuous; spore dust darker brown; underside of spore case not developing furrows 20

20) Mature mushroom usually baseball- to softball-sized; outer rind fairly tough, 1–2 mm thick; capillitial threads spiny .... *Mycenastrum corium*, p. 290
20) Mature mushroom usually softball- to basketball-sized; outer rind thin and fragile, <1 mm thick; capillitial threads not spiny .... *Calvatia gigantea*, p. 129

21) Mature mushroom shaped like an inverted pear due to the conspicuous sterile base; outer surface with fragile, tiny spines that rub off readily .... *Lycoperdon perlatum*, p. 266
21) Mature mushroom more or less spherical (sterile base less conspicuous); outer surface densely spiny with soft spines measuring up to 5 mm long 22

22) Growing in woods or in disturbed ground areas; outer skin sloughing off in chunks and patches (see p. 266) .... *Lycoperdon marginatum*, p. 266
22) Growing in grass; outer skin not sloughing off as above .... *Vascellum curtisii*, p. 387

O Key to Cup Mushrooms

1) Cup brightly colored (red, orange, yellow) 2
1) Cup not brightly colored 8

2) Cup bright yellow, very tiny (<5 mm across); growing in clusters on wood .... *Bisporella citrina*, p. 106
2) Cup red or orange, often (but not always) larger than above; growing on wood or terrestrially, in clusters or not 3

3) Cup orange 4
3) Cup red 5

4) Cups frequently split down one side; dull orange; paraphyses with curved ends........................ .... *Otidea onotica*, p. 292
4) Cups not usually split down one side; bright orange; paraphyses with club-shaped ends.......... .... *Aleuria aurantia*, p. 88

5) Cup goblet-shaped, with a long stem; about 1 cm wide at maturity; outer surface and margin of cup covered with conspicuous white hairs .... *Microstoma floccosum*, p. 277
5) Cup not goblet-shaped, with or without a stem; size varying; hairs if present brown and confined to the margin of the cup 6

6) Mature cup 2–7 cm across; stem absent; found in spring.............. *Sarcoscypha austriaca*, p. 353
6) Mature cup <2.5 cm across; stem absent or present; found in spring or summer 7

7) Stem absent; margin of cup fringed with eyelash-like brown hairs; usually found on wet logs... .... *Scutellinia scutellata*, p. 357
7) Stem usually present; margin of cup not fringed with hairs; usually found on hardwood sticks or growing terrestrially .... *Sarcoscypha occidentalis*, p. 353

8) Either the entire cup or the inner flesh of the cup gelatinous 9
8) Cup not gelatinous 10

9) Cup ear-shaped to amorphous, medium brown; entire mushroom gelatinous.......................... .... *Auricularia auricula*, p. 105
9) Cup goblet-shaped, dark brown with an orangish to tan upper surface; interior of mushroom gelatinous .... *Galiella rufa*, p. 179

10) Cup very tough and leathery, <1.5 cm across, with concentric zones of white and brown or gray shades; growing on wood .... *Poronidulus conchifer*, p. 325
10) Cup soft- or brittle-fleshed but not tough and leathery, larger than above, not zoned; habitat varying 11

11) Cup more or less black, deeply goblet-shaped, thin-fleshed; growing in clusters, in spring........ .... *Urnula craterium*, p. 387
11) Not with the above combination of characters 12

12) Cup dull yellowish to dull orangish, often split down one side; growing in clusters .... *Otidea onotica*, p. 292
12) Cup variously colored, not split down one side, growing in clusters or not 13

13) Outer surface and margin of cup covered with prominent brown hairs; inner surface whitish to pale bluish; mature cup 2–3 cm across .... *Humaria hemisphaerica*, p. 207
13) Prominent brown hairs absent; colors and size varying 14

14) Clearly defined stem present below the cup 15
14) Stem absent or very rudimentary 17

15) Stem lacking prominent ribs, finely hairy, brown.............................. *Helvella macropus*, p. 203
15) Stem with prominent ribs, bald, whitish... 16

16) Ribs on stem extending far onto the undersurface of the cup; stem ribbed and usually pocketed as well .... *Helvella acetabulum*, p. 201
16) Ribs not extending onto the undersurface of the cup; stem ribbed but not pocketed .... *Helvella queletii*, p. 204

17) Cup growing on wood; attached tightly and broadly so that only the very edge can be easily lifted from the wood; surface sticky; brown, with or without a hint of purple.................................. .... *Pachyella clypeata*, p. 293
17) Cup if growing on wood attached only under the center of the cup so that its edges are easily lifted to expose the undersurface; upper surface dry; color varying.. 18

18) Cup growing in indoor settings or in garages, on concrete rubble, and in coal bins; upper surface yellow to brown at maturity; undersurface whitish to pale tan .... *Peziza domiciliana*, p. 300
18) Growing in woods; colors varying 19

19) Flesh when squeezed exuding a yellow juice that stains fingers and white paper....................... .... *Peziza succosa*, p. 301
19) Flesh not exuding a yellow-staining juice.. 20

20) Ascus tips blue in Melzer's reagent; flesh brittle; upper surface smooth or slightly wrinkled near the center at maturity 21
20) Ascus tips not blue in Melzer's; flesh brittle or not; upper surface wrinkled, at least over the center, at maturity 22

21) Growing on wood or woodchips; undersurface white and minutely fuzzy; appearing from spring to fall; spores smooth at maturity .... *Peziza repanda*, p. 301
21) Usually growing near but not directly from wood; undersurface brownish and finely hairy; appearing in early summer; spores roughened to warty at maturity .....*Peziza badioconfusa*, p. 300

22) Widely distributed; not associated with deadwood; spores ellipsoid; usually becoming wrinkled over the center with maturity .... *Disciotis venosa*, p. 169
22) Primarily found in the northern Midwest; often found near stumps and well-rotted logs; spores fusiform, with prominent apiculi; becoming wrinkled or not 23

23) Apiculi long and pointed; cup usually reddish brown .... *Gyromitra perlata*, p. 195
23) Apiculi with distinctive, scooped-out ends; cup usually yellowish brown .... *Gyromitra leucoxantha*, p. 194

P Key to Morels, False Morels, and Saddles

1) Flesh gelatinous; cap irregular and lumpy, yellowish to greenish; stem yellowish and sticky .... *Leotia lubrica*, p. 257
1) Flesh not gelatinous; neither cap nor stem as above 2

2) Stem completely hollow, or hollow with wispy cottony fibers inside; cap with fairly regular pits and ridges, or longitudinally wrinkled, or fairly smooth (never lobed, saddle-shaped, convoluted, or brain-like); without reddish or reddish-brown shades; found in spring 3
2) Stem hollow, solid, or chambered; cap not regularly pitted and ridged; cap lobed, saddle-shaped, convoluted, brain-like, or irregular; reddish shades present or absent; found in spring, summer, and fall 10

3) Cap attached to the stem only at the very top, like a thimble sitting atop a pencil (slice the mushroom in half to view it in longitudinal section) 4
3) Cap more or less fully attached to the stem, or attached about halfway down 5

4) Cap smooth or with vague, irregular wrinkles; mushroom 3–10 cm tall when mature; asci 8-spored; spores 21–26 µm long .... *Verpa conica*, p. 388
4) Cap deeply and prominently wrinkled; mushroom often >10 cm tall when mature; asci 2-spored; spores 54–80 µm long .... *Verpa bohemica*, p. 388

5) Ridges darkening to dark brown or nearly black with maturity 6
5) Ridges not darkening with maturity 8

6) Cap attached to the stem roughly halfway up, with a substantial portion hanging free; mature stem often long in proportion to cap; stem often fragile .... *Morchella punctipes*, p. 280
6) Cap fully attached to the stem; stem not long in proportion to cap, not fragile 7

7) Found in the northern Midwest (from about 44° N northward); mushroom 4–8 cm high; spores 20–22 µm long .... *Morchella septentrionalis*, p. 280
7) Found throughout the Midwest; mushroom 5–14 cm high or more; spores 22–27 µm long..... .... *Morchella angusticeps*, p. 277

8) Mature mushroom fairly small (3–10 cm high); pits and ridges primarily vertically arranged; distributed primarily below the Great Lakes .... *Morchella diminutiva*, p. 278
8) Mature mushroom often larger than above; pits and ridges more randomly arranged; distributed throughout the Midwest 9

9) Pits and ridges contorted, asymmetrical, and irregular (see p. 279); ridges often remaining flattened or widely rounded into maturity; often (but not always) found in sandy soil........ .... *Morchella prava*, p. 279
9) Pits and ridges not appearing contorted and irregular; ridges becoming sharpened with maturity; found in a wide variety of soils .... *Morchella esculentoides*, p. 278

10) Most (but not all) species found in spring; cap reddish to reddish brown or brown (but if the cap is brown, without reddish shades, then the stem is over 1.5 cm thick) 11
10) Most species found in summer and fall (occasionally in late spring); cap white, gray, or brown (but if the cap is brown, then the stem is about 1 cm thick at maturity) 15

11) Cap saddle-shaped; found in fall; growing from deadwood .... *Gyromitra infula*, p. 193
11) Cap not saddle-shaped; found in spring; not growing from deadwood 12

12) Cap brain-like, reddish; stem 1–3 cm thick; found in the northern Midwest .... *Gyromitra esculenta*, p. 193
12) Cap not brain-like and reddish, or if brain-like and reddish, then stem 2–10 cm thick; variously distributed 13

13) Cap blocky and squarish, brown (rarely slightly reddish brown); mature spores with a large knob at each end .... *Gyromitra korfii*, p. 194
13) Cap not blocky and squarish, reddish brown to red; mature spores with small, finger-like extensions at each end 14

14) Cap tightly wrinkled, without lobes or seam-like lines; undersurface never exposed .... *Gyromitra caroliniana*, p. 192
14) Cap loosely wrinkled, often somewhat lobed, with seam-like lines stitching the lobes together; undersurface exposed in places .... *Gyromitra brunnea*, p. 192

15) Cap and stem buff to white; stem elaborately ribbed and pocketed .... *Helvella crispa*, p. 202
15) Cap not white or buff, or if so, then stem not ribbed and pocketed; stem varying 16

16) Cap gray, saddle-shaped; stem ribbed .... *Helvella sulcata*, p. 204
16) Cap varying; stem not ribbed 17

17) Cap brown to tan; margin never curled upward and inward; undersurface bald or nearly so .... *Helvella elastica*, p. 202
17) Cap whitish to buff or tan; margin often curled upward and inward, at least when young; undersurface finely grainy .... *Helvella latispora*, p. 203

Q Key to Club and Coral Mushrooms

1) Mushroom club-shaped or roughly finger-shaped, with a hard outer surface that is black or dark reddish brown (or is sometimes covered, in spring, with a bluish to whitish powder); flesh very tough 2
1) Mushroom not club-shaped or finger-shaped, or if club-shaped, then mushroom soft-fleshed and not black 4

2) Lower stem yellow, attached to long yellow cords that lead underground................................ .... *Elaphocordyceps ophioglossoides*, p. 170
2) Lower stem not yellow, not attached to yellow cords 3

3) Usually growing on sticks and small logs; mushroom club-shaped; surface developing a fine network of cracks .... *Xylaria longipes*, p. 395
3) Usually growing from deadwood near the bases of stumps; mushroom irregularly shaped (more or less finger-like); surface becoming roughened and pimply .... *Xylaria polymorpha*, p. 396

4) Mushroom shaped like a fan or spatula, with a brown stem and a tan to whitish or yellowish head; on wood or debris of conifers .... *Spathulariopsis velutipes*, p. 359
4) Not completely as above 5

5) Mushroom shaped like a club or cylinder, usually unbranched (however, mushrooms may be loosely or tightly packed together at their bases) 6
5) Mushroom shaped more or less like a coral or head of cauliflower or rosette, with distinct branches 11

6) Mushroom bright orange; surface hard and pimply; arising from the pupae of dead insects, which may be buried in deadwood or underground .... *Cordyceps militaris*, p. 151
6) Not completely as above 7

7) Usually growing in tightly packed clusters; mushrooms cylindric, 3–12 cm high; whitish to translucent .... *Clavaria vermicularis*, p. 137
7) Not completely as above 8

8) Mushroom bright yellow to bright orange 9
8) Mushroom orangish buff to brownish orange or reddish brown 10

9) Growing on wood, densely gregariously; mushrooms 1–2 cm high .... *Calocera cornea*, p. 127
9) Growing terrestrially in clusters with fused bases; mushrooms 5–15 cm high .... *Clavulinopsis fusiformis*, p. 140

10) Mature mushroom usually broadly club-shaped; surface negative with KOH .... *Clavariadelphus americanus*, p. 138
10) Mature mushroom with an enlarged, flattened apex; surface bright yellow with KOH .... *Clavariadelphus unicolor*, p. 138

11) Lilac to purple shades present (aside from purplish-brown bruising) when mushroom is fresh and young 12
11) Lilac to purple shades absent 14

12) Young branches yellowish to olive yellow above, with pale purple bases; branching frequent and repeated; iron salts green on branches .... *Ramaria fennica*, p. 331
12) Branches lilac to purple; branching sparse to frequent; iron salts negative on branches 13

13) Branches purple; basidia 4-spored; clamp connections absent .... *Clavaria zollingeri*, p. 137
13) Branches lilac to dull purple; basidia 2-spored; clamp connections present .... *Clavulina amethystinoides*, p. 139

14) Growing on wood 15
14) Growing terrestrially........ 16

15) Branch tips pyxidate: crowned with a shallow depression and 3–6 points; branches branching frequently; surfaces not bruising........ *Artomyces pyxidatus*, p. 104
15) Branch tips forked, pointed, or blunt but not pyxidate; branches mostly straight and ascending; surfaces often bruising and discoloring purplish brown .... *Ramaria stricta*, p. 333

16) Consistency tough and leathery to rubbery (try tearing the mushroom apart); surface whitish to dirty yellowish (or greenish when algae are present on old specimens), without concentric zones of texture or color........ *Tremellodendron pallidum*, p. 374
16) Not completely as above........ 17

17) Mushroom consisting of numerous flattened lobes or sections arising from a central location; surfaces white when fresh; consistency gelatinous but fairly firm .... *Tremella reticulata*, p. 374
17) Not completely as above........ 18

18) Mushroom shaped like a rosette, or more or less like a large head of cauliflower........ 19
18) Mushroom shaped more or less like a coral with branched arms........ 20

19) Mushroom 10–40 cm across; fragrant; found near the bases of trees .... *Sparassis spathulata*, p. 358
19) Mushroom 5–12 cm across; odorless; terrestrial but not always near the bases of trees .... *Podoscypha aculeata*, p. 321

20) Fresh mushroom white or whitish, sometimes becoming slightly yellowish or pinkish with age; iron salts negative on branches........ 21
20) Fresh mushroom more highly colored than above; iron salts green on branches........ 22

21) Branch tips cristate: flattened and featuring several tiny points; basidia 2-spored .... *Clavulina cristata*, p. 139
21) Branch tips bluntly pointed, not cristate; basidia 4-spored........ *Ramariopsis kunzei*, p. 333

22) Branches mostly straight and ascending; surfaces often bruising and discoloring purplish brown........ *Ramaria stricta*, p. 333
22) Branches frequently branched; surfaces not bruising purplish brown........ 23

23) Branches densely packed, pinkish to purplish; branch tips also pinkish to purplish; branches fairly short, reminiscent of broccoli .... *Ramaria botrytis*, p. 331
23) Branches not densely packed, coral pink when young, contrasting with clear yellow branch tips; branches fairly long, not reminiscent of broccoli........ *Ramaria formosa*, p. 332

R Key to Miscellaneous Other Mushrooms

1) Mushroom shaped more or less like a *Russula* (pp. 338–52) or *Lactarius* (pp. 230–51) but partially or completely covered with a crust-like, minutely pimply coating 2
1) Mushroom not as above 3

2) Crust-like coating greenish yellow, usually limited to the undersurface of the cap .... *Hypomyces luteovirens*, p. 219
2) Crust-like coating orange, usually covering the entire mushroom .... *Hypomyces lactifluorum*, p. 219

3) Mushroom appearing like a tiny bird's nest, complete with "eggs" 4
3) Mushroom not appearing like a bird's nest 7

4) Interior of nest prominently lined .... *Cyathus striatus*, p. 166
4) Interior of nest not lined 5

5) Nest yellow to brownish yellow; eggs whitish .... *Crucibulum laeve*, p. 165
5) Nest brown to black; eggs silvery to blackish 6

6) Nest clearly defined, goblet-shaped; outer surface hairy .... *Cyathus stercoreus*, p. 166
6) Nest not clearly defined (eggs piled on the broken remains of a ruptured encasement); outer surface, if visible, powdery to velvety .... *Nidularia pulvinata*, p. 291

7) Mushroom appearing a bit like a large black eye, 2–7 cm across, stuck to a log, with a felt-like outer sheath that surrounds the "eye" like an "eyelid"; surface tough and pimply .... *Camarops petersii*, p. 130
7) Mushroom not appearing like a large black eye 8

8) Mushroom shaped like a fan or spatula, with a brown stem and a tan to whitish or yellowish head; on wood or debris of conifers .... *Spathulariopsis velutipes*, p. 359
8) Mushroom not completely as above 9

9) Mushroom covered near the top with a malodorous olive to brown spore slime (which is often removed by insects); flesh spongy and porous; arising from a partially buried egg-like structure that may leave a sac-like volva at the base of the stem 10
9) Mushroom never covered with malodorous spore slime; flesh not spongy and porous; not arising from an egg-like structure 15

10) Mushroom orange to red or yellow overall 11
10) Mushroom not orange, red, or yellow 13

11) Mushroom with 3–5 arms that arise from a shared stem and are fused at their tips .... *Pseudocolus fusiformis*, p. 329
11) Mushroom shaped more or less like a spike or cylinder 12

12) Mushroom with a flimsy but clearly separated head-like structure bearing the spore slime........ .... *Phallus rubicundus*, p. 304
12) Mushroom without a clearly separated head-like structure.................... *Mutinus elegans*, p. 281

13) Cap developing a laced "skirt" that hangs downward around the stem..................................... .... *Phallus duplicatus*, p. 302
13) Cap without a laced skirt..14

14) Mature cap fairly smooth under the spore slime; often developing a lip-like central perforation at the top.. *Phallus ravenelii*, p. 303
14) Mature cap deeply pocketed and pitted under the spore slime; only occasionally developing a central perforation at the top... *Phallus hadriani*, p. 303

15) Flesh gelatinous..16
15) Flesh not gelatinous.. 23

16) Mushroom white to whitish (possibly yellowing somewhat with old age) 17
16) Mushroom not white..19

17) Mushroom terrestrial; appearing like a set of flattened fingers arising from a central structure.... .... *Tremella reticulata*, p. 374
17) Mushroom growing on wood; not appearing like a set of flattened fingers.............................18

18) Mushroom composed of graceful, nearly translucent lobes that are usually fused into a structure about 5–10 cm across; gloeocystidia absent...................................... *Tremella fuciformis*, p. 373
18) Mushroom composed of multiple opaque globs that fuse together to cover large areas of the log; gloeocystidia present... *Ductifera pululahuana*, p. 170

19) Mushroom yellow, composed of lobes or brain-like globs .... *Tremella mesenterica*, p. 373
19) Mushroom brown to black, varying in structure.. 20

20) Mushroom black; appearing like a spreading patch of globs or lobed structures; surface with minute pimples .... *Exidia glandulosa*, p. 175
20) Mushroom brown; varying in structure; surface without pimples 21

21) Mushroom developing distinctive concave depressions that are rimmed by thin ridges (see p. 175).. *Exidia recisa*, p. 175
21) Mushroom not developing rimmed depressions... 22

22) Mushroom appearing like a densely packed cluster of gelatinous leaves; spores broadly ellipsoid to subglobose; basidia longitudinally septate; infrequently encountered.................................. .... *Tremella foliacea*, p. 373
22) Mushroom appearing like a gelatinous ear or leaf, sometimes clustered tightly but often growing alone or gregariously; spores allantoid; basidia transversely septate; commonly encountered..... .... *Auricularia auricula*, p. 105

23) Cap thin, with an upper surface that features alternating zones of colors (browns, reds, tans) and a smooth undersurface; growing in shelving clusters .... *Stereum ostrea*, p. 361
23) Cap absent, or if present, then not zoned; undersurface smooth or wrinkled; growth pattern varying 24

24) Mushroom yellow to orange 25
24) Mushroom whitish to pink.. 26

25) Mushroom a single, spreading patch of wrinkled orange spore-bearing surface .... *Phlebia radiata*, p. 307
25) Individual mushrooms usually clearly separated, patch-like, or, more frequently, with wavy, thin, orange to orangish-yellow caps with smooth undersurfaces........... *Stereum complicatum*, p. 360

26) Mushroom with a well-developed cap that features a bald, pink upper surface and a deeply wrinkled, whitish undersurface .... *Phlebia incarnata*, p. 306
26) Mushroom without a well-developed cap, or with a rudimentary, woolly cap consisting of a folded-over edge; spreading surface (or undersurface of cap) pinkish to whitish, wrinkled .... *Phlebia tremellosa*, p. 307

5 THE MUSHROOMS

ABORTIPORUS BIENNIS (*BULLIARD*) SINGER

Ecology: Saprobic on the wood of hardwoods; growing alone or gregariously around the bases of stumps and living trees; causing a white rot in deadwood and a white trunk rot in living wood; summer and fall; widely distributed. **Cap:** Often irregular and covered with the pore surface, but when definable up to 20 cm across; kidney-shaped to semicircular or irregular in outline; whitish to pale brown or reddish brown; sometimes with concentric zones; finely velvety or bald. **Pore Surface:** Whitish, bruising and discoloring reddish or pinkish brown; pores angular to maze-like or irregular, 1–4 per mm; tubes to 6 mm deep. **Stem:** Often absent or poorly defined, but when present up to 6 cm long; whitish; velvety. **Flesh:** White to pinkish or pale tan; exuding a pinkish juice when squeezed; 2-layered in mature specimens; tough. **Chemical Reactions:** KOH negative on flesh. **Spore Print:** White. **Microscopic Features:** Spores 5–8 × 3–5 µm; smooth; broadly ellipsoid; inamyloid. Chlamydospores often present; globose; 5–9 µm. Gloeocystidia infrequent to numerous; variously shaped. **Comments:** Some authors give a separate species name, *Abortiporus distortus*, to the gnarled form that lacks a clearly defined cap and stem. Both forms are illustrated.

AGARICUS ARVENSIS SCHAEFFER

Ecology: Saprobic; growing alone, scattered, or gregariously in grassy places (lawns, fields, and so on); summer and fall; widely distributed. **Cap:** 7–20 cm; convex at first, often with a somewhat flattened center; later broadly convex or flat; dry; white or pale yellowish when young; developing appressed fibers or fine scales (especially in dry weather); bruising yellow; the margin often with hanging partial veil remnants. **Gills:** Free from the stem; crowded; whitish at first, becoming brown without a pink stage. **Stem:** 5–15 cm long; 1–3 cm thick; equal, or slightly bulbous; bald, or with scales below the ring; white; sometimes bruising yellow; with a persistent, large ring that is often "cogwheeled" on the lower surface. **Flesh:** Thick and white throughout; not changing color when exposed, or yellowing slightly; not yellowing in stem base. **Odor and Taste:** Odor sweet (reminiscent of anise or almonds) when young and fresh, becoming less distinctive; taste pleasant. **Chemical Reactions:** Cap yellow with KOH. **Spore Print:** Brown. **Microscopic Features:** Spores 7–9 × 4.5–6 µm; ellipsoid; smooth. **Comments:** Edible, but some people may be sensitive to it. Sometimes called the "horse mushroom." Compare with *Agaricus xanthodermus* (p. 84), which has bright yellow flesh in the stem base and a strongly unpleasant odor when the stem base is crushed; also compare with the white form of *Stropharia rugosoannulata* (p. 364).

AGARICUS CAMPESTRIS LINNAEUS

Fairy ring

Ecology: Saprobic; growing alone, gregariously, or sometimes in fairy rings in meadows, fields, lawns, and grassy areas; late summer to early winter; widely distributed and common. **Cap:** 3–11 cm; convex to broadly convex, occasionally nearly flat; whitish; bald and glossy to silky to nearly woolly or scaly. **Gills:** Free from the stem; deep pink becoming brown in maturity; crowded; covered with a thin white partial veil when in the button stage. **Stem:** 2–6 cm long; 1–2.5 cm thick; more or less equal; sometimes tapering slightly to base; with a quickly collapsing white ring; whitish; not bruising. **Flesh:** Thick and white throughout; unchanging or very rarely discoloring pinkish in wet weather. **Odor and Taste:** Not distinctive. **Chemical Reactions:** Cap surface negative with KOH. **Spore Print:** Brown. **Microscopic Features:** Spores: 5.5–10 × 4–7 µm;

ellipsoid; smooth. **Comments:** Edible and good. Sometimes called the "meadow mushroom." The habitat in grass, whitish cap, squatty stature, pink immature gills, and lack of bruising reactions are good field characters. *Agaricus porphyrocephalus* (p. 83) is similar but features a brown, hairy to scaly cap.

Photo by Rick Kerrigan

KOH on cap

AGARICUS PLACOMYCES PECK

Ecology: Saprobic; growing scattered or gregariously under hardwoods and in mixed woods; summer and fall; widely distributed but more common in the northern Midwest. **Cap:** 5–12 cm, convex to broadly convex or nearly flat in age; dry; covered with brownish fibers and scales, especially over the center; whitish underneath the scales, or pinkish in wet weather. **Gills:** Free from the stem; crowded; pale grayish pink at first, becoming brown; at first covered by a partial veil that develops brownish to yellowish droplets. **Stem:** 6–15 cm long; 1–1.5 cm thick; more or less equal, or with a slightly enlarged (but not abruptly bulbous) base; bald; white; bruising yellow, especially at the base; with a persistent ring. **Flesh:** White; bright yellow in the base when sliced. **Odor and Taste:** Taste not distinctive, or somewhat unpleasant; odor usually unpleasant (phenolic), but sometimes not distinctive. **Spore Print:** Brown. **Chemical Reactions:** Cap surface yellow with KOH. **Microscopic Features:** Spores 5–7 × 3.5–5 µm; broadly ellipsoid; smooth. **Comments:** Poisonous. Compare with *Agaricus pocillator* (below), which is skinnier, features a small, abrupt bulb at the base of the stem, and is more common south of the Great Lakes.

AGARICUS POCILLATOR MURRILL

Ecology: Saprobic; growing alone or gregariously under hardwoods and in mixed woods; summer and fall; widely distributed below the Great Lakes. **Cap:** 3–10 cm; convex to broadly convex or nearly flat in age, sometimes with an obscure, darker bump; dry; whitish to dingy, developing vaguely concentric brownish to grayish scales toward the center; sometimes pinkish in wet weather. **Gills:** Free from the stem; close; white, becoming pinkish, then brown; at first covered by a whitish partial veil that does not usually develop dark droplets. **Stem:** 4–8 cm long; 0.5–1 cm thick; more or less equal; with a small bulbous base that bruises yellow; with a ring that typically persists into maturity. **Flesh:** White; bright yellow in the stem base. **Odor and Taste:** Taste not distinctive, or somewhat

unpleasant; odor often unpleasant (phenolic), but sometimes not distinctive. **Spore Print:** Brown. **Chemical Reactions:** Cap surface and flesh yellow with KOH. **Microscopic Features:** Spores 4.5–6 × 3–3.8 µm; ellipsoid; smooth. **Comments:** Poisonous. Compare with *Agaricus placomyces* (p. 82).

AGARICUS PORPHYROCEPHALUS F. H. MØLLER

Ecology: Saprobic; growing alone, scattered, or gregariously in meadows, fields, lawns, and grassy areas; summer and fall; widely distributed. **Cap:** 3–8 cm; convex to broadly convex; brownish underneath brown to purplish-brown fibers and scales; dry; the margin sometimes adorned with hanging remnants of the partial veil. **Gills:** Free from the stem; close or crowded; pink becoming brown in maturity; covered with a thin white partial veil when in the button stage. **Stem:** 3–6 cm long; 1–2 cm thick; more or less equal, or tapering slightly to base; with a quickly collapsing white ring; whitish to brownish; bald or finely hairy. **Flesh:** Whitish; not changing, or changing to pinkish when sliced; not yellowing in the base of the stem. **Odor and Taste:** Pleasant; not distinctive. **Chemical Reactions:** Cap surface negative with KOH. **Spore Print:** Brown. **Microscopic Features:** Spores: 5–7 × 3–4.5 µm; ellipsoid. **Comments:** Compare with *Agaricus campestris* (p. 81).

AGARICUS SYLVICOLA (VITTADINI) PECK

Ecology: Saprobic; growing alone, scattered, or gregariously in woods or at the edges of woods; summer and fall; widely distributed. **Cap:** 5–18 cm; convex at first, becoming broadly convex or flat; dry; whitish, sometimes developing yellowish stains; bald or with innate, appressed fibers at maturity; bruising yellow, especially along the margin. **Gills:** Free from the stem; close; whitish at first, becoming pinkish to pinkish gray and eventually brown; when young covered by a whitish or yellowish-stained partial veil that usually features patches or a "cogwheel" pattern. **Stem:** 5–20 cm long; up to 2.5 cm thick; equal, or with a slightly to substantially and abruptly swollen base; bald or silky below the ring; white, often developing yellowish stains; usually bruising yellowish; with a persistent, large ring. **Flesh:** Thick and white throughout; often yellowing slightly when sliced, but not turning dramatically and instantly yellow in the base of the stem. **Odor and Taste:** Odor sweet (reminiscent of anise or almonds) when young and fresh, becoming less distinctive; taste pleasant. **Chemical Reactions:** Cap yellow with KOH. **Spore Print:** Brown. **Microscopic Features:** Spores 5–7.5 × 3.5–4.5 µm; ellipsoid; smooth. **Comments:** Poisonous for some people. The woodland habitat, tall stature, smooth whitish cap, yellow staining, and sweet odor are good field characters for this species group.

KOH on cap

AGARICUS XANTHODERMUS GENERVIER

Ecology: Saprobic; growing scattered or in large groups, sometimes clustered together; in grass and in cultivated areas; summer and fall; widely distributed. **Cap:** 6–20 cm; round to irregularly convex, becoming broadly convex or nearly flat; whitish, or with brownish colorations, especially toward the center; dry; bald but sometimes becoming slightly scaly in age; usually bruising yellow when rubbed, especially near the margin, the bruised areas then changing to brownish after some time has elapsed; the margin inrolled when young. **Gills:** Free from the stem; white at first, then pinkish, and finally brown; close; at first covered by a white or yellowed partial veil that has patches of tissue on its underside. **Stem:** 5–18 cm long; 1–3 cm thick; more or less equal; sometimes enlarged at the base; bald; whitish, bruising yellow (then brownish); sometimes brownish in age; with a large, flaring, thick ring on the upper portion. **Flesh:** White and thick; yellowing when crushed; bright yellow in the base of the stem. **Odor and Taste:** Odor unpleasant and phenolic, but sometimes faint. Taste mild or unpleasant. **Chemical Reactions:** Cap surface yellow with KOH. **Spore Print:** Brown. **Microscopic Features:** Spores 4.5–6 × 3–4.5 µm; ellipsoid; smooth. **Comments:** Poisonous. Compare with *Agaricus arvensis* (p. 81), and with the white form of *Stropharia rugosoannulata* (p. 364).

AGROCYBE EREBIA (FRIES) KÜHNER

Ecology: Saprobic; growing alone or gregariously on the ground in woods under hardwoods or conifers; summer and fall; widely distributed but more common in the northern Midwest. **Cap:** 2–5 cm; convex, becoming broadly convex to flat, often with a low central bump; dark brown, fading slowly to dull brown; sticky when fresh and young, but soon drying out; bald; often with whitish partial veil remnants on the margin. **Gills:** Attached to the stem or, more typically, beginning to run down it; pale brownish, becoming rusty brown; close or nearly distant. **Stem:** 3–7 cm long; up to 1 cm thick; more or less equal; whitish, becoming brownish from the base up; with a pale, thin ring that may collapse or disappear by maturity. **Flesh:** Whitish to brownish; thin. **Odor and Taste:** Not distinctive. **Spore Print:** Brown. **Microscopic Features:** Spores 11–15.5 × 5–6.5 µm; ellipsoid with a snout-like end; with a pore at one end; smooth. **Comments:** The sticky brown cap, gills that run down the stem, fragile ring, and brown spore print are good field characters for this species.

AGROCYBE MOLESTA (LASCH) SINGER

Spores

Ecology: Saprobic, decomposing grass litter; growing alone or gregariously in lawns and other grassy areas; spring and early summer; widely distributed. **Cap:** 4–9 cm; convex, becoming broadly convex to flat; creamy white, discoloring somewhat, or sometimes pale yellow brown to brownish; bald; often developing cracks in age and in dry weather; with whitish partial veil remnants on the margin. **Gills:** Attached to the stem; close; whitish at first, becoming brown; at first covered by a whitish partial veil. **Stem:** 4–10 cm long; 0.5–1.5 cm thick; more or less equal; white or brownish; with a thin ring that often disappears. **Flesh:** White; unchanging when sliced. **Odor and Taste:** Odor not distinctive, or mealy; taste mild, mealy, or slightly bitter to disagreeable. **Chemical Reactions:** KOH negative on cap surface. **Spore Print:** Brown. **Microscopic Features:** Spores 10–14 × 6.5–8 µm; ellipsoid; smooth; slightly truncated; with a pore at one end. Cystidia usually present, but highly variable. **Comments:** Also known as *Agrocybe dura*. This member of the *Agrocybe praecox* group (p. 86) is easily identified on the basis of its habitat in grass, its white colors, and its long spores. Compare with *Stropharia coronilla* (p. 362), which has a purple-brown to black spore print, a persistent ring that is grooved on the upper surface, and darker cap colors.

AGROCYBE PEDIADES (FRIES) FAYOD

Ecology: Saprobic; growing alone or gregariously in lawns, meadows, and other grassy areas (and sometimes on woodchips, dung, or sand); summer; common and widely distributed. **Cap:** 1–4 cm; convex, broadly convex, or nearly flat; brownish yellow or paler; bald; dry or sticky; occasionally with whitish partial veil remnants on the margin. **Gills:** Attached to the stem; close or nearly distant; pale grayish brown becoming brown to rusty or cinnamon brown in maturity; when young covered

by an ephemeral white partial veil. **Stem:** 2–6 cm long; 1.5–5 mm thick; more or less equal; bald; colored like the cap. **Flesh:** Pale yellowish to whitish; insubstantial. **Odor and Taste:** Mealy, or not distinctive. **Spore Print:** Brown. **Chemical Reactions:** Cap surface red to pink with KOH. **Microscopic Features:** Spores 9–13 × 6.5–8 µm; smooth; ellipsoid but slightly truncated. Cystidia fusoid-ventricose with pointed or slightly swollen tips. **Comments:** The partial veil, which is rarely recorded, disappears very quickly. The small proportions and the KOH reaction will separate this species from the *Agrocybe praecox* group (below). Also compare with *Panaeolus foenisecii* (p. 293).

AGROCYBE PRAECOX (PERSOON) FAYOD

Ecology: Saprobic on woody debris; growing alone or gregariously; spring, summer, and fall; widely distributed. **Cap:** 4–12 cm; convex, becoming broadly convex or flat, often with a low central bump; bald and smooth, but sometimes developing cracks in age; color ranging from whitish to yellow brown, brownish, or brown; sometimes with whitish partial veil remnants on the margin. **Gills:** Attached to the stem or pulling away from it; close; whitish at first, becoming brown to cinnamon brown; at first covered by a white partial veil. **Stem:** Dimensions variable, but not often wider than 1.5 cm or longer than 10 cm; more or less equal; whitish or pale brownish; with a thin, whitish ring that often disappears; with white rhizomorphs attached to the base. **Flesh:** Whitish; not particularly thick in the cap. **Odor and Taste:** Mealy. **Spore Print:** Brown. **Chemical Reactions:** KOH on cap surface negative to orangish or yellowish. **Microscopic Features:** Spores 8–11 × 5–6 µm; ellipsoid; smooth; with a pore at one end; slightly truncated. Cystidia present, but highly variable. **Comments:** Flynn and Miller (1990) determined three biological species in the *Agrocybe praecox* group that occur in the Midwest (of five biological species worldwide): *Agrocybe molesta* (p. 85); "Species III," decomposing naturally occurring wood litter in hardwood forests (possibly corresponding with the traditional species *Agrocybe acericola*) in spring and summer; and "Species

Spore print

I," decomposing woodchips in urban habitats in spring, summer, and fall. Compare with *Stropharia hardii* (p. 363), which has purplish-brown gills at maturity and a purple-brown spore print.

ALBATRELLUS CAERULEOPORUS (PECK) POUZAR

Photo by Walt Sturgeon

Ecology: Mycorrhizal with hemlock; often appearing in low, wet woods; growing alone or gregariously; summer and fall; widely distributed where hemlocks occur. **Cap:** 2–7 cm; more or less circular in outline; convex, flat, or irregular; occasionally fused with other caps; dry; bald, finely velvety, or with tiny scales in patches; blue, gray, or grayish blue at first, becoming brown, brownish, or orangish brown. **Pore Surface:** Running down the stem; pale blue or gray, becoming grayish or brownish; 2–3 angular pores per mm; tubes to 5 mm deep. **Stem:** 2.5–7 cm long; up to 2 cm wide; sometimes a little off-center; blue, discoloring to grayish or brownish with age; smooth or rugged. **Flesh:** Whitish; fairly soft when fresh. **Odor and Taste:** Odor not distinctive; taste mild or slightly acrid. **Spore Print:** White. **Microscopic Features:** Spores 4–6 × 3–5 µm; smooth; broadly ellipsoid or subglobose; inamyloid. Clamp connections absent. **Comments:** When fresh, this species is fairly unmistakable, but older, brownish specimens are frequently encountered.

ALBATRELLUS CRISTATUS (SCHAEFFER) KOTLABA & POUZAR

Photo by Bob Zordani

Ecology: Mycorrhizal with oaks and other hardwoods; growing alone or scattered; summer and fall; widely distributed. **Cap:** 5–20 cm across; circular or irregular in outline; convex, flat, or irregular; dry; bald or somewhat velvety or leathery; sometimes becoming cracked with age; yellowish to yellowish brown; often discoloring and bruising olive or greenish, especially near the margin. **Pore Surface:** Running down the stem; white, or eventually greenish to yellowish; pores small (1–3 per mm) and angular; tubes 1–5 mm deep. **Stem:** 3–6 cm long; 1–2.5 cm wide; central or somewhat off-center; yellowish; dry. **Flesh:** White; olive to greenish around larval tunnels; sometimes slowly staining olive to greenish or even bluish when sliced; thick. **Chemical Reactions:**

KOH on flesh slowly reddish; negative to greenish or yellowish on cap. **Spore Print:** White. **Microscopic Features:** Spores 5–6 × 4–5 µm; smooth; subglobose. Clamp connections absent. **Comments:** This is the most common hardwood-associated *Albatrellus* in the Midwest. Two *conifer*-associated species of *Albatrellus* that do *not* stain green are sometimes reported from the Midwest (although we have never seen them here): *Albatrellus ovinus*, with a whitish to buff cap that turns yellowish in KOH; and *Albatrellus confluens*, with a pinkish-buff cap that turns purple in KOH.

ALEURIA AURANTIA (PERSOON) FUCKEL

Ecology: Saprobic; usually growing in clusters, often in clayey soil or disturbed ground; summer and fall; widely distributed. **Fruiting Body:** Cup-shaped, often becoming flattened or irregularly shaped as a result of the clustered growth habit; reaching widths of 10 cm, but often smaller; bright orange and bald above; undersurface usually whitish and fuzzy when young, but at maturity often orange and bald; without a stem; flesh orangish and brittle. **Odor:** Not distinctive. **Microscopic Features:** Spores 18–24 × 9–11 µm; becoming warty and reticulate by maturity; ellipsoid; usually with 2 oil droplets and a prominent apiculus at each end. Paraphyses with clavate to subcapitate apices; with yellowish to orangish contents. **Comments:** Compare with *Otidea onotica* (p. 292), which features dull orangish shades, is often slit down one side, and differs microscopically.

AMANITA ABRUPTA PECK

Ecology: Mycorrhizal with hardwoods or conifers; summer and fall; widely distributed. **Cap:** 4–10 cm; convex, expanding to plano-convex or flat; dry; white; covered with small to large, conical, white to off-white warts that are randomly distributed, but are smaller and denser near the margin; the margin not lined. **Gills:** Free from the stem or slightly attached to it; close; white to cream. **Stem:** 6–12 cm long; 0.5–1.5 cm thick; tapering slightly to apex; white; bald or somewhat shaggy; with a prominent, large, abrupt basal bulb that usually features a flattened upper edge and chiseled sides; with a thick, persistent, skirt-like ring. **Flesh:** White; not staining on exposure. **Odor:** Not distinctive. **Chemical Reactions:** KOH on the cap surface negative to slightly pinkish. **Spore Print:**

White. **Microscopic Features:** Spores 6.5–9.5 × 5.5–8.5 µm; globose or broadly ellipsoid; smooth; amyloid. **Comments:** No *Amanita* should be eaten. Compare with *Amanita cokeri* (p. 91).

AMANITA BISPORIGERA ATKINSON

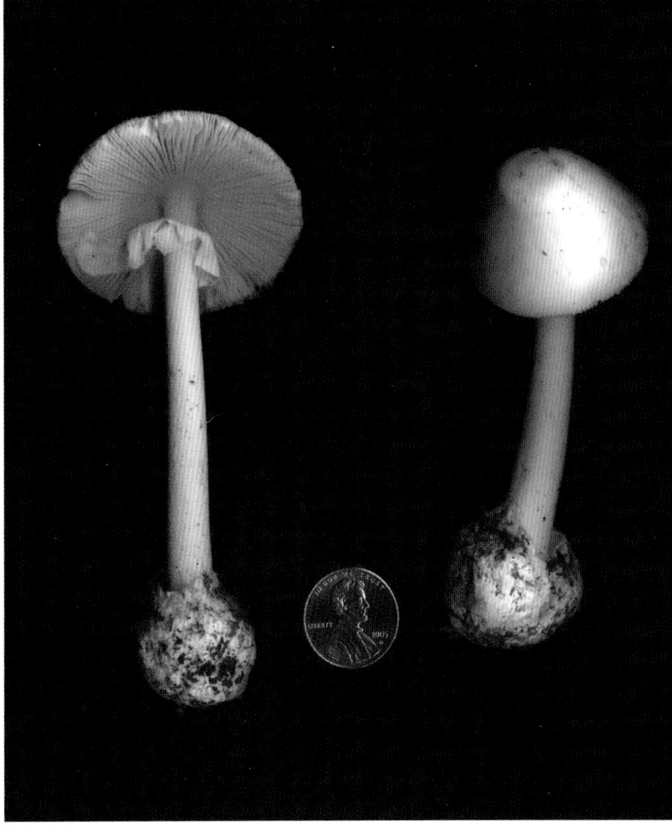

Ecology: Mycorrhizal with oaks and other hardwoods; summer and fall; widely distributed. **Cap:** 5–12 cm; almost oval at first, becoming convex, then broadly convex to nearly flat in age; bald; dry; stark white, sometimes discoloring toward the center in age; the margin not lined. **Gills:** Attached or free from the stem; close; white. **Stem:** 7.5–20 cm long; 0.5–2 cm thick; more or less equal, or tapering somewhat to apex and flaring to an enlarged base; bald or shaggy; white; with a persistent skirt-like ring that almost always remains into maturity; with a white, sac-like volva encasing the base, which may be underground. **Flesh:** White throughout. **Odor:** Not distinctive, or foul and unpleasant when old. **Spore Print:** White. **Chemical Reactions:** KOH on cap surface yellow. **Microscopic Features:** Spores 7–10 × 6.5–8.5 µm; smooth; broadly ellipsoid or subglobose; amyloid. Basidia 2-spored or 4-spored (possibly 2-spored early in the season and 4-spored as the season progresses). **Comments:** Deadly poisonous. Sometimes called the "destroying angel." Since it is so common and attractive, this species should be learned by all who forage for edible mushrooms. Compare with *Leucoagaricus naucinus* (p. 261) and with *Volvopluteus gloiocephalus* (p. 391).

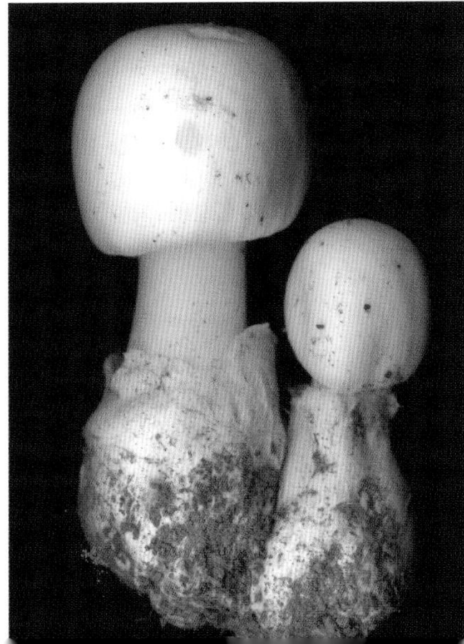

Photo by Martin Livezey

AMANITA BRUNNESCENS ATKINSON

Ecology: Mycorrhizal with hardwoods or conifers; summer and fall; widely distributed. **Cap:** 4–15 cm, convex at first, becoming broadly convex with a central bump, flat, or even shallowly depressed in age; sticky at first or when wet; deep brown to mottled brown and white (or nearly whitish overall in *Amanita brunnescens* var. *pallida*); often with a darker center; often streaked; usually with a few scattered white to grayish or tan warts; the margin sometimes faintly lined. **Gills:** Free from the stem; close or crowded; white; sometimes discoloring brownish or reddish brown. **Stem:** 5–15 cm long; 1–2 cm thick; tapering to apex; bald; with a relatively persistent, skirt-like ring that sometimes collapses against the stem; usually ending in an abrupt basal bulb that is typically "chiseled" or split vertically in one or more places; discoloring and bruising reddish brown, especially near the base. **Flesh:** White throughout; firm; sometimes discoloring or bruising reddish brown. **Chemical Reactions:** KOH on cap surface negative. **Spore Print:** White. **Microscopic Features:** Spores 7–10 µm; smooth; globose; amyloid. **Comments:** No *Amanita* should be eaten. Compare with *Amanita spreta* (p. 99).

AMANITA CECILIAE (BERKELEY & BROOME) BAS

Ecology: Mycorrhizal with hardwoods and conifers; growing alone, scattered, or gregariously; summer and fall; widely distributed. **Cap:** 5–12 cm; convex, expanding to broadly convex or nearly flat; brown overall, but usually darker in the center; with large grayish patches; the margin strongly lined at maturity. **Gills:** Free from the stem or slightly attached to it; crowded; whitish. **Stem:** 7–18 cm long; up to 2 cm thick; tapering slightly to apex; whitish; bald or finely hairy; without a ring; without a swollen base; with a whitish to grayish volva that falls apart, leaving flakes, patches, or a grayish zone of tissue on the stem base. **Flesh:** White; unchanging when sliced. **Odor:** Not distinctive. **Spore Print:** White. **Chemical Reactions:** KOH on cap surface negative. **Microscopic Features:** Spores 9–12 µm; subglobose; smooth; inamyloid. **Comments:** The lined brown cap with gray patches, ringless stem, and fragile gray volva are good field characters. Compare with *Amanita vaginata* (p. 100).

AMANITA CITRINA
(SCHAEFFER) PERSOON

Ecology: Mycorrhizal with hardwoods and conifers (especially pines); summer and fall; widely distributed. **Cap:** 5–12 cm, convex to broadly convex or flat in age; sticky when wet; with small, grayish, yellowish, or whitish patches or warts (at least when young); surface pale greenish yellow (also with lavender shades in one form), fading to nearly white; the margin not lined. **Gills:** Free from the stem; crowded; white, sometimes yellowish in age. **Stem:** 6–12 cm long; 1–1.5 cm thick; more or less equal above an abruptly bulbous base; the base with a whitish volva that adheres tightly (and is not sac-like) and features a rim or gutter on the upper edge; sometimes with a longitudinally "chiseled" or split basal bulb; with a fairly persistent white or yellowish, skirt-like ring. **Flesh:** White; unchanging when sliced. **Odor:** Not distinctive, or faintly of potatoes. **Spore Print:** White. **Microscopic Features:** Spores 7–10 µm; smooth; globose; amyloid. **Comments:** No *Amanita* should be eaten. The rimmed basal bulb and greenish colors define this species.

AMANITA COKERI
(GILBERT & KÜHNER) GILBERT

Ecology: Mycorrhizal with hardwoods or conifers; summer and fall; widely distributed below the Great Lakes. **Cap:** 7–15 cm; oval or convex, expanding to convex or plano-convex; dry, or sticky when wet; white; covered with fairly large, pointed, white to brownish warts; the margin not lined. **Gills:** Free from the stem or slightly attached to it; close or crowded; white to cream. **Stem:** 10–20 cm long; 1–2 cm thick; tapering slightly to apex; white; bald or somewhat shaggy; with a fairly large basal bulb that is shallowly rooted; with more or less concentric zones of distinctive, down-turned scales on the upper bulb and lower stem; with a thick, persistent ring that is often double or double-edged. **Flesh:** White; not staining on exposure. **Odor:** Not distinctive. **Chemical Reactions:** KOH on cap surface negative. **Spore Print:** White. **Microscopic Features:** Spores 11–14 × 6–9 µm; ellipsoid; smooth; amyloid. **Comments:** No *Amanita* should be eaten. Compare with *Amanita abrupta* (p. 88), which has an abruptly bulbous stem base that does not feature concentric zones of down-turned scales.

AMANITA FARINOSA SCHWEINITZ

Ecology: Mycorrhizal with hardwoods or conifers; sometimes found in grassy areas; early spring to late fall; widely distributed. **Cap:** 2.5–6.5 cm; oval at first, becoming convex or nearly flat, sometimes with a shallow central depression; dry; the surface dusted with fine, mealy powder that rubs off easily; occasionally with the powder gathered into a few scattered warts or patches; the margin lined; brownish gray to brownish. **Gills:** Free from the stem or slightly attached to it; close; whitish. **Stem:** 3–6.5 cm long; 0.5–1 cm thick; more or less equal above a very slight basal bulb; covered with powder like the cap; white to dirty grayish; without a ring; typically with a slight band of dense powder at the rim of the bulb, but without a sac-like volva; solid or partially hollow in age. **Flesh:** White; not changing on exposure. **Odor:** Not distinctive. **Spore Print:** White. **Microscopic Features:** Spores 5.5–8 × 6–8 µm; smooth; globose to broadly ellipsoid; inamyloid. **Comments:** No *Amanita* should be eaten. Compare with *Amanita vaginata* (p. 100).

AMANITA FLAVOCONIA ATKINSON

Ecology: Mycorrhizal with hardwoods and conifers; summer and fall; widely distributed. **Cap:** 2.5–7.5 cm, oval to convex at first, becoming broadly convex to nearly flat; sticky when fresh; bright yellow to bright orange, but often fading with age or in direct sunlight; with scattered yellow warts that disappear easily; margin not lined, or lined faintly. **Gills:** Free from the stem or slightly attached to it; close; white, sometimes with yellow edges. **Stem:** 4–10 cm long; 0.5–1.5 cm thick; more or less equal above a slightly enlarged base; with a persistent, skirt-like ring; yellow; with fragile, powdery, yellow volval remnants at the base (and often scattered on the soil surrounding the base). **Flesh:** White; unchanging when sliced. **Spore Print:** White. **Microscopic Features:** Spores 7–11 × 3.5–5 µm; smooth; ellipsoid; amyloid. **Comments:** No *Amanita* should be eaten. *Amanita frostiana* is very similar, but features a rimmed basal bulb and inamyloid spores. Compare with *Amanita flavorubescens* (p. 93), which is more robust and stains reddish.

AMANITA FLAVORUBESCENS ATKINSON

Ecology: Mycorrhizal with hardwoods, especially oaks; occasionally found in urban habitats; spring through fall; widely distributed. **Cap:** 5–14 cm; oval at first, becoming convex or nearly flat; sticky at first or when wet; yellow to yellow brown; adorned with yellow warts; margin lined or not lined. **Gills:** Free from the stem or slightly attached to it; close; white. **Stem:** 6–12 cm long; 1–2 cm thick; more or less equal above a slightly swollen base; with a persistent, skirt-like ring that sometimes features yellow stains; bald or somewhat shaggy below the ring; white, discoloring and staining reddish; base with a yellow volva that breaks up and becomes indistinct, leaving yellow remnants on the soil. **Flesh:** White; staining slowly reddish in the stem when sliced. **Spore Print:** White. **Microscopic Features:** Spores 8–10 × 5–6 µm; smooth; ellipsoid; amyloid. **Comments:** No *Amanita* should be eaten. Compare with *Amanita flavoconia* (p. 92) and with *Amanita rubescens* (p. 97).

AMANITA FULVA (SCHAEFFER) FRIES

Ecology: Mycorrhizal with hardwoods or conifers; summer and fall; widely distributed. **Cap:** 4–10 cm; oval at first, becoming convex or nearly flat, with a central bump; sticky at first or when wet; tawny; sometimes with a few scattered white to tawny patches; the margin prominently lined or grooved. **Gills:** Free from the stem or slightly attached to it; close; white. **Stem:** 7–16 cm long; 0.5–1.5 cm thick; slightly tapering to apex; bald; without a ring; the base enclosed in a sac-like, white volva that fits loosely around the stem and often discolors tawny brown. **Flesh:** White; unchanging when sliced. **Spore Print:** White. **Microscopic Features:** Spores 8–10 µm; smooth; globose; inamyloid. **Comments:** No *Amanita* should be eaten. Compare with *Amanita vaginata* (p. 100).

Photo by Melissa Bochte

AMANITA JACKSONII POMERLEAU

Ecology: Mycorrhizal with oaks and pines; summer and fall; widely distributed. **Cap:** 8–12 cm; oval at first, becoming convex, typically with a central bump; sticky; brilliant red or orange, fading to yellow on the margin; typically without warts or patches; the margin lined for about 40–50% of the cap's radius. **Gills:** Free from the stem or slightly attached to it; crowded; yellow to orange yellow; not bruising. **Stem:** 9–14 cm long; 1–1.5 cm thick; slightly tapering to apex; yellow; with orange to reddish fibers, often in zones; not bruising; with a yellow to orange, skirt-like ring; with a large (4–7 cm high and 4 mm thick), white, sac-like volva. **Flesh:** Whitish to pale yellow; not staining on exposure. **Spore Print:** White. **Microscopic Features:** Spores 7–10 µm; broadly ellipsoid; smooth; inamyloid. **Comments:** No *Amanita* should be eaten. This is the most widespread midwestern version of the well-known European species *Amanita caesarea*. An unnamed yellow version (see illustration) with larger spores is frequently found in Illinois and Indiana in oak-hickory woods; it is otherwise similar to *Amanita jacksonii*.

AMANITA MULTISQUAMOSA PECK

Ecology: Mycorrhizal with hardwoods; summer and fall; widely distributed. **Cap:** 5–10 cm; convex at first, becoming broadly convex to flat in age; sticky when fresh; pale whitish, with a yellowish-tan center, or sometimes whitish overall; with numerous whitish warts; the margin lined for 1 cm or so. **Gills:** Slightly attached, or free from the stem; close; white. **Stem:** 6–15 cm long; 1–1.5 cm thick; frequently tapering to apex; bald above the ring, and slightly scaly below it; whitish; terminating in a rimmed, collar-like basal bulb that features concentric shaggy rings below the rim, and a pinched-off bottom. **Flesh:** White; unchanging when sliced. **Spore Print:** White. **Microscopic Features:** Spores 8–11 × 6–8 µm; ellipsoid; smooth; inamyloid. **Comments:** Compare with *Amanita russuloides* (p. 98), which is straw yellow, has fewer warts, and features a more prominently lined cap margin.

AMANITA MUSCARIA VAR. GUESSOWII VESELÝ

Photo by Ron Kerner

Ecology: Mycorrhizal with hardwoods and conifers; growing alone or gregariously, often in troops or arcs; summer and fall; widely distributed but more common in northern areas. **Cap:** 4–16 cm, convex at first, becoming broadly convex to flat; bald underneath the warts; sticky when fresh; pale yellow to orange yellow, fading with age; with many cottony white warts; the margin usually slightly lined. **Gills:** Free from the stem; white; crowded. **Stem:** 4–15 cm long; 1–3 cm thick; more or less equal above an enlarged base; typically somewhat shaggy; white; with a persistent, whitish, skirt-like ring; with prominent, concentric, rim-like bands at the top of the base. **Flesh:** White; unchanging when sliced. **Spore Print:** White. **Microscopic Features:** Spores 9–13 × 6–8 µm; smooth; broadly ellipsoid; inamyloid. **Comments:** Poisonous. Also known as *Amanita muscaria* var. *formosa*. The stem base is the most distinctive identifying feature. Compare with *Amanita parcivolvata* (below).

AMANITA PARCIVOLVATA (PECK) GILBERT

Ecology: Mycorrhizal with oaks and often reported under pines in "mixed woods"; growing alone or gregariously; common in grassy, disturbed-ground settings, but also found in woods; spring through fall; widely distributed. **Cap:** 3–12 cm; convex to broadly convex, flat, or shallowly depressed; sticky when fresh; bald underneath yellowish warts or patches that can disappear with maturity; red to orange red, fading fairly quickly from the margin inward; the margin lined, at least by maturity. **Gills:** Free from the stem or nearly so; crowded; creamy to pale yellow; dusted. **Stem:** 3–12 cm long; up to about 1.5 cm thick; tapering slightly to the apex; pale yellow; without a ring; base with powdery, indistinct, flaky whitish to yellowish volval remnants. **Flesh:**

Photo by Dan Molter

Photo by Walt Sturgeon

Pale yellow; unchanging. **Odor:** Not distinctive. **Spore Print:** White. **Microscopic Features:** Spores 9.5–14 × 6–8 µm; smooth; ellipsoid to nearly cylindric; inamyloid. **Comments:** No *Amanita* should be eaten. Compare with *Amanita muscaria* var. *guessowii* (p. 95), which has a ring and multiple concentric bands of shagginess around its base.

AMANITA PELIOMA BAS

Ecology: Mycorrhizal with oaks and perhaps with other hardwoods or conifers; solitary; summer and fall; widely distributed in the lower Midwest. **Cap:** 4–9 cm; convex to broadly convex or nearly flat; moist or dry; covered with powdery material that comes off on handling; whitish to grayish or brownish buff, or with olive hues; the margin not lined, but often somewhat shaggy. **Gills:** Free from the stem or nearly so; crowded; creamy becoming brownish (the color of café au lait) or olive buff. **Stem:** 9–15 cm long; up to 1.5 cm thick; tapering slightly to the apex; colored like the cap and covered with similar powdery material; with a large, skirt-like, fragile, whitish ring that usually disappears; terminating in a turnip-shaped basal bulb that often features a tapering "root"; with powdery, indistinct volval remnants; stained bluish to greenish blue near the base. **Flesh:** White; unchanging when sliced. **Odor:** Not distinctive. **Spore Print:** White. **Microscopic Features:** Spores 8–13.5 × 5–9 µm; smooth; broadly ellipsoid; amyloid. **Comments:** No *Amanita* should be eaten. This is the only *Amanita* species with gills the color of café au lait and a blue-staining stem base. Compare with *Amanita polypyramis* (below), which has whitish to buff gills and does not stain blue on the stem.

AMANITA POLYPYRAMIS (BERKELEY & M. A. CURTIS) SACCARDO

Ecology: Mycorrhizal with conifers (especially pines) and hardwoods (especially oaks); solitary; summer and fall; southern Midwest. **Cap:** 7–21 cm; convex to broadly convex or nearly flat; moist or dry; covered with a powdery layer that soon becomes aggregated into soft warts or patches; whitish; the margin not lined, but often hung with veil material. **Gills:** Free from the stem or nearly so; crowded; creamy or dirty buff. **Stem:** 7–20 cm long; up to 3.5 cm thick; taper-

Photo by Patrick Harvey

ing slightly to the apex; colored like the cap and covered with powdery material, at least when young; with a large, skirt-like, fragile, whitish ring that often disappears; terminating in an abrupt, more or less round basal bulb; with powdery, indistinct volval remnants. **Flesh:** White; unchanging. **Odor:** Strong, reminiscent of rotting meat. **Spore Print:** White. **Microscopic Features:** Spores 9–14 × 5–10 µm; smooth; broadly ellipsoid; amyloid. **Comments:** No *Amanita* should be eaten. Compare with *Amanita pelioma* (p. 96).

Photo by Patrick Harvey

AMANITA RUBESCENS PERSOON

Ecology: Mycorrhizal with oaks and other hardwoods and sometimes with conifers; late spring, summer, and fall; widely distributed. **Cap:** 4–12 cm; convex to broadly convex or flat in age; dry or slightly sticky; with yellow warts when young, but the warts soon fade to pinkish, grayish or dull tan; surface pale bronze to brownish when young, becoming flushed with red shades, and eventually reddish brown to tan or brown; the margin not lined. **Gills:** Free from the stem or narrowly attached to it; close; white, sometimes discoloring reddish. **Stem:** 5–14 cm long; 1.5–3 cm thick; more or less equal above a slightly enlarged base; with a fragile, skirt-like ring that typically persists into maturity; without volval remnants, but sometimes with a few indistinct volval scales or zones; white, becoming stained pinkish to dirty red; bald. **Flesh:** White; staining and discoloring slowly pale pinkish red, especially around worm holes. **Spore Print:** White. **Chemical Reactions:** KOH on cap surface negative. **Microscopic Features:** Spores 7.5–10.5 × 5–7 µm; smooth; ellipsoid; amyloid. **Comments:** No *Amanita* should be eaten. According to *Amanita* expert Rod Tulloss (Tulloss and Lindgren 1994), the species described here is not the same as the true European *Amanita rubescens*. A whitish variety, *Amanita rubescens* var. *alba* (see Kuo and Methven 2010), is also common in the Midwest's oak-hickory forests. The blushing amanitas are often parasitized by *Hypomyces hyalinus* (see Kuo and Methven 2010). Compare with *Leucoagaricus americanus* (p. 260).

AMANITA RUSSULOIDES PECK

Ecology: Mycorrhizal with conifers and hardwoods, but especially fond of oaks; often found in grassy areas; summer and fall; fairly widely distributed. **Cap:** 4–12 cm; convex to broadly convex, flat, or shallowly depressed in age; thin-fleshed; sticky when fresh, but soon dry; pale dull yellow to straw yellow; with a few whitish to grayish warts that often disappear entirely; the margin grooved and pimply for 1–3 cm. **Gills:** Free from the stem or nearly so; crowded; white to creamy. **Stem:** 5–12 cm long; up to 2 cm thick; tapering slightly to apex; whitish to yellowish; with a fragile whitish ring that can appear fairly high on the stem or nearly at the bottom and often disappears entirely; terminating in a small basal bulb; with fragile white volval remnants that form a few vague rings or, fairly often, a collar-like rim. **Flesh:** White; unchanging when sliced. **Spore Print:** White. **Chemical Reactions:** KOH on cap surface pinkish orange. **Microscopic Features:** Spores 7.5–10 × 5–7 µm; smooth; broadly ellipsoid; inamyloid. **Comments:** No *Amanita* should be eaten. Compare with *Amanita multisquamosa* (p. 94).

AMANITA SALMONESCENS TULLOSS

Ecology: Mycorrhizal with oaks; growing alone, scattered, or gregariously; summer and fall; distribution uncertain (see comments). **Cap:** 3.5–8.5 cm; convex, expanding to plano-convex or flat, sometimes with a central depression; whitish, discoloring pinkish or reddish brown; covered with white to gray warts; the margin not lined, or lined slightly at maturity. **Gills:** Free from the stem or slightly attached to it; crowded or close; white to cream, sometimes discoloring slightly brownish. **Stem:** 2–7 cm long; 1 cm thick; tapering slightly, then flaring at apex; white, often bruising pink; with an elongated bulb at the bottom that is ringed by loosely concentric circles of universal veil material; with a skirt-like ring that often collapses against the stem and typically discolors pinkish to brownish salmon. **Flesh:** White; sometimes pinkish around insect-damaged areas. **Odor:** Not distinctive. **Spore Print:** White. **Microscopic Features:** Spores 6.5–9 × 4.5–6 µm; ellipsoid; smooth; amyloid. **Comments:** No *Amanita* should be eaten. This species is recorded from New Jersey, North Carolina, and Illinois. *Amanita rubescens* var. *alba* can appear similar but is usually more robust and features more prominent warts.

AMANITA SP. (UNNAMED): THE LITTLE BROWN AMANITA

Ecology: Mycorrhizal with white oaks, appearing in oak-hickory woods; often growing in moss; June and July; common in Illinois, and probably to be expected throughout the Midwest where white oaks occur. **Cap:** 15–40 mm; convex becoming plano-convex; pale brown to grayish brown with a darker center; somewhat radially streaked; the margin not lined; usually without universal veil remnants, but occasionally with a few whitish to grayish patches. **Gills:** Free from the stem; crowded; white. **Stem:** 3–6 cm long; under 1 cm thick; more or less equal above a small, nearly round basal bulb measuring about 10–15 mm across; whitish; sometimes discoloring a little brownish on handling; bald; with a thin, high, white ring that flares upward or hangs skirt-like; with an adherent white volva that extends above the bulb for a few millimeters. **Flesh:** White; unchanging when sliced. **Odor:** Not distinctive. **Spore Print:** White. **Chemical Reactions:** KOH on cap surface negative. **Microscopic Features:** Spores 6.5–9.5 µm; globose; smooth; amyloid. **Comments:** No *Amanita* should be eaten. This apparently unnamed species is quite small and easily overlooked.

AMANITA SPRETA (PECK) SACCARDO

Ecology: Mycorrhizal with hardwoods or conifers; summer and fall; widely distributed but more common in the southern Midwest. **Cap:** 5–11 cm; convex, expanding to plano-convex or flat; grayish brown, but often darker over the center; with small, dark streaks that radiate outward; usually bald but occasionally featuring a whitish patch; the margin lined faintly or strongly at maturity. **Gills:** Free from the stem or slightly attached to it; crowded or close; whitish. **Stem:** 5–10 cm long; up to 2 cm thick; tapering slightly to apex; whitish, sometimes discoloring a little brownish; with a white, skirt-like ring that may discolor brownish; with a slightly enlarged but not bulbous base that is set in a sac-like, flaring, white volva. **Flesh:** White; unchanging when sliced. **Odor:** Not distinctive. **Spore Print:** White. **Chemical Reactions:** KOH on cap surface negative. **Microscopic Features:** Spores

8.5–10 × 6–7 µm; ellipsoid; smooth; inamyloid. **Comments:** No *Amanita* should be eaten. Compare with *Amanita brunnescens* (p. 90), which lacks the flaring volva and has a stem that stains brown.

AMANITA THIERSII BAS

Ecology: Saprobic in grasses; growing alone, scattered, gregariously, or in arcs and fairy rings in lawns and meadows; summer; south of the Great Lakes (see comments). **Cap:** 5–20 cm; convex, becoming broadly convex or nearly flat; covered with powdery, shaggy, sticky universal veil material; white; the margin hung with veil remnants. **Gills:** Nearly free; close; white. **Stem:** 8–20 cm long; 1–2 cm wide; covered with shagginess like the cap; with a skirt-like white ring; volva powdery and indistinct. **Flesh:** White; unchanging when sliced. **Spore Print:** White. **Microscopic Features:** Spores 7–10 µm; globose; smooth; amyloid. **Comments:** No *Amanita* should be eaten. Unlike most species in the genus, *Amanita thiersii* is saprobic and not associated with trees. Originally documented from Texas, it has since expanded its range (Wolfe, Kuo, and Pringle 2012); it is now quite common in central and southern Illinois and Indiana, and we have seen photos of it from Ohio. It has not been reported from the Chicago area or from the northern Midwest. Compare with *Chlorophyllum molybdites* (p. 135).

AMANITA VAGINATA (BULLIARD) FRIES

Ecology: Mycorrhizal with hardwoods and conifers; found in woods or in disturbed-ground settings in urban areas, picnic areas, and so on; late spring, summer, and fall; widely distributed. **Cap:** 3–10 cm; oval, becoming convex or nearly flat, but often retaining a central bump; sticky at first or when wet; gray to grayish brown; sometimes with a few scattered white to grayish patches; the margin prominently lined or grooved. **Gills:** Free from the stem or slightly attached to it; close; white. **Stem:** 7–15 cm long; 0.5–2 cm thick; slightly tapering to apex; without a ring; the base enclosed in a sac-like, flaring, white volva that fits loosely around the stem and sometimes discolors grayish or reddish brown. **Flesh:** White; unchanging when sliced. **Spore Print:** White. **Microscopic Features:** Spores 8–12 µm; smooth; nearly round; inamyloid. **Comments:** No *Amanita* should be eaten. "*Amanita vaginata*" represents a group of poorly understood species in North America. The version we are describing here is

Photo by Lisa K. Suits

frequently encountered in urban settings throughout the Midwest. Compare with *Amanita fulva* (p. 93), which is similar but features a tawny cap—and with *Amanita ceciliae* (p. 90), which has a grayish, flimsy volva and usually features grayish patches on the cap. *Amanita sinicoflava* is also similar; it features an olive-yellow cap and a volva that stains gray to black.

AMPULLOCLITOCYBE CLAVIPES (PERSOON) REDHEAD, LUTZONI, MONCALVO, & VILGALYS

Photo by Dan Molter

Ecology: Saprobic; growing alone, scattered, or gregariously; found primarily under conifers, but sometimes reported under hardwoods; late summer and fall; widely distributed. **Cap:** 2–9 cm; at first flat with a slightly underturned margin, becoming centrally depressed or vase-shaped, with an uplifted margin; bald; moist or dry; brown to grayish brown or olive brown. **Gills:** Running down the stem; close or nearly distant; whitish or creamy. **Stem:** 3.5–6 cm long; up to 3.5 cm thick at the base; often bulbous at the bottom, but sometimes more or less equal; minutely hairy; buff or pale brownish. **Flesh:** Whitish. **Odor and Taste:** Odor usually fragrant and fruity; taste mild. **Spore Print:** White. **Chemical Reactions:** KOH on cap surface negative. **Microscopic Features:** Spores 6–8.5 × 3.5–5 µm; ovoid, or irregularly ellipsoid; smooth; inamyloid. Cystidia absent. Pileipellis a cutis. Clamp connections present. **Comments:** Also known as *Clitocybe clavipes*. The relatively recent genus *Ampulloclitocybe* was established to reflect the fact that DNA studies (Redhead et al. 2002) have placed this mushroom and closely related species far from the bulk of the genus *Clitocybe*.

ARMILLARIA GALLICA MARXMÜLLER & ROMAGNESI

Ecology: Saprobic (usually not parasitic); growing alone, gregariously, or in loose clusters on the deadwood of hardwoods and occasionally conifers; usually appearing terrestrial (but actually attached to roots), but sometimes fruiting from the bases of trees and stumps; late summer and fall; widely distributed. **Cap:** 2–6 cm; convex, becoming broadly convex or flat in age; dry or sticky; tan to pinkish brown or tawny brown; usually with fine yellowish hairs; often with white partial veil material on the margin. **Gills:** Beginning to run down the stem; nearly distant; whitish, sometimes bruising or discoloring pinkish to brownish. **Stem:** 5–10 cm long; 0.5–1 cm thick at apex; with a swollen base that often stains yellow; whitish; with a yellow ring zone

or an ephemeral, flimsy ring (but usually without a well-developed, membranous, persistent ring); attached to black rhizomorphs. **Flesh:** Whitish. **Odor and Taste:** Odor sweet; taste mild to bitter. **Spore Print:** White. **Microscopic Features:** Spores 7–9.5 × 4.5–6 µm; smooth; more or less ellipsoid; inamyloid. Basidia with basal clamps. **Comments:** Edible when not bitter, but compare with *Galerina marginata* (p. 178). The terrestrial, solitary to scattered growth pattern and the sometimes-swollen stem base are tentative field characters for identifying this species.

ARMILLARIA MELLEA (VAHL) KUMMER

Ecology: Pathogenic and parasitic on the wood of hardwoods (and occasionally on conifers); also sometimes saprobic on deadwood; causing a white, pulpy rot in the wood; spreading through wood, and from tree to tree, by means of long black rhizomorphs; mushrooms typically appearing in large clusters on wood in the fall after rains; widely distributed. **Cap:** 3–15 cm, convex, becoming broadly convex or flat in age; the margin often arched in maturity; dry or tacky; color extremely variable, but typically honey yellow; bald, or with a few tiny dark scales concentrated near the center. **Gills:** Attached or beginning to run down the stem; nearly distant; whitish, sometimes bruising or discoloring darker; at first covered by a whitish, membranous partial veil. **Stem:** 5–20 cm long; 0.5–3.5 cm thick; tapering to base due to clustered growth pattern; tough and fibrous; bald and pale near apex, darker and nearly hairy below; with a persistent ring at maturity. **Flesh:** Whitish to watery tan. **Odor and Taste:** Odor not distinctive; taste mild to bitter. **Chemical Reactions:** KOH negative on cap surface. **Spore Print:** White. **Microscopic Features:** Spores 7–9 × 6–7 µm; smooth; more or less ellipsoid; inamyloid. Basidia lacking basal clamps. **Comments:** Edible, but compare with *Galerina marginata* (p. 178). The clustered-on-wood growth, the persistent and membranous ring, the relatively bald cap, and the honey-yellow colors are good field characters. *Armillaria solidipes* (formerly known as *Armillaria ostoyae*) grows primarily on the wood of conifers; it features a darker, browner, scalier cap and a less persistent ring.

ARMILLARIA TABESCENS (SCOPOLI) EMEL

Ecology: Parasitic and/or saprobic on hardwood roots, especially those of oaks and maples; growing in large clusters at the bases of trees, or appearing to be terrestrial but actually growing from buried wood; late summer and fall; widely distributed. **Cap:**

1–4 cm; convex, becoming broadly convex or flat in age; the margin often arched in maturity; dry; tan to tawny brown or cinnamon brown, or sometimes yellow; covered with small, dark scales, which are concentrated near the center. **Gills:** Beginning to run down the stem; nearly distant; whitish, sometimes bruising or discoloring pinkish to brownish; not covered by a partial veil when young. **Stem:** 7.5–20 cm long; 0.5–1.5 cm thick; tapering to base; bald and pale near apex, darker and silky below; without a ring or ring zone. **Flesh:** Whitish to watery tan; sometimes insubstantial in stem. **Odor and Taste:** Odor not distinctive; taste mild to bitter. **Chemical Reactions:** KOH red on cap surface. **Spore Print:** White. **Microscopic Features:** Spores 8–10 × 5–7 µm; smooth; ellipsoid; inamyloid. Basidia with basal clamps. **Comments:** Edible when not bitter, but compare with *Galerina marginata* (p. 178). The colors, the complete absence of a partial veil, and the clustered growth pattern are good field characters for this species.

ARRHENIA EPICHYSIUM (PERSOON) REDHEAD, LUTZONI, MONCALVO, & VILGALYS

Ecology: Parasitic on moss; growing alone, gregariously, or in clusters on mossy deadwood of hardwoods and conifers; spring through fall; widely distributed. **Cap:** 1.5–5 cm across; plano-convex at first, becoming centrally depressed or vase-shaped; bald; the margin inrolled at first and later lined, often nearly to the center; blackish to dark grayish brown, fading markedly as it dries out and eventually becoming pale grayish brown. **Gills:** Running down the stem; close or nearly distant; pale gray. **Stem:** Up to 3 cm long and 3 mm thick; more or less equal; dry; bald or minutely hairy; colored like the cap but not fading as quickly. **Flesh:** Insubstantial; watery grayish. **Odor and Taste:** Not distinctive. **Chemical Reactions:** KOH negative on cap surface.

Spore Print: White. **Microscopic Features:** Spores 7–9 × 4–5 µm; smooth; ellipsoid; inamyloid. Cystidia absent. Clamp connections present. **Comments:** Also known as *Omphalina epichysium*. The dark colors, the depressed cap, and the gills that run down the stem are field characters for this species, but microscopic analysis may be required for confident identification.

Photo by Andy Methven

ARTOMYCES PYXIDATUS (PERSOON) JÜLICH

Ecology: Saprobic; growing alone or gregariously on the deadwood of hardwoods (especially the wood of aspens, tulip tree, willows, and maples); spring, summer, and fall; widely distributed. **Fruiting Body:** 4–13 cm high; 2–10 cm wide; repeatedly branched. **Branches:** 1–5 mm thick; smooth; whitish to pale yellowish at first, sometimes darkening to pale tan or developing pinkish hues; tips crowned with a shallow depression and 3–6 points, colored like the branches or becoming brownish. **Base:** 1–3 cm long; under 1 cm thick; whitish, pinkish, or brownish; finely fuzzy. **Flesh:** Whitish; fairly tough and pliable. **Odor and Taste:** Odor not distinctive; taste mild or peppery-acrid. **Spore Print:** White. **Chemical Reactions:** Iron salts negative to grayish or brownish on branches and base. **Microscopic Features:** Spores 4–5 × 2–3 µm; ellipsoid; very minutely pitted; amyloid. Cystidia variously shaped; often scarcely projecting. Gloeoplerous hyphae scattered in the subhymenium; occasionally rising to the hymenium to form gloeocystidia. Clamp connections present. **Comments:** Also known as *Clavicorona pyxidata*. The growth directly from rotting wood and the characteristic crowned branch tips are good field characters.

ASTEROPHORA LYCOPERDOIDES (BULLIARD) DITMAR

Ecology: Parasitic on species of *Russula* and *Lactarius*, especially *Russula dissimulans* (p. 341) and closely related species, and usually appearing when the host has begun to blacken and decay; found in a variety of forests, since the hosts are mycorrhizal with both hardwoods and conifers; summer and fall; widely distributed. **Cap:** 1–2.5 cm; convex or nearly round; dry; at first whitish and a little bit roughened or lumpy, becoming brownish and powdery. **Gills:** Usually poorly formed and vein-like; attached to the stem; thick; distant; whitish or grayish. **Stem:** 2–5 cm long; up to 1 cm thick; more or less equal; dry; bald or velvety; whitish to brownish. **Flesh:** White; unchanging when sliced. **Odor and Taste:** Mealy. **Spore Print:** Often hard to obtain; white. **Microscopic Features:** Basidiospores when present 5–6 × 3.5–4 µm; smooth; ellipsoid; inamyloid. Chlamydospores 14–17 × 12–16 µm; spiny. **Comments:** Easily identified due to its distinctive ecology and appearance.

AURICULARIA AURICULA (LINNAEUS) UNDERWOOD

Ecology: Saprobic on the deadwood of conifers and hardwoods, especially hickories; spring, summer, and fall (sometimes even in winter, when the weather is warm); widely distributed. **Fruiting Body:** Wavy and irregular; typically ear-shaped; 2–15 cm; gathered together and attached at a central or lateral position; fertile surface (usually the "downward" one) gelatinous, tan to brown; sterile surface (usually the "upper" one) silky to downy, veined, irregular, brown; flesh thin, gelatinous-rubbery. **Spore Print:** White. **Microscopic Features:** Spores 12–19 × 4–8 µm; allantoid; smooth. Basidia cylindric; transversely 3-septate. **Comments:** Compare with *Exidia recisa* (p. 175) and *Tremella foliacea* (p. 373).

AURISCALPIUM VULGARE GRAY

Ecology: Saprobic on the cones of conifers, especially pines; growing alone or gregariously (up to 4 or 5 mushrooms per cone); late fall and early winter; widely distributed but not common in the Midwest. **Cap:** 1–3 cm across; broadly convex or flat; kidney-shaped or almost circular in outline; dry; hairy, sometimes becoming bald with age; reddish brown to dark brown or nearly black. **Undersurface:** Spines 1–3 mm long; white at first, becoming brownish; crowded. **Stem:** 2–7 cm long; up to 3 mm thick; usually somewhat off-center or lateral; tough; reddish brown to dark brown; hairy; sometimes attached to a spongy underground portion when the cone is buried in duff. **Flesh:** Whitish to brownish; tough and thin. **Odor and Taste:** Odor not distinctive; taste mild or slightly bitter. **Spore Print:** White. **Chemical Reactions:** KOH on cap and stem instantly black. **Microscopic Features:** Spores 3.5–6 µm; broadly ellipsoid to subglobose; smooth, or becoming finely spiny when mature; amyloid. **Comments:** Tiny but distinctive, this fungus is easily identified but unfortunately somewhat rare in the Midwest.

AUSTROBOLETUS GRACILIS (PECK) WOLFE

Ecology: Mycorrhizal with hemlock and other conifers; growing alone or scattered; summer and fall; primarily northern in distribution. **Cap:** 3–10 cm; convex to broadly convex in age; dry; bald or felty; sometimes becoming cracked; margin even; reddish brown to cinnamon to dull yellow brown. **Pore Surface:** Whitish becoming pinkish to flesh-colored or pinkish brown; bruising brownish; pores circular, 1–2 per mm; tubes to 2 cm deep. **Stem:** 7–18 cm long; 0.5–1 cm thick; gracefully narrowing to apex, or more or less equal; colored like the cap or paler; sometimes slightly curved; frequently longitudinally grooved; white at the base. **Flesh:** White or pinkish; unchanging when sliced. **Odor and Taste:** Taste mild to slightly acidic; odor not distinctive. **Chemical Reactions:** Ammonia flashing blue green, then resolving to purplish gray on cap surface; purplish to pinkish on flesh. KOH orangish brown on cap; orangish on flesh. Iron salts negative on cap; green on flesh. **Spore Print:** Rosy brown. **Microscopic Features:** Spores 10–17 × 5–8 µm; minutely pitted; ellipsoid. **Comments:** Also known as *Tylopilus gracilis.*

BISPORELLA CITRINA (BATSCH) KORF & S. E. CARPENTER

Ecology: Saprobic on decaying logs and stumps of hardwoods and conifers; growing in dense clusters; summer and fall; widely distributed. **Fruiting Body:** Cup-shaped to disc-shaped; up to 3 mm across; bald and smooth above and below; with a tiny tapering stem, or nearly without a stem; uniformly bright yellow. **Microscopic Features:** Spores 9–14 × 3–5 µm; ellipsoid; with an oil droplet at each end; smooth; often septate by maturity. Paraphyses narrowly cylindric, with rounded or slightly clavate apices. **Comments:** Quite common and widespread. *Bisporella citrina* can appear on almost any sort of deadwood, including fence posts, garden gates, and so on. Some jelly fungi in the genus *Dacrymyces* can appear similar, but they have more gelatinous fruiting bodies and differ substantially under the microscope.

BJERKANDERA ADUSTA (WILDENOW) KARSTEN

Ecology: Saprobic on the deadwood of hardwoods and, rarely, conifers; causing a white rot; annual; appearing almost year-round; widely distributed. **Cap:** Bracket-like to shelf-like (and usually fused laterally with other caps), or appearing merely as a turned-over edge above a spreading pore surface, or occasionally lacking a cap entirely; semicircular to irregular in outline; convex to flat; to about 10 cm wide and 6 cm deep; velvety to finely hairy, becoming bald with maturity; whitish to grayish, tan, or brownish; sometimes zoned; when mature with a brown to black margin. **Pore Surface:** Gray to black; sometimes bruising darker black; with 6–7 tiny angular pores per mm; tubes to 2 mm deep. **Stem:** Absent. **Flesh:** Whitish to faintly brownish; tough and corky or leathery. **Odor and Taste:** Odor fragrant, or not distinctive; taste sour, or not distinctive. **Chemical Reactions:** KOH negative on all surfaces. **Spore Print:** White. **Microscopic Features:** Spores 4–6 × 2.5–3.5 µm; smooth; ellipsoid; inamyloid; hyaline in KOH. Setae absent. Cystidia absent. Hyphal system monomitic; hyphae with abundant clamp connections. **Comments:** The dark gray to black pore surface, which contrasts with the paler cap, is distinctive.

BOLBITIUS RETICULATUS (PERSOON) RICKEN

Ecology: Saprobic, decomposing the deadwood of hardwoods (logs, sticks, woodchips, and so on); growing alone or scattered; summer and fall; widely distributed. **Cap:** 1.5–5 cm; broadly bell-shaped to broadly convex, becoming flat; fragile; purple, grayish, or lilac gray; the center usually darker than the edge; sticky; bald; strongly lined, often nearly all the way to the center. **Gills:** Free from the stem or very narrowly attached to it; close or nearly crowded; whitish, becoming faintly pinkish, then rusty cinnamon. **Stem:** 3–7 cm long; up to about 0.5 cm thick; equal; hollow; finely scaly, powdery, or finely hairy; white. **Flesh:** Insubstantial; whitish. **Odor and Taste:** Not distinctive. **Spore Print:** Rusty brown. **Microscopic Features:** Spores 9–13 × 4–6 µm; ellipsoid; smooth;

with a pore at one end. Brachybasidioles present on gills. Pileipellis a hymeniform trichoderm. **Comments:** The lined purplish cap, relatively small size, rusty-brown spore print, and habitat on wood define this species.

BOLBITIUS TITUBANS (BULLIARD) FRIES

Ecology: Saprobic; growing alone, scattered, or gregariously on dung, in grass, on straw, and in woodchips; spring through fall; widely distributed. **Cap:** 1.5–5 cm; egg-shaped or nearly round when young, expanding to broadly bell-shaped or broadly convex, and eventually flat with a central bump; fragile; slimy when fresh; yellow or greenish yellow, often fading to grayish or pale tan but (usually) retaining a yellowish center; bald; usually strongly lined by maturity, often nearly all the way to the center; sometimes developing a pocketed or veined cap surface as the slime dries out. **Gills:** Free from the stem or narrowly attached to it; close; fragile and soft; whitish or pale yellowish, becoming rusty cinnamon; often gelatinizing somewhat in wet weather. **Stem:** 3–12 cm long; up to nearly 1 cm thick; equal or tapering to the apex; hollow; fragile; finely scaly, powdery, finely hairy, or more or less bald; white with a yellowish apex and/or base, or yellowish overall. **Flesh:** Insubstantial; yellowish. **Odor and Taste:** Not distinctive. **Chemical Reactions:** KOH on cap surface negative to dark gray. **Spore Print:** Rusty brown. **Microscopic Features:** Spores 10–16 × 6–9 µm; more or less ellipsoid, with a truncated end; smooth; with a pore. Brachybasidioles and abruptly clavate cheilocystidia present. **Comments:** "*Bolbitius vitellinus*" was traditionally separated from *Bolbitius titubans* on the basis of its thicker flesh, less striate cap, and whiter stem, but mycologists have recently synonymized the two species.

Photo by Walt Sturgeon

BOLETELLUS CHRYSENTEROIDES (SNELL) SNELL

Ecology: Associated with oaks and hemlock; presumably mycorrhizal, but often found growing from or near well-decayed oak stumps; usually growing alone; summer and fall; fairly widely distributed from roughly the Mississippi Valley eastward. **Cap:** 2–10 cm; convex, becoming broadly convex in age; dry; finely velvety to nearly bald; sometimes becoming cracked with age; dark brown to nearly black at first, becoming medium brown or eventually pale brown. **Pore Surface:** Bright to dull yellow, becoming olive yellow; bruising slowly blue and eventually brown; 1–2 round to angular pores per mm; tubes to about 1 cm deep. **Stem:** 2–3 cm long; up to 1.5 cm thick; more or less equal; at first punctuated by brownish, *Leccinum*-like scabers that later become aggregated into hairy or subscaly clusters that sometimes approximate the appearance of reticulation; yellowish to brownish at first, becoming reddish to purplish red in the midportion with age. **Flesh:** Pale yellow to whitish, or with age reddish in the midportion of the stem and around damaged areas; changing to bluish or blue when sliced. **Odor and Taste:** Not distinctive. **Spore Print:** Olive brown. **Microscopic Features:** Spores 10–17 × 5–8 µm; longitudinally twisted-grooved; ellipsoid; yellow in KOH. Pileipellis a trichoderm; terminal elements often elongated. **Comments:** Compare with *Boletus chrysenteron* (p. 114) and *Boletellus pseudochrysenteroides* (below).

BOLETELLUS PSEUDOCHRYSENTEROIDES A. H. SMITH & THIERS

Photo by Martin Livezey

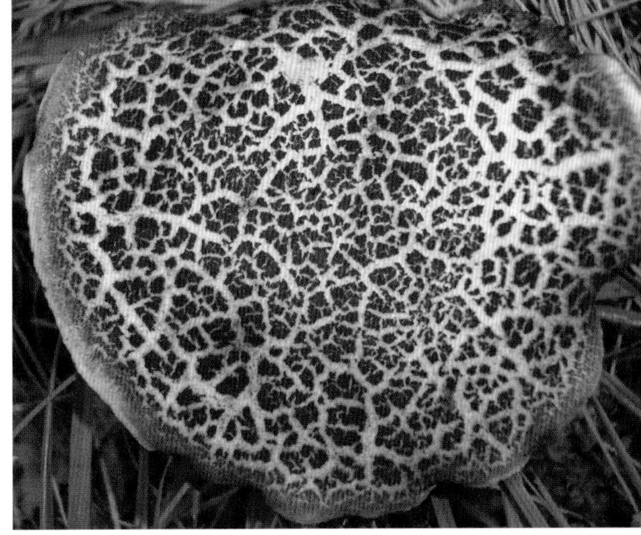

Ecology: Mycorrhizal with hardwoods, especially beech and oaks; growing alone or scattered; summer and fall; widely distributed. **Cap:** 3–10 cm; convex, becoming broadly convex or nearly flat in age; dry; soft; velvety; soon becoming prominently cracked, with whitish to pinkish flesh showing in the cracks; dark red, becoming olivaceous or remaining reddish to maturity, without olive shades. **Pore Surface:** Yellowish, becoming darker yellow to olive and eventually blackish; bruising blue, then brown, or bruising blackish; pores angular, 1–1.5 mm wide; tubes to 12 mm deep. **Stem:** 6–10 cm long; 1–2 cm thick; more or less equal; dry; solid; finely hairy or scruffy; yellow at the apex, but elsewhere colored like the cap or paler; sometimes bruising dark brown; basal mycelium dense and whitish to yellowish. **Flesh:** Pale to bright yellow in the cap, quickly staining blue on exposure; dark red in the stem and bluing somewhat, especially in the base. **Odor and Taste:** Not distinctive. **Chemical Reactions:** Ammonia yellowish on cap; orangish on flesh. KOH negative or slightly grayish on cap; orangish on flesh. Iron salts blackish on cap; dingy yellowish to olive on flesh. **Spore Print:** Dark olive gray to brown. **Microscopic Features:** Spores 11–14 × 5.5–8 µm; finely grooved; ellipsoid. **Comments:** Compare with *Boletus chrysenteron* (p. 114), which has a brownish cracked cap with pinkish flesh showing in the cracks, and smooth spores—and with *Boletellus chrysenteroides* (pp. 108–9, above), which is more brown and has a distinctive stem surface. *Boletellus intermedius* has a cap that is reddish when young, but soon becomes olive brown to olive gray.

Photo by Martin Livezey

Spores

BOLETELLUS RUSSELLII (FROST) GILBERT

Ecology: Mycorrhizal with oaks and other hardwoods, or occasionally with conifers; growing alone or scattered; summer and fall; widely distributed. **Cap:** 3–13 cm; convex, becoming broadly convex in age; dry; finely velvety to nearly bald, often becoming cracked and patchy with age; yellowish brown to reddish brown or olive gray; with a strongly incurved margin. **Pore Surface:** Yellow to greenish yellow; not bruising; pores angular, about 1 mm wide; tubes to 1.5 cm deep. **Stem:** 10–20 cm long; 1–2 cm thick; more or less equal; deeply furrowed and lacerated longitudinally (very coarsely reticulate); solid and rather tough; reddish brown to brown. **Flesh:** Pale yellow throughout; not bruising when exposed. **Odor and Taste:** Not distinctive. **Chemical Reactions:** Ammonia reddish on cap; negative on flesh. KOH negative on cap; negative to reddish on flesh. Iron salts olive gray on cap; negative on flesh. **Spore Print:** Olive brown. **Microscopic Features:** Spores 15–20 × 7–11 µm; deeply grooved and wrinkled; ellipsoid. Pileipellis a trichoderm with bundled terminal elements. **Comments:** Edible and good. Compare with *Boletus projectellus* (p. 121), which has a deeply ridged (but not coarsely lacerated-reticulate) stem and smooth spores.

BOLETUS ATKINSONII PECK

Ecology: Mycorrhizal with hardwoods, especially oaks and beech; growing alone, scattered, or gregariously; summer and fall; widely distributed. **Cap:** 4–20 cm; convex, becoming broadly convex or almost flat; dry; finely roughened; somewhat wrinkled; often becoming cracked in age; grayish brown to yellowish brown; fading with age. **Pore Surface:** White when young, becoming yellowish or brownish yellow; not bruising; pores "stuffed" when young; at maturity with 1–3 round pores per mm; tubes 5–12 mm deep. **Stem:** 5–12 cm long; 1–3 cm thick; more or less equal, or club-shaped (especially when young); dry; solid;

whitish or brownish; prominently reticulate with whitish to brownish reticulation. **Flesh:** White; not staining when sliced. **Odor and Taste:** Not distinctive. **Chemical Reactions:** Ammonia flashing purple to magenta, then resolving to purplish or brownish on cap surface; negative on flesh. KOH brown to pale orange on cap surface (sometimes flashing purplish first); negative on flesh. Iron salts negative on cap surface and flesh. **Spore Print:** Yellowish brown. **Microscopic Features:** Spores 10–14 × 3.5–5 µm; smooth; subfusoid to fusoid. Pileipellis a trichoderm. **Comments:** Edible and excellent. The ammonia reaction is a reliable identification character. Often misidentified as "*Boletus edulis*," which is a European species. An unnamed, spruce-associated species with an orangish-brown, greasy cap can be found in the northern Midwest; it is also frequently labeled "*Boletus edulis*." Compare with *Boletus variipes* (p. 124) and *Boletus* cf. *reticulatus* (p. 122).

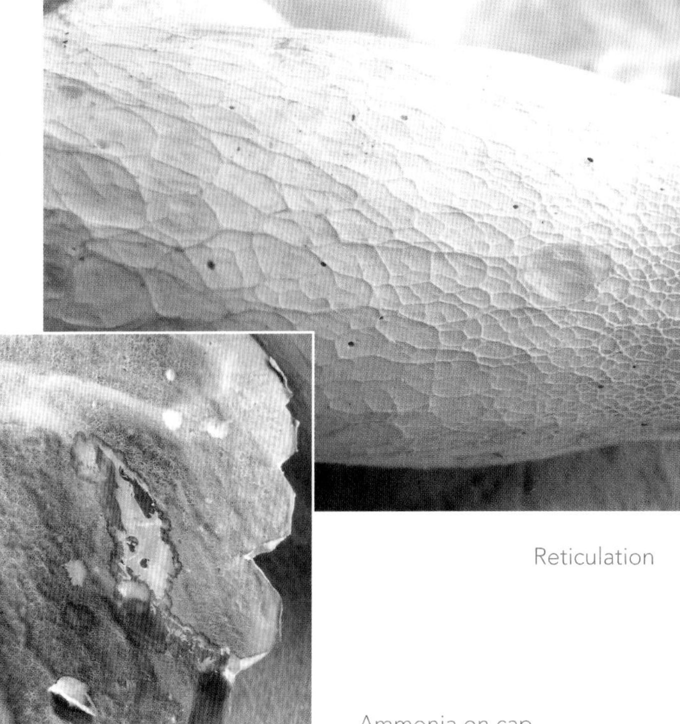

Reticulation

Ammonia on cap

BOLETUS AURIPES PECK

Ecology: Mycorrhizal with oaks and other hardwoods; growing alone, scattered, or gregariously; summer and fall; widely distributed but perhaps rare or even absent in the northern Midwest. **Cap:** 6–20 cm; convex, becoming broadly convex; dry; finely velvety or nearly bald; yellow brown or golden when in the button stage, becoming brown or yellowish brown, and eventually fading. **Pore Surface:** Bright to medium yellow, becoming brownish yellow or olive; not bruising; 2–3 pores per mm; tubes to 2 cm deep. **Stem:** 5–12 cm long; up to 3 cm thick; more or less equal, or with a swollen bottom half (especially when young); usually finely reticulate over at least the top portion; bright yellow becoming brownish yellow; often discoloring brownish with age. **Flesh:** Yellow; not staining on exposure, but sometimes becoming deeper yellow. **Odor and Taste:** Not distinctive. **Chemical Reactions:** Ammonia yellowish or negative on cap and flesh. KOH negative or yellowish on cap and flesh. Iron salts negative on cap and flesh. **Spore Print:** Yellow brown, sometimes with an olive tinge in a fresh print. **Microscopic Features:** Spores

9.5–15 × 3.5–5 µm; smooth; subfusiform. Pileipellis a trichoderm. **Comments:** The strikingly yellow and finely reticulate stem, brown cap, and lack of bruising or staining make good field characters.

BOLETUS AURIPORUS PECK

Ecology: Mycorrhizal with oaks and other hardwoods; growing alone, scattered, or gregariously; summer and fall; widely distributed. **Cap:** 2–8 cm; convex, becoming broadly convex or almost flat; sticky when fresh; finely hairy or velvety; pinkish brown, fading in age; margin with a tiny extending sterile portion. **Pore Surface:** Bright yellow; frequently bruising pinkish to reddish, especially in maturity; 1–3 pores per mm; tubes to 15 mm deep. **Stem:** 4–12 cm long; 0.5–1.5 cm thick; more or less equal; sticky when fresh; yellow above, pinkish brown and streaked-looking below; adorned with tiny yellow fibers when young and fresh; basal mycelium white; without reticulation. **Flesh:** White or pale yellow; not staining on exposure. **Odor and Taste:** The flesh tastes mild; the sticky to slimy material on the cap and stem is acidic (like putting your tongue on a 9-volt battery). Odor not distinctive. **Chemical Reactions:** Ammonia negative on cap and flesh. KOH negative to yellowish on cap and flesh. Iron salts negative to yellowish on cap and flesh; dark green to blue on pore surface. **Spore Print:** Olive brown. **Microscopic Features:** Spores 11–16 × 4–6 µm; smooth; subfusoid. Pileipellis a cutis. **Comments:** Compare with *Boletus innixus* (p. 118). *Boletus viridiflavus* is virtually identical but features an olive cap.

BOLETUS BADIUS (FRIES) FRIES

Ecology: Mycorrhizal; growing alone or scattered, on the ground or from well-decayed wood; under hemlock and other conifers, or occasionally in beech-maple or birch woods; summer through fall; appearing in the northern Midwest. **Cap:** 3–10 cm; convex, becoming broadly convex or almost flat; sticky or slimy when fresh and young but soon dry; finely velvety or bald; color variable but typically reddish brown; margin often with a tiny extending sterile portion. **Pore Surface:** Pale yellow, becoming olive; bruising promptly grayish to bluish or greenish blue; 1–2 pores per mm; tubes to 15 mm deep. **Stem:** 4–9 cm long; 1–2 cm thick; more or less equal; solid; yellowish at the apex; colored like the cap or paler below; often with broad, shallow wrinkles when young; basal mycelium white; without reticulation. **Flesh:** Whitish, often staining yellowish on exposure, and weakly bluish over the tubes, but sometimes not staining. **Odor and Taste:** Not distinctive. **Chemical Reactions:** Ammonia negative, maroon, or blackish (sometimes with an olive ring of color, or first flashing green) on cap surface; negative to brownish on flesh. KOH blackish maroon on cap surface; pale orangish on flesh; golden brown on pore surface. Iron salts dull bluish green on cap surface; pale yellow to olive on flesh. **Spore Print:** Olive. **Microscopic Features:** Spores variable in size but typically 12–15 × 3.5–4.5 µm; smooth; subfusiform. Pileipellis a cutis. **Comments:** *Boletus badius* is a European species; there may be several unnamed North American representatives of the group.

BOLETUS BICOLOR PECK

Ecology: Mycorrhizal with oaks and other hardwoods; growing alone, scattered, or gregariously; summer and fall; widely distributed. **Cap:** 5–15 cm, convex to broadly convex in age, sometimes irregular; dry; bald, like soft leather; becoming cracked; deep brick red to pinkish red, sometimes yellowish near the margin. **Pore Surface:** Bright yellow; sometimes with reddish stains; bruising blue quickly or slowly; pores round, 1–2 per mm; tubes shallow (usually measuring under 1 cm long even in large specimens). **Stem:** 5–10 cm long; 1–3 cm thick; more or less equal; solid; smooth overall, or reticulate near the apex; yellow at apex; colored like the cap below. **Flesh:** Yellow throughout; bruising slowly pale blue when exposed. **Odor and Taste:** Odor not distinctive, or strongly of beef bouillon or curry; taste mild or slightly acidic. **Chemical Reactions:** Ammonia negative to yellowish on cap; negative to brownish on flesh. KOH negative to yellowish on cap; pale orange to brownish on flesh. Iron salts blackish on cap; gray to olive on flesh. **Spore Print:** Olive brown. **Microscopic Features:** Spores 8–12 × 3.5–5 µm; smooth; subfusiform. Pileipellis a cutis. **Comments:** Study of many collections has led us to believe that the odor, extent of reticulation, and promptness of bruising are extremely variable for this species. *Boletus campestris* (p. 114) is similar but much smaller.

BOLETUS CAMPESTRIS A. H. SMITH & THIERS

Ecology: Mycorrhizal with oaks and other hardwoods; found in open, grassy areas or in denser woods; summer and fall; widely distributed. **Cap:** 2–4 cm; convex, becoming broadly convex or nearly flat in age; dry; bald or finely velvety; the surface cracking up slightly by maturity, especially toward the margin; rosy red to brick red, fading somewhat. **Pore Surface:** Yellow, becoming greenish yellow; bruising fairly quickly blue to blue green; 1–3 circular to angular pores per mm; tubes to about 1 cm deep. **Stem:** 3–7 cm long; 0.5–1 cm thick; more or less equal; yellow above; usually colored like the cap below; not reticulate; solid; with yellowish basal mycelium. **Flesh:** Yellow; staining blue to greenish blue on exposure. **Odor and Taste:** Not distinctive. **Chemical Reactions:** Ammonia negative on cap and flesh. KOH orange or yellow on cap (sometimes fleetingly dark gray first); dull orange on flesh. Iron salts negative to dull orange on cap; negative on flesh. **Spore Print:** Olive brown. **Microscopic Features:** Spores 11–15 × 4.5–7 µm; smooth; subfusoid. Pileipellis a trichoderm. **Comments:** This species is often found under oaks in urban settings. Compare with *Boletus bicolor* (p. 113). *Boletus rubellus* is a very similar European species that some mycologists list as occurring in the Midwest; it has larger pores, a tapered stem base, and much narrower spores (3–5 µm wide).

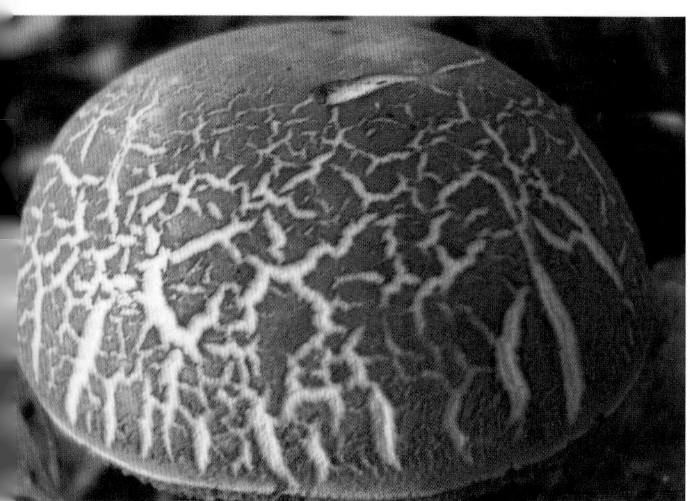

Photo by Martin Livezey

BOLETUS CHRYSENTERON BULLIARD

Ecology: Mycorrhizal with oaks and other hardwoods; growing scattered or gregariously; summer and fall; widely distributed. **Cap:** 3–8 cm; convex, becoming broadly convex or almost flat; dry; finely velvety when young; becoming cracked in age (usually conspicuously so), with reddish to pinkish flesh showing in the cracks, especially toward the margin; brown to olive brown, or rarely reddish brown overall; marginal area often reddish in age. **Pore Surface:** Yellow when young, becoming brownish or olive; sometimes with reddish areas in age; bruising blue (sometimes slowly); with 1–2 angular pores per mm;

tubes to 1 cm deep. **Stem:** 4–7 cm long; 0.5–1 cm thick; more or less equal, or tapering to base; solid; yellow above, reddish below; purplish red at base; basal mycelium white to yellowish; not reticulate, but sometimes with a few ridges; bruising blue green. **Flesh:** White when young, yellow in age; staining slowly bluish on exposure. **Odor and Taste:** Not distinctive. **Chemical Reactions:** Ammonia negative to brownish on cap and flesh. KOH negative to brown on cap; negative to brownish or orangish on flesh. Iron salts olive on cap; negative to yellow or olive on flesh. **Spore Print:** Olive brown. **Microscopic Features:** Spores 9–13 × 3.5–4.5 µm; smooth; subfusiform. Pileipellis a trichoderm. **Comments:** Compare with *Boletellus chrysenteroides* (p. 108–9) and *Boletellus pseudochrysenteroides* (p. 109). *Boletus truncatus* is virtually indistinguishable without a microscope; its spores are larger (10–15 × 5–7 µm) and frequently truncated, with a small apical pore.

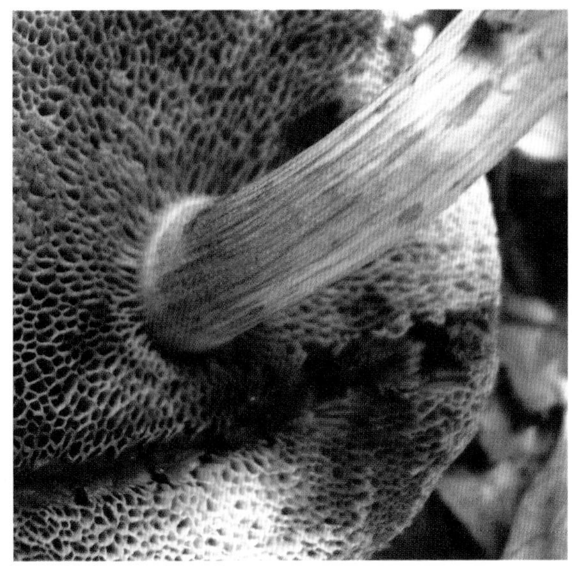

Photo by Martin Livezey

BOLETUS CURTISII BERKELEY

Ecology: Mycorrhizal with oaks and other hardwoods; growing alone, scattered, or gregariously; summer and fall; primarily southern in distribution but recorded from Missouri, Michigan, and Illinois. **Cap:** 3–9 cm; convex, becoming broadly convex or almost flat; very sticky when fresh; bald; bright yellow or orangish yellow; staining waxed paper or paper collection bags yellow; the margin with a pale, overhanging portion. **Pore Surface:** Often depressed around the stem or receding from it; whitish to pale yellow when young, becoming yellowish brown; not bruising; 2–3 pores per mm; tubes 6–12 mm deep. **Stem:** 6–12 cm long; 0.5–1.5 cm thick; more or less equal; sticky; bald or with tiny fibers near the apex; yellow; basal mycelium white and prominent. **Flesh:** Whitish; not staining on exposure. **Odor and Taste:** Not distinctive. **Chemical Reactions:** Ammonia negative on cap and flesh. KOH negative to pale olive on cap; orangish on flesh. Iron salts negative on cap; bluish gray on flesh. **Spore Print:** Rusty brown. **Microscopic Features:** Spores 9.5–17 × 4–6 µm; smooth; subfusoid. **Comments:** This distinctive species is almost *Suillus*-like.

Photo by Dan Molter

BOLETUS FROSTII RUSSELL

Ecology: Mycorrhizal with oaks and other hardwoods; growing alone, scattered, or gregariously; summer and fall; widely distributed. **Cap:** 5–15 cm, convex at first, becoming broadly convex in age; sticky or thinly slimy when fresh; bald; smooth or very finely and shallowly pockmarked; beautifully bright red, developing yellowish areas with age. **Pore Surface:** Dark to pale red; bruising promptly dark blue; often exuding yellowish droplets when young; 2–3 pores per mm; tubes yellowish to olive, to 15 mm deep. **Stem:** 4–12 cm long; up to 3.5 cm thick; more or less equal; coarsely and prominently reticulate over the entire length; red, or occasionally with yellow areas; often bruising blue. **Flesh:** Whitish to yellow; bluing when sliced. **Odor and Taste:** Not distinctive. **Chemical Reactions:** Ammonia negative on cap; grayish or yellowish on flesh. KOH black or grayish, then orangish on cap; grayish orange on flesh. Iron salts negative or yellowish on cap and flesh. **Spore Print:** Olive brown. **Microscopic Features:** Spores 11–15 (–18) × 4–5 µm; smooth; subfusiform. Pileipellis a tangled layer of gelatinized hyphae. **Comments:** When fresh, this striking bolete is hard to confuse with anything else.

BOLETUS HORTONII A. H. SMITH & THIERS

Ecology: Mycorrhizal with oaks and perhaps with other hardwoods; growing alone, scattered, or gregariously (sometimes densely so); early summer through fall; widely distributed. **Cap:** 3–14 cm; convex, becoming broadly convex; dry or greasy; conspicuously, tightly wrinkled; bald; reddish brown to cinnamon or medium brown, but often fading in age. **Pore Surface:** Yellow, becoming dull yellow or olive; not typically bruising, but sometimes bruising slowly cinnamon or bluish; with 2–3 pores per mm; tubes to about 1 cm deep. **Stem:** 6–10 cm long; 1–2 cm thick; more or less equal, or enlarging slightly to base; dry; yellow at the apex; elsewhere pale yellow to tan, sometimes flushed reddish; adorned with minute scabers that are initially yellow and concolorous with the surface, but often turn reddish with age or handling; basal mycelium whitish. **Flesh:** White to yellowish; not typically staining on exposure, but sometimes bluing slowly and weakly. **Odor and Taste:** Not distinctive. **Chemical Reactions:** Ammonia green (or flashing green and then resolving to brownish or gray) on cap; negative on flesh. KOH blackish to brownish or negative on cap; negative to orangish on flesh. Iron salts negative to pale olive on cap; negative to bluish gray on flesh.

Spore Print: Olive brown. **Microscopic Features:** Spores 12–15 × 3.5–4.5 µm; smooth; subfusiform. Pileipellis a trichoderm with tubular terminal elements and, often, inflated subterminal elements. **Comments:** Edible and good. Compare with *Leccinum subglabripes* (p. 255), which is very similar but has a smooth, rather than tightly wrinkled, cap surface. The stature and the minute scabers on the stem suggest the possibility that *Boletus hortonii* belongs in *Leccinum* or *Leccinellum* with *Leccinum subglabripes* and *Boletus longicurvipes* (p. 118); however, the pileipellis structure and the ammonia reaction of *Boletus hortonii* are not found elsewhere in either *Leccinum* or *Leccinellum*.

BOLETUS ILLUDENS PECK

Ecology: Mycorrhizal with oaks; growing scattered or gregariously; summer and fall; widely distributed. **Cap:** 3–9 cm; convex, becoming broadly convex or nearly flat; dry; bald or finely velvety; margin even; brownish to yellowish brown, reddish brown, or cinnamon. **Pore Surface:** Yellow, becoming olive yellow or brownish yellow with maturity; not bruising; pores primarily angular, 1–2 mm wide; tubes to 16 mm deep. **Stem:** 3–9 cm long; 0.5–1.5 cm thick; often tapered downward; dry; solid and tough; widely and coarsely reticulate near the apex (and often for half or more of the stem's length); whitish to pale brownish; basal mycelium whitish to yellowish. **Flesh:** Pale yellow; not staining on exposure. **Odor and Taste:** Not distinctive. **Chemical Reactions:** Ammonia flashing blue green on cap, then resolving to brownish with a greenish ring; negative on flesh. KOH dark brown or pale orange on cap; negative on flesh. Iron salts bluish gray on cap; bluish gray on flesh. **Spore Print:** Olive to olive brown. **Microscopic Features:** Spores 10–14 × 4–5 µm; smooth; subfusiform. Pileipellis a trichoderm with scattered or frequent inflated elements. **Comments:** Edible. *Boletus tenax* is virtually identical (and also turns green with ammonia) but features a stubbier, more dramatically tapering stem; its pileipellis lacks inflated elements.

BOLETUS INEDULIS MURRILL

Ecology: Mycorrhizal with hardwoods (especially oaks); growing alone or gregariously; summer and fall; widely distributed and common. **Cap:** 4–12 cm; convex, becoming broadly convex or nearly flat in age; dry; bald, or finely velvety when young; sometimes cracked in age; margin inrolled, with a narrow overhanging sterile portion; whitish to pale tan. **Pore Surface:** Yellow, becoming olive yellow; bruising

blue; pores circular, 1–3 per mm; tubes to 16 mm deep. **Stem:** 5–12 cm long; 1–2 cm thick; tapered upward or nearly equal; yellowish at apex, reddish below; bruising blackish brown in the lower portion; occasionally faintly reticulate near the apex. **Flesh:** White to yellowish; staining blue on exposure. **Odor and Taste:** Odor not distinctive; taste bitter. **Chemical Reactions:** Ammonia negative on cap and flesh. KOH negative to pale orange on cap; orangish on flesh. Iron salts grayish on cap; negative on flesh. **Spore Print:** Olive brown. **Microscopic Features:** Spores 9–13 × 3.3–4.5 µm; smooth; subfusiform. Pileipellis a trichoderm.

BOLETUS INNIXUS FROST

Ecology: Mycorrhizal with oaks and other hardwoods; growing alone, gregariously, or (more typically) in small fused clusters; summer and fall; widely distributed. **Cap:** 3–8 cm; convex, becoming broadly convex; dry or somewhat tacky when wet; bald; sometimes cracking in age; brown or reddish brown, fading to cinnamon tan. **Pore Surface:** Bright yellow; not bruising; with 1–3 pores per mm when young, but pores up to 2 mm across in age; tubes to 1 cm deep. **Stem:** 3–6 cm long; 1–1.5 cm thick at apex; usually bulbous, with a small rooting projection below the bulb; dry, or often slimy near the base; bald; not reticulate; yellowish, with brownish streaks; basal mycelium yellow. **Flesh:** White to yellow; often staining somewhat pinkish in the cap on exposure, or brownish in the stem. **Odor and Taste:** Not distinctive. **Chemical Reactions:** Ammonia flashing green, then resolving to dull orangish or reddish (sometimes with a greenish ring) on cap; pinkish to orangish on flesh. KOH dark red to reddish brown on cap; pinkish to orangish on flesh. Iron salts pale olive on cap; negative to grayish on flesh. **Spore Print:** Olive brown. **Microscopic Features:** Spores 8–11 × 3–5 µm; smooth; subfusiform. Pileipellis a cutis. **Comments:** Also known as *Boletus caespitosus*. Compare with *Boletus auriporus* (p. 112), which has a sticky stem that is not usually bulbous, and a pinkish-brown cap that does not turn green with ammonia.

BOLETUS LONGICURVIPES SNELL & A. H. SMITH

Ecology: Mycorrhizal with oaks; growing alone, scattered, or gregariously; summer and fall; widely distributed but more common below the Great Lakes. **Cap:** 2–8 cm across; convex, becoming broadly convex; sticky; bald; brownish orange when young, fading to dull orangish brown, reddish brown, or yellowish; sometimes developing olive hints; often becoming pitted or ridged over the center; with a tiny (about 1 mm or less) overhanging margin. **Pore Surface:** Depressed at the stem; pale yellowish, becoming greenish gray; with 2–3 round pores per mm; tubes

KOH on cap

Photo by Dan Molter

to 2 cm long. **Stem:** 5–10 cm long; 1–2 cm wide; more or less equal; often curved; whitish above, pinkish brown below; finely scabrous with whitish to pinkish, reddish, or reddish-brown scabers. **Flesh:** White or yellowish; not changing when sliced. **Odor and Taste:** Not distinctive. **Spore Print:** Dull olive to light brown. **Chemical Reactions:** Ammonia pinkish red on cap surface; negative on flesh. KOH bright cherry red on cap surface; negative on flesh. Iron salts bluish on cap; bluish on flesh. **Microscopic Features:** Spores subfusoid; inamyloid; yellowish in KOH; smooth; 13–18 × 4–6.5 µm. Pileipellis a semigelatinized trichoderm with occasional inflated elements. **Comments:** Several contemporary DNA studies suggest this species may belong in *Leccinum* or *Leccinellum*. Compare with *Leccinum subglabripes* (p. 255), which has inconspicuous, pale scabers and a different pileipellis, and does not turn bright red with KOH.

BOLETUS LURIDUS SCHAEFFER

Ecology: Mycorrhizal with oaks and other hardwoods; growing alone, scattered, or gregariously; summer and fall; widely distributed. **Cap:** 5–20 cm, convex, becoming broadly convex in age; dry or slightly sticky in wet weather; finely velvety or bald; variable in color but frequently olive brown, brown, reddish brown, or yellowish; bruising blackish or blue. **Pore Surface:** Yellow or red when very young; red to orange at maturity; bruising blue; 1–3 pores per mm; tubes yellowish to olive, to 15 mm deep. **Stem:** 4–15 cm long; up to 3 cm thick; tapering a little to the apex; prominently reticulate with vertically elongated, reddish reticulation; often with a velvety base; yellowish above and reddish below; sometimes brownish or purple red near the base; bruising and discoloring blue. **Flesh:** Whitish to yellow; sometimes reddish in the stem; bluing when sliced. **Odor and Taste:** Not distinctive. **Chemical Reactions:** Ammonia negative on cap; negative (but erasing blue) on flesh. KOH dark red to black on cap; orange to yellow on flesh. Iron salts olive to grayish on cap; negative (but erasing blue) on flesh. **Spore Print:** Olive brown.

Microscopic Features: Spores variable but usually 11–15 × 5–7 µm; smooth; broadly subfusiform to nearly ellipsoid. Pileipellis a trichoderm. **Comments:** *Boletus luridus* is a European species that may have several North American representatives requiring further study and documentation.

BOLETUS PALLIDUS FROST

Ecology: Mycorrhizal with oaks and other hardwoods; growing alone, gregariously, or in small clumps; summer and fall; widely distributed. **Cap:** 4–15 cm; convex, becoming broadly convex or nearly flat in age; dry; bald or very finely velvety; sometimes becoming finely cracked in age; the margin often with a tiny overhanging sterile portion; whitish to buff or pale tan, sometimes developing rose shades. **Pore Surface:** Whitish to yellowish when young, becoming yellow to greenish yellow; bruising bluish, then brownish, or not bruising; pores circular, becoming angular, 1–2 per mm; tubes to 2 cm deep. **Stem:** 5–12 cm long; 1–2.5 cm thick; more or less equal; white; sometimes yellowish at apex, sometimes with pale reddish colors below in age; sometimes developing brownish streaks; not reticulate; basal mycelium white. **Flesh:** Whitish to pale yellow; typically staining slowly and erratically pale blue on exposure, especially above the tubes—but often not staining, or staining pinkish. **Odor and Taste:** Not distinctive. **Chemical Reactions:** (Note: Chemical reactions for this species are shown on p. 12.) Ammonia gray to reddish, purple, or negative on cap; greenish on flesh. KOH rusty orange to negative on cap; orangish on flesh. Iron salts negative to blue green or grayish on cap and flesh. **Spore Print:** Olive to olive brown. **Microscopic Features:** Spores 9–15 × 3–5 µm; smooth; subfusoid. Pileipellis a cutis. **Comments:** Edible and good. As the description indicates, *Boletus pallidus* is very variable in its features; it may represent a species group.

BOLETUS PARASITICUS

Ecology: Parasitic on *Scleroderma citrinum* (p. 355), which is mycorrhizal with hardwoods and conifers; most frequently found, in our midwestern experience, in hemlock bogs; growing alone or in small clusters; summer and fall; widely distributed in the Midwest, but more common where hemlock occurs. **Cap:** 2–8 cm; convex, becoming broadly convex; dry; bald; margin rolled under when young; yellowish brown to olive. **Pore Surface:** Yellow to olive; not bruising but sometimes aging dirty brown to reddish brown; pores 1–2 mm wide; tubes to 6 mm deep. **Stem:** 3–6 cm long; 0.5–1.5

cm thick; more or less equal; often curved; dry; solid; colored more or less like the cap; covered with tiny yellowish-brown fibers. **Flesh:** Pale yellow; not staining on exposure. **Odor and Taste:** Not distinctive. **Chemical Reactions:** Ammonia red to reddish brown on cap. KOH red to reddish brown on cap; negative on flesh; cinnabar orange on stem surface. Iron salts negative on cap and flesh. **Spore Print:** Olive brown. **Microscopic Features:** Spores 12–18.5 × 3.5–5 µm; smooth; subfusoid. Pileipellis a cutis with scattered inflated elements. **Comments:** Easily recognized due to its ecology.

BOLETUS PROJECTELLUS (MURRILL) MURRILL

Ecology: Mycorrhizal with pines; growing alone, scattered, or gregariously; late summer and fall; widely distributed. **Cap:** 3–12 cm; convex, becoming broadly convex or nearly flat; dry; finely velvety or bald; often cracking with age; reddish brown to purplish brown or brown; with a projecting sterile margin that may become somewhat tattered. **Pore Surface:** Often depressed around stem; yellow to olive yellow; not bruising; with round pores measuring 1–2 mm across at maturity; tubes to about 2.5 cm deep. **Stem:** 7–15 cm long; 1–2 cm thick; slightly tapered to apex, or more or less equal; dry; solid; buff to pinkish brown or reddish brown; coarsely but shallowly ridged and/or reticulate over the top half or nearly overall; when fresh, often sticky, especially toward the base; basal mycelium prominent and white. **Flesh:** Whitish to pinkish; not staining, or staining slowly and faintly brownish on exposure. **Odor and Taste:** Not distinctive. **Chemical Reactions:** Ammonia black on cap; gray on flesh. KOH mahogany on cap; yellow on flesh. Iron salts dull gray on cap; greenish on flesh. **Spore Print:** Olive brown. **Microscopic Features:** Spores 18–33 × 7.5–12 µm; smooth; subfusoid; with thick walls. Pileipellis a cutis. **Comments:** The long stem with prominent ridges and the overhanging sterile margin are good identifying features. Compare with *Boletellus russellii* (p. 110).

BOLETUS PSEUDOSENSIBILIS A. H. SMITH & THIERS

Ecology: Mycorrhizal with oaks and other hardwoods; growing alone, scattered, or gregariously; summer and fall; widely distributed. **Cap:** 6–14 cm; convex, becoming broadly convex or almost flat; dry; bald; in age becoming somewhat cracked, with yellow flesh showing through the cracks; reddish brown, fading to yellowish brown. **Pore Surface:** Bright yellow; when young not bruising, or bruising faintly, but later bruising more readily blue, then brown; 1–3 pores per mm at maturity;

tubes shallow (5–8 mm deep). **Stem:** 8–16 cm long; 1.5–3 cm thick; more or less equal, or enlarging to base; dry; solid; yellow overall, with reddish tinges toward the base that persist with maturity; not reticulate. **Flesh:** Whitish to pale yellow in the cap; deep yellow or red in the stem; staining quickly blue on exposure. **Odor and Taste:** Not distinctive. **Chemical Reactions:** Ammonia flashing blue, then resolving to purplish gray on cap; negative to grayish on flesh. KOH yellow to orange on cap surface; brownish to orangish on flesh. Iron salts grayish on cap; grayish olive on flesh. **Spore Print:** Olive brown. **Microscopic Features:** Spores 9–12 × 3–4 µm; smooth; subfusoid. Pileipellis a cutis. **Comments:** The shallow tubes, blue staining, and ammonia reaction are good identification characters.

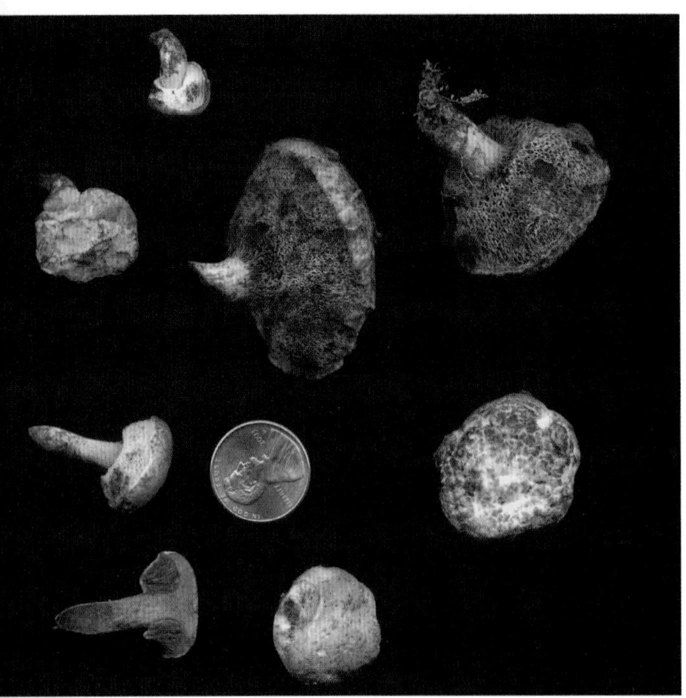

BOLETUS PSEUDOSULPHUREUS KALLENBACH

Ecology: Mycorrhizal with hardwoods; growing alone, scattered, or gregariously; late spring, early summer, or summer; widely distributed. **Cap:** 4–9 cm; cushion-shaped, becoming convex, broadly convex, or almost flat; dry; finely velvety when young, becoming bald, or cracked with age; bright yellow, developing orangish to reddish discolorations; bruising promptly blue to black; the margin with an overhanging sterile portion up to 1 mm wide. **Pore Surface:** Bright yellow, becoming olive; bruising promptly blue or greenish; 2–3 pores per mm at maturity; tubes to about 1 cm deep. **Stem:** 8–12 cm long; 1–1.5 cm thick; more or less equal; dry; solid; yellow above, reddish below, or occasionally yellow overall; bald; not reticulate; bruising greenish to bluish, then grayish brown. **Flesh:** Yellow; often red in the stem base; staining quickly blue on exposure. **Odor and Taste:** Not distinctive. **Chemical Reactions:** Ammonia negative on cap. KOH orange to red on cap and flesh. Iron salts gray to grayish olive on cap. **Spore Print:** Olive brown. **Microscopic Features:** Spores 10–14 × 4.5–6 µm; smooth; broadly fusiform. Pileipellis a trichoderm.

BOLETUS CF. RETICULATUS SCHAEFFER

Ecology: Mycorrhizal with oaks; growing scattered or gregariously (occasionally clustered); late May to August; Douglas and Lawrence Counties in Illinois (probably to be expected throughout the lower Midwest). **Cap:** 7–18 cm, convex in the button stage, expanding to broadly convex in age; dry; with the texture of well-worn leather; bald, but often breaking up and developing deep and prominent cracks; whitish to pale brown, becoming brownish to pale brown or yellow brown in age; not bruising or discoloring; the margin inrolled when young, splitting with age, typically without a sterile projection. **Pore Surface:** Whitish to dirty gray when young; becoming pale buff, then olive, then brownish; young pore surface bruising yellowish to brownish; older surfaces bruising brownish or not bruising; the pores "stuffed" until the mushroom is quite old; tubes colored like the pore surface, extending to 12 mm deep; eventually receding from the stem. **Stem:** 4–10 cm long; 2–4 cm thick; swollen and club-shaped when young, becoming club-shaped or more or less equal; finely reticulate (over the whole stem or, more often, only near the apex); the reticulation typically white but occasionally brownish; often developing fissures and "peeling" sections; whitish; sometimes appearing to stain brownish when handled; solid. **Flesh:** White; thick throughout; not staining on exposure. **Odor and Taste:** Pleasant, but not distinctive. **Chemical Reactions:** Ammonia negative to orangish tan on cap; negative on flesh. KOH negative to orangish tan on cap; negative on flesh. Iron salts negative on cap and flesh. **Spore print:** Olive brown. **Microscopic Features:** Spores 10–13 × 3–4 µm; smooth; subfusiform. Pileipellis a cutis. **Comments:** Edible and delicious. This is a summer-fruiting member of the "*Boletus edulis*" complex, roughly matching the European species *Boletus reticulatus* (also known as *Boletus aestivalis*). Compare with *Boletus atkinsonii* (p. 110), which features a distinctive ammonia reaction, and with *Boletus variipes* (p. 124), which appears in the fall.

BOLETUS SPADICEUS VAR. GRACILIS
A. H. SMITH & THIERS

Ecology: Mycorrhizal with oaks and other hardwoods; growing alone, scattered, or gregariously; summer and fall; widely distributed. **Cap:** 2–8 cm; convex, becoming broadly convex or almost flat; dry; finely velvety; yellowish brown to dull brown or reddish brown. **Pore Surface:** Yellow, becoming olive yellow; sometimes bruising reddish brown; pores angular, especially near the stem, 1–2 mm wide; tubes to about 1.5 cm deep. **Stem:** 3–6 cm long; up to 1 cm thick; more or less equal; solid; yellowish underneath fine reddish-brown hairs and granules; not reticulate; basal mycelium yellow. **Flesh:** Whitish in the cap; yellow

Ammonia on cap

in the stem; not staining on exposure, or staining faintly bluish. **Odor and Taste:** Pleasant; not distinctive. **Chemical Reactions:** Ammonia flashing green to blue green on cap, then resolving to reddish brown; flashing greenish on flesh, then resolving to negative. KOH purple on cap; orangish on flesh. Iron salts olive on cap; olive on flesh. **Spore Print:** Olive brown. **Microscopic Features:** Spores 9–13 × 3.5–4.5 µm; smooth; subfusiform; yellow in KOH. Pileipellis a tangled layer of cylindric hyphae with rounded to subacute apices. **Comments:** The skinny, nonreticulated stem and ammonia reaction are good identification characters. In the northern Midwest *Boletus spadiceus* var. *spadiceus* is similar but stockier; it is associated with conifers.

BOLETUS SUBVELUTIPES PECK

Ecology: Mycorrhizal with hardwoods; growing alone, scattered, or gregariously; summer and fall; widely distributed. **Cap:** 5–10 cm; convex, becoming broadly convex; dry; bald or finely velvety; variable in color (brown, red, reddish brown, orangish, cinnamon, olive, olive brown, yellowish, yellow brown) but not pallid or whitish when fresh; sometimes bruising dark blue to blackish. **Pore Surface:** Red or orange red; frequently yellow or pale orange at the margin; bruising instantly dark blue to blackish; pores circular, fairly small (1–3 per mm); tubes yellow, to about 2 cm deep. **Stem:** Up to about 10 × 2 cm; more or less equal; dry; solid; not reticulate; with a variously colored (whitish, yellowish, reddish, rusty brown) velvety, fuzzy covering over the base (sometimes obscured by leaves or substrate) that occasionally extends up the stem for half its length or more; bruising dark blue to blackish. **Flesh:** Whitish to yellowish or bright yellow; staining quickly blue on exposure. **Odor and Taste:** Not distinctive. **Chemical Reactions:** Variable and unreliable for identification (see comments). **Spore Print:** Olive brown. **Microscopic Features:** Spores 14–20 × 5–8 µm; smooth; subfusiform. Pileipellis a cutis. **Comments:** The red-pored, blue-staining, nonreticulate, hardwood-associated species of *Boletus* in the Midwest are confusing and poorly understood. We have applied the name "*Boletus subvelutipes*" to the group, but, as the ranges and variability in the description demonstrate, there are probably several species involved.

BOLETUS VARIIPES PECK

Ecology: Mycorrhizal with oaks and other hardwoods; growing alone, scattered, or gregariously; late summer and fall; widely distributed. **Cap:** 6–20 cm; convex, becoming broadly convex or almost flat; dry; finely velvety at first; often becoming minutely cracked in age; tan to brownish or pale grayish brown. **Pore Surface:**

White when young, becoming yellowish or olive; not bruising; pores "stuffed" when young; 1–2 pores per mm at maturity; tubes 1–3 cm deep. **Stem:** 8–15 cm long; 1–3.5 cm thick; swollen in the middle, more or less equal, or enlarging to base; dry; solid; whitish or grayish brown; usually fairly prominently reticulate with whitish or brownish reticulation, or at times only finely reticulate. **Flesh:** White; not staining on exposure. **Odor and Taste:** Not distinctive. **Chemical Reactions:** Ammonia dark yellow with a purplish ring on cap; negative to grayish on flesh. KOH similar to ammonia on cap; grayish on flesh. Iron salts negative to pale olive on cap; gray to yellowish on flesh. **Spore Print:** Olive brown. **Microscopic Features:** Spores 9–18 × 4–6 µm; smooth; subfusiform. Pileipellis a trichoderm. **Comments:** Edible and very good. Compare with *Boletus atkinsonii* (p. 110) and *Boletus* cf. *reticulatus* (p. 122).

BOLETUS VERMICULOSUS PECK

Ecology: Mycorrhizal with oaks; growing alone, scattered, or gregariously in oak-hickory forests; June and July; central Illinois, possibly widely distributed in the Midwest (see comments). **Cap:** 4–13 cm; convex, becoming broadly convex; dry; dull; soft; olive brown to medium brown or dark brown, fading to tan; often with a yellowish margin when young, but not yellow overall in any stage of development; when fresh, bruising blue to black. **Pore Surface:** Dark red brown to maroon when young, but quickly fading to dull brownish orange; bruising promptly dark blue or black; pores round, 2–3 per mm; tubes dull yellowish, to about 2 cm deep. **Stem:** 7–10 cm long; up to about 2 cm thick; slender; more or less equal; covered with tiny tufts of fibers that become brownish when handled (reminiscent of the scabers on *Leccinum subglabripes*, p. 255); brownish overall, with a yellowish apex and sometimes a pale reddish zone; not reticulate; basal mycelium whitish. **Flesh:** Whitish or yellowish in cap; yellowish in upper stem; staining sky blue in cap and red in stem when sliced. **Odor and Taste:** Not distinctive. **Chemical Reactions:** Ammonia reddish on cap; orangish on flesh. KOH dark red on cap; orange on flesh. Iron salts greenish on cap; negative on flesh. **Spore Print:** Olive brown. **Microscopic Features:** Spores 11–12 × 3–4 µm; smooth; subfusiform; yellowish in KOH. Pileipellis a trichoderm. **Comments:** Here we have described the *vermiculosus*-like species of *Boletus* from our area (central Illinois), and we have opted to treat *Boletus vermiculosus* in a wide sense, although several closely related species have been described.

Spores

BONDARZEWIA BERKELEYI (FRIES) BONDARTSEV & SINGER

Ecology: Parasitic on hardwoods (especially oaks); causing a white, stringy butt rot; also saprobic on the deadwood of hardwoods; growing alone or gregariously at the bases of trees; summer and fall; widely distributed. **Fruiting Body:** 25–80 cm across; consisting of 1–5 caps arising from a single gnarled stem. **Individual Caps:** 6–25 cm across; kidney-shaped or irregular in outline; convex, flat, or with a central depression; dry; velvety or leathery, sometimes radially wrinkled (but not scaly) or with vague, semiconcentric zones of texture or color; whitish to cream-colored, yellowish, or pale tan; not bruising. **Pore Surface:** Running down the stem; whitish; not bruising, or bruising very faintly brownish; pores angular, 0.5–2 mm across; tubes to 1 cm deep. **Stem:** 4–10 cm long; 3–5 cm wide; central or somewhat off-center; yellowish to pale brownish; dry; tough. **Flesh:** White; thick; not discoloring or bruising. **Chemical Reactions:** KOH pale reddish orange on cap; yellowish on flesh. **Spore Print:** White. **Microscopic Features:** Spores 7–9 × 6–8 µm; globose to subglobose; amyloid; ornamented with many ridges and spines reaching lengths of 1 µm or longer. Cystidia absent. Hyphal system dimitic. **Comments:** The large size, pale colors, and lack of bruising or staining reactions are good field characters.

CALLISTOSPORIUM LUTEO-OLIVACEUM (BERKELEY & CURTIS) SINGER

Ecology: Saprobic on well-decayed wood of conifers and perhaps on the deadwood of hardwoods; growing alone or gregariously; occasionally on wood so far decayed that the mushrooms appear terrestrial, and sometimes on buried wood; summer and fall; widely distributed. **Cap:** Usually 1.5–3 cm, but sometimes as large as 6 cm; convex, becoming plano-convex or flat; at first very finely dusted, but soon bald; somewhat moist when fresh; dark olive to olive yellow, changing color markedly as it dries out, eventually becoming yellowish or cinnamon. **Gills:** Attached to the stem, sometimes by means of a notch; close; yellow or golden yellow. **Stem:** 3–6 cm long; up to about 5 mm thick (occasionally thicker); when young finely dusted overall, becoming bald over the upper half with age; hollowing; often grooved or flattened; colored like the cap; basal mycelium white. **Flesh:** Thin; insubstantial; colored like the cap or paler. **Odor and Taste:** Odor pungent, fruity, or not distinctive; taste mild or a little bitter. **Chemical Reactions:** KOH on cap purplish red. **Spore Print:** White. **Microscopic Features:** Spores 5–6.5 × 3–4.5 µm; broadly ellipsoid; smooth; inamyloid, turning purple in a KOH mount. Pleurocystidia absent; cheilocystidia inconspicuous, about the length of the basidia, clavate to contorted or branched. Pileipellis a cutis, with clavate cystidia (especially in young specimens). **Comments:** The dramatic KOH reaction helps in identifying this species.

CALOCERA CORNEA (BATSCH) FRIES

Ecology: Saprobic; growing scattered to gregariously on the barkless wood of oaks and other hardwoods; summer and fall; widely distributed. **Fruiting Body:** Cylindric, with rounded to sharpened tips; occasionally shallowly forked near the tip; to about 2 cm high and 3 mm thick; bald and slick; firm but gelatinous; orangish yellow. **Spore Print:** White to yellowish. **Microscopic Features:** Spores 7–11 × 3–4.5 µm; cylindric to allantoid; smooth; aseptate or frequently faintly 1-septate by maturity. Basidia Y-shaped; up to 25 × 3 µm.

Basidia

CALOCYBE CARNEA (BULLIARD) DONK

Ecology: Saprobic; growing alone, scattered, gregariously, or in small clusters in grassy areas; usually found in cultivated (rather than woodland) areas; summer and fall; widely distributed but not common. **Cap:** 1.5–4 cm; convex, becoming broadly convex, flat, or shallowly depressed; the margin inrolled at first; dry; bald; pink to pinkish brown. **Gills:** Attached to the stem, sometimes by means of a notch, or nearly free from the stem in maturity; close or crowded; white. **Stem:** 2–5 cm long; under 1 cm thick; becoming hollow with age; bald or with white hairs and fuzz, especially basally; colored like the cap. **Flesh:** Whitish, thin. **Odor and Taste:** Not distinctive, or mealy. **Chemical Reactions:** KOH negative on cap. **Spore Print:** White. **Microscopic Features:** Spores 4–6.5 ×

2–3.5 µm; ellipsoid; smooth; inamyloid. Cystidia absent. Pileipellis a cutis. Clamp connections present. **Comments:** The pink cap and stem, white gills, and habitat in grass are good field characters.

Photo by Patrick Harvey

CALOSTOMA CINNABARINUM CORDA

Ecology: Mycorrhizal with oaks; growing alone or gregariously, often in moss beds or in low-lying, wet areas; spring through fall; widely distributed, but apparently more common at higher elevations. **Fruiting Body:** At first appearing like a raised gelatinous egg or lump, with a translucent outer layer and a red inner layer; later appearing like a bald or dusted, pinkish to red balloon with a central pore, raised on a shaggy reddish to reddish-brown stem that is surrounded by the deciduous, gelatinous material (often containing reddish chunks); finally appearing like a pinkish to reddish, perforated balloon about 2 cm across, atop a shaggy or even coarsely reticulate stem that is 2–4 cm long and 1–2 cm thick; spore mass within the ball white, becoming buff or yellowish at maturity. **Microscopic Features:** Spores 14–28 × 6–11 µm; ellipsoid; finely reticulate. **Comments:** Odd and unmistakable.

CALVATIA CRANIIFORMIS (SCHWEINITZ) FRIES

Ecology: Saprobic; terrestrial; growing alone or gregariously; usually found in grass on lawns and in meadows, but also found growing from leaf litter in woods, ditches, and edges of woods; summer; widely distributed. **Fruiting Body:** 8–20 cm across; 6–20 cm tall; skull-shaped, roundish, or shaped like an inverted pear; white to tan; bald; outer skin cracking and flaking with age; flesh divided into a basal area (the sterile base) and a larger main area; flesh whitish, becoming yellowish and eventually turning into brown spore dust. **Microscopic Features:** Spores 2.5–3.5 µm; globose; nearly smooth; with or without a short tail; inamyloid. Capillitial threads 2–7.5 µm wide; thick-walled; pitted. **Comments:** Edible when fresh and young. *Calvatia cyathiformis* (p. 129) can appear similar but has purple spore powder and usually features a less prominent sterile base.

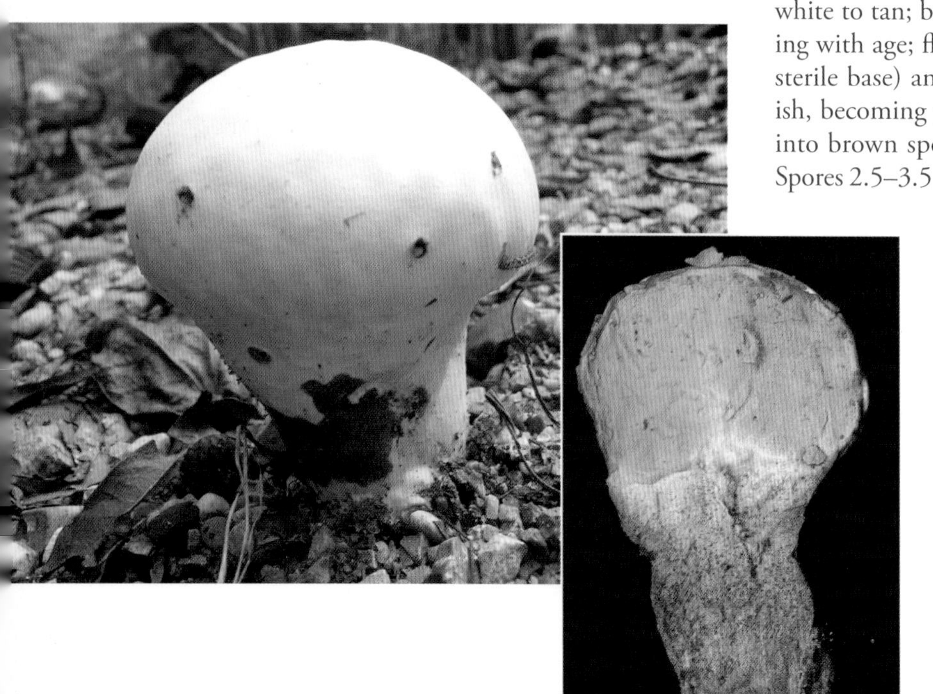

CALVATIA CYATHIFORMIS (BOSC) MORGAN

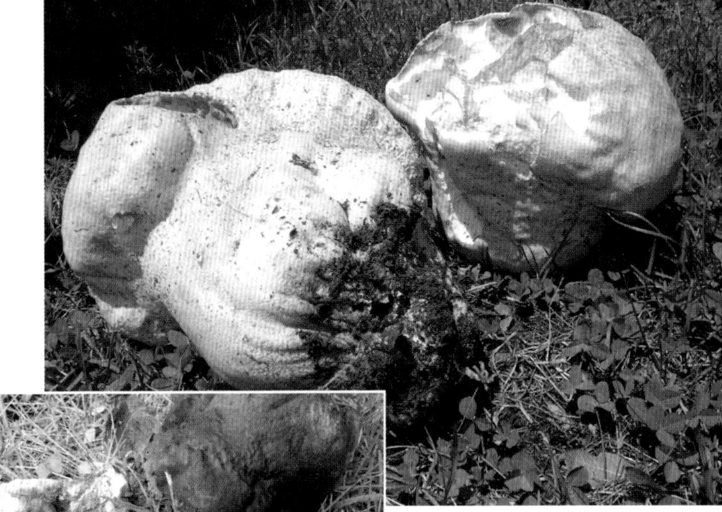

Ecology: Saprobic; growing alone, scattered or gregariously in grass (lawns, meadows, and so on); often appearing in fairy rings; summer and fall; widely distributed. **Fruiting Body:** 5–20 cm; vaguely round at first, becoming pear-shaped or round with a flattened top and narrowed base; whitish to tan or brownish; bald; sterile base usually fairly well developed; flesh white, becoming yellowish, then dull purple to purplish brown and powdery. **Microscopic Features:** Spores 3.5–7.5 µm; globose, spiny or warty to nearly smooth. Capillitial threads 3–7.5 µm wide; thick-walled; minutely pitted. **Comments:** Edible when fresh and young. Compare with *Calvatia craniiformis* (p. 128). *Calvatia fragilis* also features purple spore powder, but it is smaller (measuring 4–9 cm) and features a less prominent sterile base.

CALVATIA GIGANTEA (BATSCH) LLOYD

Ecology: Saprobic; terrestrial; growing alone or gregariously in grass, often at the edges of meadows, in drainage ditches, or under brush; late summer and early fall; widely distributed. **Fruiting Body:** Shaped like a ball, or nearly so; up to 60 cm or more across; white when fresh, becoming yellowish or olive brown; finely velvety when young, but soon bald; soft; interior white and fleshy, becoming yellowish or greenish yellow and eventually turning into brownish spore dust; the outer surface eventually falling away in pieces; often with a small cord at the point of attachment to the ground. **Microscopic Features:** Spores 3–5.5 × 3–5 µm; globose or subglobose; minutely spiny or nearly smooth. Capillitial threads 2–9 µm wide; thick-walled; occasionally branched; septate. **Comments:** Edible when fresh. Smaller specimens should be compared with *Calvatia craniiformis* (p. 128) and *Calvatia cyathiformis* (above), both of which have sterile bases.

Photo by
Patrick Harvey

CALVATIA RUBROFLAVA (CRAGIN) MORGAN

Ecology: Saprobic; growing alone, scattered, or gregariously in grass (lawns and gardens) as well as in woods, ditches, and edges of woods; summer and fall; widely distributed. **Fruiting Body:** 2–10 cm across, 1.5–5 cm high; round overall, or pinched below; often with ridges and furrows in the lower half; sterile base usually present; outer surface white at first, bruising yellow and quickly becoming yellow overall, and eventually reddish brown; flesh white, bruising yellow to orange, and eventually turning to brownish spore powder. **Microscopic Features:** Spores 3–5 µm; globose; minutely roughened; with a short tail. Capillitial threads 2–7 µm wide; thick-walled; deeply pitted. **Comments:** The yellow bruising makes this puffball unique.

CAMAROPS PETERSII (BERKELEY & CURTIS) NANNFELDT

Ecology: Saprobic on the barkless wood of fallen oaks; growing alone or in small groups; late summer and fall. **Fruiting Body:** 2–7 cm wide; up to about 2 cm high; subcircular or broadly elliptical in outline; cushion-shaped, with a somewhat narrowed base; upper surface black and shiny, covered with pimple-like dots (and covered with black slime when the mushroom is producing spores); encased in a black, felt-like veil that soon ruptures and becomes a sheath around the sides of the fruiting body, with a ragged upper edge; interior tough and brownish, filled with black channels and pockets but not featuring concentric zones. **Microscopic Features:** Spores 6–8.5 × 3–4.5 µm smooth; broadly ellipsoid at one end and broadly fusiform at the other; with a tiny pore at the narrowed end; purplish gray in KOH. **Comments:** This unmistakable fungus almost looks like a hard black eye with felty eyelids.

CANTHARELLUS APPALACHIENSIS R. H. PETERSEN

Ecology: Mycorrhizal; growing alone, gregariously, or in small clusters under hardwoods or in mixed woods; summer and fall; common from about the Mississippi River valley eastward. **Cap:** 1–5 cm; convex, with an inrolled margin, becoming broadly convex or flat with an inrolled, uplifted, or irregular and wavy margin; shallowly depressed in the middle at maturity (but the disc does not become perforated); bald or with tiny appressed fibers; moist when fresh; brown at first, but soon developing yellow undertones and eventually becoming yellowish to yellowish brown overall, with a brown spot over the center. **Undersurface:** With well-developed false gills that run down the stem; yellow throughout development; often with cross-veins at maturity. **Stem:** 1.5–5 cm long; up to about 1 cm thick; fairly slender; tapering downward; more or less bald; brown at first and remaining brownish or yellow brown. **Flesh:** Pale or brownish; unchanging when sliced. **Odor and Taste:** Odor like apricots, or not distinctive; taste not distinctive. **Chemical Reactions:** Iron salts dull red on flesh and undersurface. **Spore Print:** Buff. **Microscopic Features:** Spores 7.5–9 × 4.5–5.5 µm; smooth; more or less ellipsoid; inamyloid; yellowish in KOH. **Comments:** Edible and good. *Cantharellus appalachiensis* is the only midwestern chanterelle that turns red with iron salts. In the absence of the chemical test, the darker, browner colors, yellow gills, and slender stem usually separate it easily.

CANTHARELLUS CIBARIUS FRIES

Ecology: Mycorrhizal with hardwoods, especially oaks; growing alone, scattered, or gregariously in summer and fall; widely distributed. **Cap:** 1.5–15 cm across; more or less convex when young (often with an inrolled margin); becoming flat or shallowly depressed, with a wavy and irregular margin; tacky when wet; bald or with a few tiny appressed fibers; pale yellow to egg-yolk yellow to almost orange. **Undersurface:** With well-developed false gills that sometimes feature cross-veins; running deeply down the stem; colored like the cap or paler (whitish in one variety); sometimes staining brownish to orangish. **Stem:** 2.5–8 cm long; 1–2 cm thick; extremely variable in shape (from thin, more or less equal, and graceful to thick, stocky, and nearly club-shaped);

bald below the false gills; colored like the cap or paler; sometimes bruising brownish to orangish. **Flesh:** White; solid; unchanging when sliced. **Odor and Taste:** Taste not distinctive, or slightly peppery; odor fragrant and sweet, like apricots. **Chemical Reactions:** Iron salts fleetingly reddish, then pinkish gray to gray on flesh; dark gray on false gills. Ammonia negative on all surfaces. **Spore Print:** Pale yellow to creamy white. **Microscopic Features:** Spores 7–11 × 4.5–6 µm; smooth; ellipsoid; inamyloid; hyaline in KOH. **Comments:** Edible and very good—but compare carefully with *Omphalotus illudens* (p. 292), *Hygrophoropsis aurantiaca* (p. 215), and *Cortinarius hesleri* (p. 156). The description above represents a compilation of midwestern, *cibarius*-like chanterelles, several of which are likely to be separated as distinct species.

Photo by Dan Molter

CANTHARELLUS CINNABARINUS (SCHWEINITZ) SCHWEINITZ

Ecology: Mycorrhizal with hardwoods (especially beech, hickories, and aspens); growing alone, scattered, or gregariously; summer and fall; widely distributed. **Cap:** 1–5 cm across; convex to flat when young, becoming flat or shallowly vase-shaped; bald; the margin inrolled when young, expanding and becoming wavy; flamingo pink to cinnabar red or reddish orange. **Undersurface:** With well-spaced, well-developed false gills that run down the stem; colored like the cap or slightly paler. **Stem:** 1–4 cm long; 0.5–1.5 cm wide; equal or tapering slightly to the base; colored like the cap or paler. **Flesh:** Whitish or tinged with the cap color; not changing color when sliced. **Odor and Taste:** Odor sweet and fragrant; taste mild to slightly peppery. **Chemical Reactions:** Iron salts negative to very pale gray on flesh; negative to very pale gray on undersurface. **Spore Print:** Whitish or pinkish. **Microscopic Features:** Spores 6–11 × 4–6 µm; smooth; ellipsoid; inamyloid; hyaline to ochraceous in KOH. **Comments:** Edible. Easily distinguished from other chanterelles on the basis of its colors.

CANTHARELLUS IGNICOLOR R. H. PETERSEN

Ecology: Saprobic and/or mycorrhizal; growing alone or gregariously in moss or sphagnum in conifer bogs and under hardwoods in damp, shady areas; summer and fall; widely distributed. **Cap:** Up to 5 cm wide; convex when very young but soon developing a central depression and, eventually, becoming perforated in the center and vase-shaped overall; with a wavy and often irregular margin at maturity; slightly sticky or waxy when fresh; bald, or with tiny appressed fibrils; yellow, brownish yellow, or orange, but often fading to dull yellowish. **Undersurface:** With well-developed false gills that run down the stem; creamy to pale yellow, pinkish, or very pale tan. **Stem:** Up to 6 cm long; to 1.5 cm thick; equal or tapering to base; becoming hollow; bald; yellow or orange. **Odor and Taste:** Not distinctive. **Spore Print:** Whitish or pale pinkish yellow. **Chemical Reactions:** Iron salts grayish on undersurface and flesh. **Microscopic Features:** Spores 9–13 × 6–9 µm; ellipsoid; smooth. **Comments:** According to a DNA study (Dahlman, Danell, and Spatafora 2000), this species belongs in the genus *Craterellus*, but an official transfer has not yet been made.

CANTHARELLUS LATERITIUS (BERKELEY) SINGER

Ecology: Mycorrhizal with oaks; growing alone, scattered, or gregariously; summer and fall; widely distributed. **Cap:** 2–10 cm across; flat, becoming shallowly vase-shaped with a wavy margin; bald; bright orange yellow to egg-yolk yellow; bruising reddish brown and occasionally blackening at the margin when old. **Undersurface:** Smooth or with shallow wrinkles; colored like the cap. **Stem:** 2–10 cm long; 0.5–2.5 cm thick; tapering to the base; colored like the cap or paler. **Flesh:** Whitish to yellowish; soft. **Odor and Taste:** Taste not distinctive; odor usually strong, fragrant and sweet. **Chemical Reactions:** Iron salts pinkish gray to gray on flesh; dark gray on undersurface. **Spore Print:** Pale pinkish yellow. **Microscopic Features:** Spores 7.5–12.5 × 4.5–6.5 µm; smooth; ellipsoid; inamyloid; hyaline to ochraceous in KOH. **Comments:** Edible. *Cantharellus confluens*, found in the southeastern Midwest, is nearly identical but features a stem that gives rise to several confluent caps. Occasionally one encounters forms of *Cantharellus lateritius* with wrinkled undersurfaces that almost approximate false gills and seem intermediate between this species and the *cibarius*-like species.

CANTHARELLUS MINOR PECK

Ecology: Mycorrhizal with hardwoods (especially oaks); growing alone or scattered, usually in moss; summer and fall; widely distributed. **Cap:** 0.5–3 cm across; convex, becoming shallowly vase-shaped with an arched and wavy margin; not developing a central perforation; egg-yolk yellow to orange yellow; bald and often somewhat waxy. **Undersurface:** With well-developed false gills that run down the stem; colored like the cap. **Stem:** 15–40 mm long; 1–7 mm wide; slender; equal or tapering slightly to

base; becoming hollow; colored like the cap or paler. **Flesh:** Insubstantial; pale yellowish to orangish. **Odor and Taste:** Taste not distinctive; odor sweet and fragrant. **Chemical Reactions:** Iron salts negative on flesh and undersurface. **Spore Print:** Pale yellowish. **Microscopic Features:** Spores 6–11.5 × 4–6.5 µm; smooth; more or less ellipsoid; inamyloid; hyaline to ochraceous in KOH. **Comments:** Compare with *Cantharellus ignicolor* (p. 132), which is usually somewhat larger and develops a perforation in the center of the cap. Occasional miniature forms of chanterelles in the *cibarius* group are stockier and feature shorter, thicker stems.

CERRENA UNICOLOR (BULLIARD) MURRILL

Ecology: Saprobic on the deadwood of hardwoods (very rarely reported on conifers); causing a white rot; annual; growing in overlapping clusters; found year-round but especially common in spring and early summer; widely distributed. **Fruiting Body:** Sometimes lacking a cap (especially when growing on the undersides of logs), appearing like a pore surface that lost its mushroom, but more commonly with a kidney-shaped to fan-shaped cap 3–10 cm across; upper surface velvety to hairy, whitish to brownish, but often appearing green from algae; usually with concentric zones of texture and/or color. **Pore Surface:** Whitish when young, becoming gray; pores maze-like or slot-like, becoming tooth-like with age; tubes to 4 mm deep. **Flesh:** Whitish; with a dark line just beneath the cap surface; leathery. **Spore Print:** White. **Microscopic Features:** Spores 5–7 × 2.5–4 µm; smooth; long-ellipsoid; inamyloid; hyaline in KOH. Hyphal system trimitic. **Comments:** The relationship of *Cerrena unicolor* to the horntail wasp and the ichneumonid wasp is fascinating; see Kuo and Methven (2010, 43) for details.

CHALCIPORUS PIPERATUS (BULLIARD) BATAILLE

Ecology: Mycorrhizal with conifers; growing alone, scattered, or gregariously; summer and fall; northern Midwest. **Cap:** 2–5 cm (rarely to 10 cm); convex, becoming broadly convex; sticky when fresh, but soon dry; bald; dull reddish brown to dull pinkish tan, fading to tan. **Pore Surface:** Cinnamon brown to reddish brown, becoming dull coppery reddish at maturity; bruising brown; usually with 1–2 pores per mm; tubes to 1 cm deep; often with wide pores near the stem that create fine lines at the stem apex. **Stem:** 2–8 cm long; up to 1.5 cm thick; more or less equal; dry; solid; colored like the cap; bald; base with bright to dull yellow mycelium. **Flesh:** Yellowish to pinkish in the cap; brighter yellow in the stem; not staining on exposure, or staining brownish to grayish. **Odor and Taste:** Odor not distinctive; taste strongly peppery. **Chemical Reactions:** Ammonia grayish to dull olive on cap; negative to pinkish gray on flesh. KOH negative to gray on cap and flesh. Iron salts negative on cap and flesh. **Spore Print:** Brown to reddish brown. **Microscopic Features:** Spores 8–11 × 4–5 µm; smooth; subfusoid. Pileipellis a cutis. **Comments:** The bitter-tasting flesh, yellow stem base, and brownish-red color of the pore surface are good identifying features. *Chalciporus piperatoides* is similar but stains and bruises blue.

CHLOROPHYLLUM MOLYBDITES (G. MEYER) MASSEE

Ecology: Saprobic; growing gregariously in lawns and meadows, often in troops or fairy rings; summer and fall; widely distributed. **Cap:** 10–40 cm; convex to conical when young, becoming convex to broadly convex or nearly flat in age; dry; nearly bald at first, but soon becoming scaly, with brown to pinkish-brown scales that are uplifted or flat, and concentrated near the center in age; whitish to tan or yellowish white. **Gills:** Free from the stem; close; white when young, becoming grayish green to brownish green (but sometimes remaining whitish until well into maturity). **Stem:** 5–25 cm long; 1.5–2.5 cm thick; more or less equal, sometimes slightly enlarged toward base; bald; firm; white, sometimes discoloring slightly brownish; with a persisting, double-edged ring. **Flesh:** White throughout, not staining when sliced, or staining reddish brown to pale pinkish red or almost orange in the stem base; thick. **Odor and Taste:** Not distinctive. **Spore Print:** Dull green. **Microscopic Features:** Spores 8–13 × 6.5–9 µm; smooth; ellipsoid; dextrinoid; with a small pore. Cheilocystidia abundant; mostly clavate to fusoid-ventricose. Pileipellis a cutis of interwoven, narrow elements. **Comments:** Poisonous. This mushroom causes more mushroom poisonings than any other North American species. Crucial identifying features are the fairly large size, the growth in grass, the green spore print, and the brownish-green mature gills.

Spore print

Photo by Martin Livezey

CHLOROPHYLLUM RHACODES (VITTADINI) VELLINGA

Ecology: Saprobic; typically growing in troops or fairy rings in disturbed-ground areas like roadsides, gardens, the edges of fields, and so on, often in the vicinity of conifers; fall; widely distributed. **Cap:** 5–20 cm; dry; convex to nearly round when young; becoming flat or very broadly bell-shaped; at first bald and brownish but soon breaking up so that the center remains smooth (or cracked) and brown, but the rest of the surface consists of shaggy scales with brownish tips over a whitish background. **Gills:** Free from the stem; close; white or, in maturity, pale brownish. **Stem:** 10–20 cm long; 1–3 cm thick; with a bulbous base that sometimes has a prominent rim at the top of the bulb; bald; white, bruising and discoloring brownish; with a high, double-edged, moveable ring. **Flesh:** Whitish throughout, but typically turning pinkish orange, then slowly brownish when sliced (especially near the apex of the stem); thick. **Spore Print:** White. **Odor and Taste:** Pleasant; not distinctive. **Microscopic Features:** Spores 6–13 × 5–9 µm; smooth; ellipsoid; dextrinoid; with a small pore. Cheilocystidia broadly clavate to clavate. Pileipellis with clavate to capitate terminal elements. **Comments:** Compare with *Chlorophyllum molybdites* (p. 135), which has scales that are less brown and features a green spore print and mature gills; also compare with *Macrolepiota procera* (p. 268).

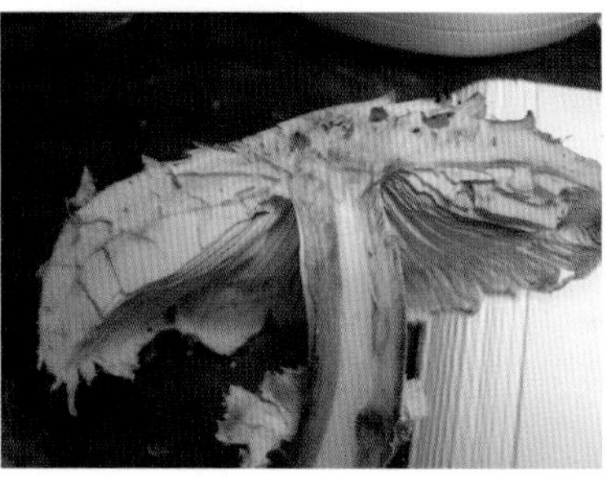

CHROOGOMPHUS OCHRACEUS (KAUFFMAN) O. K. MILLER

Ecology: Mycorrhizal with conifers, especially pines; growing alone, scattered, or gregariously; summer and fall; widely distributed but more common where conifers occur naturally. **Cap:** 2–12 cm wide; convex, occasionally with a central point; bald; slimy when fresh and young, but often dry and shiny or silky when collected; color ranging from yellowish to orangish, reddish, purplish red, or reddish brown—

Photo by Andy Methven

usually darker with maturity. **Gills:** Running down the stem; distant or nearly so; pale yellowish at first, becoming grayish cinnamon and finally blackish as the spores mature. **Stem:** 3.5–18 cm long; up to 2.5 cm wide; tapering to base; yellowish to pale orangish; sometimes with scattered orangish to reddish fibers; often with a wispy ring zone from the collapsed partial veil. **Flesh:** Pinkish above, yellowish in the stem. **Odor and Taste:** Not distinctive. **Spore Print:** Dark gray to black. **Microscopic Features:** Spores 14–22 × 6–7.5 µm; smooth; narrowly ellipsoid to subfusoid. Cystidia long-cylindric, subutriform, or narrowly clavate; with thin walls (under 1 µm thick). **Comments:** Often called "*Chroogomphus rutilus*," but recent study (Miller 2003) indicates that the species is strictly European. *Chroogomphus vinicolor* can appear nearly identical but features thick-walled cystidia.

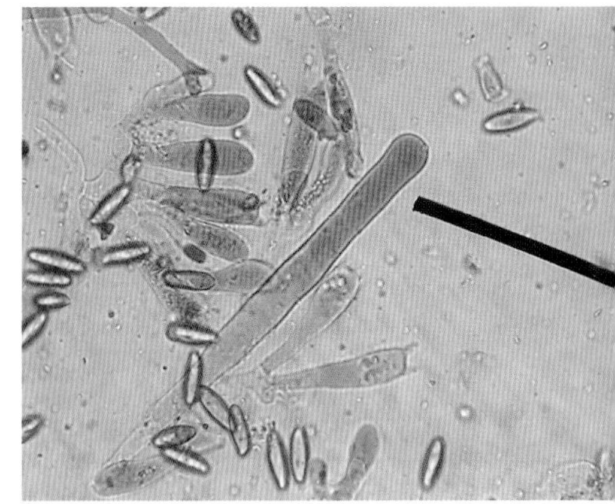

Cystidia

CLAVARIA VERMICULARIS (SWARTZ) FRIES

Ecology: Saprobic; growing in clusters, often with fused bases, or occasionally growing gregariously; found in woods under hardwoods or conifers, especially in moss and in moist areas; summer and fall; widely distributed. **Fruiting Body:** 3–12 cm high; 1–5 mm wide; cylindric and unbranched, or occasionally developing a few branches at the tip; sometimes flattened or grooved; dry or moist; white or translucent and whitish; often curved; usually with a somewhat pointed tip that discolors yellowish or pale brownish. **Flesh:** White; thin. **Odor and Taste:** Not distinctive. **Spore Print:** White. **Chemical Reactions:** Iron salts negative on all surfaces. KOH negative on all surfaces. **Microscopic Features:** Spores 4.5–7 × 2.5–4 µm; ellipsoid; smooth; with an apiculus. Basidia 4-sterigmate. Clamp connections absent.

CLAVARIA ZOLLINGERI LÉVEILLÉ

Ecology: Saprobic; almost always found in moss under hardwoods; growing alone or in groups; summer and fall; widely distributed. **Fruiting Body:** 2–10 cm high; individual elements usually sharing a common base, branching occasionally, 2–6 mm wide; surface purple to pinkish purple, fading somewhat; tips rounded or irregular; base whitish. **Flesh:** Brittle; purplish; thin. **Odor and Taste:** Not distinctive, or mildly radish-like. **Spore Print:** White. **Chemical Reactions:** Iron salts negative on all surfaces. **Microscopic Features:** Spores 4–7 × 3–5.5 µm; ellipsoid; smooth; with an apiculus; inamyloid. Basidia 4-sterigmate. Clamp connections absent.

Photo by Dan Molter

Photo by Joe McFarland

CLAVARIADELPHUS AMERICANUS (CORNER) METHVEN

Ecology: Mycorrhizal with oaks and pines; growing scattered or gregariously; summer and fall; widely distributed. **Fruiting Body:** 3–15 cm high; up to about 3 cm wide at the apex; cylindric or narrowly club-shaped at first, becoming more broadly club-shaped with age; dry; initially smooth, becoming shallowly wrinkled; orangish buff when young, darkening to orangish brown or cinnamon brown. **Flesh:** Whitish; sometimes staining brownish in places when sliced. **Odor and Taste:** Not distinctive. **Chemical Reactions:** KOH negative on surfaces; iron salts greenish. **Spore Print:** White. **Microscopic Features:** Spores 8–12 × 4–6 µm; broadly ovoid; smooth. **Comments:** *Clavariadelphus pistillaris* is nearly identical but associates exclusively with beeches. Compare with *Clavariadelphus unicolor* (below), which develops a flattened apex and turns yellow with KOH.

CLAVARIADELPHUS UNICOLOR (BERKELEY & RAVENEL) CORNER

Ecology: Mycorrhizal with hardwoods or conifers, particularly oaks and pines; growing alone, scattered, gregariously, or in small clusters; fall; widely distributed. **Fruiting Body:** 3–10 cm high; 2–6 cm wide; cylindric or club-shaped when young, later enlarging at the top and appearing cut off and flattened; surface smooth or broadly wrinkled; pinkish to reddish brown; sometimes bruising darker brown. **Flesh:** White; soft; sometimes staining brownish orange on exposure. **Odor and Taste:** Not distinctive. **Chemical Reactions:** KOH bright yellow on surfaces; iron salts greenish. **Spore Print:** White. **Microscopic Features:** Spores 8.5–11.5 × 4.5–6 µm; broadly ellipsoid; smooth. **Comments:** Compare with *Clavariadelphus americanus* (above).

CLAVULINA AMETHYSTINOIDES (PECK) CORNER

Ecology: Mycorrhizal; found under conifers and hardwoods; growing alone, scattered, or gregariously but not in clusters; often in moss or in moist areas; summer and fall; southern Midwest. **Fruiting Body:** 2–6 cm high; usually moderately and irregularly branched, antlered, or lobed, but sometimes branched sparingly or not at all; when branched up to 4 cm wide. **Branches:** Fairly smooth, or finely rugged (but bald); fleshy tan to drab lilac or drab purple; tips colored like the sides, bluntly to sharply pointed or occasionally vaguely "cristate" with multiple sharp points. **Base:** Up to about 3 cm long; velvety at the base; colored and textured like the branches. **Flesh:** Colored like the surfaces; brittle in the branches and tougher in the stem. **Odor and Taste:** Not distinctive. **Spore Print:** White. **Chemical Reactions:** Iron salts negative on branches. **Microscopic Features:** Spores 7.5–8.5 × 6–7.5 µm; subglobose or broadly ellipsoid; smooth; with an apiculus. Basidia 2-sterigmate with long, incurved sterigmata. Clamp connections present. **Comments:** Compare with *Clavaria zollingeri* (p. 137), which is more branched and more purple.

CLAVULINA CRISTATA (HOLMSKJOLD) SCHRÖTER

Ecology: Mycorrhizal with conifers and perhaps with hardwoods; growing alone, gregariously, or in clusters; summer and fall; widely distributed but more common where conifers occur naturally. **Fruiting Body:** 2–10 cm high; 3–10 cm wide; sparingly to (more commonly) repeatedly branched. **Branches:** 2–5 mm thick; smooth; white, sometimes becoming pinkish to pale pinkish brown with age; tips colored like the sides, flattened and "cristate" with several sharp points; often parasitized (see comments) and becoming dark gray to black from the base upward, or eventually blackish overall. **Base:** When present 0.5–3 cm long; up to about 0.5 cm wide; white. **Flesh:** Whitish; fairly brittle. **Odor and Taste:** Not distinctive. **Spore Print:** White. **Chemical Reactions:** Iron salts negative on branches. **Microscopic Features:** Spores 7–11 × 6.5–10 µm; subglobose; smooth; with an apiculus. Basidia 2-sterigmate with long (5–7 µm), incurved sterigmata. Clamp connections present. **Comments:** This species is frequently attacked by a parasite, *Helminthosphaeria clavariarum*, rendering it partially or completely gray to black. Compare with *Ramariopsis kunzei* (p. 333) and *Tremellodendron pallidum* (p. 374).

Photo by Patrick Harvey

CLAVULINOPSIS FUSIFORMIS (SOWERBY) CORNER

Ecology: Presumably saprobic; growing in dense clusters with fused bases, or occasionally gregariously; in woods under hardwoods or conifers, sometimes in grass; summer and fall; widely distributed. **Fruiting Body:** 5–15 cm high; up to 1.5 cm wide; cylindric and unbranched; often flattening; sometimes grooved; dry; bright or pale yellow, or orange yellow; fading with age; white at the extreme base; usually with a somewhat pointed tip. **Flesh:** Yellow; thin. **Odor and Taste:** Odor not distinctive; taste bitter. **Chemical Reactions:** KOH negative on surfaces. **Spore Print:** White. **Microscopic Features:** Spores 5–9 × 4.5–9 µm; subglobose or broadly ellipsoid; smooth; with a prominent apiculus 1–2 µm long. Basidia 4-sterigmate. Clamp connections present. **Comments:** *Clavulinopsis laeticolor* is a similar but smaller species (1–7 cm high) that does not grow in clusters.

KOH on cap

CLIMACODON PULCHERRIMUS (BERKELEY & CURTIS) NIKOLAJEVA

Ecology: Saprobic on the deadwood of hardwoods (and occasionally conifers); causing a white rot; growing alone, gregariously, or in shelving clusters; summer; widely distributed. **Cap:** 4–11 cm across; broadly convex to flat; fan-shaped or semicircular in outline; dry; matted-hairy to woolly; whitish to pale tan or faintly orangish. **Undersurface:** Composed of spines up to 8 mm long, fairly tightly packed, whitish to faintly orangish when fresh, but often darkening or drying to reddish brown, with age often sticking together. **Stem:** Absent. **Flesh:** White; unchanging when sliced; somewhat fibrous. **Odor and Taste:** Not distinctive. **Chemical Reactions:** KOH pink to red on flesh and cap. **Spore Print:** White. **Microscopic Features:** Spores 4–6 × 1.5–3 µm; smooth; ellipsoid; inamyloid. Cystidia absent. Hyphal system monomitic. Hyphae of the context and pileipellis frequently with 1–4 clamp connections at septa. **Comments:** Field characters for this rare species include the whitish spines that darken to reddish brown, the woolly cap surface, and the KOH reaction.

CLIMACODON SEPTENTRIONALIS (FRIES) KARSTEN

Photo by Ron Kerner

Ecology: Parasitic on hardwoods, especially green ash, sugar maple, and beech; growing in large shelf-like clusters in the wounds of living trees, or on recently dead stumps or trunks; summer and fall; widely distributed. **Caps:** Up to 30 cm across and 5 cm thick at the base; convex, flat, or shallowly depressed; kidney-shaped or semicircular in outline; sticky or dry; hairy or roughened; whitish, becoming yellowish with age; sometimes with fine concentric zones of texture. **Undersurface:** Spines 1–2.5 cm long; tightly packed; white at first, becoming yellowish with age. **Stem:** Absent, but caps often share a whitish basal plate. **Flesh:** White; tough; unchanging when sliced; zoned. **Odor and Taste:** Taste mild when young but bitter or unpleasant in age; odor

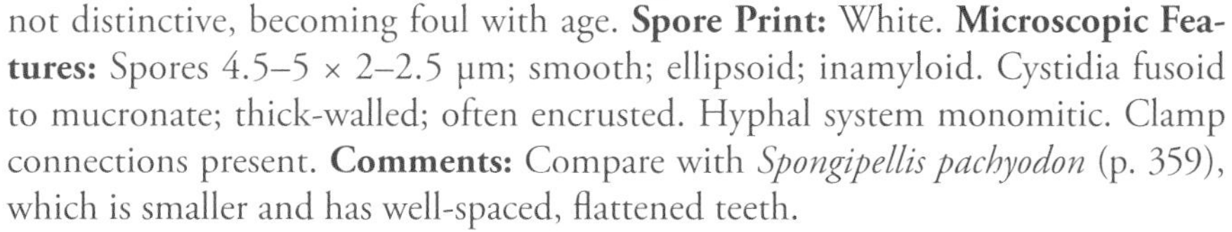

not distinctive, becoming foul with age. **Spore Print:** White. **Microscopic Features:** Spores 4.5–5 × 2–2.5 µm; smooth; ellipsoid; inamyloid. Cystidia fusoid to mucronate; thick-walled; often encrusted. Hyphal system monomitic. Clamp connections present. **Comments:** Compare with *Spongipellis pachyodon* (p. 359), which is smaller and has well-spaced, flattened teeth.

CLITOCYBE ECCENTRICA PECK

Ecology: Saprobic; growing gregariously or, more often, in clusters on wood (primarily the wood of hardwoods) or woody debris; late May through fall; widely distributed. **Cap:** 1–6 cm; convex, becoming flat or shallowly vase-shaped; dry; bald; whitish to pale brownish; usually changing color markedly as it dries out; the margin frequently inrolled. **Gills:** Running down the stem; fairly crowded; white or buff. **Stem:** 3–5 cm long; up to 7 mm thick; often somewhat off-center; more or less equal; dry; bald or finely hairy above, densely hairy at the extreme base; with white rhizomorphs attached. **Flesh:** Thin; watery or pale. **Odor and Taste:** Taste not distinctive, or bitter; odor not distinctive, or somewhat fragrant. **Spore Print:** White to creamy. **Chemical**

Reactions: KOH on cap surface yellowish to yellow. **Microscopic Features:** Spores 4.5–6 × 2.5–3.5 µm; ellipsoid; smooth; inamyloid. Clamp connections present. **Comments:** Compare with *Melanoleuca melaleuca* (p. 276), which is darker brown and grows in grass.

CLITOCYBE NUDA (BULLIARD) H. E. BIGELOW & A. H. SMITH

Ecology: Saprobic; growing alone, scattered, gregariously, or in clusters in organic debris, in woods or in urban settings; late summer and fall (also over winter during warm spells); widely distributed. **Cap:** 4–20 cm; convex, with an inrolled margin when young, becoming broadly convex to nearly flat—or with an uplifted, wavy margin in age; bald; slightly tacky when moist; sometimes finely cracked over the center; usually dull purple, or purplish with brown shades when fresh, fading to brownish, flesh-colored, tan, or paler—but sometimes brown or buff from the beginning. **Gills:** Attached to the stem, sometimes by a notch, or beginning to run down it; close or crowded; pale lavender to lilac, fading to buff, pinkish buff, or brownish. **Stem:** 3–10 cm long; 1–3 cm thick at apex; equal, or enlarged at the base; dry; finely hairy, and/or mealy near the apex; pale purple or colored like the gills; becoming brownish in age; base often covered with lilac to buff mycelium. **Flesh:** Thick; soft; purplish to lilac buff or whitish. **Odor and Taste:** Taste not distinctive, pleasant, or slightly bitter; odor fragrant. **Spore Print:** Pinkish. **Microscopic Features:** Spores 5.5–8 × 3.5–5 µm; ellipsoid; roughened or sometimes nearly smooth; inamyloid. Cystidia absent. Pileipellis a cutis. Clamp connections present. **Comments:** Also known as *Lepista nuda* and frequently called the "blewit." Edible but not very good, and easily confused with poisonous species.

CLITOCYBE ODORA (BULLIARD) KUMMER

Ecology: Saprobic; growing scattered or gregariously on hardwood litter; summer and fall; widely distributed. **Cap:** 2–11 cm; convex, with an inrolled margin at first, becoming flat or shallowly vase-shaped; dry; bald or finely hairy; blue green to greenish, sometimes with a paler central area; fading quickly; in dry weather sometimes whitish; the margin often lined at maturity. **Gills:** Attached to the stem or running down it; close or crowded; whitish to pinkish buff.

Stem: 2–8 cm long; up to 15 mm thick; more or less equal; dry; finely hairy; whitish; with copious white mycelium at the base. **Flesh:** Thin; whitish. **Odor and Taste:** When fresh, strongly anise-like. **Chemical Reactions:** KOH on cap surface erasing green to pale orange. **Spore Print:** Pinkish to creamy. **Microscopic Features:** Spores 6–9 × 3.5–5.5 µm; ellipsoid; smooth; inamyloid. Cystidia absent. Clamp connections present. **Comments:** When fresh, this mushroom is easily identified by the green color and the strong odor of anise.

CLITOCYBE SUBCONNEXA MURRILL

Ecology: Saprobic; growing scattered or, more commonly, in clusters in leaf debris or conifer duff; appearing under hardwoods or conifers in a variety of diverse ecosystems; summer and fall; widely distributed. **Cap:** 3–9 cm; convex, with an inrolled margin, becoming plano-convex or flat, with an even margin; bald or with a satiny whitish sheen; dry; soft; white to buff, developing watery spots with age; the margin sometimes becoming lined and ridged with maturity. **Gills:** Broadly attached to the stem or beginning to run down it; crowded; buff. **Stem:** 2–8 cm long; up to 1.5 cm thick; more or less equal; bald or with a satiny whitish sheen; buff to grayish or watery brownish where handled; basal mycelium white, often copious. **Flesh:** Whitish; not changing when sliced; fairly brittle. **Odor and Taste:** Odor fragrant, or not distinctive. Taste mild or slightly bitter. **Chemical Reactions:** KOH negative on cap. **Spore Print:** Pinkish (sometimes nearly white). **Microscopic Features:** Spores 4.5–6 × 3–3.5 µm; ellipsoid; finely warty; inamyloid. Cystidia absent. Pileipellis a cutis. Clamp connections present. **Comments:** Compare with *Hygrophorus sordidus* (p. 216) and with *Rhodocollybia maculata* (p. 336).

CLITOCYBULA ABUNDANS (PECK) SINGER

Ecology: Saprobic; growing in dense clusters on the deadwood of conifers and hardwoods (especially paper birch); summer and fall; fairly widely distributed but more common in the northern Midwest. **Cap:** 1–4 cm; convex, becoming plano-convex to flat, with a central depression or "belly button"; bald, but with innate, radiating fibers; moist when fresh; the margin not lined, but often splitting in age; pale grayish brown centrally, grayish buff toward the margin. **Gills:** Broadly attached to the stem or just beginning to run down it; close; sometimes with cross-veins; white. **Stem:** 2–6 cm long; up to 4 mm thick; more or less equal; bald, or silky near the apex; whitish; hollowing. **Flesh:** Insubstantial; watery whitish. **Odor and Taste:** Not distinctive. **Chemical Reactions:** KOH negative on cap. **Spore Print:** White. **Microscopic Details:** Spores 4.5–6.5 × 3.5–5 µm; ellipsoid; smooth; amyloid. Cheilocystidia clavate to irregular and oblique. Pileipellis a cutis with pileocystidia in the area over the disc. Clamp connections present.

CLITOCYBULA LACERATA (SCOPOLI) MÉTROD

Ecology: Saprobic; growing alone, scattered, gregariously, or in loose clusters on the wood of spruces, paper birch, and oaks (but often attached to buried wood and appearing terrestrial); summer and fall; widely distributed. **Cap:** 2–6 cm; convex, with an inrolled margin, becoming more or less flat, with a shallow central depression and a wavy margin that is not lined, but often splits radially; streaked; with appressed radiating fibers; moist; gray to gray brown. **Gills:** Broadly attached or beginning to run down the stem; distant or nearly so; with numerous cross-veins; white, sometimes discoloring grayish. **Stem:** 1.5–5 cm long; up to 5 mm thick; more or less equal, or flared at the apex; bald; hollow; whitish to gray. **Flesh:** Thin; white. **Odor and Taste:** Not distinctive, or slightly unpleasant. **Chemical Reactions:** KOH negative on cap. **Spore Print:** White. **Microscopic Features:** Spores 6–8 × 4.5–6 µm; ellipsoid; smooth; amyloid. Cystidia absent. Pileipellis a cutis, with pileocystidia in the area over the disc. Clamp connections present. **Comments:** The streaked cap, the white gills with cross-veins, the fairly small size, and the tendency to grow gregariously or in very loose clusters are good field characters. Compare with *Megacollybia rodmani* (p. 275).

Photo by Andy Methven

CLITOPILUS PRUNULUS (SCOPOLI) KUMMER

Ecology: Saprobic; growing alone, scattered, or gregariously under hardwoods or conifers, in grassy areas and open woods; summer and fall; widely distributed. **Cap:** 3–12 cm; convex, with an inrolled margin, becoming flat or irregular, often with a wavy margin; dry; finely suede-like; white, buff, or pale grayish. **Gills:** Running down the stem; close or almost distant; whitish at first, then pinkish. **Stem:** 3–8 cm long; up to 1.5 cm thick; sometimes off-center;

equal; solid; bald; dry; white or pale grayish. **Flesh:** Fairly firm; white. **Odor and Taste:** Strongly mealy. **Chemical Reactions:** KOH negative on cap. **Spore Print:** Pink to brownish pink. **Microscopic Features:** Spores 9–12 × 4–7 µm; subfusiform; angular in end view; ridged lengthwise; inamyloid. **Comments:** Compare with *Clitocybe subconnexa* (p. 143), which has crowded, white mature gills and a white spore print.

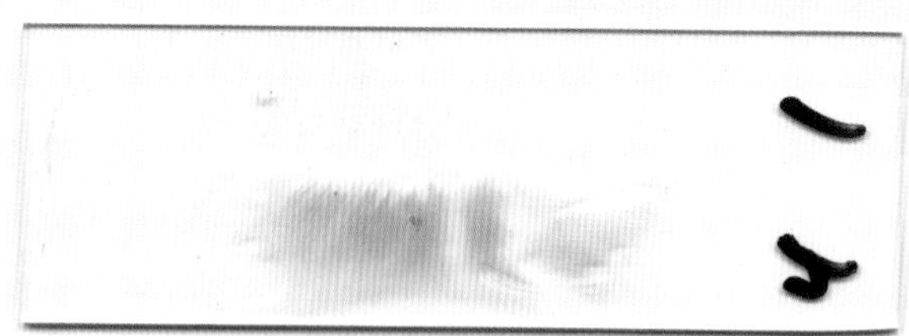

Spore print

COLLYBIA COOKEI (BRESÀDOLA) ARNOLD

Ecology: Saprobic; growing on the remains of decayed mushrooms or on humus (occasionally on well-rotted wood); under hardwoods or conifers; summer and fall; fairly widely distributed. **Cap:** 2–9 mm across; convex, with a somewhat inrolled margin when young, becoming broadly convex to flat, with or without a shallow central depression; dry or moist; bald; whitish to buff. **Gills:** Attached to the stem; close or almost distant; whitish. **Stem:** 1–6 cm long; 1–2 mm thick; equal; dry; whitish; becoming hollow; attached at the base to sclerotia that are more or less round, are yellowish to orangish yellow, and measure 4–10 mm. **Flesh:** Whitish; thin. **Spore Print:** White. **Microscopic Features:** Spores 4.5–6 × 3–3.5 µm; smooth; more or less ellipsoid; inamyloid. Cystidia absent. Pileipellis a cutis with scattered pileocystidia. **Comments:** *Collybia tuberosa* is nearly identical but features ellipsoid, reddish-brown sclerotia that resemble apple seeds.

Sclerotia

Photo by Walt Sturgeon

COLTRICIA CINNAMOMEA (JACQUIN) MURRILL

Ecology: Mycorrhizal with hardwoods; growing alone or in small groups, often in moss and along paths; summer and fall; widely distributed. **Cap:** 1–5 cm; more or less round in outline; flat or vase-shaped; dry; silky-shiny when fresh; cinnamon brown, usually with concentric bands of colors; the margin straight and thin, some-

times eroding in age. **Pore Surface:** Yellowish brown to brown or cinnamon brown; running down the stem or not; pores angular to circular, 2–3 per mm; tubes 3 mm deep at most; not bruising. **Stem:** 1–5 cm long; 1–4 mm thick; dry; brown to cinnamon brown; velvety; more or less equal; tough. **Flesh:** Rusty brown to orange; thin; tough. **Chemical Reactions:** Flesh instantly black with KOH. **Spore Print:** Yellowish brown. **Microscopic Features:** Spores 6–10 × 4.5–7 µm; smooth; ellipsoid; weakly dextrinoid. Setae absent. Hyphal system monomitic. Clamp connections absent.

CONNOPUS ACERVATUS (FRIES) K. W. HUGHES, D. A. MATHER, & R. H. PETERSEN

Ecology: Saprobic; growing in dense clusters on conifer stumps (and sometimes from buried conifer wood, appearing terrestrial); summer and fall; northern Midwest. **Cap:** 1–5 cm; convex, becoming plano-convex; bald; reddish brown and moist when young and fresh, but soon fading to brownish or pinkish buff (often passing through a 2-toned stage). **Gills:** Attached to the stem broadly or narrowly; close or crowded; whitish when young, developing pink tones. **Stem:** 2–12 cm long; up to about 6 mm thick; more or less equal; dry; hollow; bald except for whitish fuzz near the base; reddish brown to purplish brown; not fading as quickly as the cap. **Flesh:** Thin; whitish. **Odor and Taste:** Odor not distinctive; taste mild or bitter. **Spore Print:** White. **Microscopic Features:** Spores: 5.5–7 × 2.5–3 µm; smooth; ellipsoid or nearly cylindric; inamyloid. Pleurocystidia absent. Cheilocystidia variously shaped; often with protrusions or lobes. Pileipellis a cutis. **Comments:** Also known as *Collybia acervata* and *Gymnopus acervatus*. A recent DNA study (Hughes, Mather, and Petersen 2010) found support for placement of this species in its own genus.

CONOCYBE APALA (FRIES) ARNOLDS

Ecology: Saprobic; growing scattered or gregariously in grassy areas (lawns, meadows, and pastures); summer and fall (especially common in muggy weather); widely distributed. **Cap:** 1–3 cm; conical when young, becoming broadly conical with an uplifted marginal edge; dry; finely lined from the margin nearly to the center; whitish or creamy buff, sometimes with a slightly darker center. **Gills:** Attached to the stem or nearly free from it; close; pale at first but soon cinnamon brown or pinkish brown. **Stem:** 3–11 cm long; only a few millimeters thick; extremely fragile; hollow; more or less equal; whitish; bald or with tiny hairs on the upper half. **Flesh:** Insubstantial. **Odor and Taste:** Not distinctive. **Chemical Reactions:** KOH pinkish gray to lilac gray on cap. **Spore Print:** Cinnamon brown or reddish brown. **Microscopic Features:** Spores 10–14 × 7–9 µm; ellipsoid, with a truncated end; smooth; with a pore. Pleurocystidia absent. Cheilocystidia lecythiform. Pileipellis hymeniform. **Comments:** Also known as *Conocybe lactea* and *Conocybe albipes*. A wilted-looking form of this mushroom is sometimes found; it was previously known as *Gastrocybe lateritia* (see Kuo and Methven 2010), but recent research (Hallen, Watling, and Adams 2003) indicates it is not a separate species.

COPRINELLUS DISSEMINATUS (PERSOON) J. E. LANGE

Spore print

Ecology: Saprobic; growing in clusters, often by the hundreds, on decaying wood, especially near the bases of stumps; spring, summer, and fall; widely distributed. **Cap:** Minute to 2 cm; oval when young, expanding to broadly convex or bell-shaped; when young almost white, with a brownish center; with age darkening to grayish or grayish brown with a brownish center; paler toward the margin; bald, or very finely granular-hairy when young; lined or grooved from the margin nearly to the center. **Gills:** Attached to the stem or free from it; white at first, but soon gray, then blackish; not deliquescing; close or almost distant. **Stem:** 1.5–4 cm long; 1–2 mm thick; equal; smooth; often curved; white; hollow. **Flesh:** Very thin; fragile. **Odor and Taste:** Not distinctive. **Spore Print:** Black or blackish brown. **Microscopic Features:** Spores 6.5–10 × 4–6 µm; ellipsoid; smooth; with a central pore. Cheilocystidia cylindric; pleurocystidia absent. Pileipellis an epithelium with pileocystidia. Veil elements subglobose. **Comments:** Also known as *Coprinus disseminatus.*

COPRINELLUS DOMESTICUS (BOLTON) VILGALYS, HOPPLE, & JACQ. JOHNSON

Ecology: Saprobic; growing gregariously or in small clusters (occasionally alone) on decaying hardwood logs; summer and fall; widely distributed. **Cap:** Up to 7 cm across; oval when young, expanding to convex or conical; when young, honey yellow centrally and whitish toward the margin; in age, gray with a brownish center; covered with whitish to brownish universal veil fragments in the form of small scales or granules; finely grooved or lined from the margin nearly to the center. **Gills:** Attached to the stem or free from it; white at first, but soon gray, then blackish; eventually deliquescing; close. **Stem:** 4–10 cm long; up to 1 cm thick; equal, with a slightly swollen base; bald; white; hollow; sometimes with a volva-like rim at the base; usually arising from a mat of orange fibers. **Flesh:** Very thin; fragile. **Odor and Taste:** Not distinctive. **Chemical Reactions:** KOH negative on cap surface. **Spore Print:** Black or blackish brown. **Microscopic Features:** Spores 6–9 × 3.5–5 µm; ellipsoid; smooth; with an eccentric pore. Pleurocystidia subglobose to subcylindric; cheilocystidia variously shaped. Pileipellis an epithelium. Veil elements allantoid to nearly subglobose. **Comments:** *Coprinellus radians* is a similar species with slightly larger spores. The distinctive mat of orange fibers from which these species grow is called an *ozonium.*

COPRINELLUS MICACEUS (BULLIARD) VILGALYS, HOPPLE, & JACQ. JOHNSON

Ecology: Saprobic; growing in clusters on decaying wood (the wood may be buried, causing the mushrooms to appear terrestrial); frequently urban, but also found in woods; spring, summer, and fall; widely distributed. **Cap:** 2–15 cm, oval when young, expanding to broadly convex or bell-shaped, sometimes with a curled-up and/or tattered margin; honey brown, tawny, amber, or sometimes paler; becoming paler with age, especially toward the margin; buttons covered with mica-like granules that frequently wash off with rain or dew; the margin lined or grooved, usually halfway toward the center or more. **Gills:** Attached to the stem or free from it; pale, becoming brown, then black; deliquescing, but usually not completely; close or crowded. **Stem:** 2–8 cm long; 3–6 mm thick; equal; bald or very finely hairy or granulated; white; fibrous; hollow. **Flesh:** White to pale throughout; thin; soft. **Odor and Taste:** Not distinctive. **Spore Print:** Black. **Microscopic Features:** Spores 7–11 × 4–7 µm; subellipsoid to mitriform; smooth; with a central pore. Pleurocystidia and cheilocystidia ellipsoid to ovoid or subclavate. Pileipellis an epithelium. Veil elements subglobose to cylindric; chained. **Comments:** Also known as *Coprinus micaceus.*

COPRINOPSIS ATRAMENTARIA (BULLIARD) REDHEAD, VILGALYS, & MONCALVO

Photo by Dan Molter

Ecology: Saprobic; growing in clusters on decaying wood (the wood may be buried, causing the mushrooms to appear terrestrial); often growing from senescent roots around stumps; frequently urban, but also found in woods; spring, summer, and fall; widely distributed. **Cap:** Oval when young, expanding to conical-convex; up to 10 cm across; often with a curled-up and/or tattered margin when mature; lead gray, grayish, or gray brown; bald, or finely scaly to slightly scruffy over the center; faintly grooved or lined. **Gills:** Attached to the stem or free from it; whitish, becoming black; deliquescing; close or crowded. **Stem:** 8–15 cm long; 6–12 mm thick; equal; bald or finely hairy; sometimes sheathed with veil toward the base; white; fibrous; hollow. **Flesh:** White to pale gray throughout; thin; soft. **Odor and Taste:** Not distinctive. **Spore Print:** Black. **Microscopic Features:** Spores 6.5–10.5 × 4–6.5 µm; ellipsoid; smooth; with a central pore. Cystidia cylindric to utriform. Pileipellis a cutis. Veil elements tubular. **Comments:** Also known as *Coprinus atramentarius.*

Photo by Ron Kerner

COPRINOPSIS LAGOPUS (FRIES) REDHEAD, VILGALYS, & MONCALVO

Ecology: Saprobic; growing alone or gregariously (sometimes densely so) on decaying wood or on woody debris (sometimes appearing terrestrial) in forests or, occasionally, in urban settings; spring, summer, and fall; widely distributed. **Cap:** Up to 4 cm across when mature and expanded; oval and tiny when young, expanding to broadly convex or bell-shaped and eventually more or less flat; gray to black; at first covered with a dense coating of silvery hairs (a universal veil) that break up into patches as the mushroom grows and may eventually disappear; the finely lined margin split-

ting as the gills dissolve. **Gills:** Attached to the stem; crowded; pale at first, but soon gray, then blackish; deliquescing or merely deteriorating and collapsing in dry weather. **Stem:** Up to 2 cm long and 0.5 cm thick; equal; hollow; fragile; white; densely hairy at first (especially near the base), but sometimes nearly bald by maturity. **Flesh:** Insubstantial. **Odor and Taste:** Not distinctive. **Spore Print:** Black. **Microscopic Features:** Spores 10–14 × 6–8.5 µm; ellipsoid; smooth; dark-dextrinoid; with a wide (1.5–2 µm) central pore. Cystidia enormous; variously shaped. Pileipellis a cutis. Veil composed of elongated, often semi-inflated allantoid elements. **Comments:** Also known as *Coprinus lagopus*. Several species are virtually identical and must be separated with microscopic analysis.

COPRINOPSIS VARIEGATA (PECK) REDHEAD, VILGALYS, & MONCALVO

Ecology: Saprobic; growing gregariously or in clusters on decaying hardwood logs; summer and fall; widely distributed. **Cap:** To 7.5 cm across; oval when young, expanding to bell-shaped; when young whitish, in age gray to grayish brown; covered with large, loose scales and patches that are whitish to yellowish tan; the margin not prominently lined. **Gills:** Attached to the stem or free from it; white at first, but soon grayish or purplish gray, then black; eventually deliquescing; crowded. **Stem:** 4–12 cm long; up to 1 cm thick; more or less equal; felty or woolly; white; hollow; sometimes with partial veil remnants attached or with a sheathed appearance but rarely with a well-developed ring when mature; the base attached to brown mycelial strands. **Flesh:** Thin; whitish. **Odor and Taste:** Not distinctive, or somewhat foul. **Spore Print:** Black or blackish brown. **Microscopic Features:** Spores 7.5–10 × 4–5 µm; ellipsoid; smooth; with a central pore. Cystidia elliptical to clavate or fat-lageniform. Pileipellis a cutis. Veil elements cylindric. **Comments:** Also known as *Coprinus variegatus* and *Coprinus quadrifidus*.

COPRINUS COMATUS (O. F. MÜLLER) PERSOON

Ecology: Saprobic; growing alone or in clusters, lines, or fairy rings on lawns, woodchips, or hard-packed ground; summer and fall; widely distributed. **Cap:** 3–15 cm; oval to rounded-cylindric when young, expanding to bell-shaped with a lifting margin; in age turning to black "ink" from the margin inward; dry; whitish with a brownish center; with large, shaggy scales; margin lined at maturity. **Gills:** Free from the stem; white, becoming pinkish, then black; deliquescing; very crowded. **Stem:** 5–20 cm long; 1–2 cm thick; frequently tapering to apex; bald or silky; white; easily separable from cap; hollow, with a string-like strand of fibers hanging inside. **Flesh:** White throughout; soft. **Odor and Taste:** Not distinctive. **Spore Print:** Black. **Microscopic Features:** Spores 9–13 × 7–9 µm; ellipsoid; smooth; with a central to slightly eccentric pore. Pleurocystidia absent. Cheilocystidia variously shaped. Pileipellis cutis-like. Veil elements cylindric. **Comments:** Often called the "shaggy mane." Edible and good when collected in the button stage (when the gills are still white), but compare it carefully with *Amanita thiersii* (p. 100) and *Chlorophyllum molybdites* (p. 135), which also grow in lawns and meadows. The deliquescing gills of *Coprinus comatus* are illustrated on page 397. The strand of fibers in the stem is diagnostic for the genus *Coprinus*, as it has been recently defined by DNA studies.

CORDYCEPS MILITARIS (LINNAEUS) LINK

Ecology: Parasitic on buried larvae and pupae of insects (primarily moths and butterflies), but appearing to arise from stumps and logs; growing alone or gregariously; summer and fall; widely distributed. **Fruiting Body:** 2–8 cm long; up to about 0.5 cm wide; club-shaped, with the top wider than the base; the upper portion orange and pimply, the lower portion smooth and orange to pale orange, often curved; narrowing at the base; flesh pale, watery orange, with an outer cortex. **Microscopic Features:** Spores segmented and thread-like; breaking into ellipsoid segments 2–4.5 × 1–1.5 µm. **Comments:** Compare with *Clavulinopsis fusiformis* (p. 140), which grows in clusters on forest litter and does not feature a pimply surface.

Photo by Dan Molter

CORTINARIUS ARMILLATUS (FRIES) FRIES

Ecology: Mycorrhizal with paper birch; growing alone, scattered, or gregariously; summer and fall; northern Midwest. **Cap:** 5–15 cm; convex or bell-shaped, becoming broadly convex, broadly bell-shaped, or nearly flat; dry; bald, finely hairy, or very finely scaly over the center at maturity; yellow brown to reddish brown, often with a deeper, brick-red center; sometimes fading to dull tan. **Gills:** Attached to the stem; close or nearly distant; pale dirty yellowish to pale cinnamon at first, becoming rusty brown with maturity; covered by a whitish cortina when young. **Stem:** 7–15 cm long; up to 2.5 cm thick; swollen at the base; dry; bald or finely silky; whitish to pale brownish; encircled by 2–4 orange-red, concentric bands; with a rusty ring zone above the bands; basal mycelium whitish. **Flesh:** Whitish to pale brownish. **Odor:** Not distinctive, or radish-like. **Chemical Reactions:** KOH on black on cap surface; purple on orange areas of the stem. **Spore Print:** Rusty brown. **Microscopic Features:** Spores 9–12 × 5–7 µm; ellipsoid; finely warty; moderately to strongly dextrinoid; with thick (about .75 µm) walls. Cystidia absent. Pileipellis a cutis. **Comments:** The association with paper birch and the 2–4 red bracelets on the stem are good field characters.

CORTINARIUS BOLARIS (PERSOON) FRIES

Ecology: Mycorrhizal with hardwoods (perhaps exclusively with beech and oaks, though it is sometimes reported under conifers), often in wet areas; growing alone, gregariously, or in small troops; summer and fall; widely distributed. **Cap:** 2.5–8 cm; convex or broadly bell-shaped at first, becoming broadly convex, broadly bell-shaped, or nearly flat; dry; covered with red to brownish-red appressed scales that become more separated as the cap expands, revealing the whitish to yellowish or pinkish flesh beneath. **Gills:** Attached to the stem; close or crowded; dirty yellowish to dull cinnamon at first, becoming cinnamon to rusty; covered by a whitish cortina when young. **Stem:** 4–10 cm long; up to 1.5 cm thick; more or less equal; dry; whitish underneath stretched-out red scales or irregular bands; discoloring and bruising rusty orange to red near the base; usually with a rusty ring zone above the scales and bands. **Flesh:** Whitish, becoming slowly yellowish when sliced and exposed to air. **Odor and Taste:** Not distinctive. **Chemical Reactions:** KOH black on cap. **Spore Print:** Rusty brown. **Microscopic Features:** Spores 6–8 × 5–6 µm; subglobose to ovoid; moderately verrucose. Pleurocystidia absent. Marginal cells clavate to subclavate. Pileipellis a cutis; elements occasionally clamped.

Photo by Noah Siegel

CORTINARIUS CAPERATUS (PERSOON) FRIES

Ecology: Mycorrhizal with conifers (sometimes also with hardwoods, and bushes in the blueberry family); growing alone or, more often, gregariously; summer and fall; widely distributed but more common where conifers occur naturally. **Cap:** 5–15 cm; convex, becoming broadly convex, flat, or somewhat bell-shaped; dry; usually wrinkled; when young with a grayish to whitish, tissue-like coating of fibers, especially over the center; pale yellowish at first, but soon yellowish brown, often with a pale margin. **Gills:** Attached to the stem; close; pale at first, becoming brown or cinnamon brown; the faces sometimes somewhat mottled or striped; covered by a white partial veil when young. **Stem:** 5–13 cm long; 1–2.5 cm thick at the apex; equal or slightly swollen at the base; dry; usually rough or shaggy near the apex; whitish or pale tan; with a thick white ring at the midsection; sometimes with a whitish covering near the base. **Flesh:** Whitish, grayish, or pale lilac. **Odor:** Not distinctive. **Spore Print:** Rusty brown. **Microscopic Features:** Spores 10–15 × 7–10 µm; ellipsoid or nearly amygdaliform; moderately verrucose. Cystidia absent. Pileipellis a cutis. **Comments:** Also known as *Rozites caperata*. Edible, but compare carefully with species of *Amanita* (pp. 88–101). Field characters include the colors, the pasted-tissue texture of the young cap surface, the thick white ring, and the rusty-brown spore print.

CORTINARIUS COLLINITUS (PERSOON) FRIES

Ecology: Mycorrhizal with conifers or hardwoods; growing scattered or gregariously; summer and fall; widely distributed. **Cap:** 3–9 cm; broadly conic to bell-shaped when young, becoming broadly bell-shaped or nearly convex; thickly slimy; bald; variable in color, ranging from fairly dark purplish brown when young and fresh to orangish brown or yellowish

brown; the margin finely lined. **Gills:** Attached to the stem; close; lilac to pale purple at first, becoming brownish or rusty brown; often with whitish edges. **Stem:** 8–10 cm long; to nearly 2 cm thick; equal or tapering a little to the base; covered with lilac to purple slime when fresh; the slime often remaining as purplish patches, especially over the lower half, or disappearing to leave a whitish surface; often with a rusty ring zone. **Flesh:** Whitish to purplish. **Odor and Taste:** Not distinctive. **Chemical Reactions:** KOH negative on cap and on flesh. **Spore Print:** Rusty brown to medium brown. **Microscopic Features:** Spores 12–16.5 × 6.5–8 µm; football-shaped; moderately to strongly verrucose. Cystidia absent. Marginal cells present. Pileipellis an ixocutis with conspicuously clamped elements. **Comments:** "*Cortinarius collinitus*" represents a large group of species in need of contemporary study, and several midwestern versions exist.

CORTINARIUS CORRUGATUS PECK

Ecology: Mycorrhizal with beech and other hardwoods; growing alone, scattered, or gregariously; summer and fall; widely distributed. **Cap:** 4–10 cm; bell-shaped to convex or widely conical at first, becoming broadly convex to broadly bell-shaped; slimy when fresh or wet, but often merely tacky or even dry when collected; bald, but distinctively corrugated-wrinkled except in the very center; orange brown to reddish brown or yellowish brown. **Gills:** Attached to the stem; close; whitish, grayish, or pale lilac at first, becoming cinnamon to rusty with a slight hint of lilac; cortina ephemeral. **Stem:** 7–12 cm long; up to 2 cm thick; more or less equal, terminating in a slightly rounded bulb; dry; finely silky; whitish to yellowish or pale brownish; often with rusty, slimy veil material around the bulb. **Flesh:** Whitish; becoming yellowish to rusty in places when exposed. **Odor and Taste:** Not distinctive. **Chemical Reactions:** KOH dark red to black on cap. **Spore Print:** Rusty brown. **Microscopic Features:** Spores 10–15 × 7–10 µm; amygdaliform; moderately to strongly verrucose. Pleurocystidia absent. Marginal cells clavate to subclavate. Pileipellis a slightly gelatinized cutis of encrusted elements. **Comments:** Compare with *Psathyrella delineata* (p. 327), which grows from wood and features partial veil remnants on the cap margin as well as a purple-black spore print.

CORTINARIUS CROCEUS (SCHAEFFER) GRAY

Spore print

Ecology: Mycorrhizal with conifers; growing alone or scattered, often in dry areas; summer and fall; widely distributed. **Cap:** 1.5–8 cm; convex or nearly conical at first, becoming broadly convex, flat, or broadly bell-shaped, sometimes with a sharp central bump; dry; silky; yellowish brown to olive brown, often aging to dark brown, especially over the center; the margin often more yellowish. **Gills:** Attached to the stem, but often pulling away from it in age; close or crowded; yellow to orangish at first, becoming cinnamon to rusty; covered by a yellowish cortina when young; sometimes spotting and discoloring reddish brown. **Stem:** 3–7 cm long; up to 1 cm thick at the apex; more or less equal; dry; silky with brownish fibers; yellowish above, sometimes olive brown to reddish brown below; sometimes with a rusty ring zone; basal mycelium pale yellow. **Flesh:** Yellowish. **Odor:** Usually radish-like. **Chemical Reactions:** KOH red, then dark red to black on cap. **Spore Print:** Rusty brown. **Microscopic Features:** Spores 6.5–9 × 4.5–6 µm; ellipsoid; slightly to moderately roughened. Some basidia with reddish to purplish or reddish brown contents in KOH. Cystidia absent. Pileipellis a cutis. **Comments:** Also known as *Dermocybe crocea*.

CORTINARIUS DISTANS PECK

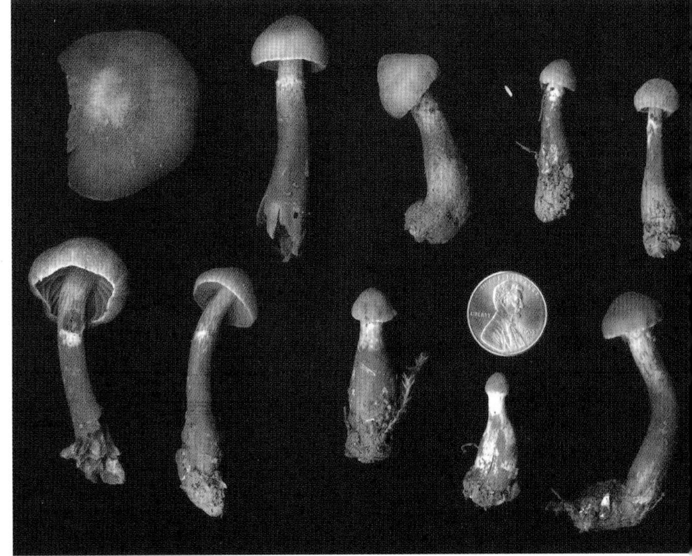

Ecology: Mycorrhizal with hardwoods, especially oaks and hickories; growing alone or gregariously; common in spring and early summer but appearing through fall; widely distributed. **Cap:** 2–7 cm; bell-shaped to conical, becoming broadly bell-shaped or convex; moist when fresh; usually finely grainy or scaly, at least when young; orangish brown, changing color markedly as it dries out and becoming dull orangish tan; the margin at first whitish, often splitting in age. **Gills:** Attached to the stem, often by a notch; distant; pale brownish to nearly yellowish at first, becoming cinnamon brown; initially covered by a white cortina. **Stem:** 4–8 cm long; up to 1.5 cm thick; equal or club-shaped (especially when young); finely silky; brownish, with a paler apex when young; often with a white ring zone; basal mycelium whitish. **Flesh:** Whitish when young but soon brownish;

becoming crumbly in the stem with age. **Odor:** Radish-like, sweetish and fragrant, or not distinctive. **Chemical Reactions:** KOH slowly dark reddish brown on cap. **Spore Print:** Rusty brown. **Microscopic Features:** Spores 6–9 × 4–6 µm; ellipsoid, often with one subfusoid end; moderately to finely ornamented; dextrinoid. Cystidia absent. Pileipellis a cutis. **Comments:** Often one of the first gilled mushrooms to appear in the spring. The conical to bell-shaped cap and distant gills are good field characters.

CORTINARIUS HESLERI AMMIRATI, NISKANEN, LIIMATAINEN, & MATHENY

Ecology: Mycorrhizal with oaks and perhaps with beech; growing alone, scattered, or gregariously; late spring and summer; widely distributed. **Cap:** 3–9 cm; convex or nearly conical at first, becoming broadly convex, nearly flat, or (frequently) broadly bell-shaped; dry; silky, occasionally becoming more or less bald with age; bright reddish orange when fresh, sometimes fading to pale orange or brownish orange. **Gills:** Attached to the stem; close; colored like the cap, becoming cinnamon to rusty orange; covered by an orange cortina when young. **Stem:** 2–10 cm long; up to 1.5 cm thick at the apex; more or less equal; dry; silky; pale orangish above, colored like the cap below; often darkening to reddish brown near the base or when handled; sometimes with a rusty ring zone; basal mycelium when fresh pastel orange. **Flesh:** Pale orangish overall; deep orange in the stem base. **Odor:** Mild or radish-like. **Chemical Reactions:** KOH purple or purplish black on cap. **Spore Print:** Rusty brown. **Microscopic Features:** Spores 8–10 × 5–6 µm; usually football-shaped but sometimes broadly ellipsoid; roughened with fairly prominent, widely spaced bumps. Cystidia absent. Pileipellis a cutis. Contextual and lamellar elements pinkish purple to purplish in KOH. **Comments:** Compare with *Hygrophoropsis aurantiaca* (p. 215), which has a white spore print and usually associates with conifers; with *Cantharellus cibarius* (p. 131), which has false (rather than true) gills, has a pale spore print, and is usually more yellow than orange; and with *Omphalotus illudens* (p. 292), which grows from wood and features gills that run down the stem along with a white spore print. *Cortinarius marylandensis* is a similar, bright red species.

CORTINARIUS INFRACTUS (PERSOON) FRIES

Ecology: Mycorrhizal with hardwoods or (less frequently) with conifers; growing alone, scattered, or gregariously; late summer and fall; widely distributed. **Cap:** 4–10 cm; convex, becoming broadly convex to nearly flat, or broadly bell-shaped;

sticky when fresh; bald; generally grayish olive to olive brown, but sometimes developing rusty to orangish-brown shades. **Gills:** Attached to the stem; close; brownish olive to olive gray at first (sometimes with a purplish tint), becoming rusty brown. **Stem:** 4–9 cm long; up to about 2.5 cm thick; club-shaped; dry; pale olive to whitish, discoloring brownish, or with purplish shades near the apex when young; often adorned with rusty cortina remnants when mature. **Flesh:** Whitish, or with purplish shades in the stem. **Odor and Taste:** Odor not distinctive; taste bitter. **Chemical Reactions:** KOH dark gray on cap; gray on flesh. **Spore Print:** Rusty brown. **Microscopic Features:** Spores 7–8 × 5–6 µm; subglobose to broadly ellipsoid; moderately to strongly verrucose. Basidia green in KOH. Cystidia absent; marginal cells present. Pileipellis an ixocutis of clamped elements. **Comments:** The olive tinges in the cap and gills, along with the bitter taste, are good field characters for tentative identification.

CORTINARIUS IODEOIDES KAUFFMAN

Ecology: Mycorrhizal with oaks and perhaps with other hardwoods; growing alone, scattered, or gregariously; fall; widely distributed. **Cap:** 2–5 cm; convex to broadly convex or slightly broadly bell-shaped; slimy; bald; lilac to purple, fading to pinkish gray or yellowish and sometimes developing yellowish spots. **Gills:** Attached to the stem; close; lilac when very young, but soon white, eventually becoming cinnamon to rusty; covered by a cortina when young. **Stem:** 2–6.5 cm long; to 1 cm thick; white, but when young covered (at least near the base) by a lilac to purple veil of slime; more or less club-shaped, especially when young; often with a rusty ring zone. **Flesh:** Purplish to white; soft. **Odor and Taste:** Cap slime bitter. Odor not distinctive. **Chemical Reactions:** KOH on cap surface erasing purple to pinkish. **Spore Print:** Rusty brown. **Microscopic Features:** Spores 7–8 × 4–5 µm; ellipsoid; slightly verrucose. Cystidia absent. Pileipellis an ixolattice. **Comments:** *Cortinarius iodes* is nearly identical but features larger spores; the slime on its cap is not bitter. Compare with *Inocybe lilacina* (p. 223).

CORTINARIUS MUCOSUS (BULLIARD) J. J. KICKX

Ecology: Mycorrhizal with pines and other conifers; growing alone, scattered, or gregariously; late summer and fall; widely distributed. **Cap:** 4–12 cm; convex, becoming broadly convex or nearly flat; slimy when fresh; bald; brownish orange, fading to orangish or yellowish with age. **Gills:** Attached to the stem; close or nearly crowded; creamy at first, becoming cinnamon to rusty brown. **Stem:** 4–10 cm long; up to about 2.5 cm thick; more or less equal; white; covered with a glutinous slime veil when fresh and young, but eventually more or less dry; often with rusty fibrils or a ring zone. **Flesh:** Whitish. **Odor and Taste:** Not distinctive. **Chemical Reactions:** KOH blackish red on cap. **Spore Print:** Rusty brown. **Microscopic Features:** Spores 11–17 × 5–7.5 µm; amygdaliform; moderately to strongly verrucose. Cystidia absent; marginal cells occasional. Pileipellis an ixocutis of clamped elements. **Comments:** The slimy brownish-orange cap, *Russula*-like stature, slimy stem, and preference for pines are good field characters.

CORTINARIUS OLEARIOIDES ROB. HENRY

Ecology: Mycorrhizal with hardwoods, especially oaks and beech; growing scattered or gregariously; fall; widely distributed. **Cap:** 5–15 cm; convex, becoming broadly convex or nearly flat; sticky when fresh; silky to bald; bright yellow when fresh and young, maturing to orange brown or yellowish brown. **Gills:** Attached to the stem; close; bright yellow at first, becoming orangish rusty brown. **Stem:** 4–10 cm long; up to about 3 cm thick above; more or less equal above a swollen, rimmed basal bulb; pale to bright yellow, discoloring brownish; dry; bald or slightly hairy in places; often with rusty fibrils or a ring zone. **Flesh:** Pale yellow to whitish. **Odor and Taste:** Odor not distinctive, or fruity, or potato-like; taste not distinctive. **Chemical Reactions:** KOH red on cap; reddish on flesh. **Spore Print:** Rusty brown. **Microscopic Features:** Spores 9–12 × 5–6.5 µm; limoniform; coarsely and moderately to strongly verrucose. Cystidia absent. Pileipellis an ixocutis of clamped elements. **Comments:** Also known as *Cortinarius subfulgens*. As is the case for all the yellow to orange or brownish *Cortinarius* species with basal bulbs, the color of the young gills (yellow) and the morphology of the spores (p. 158) are crucial for identification.

CORTINARIUS RUBRIPES PECK

Ecology: Mycorrhizal with hardwoods, especially oaks; growing alone, scattered, or gregariously; summer and fall; widely distributed. **Cap:** 2.5–12 cm; convex, becoming broadly convex, flat, or broadly bell-shaped; moist, becoming dry; bald or silky; purplish cinnamon at first, changing to reddish brown or cinnamon brown as it dries out. **Gills:** Attached to the stem; fairly well spaced; pale purplish when young, becoming cinnamon to rusty; at first covered by a cortina. **Stem:** 3–9 cm long; 0.5–2.5 cm thick at the apex; somewhat swollen at the base; dry or moist; bald or finely silky; pale purplish to brownish, with a fiery orange or bright to brick-red base; basal mycelium also brightly colored; sometimes with a rusty ring zone. **Flesh:** Whitish or dingy brownish. **Odor:** Fragrant, or not distinctive. **Chemical Reactions:** KOH gray to purplish on cap; instantly dark blue to dark purple on orange surfaces. **Spore Print:** Rusty brown. **Microscopic Features:** Spores 7–10 × 4–5.5 µm; ellipsoid, often with 1 subfusoid end; weakly to moderately roughened. Cystidia absent. Pileipellis a cutis. **Comments:** The quickly fading purple shades and the bright orange stem base are good field characters.

CORTINARIUS SEMISANGUINEUS (FRIES) GILLET

Ecology: Mycorrhizal with conifers, especially pines; growing alone or scattered, often in moss; summer and fall; widely distributed but more common where conifers occur naturally. **Cap:** 1.5–7 cm; more or less convex at first, becoming broadly convex, flat, or broadly bell-shaped, sometimes with a sharp central bump; dry; silky; yellowish brown to cinnamon brown, often darker over the center. **Gills:** Attached to the stem, but often pulling away from it in age; close; blood red, becoming cinnamon to rusty; covered by a yellowish cortina when young. **Stem:** 2.5–10 cm long; up to 1.5 cm thick at the apex; more or less equal; dry; silky; usually pale yellowish, but often darker or reddish toward the base; often with a rusty ring zone. **Flesh:** Whitish or pale yellowish. **Odor:** Mild or radish-like. **Chemical Reactions:** KOH purple to purplish black or black on cap. **Spore Print:** Rusty brown. **Microscopic Features:** Spores 6–9 × 4–5 µm; ellipsoid; slightly roughened. Cystidia absent. Pileipellis a cutis. **Comments:** Also known as *Dermocybe semisanguinea*. The combination of the blood-red gills and brown cap is distinctive.

CORTINARIUS TORVUS (FRIES) FRIES

Ecology: Mycorrhizal with hardwoods, including beech and oaks; growing scattered to gregariously; spring, summer, and fall; widely distributed. **Cap:** 3–8 cm; convex or irregular at first, becoming broadly convex, broadly bell-shaped, or nearly flat; dry; very finely silky or, in age, nearly bald; quite variable in color but generally lilac brown when young, fading markedly as it dries out to grayish lilac (often reminiscent of *Lactarius argillaceifolius*, p. 232) or silvery, and eventually to a wishy-washy tan; the margin inrolled well into maturity. **Gills:** Attached to the stem; nearly distant; brownish purple when young, becoming rusty brown; covered by a whitish cortina when young. **Stem:** 4–10 cm long; up to 1.5 cm thick at the apex; tapering to a club-shaped, swollen base; dry; pale purple above when fresh and young but later silvery to whitish or faintly brownish; sheathed or "booted" from the base with whitish to lilac-gray veil material that often terminates in a folded-over, fragile ring. **Flesh:** Whitish, or with purple to gray shades in the stem. **Odor:** Strong and sickly sweet. **Chemical Reactions:** KOH negative to gray or nearly black on cap; grayish to gray on flesh. **Spore Print:** Rusty brown. **Microscopic Features:** Spores 8–11.5 × 4.5–6 µm; ellipsoid, with a narrowed apicular end; weakly to moderately verrucose. Cystidia absent, but subclavate, septate marginal cells present. Pileipellis a cutis of occasionally encrusted elements. **Comments:** The sheathed stem, well-spaced purple gills, and sickly sweet odor are good field characters. Compare with *Laccaria ochropurpurea* (p. 227).

CORTINARIUS VIBRATILIS (FRIES) FRIES

Ecology: Mycorrhizal with hardwoods and with conifers; often found in mossy, wet places; growing alone or gregariously; fall; widely distributed. **Cap:** 2–5 cm; convex, becoming broadly convex, nearly flat, or broadly bell-shaped; slimy when fresh; yellow to orangish yellow or nearly orange; the margin usually paler; bald. **Gills:** Attached to the stem; close; whitish to yellowish white at first, becoming cinnamon to rusty brown. **Stem:** 3–7 cm long; up to about 1 cm thick; usually with a somewhat swollen basal bulb, at least when young; white; covered with a glutinous slime veil when fresh and young, but soon more or less dry, or slimy only at the base; often with rusty fibrils or a faint ring zone. **Flesh:** Whitish. **Odor and Taste:** Odor not distinctive, or slightly foul; taste extremely bitter. **Chemical Reactions:** KOH negative on cap. **Spore Print:** Rusty brown. **Microscopic Features:** Spores 6–7.5 × 4–5 µm; ellipsoid; very slightly verrucose (appearing almost smooth). Cystidia absent. Pileipellis an ixocutis of clamped elements. **Comments:** "*Cortinarius vibratilis*" is likely a species group. The very bitter taste is a good field character when combined with the slimy yellow cap, whitish young gills, and small bulb on the stem base.

CORTINARIUS VIOLACEUS (LINNAEUS) S. F. GRAY

Ecology: Mycorrhizal with hardwoods or conifers (see comments regarding varieties of this species); growing alone, scattered, or gregariously; fall; widely distributed. **Cap:** 4–12 cm; convex, becoming broadly convex, nearly flat, or slightly bell-shaped; dry; densely hairy, becoming fuzzy or scaly; deep purple, becoming brownish purple and eventually dark brown. **Gills:** Attached to the stem; nearly distant; dark purple at first, becoming grayish to blackish, and eventually rusty brown; covered by a purple cortina when young. **Stem:** 6–16 cm long; up to 2 cm thick; equal above a swollen or club-shaped base; dry; purple and finely hairy when young, becoming purplish gray to nearly black or brown, with a sheen; becoming hollow. **Flesh:** Purple to lilac or purplish gray. **Odor:** Sweet and slightly fragrant, or not distinctive. **Chemical Reactions:** KOH red on cap and on flesh. **Spore Print:** Rusty brown. **Microscopic Features:** Spores 11.5–14.5 (–18) × 7–9 µm; ellipsoid to amygdaliform; moderately verrucose. Cystidia fusoid-ventricose with a long neck, or sometimes irregularly cylindric; with purple to reddish contents in a KOH mount when fresh, but with brown contents after drying. Pileipellis a cutis with

Photo by Dan Molter

fascicles of upright elements. **Comments:** Young, purple specimens and old, brown specimens can look so different that it can be hard to believe they represent the same species. According to some authors, *Cortinarius violaceus* should be divided into two varieties (or subspecies, or species, depending on the author): var. *violaceus*, associating with various hardwoods and featuring amygdaliform spores, and var. *hercynicus*, associating with conifers and featuring ellipsoid spores.

CRATERELLUS CALYCULUS (BERKELEY & CURTIS) BURT

Ecology: Saprobic or possibly mycorrhizal; growing alone or gregariously in moss under hardwoods in damp, shady areas; summer and fall; widely distributed. **Cap:** Up to 1 cm wide; flat or very shallowly vase-shaped; typically without a perforated center; dry; matted-hairy to finely scaly, or more or less bald; dark brown to blackish, fading; the margin uplifted and sometimes "crisped" or irregular. **Undersurface:** Smooth or slightly wrinkled; gray; running down the stem. **Stem:** Up to 3 cm long; 1–3 mm thick; equal or tapering to base; solid; smooth; colored like the cap. **Odor and Taste:** Not distinctive. **Spore Print:** White. **Microscopic Features:** Spores 10–11.5 × 7–8 µm; ellipsoid; inamyloid; smooth. Clamp connections absent. **Comments:** Easily distinguished from most other species of *Craterellus* on the basis of its size and/or colors.

CRATERELLUS FALLAX A. H. SMITH

Ecology: Mycorrhizal with various hardwoods and conifers (including oaks, hemlock, and Virginia pine); growing alone, scattered, or gregariously; early summer through early fall; widely distributed. **Fruiting Body:** 2–7 cm wide; up to 10 cm high; tubular at first, becoming deeply vase-shaped; the upper edge rolled under when young and often partly rolled under in maturity; thin-fleshed; without a clearly defined cap and stem. **Upper (Inner) Surface:** Black to dark gray; bald or, more commonly, roughened or finely scaly with dark fibers and scales over a paler grayish or grayish-brown base color. **Under (Outer) Surface:** Smooth or very shallowly wrinkled; rarely with a few deeper folds near the cap margin; blackish, becoming dusted with the spore color at maturity (salmon-tinged or yellowish). **Flesh:** Thin and

brittle; blackish. **Odor and Taste:** Taste mild; odor not distinctive, or somewhat sweet and fragrant. **Spore Print:** Salmon-tinged or yellowish. **Microscopic Features:** Spores 8–14 × 5–9 µm; smooth; ellipsoid. Clamp connections absent. **Comments:** Edible and very good. Often called the "black trumpet." Compare with *Craterellus foetidus* (below). *Craterellus fallax* is sometimes treated as "*Craterellus cornucopioides*," but a recent DNA study (Matheny et al. 2010) supports the idea that the latter species is European.

CRATERELLUS FOETIDUS A. H. SMITH

Ecology: Mycorrhizal with hardwoods (but possibly also saprobic); growing gregariously or, more commonly, in fused clusters of 2–4 mushrooms; under oaks and other hardwoods; early summer through fall; widely distributed. **Fruiting Body:** Up to 10 cm tall; 3–7 cm wide; thin-fleshed; tubular at first, but soon shaped like an inverted vase or trumpet; the upper edge rolled under when young, becoming wavy and irregular in age; without a clearly differentiated stem and cap. **Upper Surface:** Color variable and dependent on conditions, but typically watery gray; bald or slightly roughened; sometimes slightly scaly near the margin. **Undersurface**: Becoming veined or prominently wrinkled with gill-like folds toward the cap margin; gray, or with a pinkish dusting. **Odor and Taste:** Odor sickeningly strong and sweet in fresh, mature specimens; taste not distinctive. **Spore Print:** White. **Microscopic Features:** Spores 8–10 × 5–6 µm; ellipsoid; smooth. Clamp connections absent. **Comments:** Edible and good. Compare with *Craterellus fallax* (p. 162), which lacks well-developed wrinkles and folds on its undersurface, does not usually grow in clusters, and is usually less substantial.

CRATERELLUS TUBAEFORMIS (FRIES) QUÉLET

Ecology: Mycorrhizal and/or saprobic; growing alone, gregariously, or in clusters in moss or on well-decayed, moss-covered logs in conifer bogs; summer and fall; northern Midwest. **Cap:** 1–5 cm wide; convex at first, soon becoming vase-shaped and eventually becoming perforated on the center; with a wavy and irregular margin when mature; smooth or somewhat roughened; sticky or waxy when fresh; dark yellowish brown to blackish brown (rarely completely yellow), fading with age. **Undersurface:** With well-developed false gills that fork frequently and have cross-veins; yellowish gray, becoming brownish. **Stem:** 3–8 cm long; to 1 cm wide; more or less equal; becoming hollow; bald; yellow. **Flesh:** Thin; pale; insubstantial. **Odor and Taste:** Taste mild; odor not distinctive, or slightly fragrant. **Spore Print:** White to buff or yellowish. **Microscopic Features:** Spores 8–13 × 5.5–10 µm; smooth; ellipsoid. Clamp connections present. **Comments:** Edible and good. Also known as *Cantharellus tubaeformis*.

CREPIDOTUS APPLANATUS (PERSOON) KUMMER

Ecology: Saprobic; growing gregariously or, more commonly, in overlapping clusters on dead hardwood stumps and logs; summer and fall; widely distributed. **Cap:** 1–4 cm; shell-shaped or petal-shaped; somewhat flabby; bald, or finely velvety toward the point of attachment; the margin often slightly lined; white, becoming brownish to pale cinnamon brown; fading markedly as it dries out. **Gills:** Close or crowded; whitish, becoming dull brown in maturity. **Stem:** Absent. Rarely, when conditions force the mushroom to grow straight upward rather than in a shelf-like position, the cap may be nearly circular, creating the illusion of a rudimentary "stem" where the mushroom attaches to the wood. **Flesh:** Soft; thin. **Odor and Taste:** Not distinctive. **Spore Print:** Brown. **Microscopic Features:** Spores 4–6 µm; globose; very finely punctate or roughened (often hard to discern even with oil immersion). Cheilocystidia variously shaped. Pileipellis a cutis with occasional erect elements. Clamp connections present. **Comments:** Compare with *Hohenbuehelia angustata* (p. 205).

CREPIDOTUS CROCOPHYLLUS (BERKELEY) SACCARDO

Ecology: Saprobic; growing alone, scattered, or gregariously on the deadwood of hardwoods (and occasionally on the wood of conifers); summer and fall; widely distributed. **Cap:** 1–5 cm across; semicircular, shell-shaped, or fan-shaped; broadly convex and remaining so; whitish to dull brownish or yellowish underneath orangish-brown to reddish-brown fibrils that may become aggregated into small scales; the fibrils sometimes sparse; often with orangish fuzz near the point of attachment to the substrate. **Gills:** Crowded, close, or nearly distant; when young orange to orangish (rarely whitish to yellowish); becoming brown with maturity. **Stem:** Absent. **Flesh:** Soft; thin; whitish. **Odor and Taste:** Odor not distinctive; taste mild or slightly bitter. **Chemical Reactions:** KOH negative to slowly reddish on cap; on gills deep red. **Spore Print:** Brown. **Microscopic Features:** Spores 4.5–8 µm; globose or subglobose; very finely punctate or roughened (often hard to discern even with oil immersion). Pleurocystidia absent. Cheilocystidia clavate, cylindric, or subutriform. Pileipellis a cutis of clamped, smooth or encrusted elements. **Comments:** When fresh, the orange gills, when combined with the brownish cap, are distinctive. *Phyllotopsis nidulans* (p. 313) is orange overall.

CRINIPELLIS ZONATA (PECK) PATOUILLARD

Ecology: Saprobic; growing alone or in small clusters on small sticks and other hardwood debris; summer and fall; widely distributed. **Cap:** 1–2.5 cm; convex or nearly flat; usually with a distinctive small depression over the center; densely hairy; dry; tawny brown; with obscurely concentric zones of color and texture. **Gills:** Free from the stem or nearly so; close; white; not discoloring. **Stem:** 2.5–5 cm long; 1–2 mm thick; equal; dry; densely hairy; hollow; colored like the cap or darker. **Flesh:** Whitish in cap; insubstantial. **Odor and Taste:** Taste mild or slightly mealy; odor not distinctive. **Chemical Reactions:** KOH black on cap. **Spore Print:** White. **Microscopic Features:** Spores 4–6 × 3–5 µm; smooth; ellipsoid. **Comments:** The densely hairy, tawny-brown cap and stem, white spore print, small size, and habitat on hardwood debris are good field characters.

CRUCIBULUM LAEVE (HUDSON) KAMBLY

Photo by Lisa K. Suits

Ecology: Saprobic; growing alone, scattered, or densely gregariously on woodland debris (sticks, leaves, nutshells, needles, and so on), woodchips, old furniture, dung, and so on (but not typically on bare soil or on larger logs); spring through fall; widely distributed. **Fruiting Body:** 5–8 mm high; up to 15 mm across; at first cushion-shaped to round, and closed by a yellowish "lid"; later becoming cup-shaped, with the lid disappearing; outer surface yellowish at first, remaining yellow or darkening to nearly brown, velvety or nearly bald; inner surface smooth and shiny, whitish to grayish. **Peridioles:** To 2 mm wide; shaped like flattened circles or ellipses; tough; attached by tiny cords; pale. **Microscopic Features:** Spores 7–10 × 3–6 µm; smooth; ellipsoid. **Comments:** This is the most common woodland bird's-nest fungus in the Midwest.

CYATHUS STERCOREUS (SCHWEINITZ) DE TONI

Ecology: Saprobic; growing gregariously or in dense clusters on woodchips, organic debris (straw, sawdust, and so on), manured soil, or dung; summer and fall (or over winter in greenhouses); widely distributed. **Fruiting Body:** Typically about 1 cm high and a little less than 1 cm wide at the top; goblet-shaped; outer surface brown to reddish brown, hairy and shaggy when young (but sometimes becoming bald with age); inner surface bald and shiny, dark brown to black; "lid" typically whitish, soon disappearing. **Peridioles:** To 1 or 2 mm wide; lens-shaped; attached by cords, but the cords can be very difficult to find, especially for the peridioles near the top of the pile. **Microscopic Features:** Spores extremely variable in shape and size but generally quite large (18–40 × 18–30 µm); smooth; globose to oval; thick-walled. **Comments:** Compare with *Cyathus striatus* (below), which has a prominently lined inner surface.

CYATHUS STRIATUS (HUDSON) WILDENOW

Ecology: Saprobic; growing scattered or gregariously on forest debris in open woods, but almost never terrestrial; also frequently found on woodchips in urban settings; summer and fall; widely distributed. **Fruiting Body:** Typically 7–10 mm high and 6–8 mm wide, but somewhat variable in size; vase-shaped; outer surface grayish buff to dark brown, shaggy to woolly, with tufts of hairs; inner surface distinctly grooved or lined (otherwise bald) and shiny; "lid" typically white, disappearing with maturity. **Peridioles:** To 2 mm wide; often roughly triangular; sheathed; attached by cords. **Microscopic Features:** Spores 15–20 × 8–12 µm; smooth; ellipsoid; notched. **Comments:** Compare with *Cyathus stercoreus* (above).

CYSTODERMELLA CINNABARINA (ALBERTINI & SCHWEINITZ) HARMAJA

Ecology: Saprobic; growing alone, gregariously, or in loose clusters under conifers and occasionally under hardwoods (sometimes fruiting from well-rotted wood); summer and fall; widely distributed. **Cap:** 3–8 cm; dry; egg-shaped or convex at first, becoming broadly convex, broadly bell-shaped, or nearly flat; covered with mealy, granular scales; cinnabar red to orange or rusty cinnamon. **Gills:** Attached to the stem but pulling away from it by maturity; close or crowded; white; at first covered by the partial veil. **Stem:** 3–6 cm long; up to 1.5 cm thick; more or less club-shaped; dry; bald and whitish to pale cinnamon near the apex but sheathed with cinnabar granular scales from the base upward, the sheath terminating in a flimsy ring zone; the granules often wearing away as the mushroom matures, exposing a coarse, whitish surface below. **Flesh:** Whitish; unchanging. **Odor and Taste:** Taste mild, slightly oily, or mealy; odor similar. **Chemical Reactions:** KOH dark purple to black on cap. **Spore Print:** White. **Microscopic Features:** Spores 4–5 × 2.5–3 µm; ellipsoid; smooth; inamyloid. Cheilocystidia elongated fusoid-ventricose; often apically encrusted. Pleurocystidia absent, or present and comparable to cheilocystidia. Pileipellis elements with rusty-brown walls in KOH; chained together; variously sized and shaped. **Comments:** Distinguishing features include the reddish-orange granular covering on the fresh cap and stem, and the white spore print. Compare with *Cystodermella granulosa* (below), which is usually brown but is occasionally orangish and which lacks cheilocystidia.

CYSTODERMELLA GRANULOSA (BATSCH) HARMAJA

Ecology: Saprobic; growing scattered or gregariously under hardwoods or conifers, often on waste ground, moss, or barren places; summer and fall; widely distributed. **Cap:** 1–5 cm; dry; at first convex, with an inrolled margin, densely covered with conical granules and warts; in maturity broadly convex or flat, the granules sometimes less prominent; color ranging from tawny brown to brick red or cinnamon brown, or occasionally orangish brown; often fading substantially when exposed to sunlight. **Gills:** Attached to the stem; close; whitish or yellowish. **Stem:** 2–6 cm long; up to 1 cm thick; equal; solid or hollow; dry;

covered with granules and scales below but bald near the apex; colored like the cap. **Flesh:** Whitish; unchanging. **Odor and Taste:** Not distinctive. **Spore Print:** White. **Microscopic Features:** Spores 3.5–5 × 2–3 µm; ellipsoid; smooth; inamyloid. Cheilocystidia absent. Pileipellis elements with rusty-brown walls in KOH; chained together; variously sized and shaped. **Comments:** Compare with *Cystodermella cinnabarina* (p. 167). *Leucopholiota decorosa* (p. 264) can appear similar but grows on wood and features notched gills.

KOH on cap

DAEDALEA QUERCINA (LINNAEUS) PERSOON

Ecology: Saprobic; growing alone or in small groups with fused caps on decaying oak wood (occasionally on the wood of other hardwoods); annual or perennial; causing a brown rot of the heartwood; summer and fall (or over winter or in spring when perennial); widely distributed, but less common west of the Mississippi. **Cap:** 4–20 cm; broadly convex to more or less flat; fan-shaped in outline; dry; bald or finely fuzzy (generally smoother toward the margin); whitish when fresh, but grayish, brown, or black in age (often darker toward the point of attachment in specimens that are several years old). **Pore Surface:** Maze-like, with thick walls (about 1–3 mm wide); occasionally developing pore-like or gill-like areas; whitish when fresh, becoming dingy yellowish or pale tan; not bruising; tubes to 4 cm deep. **Stem:** Absent. **Flesh:** Whitish, or with age brownish; very tough. **Spore Print:** White. **Chemical Reactions:** All parts dark gray to black with KOH. **Microscopic Features:** Spores: 5–6 × 2–3.5 µm; smooth; cylindric to ellipsoid. Hyphal system trimitic. **Comments:** Compare with *Daedaleopsis confragosa* (below) and with *Lenzites betulina* (p. 257).

DAEDALEOPSIS CONFRAGOSA (BOLTON) SCHRÖTER

Ecology: Saprobic; growing alone or gregariously on decaying hardwood logs and stumps, or rarely from the wounds of living hardwoods; partial to birches, willows, and many other hardwoods, but only rarely appearing on oaks; very rarely on conifer wood; producing a white rot; summer through winter; widely distributed. **Cap:** 5–15 cm; broadly convex to more or less flat; fan-shaped or nearly round in outline;

dry; bald or minutely hairy; pale grayish to brown or reddish brown (occasionally whitish); typically with zones of color. **Pore Surface:** White, becoming dingy brownish in age; typically with elongated, maze-like pores and fairly thin walls between the pores, but sometimes with more or less round pores, or rarely with the pores elongated so much that they appear like gills; when fresh, bruising salmon pink to reddish. **Stem:** Absent. **Flesh:** White, or pinkish to brownish; very tough. **Spore Print:** White. **Chemical Reactions:** All parts dark gray to black with KOH. **Microscopic Features:** Spores: 7–11 × 2–3 µm; smooth; cylindric to ellipsoid. Hyphal system trimitic. **Comments:** This polypore is quite variable in its appearance. Compare with *Daedalea quercina* (p. 168), which has substantially thicker walls between the pores, does not bruise red, and favors oaks. Also compare with *Trametes elegans* (p. 370), which has a whitish cap, a pore surface that features maze-like, gill-like, and "normal" pores that do not bruise reddish, and a yellowish KOH reaction.

DISCIOTIS VENOSA (PERSOON) ARNOULD

Ecology: Possibly mycorrhizal and/or saprobic; found primarily under hardwoods, in beech-maple and oak-hickory forests; growing alone, scattered, or gregariously; spring (usually found during morel season); widely distributed. **Fruiting Body:** 4–21 cm across; shaped more or less like a cup when young, often with a curled-in edge; in age flattening and becoming irregularly saucer-shaped; upper surface yellowish brown to brown or reddish brown, smooth at first but soon becoming wrinkled or veined, especially over the center; undersurface whitish to pale tan, often dotted with brown scales, rough or finely hairy; pinched together in the center to form a very short pseudostem that is buried in the ground; flesh brittle and pale brownish. **Microscopic Features:** Spores 22–25 × 12–15 µm; smooth; ellipsoid; contents homogeneous. Asci 8-spored; inamyloid. **Comments:** This fungus is closely related to true morels (pp. 277–80), but it should not be eaten.

Microscopic analysis may be required for identification. Compare with *Gyromitra perlata* (p. 195), *Gyromitra leucoxantha* (p. 194), *Peziza repanda* (p. 301), and *Peziza badioconfusa* (p. 300), all of which also appear in spring.

DUCTIFERA PULULAHUANA (PATOUILLARD) DONK

Ecology: Saprobic on decaying hardwood logs (typically appearing after the bark has disappeared); late spring, summer, and fall; from about the Great Lakes southward. **Fruiting Body:** A mass of individual whitish, jelly-like globs growing in close proximity and often fusing together to form structures reminiscent of exposed brains; individual globs up to about 3 cm across, irregularly shaped but frequently roughly fan-shaped; stemless; flesh thick and gelatinous. Older specimens may discolor somewhat yellowish, brownish, or even pinkish to purplish. **Microscopic Features:** Spores 9–12 × 4.5–7 µm; allantoid or broadly ellipsoid. Basidia longitudinally septate. Gloeocystidia present. **Comments:** This fungus is the most common jelly fungus in our area (central Illinois). Compare with *Tremella fuciformis* (p. 373).

ELAPHOCORDYCEPS OPHIOGLOSSOIDES (EHRHART) G. H. SUNG, J. M. SUNG, & SPATAFORA

Ecology: Parasitic on underground "false truffles" in the genus *Elaphomyces*, but appearing to be terrestrial; late summer and fall; widely distributed. **Fruiting Body:** 2–8 cm long; up to 1 cm wide; club-shaped, with the top wider than the base; without a clearly defined head, but with the upper portion reddish brown and bald when young, becoming blackish and roughened or pimply (use a hand lens) with maturity; lower portion bald throughout development, yellow to brownish or blackish, rooting; base attached to yellow cords that lead to the underground *Elaphomyces* fruiting body; flesh whitish and tough. **Microscopic Features:** Spores segmented and thread-like; breaking into ellipsoid segments 2–5 × 1.5–2 µm. **Comments:** Also known as *Cordyceps ophioglossoides*.

Photo by Noah Siegel

ENTOLOMA ABORTIVUM (BERKELEY & M. A. CURTIS) DONK

Abortive forms parasitizing *Armillaria mellea*

Ecology: Parasitic on species of *Armillaria* (pp. 101–3), and also saprobic; growing scattered or gregariously near decaying wood, or in leaf litter near decaying wood; usually encountered with *Armillaria* species fruiting in the vicinity; late summer and fall; widely distributed. **Cap:** 4–10 cm; convex, with an inrolled margin, expanding to flat, broadly convex, or with a central bump; bald, or with appressed fibers; dry; gray to grayish brown. **Gills:** Attached to the stem or beginning to run down it; close or crowded; pale grayish at first, later becoming pink from maturing spores. **Stem:** 3–10 cm long; 0.5–2 cm thick; occasionally somewhat off-center; typically with an enlarged base; solid; bald or finely hairy; with white basal mycelium and threads. **Flesh:** Thick; white. **Odor and Taste:** Mealy. **Spore Print:** Pink. **Microscopic Features:** Spores 7–9 × 6.5–8 µm; angular and irregular; 5- to 8-sided. Cystidia absent. Pileipellis an ixocutis. Clamp connections present. **"Aborted" Form:** An irregular ball of tissue 2–10 cm high; white; with pinkish areas inside; microscopically containing hyphae from *Entoloma abortivum* as well as *Armillaria* species. **Comments:** A 2001 study (Czederpiltz, Volk, and Burdsall) determined that *Entoloma abortivum* attacks *Armillaria* fruitings to create the "aborted" form, rather than the other way around, as was previously supposed.

ENTOLOMA GRISEUM PECK

Ecology: Saprobic; growing alone, scattered, or gregariously under hardwoods or conifers in low, wet woods; spring (but see comments); possibly widely distributed. **Cap:** 3–9 cm; convex, with a slight central bump, becoming broadly convex or nearly flat; at first firm, but soon fragile and thin; tacky but not slimy when fresh, becoming dry and silky; brownish gray, fading to buff as it dries out, often resulting in a mottled appearance; the margin not prominently lined but sometimes faintly lined when wet. **Gills:** Attached to the stem; close; whitish or very pale

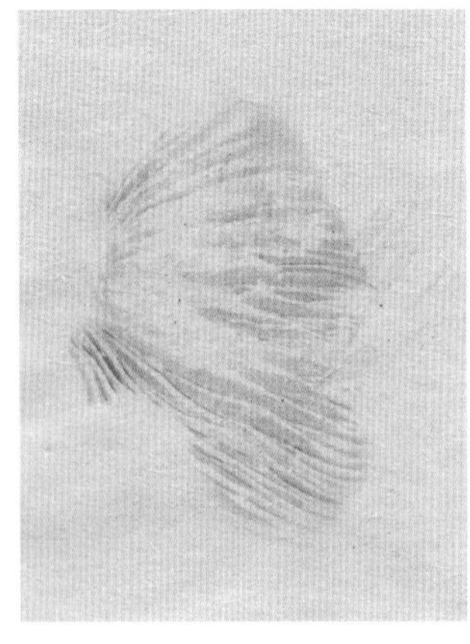
Spore print

gray at first, becoming pink with maturity. **Stem:** 3–9 cm long; 4–12 mm thick; more or less equal; fairly dry; bald; whitish to pale grayish; developing hollow areas. **Flesh:** Thin; fragile; whitish to grayish. **Odor and Taste:** Mealy. **Chemical Reactions:** KOH negative on cap. **Spore Print:** Pink. **Microscopic Features:** Spores 7–10 × 6.5–8 µm; 5- and 6-sided; angular; inamyloid. Cystidia absent. Pileipellis a cutis. Clamp connections absent. **Comments:** The fragile, flat cap that develops a silky sheen will help separate *Entoloma griseum* from *Entoloma vernum* (p. 174), which also appears in spring. *Entoloma griseum* may represent a species cluster. In our experience it fruits in spring in low, wet woods, but it has also been described as occurring in summer and fall in the northern Midwest in upland woods. *Entoloma griseum* (Peck, 1893) Hesler, 1967 is a different species, now known as *Entoloma squamatum*.

Photo by Walt Sturgeon

ENTOLOMA INCANUM (FRIES) HESLER

Ecology: Saprobic; growing alone, scattered, or gregariously under hardwoods or conifers in woods, or in grassy areas, moss, leaf litter, or disturbed soil (ditches, paths, roadbeds, and so on); summer and fall; widely distributed. **Cap:** 1–5 cm; convex, with a central depression or a "navel"; dry to greasy; bald or finely silky; yellow green becoming deep green, then fading to greenish, yellowish, or brownish; the margin becoming lined. **Gills:** Attached to the stem; nearly distant; at first whitish or colored like the cap, becoming pink with maturity; bruising green to blue green. **Stem:** 2–6 cm long; 1–4 mm thick; more or less equal; dry or greasy; bald; hollow; colored like the cap, or more brightly colored; bruising darker green to blue green; basal mycelium white. **Flesh:** Thin; fragile; yellowish to greenish; darkening to dark green or blue green when bruised. **Odor and Taste:** Odor of mice; taste not distinctive. **Spore Print:** Pink. **Microscopic Features:** Spores 8.5–11 × 7–8 µm; mostly 6-sided; angular; inamyloid. Pleurocystidia absent. Cheilocystidia absent or present and then clavate, to about 70 × 12 µm. Pileipellis a cutis with cystidioid terminal elements. Clamp connections absent. **Comments:** Also known as *Leptonia incana*. When fresh, the green colors make this species fairly unmistakable, but older, faded specimens can be baffling.

ENTOLOMA MURRAYI (BERKELEY & M. A. CURTIS) SACCARDO

Photo by Charya Peou

Ecology: Saprobic; growing alone, scattered, or gregariously under hardwoods or conifers in swamps and wet woods; summer and fall; widely distributed. **Cap:** 1–3 cm; conical or bell-shaped, with a sharply pointed center; silky; bright yellow, fading in age; dry or somewhat sticky when fresh. **Gills:** Attached to the stem; almost distant; pale yellow at first, eventually pinkish. **Stem:** 5–10 cm long; 2–4 mm thick; fragile; dry; bald; yellow; with white mycelium at the base. **Flesh:** Thin; fragile; colored like the cap. **Spore Print:** Pink. **Microscopic Features:** Spores 9–12 × 8–10 µm; 4-sided; angular; inamyloid. Cystidia absent. **Comments:** *Entoloma luteum* is similar but more drab and less pointy. Compare with *Entoloma salmoneum* (p. 174), which is salmon orange when fresh.

ENTOLOMA RHODOPOLIUM (FRIES) KUMMER

Ecology: Saprobic; growing alone, scattered, or gregariously under hardwoods; late summer and fall; widely distributed. **Cap:** 5–12 cm; convex, sometimes with a slight central bump, becoming broadly convex, broadly bell-shaped, or nearly flat; sticky when fresh; tan to yellow brown or grayish brown, fading and drying out to grayish or almost whitish; the margin lined, at least by maturity. **Gills:** Attached to the stem; close or nearly distant; white at first, becoming pink with maturity. **Stem:** 4–10 cm long; 6–12 mm thick; more or less equal; fairly dry; bald, or very finely hairy at the apex; white; becoming hollow. **Flesh:** Thin; fragile; whitish. **Odor and Taste:** Mealy, or not distinctive. **Chemical Reactions:** KOH negative on cap. **Spore Print:** Pink. **Microscopic Features:** Spores 6.5–11 × 7–9 µm; 6-, 7-, and 8-sided; angular; inamyloid. Cystidia absent. Pileipellis a cutis. Clamp connections present. **Comments:** *En-*

toloma rhodopolium is the most common fall *Entoloma* in the Midwest's hardwood forests. The taxonomy of the *rhodopolium* group is problematic, and it is unclear whether our species is actually the same as the original European species.

Photo by Noah Siegel

ENTOLOMA SALMONEUM (PECK) SACCARDO

Ecology: Saprobic; growing alone or scattered in leaf litter under hardwoods, or in moss under conifers; frequently on rotting, moss-covered conifer logs; summer and fall; widely distributed. **Cap:** 1–4 cm; conical or bell-shaped, with a sharply pointed center; bald; salmon pink or salmon orange, fading to dirty yellowish; sticky when fresh. **Gills:** Attached to the stem; almost distant; salmon orange, remaining so longer than the cap. **Stem:** 4–10 cm long; 2–6 mm thick; hollow; fragile; bald; colored like the cap, or with a greenish tinge; with white mycelial threads at the base. **Flesh:** Thin; fragile; colored like the cap. **Spore Print:** Pink. **Microscopic Features:** Spores 10–12 × 10–12 µm; angular, nearly square. **Comments:** Also known as *Nolanea salmonea* and *Nolanea quadrata*. Compare with *Entoloma murrayi* (p. 173).

ENTOLOMA VERNUM LUNDELL

Ecology: Saprobic; growing alone, scattered, or in little groups; terrestrial under hardwoods (especially tulip trees) or conifers; spring; widely distributed. **Cap:** 2–5 cm; conical or bell-shaped, with a pointed center, sometimes flattening with age but retaining a central point; bald or finely silky; dark to light brown or tan; dry or somewhat sticky when fresh. **Gills:** Attached to the stem at first, but eventually receding from it to appear free; almost distant; eventually dark pink. **Stem:** 2.5–10 cm long; 3–10 mm thick; faintly longitudinally ridged; fragile and easily splitting; colored like the cap or paler; with white basal mycelium. **Flesh:** Thin; fragile. **Odor and Taste:** Mealy, or not distinctive. **Spore Print:** Pink. **Microscopic Features:** Spores 8–12 × 7–9 µm; 5-sided to 6- or 7-sided. Cystidia absent. Pileipellis a cutis; elements encrusted. Clamp connections present. **Comments:** Reported as poisonous. This species (which may be a species group) is often encountered by morel hunters. Compare with *Entoloma griseum* (p. 171).

Photo by Dan Molter

EXIDIA GLANDULOSA (BULLIARD) FRIES

Ecology: Saprobic; growing on recently fallen hardwood sticks and branches (especially on the wood of oaks); commonly encountered in spring and again in fall, but not infrequently appearing during summer cold spells or winter warm spells; widely distributed. **Fruiting Body:** Individual fruiting bodies are 1–2 cm across, but are typically fused into large patches (often over 50 cm long); gelatinous; lobed and brain-like; reddish black to black; surface slightly roughened with small pimples. **Odor and Taste:** Not distinctive. **Microscopic Features:** Spores 10–16 × 3–5 µm; allantoid; smooth. Basidia longitudinally septate (cruciate). Clamp connections present.

EXIDIA RECISA (DITMAR) FRIES

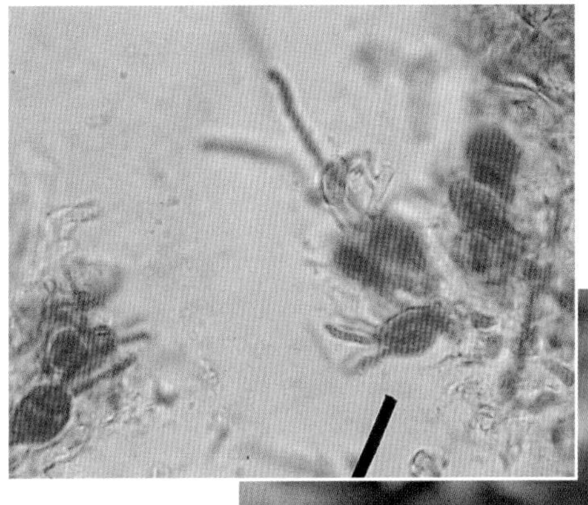

Basidia

Ecology: Saprobic; growing on recently fallen hardwood branches and logs, or on dead branches of standing trees; spring through fall; widely distributed. **Fruiting Body:** Individual fruiting bodies are 1–3 cm across but are often clustered together; gelatinous but fairly firm; lobed or with distinctive concave depressions outlined by fairly sharp edges; brown to amber brown, with blackening wrinkles and edges at maturity; surface bald or slightly roughened. **Odor and Taste:** Not distinctive. **Microscopic Features:** Spores 10.5–14 × 3.5–5 µm; allantoid; smooth. Basidia longitudinally septate (cruciate), with elongated sterigmata. Clamp connections present. **Comments:** Compare with *Auricularia auricula* (p. 105), which does not usually develop edged concave depressions and which features transversely 3-septate basidia.

Spores

Individually discrete tubes

FISTULINA HEPATICA (SCHAEFFER) WITHERING

Ecology: Saprobic and sometimes weakly parasitic on the wood of hardwoods (especially oaks); causing a brown rot; annual; growing alone or in small groups near the bases of trees and on stumps; summer and fall; widely distributed. **Cap:** Up to 30 cm across; irregular in shape, but often fan-shaped or tongue-like; sometimes fused laterally with other caps; finely bumpy, velvety, or bald; the margin lobed; red, reddish orange, or liver-colored. **Pore Surface:** Whitish or pale pinkish, becoming reddish brown in age; bruising reddish brown; tubes individually discrete and separated (use a hand lens), to 1.5 cm long. **Stem:** Absent or rudimentary and lateral; colored like the cap; firm. **Flesh:** Whitish, streaked with reddish areas; thick; soft; watery; exuding a reddish juice when squeezed. **Odor and Taste:** Odor not distinctive; taste sour or acidic. **Spore Print:** Pinkish to pinkish brown. **Microscopic Features:** Spores 3.5–4.5 × 2.5–3 µm; smooth; ovoid; inamyloid. True cystidia absent. Hyphal system monomitic.

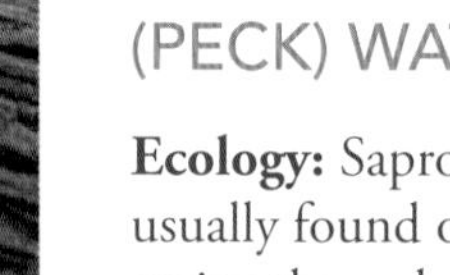

FLAMMULASTER ERINACEELLUS (PECK) WATLING

Ecology: Saprobic on the deadwood of hardwoods; usually found on fallen, well-decayed, barkless logs; spring through fall; widely distributed. **Cap:** 1–4 cm; convex becoming flat; dry; densely covered with granular scales that often become powdery; dark brown to dark rusty brown; the margin sometimes hung with remnants of the partial veil. **Gills:** Attached to the stem; close; whitish at first, becoming brownish; often with frayed-looking edges. **Stem:** 3–4 cm long; under 5 mm thick; equal; covered with granular scales like the cap, but often less densely, revealing the paler color of the stem surface underneath; usually featuring a ring zone. **Flesh:** Insubstantial. **Odor and Taste:** Odor not distinctive; taste mild, bitter, or metallic. **Spore Print:** Pale cinnamon brown. **Chemical Reactions:** KOH red, then black on cap; dark reddish brown on flesh. Iron salts olive on flesh. **Microscopic Features:** Spores 6–9 × 4–5 µm; smooth; more or less ellipsoid; inamyloid. Pleurocystidia absent. Cheilocystidia abundant, with bulbous, capitate ends. Pileipellis cellular. **Comments:** Compare with *Pluteus granularis* (p. 318), which features free gills and a pink spore print, and with *Cystodermella granulosa* (p. 167), which grows on the ground and has a white spore print.

FLAMMULINA VELUTIPES (CURTIS) SINGER

KOH on cap

Ecology: Saprobic on the stumps, logs, roots, and living wood of hardwoods; sometimes appearing terrestrial but actually attached to buried wood; fall to spring; widely distributed. **Cap:** 1–7 cm; convex, becoming broadly convex to flat; moist and sticky when fresh; bald; color fairly variable—dark orange brown to yellowish brown, often fading with maturity. **Gills:** Attached to the stem; whitish to pale yellow; crowded or close. **Stem:** 2–11 cm long; 3–5 mm thick; equal or larger toward base; tough; pale to yellowish brown or orange brown when young; covered with a velvety coating that darkens from the base upward, becoming rusty brown to dark brown or black. **Flesh:** Whitish to yellowish; thin. **Chemical Reactions:** KOH bright red on cap. **Spore Print:** White. **Microscopic Features:** Spores 6.5–9 × 3–5 µm; smooth; more or less ellipsoid; inamyloid. **Comments:** Edible, but tough. Despite appearances, the commercially produced "enoki" mushroom found in many grocery stores is a cultivated form of this mushroom. Compare with *Xeromphalina tenuipes* (p. 393), which has a dry cap and a brownish-orange fuzzy stem that does not darken.

FOMES FOMENTARIUS (LINNAEUS) J. KICKX

Ecology: Parasitic and saprobic on the living wood or deadwood of hardwoods (especially paper birch and beech); causing a white rot; growing alone or gregariously; perennial; northern Midwest. **Cap:** Up to about 20 cm across; shell-shaped to hoof-shaped; with a dull, woody upper surface that is zoned with gray and brownish gray. **Pore Surface:** Brownish; 2–5 round pores per mm; yearly tube layers indistinct, brown, becoming stuffed with whitish material. **Stem:** Absent. **Flesh:** Brownish; thin; hard. **Microscopic Features:** Spores 12–20 × 4–7 µm; cylindric; inamyloid; smooth. Hyphal system trimitic. **Comments:** Compare with *Ganoderma applanatum* (p. 180).

Photo by Walt Sturgeon

FOMITOPSIS PINICOLA (SWARTZ) KARSTEN

Ecology: Saprobic on the deadwood of conifers and sometimes hardwoods (including paper birch and aspens); also sometimes parasitic on living trees; causing a brown cubical rot; growing alone or gregariously; perennial; northern Midwest. **Cap:** Up to about 40 cm across; semicircular or fan-shaped; convex or hoof-shaped; bald, becoming wrinkled with age; appearing varnished toward the margin (and overall when very young); red to dark brownish red (or brown to black toward the point of attachment or when mature), with a white to yellow marginal area. **Pore Surface:** Cream-colored; not bruising significantly; with 3–6 round pores per mm; annual tube layers usually fairly distinct, up to 8 mm deep. **Stem:** Absent. **Flesh:** Whitish; leathery to woody. **Odor:** Musty and strong when fresh. **Chemical Reactions:** KOH on flesh red to dark brownish red. **Microscopic Features:** Spores 6–9 × 3.5–4.5 µm; cylindric; inamyloid; smooth. Hyphal system trimitic. **Comments:** This fungus is one of the most prevalent and important decomposers in coniferous forests, producing brown rot residues that are essential to soils. Compare with *Ganoderma tsugae* (p. 181), which is annual and features corky, rather than woody, flesh.

GALERINA MARGINATA (BATSCH) KÜHNER

Ecology: Saprobic on the rotting wood of fallen hardwoods and conifers; growing gregariously or in clusters (rarely alone); most frequent in fall, but often encountered in spring, and not infrequently found in summer and during winter warm spells; widely distributed. **Cap:** 1–4 cm; convex or nearly flat, sometimes slightly bell-shaped; sticky when fresh or wet, otherwise tacky or dry; bald; brown to tawny brown, sometimes fading to yellowish or tan; the margin finely lined when fresh and moist. **Gills:** Attached to the stem or running slightly down it, but sometimes pulling away from the stem in age; close; yellowish at first, eventually becoming rusty brown or brownish as the spores mature; not bruising; at first covered with a whitish partial veil. **Stem:** 2–10 cm long; 3–6 mm thick; more or less equal; dry;

hollow; finely shaggy below; with a ring that is often fragile and collapsed, or with a ring zone (though specimens are sometimes found in which all evidence of the partial veil has disappeared); the ring white at first but soon dusted with rusty-brown spores; darkening below in age; sometimes with whitish mycelial threads. **Flesh:** Insubstantial; watery brown. **Odor:** Mild or slightly mealy. **Chemical Reactions:** KOH red on cap. **Spore Print:** Rusty brown. **Microscopic Features:** Spores 8–11 × 5–6.5 µm; roughened or wrinkled; ellipsoid. Cystidia fusoid-ventricose, with long necks. Pileipellis an ixocutis. **Comments:** Deadly. This species should be learned by anyone collecting edible mushrooms in the Midwest. Hallmark features include the rusty-brown spore print, the growth on wood (often in clusters), the thin ring or ring zone (which may disappear), and the brown to tawny cap, which often fades. Also sometimes called *Galerina autumnalis*. Compare with species of *Armillaria* (pp. 101–3), which have white spore prints, and with species of *Hypholoma* (pp. 217–18), which have purple-brown spore prints.

Spore print

GALIELLA RUFA (SCHWEINITZ) NANNFELDT & KORF

Ecology: Saprobic on decaying hardwood sticks and logs; growing in clusters; spring and summer; widely distributed. **Fruiting Body:** Closed up and urn-like at first; becoming goblet-shaped; 2–4 cm across; upper surface orangish tan to reddish brown, tough-skinned, and bald; undersurface blackish, finely velvety; stem absent or rudimentary; flesh gelatinous and rubbery. **Microscopic Features:** Spores 20 × 10 µm; ellipsoid with narrowed ends; warty. **Comments:** Also known as *Bulgaria rufa*. Reminiscent of a deep, chocolate peanut butter cup when mature, this fungus is very common in early summer.

GANODERMA APPLANATUM (PERSOON) PATOUILLARD

KOH on flesh and tubes

Photo by Melissa Bochte

Ecology: Saprobic and sometimes parasitic; growing alone or in groups on decaying logs and stumps, or from the wounds of injured living trees; producing a white to straw-colored rot of sapwood and heartwood; found on most species of hardwoods and on many conifers; perennial; common and widely distributed. **Cap:** 5–50 cm across; more or less fan-shaped, semicircular, or irregular; with a dull, unvarnished outer crust; often furrowed in zones; brownish to grayish brown. **Pore Surface:** White, becoming dirty yellowish or dingy brownish to olive in age; bruising slowly brown; with 4–6 tiny (nearly invisible to the naked eye) circular pores per mm; tubes in annual layers, separated by brown tissue, with each layer 4–12 mm deep. **Stem:** Usually absent; if present, lateral and stubby. **Flesh:** Brown to cinnamon brown; very tough. **Chemical Reactions:** Flesh and tubes black with KOH. **Spore Print:** Brown or reddish brown. **Microscopic Features:** Spores 8–12 × 6.5–8 µm; more or less ellipsoid, with a truncated end; under oil immersion ornamented, double-walled, with a series of "pillars" between the walls; inamyloid. Cystidia and setae absent. Hyphal system trimitic. **Comments:** Sometimes called the "artist's fungus" because drawings made on the brown-bruising pore surface will last for decades. Compare with *Fomes fomentarius* (p. 177), common in the northern Midwest (especially on the wood of paper birch), which features a brownish pore surface that does not bruise; also compare with *Perenniporia fraxinophila* (p. 299).

GANODERMA LUCIDUM (CURTIS) KARSTEN

Ecology: Parasitic on living hardwoods and saprobic on the deadwood of hardwoods; causing a white butt and root rot; growing alone or gregariously, usually near the base of the tree; annual; widely distributed. **Cap:** 2–30 cm; at first irregularly knobby or elongated, but by maturity more or less fan-shaped; with a shiny, varnished surface often roughly arranged into lumpy zones; red to reddish brown when mature; when young often with zones of bright yellow and white toward the margin. **Pore Surface:** Whitish, becoming dingy brownish in age; usually bruising brown; with 4–7 tiny (nearly invisible to the naked eye) circular pores per mm; tubes to 2 cm deep. **Stem:** Sometimes absent, but more commonly present; 3–14 cm long; up to 3 cm thick; twisted; equal or irregular; varnished and colored like the cap; often distinctively angled away from one side of the cap. **Flesh:** Brownish; fairly soft when young, but soon tough. **Spore Print:** Brown. **Chemical Reactions:** KOH black or blackish on all surfaces. **Microscopic Features:** Spores 9–12 × 5.5–8 µm; more or less ellipsoid, sometimes with a truncated end; under oil immersion ornamented, appearing double-walled, with a row of "pillars" between the walls. Setae and cystidia absent. Hyphal system dimitic. **Comments:** Compare with *Ganoderma tsugae* (below), which is very similar but grows on the wood of conifers, and with *Fomitopsis pinicola* (p. 178). A brown-and-yellow form of *Ganoderma lucidum* (illustrated) is often found infecting honey locust trees; whether or not it constitutes a separate species is unclear.

GANODERMA TSUGAE MURRILL

Ecology: Parasitic on living conifers (principally hemlock) and saprobic on the deadwood of conifers; producing a white butt rot of the heartwood; growing alone or gregariously; annual; widely distributed. **Cap:** 5–30 cm; at first irregularly knobby or elongated, but by maturity more or less fan-shaped; with a shiny, varnished surface often roughly arranged into lumpy zones; red to reddish brown when mature; when young often with zones of bright yellow and white toward the margin; occasionally with bluish tints. **Pore Surface:** White, becoming dingy brownish in age; usually bruising brown; with 4–6 tiny (nearly invisible to the naked eye) circular pores per mm; tubes to 2 cm deep. **Stem:** Sometimes absent, but more commonly present; 3–14 cm long; up to 3 cm thick; twisted; equal or irregular; varnished and colored like the cap; often distinctively angled away from one side of the cap. **Flesh:** Whitish; fairly soft when young, but soon tough. **Spore Print:** Brown. **Microscopic Features:** Spores 13–15 × 7.5–8.5 µm; more or less ellip-

soid, sometimes with a truncated end; under oil immersion ornamented, appearing double-walled, with a row of "pillars" between the walls. Setae and cystidia absent. Hyphal system dimitic. **Comments:** Compare with *Fomitopsis pinicola* (p. 178) and with *Ganoderma lucidum* (p. 180).

GEASTRUM MORGANII LLOYD

Ecology: Saprobic; growing alone or gregariously under hardwoods; often found near rotting stumps; fall; possibly widely distributed. **Fruiting Body:** At first a bulb-shaped ball 1–2 cm across, partially submerged in the substrate, with a reddish to purplish or orangish covering that often separates in places to reveal a paler surface underneath; with maturity the outer skin peeling back to form 5–7 pinkish buff arms that bruise slowly reddish when handled and often develop cracks and fissures (sometimes cracking deeply and uniformly to create a small saucer like that of *Geastrum triplex*, p. 183); spore case more or less round, bald or faintly felty, brown to brownish, with a grooved (or at least wrinkled) conical beak; 2–3 cm across when arms are opened; interior of spore case initially solid and white but soon powdery and brown. **Microscopic Features:** Spores 3.5–4.5 µm; globose; spiny. Capillitial threads 4–8 µm wide; hyaline to brownish in KOH; not encrusted. **Comments:** This rare species is apparently limited to the Midwest. Compare with *Geastrum saccatum* (below) and *Geastrum triplex* (p. 183), neither of which has a prominently lined beak, arms that bruise reddish, or a reddish to purplish covering when in the button stage. The illustrated collection was made by our friend John Steinke, an amateur mycologist in Wisconsin who has an astounding knack for always finding the coolest mushrooms of the foray.

GEASTRUM SACCATUM FRIES

Ecology: Saprobic; growing alone or gregariously under hardwoods or conifers; often appearing around stumps; spring through fall; widely distributed. **Fruiting Body:** At first a bald, egg-shaped ball with a pointed beak, 2–3 cm wide, attached to the substrate by a point at the base; with maturity the outer skin peeling back to form 4–9 more or less triangular, buff-colored arms; spore case up to 2 cm wide, more or less round, bald, brownish to purplish brown, with a smooth conical beak that is surrounded by a circular ridge or depression (often resulting in a pale area);

2–5 cm across when arms are opened; interior of spore case initially solid and white but soon powdery and medium brown. **Microscopic Features:** Spores 3.5–4.5 µm; globose; spiny. Capillitial threads 4–8 µm wide; yellowish to brownish in KOH; slightly encrusted. **Comments:** Compare with *Geastrum triplex* (below), which is larger and features thick arms that crack and bend distinctively, and with *Geastrum morganii* (p. 182), which bruises reddish and features a reddish covering when in the button stage.

GEASTRUM TRIPLEX JUNGHUHN

Ecology: Saprobic; growing alone or gregariously under hardwoods; summer and fall; widely distributed. **Fruiting Body:** At first a bald, egg-shaped ball with a prominent pointed beak, 1–5 cm wide, attached to the substrate by a point at the base; with maturity the outer skin peeling back to form 4–8 more or less triangular, buff-colored arms that are thick and usually develop fissures and cracks, frequently splitting to form a saucer-like structure that holds the spore case aloft; spore case more or less round, bald, brownish, with a fuzzy, conical beak that is often surrounded by a pale area; 5–10 cm across when arms are opened; interior of spore case initially solid and white but soon powdery and brown. **Microscopic Features:** Spores 3.5–4.5 µm; globose; spiny. Capillitial threads 3–6 µm wide; yellowish in KOH; encrusted. **Comments:** Compare with *Geastrum saccatum* (p. 182) and *Geastrum morganii* (p. 182).

GERRONEMA STROMBODES (BERKELEY & MONTAGNE) SINGER

Ecology: Saprobic on the deadwood of hardwoods and conifers; growing alone, gregariously, or, more often, in clusters; late spring through fall; southern Midwest. **Cap:** 2.5–10 cm across; plano-convex at first, becoming centrally depressed or shallowly vase-shaped; tacky; with innate, brown to grayish-brown, pressed-down fibers that uniformly cover the surface when young but begin to be stretched out and streaked-looking with age, exposing a pale yellowish surface; margin becoming wavy with age. **Gills:** Running down the stem; distant; yellowish white to pale yellow. **Stem:** Up to 6 cm long and 8 mm thick; more or less equal; dry; minutely hairy; whitish, yellowish,

or pale grayish. **Flesh:** Thin; whitish to yellowish. **Odor and Taste:** Taste mild or somewhat bitter; odor mild or faintly sweetish. **Chemical Reactions:** KOH negative on cap. **Spore Print:** White. **Microscopic Features:** Spores 7.5–9 × 4–5 µm; smooth; ellipsoid; inamyloid. Cystidia absent. Clamp connections present. **Comments:** Young and mature stages of this mushroom can appear very different as the fibrils on the cap surface become stretched out.

GLOEOPORUS DICHROUS (FRIES) BRESÀDOLA

Ecology: Saprobic on the deadwood of hardwoods and, rarely, conifers; sometimes reported on the decaying fruiting bodies of other polypores (including *Ganoderma applanatum*, p. 180); causing a white rot; usually growing gregariously; annual; spring through fall; widely distributed. **Cap:** Often present and fairly well developed, but sometimes absent or present merely as a turned-over edge above the pore surface; shelf-like and fused laterally with other caps, or kidney-shaped to semicircular; up to about 6 cm wide individually; velvety to finely hairy or nearly bald when mature; with or without concentric zones of texture; creamy to white, but in old age sometimes becoming green as a result of algae. **Pore Surface:** Reddish brown to orange brown when young, becoming browner with age (and purplish brown when dried); with concentric bands of color shades; often covered with a whitish bloom; with 4–6 round to angular pores per mm; tubes up to about 1 mm deep, gelatinous to rubbery, separable as a layer when fresh (use tweezers or a sharp knife point). **Stem:** Absent. **Flesh:** White; cottony to tough; thin. **Odor and Taste:** Not distinctive. **Chemical Reactions:** KOH negative to yellowish or orangish on flesh and cap. **Microscopic Features:** Spores 3.5–5.5 × 0.7–1.5 µm; smooth; allantoid; inamyloid. Setae absent. Hyphal system monomitic, with prominent clamp connections. **Comments:** The brown to reddish-brown pore surface and the rubbery, separable tube layer are good field characters.

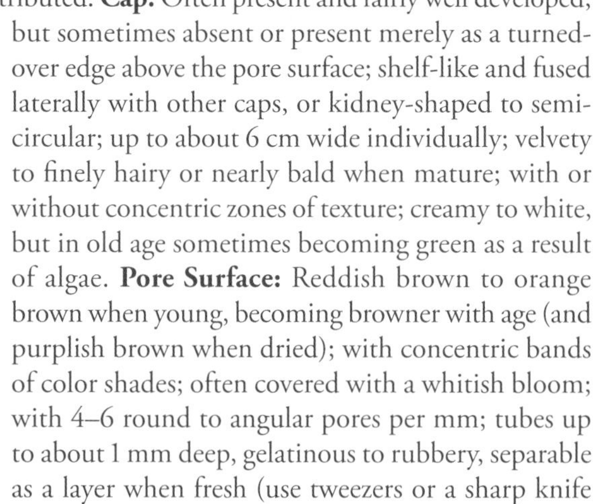

GOMPHUS FLOCCOSUS (SCHWEINITZ) SINGER

Ecology: Mycorrhizal with conifers (especially firs); growing alone, scattered, or gregariously; summer and fall; northern Midwest and Ohio. **Fruiting Body:** Vase-shaped and fleshy, developing a deep central depression; 5–15 cm across; up to 30 cm high but usually shorter (up to 15 cm high); single (very rarely with 2 or 3 caps sharing a stem). **Upper Surface:** Cinnamon to pale orange, or reddish orange to orange or nearly scarlet; covered with soft scales that become more prominent as the mushroom matures. **Undersurface:** Shallowly to deeply wrinkled; cream color or darker; often yellow near the cap edge when young; sometimes bruising purplish; running down the stem. **Stem:** 1–3 cm wide; not distinctly separate from the cap; colored like the undersurface; sometimes with yellow shades; bald. **Flesh:** White; fibrous; sometimes bruising and discoloring brownish. **Odor and Taste:** Taste sweet and slightly sour; odor not distinctive. **Spore Print:** Cinnamon to pale brownish yellow. **Microscopic Features:** Spore 11–20 × 6–10 µm; wrinkled or warty; more or less ellipsoid; cyanophilic.

GRIFOLA FRONDOSA (DICKSON) S. F. GRAY

Photo by Patrick Harvey

Ecology: Weakly parasitic on living oaks and other hardwoods; also saprobic on decaying wood; causing a white butt rot; fruiting in large clusters of rosettes near the bases of trees; often reappearing in the same place in subsequent years; summer and fall; widely distributed. **Fruiting Body:** 15–60 cm broad or more; composed of multiple caps sharing a branched, stem-like structure. **Caps:** 2–10 cm across; more or less fan-shaped; gray brown (often with vague concentric zones); finely velvety or bald; with wavy margins. **Pore Surface:** Running down the stem, often nearly to the ground; lavender gray when young, becoming dirty whitish to yellowish; with 2–4 angular pores per mm; tubes to 5 mm deep. **Stem:** Branched; whitish; tough; often off-center. **Flesh:** Firm; white. **Odor and Taste:** Mild; pleasant. **Spore Print:** White. **Microscopic Features:** Spores 5–7 × 3.5–5 µm; smooth; broadly ellipsoid; inamyloid. Cystidia absent. Hyphal system dimitic. **Comments:** Sometimes called the "hen of the woods." Edible and good, but some people (including one of us) are sensitive to it and experience minor gastrointestinal discomfort. Compare with *Meripilus sumstinei* (p. 276), which has larger individual caps and bruises black, and with *Polyporus umbellatus* (p. 324), which has small, more clearly defined, individual caps.

GYMNOPILUS FULVOSQUAMULOSUS HESLER

Ecology: Saprobic on the deadwood of hardwoods; growing alone, gregariously, or in small clusters; summer and fall; widely distributed. **Cap:** 3–13 cm; convex, becoming plano-convex or nearly flat; dry; covered with prominent tawny scales composed of aggregated fibrils; ground color under the scales pale yellow; the margin somewhat inrolled, at least when young. **Gills:** Attached to the stem or beginning to run down it; close; pale to medium yellow, developing cinnamon to rusty spots and eventually becoming rusty overall; when very young covered by a cortina-like partial veil. **Stem:** 3–8 cm long; up to 1.5 cm thick; more or less equal, or with a slightly swollen base; pale yellow when young, discoloring rusty brown with age or on handling; finely hairy; with a very ephemeral and easily disappearing ring or ring zone near the apex. **Flesh:** Whitish to pale yellow. **Odor and Taste:** Taste bitter; odor not distinctive. **Spore Print:** Rusty brown to orange brown. **Chemical Reactions:** KOH red on cap surface, black on the pigmented scales. Iron salts slowly olive on flesh. **Microscopic Features:** Spores 7–10 × 5–5.5 µm; warty; ellipsoid; dextrinoid. Pleurocystidia and cheilocystidia both present; variously shaped. Pileipellis a tangled cutis with elements occasionally aggregated into upright bundles. **Comments:** Compare with *Pholiota squarrosoides* (p. 310), which features a (plain) brown spore print and a somewhat sticky cap surface, and does not taste bitter or react to KOH.

Photo by Patrick Harvey

GYMNOPILUS LIQUIRITIAE (PERSOON) KARSTEN

Ecology: Saprobic on the rotting wood of fallen hardwoods or, in northern areas, conifers; growing alone or gregariously; summer and fall; widely distributed. **Cap:** 2–8 cm; convex or nearly flat, sometimes slightly bell-shaped; dry; bald; rusty brown to orange; the margin sometimes finely lined at maturity. **Gills:** Attached to the stem, but sometimes pulling away from it in age; close or crowded; yellowish or pale orange at first, eventually orange; sometimes with reddish-brown spots. **Stem:** 3–7 cm long; 3–8 mm thick; more or less equal, or tapering in either direction; sometimes somewhat off-center; bald or finely hairy; whitish to pale orange; basal mycelium yellow to rusty. **Flesh:** Pale orange to pale yellow. **Odor and Taste:** Taste very bitter; odor mild, fragrant, or like that of raw potatoes. **Spore Print:** Rusty brown. **Chemical Reactions:** KOH dark red on cap. **Microscopic Features:** Spores 7–8.5 × 4–5.5 µm; roughened with very tiny spines; ellipsoid; dextrinoid. Pleurocystidia and cheilocystidia variously shaped. **Comments:** Common in the Midwest and characterized by a cap that lacks scales, the lack of a ring on the stem, and spiny spores. This fungus produces massive quantities of spores, which cover the substrate and all nearby mushrooms with a rusty powder.

Photo by Patrick Harvey

GYMNOPILUS LUTEUS (PECK) HESLER

Ecology: Saprobic on the deadwood of hardwoods; growing alone, gregariously, or in small clusters; summer and fall; widely distributed. **Cap:** 5–10 cm; convex or nearly flat; dry; silky or finely hairy (occasionally with minute scales over the center); yellow to orange yellow. **Gills:** Attached to the stem; close; yellow, becoming rusty with maturity. **Stem:** 4–8 cm long; up to 1.5 cm thick; more or less equal; not typically swollen in the middle at maturity; colored like the cap but developing rusty stains when handled or with age; finely hairy; usually with a fragile ring or ring zone near the apex. **Flesh:** Pale yellow. **Odor and Taste:** Taste bitter; odor not distinctive. **Spore Print:** Rusty brown to orange brown. **Chemical Reactions:** KOH red on cap. **Microscopic Features:** Spores 6–9 × 4.5–5.5 µm; warty; ellipsoid; dextrinoid. Pleurocystidia and cheilocystidia variously shaped.

Photo by Dan Molter

Photo by Walt Sturgeon

GYMNOPILUS SAPINEUS (FRIES) MURRILL

Ecology: Saprobic on the deadwood of conifers (especially pines); growing alone, gregariously, or in small clusters; summer and fall; widely distributed. **Cap:** 2–8 cm; convex or nearly flat, sometimes slightly bell-shaped; dry; bald, finely hairy, or decidedly but minutely scaly; yellowish to tawny or reddish brown. **Gills:** Attached to the stem; close; yellow, yellowish, or whitish at first, developing rusty-brown spots and eventually becoming rusty brown overall. **Stem:** 3–7 cm long; under 1 cm thick; more or less equal; bald or finely hairy; colored like the cap, but paler; usually darkening to brown from the base up with age; with whitish to yellowish basal mycelium. **Flesh:** Whitish or pale yellow. **Odor and Taste:** Taste bitter or, more rarely, mild; odor not distinctive. **Spore Print:** Rusty brown to orange brown. **Chemical Reactions:** KOH dark red, then black on cap. **Microscopic Features:** Spores 6.5–10 × 4–5.5 µm; warty; ellipsoid; dextrinoid. Pleurocystidia and cheilocystidia variously shaped. **Comments:** *Gymnopilus penetrans* is sometimes separated on the basis of its less scaly cap, but a DNA study (Guzmán-Dávalos et al. 2003) suggests the possibility that it is not a phylogenetically distinct species.

GYMNOPUS DICHROUS (BERKELEY & M. A. CURTIS) HALLING

Ecology: Saprobic; growing scattered, gregariously, or in clusters on sticks, logs, and stumps of oaks, beech, and other hardwoods; late spring through fall; widely distributed. **Cap:** 1–5 cm; convex with an incurved margin when young, becoming broadly convex, flat, or shallowly depressed; dry; bald; brown to orangish brown or reddish brown at first, fading to pinkish buff or tan; usually becoming radially wrinkled and developing a lined margin; in age or in dry conditions sometimes splitting radially. **Gills:** Narrowly attached to the stem or nearly free from it; close or nearly distant; whitish when young, darkening to pinkish buff; sometimes stained and spotted reddish brown when old. **Stem:** 1–5 cm long; up to about 5 mm thick; more or less equal; dry; tough; finely hairy or finely velvety; buff above, but colored like the cap or darker below; with a slight, fuzzy, swollen knob at the point of attachment to the wood. **Flesh:** Whitish to brownish; thin; tough. **Odor and Taste:** Not distinctive. **Chemical Reactions:** KOH olive on cap surface. **Spore Print:** White. **Microscopic Features:** Spores 10–12 × 3–4.5

µm; smooth; lacrymoid to ellipsoid; inamyloid. Cheilocystidia usually abundant, but soon collapsing and often difficult to differentiate; swollen. Pileipellis a cutis of brownish, frequently encrusted (in bands or spirals) elements. **Comments:** *Gymnopus subnudus* is a similar species appearing on leaf litter rather than wood; it lacks the small knob at the base of the stem and differs microscopically.

GYMNOPUS DRYOPHILUS (BULLIARD) MURRILL

Ecology: Saprobic; growing alone, scattered, or gregariously under hardwoods or conifers; frequently arising from twigs or leaf litter; summer and fall; widely distributed. **Cap:** 1–7.5 cm, convex, with an incurved margin when young, becoming broadly convex to flat; moist; bald; dark reddish brown to brown when young, becoming tan to orangish brown or paler. **Gills:** Attached to the stem or free from it; whitish; crowded. **Stem:** 1–10 cm long; 2–7 mm thick; equal (occasionally slightly flared to base); dry; pliant and fibrous; bald; whitish above, light buff below, becoming darker; soon hollow; with thin white rhizomorphs attached to the base. **Flesh:** Whitish; thin. **Odor and Taste:** Not distinctive. **Chemical Reactions:** KOH varying from negative to dark gray or pale olive on cap. **Spore Print:** White to creamy or pale yellowish white. **Microscopic Features:** Spores: 5–6.5 × 2.5–3.5 µm; smooth; ellipsoid; inamyloid. Cheilocystidia clavate, subclavate, cylindric, or irregular; often with lobes or coralloid projections. Pileipellis a cutis of branched and swollen, interwoven hyphae. **Comments:** Also known as *Collybia dryophila*. Compare with *Gymnopus subsulphureus* (p. 191), which appears in spring and features a clear yellow cap and gills, as well as pinkish rhizomorphs, and with *Rhodocollybia butyracea* (p. 336), which grows only under conifers, is a bit stockier, often features finely jagged gill edges, and has dextrinoid spores.

GYMNOPUS LUXURIANS (PECK) MURRILL

Ecology: Saprobic; growing gregariously or in tight clusters in woodchips, or on lawns (fruiting from dead, buried roots); summer and fall; widely distributed. **Cap:** 2–12 cm, convex, with an incurved margin when young, becoming broadly convex or flat; dry or tacky; bald; dark reddish brown when young, fading to tan; often somewhat streaked-looking. **Gills:** Attached to the stem, often by means of a notch; whitish when young, darkening with maturity to pinkish tan; close. **Stem:** 4–10

cm long; up to about 1 cm thick; more or less equal, but often with an enlarged base; dry; tough; often twisted; somewhat longitudinally ridged; finely hairy or finely dusted; whitish above, buff to brownish below; darkening with age; often with whitish rhizomorphs attached to the base. **Flesh:** Whitish to pale pinkish tan. **Odor and Taste:** Odor not distinctive, or slightly fragrant; taste not distinctive, or slightly bitter. **Spore Print:** Creamy white. **Chemical Reactions:** KOH negative to pale olive gray on cap. **Microscopic Features:** Spores: 6.5–10 × 3–5.5 µm; smooth; lacrymoid to ellipsoid; inamyloid. Cheilocystidia variously shaped; often with broad protrusions or branches. Pileipellis a tangled cutis of encrusted elements. **Comments:** Also known as *Collybia luxurians*.

GYMNOPUS SEMIHIRTIPES (PECK) HALLING

KOH on cap

Ecology: Saprobic; growing alone, scattered, gregariously, or in clusters on leaf litter and woody debris under hardwoods; spring and early summer; widely distributed. **Cap:** 0.5–2 cm; convex, becoming broadly convex or nearly flat; dry; bald; sometimes becoming wrinkled over the center; orangish brown to reddish brown when young and fresh, but quickly fading to pinkish tan or buff, with a darker center. **Gills:** Attached to the stem or nearly free from it; nearly distant; whitish. **Stem:** 2–5 cm long; up to about 3 mm thick at the apex; more or less equal; dry; densely hairy over the lower portion with reddish-brown to purplish-brown hairs, but bald above; reddish brown. **Flesh:** Whitish; thin. **Odor and Taste:** Not distinctive. **Chemical Reactions:** Ammonia or KOH promptly olive, green, or black on cap and stem surface. **Spore Print:** White. **Microscopic Features:** Spores 7.5–9 × 3–4.5 µm; smooth; lacrymoid to ellipsoid; inamyloid. Cheilocystidia rare or absent. Hyphae of stem encrusted with dark brown material in a water mount. **Comments:** *Gymnopus spongiosus* is a similar species appearing in late summer and fall; its stem is fuzzy nearly all the way to the apex. Compare with *Gymnopus dichrous* (p. 188), which lacks the spongy, hairy stem.

GYMNOPUS SUBSULPHUREUS (PECK) MURRILL

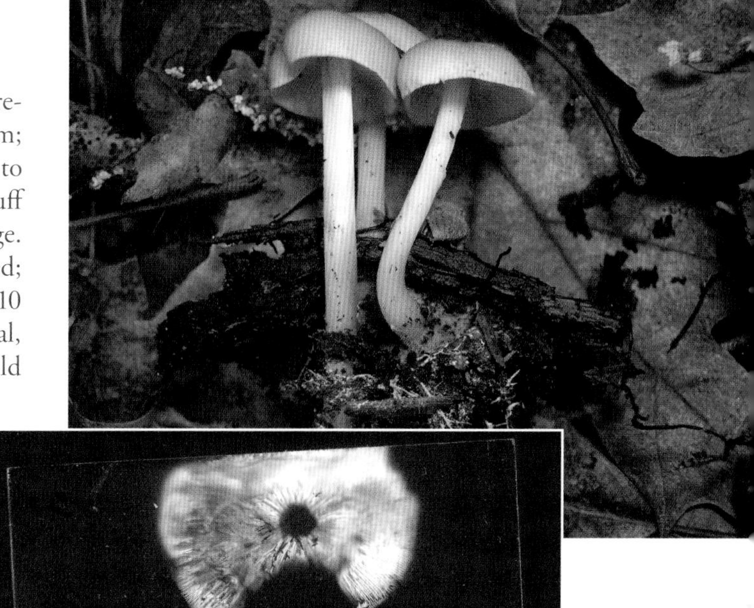

Ecology: Saprobic; growing alone, scattered, or gregariously; spring; widely distributed. **Cap:** 1–4 cm; convex, becoming plano-convex; bald; moist; pale to bright yellow; fading markedly as it dries out to buff or yellowish, often passing through a 2-toned stage. **Gills:** Attached to the stem narrowly; very crowded; yellow to yellowish (rarely nearly white). **Stem:** 2–10 cm long; up to about 7 mm thick; more or less equal, with a small basal bulb; dry to greasy; hollow; bald except for whitish fuzz near the base; yellow; base attached to pinkish rhizomorphs. **Flesh:** Thin; whitish to yellowish. **Odor and Taste:** Odor not distinctive; taste mild or slightly bitter. **Chemical Reactions:** KOH negative on cap. **Spore Print:** White. **Microscopic Features:** Spores: 5–6.5 × 2.5–3.5 µm; smooth; ellipsoid; inamyloid. Cheilocystidia variously shaped; often with protrusions or lobes. Pileipellis a cutis of nonencrusted elements. **Comments:** Compare with *Gymnopus dryophilus* (p. 189) and with *Marasmius strictipes* (p. 274).

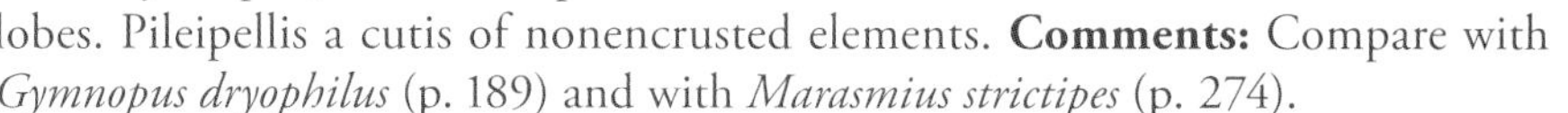

Spore print

GYRODON MERULIOIDES (SCHWEINITZ) SINGER

Ecology: Found under both white and green ash trees; involved in symbiosis with the leafcurl ash aphid, *Meliarhizophagus fraxinifolii* (see comments); growing alone, scattered, or gregariously; summer and fall; widely distributed. **Cap:** 5–20 cm, nearly convex when young, becoming wavy and nearly vase-shaped, or more or less flat; often irregular in development; light to dark brown, sometimes reddish brown; dry, or tacky when wet; softly leathery; sometimes bruising darker brown. **Pore Surface:** Running down the stem; pores elongated radially (sometimes appearing almost like gills), with many cross-veins; yellow to olive, bruising brownish to olive to almost blue (sometimes not bruising); not easily separable. **Stem:** 2–4 cm long; 0.5–2.5 cm thick; usually not central; yellowish above, brown below; bruising darker brown. **Flesh:** Whitish to yellowish; sometimes bluing slowly when exposed. **Odor and Taste:** Not distinctive. **Chemical Reactions:** Ammonia purplish red on cap; orangish to negative on flesh. KOH dark orange on cap; orange on flesh. Iron salts pale orange on cap; bluish gray on flesh. **Spore Print:**

Olive brown. **Microscopic Features:** Spores 7–10 × 6–7.5 µm; smooth; ellipsoid to ovate. Pleurocystidia lageniform. Pileipellis a cutis. **Comments:** Also known as *Boletinellus merulioides*. This mushroom's mycelium forms little knots of tissue that surround and protect the leafcurl ash aphid; in exchange, the aphid's honeydew gives nutrients to the fungus. *Paragyrodon sphaerosporus* (p. 296) can look superficially similar but bruises brown and features much smaller pores that are not radially arranged, along with a volva-like ring at the base of the stem and globose spores.

GYROMITRA BRUNNEA UNDERWOOD

Ecology: Possibly saprobic and/or mycorrhizal; found under oaks and other hardwoods; spring; widely distributed. **Cap:** 4–8 cm across; variable in shape, but often featuring 2–4 loosely arranged lobes raised and pinched together in a saddle-shaped formation; usually with fairly well-defined "seams" joining the lobes; tan to reddish brown; undersurface whitish, exposed in places, frequently ingrown with stem where contact occurs. **Flesh:** Whitish or flushed rose; brittle; chambered; usually thick in the stem. **Stem:** 2–9 cm long; pale pinkish tan to pure white in age; generally not round in cross section; bald; sometimes discoloring grayish on handling. **Microscopic Features:** Spores 24–30 × 13.5–15 µm; with 1–3 oil droplets; ellipsoid; developing one to several apical projections at each end. Paraphyses with subclavate apices; with orangish to reddish contents. **Comments:** Not recommended for the table. Also known by the European name *Gyromitra fastigiata*. Compare with *Gyromitra caroliniana* (below), which has a cap that is not lobed and lacks "seams"; additionally, its cap is more tightly adjoined to the stem, so that the whitish undersurface is almost never visible.

GYROMITRA CAROLINIANA (BOSC) FRIES

Ecology: Possibly saprobic and/or mycorrhizal; found under hardwoods, usually around dead trees and stumps; spring; distributed below the Great Lakes, especially in the Mississippi and Ohio watersheds. **Cap:** 5–10+ cm across; variable in shape but usually more or less round; surface tightly wrinkled, without lobes or "seams"; dark red to brownish red or reddish brown; tightly adjoined to the stem; pale undersurface usually not exposed. **Flesh:** Whitish; brittle; chambered; without a central cavity; in the cap forming structures reminiscent of broccoli pieces. **Stem:** 6–10 cm long or larger (often massive); whitish to pure white; bald; developing longitudinal wrinkles and folds with maturity; sometimes discoloring grayish on handling. **Microscopic Features:** Spores 30–32.5 × 11.5–14 µm; with 1 large oil droplet and 2–3 smaller ones; ellipsoid; finely reticulate; developing up to 6 apical projections at each end. Paraphyses with clavate to subclavate apices; with orangish to reddish contents. **Comments:** Not recommended for the table. Compare with *Gyromitra brunnea* (p. 192).

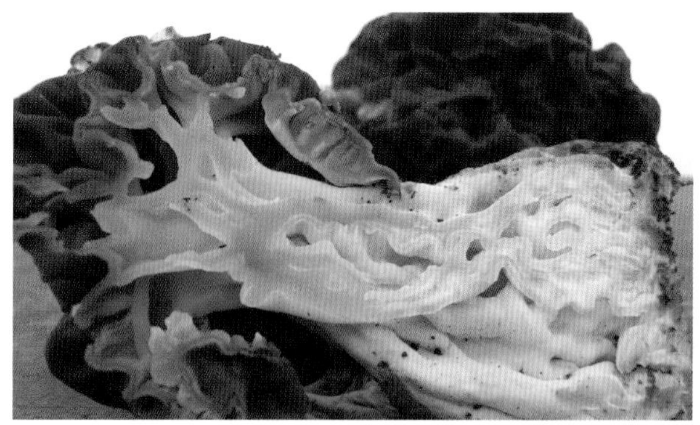

GYROMITRA ESCULENTA (PERSOON) FRIES

Ecology: Possibly saprobic and/or mycorrhizal; found under conifers; spring; northern Midwest. **Cap:** 3–12 cm across; irregular and variable in shape, but often brain-like and somewhat lobed (but usually not saddle-shaped); pinkish tan to reddish brown, darkening to nearly black in age and under prolonged direct sunlight; pale underside generally not exposed; margin usually curved inward. **Flesh:** Thin; brittle; chambered; whitish to watery tan. **Stem:** 3–7 cm high; up to 3 cm thick; pale yellowish tan to pinkish or reddish; often with a few deep grooves; bald; often with a somewhat waxy texture. **Microscopic Features:** Spores 18–30 × 10–13 µm; smooth; ellipsoid; smooth; with 2 small polar oil droplets. Paraphyses with clavate to subclavate apices; with reddish to orangish contents. **Comments:** Poisonous.

GYROMITRA INFULA (SCHAEFFER) QUÉLET

Ecology: Saprobic; usually found growing alone or gregariously from well-rotted, moss-covered wood, but sometimes found growing on the ground; fall; northern Midwest. **Cap:** 3–5 cm across; usually more or less saddle-shaped, with 2 prominently raised lobes (rarely with 3 or 4 lobes); color variable, ranging from tan to yellowish brown or reddish brown; underside paler, sometimes ingrown with stem where contact occurs. **Flesh:** Thin and brittle; chambered. **Stem:** 1–12 cm tall; up to 2 cm wide; not ribbed; bald; whitish, or tinged with the cap color. **Microscopic Features:** Spores 17–26 × 7–10 µm; oblong to ellipsoid; with 2 large oil droplets; with a blunt apiculus at each end. Paraphyses clavate to capitate; with reddish

to orangish contents. **Comments:** Poisonous. *Gyromitra ambigua* is very similar but is a little darker and more purple; it also features somewhat larger spores.

GYROMITRA KORFII (RAITVIR) HARMAJA

Ecology: Saprobic; found under various hardwoods, often near stumps or dying trees; spring; widely distributed but less common in the southern Midwest. **Cap:** 5–10 cm across; variable in shape but usually blocky and squarish; loosely wrinkled to convoluted; tan to brown (rarely cinnamon or tawny); margins incurved and tightly affixed, often ingrown with the stem where contact occurs; pale undersurface rarely slightly exposed. **Flesh:** Whitish; brittle; chambered. **Stem:** 3–6 cm high; up to 6 cm thick; pale tan to white; massive; bald; developing broad longitudinal ribs or waves. **Microscopic Features:** Spores 25–30 × 10.8–12.6 µm; subfusiform; with a knob at each end (the broad, blunt apiculi develop with maturity and are often absent on immature spores); usually with 1 large oil droplet and 2 smaller, polar droplets. Paraphyses with clavate apices; with golden to reddish or orangish contents. **Comments:** Not recommended for the table. Also known as *Gyromitra gigas*, according to some mycologists. Below the Great Lakes *Gyromitra korfii* should be compared with *Gyromitra brunnea* (p. 192), which is less blocky and usually features a lobed cap.

GYROMITRA LEUCOXANTHA (BRESÀDOLA) HARMAJA

Ecology: Saprobic; growing alone or gregariously; terrestrial, but usually appearing near rotted wood and stumps; found under hardwoods and conifers; spring; northern Midwest. **Fruiting Body:** Cup-shaped or bowl-shaped when young; flattening out with maturity and becoming irregularly saucer-shaped; to 10 cm across; upper surface yellow to yellowish brown or orangish brown; smooth at first but usually becoming wrinkled or bumpy, at least over the center; undersurface whitish and very finely hairy, sometimes bruising brownish; rudimentary stem (often present) to 5 cm long and 3 cm wide, whitish, continuous with undersurface; flesh 2–3 mm thick, watery whitish. **Microscopic Features:** Spores 28–40 × 12–16 µm; with 1 or 2 oil droplets; smooth or roughened; when mature, with blunt, "scooped-out" apiculi at each end, extending up to 4 µm (best seen in a water mount). Paraphyses with clavate apices; with orangish granular contents. **Comments:** Also known as *Discina leucoxantha*. Compare with *Gyromitra perlata* (below), which is usually more reddish and less yellow and which has pointed, rather than scooped-out, apiculi; also compare with *Disciotis venosa* (p. 169), which is more brown, lacks a pseudostem, and has ellipsoid spores with homogeneous contents.

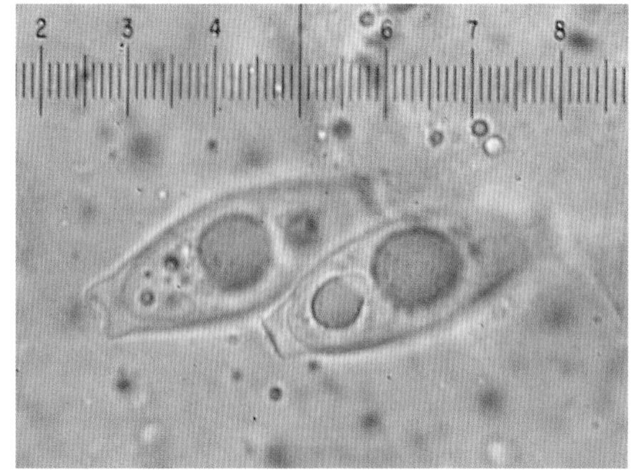

Spores

GYROMITRA PERLATA (FRIES) HARMAJA

Ecology: Saprobic; growing alone or gregariously; terrestrial, but usually appearing near or on rotted wood and stumps; found under conifers or hardwoods; spring; fairly widely distributed, but much more common from the Great Lakes northward. **Fruiting Body:** Cup-shaped or bowl-shaped when young; flattening out with maturity, becoming irregularly saucer-shaped; to 7 cm across; upper surface reddish brown, darkening to dark brown or blackish (especially in raised areas), smooth or, more frequently, wavy to wrinkled or bumpy; undersurface whitish to pale grayish brown, bald or very finely hairy; stem when present to 5 cm long and 3 cm wide, whitish, continuous with undersurface, usually broadly ribbed. **Microscopic Features:** Spores 27.5–45.5 × 11.5–16 µm; fusiform; usually with 1 prominent oil droplet (but sometimes with 2 or 3 droplets); smooth or roughened; at maturity with pointed apiculi extending up to 5.5 µm (best seen in a water mount). Paraphyses with clavate to subcapitate apices; with orangish to orange-brown granular contents. **Comments:** Also known as *Discina perlata*. DNA studies (including our own unpublished findings) confirm the idea that the cup-like species traditionally placed in the genus *Discina* actually belong in *Gyromitra*. Compare with *Gyromitra leucoxantha* (p. 194), which is less red and which features spores with scooped-out apiculi; also compare with *Disciotis venosa* (p. 169), which is less red, lacks the pseudostem, and has substantially different spores.

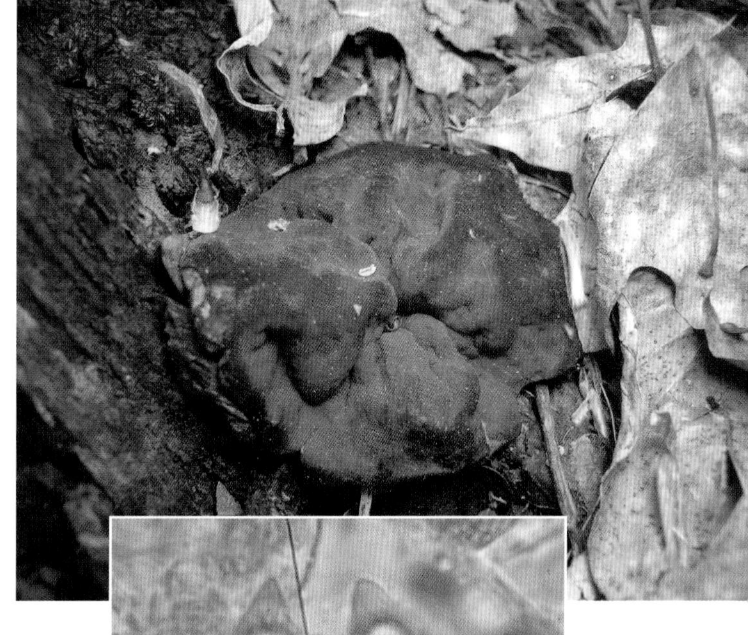

Spores

Spore print

GYROPORUS CASTANEUS (BULLIARD) QUÉLET

Ecology: Mycorrhizal with hardwoods; growing scattered or gregariously; summer and fall; widely distributed. **Cap:** 3–10 cm; convex, becoming broadly convex or nearly flat in age; dry; bald or slightly velvety; margin even, but often splitting in places at maturity; chestnut brown to yellowish brown or orange brown. **Pore Surface:** White to cream or yellowish; not bruising; 1–3 round pores per mm; tubes to 8 mm deep. **Stem:** 3–9 cm long; 0.5–1.5 cm thick; more or less equal, but sometimes tapering to apex and/or base; brittle; hollowing; colored like the cap or slightly paler; not bruising; not reticulate. **Flesh:** White; brittle; not staining on exposure. **Odor and Taste:** Not distinctive. **Chemical Reactions:** Ammonia negative on cap and flesh. KOH negative or yellow on cap; negative on flesh. Iron salts negative on cap and flesh. **Spore Print:** Pale yellow. **Microscopic Features:** Spores 8–13 × 5–6 µm; smooth; ellipsoid to oval. Pileipellis a trichoderm. **Comments:** Edible and good when dried and reconstituted. The colors, along with the hollowing brittle stem and the yellow spore print, are good field characters. Compare with *Gyroporus purpurinus* (p. 197), which is very similar but purplish red.

GYROPORUS CYANESCENS (BULLIARD) QUÉLET

Ecology: Mycorrhizal with hardwoods; growing alone or scattered, usually in sandy soil, especially in disturbed ground (roadbeds, and so on); summer and fall; northern Midwest from the Great Lakes northward. **Cap:** 4–12 cm; convex, becoming broadly convex or, sometimes, nearly flat in age; dry; coarsely roughened or almost matted-scaly; straw-colored or paler; bruising greenish yellow, then blue. **Pore Surface:** White to yellowish; bruising greenish yellow, then blue; 1–2 round pores per mm; tubes to 10 mm deep. **Stem:** 4–10 cm long; 1–2.5 cm thick; more or less equal, or swollen; brittle; soon hollowing; colored like the cap or slightly paler; not reticulate; textured like the cap, or bald in age; bruising greenish yellow, then blue. **Flesh:** White to pale yellow; brittle; bruising greenish yellow, then blue on exposure. **Odor and Taste:** Not distinctive. **Spore Print:** Pale yellow. **Microscopic Features:** Spores 8–10 × 5–6 µm; smooth; ellipsoid. Pileipellis a collapsing trichoderm. **Comments:** Edible. The straw colors, brittle consistency, dramatic bluing, and yellow spore print are good identifying features.

GYROPORUS PURPURINUS (SNELL) SINGER

Ecology: Mycorrhizal with hardwoods (but sometimes reported under conifers); growing alone, scattered, or gregariously; summer and fall; widely distributed. **Cap:** 2–8 cm; convex, becoming broadly convex or nearly flat in age; dry; bald or slightly velvety; sometimes becoming slightly cracked in age; purplish red. **Pore Surface:** Whitish at first, becoming pale yellow; not bruising; 1–4 round pores per mm; tubes to 8 mm deep. **Stem:** 3–6 cm long; 0.5–1 cm thick; more or less equal, but sometimes tapering to apex; dry; brittle; hollowing; colored like the cap; not bruising; not reticulate. **Flesh:** White; not staining on exposure. **Odor and Taste:** Not distinctive. **Chemical Reactions:** Ammonia negative on cap surface and flesh. KOH negative or slowly reddish on cap, negative to yellow on flesh. Iron salts negative on cap and flesh. **Spore Print:** Yellow. **Microscopic Features:** Spores 8–11 × 5–7 µm; smooth; ellipsoid to oval. Pileipellis a trichoderm. **Comments:** Edible. Compare with *Gyroporus castaneus* (p. 196).

HAPALOPILUS NIDULANS (FRIES) KARSTEN

Ecology: Saprobic; growing alone or in small groups on decaying hardwood logs and sticks; causing a white rot; late spring to fall; widely distributed. **Cap:** 2.5–6 cm across; irregularly bracket-shaped or kidney-shaped; convex; bald or finely hairy; dull orange to dull cinnamon. **Pore Surface:** Dull orange to dull cinnamon; not bruising; with 2–4 angular pores per mm; tubes to 1 cm deep. **Stem:** Absent. **Flesh:** Dull orange or paler; watery and soft at first, but later tough and hard. **Chemical Reactions:** All parts purple to lilac with KOH. **Spore Print:** White. **Microscopic Features:** Spores 3.5–5 × 2–3 µm; smooth; ellipsoid to cylindric; inamyloid. Hyphal system monomitic, with conspicuous clamp connections. **Comments:** The KOH reaction of this fungus is stunning.

KOH on flesh

HARRYA CHROMAPES (FROST) HALLING, NUHN, OSMUNDSON, & MANF. BINDER

Ecology: Mycorrhizal with a wide variety of hardwoods and conifers, appearing in diverse ecosystems; growing alone, scattered, or gregariously; summer and fall; widely distributed. **Cap:** 3–11 cm across; convex, becoming broadly convex or flat; dry or tacky; bald or very finely hairy; occasionally somewhat pitted; when young pink to pale red, fading to pinkish tan, tan, or yellowish; without an overhanging margin. **Pore Surface:** Depressed at the stem; whitish, becoming pinkish, and finally brownish; not bruising; with 1–3 round or angular pores per mm; tubes to 1.5 cm long. **Stem:** 4–17 cm long; 1–2.5 cm wide; at maturity more or less equal, or tapering to apex; whitish to pinkish above; chrome yellow at the base; densely scabrous with pink to reddish-brown scabers. **Flesh:** White or faintly pinkish; unchanging when sliced and exposed to air, or bluing slightly. **Odor and Taste:** Not distinctive. **Spore Print:** Pinkish brown to cinnamon brown. **Chemical Reactions:** Ammonia yellow on cap surface. KOH brownish on cap surface and on flesh. Iron salts greenish on flesh. **Microscopic Features:** Spores subfusoid; inamyloid; yellowish in KOH; smooth; 11–17 × 4–6 µm. Pileipellis a tangled cutis. **Comments:** Previously known as *Tylopilus chromapes* and *Leccinum chromapes*, this distinctive bolete was recently placed in a new genus, *Harrya*, based on its DNA (Halling et al. 2012).

Photo by Noah Siegel

HEBELOMA ALBIDULUM PECK

Ecology: Mycorrhizal with hardwoods (possibly also associated with berry bushes); growing scattered or gregariously; fall; widely distributed but not common. **Cap:** 2.5–7 cm; convex, becoming broadly convex, broadly bell-shaped, or nearly flat; sticky when very fresh; bald; white to off-white when fresh, but sometimes discoloring yellowish with age. **Gills:** Attached to the stem, often by a notch; close; white when young, becoming cinnamon brown to brown. **Stem:** 4–8 cm long; 3–7 mm thick; more or less equal, or not infrequently with a small basal bulb that may be buried underground; silky to finely scaly near the apex; whitish. **Flesh:** Whitish in the cap; brownish in the stem. **Odor and Taste:** Radish-like, or not distinctive. **Chemical Reactions:** KOH negative to dull olive on cap. **Spore Print:** Brown to reddish brown. **Microscopic Features:** Spores 9–12 × 6–7.5 µm; almond-shaped; finely verrucose; occasionally with a loosening perispore; weakly dextrinoid. Cheilocystidia abundant; generally cylindric, subclavate, or clavate, but occasionally with an elongated cylindric extension. Pileipellis an ixocutis. **Comments:** *Hebeloma sarcophyllum* is similar but has pinkish immature gills. Compare with *Agaricus pocillator* (p. 82) and *Agaricus silvicola* (p. 83), both of which feature rings and stain yellow.

HEBELOMA CRUSTULINIFORME (BULLIARD) QUÉLET

Ecology: Mycorrhizal with hardwoods or conifers; growing gregariously or in loose clusters, sometimes in arcs or fairy rings, in grassy areas at the edges of woods, or in woods; late summer and fall; widely distributed. **Cap:** 3–11 cm; convex, becoming broadly convex, broadly bell-shaped, or flat; sticky when fresh; bald; whitish, dirty buff, or pale tan, often with a somewhat darker central area; the margin inrolled when young. **Gills:** Attached to the stem, often by a notch; crowded; pale when young, becoming brownish; often with beads of liquid when young and fresh, and, later, with brownish spots where the beads occurred; with whitish edges. **Stem:** 4–13 cm long; 0.5–1.5 cm thick; more or less equal above a slightly swollen base; finely hairy or bald; with little flakes of tissue near the apex; without a cortina or ring zone; the base sometimes with white rhizomorphs. **Flesh:** Whitish; thick. **Odor and Taste:** Odor radish-like; taste radish-like or bitter. **Chemical Reactions:** KOH negative to gray on cap. **Spore Print:** Brown. **Microscopic Features:** Spores 9–13 × 5–7.5 µm; amygdaliform to limoniform; finely verrucose; not dextrinoid. Cheilocystidia abundant; apices subclavate to clavate; rarely basally inflated. Pileipellis an ixocutis. **Comments:** Poisonous. The beaded-spotted gills with whitish edges, the flaky (but not scaly) stem apex, and the radish-like odor are good preliminary identifying features.

Spore print

HEBELOMA MESOPHAEUM (PERSOON) QUÉLET

Ecology: Mycorrhizal with various conifers, including pines, spruces, and firs; usually growing gregariously; fall, winter (during warm spells), and spring; widely distributed. **Cap:** 2–7 cm; convex, becoming broadly convex, broadly bell-shaped, or nearly flat; sticky when fresh; bald; brown to pinkish brown over the center; often paler toward the margin; the margin with or without veil remnants. **Gills:** Attached to the stem, often by a notch; close or crowded; creamy or faintly pinkish when

young, becoming brownish. **Stem:** 2–9 cm long; up to 1 cm thick; more or less equal; silky; whitish at first, discoloring brownish to brown from the base up with maturity; sometimes with a faint or more prominent ring zone. **Flesh:** Whitish. **Odor and Taste:** Odor radish-like, or not distinctive; taste radish-like or bitter. **Chemical Reactions:** KOH negative to gray on cap. **Spore Print:** Brown to pinkish brown. **Microscopic Features:** Spores 8.5–11 × 5–7 µm; ellipsoid; very finely verrucose (nearly smooth); not dextrinoid. Cheilocystidia abundant; cylindric above a ventricose base. Pileipellis an ixocutis. **Comments:** Not recommended for the table; potentially poisonous. Key macroscopic features include the 2-toned cap, the brown spore print, the radish-like odor, and the habitat under conifers.

HEBELOMA SINAPIZANS (PAULET) SACCARDO

Ecology: Mycorrhizal with hardwoods or conifers; growing gregariously or in loose clusters, sometimes in arcs or fairy rings, in grassy areas at the edges of woods, or in woods; late summer and fall; widely distributed. **Cap:** 4–15 cm; convex or broadly convex, becoming flat; sticky when fresh; bald; with a soft, cottony margin when young; sometimes with a whitish sheen when young; cinnamon tan to darker reddish brown. **Gills:** Attached to the stem, often by a notch; close; pale clay color when young, becoming cinnamon brown to brown; sometimes with beads of liquid when young and fresh; the edges often becoming ragged as the mushroom matures. **Stem:** 4–12 cm long; 1–3 cm thick; more or less equal above a fairly abrupt, swollen base; finely mealy or dusty near the apex; developing scales below, often in more or less concentric bands; whitish, but the scales often capturing spores as the mushroom matures and thus becoming brownish; without a cortina or a ring zone. **Flesh:** Whitish; thick. **Odor and Taste:** Radish-like. **Chemical Reactions:** KOH gray on cap. **Spore Print:** Brown to pinkish brown. **Microscopic Features:** Spores 11–15 × 6.5–8 µm; sublimoniform, with a snout-like end; finely verrucose; rarely with a loosening perispore; moderately dextrinoid. Cheilocystidia abundant; clavate, subcapitate, or sometimes merely cylindric, but almost never ventricose. Pileipellis an ixotrichoderm in young specimens; later an ixocutis. **Comments:** Poisonous. The relatively thick stem that develops concentric scaly bands is distinctive.

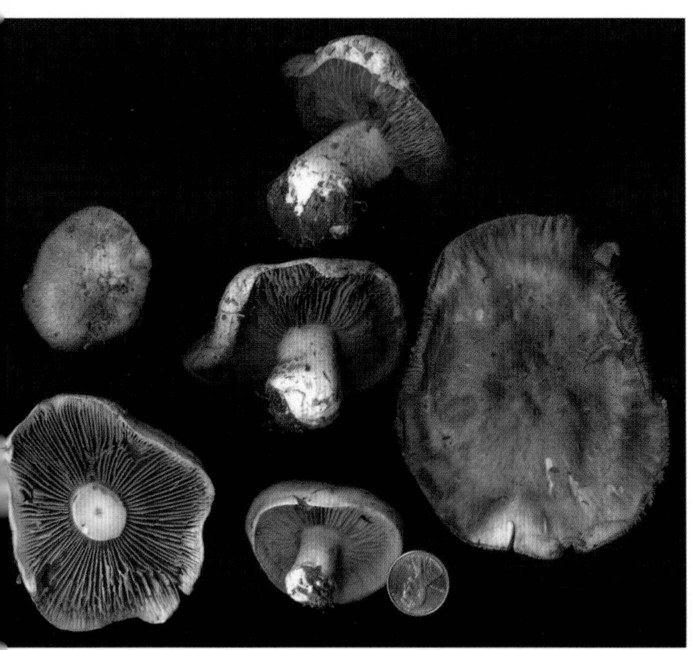

HEIMIOPORUS BETULA (SCHWEINITZ) HORAK

Ecology: Mycorrhizal with oaks and pines, especially in mixed pine-oak woods; growing alone or scattered; summer and fall; southeastern Midwest. **Cap:** 3–9 cm; convex to broadly convex in age; moist to slimy when fresh; shiny when dry; bald; often becoming pitted or wrinkled with age; yellow, orangish, reddish, or reddish brown; with a tiny sterile margin. **Pore Surface:** Often sunken at the stem in maturity; yellow, becoming greenish yellow; not bruising; with 1–2 angular pores per mm; tubes to 1.5 cm deep. **Stem:** 10–30 cm long; 1–2.5 cm thick; tapered to apex, or more or less equal; deeply and coarsely reticulate with a yellow reticulum that reddens with age; solid; yellow above and reddish below, becoming more reddish overall; basal mycelium white; base attached to white rhizomorphs. **Flesh:** Yellow, with reddish areas in the stem; not bruising when exposed. **Odor and Taste:** Not distinctive. **Spore Print:** Olive to olive brown. **Microscopic Features:** Spores 13–22 × 6–10 µm; finely pitted; narrowly ellipsoid. Pileipellis an ixotrichoderm. **Comments:** Also known as *Austroboletus betula.* Compare with *Boletus projectellus* (p. 121), which has a darker, dry cap and a stem that is prominently ridged but not lacerate-reticulate, and with *Boletellus russellii* (p. 110), which has a darker, dry cap.

HELVELLA ACETABULUM (LINNAEUS) QUÉLET

Ecology: Possibly saprobic and/or mycorrhizal; growing alone or gregariously under hardwoods or conifers; spring and early summer; widely distributed. **Cap:** 1–8 cm; cup-like; sometimes becoming flat in age; upper surface brown to yellowish brown, bald; undersurface brown to yellow brown, sometimes paler near the stem, finely hairy near the margin, with forked ribs extending from the stem, sometimes almost to the margin; the margin more or less even. **Flesh:** Thin; brittle. **Stem:** To 9 cm long and 3 cm thick; becoming broader near the cap; deeply ribbed with sharp-edged ribs that extend far onto the undersurface of the cap; cream-colored. **Micro-**

Photo by Melissa Bochte

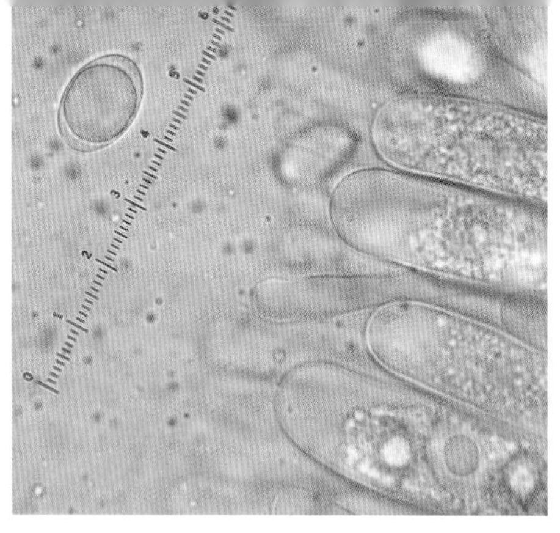

Spore, asci, and paraphyses

scopic Features:** Spores 16–18 × 11–13.5 µm; ellipsoid; smooth; with 1 central oil droplet. Paraphyses subclavate; brownish. **Comments:** Some mycologists recognize *Helvella costifera* as a distinct species based on the grayish-brown (rather than yellowish-brown) cap and with blunt-edged ribs on its stem. Compare with *Helvella queletii* (p. 204), which is grayish brown and features ribs that only extend a few millimeters onto the cap's undersurface.

Photo by Patrick Harvey

HELVELLA CRISPA (SCOPOLI) FRIES

Ecology: Possibly saprobic and/or mycorrhizal; growing alone or gregariously under conifers or hardwoods; sometimes growing from rotting wood; often found in disturbed-ground areas (pathsides, edges of woods, and so on); summer and fall; widely distributed. **Cap:** 1–5 cm across; broadly saddle-shaped and irregularly lobed; surface smooth or slightly wrinkled; white or, more typically, creamy to slightly yellowish; undersurface finely hairy, colored like the upper surface or slightly darker; the margin often curled upward, and usually not fused with the stem where contact occurs. **Flesh:** Thin; brittle; often chambered in the stem. **Stem:** 3–10 cm long; 0.5–3.5 cm wide; white or flushed slightly pinkish; deeply and ornately ribbed, with cross-veins and pockets. **Microscopic Features:** Spores 17–21 × 10–14 µm; ellipsoid; smooth; with 1 oil droplet or with 1 large central droplet and several smaller polar droplets. Paraphyses clavate; hyaline. **Comments:** Compare with *Helvella sulcata* (p. 204).

HELVELLA ELASTICA BULLIARD

Ecology: Possibly saprobic and/or mycorrhizal; growing alone or gregariously under conifers or hardwoods, on the ground, or, rarely, from rotting wood; fall; widely distributed. **Cap:** 1–5 cm across; folded over or loosely saddle-shaped; with convex lobes that sometimes fuse by maturity; upper surface tan to grayish brown, bald; undersurface whitish, or at least paler than the upper surface, bald, sometimes ingrown with the stem where contact occurs; margin when young folding downward. **Flesh:** Thin; brittle. **Stem:** 2–6 cm long; to 1 cm thick; more or less equal; creamy; bald.

Microscopic Features: Spores 19.5–22.5 × 11.5–13.5 µm; ellipsoid; with 1 central oil droplet and up to 5 small droplets at each end. Paraphyses clavate; hyaline to tan. **Comments:** Compare with *Helvella latispora* (below), which has a finely fuzzy undersurface and a young margin that curves upward rather than downward.

HELVELLA LATISPORA BOUDIER

Ecology: Possibly saprobic and/or mycorrhizal; growing scattered or gregariously under hardwoods; often along paths and roads in disturbed soil; appearing from late spring and early summer to fall; widely distributed. **Cap:** 1–4 cm across; 1–4.5 cm high; at first cup-shaped with the margin curled upward; in maturity saddle-shaped with a deep cleft, or with 3 lobes, or lobed and irregular; upper surface bald, tan to buff or whitish; undersurface fuzzy, whitish, rarely ingrown with the stem where contact occurs. **Stem:** 1–6 cm; 2–10 mm thick; more or less equal; bald or somewhat fuzzy; hollow; whitish. **Flesh:** Thin; brittle; whitish. **Spore Print:** White. **Microscopic Features:** Spores 17.5–20 × 11–13.5 µm; ellipsoid; smooth; with 1 central oil droplet and, occasionally, several smaller polar droplets. Paraphyses clavate; hyaline. **Comments:** Also known as *Helvella stevensii*. Compare with *Helvella elastica* (p. 202).

HELVELLA MACROPUS (PERSOON) KARSTEN

Ecology: Possibly saprobic and/or mycorrhizal; growing alone or gregariously on the ground under hardwoods or conifers, or on rotting wood; summer to fall; widely distributed. **Cap:** 1–5 cm; cup-shaped or disc-shaped, or occasionally nearly flat; upper surface brownish, bald; undersurface similarly colored, finely hairy (especially near the margin). **Flesh:** Thin; brownish. **Stem:** 1–5 cm long; to 0.5 cm thick; equal; occasionally with clefts near the base in age; brownish; finely hairy. **Microscopic Features:** Spores 21–24 × 10.5–12.5 µm; fusiform; smooth or slightly roughened; with 1 large central oil droplet and another smaller oil droplet at each end. Paraphyses clavate; hyaline to pale brownish. **Comments:** Compare with *Helvella queletii* (p. 204). *Helvella corium* is a similar but jet black northern species. *Helvella cupuliformis* is nearly identical to the naked eye but features ellipsoid spores.

Photo by Melissa Bochte

HELVELLA QUELETII BRESÀDOLA

Ecology: Possibly saprobic and/or mycorrhizal; growing alone or gregariously under hardwoods or conifers; spring and early summer; widely distributed. **Cap:** 1.5–6 cm across; when young often folded inward along a central axis; at maturity cup-like or saucer-shaped (but sometimes irregular); upper surface grayish brown to brown, smooth or slightly wrinkled; undersurface pale grayish brown to whitish, densely but finely fuzzy. **Flesh:** Thin; brittle. **Stem:** To 11 cm long and 4 cm thick; flaring to apex and/or base; usually deeply ribbed with round-edged ribs that terminate at the apex of the stem and do not continue more than a few millimeters onto the undersurface of the cap; whitish or very pale brown. **Microscopic Features:** Spores 17–22 × 11–14 µm; ellipsoid; smooth; with 1 central oil droplet. Paraphyses clavate; hyaline to brownish. **Comments:** Compare with *Helvella acetabulum* (p. 201) and with *Helvella macropus* (p. 203), which features a nonribbed stem.

HELVELLA SULCATA AFZELIUS

Ecology: Possibly saprobic and/or mycorrhizal; growing alone or gregariously under hardwoods or conifers, usually from rotting woody debris (around old stumps and so on); late spring through fall; widely distributed. **Cap:** 1–5 cm across; saddle-shaped, 3-lobed, or loosely and irregularly lobed; pale to dark gray, or sometimes nearly black; bald; undersurface bald, pale gray, exposed when young or in irregular caps; margin ingrown with the stem in places when mature. **Stem:** 1–6 cm long; to 2 cm wide; more or less equal; extensively ribbed, but the ribs not forming holes or pockets, and not extending onto the undersurface of the cap; whitish to grayish. **Microscopic Features:** Spores: 14–18 × 10.5–12.5 µm; ellipsoid; smooth; with 1 large oil droplet. Paraphyses clavate; hyaline to brown. **Comments:** Pale forms of this species can approximate *Helvella crispa* (p. 202), but that species has a stem that develops pockets between the ribs, a finely fuzzy undersurface, and a cap margin that curls upward. *Helvella lacunosa*, rare in the Midwest, has a black cap that is irregularly lumpy and lobed and a dark gray stem that develops extensive pockets between the ribs.

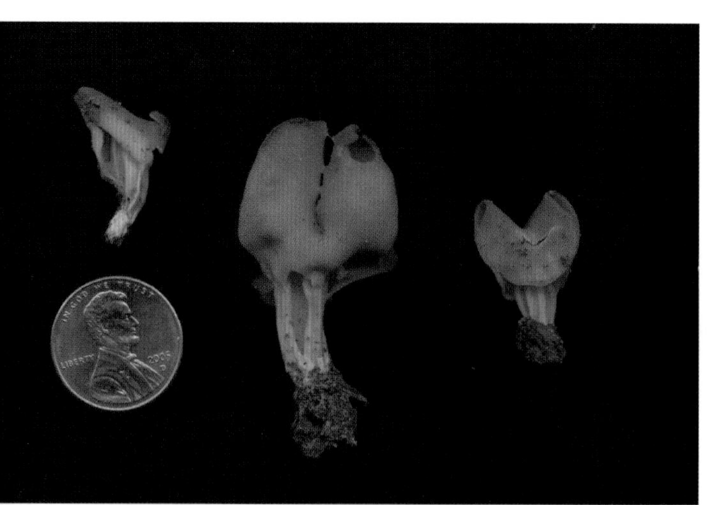

HERICIUM CORALLOIDES (SCOPOLI) PERSOON

Ecology: Saprobic; growing alone or gregariously on fallen hardwood branches and stumps; late summer and fall; widely distributed. **Fruiting Body:** 8–35 cm across; consisting of branches that arise from a more or less central core; with spines averaging about 1 cm long that hang in rows along the branches; white, or in age discoloring brownish to yellowish. **Flesh:** White; not changing when sliced. **Spore Print:** White. **Microscopic Features:** Spores 3–5 × 3–4 µm; globose or subglobose; amyloid; smooth or minutely rough. **Comments:** Edible. *Hericium americanum* is also branched but features longer spines (up to 4 cm long); *Hericium erinaceus* (below) fruits from the wounds of living trees and has longer spines and an unbranched fruiting body.

HERICIUM ERINACEUS (BULLIARD) PERSOON

Ecology: Saprobic and parasitic; growing alone; growing on deadwood or fruiting from the wounds of living oaks and other hardwoods; late summer and fall; widely distributed. **Fruiting Body:** 8–40 cm across; consisting of a single unbranched clump of soft spines measuring 1–6 cm long, hanging from a tough, hidden base that is attached to the tree; white, or in age discoloring brownish to yellowish. **Flesh:** White; not changing when sliced. **Spore Print:** White. **Microscopic Features:** Spores 4–5.5 × 5–6.5 µm; ellipsoid or subglobose; amyloid; smooth or minutely roughened. **Comments:** Edible. Compare with *Hericium coralloides* (above).

HOHENBUEHELIA ANGUSTATA (BERKELEY) SINGER

Ecology: Saprobic on well-decayed wood of hardwoods; growing gregariously; summer and fall; widely distributed. **Cap:** 1–6 cm across; convex, becoming plano-convex; fan-shaped to spoon-shaped in outline (or occasionally rolled into a fun-

nel shape); rubbery and moist; bald overall, but sometimes finely hairy when young and usually featuring whitish fuzz near the point of attachment; whitish to beige or watery brownish; the margin at first inrolled. **Gills:** Close or crowded; whitish, becoming yellowish to dull tan. **Stem:** True stem absent, but a tiny pseudostem is usually present, attached to white rhizomorphs. **Flesh:** Whitish to brownish; rubbery. **Odor and Taste:** Mealy. **Chemical Reactions:** KOH negative on cap. **Spore Print:** White. **Microscopic Features:** Spores 3–5.5 µm; broadly ovoid to subglobose or globose; smooth; inamyloid. Pleurocystidia ("metuloids") abundant; lanceolate to broadly fusoid; with thick (2–3.5 µm) walls and apical encrustations. **Comments:** Compare with *Crepidotus applanatus* (p. 164), which has a brown spore print and does not smell mealy. Cystidia of this species are illustrated on p. 16.

HOHENBUEHELIA ATROCOERULEA VAR. GRISEA
(PECK) THORN & G. L. BARRON

Ecology: Saprobic on the deadwood of hardwoods and (less often) conifers; growing gregariously or in shelf-like clusters; summer and fall; widely distributed. **Cap:** 2–5 cm across; convex, becoming plano-convex; fan-shaped to semicircular or kidney-shaped in outline; rubbery and moist; bald, or finely fuzzy in places, especially toward the point of attachment; nearly black at first, becoming blackish brown to dark brown and eventually drying out and fading to tan or beige. **Gills:** Close or nearly distant; whitish, becoming dull yellowish. **Stem:** Absent, but a tiny pseudostem is occasionally present. **Flesh:** Whitish to brownish; rubbery. **Odor and Taste:** Odor mealy or not distinctive; taste mealy. **Spore Print:** White. **Microscopic Features:** Spores 6–9 × 3–4.5 µm; ellipsoid; smooth; inamyloid. Pleurocystidia ("metuloids") lanceolate to fusoid; with thick (2–6 µm) walls; often developing heavy apical encrustations. **Comments:** *Hohenbuehelia mastrucata* (see Kuo and Methven 2010) is similar but features prominent gelatinous spines on its cap.

HOHENBUEHELIA PETALOIDES (BULLIARD) SCHULZER

Ecology: Saprobic; growing alone, gregariously, or in clusters, usually on the ground; often in the vicinity of woody debris; often found in gardens, parks, lawns, and so on, but also found in woods; summer and fall; widely distributed. **Cap:** 2–7 cm across; shoehorn-shaped, or rolled into a funnel shape; rubbery and moist; usually bald, but sometimes with fine white fuzz in places; beige to grayish brown or yellow brown. **Gills:** Running down the stem; close or crowded; whitish, becoming dull yellowish. **Stem:** Present but hard to define precisely, since it is continuous with the cap; brownish above, white and fuzzy below. **Flesh:** Whitish; rubbery. **Odor and Taste:** Mealy. **Chemical Reactions:** KOH negative on cap. **Spore Print:** White. **Microscopic Features:** Spores 5–9 × 3–5 µm; ellipsoid; smooth; inamyloid. Pleurocystidia ("metuloids") abundant; lanceolate to fusoid; with thick walls; developing apical encrustations. **Comments:** Also known as *Hohenbuehelia geogenia*. Compare with *Lentinellus micheneri* (p. 256), which features serrated gill edges and amyloid spores, and grows directly from wood. Occasional specimens of *Hohenbuehelia angustata* (p. 205) become shoehorn-shaped, but that species grows directly from wood and features smaller, globose spores.

HUMARIA HEMISPHAERICA (WIGGERS) FUCKEL

Photo by Noah Siegel

Ecology: Saprobic; growing alone or gregariously on well-decayed wood or on the ground; summer and fall; widely distributed. **Fruiting Body:** Goblet-shaped when young, becoming more broadly cup-shaped and reaching a width of 2–3 cm when mature; upper surface white or pale bluish, bald; undersurface densely hairy with prominent hairs that extend above the margin of the cup, brown; without a stem; flesh brownish or pale, brittle. **Microscopic Features:** Spores 20–24 × 10–12 µm; finely warty; ellipsoid; usually with 2 oil droplets that break up at maturity. Hairs brown in KOH, septate. **Comments:** *Jafnea semitosta* (see Kuo and Methven 2010) is similar but larger, reaching 7 cm across.

HYDNELLUM CAERULEUM (HORNEMAN) KARSTEN

Ecology: Mycorrhizal with conifers; growing alone or gregariously; summer and fall; northern Midwest. **Cap:** Usually single, but occasionally fused with other caps; 3–15 cm wide; top-shaped to convex, becoming flat or shallowly depressed; somewhat velvety; sometimes ridged or pitted; when fresh and young white to whitish or

Photo by Walt Sturgeon

Photo by Noah Siegel

Photo by Ron Kerner

very pale yellowish, but usually with a bluish cast, becoming dingy tan to brownish over the center or overall; the pale margin often bruising blue. **Undersurface:** Running down the stem; covered with crowded spines that are 3–6 mm long; whitish to pale grayish at first, becoming brownish to brown. **Stem:** 2–5 cm long; 1–3 cm thick at apex; more or less cylindric, or with a slightly swollen base; orange to orangish. **Flesh:** Whitish to orangish or brownish, with zones of blue or brown; tough but pliant. **Odor and Taste:** Mealy. **Chemical Reactions:** KOH olive green to blackish or purplish black on flesh. **Spore Print:** Brown. **Microscopic Features:** Spores 5–6.5 × 4.5–5.5 µm; subglobose to irregular; with low warts. Clamp connections absent. **Comments:** Compare with *Phellodon alboniger* (p. 306).

HYDNELLUM CONCRESCENS (PERSOON) BANKER

Ecology: Mycorrhizal with hardwoods (especially oaks); growing alone or gregariously; summer and fall; widely distributed. **Cap:** Often fused with other caps; 2–10 cm wide; plano-convex, becoming flat or shallowly depressed; finely velvety or nearly bald; not infrequently developing pits, radially arranged ridges, or elaborate outgrowths; brownish pink to pinkish brown, sometimes fading to nearly whitish; with concentric zones of texture and/or color; the fresh margin bruising dark brown to black. **Undersurface:** Running down the stem; covered with crowded spines that are 1–3 mm long; whitish at first, becoming brownish to brown. **Stem:** 2–4 cm long; 0.5–2 cm thick at apex; often swollen and velvety or spongy, especially toward the base. **Flesh:** Pinkish to brownish, often with zones of these shades; tough but pliant. **Odor and Taste:** Odor not distinctive, or mealy; taste mild or mealy. **Chemical Reactions:** KOH on flesh blue green to olive, then slowly gray to black, or promptly black. **Spore Print:** Brown. **Microscopic Features:** Spores 4–7 µm; subglobose to irregular; prominently nodulose. Clamp connections absent. **Comments:** *Hydnellum scrobiculatum* is similar but grows under conifers and features an azonate cap. Compare with *Hydnellum spongiosipes* (below), which features longer spines, a spongy, swollen stem base, an azonate, rugged, or pitted cap surface that is not ridged or decorated with outgrowths, 2-layered flesh, and tuberculate spores.

HYDNELLUM SPONGIOSIPES (PECK) POUZAR

Ecology: Mycorrhizal with oaks (especially white oak) and other hardwoods; growing alone or gregariously; summer and fall; widely distributed. **Cap:** Single or fused with other caps; 2–10 cm wide; convex, becoming broadly convex to flat; cinnamon brown to dark brown; velvety; sometimes rugged or pitted; paler areas bruising dark brown. **Undersurface:** Running down the stem; covered with crowded spines that are 4–7 mm long; pale to lilac brown; sometimes bruising dark brown; darker brown in age. **Stem:** 3–10 cm long; 1–3 cm thick at apex; club-shaped; swollen and much thicker below; spongy; dark brown; velvety. **Flesh:** 2-layered. Upper layer pale brown and fairly soft; lower layer dark brown to purplish brown and corky. **Odor and Taste:** Odor mealy or not distinctive; taste mealy or mild. **Chemical Reactions:** KOH on flesh olive green to blackish or slowly black. **Spore Print:** Brown. **Microscopic Features:** Spores 4.5–7 × 4–5.5 µm; subglobose or irregular; prominently tuberculate. Clamp connections absent. **Comments**: Compare with *Hydnellum concrescens* (pp. 208–9, above).

Photo by Ron Kerner

2-layered flesh

HYDNUM REPANDUM LINNAEUS

Ecology: Mycorrhizal with hardwoods or conifers; growing alone or gregariously; summer and fall; widely distributed. **Cap:** 2–17 cm wide; broadly convex, becoming flat with a central depression; the margin inrolled at first; dry; bald, but softly leathery; dull orange tan or paler. **Undersurface:** Running down the stem; covered with spines that are 2–7 mm long; pale or dull orange; bruising dark orange or yellowish brown. **Stem:** 3–10 cm long; 1–3 cm thick; sometimes somewhat off-center; dry; bald; whitish or colored like the cap; bruising orangish brown to brownish. **Flesh:** Whitish; often discoloring yellowish when exposed or bruised. **Odor and Taste:** Taste mild or peppery; odor mild. **Spore Print:** White. **Microscopic Features:** Spores 6.5–9 × 5.5–8 µm; broadly ellipsoid to subglobose; smooth. Clamp connections present. **Comments:** Also known as *Dentinum repandum*. Sometimes called the "hedgehog mushroom." Edible and very good. *Hydnum umbilicatum* is a very similar species found in northern conifer bogs; it features a centrally depressed, smaller cap.

HYGROCYBE CANTHARELLUS (SCHWEINITZ) MURRILL

Ecology: Saprobic under hardwoods or conifers; growing alone or gregariously; summer and fall; widely distributed. **Cap:** 1–3.5 cm; convex, remaining so or developing a central depression; dry; silky, developing tiny scales with age; reddish orange, orange, or pale orange; fading with age. **Gills:** Running down the stem; distant or nearly so; orange to yellow, but usually paler than the cap. **Stem:** 3–10 cm long; 2–8 mm thick; colored like the cap, or paler; whitish to yellowish at the base; equal; dry. **Flesh:** Colored like the cap; thin. **Odor and Taste:** Not distinctive. **Spore Print:** White. **Microscopic Features:** Spores 7–12 × 4–6 µm; smooth; ellipsoid. Gill tissue parallel. **Comments:** Compare with *Hygrocybe miniata* (p. 212), which has a scarlet cap when young and fresh, attached gills that do not run down the stem, a shorter stem, and smaller spores.

HYGROCYBE CONICA (SCHAEFFER) KUMMER

Ecology: Saprobic under hardwoods or conifers; growing alone or gregariously; spring through fall; widely distributed. **Cap:** 2–7 cm; sharply to broadly conic or sometimes convex, with a conic central point; sticky when fresh, but soon dry; bald or finely hairy in age; scarlet to reddish orange, often with olive to greenish tints; bruising and discoloring black with age. **Gills:** Nearly free from the stem; close; thick; whitish, becoming yellowish orange or olive yellow; bruising black. **Stem:** 6–11 cm long; 5–10 mm thick; colored like the cap, but white at the base; equal; moist but not sticky; splitting; often grooved lengthwise or twisted; hollow; bruising black. **Flesh:** Colored like the cap; thin; slowly blackening. **Odor and Taste:** Not distinctive. **Chemical Reactions:** KOH negative on cap. **Spore Print:** White. **Microscopic Features:** Spores 9–12 × 5.5–6.5 µm; smooth; ellipsoid. Gill tissue parallel. **Comments:** Sometimes called the "witch's hat." The colors of this mushroom are variable and range from scarlet to orange or orangish yellow. Compare with *Hygrocybe cuspidata* (below) and *Hygrocybe persistens* (p. 212), neither of which bruises black.

HYGROCYBE CUSPIDATA (PECK) MURRILL

Ecology: Saprobic under hardwoods or conifers; growing gregariously; spring through fall; widely distributed. **Cap:** 2–7 cm; conical, expanding a little in age; sticky when fresh; the margin often upturned and splitting in age; scarlet red when fresh, fading to orange. **Gills:** Free from the stem or slightly attached to it; close or almost distant; thick by maturity; pale orange or orangish yellow; often with eroded edges in age. **Stem:** 5–9 cm long; 5–10 mm thick; equal or slightly tapering to apex; dry; bald, but often becoming grooved lengthwise; becoming hollow; colored like the cap or paler; whitish near the base. **Flesh:** Yellowish or whitish; thin; sometimes turning grayish near the cap margin or in the stem base a few hours after being sliced. **Odor and Taste:** Not distinctive. **Spore Print:** White. **Microscopic Features:** Spores 8–12 × 4–6.5 µm; smooth; ellipsoid. Gill tissue parallel. **Comments:** Compare with *Hygrocybe conica* (above), which bruises and discolors black, and with *Hygrocybe persistens* (p. 212), which is yellow or orange. Some mycologists do not recognize *Hygrocybe cuspidata* as a distinct species from *Hygrocybe persistens*, since it differs primarily in color.

HYGROCYBE MINIATA (FRIES) KUMMER

Ecology: Saprobic in hardwood forests and in mixed woods; on soil or in moss; sometimes on rotting logs; growing gregariously; summer and fall; widely distributed. **Cap:** 2–4 cm; broadly convex, with an incurved margin when young; becoming broadly convex or nearly flat; dry or slightly moist; bald or minutely scaly or hairy; scarlet when young and fresh, but often fading to orange or yellow; the margin sometimes thinly lined. **Gills:** Attached to the stem, but sometimes beginning to run down it; close or almost distant; thick; colored like the cap or paler. **Stem:** 3–5 cm long; 3–5 mm thick; equal; dry; bald; colored like the cap but fading more slowly. **Flesh:** Colored like the cap or paler; thin. **Odor and Taste:** Not distinctive. **Spore Print:** White. **Microscopic Features:** Spores 6–8 × 4–5 µm; smooth; ellipsoid. Gill tissue parallel or nearly so. **Comments:** Defining features include the scarlet-colored, relatively dry, convex cap and the attached gills that do not run far down the stem. Compare with *Hygrocybe cantharellus* (p. 210).

HYGROCYBE PERSISTENS (BRTIZELMAYR) SINGER

Ecology: Saprobic under hardwoods or conifers; growing alone or scattered; spring through fall; widely distributed. **Cap:** 2–10 cm; conical when young, becoming bell-shaped with a central nipple; slimy to sticky; the margin often faintly lined when young, becoming uplifted and torn in age; yellow to orange. **Gills:** Free from the stem or narrowly attached to it; close or almost distant; thick; yellow. **Stem:** 6–8 cm long; 3–6 mm thick; more or less equal; dry, greasy, or somewhat sticky (especially on handling); often becoming grooved or split lengthwise; colored like the cap; white near the base; the base sometimes becoming grayish or blackish in age. **Flesh:** Yellowish; thin. **Odor and Taste:** Not distinctive. **Spore Print:** White. **Microscopic Features:** Spores 9–14 × 5–7.5 µm; smooth; ellipsoid. Gill tissue parallel or nearly so. **Comments:** Also known as *Hygrocybe acutoconica*. Compare with *Hygrocybe cuspidata* (p. 211) and with *Hygrocybe conica* (p. 211).

HYGROCYBE PRATENSIS (SCHAEFFER) MURRILL

Ecology: Saprobic; frequently found in open areas and grassy places, or in woods under hardwoods or conifers; growing scattered to gregariously or, occasionally, in small clusters; late spring through fall; widely distributed. **Cap:** 2–7 cm; slightly irregular to convex when young, becoming convex to flat, or with an uplifted margin; dry; with minute, appressed fibers, at least when young; orange to cinnamon orange when young and fresh, but soon fading to orangish buff; often somewhat cracked over the disc by maturity; the margin not lined. **Gills:** Running slightly down the stem; distant or nearly so; thick and waxy; creamy orangish; often with cross-veins by maturity. **Stem:** 3–8 cm long; 0.5–2 cm thick; equal; bald; dry; white, or tinged with the cap color. **Flesh:** White; brittle. **Odor and Taste:** Not distinctive. **Chemical Reactions:** KOH negative on cap. **Spore Print:** White. **Microscopic Features:** Spores 5.5–8 × 3.5–5 µm; smooth; ellipsoid or subglobose. Gill tissue interwoven. **Comments:** Also known as *Camarophyllus pratensis* and *Hygrophorus pratensis*. The dry surfaces, dull orangish colors, and distant gills that begin to run down the stem are good preliminary identification characters.

Photo by Dan Molter

HYGROCYBE PSITTACINA (SCHAEFFER) KUMMER

Ecology: Saprobic in conifer and hardwood forests; growing scattered to gregariously; frequently found on embankments along wooded roadsides; spring through fall; widely distributed. **Cap:** 1–3 cm; broadly conic to bell-shaped, becoming convex to flat; slimy, or appearing lacquered when dried out; dark green when young, but soon changing to yellowish, orangish, or pinkish; finally dingy straw yellow; the margin thinly lined at first. **Gills:** Attached to the stem; almost distant, thick and waxy; light green, becoming reddish to yellowish. **Stem:** 3–7 cm long; 2–5 mm thick; green above or completely green when young, changing to yellow or orange like the cap; slimy; equal. **Flesh:** Colored like the cap; thin. **Odor and Taste:** Not distinctive. **Spore Print:** White. **Microscopic Features:** Spores 6.5–8 × 4–5 µm; smooth; ellipsoid. Gill tissue parallel. **Comments:** Sometimes called the "parrot mushroom." When fresh and young, this species is easily recognized due to its green colors and slimy surfaces, but older specimens that have lost all trace of green can be baffling.

Photo by Dan Molter

HYGROCYBE PUNICEA (FRIES) KUMMER

Ecology: Saprobic under hardwoods or conifers; growing scattered or gregariously; spring through fall; widely distributed. **Cap:** 3–15 cm; broadly convex, soon expanding to broadly bell-shaped or bluntly conical (or eventually more or less flat); greasy or thinly sticky when fresh; smooth, or very finely rugged; dark red, fading to brownish red, orangish red, or buff. **Gills:** Narrowly attached to the stem; distant or nearly so; thick and waxy; buff to reddish or orangish; often with yellowish edges. **Stem:** 3–15 cm long; up to 1.5 cm thick; equal or slightly tapering at either end; dry; stringy; usually splitting and becoming finely hairy; a mixture of orange, yellow, and/or red; usually paler than the cap; often with a whitish base. **Flesh:** Thin; yellowish, or whitish near the center. **Odor and Taste:** Not distinctive. **Spore Print:** White. **Microscopic Features:** Spores 7–11 × 4.5–5.5 µm; smooth; ellipsoid. Gill tissue parallel. **Comments:** Compare with *Hygrocybe miniata* (p. 212), which features a convex, dry cap, a shorter and narrower stem, and smaller spores. *Hygrocybe coccinea* is a very similar but smaller species.

HYGROCYBE VIRGINEA (WULFEN) ORTON & WATLING

Spore print

Ecology: Saprobic; growing gregariously near hardwoods or conifers; often in areas that have been recently cleared and then allowed to redevelop (park edges, roadbanks, and so on), or in thick and untended grass under dense brambles and ground cover; summer and fall; widely distributed. **Cap:** 1–7 cm; convex when young, becoming broadly convex to flat, or with a shallow central depression and an uplifted margin; moist and greasy when fresh; bald; off-white, drying out to pure white from the margin inward; the margin sometimes faintly lined. **Gills:** Running down the stem or beginning to do so; distant or nearly so; thick and waxy; whitish. **Stem:** 2–9 cm long; up to 1 cm or more thick; often tapering to base; dry; bald or very finely hairy at maturity; whitish. **Flesh:** White; unchanging. **Odor and Taste:** Not distinctive. **Spore Print:** White. **Microscopic Features:** Spores 7–10 × 4.5–7 µm; smooth; ellipsoid. Gill tissue interwoven.

HYGROPHOROPSIS AURANTIACA (WULFEN) MAIRE

Ecology: Saprobic, decomposing forest litter and woody debris; usually found under conifers; occasionally growing from well-rotted wood; growing alone, scattered, or gregariously; summer and fall; widely distributed, but more common where conifers occur naturally. **Cap:** 2–10 cm; convex, becoming broadly convex, flat, or shallowly depressed; dry; very finely velvety and soft to the touch; the margin initially inrolled; color variable, but usually brown, orange, or somewhere between (occasionally nearly white or black); often with a browner center and a margin that is more orange. **Gills:** Running down the stem; close or crowded; repeatedly forked; pale to bright orange. **Stem:** 2–10 cm long; up to 1.5 cm thick; more or less equal; colored like the cap; bald or very finely velvety. **Flesh:** Thin; whitish to orangish. **Odor and Taste:** Mild. **Spore Print:** White. **Chemical Reactions:** KOH reddish on cap. **Microscopic Features:** Spores 5–8 × 3–5 µm; smooth; ellipsoid; dextrinoid, or with both inamyloid and dextrinoid spores present. Cystidia absent. Pileipellis a cutis. **Comments:** Not recommended for the table. Compare with *Cantharellus cibarius* (p. 131), which has false, rather than true, gills and does not usually associate with conifers in the Midwest; also with *Omphalotus illudens* (p. 292), which grows in dense clusters on wood, and *Cortinarius hesleri* (p. 156), which features a rusty-brown spore print and, when young, a cortina.

HYGROPHORUS OCCIDENTALIS A. H. SMITH & HESLER

Ecology: Mycorrhizal with hardwoods; growing scattered to gregariously; fall; widely distributed. **Cap:** 2–8 cm; convex when young, becoming broadly convex to flat, often with a central depression; slimy; bald, or with minute pressed-down fibers under the slime; whitish at first, but soon developing grayish to brownish shades over the center; the margin typically remaining paler. **Gills:** Attached to the stem or running down it; distant or close; white to creamy.

Stem: 2–7 cm long; 3–10 mm thick; equal above, tapering to base; slimy, at least over the lower portion; with tiny white fibers over the dry apex; white or becoming tinged with the cap color; stuffed. **Flesh:** White; unchanging. **Odor and Taste:** Not distinctive. **Chemical Reactions:** KOH golden orange on cap. **Spore Print:** White. **Microscopic Features:** Spores 6–8 × 3.5–5 µm; smooth; ellipsoid; inamyloid. Gill tissue divergent. **Comments:** Identification characters include the slimy white cap that becomes grayish to brownish over the center, the slimy stem, and the appearance under hardwoods in the fall.

HYGROPHORUS RUSSULA (SCHAEFFER) KAUFFMAN

Ecology: Mycorrhizal with oaks and other hardwoods; growing scattered or gregariously, sometimes in fairy rings or arcs; late summer and fall; widely distributed. **Cap:** 5–12 cm; convex or round when young, becoming broadly convex to flat; sticky at first, but often drying out quickly; bald, or finely hairy in places; the margin inrolled and soft or cottony, eventually unrolling; reddish to pinkish, often with streaks or spots of color; bruising yellow in places, especially near the margin. **Gills:** Attached to the stem or beginning to run down it; close; white when young, but soon developing reddish spots or becoming pinkish overall. **Stem:** 3–7 cm long; 1.5–3.5 cm thick; more or less equal; white at first but soon developing the colors of the cap; bald or finely hairy; solid. **Flesh:** White, or flushed with pink; thick; hard. **Odor and Taste:** Not distinctive. **Chemical Reactions:** KOH grayish to brownish on cap, erasing pink pigments. **Spore Print:** White. **Microscopic Features:** Spores 6–8 × 3–4.5 µm; smooth; ellipsoid. Gill tissue divergent. **Comments:** Edible but not very good. In the northern Midwest the very similar *Hygrophorus purpurascens* appears under conifers; it has a cortina-like partial veil when very young.

Photo by Melissa Bochte

HYGROPHORUS SORDIDUS PECK

Ecology: Mycorrhizal with oaks; growing gregariously; summer and fall; widely distributed. **Cap:** 8–20 cm; convex when young, becoming broadly convex or nearly flat; slimy; bald; white, sometimes developing a dingy yellowish center with age. **Gills:** Attached to the stem or beginning to run down it; nearly distant; white, unchanging or becoming slightly yellowish with age. **Stem:** 6–10 cm long; up to 3 cm thick; more or less equal above a tapered base;

dry; bald or finely hairy toward the apex; whitish, becoming a little brownish where handled. **Flesh:** White; unchanging. **Odor and Taste:** Not distinctive. **Spore Print:** White. **Chemical Reactions:** KOH negative on cap. **Microscopic Features:** Spores 6–8 × 4–5.5 µm; smooth; ellipsoid; inamyloid. Gill tissue divergent. **Comments:** Compare with *Clitocybe subconnexa* (p. 143), which has crowded gills and a satiny sheen on the cap and stem, and with *Tricholoma subresplendens* (p. 380), which has gills attached by a notch, a dryer cap, and a mealy odor.

HYPHOLOMA CAPNOIDES (FRIES) KUMMER

Ecology: Saprobic; growing in clusters on decaying conifer logs; common in red pine plantations after trimming operations; spring or late fall; widely distributed, but more common in the northern Midwest. **Cap:** 2–7.5 cm; convex to broadly convex; sometimes with an incurved margin when young; often with partial veil remnants on the margin; bald; dry; usually orange brown to cinnamon brown, but sometimes yellowish or brownish; sometimes paler toward the margin. **Gills:** Attached to the stem or pulling away from it; whitish to pale gray at first, becoming darker gray and eventually nearly purple brown; close. **Stem:** 5–10 cm long; 5–10 mm thick; usually tapering to base; bald, or with small partial veil fibrils in a ring zone near the cap; colored like the cap, paler. **Flesh:** Pale; thin. **Odor and Taste:** Not distinctive. **Spore Print:** Purple brown. **Microscopic Features:** Spores 6–7.5 × 3.5–4.5 µm; ellipsoid; smooth; with a small pore. Pleurocystidia with refractive contents. Cheilocystidia present. **Comments:** Compare with *Galerina marginata* (p. 178), which has a rusty-brown spore print and mature gills, and with *Hypholoma sublateritium* (p. 218), which has a brick-colored cap and fruits from the wood of hardwoods.

HYPHOLOMA FASCICULARE (HUDSON) KUMMER

Ecology: Saprobic; growing in clusters on decaying logs and stumps of conifers; fall and early winter, sometimes in spring; widely distributed. **Cap:** 2–5 cm; conical to convex at first, becoming broadly convex to flat; bald; dry; bright sulphur yellow to greenish yellow when fresh (but sometimes yellowish orange when young), often with a darker center; the margin occasionally with small partial veil fragments. **Gills:** Attached to the stem or pulling away from it;

Photo by Patrick Harvey

close or crowded; sulphur yellow, becoming olive or greenish yellow, eventually dusted with spores and spotted purplish brown to blackish. **Stem:** 5–12 cm long; 3–10 mm thick; more or less equal, or tapering to base, bright yellow to tawny, developing rusty-brown stains from the base upward; sometimes with a faint ring zone. **Flesh:** Thin; yellow. **Odor and Taste:** Odor not distinctive; taste bitter. **Spore Print:** Purple brown. **Microscopic Features:** Spores: 6–8 × 3.5–5 µm; ellipsoid; smooth; with a pore. Pleurocystidia ventricose to mucronate, often with a long neck; with refractive contents. Cheilocystidia fusoid-ventricose. **Comments:** The yellow colors, bitter taste, purple-brown spore print, and habitat on the wood of conifers are good field characters.

Photo by Patrick Harvey

HYPHOLOMA SUBLATERITIUM (SCHAEFFER) QUÉLET

Ecology: Saprobic; growing in clusters on decaying hardwood logs and stumps; fall; widely distributed. **Cap:** 4–10 cm; convex to broadly convex, or occasionally nearly flat in age; with an incurved margin when young; bald; dry or moist; brick red, paler on the margin. **Gills:** Attached to the stem; close or crowded; whitish to pale gray at first, becoming purple gray. **Stem:** 5–10 cm long; 0.5–1.5 cm thick; more or less equal; often twisted due to clustered growth pattern; bald or a little shaggy; sometimes with a faint ring zone near the top; whitish above, reddish below; sometimes bruising and staining yellow. **Flesh:** Firm; cream-colored. **Odor and Taste:** Odor not distinctive; taste mild to bitter. **Spore Print:** Purple brown to purple black. **Microscopic Features:** Spores 6–7.5 × 3.5–4.5 µm; ellipsoid; smooth; with an obscure pore. Pleurocystidia with refractive contents. Cheilocystidia present. **Comments:** Compare with *Galerina marginata* (p. 178), which features a rusty-brown spore print, and with *Hypholoma capnoides* (p. 217), which grows on the wood of conifers.

HYPOMYCES LACTIFLUORUM (SCHWEINITZ) TULASNE & C. TULASNE

Ecology: Parasitic on species of *Russula* and *Lactarius*; growing alone or gregariously in woods; summer and fall; widely distributed. **Fruiting Body:** A hard, orange covering; attacking the host rapidly and soon engulfing it entirely; the surface dotted with tiny pimples. **Microscopic Features:** Spores 35–50 × 4–5 µm; fusiform; warty; colorless; septate. **Comments:** Edible, but care should be taken to identify the host as an edible species.

Photo by Charya Peou

HYPOMYCES LUTEOVIRENS (FRIES) TULASNE & C. TULASNE

Ecology: Parasitic on various species of *Russula*, which have diverse habitats; summer and fall; widely distributed. **Fruiting Body:** A powdery, mold-like covering over the gills and stem of the host; yellow to yellowish green; becoming hard and pimply. **Microscopic Features:** Spores 30–36 × 4.5–5.5 µm; without septa.

Photo by Ron Kerner

HYPSIZYGUS ULMARIUS (BULLIARD) REDHEAD

Ecology: Saprobic; growing alone or in small groups from branch scars of living hardwoods (especially elms); summer and fall; widely distributed. **Cap:** 5–15 cm; convex, becoming plano-convex or nearly flat; bald, but often cracking with age to form tiny scales; whitish to pale tan. **Gills:** Attached to the stem; close or nearly distant; whitish, becoming cream. **Stem:** Sometimes slightly off-center; 5–10 cm long; 1–2.5 cm thick; dry; bald or finely hairy; whitish; solid. **Flesh:** Firm; white. **Odor and Taste:** Not distinctive. **Chemical Reactions:** KOH nega-

tive on cap. **Spore Print:** White. **Microscopic Features:** Spores 5–6 µm; globose; smooth; inamyloid. Pileipellis a cutis. Clamp connections present. **Comments:** Edible. Compare with *Pleurotus dryinus* (p. 314), which features a partial veil and a densely hairy stem and which yellows with age.

INFUNDIBULICYBE GIBBA (PERSOON) HARMAJA

Ecology: Saprobic; growing alone, scattered, or gregariously; primarily found under hardwoods (especially oaks), but sometimes reported under conifers; summer and fall; widely distributed. **Cap:** 3–9 cm; at first flat or with a central depression, becoming deeply vase-shaped; bald; dry or slightly tacky; tan, pinkish tan, or flesh-colored; fading with age; sometimes with a wavy margin in maturity. **Gills:** Running down the stem; close or crowded; white or pale cream. **Stem:** 2.5–8 cm long; up to 1 cm thick; equal; dry; bald; whitish, off-white, or a very pale version of the cap color; base often covered with white mycelium. **Flesh:** Thin; whitish. **Odor and Taste:** Taste mild; odor sweet, or not distinctive. **Spore Print:** White. **Microscopic Features:** Spores 5–9 × 3.5–6 µm; lacrymoid; smooth; inamyloid. Cystidia absent. Pileipellis a cutis. Clamp connections present. **Comments:** Also known as *Clitocybe gibba*.

INOCYBE ADAEQUATA (BRITZELMAYR) SACCARDO

Ecology: Mycorrhizal with hardwoods; growing alone, scattered, or gregariously, often in disturbed ground (pathsides, the edges of woods, and so on); summer and fall; widely distributed. **Cap:** 3–8 cm; conical to bell-shaped, becoming broadly bell-shaped; dry; radially hairy; purplish brown to reddish brown, somewhat darker over the center; the margin usually splitting and the surface usually becoming radially separated. **Gills:** Attached to the stem but sometimes pulling away from it in age; close; white, becoming brownish with maturity (and then often with whitish edges); sometimes discoloring pinkish to reddish. **Stem:** 3–8 cm long; up to 1.5 cm thick; equal, or with a swollen base; dry; hairy; whitish above, becoming pinkish to pinkish lilac below; sometimes bruising pinkish red. **Flesh:** Whitish overall, but often pinkish or pale lilac in places. **Odor:** Mildly mealy, fruity, or unpleasant. **Chemical Reactions:** KOH negative on cap. **Spore Print:** Brown. **Microscopic Features:** Spores 9–15 × 5–8 µm; more or less ellipsoid; smooth. Pleurocystidia absent. Cheilocystidia cylindric to clavate; thin-walled. **Comments:** Also known as *Inocybe jurana*. Best identified with microscopic analysis of spores and cystidia.

INOCYBE CALOSPORA QUÉLET

Cystidia

Ecology: Mycorrhizal with hardwoods; growing gregariously, often in groups of about a dozen mushrooms; summer and fall; widely distributed. **Cap:** 1–3 cm; conical at first, becoming broadly bell-shaped or flat with a pointy central bump; dry; scaly; dark brown to brown. **Gills:** Attached to the stem (sometimes by a notch) or nearly free from it; close or nearly distant; whitish to pale tan, becoming medium brown or cinnamon brown, with white edges. **Stem:** 2–6 cm long; up to 3 mm thick; more or less equal, with a small basal bulb; dry; very finely hairy; usually pale cinnamon brown to pale reddish brown (sometimes whitish or dark brown); fairly tough; basal mycelium white. **Flesh:** Yellowish to brownish; insubstantial. **Odor:** Slightly sweet and fragrant, or not distinctive. **Chemical Reactions:** KOH negative to slightly pinkish on cap. **Spore Print:** Brown. **Microscopic Features:** Spores 9.5–13.5 × 8.5–11 µm (including ornamentation); subglobose; covered with prominent spines 2–3 µm long. Pleurocystidia scattered; fusoid or clavate, often with a flattened apex; thick-walled; sparsely apically encrusted. **Comments:** Best identified with microscopic analysis of spores and cystidia.

INOCYBE FIBROSA (SOWERBY) GILLET

Spores

Ecology: Mycorrhizal; growing gregariously in hardwood lowlands; summer and fall; widely distributed. **Cap:** 4–10 cm; broadly bell-shaped, becoming broadly convex, with a central bump; dry; silky; whitish, sometimes developing yellowish stains; the margin often splitting when mature. **Gills:** Attached to the stem (sometimes by a notch) or nearly free from it; close; whitish, becoming grayish brown and eventually medium brown to cinnamon brown. **Stem:** 4–8 cm long; up to about 1.5 cm thick; more or less equal, with a slightly swollen base; dry; silky or bald; whitish, developing yellowish to grayish stains and discolorations. **Flesh:** Whitish. **Odor:** Spermatic. **Chemical Reactions:** KOH negative on cap. **Spore Print:** Dull brown.

Microscopic Features: Spores 9–13 × 5–7 µm; angular; nodulose. Pleurocystidia cylindric or subfusiform; thick-walled; sometimes apically encrusted. **Comments:** We adhere to the concept of *Inocybe fibrosa* in the sense of Kauffman (1918, 1924), which may be distinct from the European species. The large size (for the genus), the white colors, and the microscopic features are distinctive.

INOCYBE GEOPHYLLA (SOWERBY) KUMMER

Ecology: Mycorrhizal with hardwoods and conifers; growing alone, scattered, or gregariously; summer and fall; widely distributed. **Cap:** 1–4 cm; conical at first, becoming broadly bell-shaped or broadly convex; dry; silky or almost bald; whitish; the margin often splitting when mature. **Gills:** Attached to the stem, sometimes by a notch; close; whitish, becoming grayish brown and eventually medium brown; covered at first by a white cortina. **Stem:** 1–6 cm long; up to about 5 mm thick; more or less equal; dry; silky; whitish; fairly firm. **Flesh:** Whitish; insubstantial. **Odor:** Spermatic, or sometimes not distinctive. **Chemical Reactions:** KOH negative on cap. **Spore Print:** Dull brown. **Microscopic Features:** Spores 8–10 × 4.5–6 µm; more or less ellipsoid; smooth. Cystidia fusoid or fusoid-ventricose, often with a flattened apex; abundant; thick-walled; apically encrusted. **Comments:** Compare with *Inocybe fibrosa* (p. 221), which is larger and features different microscopic characters.

INOCYBE LACERA (FRIES) KUMMER

Ecology: Mycorrhizal with conifers or hardwoods; growing alone, scattered, or gregariously; summer and fall; widely distributed. **Cap:** 1.5–4 cm; convex to conical, becoming broadly convex or broadly bell-shaped; dry; densely hairy or scaly, becoming cracked and lacerated; brown; sometimes with pale remnants of the cortina along the margin. **Gills:** Attached to the stem; close or crowded; pale at first, becoming brownish with maturity (and then usually with whitish edges); at first sparsely covered by an ephemeral cortina. **Stem:** 1–4 cm long; up to 0.5 or nearly 1 cm thick; more or less equal; dry; finely hairy or bald; pale brown-

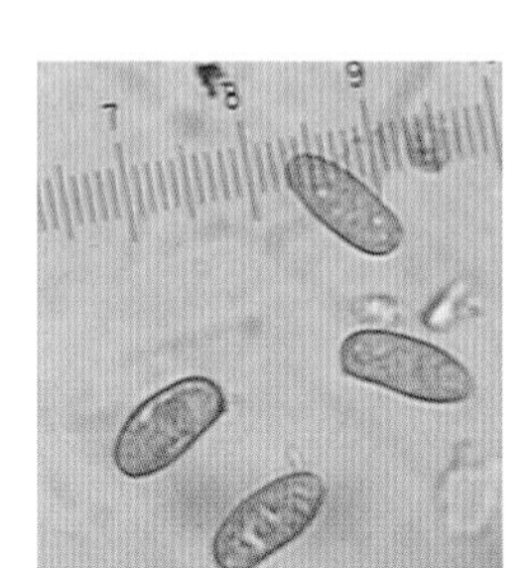

Spores

ish; rarely with a thin ring zone resulting from the cortina. **Flesh:** Whitish or tan. **Odor:** Not distinctive. **Chemical Reactions:** KOH gray on cap. **Spore Print:** Brown. **Microscopic Features:** Spores 12–17 × 4.5–6 µm; long-ellipsoid or nearly cylindric; smooth. Pleurocystidia fusiform or fusoid-ventricose; walls 1–3 µm thick; often apically encrusted. Cheilocystidia similar to pleurocystidia. **Comments:** Best identified with microscopic analysis of spores and cystidia.

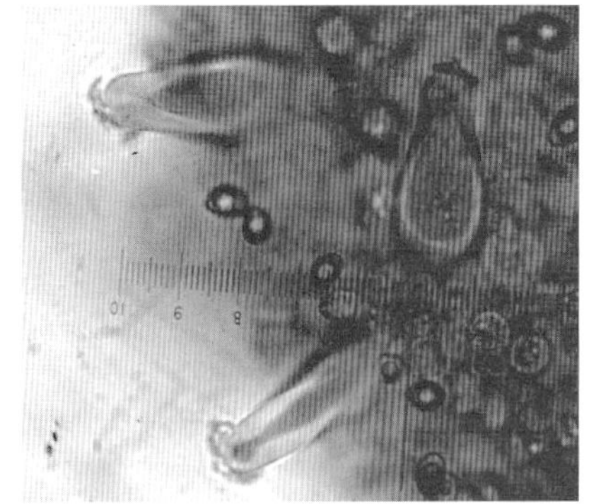

Cystidia

INOCYBE LILACINA (PECK) KAUFFMAN

Ecology: Mycorrhizal with hardwoods and conifers; growing alone, scattered, or gregariously; late summer and fall; widely distributed. **Cap:** 1.5–4 cm; conical to bell-shaped, becoming broadly bell-shaped; dry; silky or bald; purple to lilac overall, but often mottled with pinkish, whitish, or brownish hues; sometimes fading to nearly white overall when old or exposed to direct sunlight; the margin often inrolled somewhat when young, and usually splitting when mature. **Gills:** Attached to the stem, sometimes by a notch; close; whitish or pale lilac, becoming grayish brown and eventually brown with pale edges; covered at first by a white cortina. **Stem:** 3–6 cm long; up to 1 cm thick; equal, or enlarged toward the base; dry; finely hairy; lilac or whitish; the base whitish; sometimes with a faint ring zone. **Flesh:** Whitish or lilac. **Odor:** Spermatic. **Chemical Reactions:** KOH negative on cap. **Spore Print:** Brown. **Microscopic Features:** Spores 7–9 × 4–5.5 µm; more or less ellipsoid; smooth. Pleurocystidia fusoid-ventricose; abundant; thick-walled; apically encrusted. Cheilocystidia similar to pleurocystidia. **Comments:** Also known as *Inocybe geophylla* var. *lilacina*. Compare with *Cortinarius iodeoides* (p. 157), which features a rusty-brown spore print, roughened spores, and a cap that sometimes develops yellowish spots but does not usually become mottled with brownish and whitish areas.

Spores

INOCYBE RIMOSA (BULLIARD) KUMMER

Ecology: Mycorrhizal with hardwoods or conifers; growing alone, scattered, or gregariously; summer and fall; widely distributed. **Cap:** 2–8 cm; conical to bell-shaped, becoming broadly bell-shaped, usually with a sharp and distinct central bump; dry; silky or finely hairy; straw yellow to yellowish or yellowish brown; the margin splitting and the surface becoming radially separated. **Gills:** Attached to the stem but sometimes pulling away from it in age; close or crowded; whitish, becoming grayish and then brownish with maturity (sometimes developing a greenish cast). **Stem:** 3–9 cm long; up to 1 cm thick; more or less equal, without a swollen base; dry; bald or finely silky; sometimes twisted or grooved; whitish or pale yellowish. **Flesh:** Whitish; insubstantial. **Odor:** Spermatic, mealy, or not distinctive. **Chemical Reactions:** KOH negative on cap. **Spore Print:** Brown. **Microscopic Features:** Spores 9.5–14.5 × 6–8.5 µm; ellipsoid; smooth. Pleurocystidia absent. Cheilocystidia cylindric to nearly clavate; thin-walled. **Comments:** Also known as *Inocybe fastigiata*. Best identified with microscopic analysis of spores and cystidia.

INONOTUS DRYADEUS (PERSOON) MURRILL

Ecology: Parasitic on living oaks; causing a white butt rot and root rot; annual; growing alone, gregariously, or in shelving clusters; summer and fall; widely distributed. **Cap:** Up to 40 cm across; semicircular, kidney-shaped, cushion-shaped, or irregular; usually convex; finely velvety, becoming bald with age; often lumpy; buff to dull yellow, becoming brown with age; often exuding drops of amber liquid when fresh, especially along the margin; the margin thick. **Pore Surface:** Buff to yellowish when young, becoming brown; bruising slowly brown; exuding drops of amber liquid when fresh and young; with 4–6 circular to angular pores per mm; tubes to 2 cm deep. **Stem:** Absent. **Flesh:** Yellowish brown becoming reddish brown; soft, becoming leathery or corky; zoned. **Chemical Reactions:** Flesh black with KOH. **Spore Print:** Yellowish to brownish. **Microscopic Features:** Spores 6–8 × 5–7 µm; smooth; subglobose; hyaline in KOH; dextrinoid. Setae usually present, but sometimes very rare; usually curved. Hyphal system monomitic. **Comments:** The positioning at the base of the tree, dull yellow cap, and buff pore surface that bruises brown are good field characters.

ISCHNODERMA RESINOSUM (SCHRADER) KARSTEN

Ecology: Saprobic on the deadwood of hardwoods and conifers; annual; causing a whitish to yellowish rot that separates the annual rings in the wood and often smells of anise; appearing on recently fallen wood and on wood that has been down for several years, but not typically on well-rotted wood; growing alone, gregariously, or in overlapping clusters; usually appearing in fall; widely distributed. **Cap:** Usually present and well developed, but sometimes present merely as a folded-over edge above a spreading pore surface, and occasionally almost entirely absent; up to 20 cm across; irregularly bracket-shaped or kidney-shaped; broadly convex; when young quite thick and fleshy, with a pale brownish, finely velvety surface and a thick white margin that can be adorned with water droplets in wet weather; in maturity becoming dark brown, sometimes with zones of color, fairly bald, dry, and tough. **Pore Surface:** When young, whitish, soft, promptly bruising brown; in maturity pale brown and hard; with 4–6 angular or round pores per mm; tubes to 1 cm deep. **Stem:** Absent. **Flesh:** Whitish and soft at first; darkening to brownish or cinnamon brown, and becoming tougher with maturity. **Odor and Taste:** Not distinctive. **Chemical Reactions:** All parts grayish to blackish with KOH. **Spore Print:** White. **Microscopic Features:** Spores 5–7 × 1.5–2 µm; smooth; cylindric; inamyloid. Setae absent. Hyphal system dimitic, with clamp connections. **Comments:** The soft flesh when young, the quickly and conspicuously bruising pore surface, and the KOH reaction are good identification characters.

Photo by Martin Livezey

LACCARIA AMETHYSTINA (HUDSON) COOKE

Ecology: Mycorrhizal with hardwoods, especially oaks and beech; growing alone, scattered, or gregariously; late spring and summer; widely distributed. **Cap:** 0.5–3.5 cm; broadly convex to flat, or developing a central depression; the margin even or inrolled, not lined, or slightly lined at maturity; finely hairy-scaly, or nearly bald; bright grayish purple, fading to buff; changing color markedly as it dries out, often resulting in 2-toned specimens. **Gills:** Attached to the stem, or rarely beginning to run down it; distant or nearly so; thick; dark purple or colored like the cap. **Stem:** 1–7 cm long; 1–7 mm thick; equal or slightly swollen at the base; finely to coarsely hairy or scaly; colored like the cap; with lilac to whitish basal mycelium. **Flesh:** Insubstantial; colored like the cap or paler. **Odor and Taste:** Not distinctive. **Chemical Reactions:** KOH brownish on cap. **Spore Print:** White. **Microscopic Features:** Spores 7–10 µm; globose; ornamented with spines 1.5–3 µm long and over 1 µm wide at their bases; inamyloid. Basidia 4-spored, or rarely 2-spored. Cheilocystidia narrowly cylindric, subclavate, or somewhat irregular. **Comments:** The small size, thick purple gills, and purple cap that soon fades to buff are diagnostic.

LACCARIA LACCATA (SCOPOLI) COOKE

Ecology: Mycorrhizal with hardwoods or conifers; growing alone or gregariously (sometimes in loose clusters); spring, summer, and fall; widely distributed. **Cap:** Usually 1–4.5 cm across at maturity, but sometimes larger or smaller; convex, becoming flat and sometimes uplifted; often with a central depression; the margin even or lined; bald to finely hairy; orangish brown, fading to buff; color often changing markedly as it dries out. **Gills:** Attached to the stem, or beginning to run down it; distant or close; pinkish, but sometimes developing a faintly purplish cast. **Stem:** 2–10 cm long; up to 1 cm thick; equal or tapering to base; bald to finely hairy; occasionally longitudinally grooved; colored like the cap; with white basal mycelium; becoming hollow. **Flesh:** Thin; colored like the cap. **Odor and Taste:** Taste mild to slightly radish-like; odor similar. **Chemical Reactions:** KOH negative on cap. **Spore Print:** White. **Microscopic Features:**

Spores 7–10 µm; subglobose to globose; ornamented with spines 1–2 µm long and about 1 µm wide at their bases; inamyloid. Basidia 4-spored. Cheilocystidia usually present; filamentous to subclavate. **Comments:** Several species of *Laccaria* are very similar; see Key D (couplets 50–54, p. 37) for help separating them.

LACCARIA LONGIPES MUELLER

Ecology: Mycorrhizal with conifers and hardwoods; growing alone, scattered, or gregariously in sphagnum bogs; fall; northern Midwest. **Cap:** 1–8 cm; convex, becoming flat or shallowly depressed; the margin usually lined; finely hairy; orangish brown, fading with age. **Gills:** Attached to the stem; distant or nearly so; pinkish flesh color. **Stem:** 7–15 cm long; up to about 1 cm thick; equal or with a slightly enlarged base; hairy; colored like the cap; with whitish basal mycelium. **Flesh:** Thin; pinkish flesh color. **Odor and Taste:** Taste not distinctive, or slightly bitter; odor not distinctive. **Spore Print:** White. **Chemical Reactions:** KOH negative on cap. **Microscopic Features:** Spores 7–8 × 6–8 µm; globose or subglobose; ornamented with spines mostly about 1 µm long, with bases <1 µm wide; inamyloid. Basidia 4-spored. Cheilocystidia absent. Comments: Several species of *Laccaria* are very similar; see Key D (couplets 50–54, p. 37) for help separating them.

LACCARIA OCHROPURPUREA (BERKELEY) PECK

Ecology: Mycorrhizal with hardwoods and conifers; growing alone, scattered, or gregariously; especially partial to oaks and beech, but also frequently found in young plantations of eastern white pine; common; late summer and fall; widely distributed. **Cap:** 3.5–12 cm; broadly convex, becoming flat and sometimes uplifted; often with a central depression; the margin even or inrolled, not lined; nearly bald or finely hairy-scaly; light lilac brown becoming light brown, fading to buff or nearly white. **Gills:** Attached to the stem, or rarely running slightly down it; close or nearly distant; thick; dark purple; in age sometimes dusted with white from spores. **Stem:** 4.5–19 cm long; 0.5–2.5 cm thick; equal or swollen at the base; coarsely hairy or scaly; colored like the cap; with lilac basal mycelium; solid; sometimes discoloring brownish to reddish brown. **Flesh:** Thick; colored like the cap or paler. **Odor and Taste:** Not distinctive. **Chemical Reactions:** KOH fleetingly orangish on cap and stem; ammonia reaction similar. **Spore Print:** White. **Microscopic Features:** Spores 7–9 µm; subglobose to globose; ornamented with spines 1–2 µm long and 1–1.5 µm wide at their bases. Basidia 4-spored, or rarely 2-spored. Cheilocystidia narrowly cylindric, subclavate, or subcapitate. **Comments:** Compare with *Cortinarius torvus* (p. 160) and other purple-gilled, pale-capped species of *Cortinarius*, which have rusty-brown spore prints.

LACCARIA OHIENSIS (MONTAGNE) SINGER

Ecology: Mycorrhizal with hardwoods; growing scattered to gregariously; summer and fall; possibly widely distributed, though we have not seen it in northern areas. **Cap:** 0.5–2.5 cm; convex, becoming flat and sometimes uplifted; often with a central depression; usually prominently lined or grooved; bald or finely hairy; orangish brown to dull reddish brown, fading to buff; changing color markedly as it dries out; often becoming tattered and radially torn with age. **Gills:** Attached to the stem; distant; pinkish flesh color. **Stem:** 1.5–2.5 cm long; up to 2 mm thick; equal or with an enlarged base; bald or finely hairy; colored like the cap; with white basal mycelium. **Flesh:** Thin; colored like the cap. **Odor and Taste:** Not distinctive. **Spore Print:** White. **Microscopic Features:** Spores 8–9 µm; globose to subglobose; ornamented with spines 1.5–3 µm long and 1 µm across at the base; inamyloid. Basidia 4-spored. Cheilocystidia usually present; filamentous or subcapitate. **Comments:** Several species of *Laccaria* can appear similar when they are small; see Key D (couplets 50–54, p. 37) for help separating them.

LACCARIA PROXIMA (BOUDIER) PATOUILLARD

Ecology: Mycorrhizal with pines, especially in young plantations; growing scattered or gregariously; summer and fall; widely distributed. **Cap:** 1.5–7 cm; convex, becoming flat and sometimes uplifted; the margin inrolled at first; at first finely roughened, later more prominently roughened or scaly; reddish brown to orange brown. **Gills:** Attached to the stem; distant or nearly so; pinkish flesh color. **Stem:** 2.5–8 cm long; up to 1 cm thick; equal or with an enlarged base; finely or prominently hairy and shaggy; colored like the cap (sometimes with a darker base); with white basal

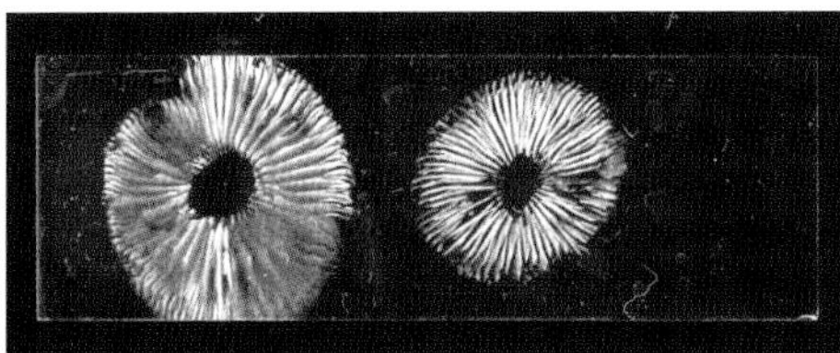

Spore print

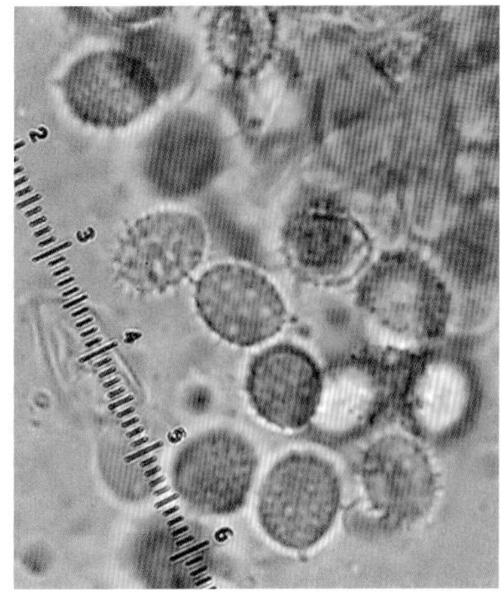

Spores

mycelium. **Flesh:** Thin; colored like the cap or paler. **Odor and Taste:** Not distinctive. **Chemical Reactions:** KOH negative on cap. **Spore Print:** White. **Microscopic Features:** Spores 8–11 × 7–9 µm; ellipsoid; spines mostly 0.5–1 µm long. Basidia 4-spored. Cheilocystidia filamentous to subclavate or subcapitate. **Comments:** Several species of *Laccaria* are very similar; see Key D (couplets 50–54, p. 37) for help separating them.

LACCARIA TRULLISSATA (ELLIS) PECK

Ecology: Mycorrhizal, usually with pines; growing scattered or gregariously in sand dunes; late summer and fall; along the Great Lakes. **Cap:** 2–7 cm; convex, becoming flat and sometimes depressed; the margin often inrolled, not lined; finely hairy to finely scaly or more prominently roughened; purplish when young but soon reddish brown, brownish, or buff. **Gills:** Attached to the stem; close or nearly distant; dark purple. **Stem:** 4–9 cm long; up to about 2.5 cm thick; usually with an enlarged base; hairy and often longitudinally lined; the surface frequently splitting near the apex; colored like the cap; with purplish basal mycelium beneath the covering of sand; often nearly entirely submerged in the sand. **Flesh:** Pale purplish or whitish. **Odor and Taste:** Not distinctive. **Spore Print:** White. **Microscopic Features:** Spores 14–20 × 5.5–8 µm; ellipsoid or broadly fusiform; roughened, but without the clearly defined, measurable spines typical of most other *Laccaria* species; inamyloid. Basidia 4-spored. Cheilocystidia absent or rare; when present filamentous. **Comments:** Nearly unmistakable due to its ecology and deep purple gills.

Photo by Ron Kerner

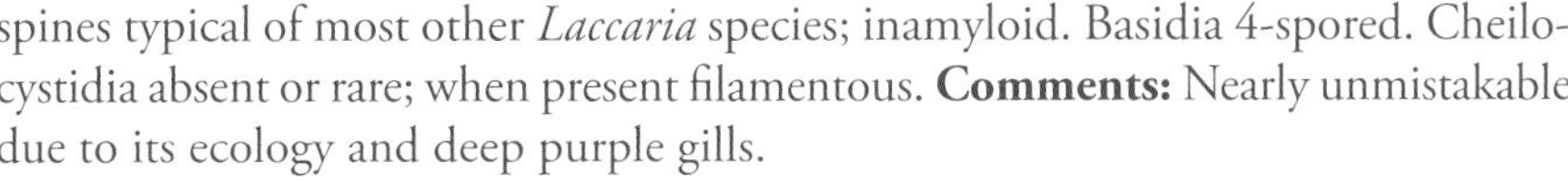

Mottled gills

LACRYMARIA VELUTINA (PERSOON) KONRAD & MAUBLANK

Ecology: Saprobic; growing alone, gregariously, or in clusters on lawns, in pastures, along roads, and in gravelly soil, usually near recently dead hardwood trees; sometimes in woods; summer through fall; widely distributed. **Cap:** 3–12 cm; convex when young, expanding to broadly convex, flat, or very broadly bell-shaped; dry; densely hairy but sometimes becoming more or less bald in age; often becoming radially wrinkled; the margin usually hung with whitish partial veil remnants, at least when young; yellow brown to cinnamon brown or orangish brown. **Gills:** Attached to the stem or free from it; crowded; pale at first, later dark brown and mottled; with whitish edges. **Stem:** 5–15 cm long; 0.5–1.5 cm thick; equal, or with a swollen base; hairy; with a fragile ring or a ring zone that is darkened by spores; white above, pale brownish below; hollow; basal mycelium white. **Flesh:** Thick; brownish. **Odor and Taste:** Not distinctive. **Chemical Reactions:** KOH negative to brownish on cap. **Spore Print:** Dark brown to nearly black. **Microscopic Features:** Spores 8–12 × 5–8 µm; ellipsoid with a snout-like end; warty; dark brown in KOH. Pleurocystidia clavate to utriform or subcylindric; often clustered in threes or fours. Cheilocystidia abundant; flexuous; subcylindric, with subcapitate to capitate apices. Pileipellis hymeniform. **Comments:** Also known as *Psathyrella velutina* and as *Lacrymaria lacrymabunda*. The hairy cap, mottled gills, and nearly black spore print are good field characters for this species. Recent DNA studies (Padamsee et al. 2008) suggest the possibility of cryptic species within the current concept of this mushroom.

Photo by Dan Molter

LACTARIUS ALLARDII COKER

Ecology: Mycorrhizal with oaks, in hardwood forests, or in pine-oak forests; growing scattered or gregariously; summer and fall; widely distributed, but more common in the southeastern Midwest. **Cap:** 4–20 cm; convex, with a shallow central depression, becoming shallowly to deeply vase-shaped; dry; bald; finely velvety to the touch, at least when young; whitish when very young or when covered with leaves, but soon becoming brownish pink to pinkish brown, and eventually darkening to brick

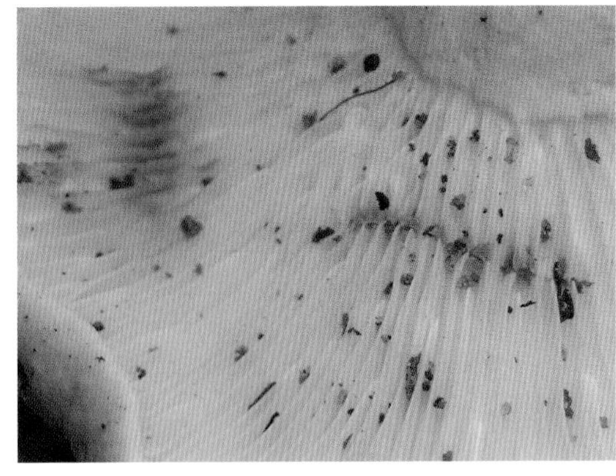

red. **Gills:** Attached to the stem or beginning to run down it; close or nearly distant; whitish, maturing to buff; staining greenish, then brown where damaged. **Stem:** 2–7 cm long; 1–3 cm thick; more or less equal; hard; bald; without potholes; white, or becoming colored like the cap; hollowing; dry. **Flesh:** White; staining purplish pink, then greenish when sliced. **Milk:** White, turning slowly greenish, then brownish; copious; sticky; staining tissues greenish, then brownish; staining white paper yellow. **Odor and Taste:** Odor fragrant, or not distinctive; taste strongly acrid. **Spore Print:** White to pale yellowish. **Microscopic Features:** Spores 7.5–10.5 × 5.5–8 µm; subglobose to broadly ellipsoid; ornamentation under 0.5 µm high, as isolated warts and rare, scattered connectors. Pileipellis a cutis-like tangle of elements that are often aggregated into upright fascicles of pileocystidia. **Comments:** Compare with *Russula compacta* (p. 340), which can appear similar but bruises brown and does not exude milk.

LACTARIUS AQUIFLUUS PECK

Ecology: Mycorrhizal with conifers (and rarely with paper birch) in boggy, wet locations; usually growing in sphagnum; summer and fall; northern Midwest. **Cap:** 3–13 cm; convex, with an inrolled margin when young, becoming broadly convex, flat, or shallowly depressed, with an even margin; dry; bald or finely velvety at first, becoming rough or subscaly; somewhat variable in color but usually some version of light brown. **Gills:** Attached to the stem or beginning to run down it; close; not infrequently forked near the stem; whitish at first, becoming dirty yellowish as the spores mature, but not spotting or staining when sliced. **Stem:** 3–10 cm long; up to 2 cm thick; more or less equal; dry; bald or very finely velvety when young; without potholes but sometimes with watery spots; very variable in color but frequently orangish, pinkish, or orangish brown; usually with a thin whitish bloom and thus darker where handled (though not actually bruising). **Flesh:** Pale pinkish or pale brownish, becoming dingy with age but not staining on exposure. **Milk**: Scant; watery; not staining tissues. **Odor and Taste:** Odor (of mature specimens, or on drying) strongly of curry or burned maple syrup; taste mild or slowly, slightly acrid. **Spore Print:** Creamy white to pale orangish yellow. **Microscopic Features:** Spores 6–9 × 5–7.5 µm; broadly ellipsoid; ornamentation up to 1 µm high as amyloid spines and ridges that form a nearly complete reticulum. Pileipellis a dense tangle of repent and erect hyphae. **Comments:** Also known under the European species name *Lactarius helvus*.

LACTARIUS AREOLATUS HESLER & A. H. SMITH

Ecology: Mycorrhizal with oaks and with hop hornbeam; growing scattered or gregariously; summer and fall; widely distributed. **Cap:** 2–7 cm; convex to bell-shaped, quickly becoming flattened or centrally depressed; moist or dry; bald at first, but soon becoming roughened-scurfy and wrinkled; dark reddish brown to orangish brown when very fresh and young, becoming burnt orange to pinkish brown or orangish brown; the margin becoming lined and/or scalloped. **Gills:** Beginning to run down the stem; close or nearly distant; creamy to pale yellowish at first, developing cinnamon spots and eventually discoloring cinnamon; not staining from the milk. **Stem:** 2–9 cm long; up to about 1 cm thick; more or less equal; bald; without potholes; colored like the cap, or paler; hollow; dry. **Flesh:** Pale orangish to pale cinnamon; brittle; not staining when sliced. **Milk:** Watery to whey-like; not staining tissues; not staining white paper. **Odor and Taste:** Odor not distinctive, or slightly to strongly fragrant (even, at times, a little reminiscent of *Lactarius camphoratus*, p. 233); taste mild. **Spore Print:** Pale yellowish. **Chemical Reactions:** Cap surface olive with KOH. **Microscopic Features:** Spores 6.5–9 × 5–7 µm; subglobose to broadly ellipsoid; ornamentation 0.5–1.0 mµ high, as isolated warts and scattered but frequent ridges that do not form a complete reticulum. Pileipellis a hyphoepithelium with terminal elements that tend to inflate and aggregate with maturity. **Comments:** Compare with *Lactarius camphoratus* (p. 233) and with *Lactarius subserifluus* (p. 247). *Lactarius rimosellus* is nearly identical but has spores with completely isolated warts.

LACTARIUS ARGILLACEIFOLIUS HESLER & A. H. SMITH

Ecology: Mycorrhizal with oaks; growing alone or gregariously; spring (it is often one of the first mycorrhizal mushrooms to appear in oak-hickory forests), summer, and fall; widely distributed. **Cap:** 3–18 cm; convex, becoming flat or shallowly vase-shaped; drab cinnamon to drab lilac brown; without zones; bald; minutely pocked and rugged; sticky when fresh. **Gills:** Beginning to run down the stem; close or crowded; cream-colored when young, becoming dingy cinnamon with age; stained slowly brown (or rarely olive to greenish) by the latex where damaged. **Stem:** 3–9 cm long; 1–3.5 cm thick; tapering to base; pale or brownish in age; dry or slightly sticky; bald; without potholes. **Flesh:** White; unchanging, or discoloring faintly tan when sliced. **Milk:** Off-white; unchanging when exposed; staining tissues brown to brownish, or rarely olive to greenish; over time staining white paper yellow. **Odor and Taste:** Odor not distinctive, or mildly fragrant; taste mild or slowly slightly acrid. **Spore Print:** Pale yellowish. **Chemical Reactions:** KOH on cap surface erasing pigments to pale orange or tan. **Microscopic Features:** Spores 8–10 × 7–8 µm; broadly ellipsoid or subglobose; ornamentation 0.5–1 µm high, composed of fairly isolated warts and ridges that sometimes form broken reticula. Pileipellis an ixolattice. **Comments:** The drab lilac-brown cap, brown-staining gills, and off-white milk are good identification characters.

LACTARIUS ATROVIRIDIS PECK

Ecology: Mycorrhizal with oaks (but sometimes reported under conifers); growing alone or gregariously; summer and fall; widely distributed. **Cap:** 3–15 cm; convex, becoming plano-convex, with a central depression; dry, or sticky in wet weather; pockmarked and rugged, sometimes smoother over the disc; various shades of green, often with darker green spots arranged concentrically over the marginal half; the margin inrolled. **Gills:** Attached or beginning to run down the stem; close; pale pinkish; often bruising and staining greenish to brownish; frequently with green tints on the edges of mature gills. **Stem:** 2–8 cm long; 1–2.5 cm thick; equal or tapering to the base; slimy when fresh, but soon dry; with many potholes; colored and textured like the cap; becoming hollow with age. **Flesh:** Whitish to pale pinkish. **Milk:** Fairly copious; creamy white; sometimes becoming greenish on exposure to air. **Odor and Taste:** Odor not distinctive; taste mild or acrid. **Chemical Reactions:** KOH dark purple magenta on cap. **Spore Print:** Cream. **Microscopic Features:** Spores 6–9 × 5.5–6.5 µm; subglobose to broadly ellipsoid; ornamentation 0.2–1.0 µm high, as amyloid warts and ridges forming a broken or partial reticulum. Pileipellis a cutis to an ixocutis; elements pink in KOH. **Comments:** Not easily mistaken for other species.

LACTARIUS CAMPHORATUS (BULLIARD) FRIES

Ecology: Mycorrhizal with conifers or hardwoods; growing alone, scattered, or gregariously, often in moss; spring, summer, and fall; widely distributed. **Cap:** 1–4 cm; convex, becoming broadly convex or centrally depressed, usually with a sharp central point; moist or dry; bald or very finely dusted; dark reddish brown, often fading to rusty brown or orangish brown; the margin sometimes becoming scalloped and/or lined with age. **Gills:** Attached to the stem or running slightly down it; close or crowded; whitish to pale pinkish, often developing reddish to cinnamon tones with maturity, but not staining from the milk. **Stem:** 1.5–6 cm long; up to about 1 cm thick; more or less equal; bald or with fuzz near the base; without potholes; colored like the cap, or paler, especially toward the apex. **Flesh:** Pale cinnamon to whitish; brittle and hard; not staining when sliced. **Milk:** Milky white when young and fresh, but sometimes whey-like or watery by maturity; not staining tissues, or, in some of our collections, staining tissues very faintly pinkish. **Odor and Taste:** Odor sometimes indistinct when fresh, but usually reminiscent of maple syrup, burned sugar, or curry, becoming stronger when the mushroom is dried; taste mild or slightly bitter. **Spore Print:** Pale yellow or whitish. **Chemical Reactions:** KOH olive on cap. **Microscopic Features:** Spores 7–8.5 × 6–7.5 µm; subglobose to broadly ellipsoid; ornamentation 0.5–1.0 µm high, as isolated warts and scattered ridges that do not form a complete reticulum. Pileipellis a hyphoepithelium. **Comments:** There are many small, burnt-orange species of *Lactarius* in the Midwest. We are using the name *Lactarius camphoratus* for the mushroom described here, but the true *Lactarius camphoratus* may be strictly European. The entire group is in need of contemporary study. When the odor of *Lactarius camphoratus* is weak, it might be confused with *Lactarius areolatus* (p. 232), which is a little larger and features a cap that becomes wrinkled, and with *Lactarius subserifluus* (p. 247), which is also a little larger and features a distinctively tough and skinny stem. *Lactarius fragilis* is similar but features watery milk (even when young), yellowish gills, and reticulate spores.

LACTARIUS CHELIDONIUM VAR. *CHELIDONIOIDES* (A. H. SMITH) HESLER & A. H. SMITH

Ecology: Mycorrhizal with pines, especially white pine and red pine in young plantations; September, October, and November; widely distributed. **Cap:** 3–12 cm; convex, becoming plano-convex to shallowly depressed or shallowly vase-shaped; sticky when fresh, but soon dry; bald or very finely appressed-fibrillose; often finely roughened; dirty bluish when young, passing through stages of yellowish brown and dull orange; often mottled with watery spots of color; readily bruising dark green; in age often green overall; without concentric zones of color, or with faint zones near the margin. **Gills:** Beginning to run down the stem; close or fairly crowded; pale yellowish when young, becoming dirty yellowish to dull orange or brownish; bruising and discoloring green. **Stem:** 2–6 cm long; 1–3 cm thick; tough; more or less equal; dry; bald; without potholes; colored like the cap or paler. **Flesh:** Sky blue in the cap; paler elsewhere; sometimes orange in the stem, especially at the base and near the cortex. **Milk:** Very scant (likely to be observed only in very young buttons); dirty yellowish to yellowish brown; staining tissues green; staining white paper yellowish. **Odor and Taste:** Odor fragrant, or not distinctive; taste mild or slowly slightly peppery. **Spore Print:** Pale buff to yellowish or orangish. **Chemical Reactions:** KOH negative on cap. **Microscopic Features:** Spores 7–9 × 5–7 µm; broadly ellipsoid; ornamentation 0.5–1 µm high, as amyloid warts and ridges forming a partial reticulum. Pileipellis an ixocutis. **Comments:** Compare with *Lactarius deliciosus* var. *deterrimus* (p. 236).

LACTARIUS CONTROVERSUS PERSOON

Ecology: Mycorrhizal with cottonwoods and other poplars (species of *Populus*, including quaking aspen and big-toothed aspen, but not the misnamed "tulip poplar," *Liriodendron tulipifera*) and with willows; growing alone or gregariously, or sometimes in dense troops; summer and fall; northern Midwest. **Cap:** 7–30 cm; at first convex, with an inrolled, slightly hairy margin; becoming flat with a central depression, or vase-shaped, with an even and bald margin; slimy to sticky when fresh, but soon dry; rugged with appressed fibers; whitish overall, but often with faint zones of pinkish or purplish, especially near the margin. **Gills:** Attached to the stem or beginning to run down it; thin; close or nearly crowded; sometimes forking near the stem; pinkish to pale pink. **Stem:** 2.5–10 cm long; 1.5–4 cm thick; more or less equal, or tapering to the base; sticky when fresh, but soon dry; usually without potholes, but occasionally with a few; bald; eventually becoming hollow; whitish. **Flesh:** White; unchanging when sliced; fairly firm. **Milk:** White; unchanging on exposure to air; not staining tissues; not staining white paper. **Odor and Taste:** Odor not distinctive, or pleasantly fragrant; taste slowly moderately to strongly acrid. **Chemical Reactions:** KOH negative to pale yellowish on cap. **Spore Print:** Creamy white or pale pinkish. **Microscopic**

Features: Spores 6–7.5 × 4.5–5 µm; ellipsoid; ornamentation under 0.5 µm high, as amyloid warts and ridges usually forming a partial or nearly complete reticulum. Pileipellis an ixocutis. **Comments:** The pink gills and association with poplars are good field characters.

LACTARIUS CORRUGIS PECK

Ecology: Mycorrhizal with oaks and perhaps with other hardwoods; growing alone, scattered, or gregariously; summer and fall; widely distributed. **Cap:** 4–20 cm; at first convex; becoming shallowly depressed; notably velvety; when young often appearing coated with a thin, grayish to whitish, felt-like material; in maturity often becoming deeply wrinkled and corrugated; usually dark brownish red to dark brick red, but sometimes purplish brown or dark brown. **Gills:** Attached to the stem or beginning to run down it; close; pale buff when young, but soon orangish to yellowish or brownish; discoloring brown where injured. **Stem:** 3–11 cm long; 1.5–3 cm thick; colored more or less like the cap, or paler; equal; when young with a felt-like coating like that on the cap; solid. **Flesh:** Whitish to yellowish; staining slowly brown when sliced. **Milk:** White; copious; unchanging when exposed to air; staining tissues brown; staining white paper brown. **Odor and Taste:** Odor not distinctive, or sometimes slightly fishy; taste mild. **Chemical Reactions:** KOH olive to brown on cap. **Spore Print:** White. **Microscopic Features:** Spores 9–13 × 8.5–12 µm; globose or subglobose; ornamentation 0.4–0.7 µm high, as widely spaced amyloid ridges forming a partial to complete reticulum. Pileipellis a lamprotrichoderm with a turf of cylindric to narrowly fusiform pileocystidia. **Comments:** Compare with *Lactarius volemus* (p. 250), which is usually more orange, lacks the felt-like coating when young, and does not usually develop a corrugated cap.

LACTARIUS DELICIOSUS VAR. DETERRIMUS (GRÖGER) HESLER & A. H. SMITH

Ecology: Mycorrhizal with conifers, especially white pine; growing alone, scattered, or gregariously in cold conifer bogs and low, wet woods; summer and fall; northern Midwest. **Cap:** 3–13 cm across; at first convex, becoming broadly convex, flat, or shallowly vase-shaped; slimy to sticky when wet, but often dry; the margin sometimes inrolled when young; smooth or slightly roughened; carrot orange or orange, with or without concentric zones of color; stained and discolored greenish at maturity. **Gills:** Beginning to run down the stem; close or crowded; orange; bruising slowly red, then green; frequently entirely greenish at maturity. **Stem:** 2–7 cm long;

1.5–2.5 cm thick; orange; more or less equal; bald; without potholes; often becoming hollow; bruising and staining like the cap. **Flesh:** Pale orangish; staining slowly deep purplish red when sliced, especially in the stem base and over the gills. **Milk:** Orange; staining tissues slowly deep red, then green. **Odor and Taste:** Odor not distinctive; taste mild to slowly slightly acrid. **Spore Print:** Pale buff. **Microscopic Features:** Spores 7.5–9 × 6–7 µm; ellipsoid; ornamentation 0.5–1.0 µm high, as amyloid warts and ridges forming a partial reticulum. Pileipellis an ixocutis. **Comments:** Edible, but not very good. This is *Lactarius deliciosus* var. *deterrimus* in the sense of Hesler and Smith (1979). However, the epithet *deterrimus* may now apply to a spruce-associated European species, while the true *Lactarius deliciosus* has been found to be strictly European as well, leaving no appropriate name for the mushroom described by Hesler and Smith. Compare with *Lactarius chelidonium* var. *chelidonioides* (p. 234) and with *Lactarius thyinos* (p. 249).

LACTARIUS FUMOSUS PECK

Ecology: Mycorrhizal with hardwoods and conifers; growing alone, scattered, or gregariously; summer and fall; widely distributed. **Cap:** 3–10 cm; at first broadly convex, becoming flat or shallowly depressed; dry; bald; dull smoky brown or paler (occasionally nearly whitish); the margin even. **Gills:** Attached to the stem or beginning to run down it; close or crowded; white, becoming pale brownish with age; when fresh, staining pink to reddish when sliced. **Stem:** 4–11 cm long; up to 1.5 cm thick; more or less equal; bald, without potholes; colored like the cap or paler; often whitish near the base; usually bruising slowly pinkish to reddish. **Flesh:** Whitish; usually staining pink to reddish when sliced, at least over time, but occasionally not staining (especially in dry, hot weather). **Milk:** White; unchanging; usually staining tissues pink to reddish. **Odor and Taste:** Odor not distinctive; taste variable, ranging from acrid (sometimes slowly) or peppery to mild. **Spore Print:** Pale cream to buff. **Chemical Reactions:** KOH negative on cap. **Microscopic Features:** Spores 6–8 µm; globose or subglobose; ornamentation 0.5–1.5 µm high, as spines and ridges forming a broken to nearly complete reticulum. Pileipellis a trichoepithelium or, in young caps, nearly a trichoderm. **Comments:** Compare with *Lactarius subvernalis* var. *cokeri* (p. 249), which is more white and is usually smaller and more acrid, and with *Lactarius imperceptus* (p. 240).

LACTARIUS GERARDII PECK

Ecology: Mycorrhizal with hardwoods (especially oaks); also sometimes reported under conifers; growing alone, scattered, or gregariously; summer and fall; widely distributed. **Cap:** 3–10.5 cm; convex, with a small point in the middle, becoming flat with an uplifted margin, with the central point often disappearing; dry; with a waxy feel; often rugged and wrinkled; yellow brown to grayish brown; the margin sometimes becoming scalloped. **Gills:** Running down the stem; quite distant; stark white. **Stem:** 3–8 cm long; 1–2.5 cm thick; more or less equal; dry; without potholes; textured and colored like the cap; sometimes with a white apex, or sometimes with the gills running into the brown coloration; becoming hollow. **Flesh:** White; thin; somewhat brittle. **Milk:** White; unchanging on exposure to air; not staining tissues, or staining them pink. **Odor and Taste:** Odor not distinctive; taste mild or slightly acrid. **Chemical Reactions:** KOH negative on cap; yellowish on flesh. **Spore Print:** White. **Microscopic Features:** Spores 7–10 × 7.5–9 µm; globose to subglobose; ornamentation 0.5–0.8 µm high, as amyloid warts and ridges forming a partial or complete reticulum. Pileipellis a trichoepithelium; terminal cells long and cystidium-like; brown in KOH. **Comments:** Compare with *Lactarius lignyotus* (p. 241), which features velvety, dark brown surfaces. A recent DNA study (Stubbe, Nuytinck, and Verbeken 2010) found several cryptic species within the traditional concept of *Lactarius gerardii*.

LACTARIUS GLAUCESCENS CROSSLAND

Ecology: Mycorrhizal with oaks and other hardwoods; growing scattered, gregariously, or sometimes in dense troops, often in moss; summer; widely distributed. **Cap:** 4–11 cm; broadly convex, becoming flat, shallowly depressed, or vase-shaped; dry; bald; soft; white or whitish, sometimes discoloring a little yellowish or brownish with age; the margin even. **Gills:** Beginning to run down the stem; very crowded; forking frequently; pale cream. **Stem:** 3–10 cm long; 1–2 cm thick; white; tapering to base; bald; without potholes; solid. **Flesh:** White; thick; hard; unchanging when sliced. **Milk:** Copious; white; changing slowly (sometimes overnight) to olive green or pastel green; staining white paper yellow overnight. **Odor and Taste:** Odor fragrant, or not distinctive; taste excruciatingly acrid. **Chemical Reactions:** KOH negative to slowly

pale orangish on cap. **Spore Print:** Creamy. **Microscopic Features:** Spores 6–9 × 5–6.5 µm; broadly ellipsoid; ornamentation <0.5 µm high (sometimes difficult to see, even with oil immersion), as isolated warts and lines. Pileipellis a hyphoepithelium with a fairly thick upper, cutis-like layer. **Comments:** Not recommended for the table. The white colors, milk that turns green, and very crowded gills are distinctive. Also known as *Lactarius piperatus* var. *glaucescens*. *Lactarius piperatus* is very similar but has milk that does not turn green. Compare with *Lactarius subvellereus* var. *subdistans* (p. 248), which has a velvety cap and distant gills, and with *Lactarius maculatipes* (p. 242), which has a pale yellow zoned cap, yellowing milk, and a stem with potholes.

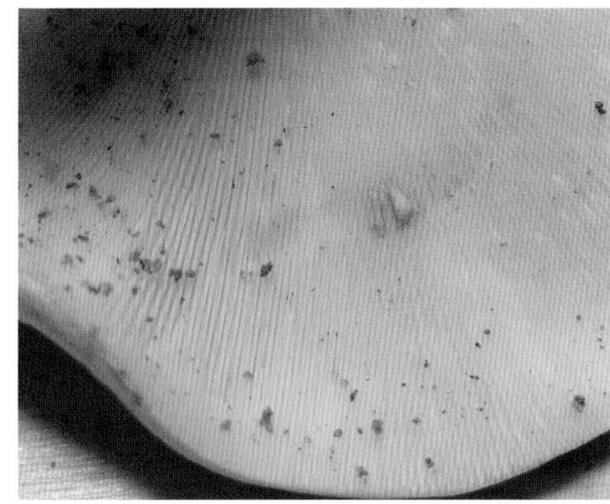

LACTARIUS HYGROPHOROIDES
BERKELEY & M. A. CURTIS

Ecology: Mycorrhizal with oaks and perhaps with other hardwoods; growing scattered or gregariously; summer; widely distributed. **Cap:** 3–10 cm; at first convex; becoming flat, with a shallow central depression, or vase-shaped; often dusted with a whitish bloom; finely velvety; dry; the margin even, slightly incurved at first; often slightly rugged; evenly colored dull orange to cinnamon orange. **Gills:** Attached to the stem or running slightly down it; distant; whitish becoming cream-colored or pale yellowish; not staining, or staining brownish where damaged, sometimes with a lavender stage. **Stem:** 3–5 cm long; 0.5–1.5 cm thick; colored like the cap or paler; more or less equal; bald or very finely velvety like the cap; solid. **Flesh:** Firm; white. **Milk:** Copious; white; unchanging or turning slightly yellowish over time; not staining surfaces, or staining them brownish, sometimes with a lavender stage; staining white paper yellow overnight. **Odor and Taste:** Not distinctive. **Spore Print:** White. **Chemical Reactions:** KOH pale olive on cap. **Microscopic Features:** Spores 7–9 × 5.5–7 µm; ellipsoid; ornamentation under 0.5 µm high, composed of isolated warts and scattered connectors occasionally forming a partial reticulum. Pileipellis a lamprotrichoderm, featuring a layer of upright pileocystidia arising from a cellular layer. **Comments:** Compare with *Lactarius volemus* (p. 250), which has close gills that always stain brown and a fishy odor.

LACTARIUS IMPERCEPTUS BEARDSLEE & BIRMINGHAM

Ecology: Mycorrhizal with oaks and possibly with other hardwoods; summer and fall; widely distributed. **Cap:** 2.5–9 cm; convex, with an incurved margin when young, becoming flat or shallowly depressed, often with a central bump; dry or moist; bald; dull brown to tan, cinnamon tan, pinkish brown, or paler; without zones of color or texture. **Gills:** Attached to the stem or beginning to run down it; close; whitish to pinkish or very pale tan; often developing cinnamon to reddish-brown stains and discolorations. **Stem:** 2.5–9 cm long; up to about 1.5 cm thick; more or less equal; dry or moist; without potholes; bald; pale at first, becoming colored like the cap. **Flesh:** Thin; pale, becoming pinkish; not changing when sliced, or turning slowly yellowish to yellow. **Milk:** Creamy; turning slightly to substantially yellowish (often very slowly) or not yellowing appreciably; not staining tissues, or staining them yellowish; staining white paper yellow. **Odor and Taste:** Odor not distinctive; taste usually acrid but sometimes weakly so. **Spore Print:** White to yellowish. **Microscopic Features:** Spores 7–9.5 × 6–8 µm; broadly ellipsoid; ornamentation 0.5–1.5 µm high, as amyloid warts and ridges that form a broken reticulum or remain scattered. Pileipellis an ixolattice or ixotrichoderm. **Comments:** Compare with *Lactarius fumosus* (p. 237), which has a smoky-brown cap and nonyellowing milk that stains surfaces pink.

LACTARIUS INDIGO (SCHWEINITZ) FRIES

Ecology: Mycorrhizal with oaks and with pines; growing alone, scattered, or gregariously; summer and fall; widely distributed. **Cap:** 5–15 cm; convex, becoming flat or vase-shaped; the margin at first inrolled; deep to medium blue when fresh; grayish or silvery blue when faded; sometimes developing brownish areas when old; with concentric zones of color, or sometimes evenly colored; sticky or slimy when fresh; bruising and discoloring deep green, especially with age. **Gills:** Attached to the stem or beginning to run down it; close; colored like the cap or a little paler; becoming nearly yellowish at maturity; staining green. **Stem:** 2–8 cm long; 1–2.5 cm thick; equal or tapering to base; sometimes a little off-center; slimy at first, but soon dry; hard; hollowing; usually with potholes on the surface; colored like the cap. **Flesh:** Whitish,

turning indigo blue when sliced; staining slowly greenish. **Milk:** Deep indigo blue; becoming dark green on exposure. **Odor and Taste:** Odor not distinctive; taste mild to slowly, slightly acrid. **Spore Print:** Cream. **Chemical Reactions:** KOH negative or yellowish on cap. **Microscopic Features:** Spores 7–10 × 5.5–7.5 µm; broadly ellipsoid to subglobose; ornamentation about 0.5 µm high, as amyloid warts and connecting lines that sometimes form a partial reticulum. Pileipellis an ixocutis. **Comments:** Edible. When fresh and blue, this species is not easily mistaken for other mushrooms.

LACTARIUS LIGNYOTUS FRIES

Ecology: Mycorrhizal with conifers, especially spruces and firs; usually terrestrial, but not infrequently found growing from well-rotted wood near the ground; late summer and fall; northern Midwest. **Cap:** 2–10 cm; convex, with a small point in the middle, becoming flat or shallowly depressed, with the central point remaining or disappearing; dry; finely velvety; often with a rugged or wrinkled surface; nearly black when young, dark brown to brown in age; the margin sometimes becoming ridged. **Gills**: Attached to the stem or beginning to run down it; close or nearly distant; white or whitish, remaining pale until old age, when pinkish to orangish hues often result from drying milk and spore maturation; occasionally with brownish edges; usually staining slowly pinkish when damaged, but sometimes not staining. **Stem:** 4–12 cm long; up to 1.5 cm thick; more or less equal; dry; textured and colored like the cap, except for a whitish base; often with small ribs at the apex. **Flesh:** White; usually changing slowly to pinkish when sliced (especially in the base of the stem), but the change is sometimes absent, slight, or very, very slow to develop. **Milk:** White; often drying pinkish; staining white paper brown over time. **Odor and Taste:** Not distinctive. **Chemical Reactions:** KOH negative on cap. **Spore Print:** Creamy white to orangish yellow. **Microscopic Features:** Spores 8–10 µm; globose or broadly ellipsoid; ornamentation 1–2 µm high, as amyloid spines and ridges forming a partial reticulum. Pileipellis an epithelium with cylindric to clavate terminal elements; brown in KOH. **Comments:** Compare with *Lactarius gerardii* (p. 238). Varieties of *Lactarius lignyotus* include var. *canadensis*, with brown gill edges and pink staining; var. *nigroviolascens* (see Kuo and Methven 2010), with purple staining; and var. *marginatus*, with brown gill edges *and* purple staining.

LACTARIUS LUTEOLUS PECK

Ecology: Mycorrhizal with hardwoods; growing scattered or gregariously; summer and fall; widely distributed. **Cap:** 2.5–8 cm; convex, becoming broadly convex or shallowly depressed; dry; finely velvety to the touch; whitish, becoming yel-

lowish to brownish with age. **Gills:** Attached to the stem or beginning to run down it; close; whitish, maturing to buff or yellowish; staining slowly dark brown where damaged. **Stem:** 2.5–6 cm long; 0.5–1 cm thick; more or less equal; finely velvety; without potholes; whitish; staining slowly dark brown. **Flesh:** White; staining slowly dark brown when sliced. **Milk:** White; copious; sticky; staining tissues slowly brown. **Odor and Taste:** Odor strong and fishy; taste not distinctive. **Chemical Reactions:** KOH negative to orangish on cap. **Spore Print:** White to creamy. **Microscopic Features:** Spores 7–9 × 5.5–7 µm; ellipsoid; ornamentation to just under 1 µm high, as isolated warts with occasional connectors forming a partial reticulum. Pileipellis a lamprotrichoderm, featuring a layer of upright pileocystidia arising from a cellular layer. **Comments:** The whitish colors, brown-staining milk, and fishy odor are good field characters.

LACTARIUS MACULATIPES BURLINGHAM

Ecology: Mycorrhizal with oaks and possibly other hardwoods; summer and fall; widely distributed. **Cap:** 3–10 cm; broadly convex, with an inrolled margin when young; becoming shallowly depressed or vase-shaped with an uplifted margin; slimy when wet; smooth or finely roughened; whitish to pale yellowish; typically with vague zones of color or texture, at least when young. **Gills:** Beginning to run down the stem; close or crowded; pale yellowish; often bruising tan. **Stem:** 3–8 cm long; 1–2 cm thick; tapering to base; slimy when fresh or wet; usually with yellowish potholes by maturity; whitish to pale yellow. **Flesh:** White; firm; changing to yellow when sliced. **Milk:** White, becoming yellow on exposure to air (usually quickly, but sometimes taking several minutes or more); staining white paper yellow. **Odor and Taste:** Odor not distinctive; taste acrid (sometimes developing slowly). **Spore Print:** Yellowish. **Chemical Reactions:** KOH greenish yellow on cap. **Microscopic Features:** Spores 6.5–9

× 6–7.5 µm; broadly ellipsoid or occasionally subglobose; ornamentation 0.5–1 µm high, as amyloid warts and connecting lines that branch into short patterns but do not form a complete reticulum. Pileipellis a very thick ixocutis. **Comments:** Not recommended for the table. Compare with *Lactarius vinaceorufescens* (p. 250), which has a pinkish-cinnamon cap and a stem that lacks potholes.

LACTARIUS PSAMMICOLA A. H. SMITH

Ecology: Mycorrhizal with oaks and possibly other hardwoods; growing alone, scattered, or gregariously; summer and fall; widely distributed. **Cap:** 4–14 cm; at first with a deep central depression and an inrolled hairy margin; later vase-shaped, with the margin typically remaining somewhat inrolled and softly leathery or finely hairy; sticky when fresh, but soon dry; roughened; with buff and orange concentric zones of color. **Gills:** Running down the stem; close; rarely forking near the stem; whitish or buff, becoming darker and dirty; sometimes bruising brownish to lilac brown. **Stem:** 1–3 cm long; 1–2 cm thick; whitish, sometimes discoloring brownish where handled; tapering to base; with potholes. **Flesh:** Thick; white; unchanging when sliced. **Milk:** White; unchanging; not staining tissues, or staining them slowly brownish to lilac brownish; slowly staining white paper yellow. **Odor and Taste:** Odor not distinctive; taste strongly acrid. **Chemical Reactions:** KOH negative on cap. **Spore Print:** Yellowish to yellow. **Microscopic Features:** Spores: 7.5–9 × 6–7.5 µm; broadly ellipsoid; ornamentation about 0.5 µm high, as isolated amyloid warts and short ridges that occasionally form a partial reticulum. Pileipellis a thick ixocutis. **Comments:** The association with oaks, strongly acrid taste, potholes on the stem, and zoned orangish cap are good field characters. *Lactarius psammicola* is one of several North American versions of the European species *Lactarius zonarius*. The group is in need of contemporary study.

LACTARIUS PUBESCENS VAR. BETULAE (A. H. SMITH) HESLER & A. H. SMITH

Ecology: Mycorrhizal with paper birch in boreal ecosystems and where the tree has been planted as an ornamental; growing scattered or gregariously; late summer and fall; northern Midwest. **Cap:** 3–10 cm across when mature; convex, becoming centrally depressed with an arched margin and, eventually, vase-shaped; whitish to pale pinkish or pale orangish pink; sticky when fresh; covered with a dense layer of appressed hairs; the margin hairy or "bearded," especially when young. **Gills:** Beginning to run down the stem; close; whitish to pinkish; sometimes stained slowly

yellowish by the milk where damaged. **Stem:** 2–8 cm long; 1–2 cm thick; more or less equal; colored like the cap; dry; bald; without potholes, but occasionally with vague brownish spots. **Flesh:** Whitish to pinkish; sometimes stained slowly yellowish by the milk where damaged. **Milk:** White; unchanging or changing slowly to yellow or yellowish, or merely drying yellow; staining white paper yellow overnight. **Odor and Taste:** Odor fragrant and sweet, not distinctive; taste acrid (sometimes slowly). **Spore Print:** White to cream. **Chemical Reactions:** KOH negative on cap. **Microscopic Features:** Spores 6–8 × 5–6.5 µm; broadly ellipsoid; ornamentation 0.5–1 µm high, composed of amyloid warts and widely spaced amyloid ridges that sometimes form a partial or nearly complete reticulum. Pileipellis a cutis of clearly defined, densely packed, cylindric hyphae, sometimes embedded in gelatinous material. **Comments:** The pale colors, the hairy cap with a "bearded" margin, the association with paper birch, and the slowly yellowish milk are good field characters. *Lactarius torminosus* is similar and also associates with birch but features a more highly colored, pinkish-orange to salmon-colored cap.

LACTARIUS QUIETUS VAR. INCANUS HESLER & A. H. SMITH

Ecology: Mycorrhizal with oaks and perhaps with other hardwoods in oak-based forests; growing alone, scattered, or gregariously; summer and fall; widely distributed. **Cap:** 3–11 cm; convex, becoming flat or shallowly vase-shaped; dry; smooth or uneven and somewhat rugged; when young often with a whitish dusting; usually zoned with shades of dark reddish brown, but sometimes becoming vaguely zoned or without zones with age. **Gills:** Attached to the stem or running slightly down it; close or nearly crowded; whitish at first, developing cinnamon stains and discolorations, but not staining from the milk. **Stem:** 4–14 cm long; up to 1.5 cm thick; more or less equal; bald; without potholes; when young with a white dusting; colored like the cap, but paler; darkening with age from the base upward; hollowing. **Flesh:** Whitish to pinkish; not changing when sliced, or staining slowly pinkish. **Milk:** White at first, becoming watery with age; sometimes slightly yellowish; not changing on exposure; not staining tissues;

often staining white paper yellow overnight. **Odor and Taste:** Odor strongly fragrant, or not distinctive; taste mild or slightly acrid. **Chemical Reactions:** KOH olive on cap. **Spore Print:** White or pale yellowish. **Microscopic Features:** Spores 6–8 × 5–7 µm; broadly ellipsoid; ornamentation 0.5–1.0 µm high, as amyloid warts and scattered ridges that occasionally form zebroid patterns but do not form a reticulum. Pileipellis a trichoderm or oedotrichoderm.

LACTARIUS SCROBICULATUS VAR. CANADENSIS (A. H. SMITH) HESLER & A. H. SMITH

Ecology: Mycorrhizal with conifers; growing alone, scattered, or gregariously; summer and fall; northern Midwest. **Cap:** 4–12 cm; broadly convex, with an inrolled and bearded margin when young, becoming shallowly vase-shaped, with the margin uplifted and smoother; sticky when young, but soon dry; covered with hairs that may darken to brownish, the hairs remaining visible in maturity; whitish at first, becoming olive buff or yellowish in age; without concentric zones of color. **Gills:** Beginning to run down the stem; crowded; often forking near the stem; whitish; bruising or staining yellowish to pale brownish. **Stem:** 3–11 cm long; 1–3.5 cm thick; equal; with many glazed yellowish or brownish potholes; whitish; bruising and discoloring yellowish or brownish. **Flesh:** Whitish; firm. **Milk:** White, promptly turning yellow on exposure to air; scanty. **Odor and Taste:** Odor not distinctive; taste mild or slowly slightly acrid. **Chemical Reactions:** KOH negative to faintly orange on cap. **Spore Print:** White or creamy. **Microscopic Features:** Spores 7–9 × 5.5–7 µm; ellipsoid; ornamentation about 0.5 µm high as amyloid warts and scattered short ridges that occasionally branch but do not form reticula. Pileipellis an ixocutis with occasional fascicles of upright hyphae. **Comments:** Recognized by the hairy whitish to yellowish cap; the milk, which turns rapidly yellow on exposure; and the association with northern conifers.

LACTARIUS SUBPALUSTRIS HESLER & A. H. SMITH

Ecology: Mycorrhizal with hardwoods, primarily with oaks but also reported under paper birch, beech, hop hornbeam, and ashes; growing alone or gregariously; summer and fall; widely distributed. **Cap:** 5–20 cm; broadly convex, with an inrolled margin when young; becoming shallowly depressed, with an uplifted margin, or shallowly vase-shaped; slimy when fresh; bald; drab gray to faintly yellowish or brownish; without concentric zones of color, or with faint zones. **Gills:** Beginning to run down the stem; close or nearly distant; creamy white when young, becoming

orangish to pale dingy tan; staining and bruising lilac and eventually purplish brown. **Stem:** 4–10 cm long; 1.5–2.5 cm thick; tough; more or less equal; usually featuring potholes; slimy when very fresh, but soon dry; whitish; developing yellowish to brownish discolorations and stains. **Flesh:** Watery whitish; firm; staining lilac when sliced. **Milk:** Watery white; staining all surfaces lilac (sometimes slowly). **Odor and Taste:** Odor not distinctive; taste mild, slightly bitter, or faintly acrid (never strongly acrid). **Spore Print:** Pale yellowish. **Chemical Reactions:** KOH yellow to orangish on cap. **Microscopic Features:** Spores 7–11 × 7–9 µm; subglobose to broadly ellipsoid; ornamentation consisting of isolated warts and ridges extending 1–2 µm high, not forming a reticulum. Pileipellis an ixocutis. **Comments:** *Lactarius uvidus* also stains lilac but is associated with aspens and paper birch in the northern Midwest, turns green with KOH, and features a drab lilac cap.

LACTARIUS SUBPLINTHOGALUS COKER

Ecology: Mycorrhizal with oaks and perhaps with other hardwoods; growing alone, scattered, or gregariously; summer and fall; widely distributed but more common below the Great Lakes. **Cap:** 3–10 cm; flat, with a central depression, or shallowly vase-shaped; the margin usually becoming scalloped or pleated by maturity, at least shallowly; smooth or somewhat wrinkled, especially in age; bald or very finely velvety; whitish to yellowish buff, eventually darkening to light brown or grayish brown. **Gills:** Beginning to run down the stem; very distant (about 1–3 mm apart at the margin); yellowish; stained salmon pink (sometimes slowly) by the milk. **Stem:** 3–8 cm long; 0.5–1.5 cm thick; equal or tapered to base; bald; colored like the cap or paler; dry; hollowing. **Flesh:** Soft; whitish; staining salmon pink when sliced. **Milk:** White; drying pink; staining tissues pink. **Odor and Taste:** Odor not distinctive; taste acrid (or sometimes mild, especially in older specimens). **Spore Print:** Creamy or buff. **Chemical Reactions:** KOH negative on cap. **Microscopic Features:** Spores 7–9.5 × 7–8 µm; subglobose; ornamentation 1.5–2.5 µm high, as amyloid spines and wide, branched ridges that do not generally form a reticulum. Pileipellis a trichoepithelium, with terminal

cells cylindric to subclavate. **Comments:** The distant gills, pink staining, pale colors, and scalloped mature cap margin are good field characters. Compare with *Lactarius subvernalis* var. *cokeri* (p. 249), which does not develop a scalloped margin and remains whitish throughout development.

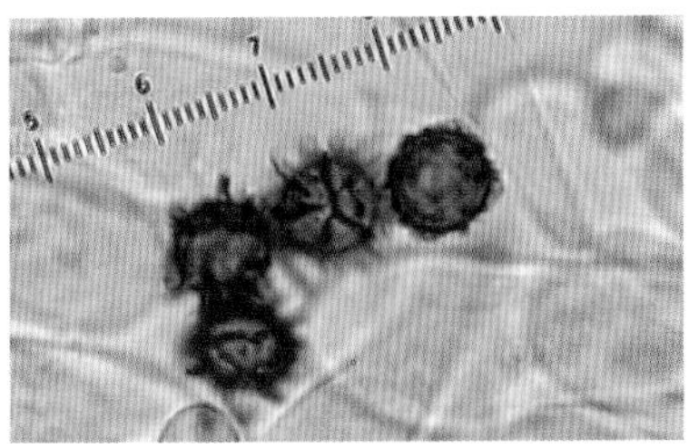

Spores

LACTARIUS SUBPURPUREUS PECK

Ecology: Mycorrhizal with hemlock; growing alone, scattered, or gregariously; summer and fall; northern Midwest and Ohio. **Cap:** 3–10 cm; at first convex; becoming flat, with a shallow central depression, or vase-shaped; dry or slightly sticky; the margin naked, sometimes lined in age; bald; zoned with concentric bands of purplish red and pale pink, but soon fading to pinkish buff; sometimes more spotted than zoned; bruising green. **Gills:** Attached to the stem or running slightly down it; nearly distant; purplish red and typically remaining so longer than the cap; bruising and spotting green. **Stem:** 3–8 cm long; 0.5–1.5 cm thick; colored like the cap or paler; more or less equal; sometimes spotted or pitted; becoming hollow. **Flesh:** Whitish to pink; staining red, and eventually green when sliced. **Milk:** Wine red; scanty. **Odor and Taste:** Odor not distinctive; taste mild to faintly peppery. **Chemical Reactions:** KOH negative on cap. **Spore Print:** Pale creamy. **Microscopic Features:** Spores 8–12 × 6.5–9 µm; broadly ellipsoid; ornamentation 0.2–0.5 µm high, as amyloid lines and warts that form zebroid patterns and, occasionally, partially reticulated areas. Pileipellis an ixocutis. **Comments:** The purplish-red to pink zoned cap, the wine-red milk, and the association with hemlock characterize this species.

LACTARIUS SUBSERIFLUUS LONGYEAR

Ecology: Mycorrhizal with oaks, primarily in oak-hickory woods; growing alone, scattered, or gregariously; June, July, and August; probably widely distributed. **Cap:** 2–7 cm; plano-convex, developing a central depression and, at the center, a sharp bump; moist or dry; bald; brownish orange to rusty orange. **Gills:** Running down the stem; well spaced; creamy to pale yellowish at first, developing cinnamon spots and eventually discoloring cinnamon. **Stem:** 5–12 cm long; 3–7 mm thick; tough and flexible; more or less equal; bald; without potholes; cinnamon to rusty brown; dry; base covered with stiff orange to whitish hairs. **Flesh:** Pale brownish to pale cinnamon; not staining when sliced. **Milk:** Watery; not staining tissues, or staining the gills cinnamon; not staining white paper. **Odor and Taste:** Odor not distinctive, or fragrant; taste mild or slightly peppery. **Spore Print:** Pale yellowish. **Chemical Reactions:** KOH olive on cap. **Microscopic Features:** Spores 6–7.5 × 6–7 µm; subglobose; ornamentation 1.0–1.5 µm high, as amyloid warts and ridges that form a partial to nearly complete reticulum. Pileipellis a hyphoepithelium. **Comments:** The tough and flexible stem is atypical for the genus and is the best field character for this species. Compare with *Lactarius camphoratus* (p. 233) and with *Lactarius areolatus* (p. 232), which features a cap that becomes wrinkled and a brittle stem.

LACTARIUS SUBVELLEREUS VAR. SUBDISTANS HESLER & A. H. SMITH

Ecology: Mycorrhizal with oaks and perhaps with other hardwoods; summer and fall; widely distributed. **Cap**: 4–15 cm; convex, with a soft, inrolled margin at first; becoming flat or shallowly depressed; dry; finely velvety; whitish; without concentric zones of color or texture. **Gills:** Attached to the stem or beginning to run down it; distant or nearly so; whitish, becoming yellowish; bruising and spotting slowly brownish. **Stem:** 2–5 cm long; up to 3.5 cm thick; more or less equal; dry; finely velvety; without potholes; whitish; sometimes bruising brownish. **Flesh:** White; changing to yellowish when sliced. **Milk:** White; changing to yellow or yellowish (often slowly, and only very slightly) on exposure; staining the gills brownish to pinkish brown; staining white paper yellow. **Odor and Taste:** Odor not distinctive; taste strongly acrid. **Spore Print:** White. **Chemical Reactions:** KOH pinkish to pale magenta on cap; orange on gills and on flesh. **Microscopic Features:** Spores 7.5–9 × 5–7 µm; broadly ellipsoid; ornamentation under 0.5 µm high, as isolated warts (sometimes nearly invisible, even with oil immersion). Pileipellis a lamprotrichoderm featuring a dense turf of upright, tapered, thick-walled pileocystidia. **Comments:** The colors, velvety feel of the surfaces, and distant gills are good field characters. Compare with *Lactarius glaucescens* (p. 238). *Lactarius deceptivus* features a cap that develops scaly areas, a cottony cap margin, close gills, and different microcharacters.

LACTARIUS SUBVERNALIS VAR. COKERI (A. H. SMITH & HESLER) HESLER & A. H. SMITH

Ecology: Mycorrhizal with hardwoods, especially oaks; growing scattered or gregariously; summer and fall; widely distributed. **Cap:** 3–6 cm; convex at first, becoming flat, centrally depressed, or shallowly vase-shaped; the margin even by maturity; dry; finely suede-like; whitish to buff, or sometimes pale brownish with maturity; more or less evenly colored; sometimes bruising pink. **Gills:** Attached to the stem or running slightly down it; often forked near the stem; close or crowded; white at first, later dingy buff; often stained salmon pink by the milk when sliced. **Stem:** 5–7 cm long; 0.5–2 cm thick; more or less equal; dry; finely suede-like; without potholes; whitish; usually bruising pink; hollowing. **Flesh:** Soft; whitish, but typically staining pink when sliced (occasionally not staining, or staining only faintly and very slowly, especially in hot, dry weather). **Milk:** White; unchanging; usually staining surfaces pink; staining white paper slightly yellow. **Odor and Taste:** Odor not distinctive; taste usually strongly acrid, but occasionally slightly acrid or even mild. **Chemical Reactions:** KOH negative on cap. **Spore Print:** Pale yellow. **Microscopic Features:** Spores 6–8 µm; globose or subglobose; ornamentation 0.5–1.5 µm high, as amyloid spines and ridges forming a partial or complete reticulum. Pileipellis a trichoepithelium or an epithelium. **Comments:** Compare with *Lactarius fumosus* (p. 237) and with *Lactarius subplinthogalus* (p. 246).

LACTARIUS THYINOS A. H. SMITH

Ecology: Mycorrhizal with conifers; growing scattered or gregariously; summer and fall; northern Midwest. **Cap:** 3–9 cm; at first convex, becoming flat, with a shallow central depression, or vase-shaped; slimy or thinly slimy when fresh; the margin arched; bald; zoned with concentric bands of carrot orange and paler orange. **Gills:** Attached to the stem or running slightly down it; close or nearly distant; orange; bruising brownish. **Stem:** 4–8 cm long; 1.5–2 cm thick; orange; more or less equal, or tapering somewhat to base; bald; hollow; sometimes slimy when young; often with a whitish sheen above; sometimes bruising dull red or brownish; sometimes with wide, shallow potholes. **Flesh:** Thin; white

to orangish. **Milk:** Orange; unchanging when exposed; slowly staining tissues red. **Odor and Taste:** Odor faintly fragrant; taste mild. **Chemical Reactions:** KOH negative on cap. **Spore Print:** Whitish to pale yellow. **Microscopic Features:** Spores 9–12 × 7.5–9 µm; broadly ellipsoid to subglobose; ornamentation 0.5–1.0 µm high, as amyloid warts and ridges forming a partial reticulum. Pileipellis an ixocutis. **Comments:** Compare with *Lactarius deliciosus* var. *deterrimus* (p. 236), which stains green.

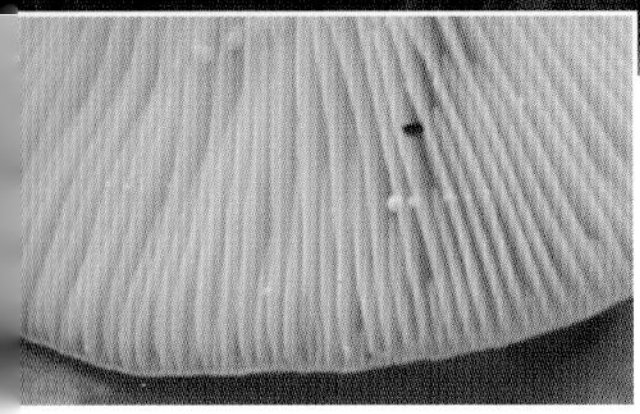

LACTARIUS VINACEORUFESCENS A. H. SMITH

Ecology: Mycorrhizal with pines (especially white pine); growing scattered or gregariously; summer and fall; widely distributed. **Cap:** 4–12 cm; broadly convex, with an inrolled margin when young; becoming shallowly depressed or vase-shaped, with an uplifted margin; slimy or sticky when fresh; bald; cinnamon pink, cinnamon, or reddish brown; typically with vague concentric zones of color, at least when young. **Gills:** Beginning to run down the stem; close; pale at first, developing pinkish to brownish stains, and often becoming reddish to reddish brown overall with age. **Stem:** 4–7 cm long; 1–2.5 cm thick; equal, or enlarging toward the base; bald; without potholes; whitish, becoming colored like the cap with age. **Flesh:** White; firm; staining yellow when sliced. **Milk:** White, becoming yellow within a few seconds on exposure to air; staining white paper yellow. **Odor and Taste:** Odor not distinctive; taste acrid or peppery (sometimes slowly so). **Chemical Reactions:** KOH olive (or sometimes negative) on cap. **Spore Print:** Whitish to yellowish. **Microscopic Features:** Spores 6.5–9 × 5–7 µm; broadly ellipsoid or subglobose; ornamentation 0.5–1 µm high, as amyloid warts and ridges that sometimes form a partial reticulum. Pileipellis an ixocutis. **Comments:** *Lactarius chrysorrheus* is very similar but is associated with hardwoods. It has a cap with more pronounced yellow colors as well as gills that do not develop reddish spots and stains. Compare with *Lactarius maculatipes* (p. 242).

LACTARIUS VOLEMUS (FRIES) FRIES

Ecology: Mycorrhizal with oaks and other hardwoods, as well as conifers; growing alone, scattered, or gregariously; summer and fall; widely distributed. **Cap:** 3–13 cm; at first convex, with an inrolled margin; becoming flat, with a central depression, shallowly vase-shaped, or (rarely) with a slight bump over the disc, the margin even; smooth or slightly wrinkled, but usually finely velvety to the touch, at least when young; brownish orange, orangish brown, or sometimes lighter or darker (approaching deep brownish red); without concentric zones of color. **Gills:** Attached to the stem or running slightly down it; close; creamy white; discoloring brown where injured; often forking near the margin. **Stem:** 5–10 cm long; 0.5–2.5 cm thick; colored like the cap or paler; equal or tapering to the base; bald; sometimes vaguely ribbed longitudinally; solid or becoming hollow. **Flesh:** White; staining slowly brown when sliced. **Milk:** White; copious; sometimes becoming brownish on exposure to air; staining tissues brown; staining white paper brown. **Odor and Taste:** Odor fishy; taste mild. **Chemical Reactions:** KOH olive on cap; orange on milk. **Spore Print:** White. **Microscopic Features:** Spores 6.5–9.5 × 5.5–9 µm; subglobose or occasionally broadly ellipsoid; ornamentation 0.4–0.8 µm high, as widely spaced amyloid ridges forming a complete reticulum. Pileipellis a lamprotrichoderm, with a turf of cylindric to narrowly fusiform pileocystidia. **Comments:** Compare with *Lactarius corrugis* (p. 236) and with *Lactarius hygrophoroides* (p. 239).

LAETIPORUS CINCINNATUS (MORGAN) BURDSALL, BANIK, & VOLK

Ecology: Parasitic and saprobic on living and dead oaks; causing a brown butt rot and root rot; growing alone or gregariously at the bases of trees; summer and fall, rarely in winter and spring; widely distributed. **Fruiting Body:** Up to 60 cm across; usually consisting of several to many caps in a rosette but very rarely consisting of a shelving array near the base of the tree. **Caps:** 5–15 cm across and up to 20 cm deep; up to 3 cm thick; fan-shaped to irregularly lobed; smooth to wrinkled; suede-like; bright to pale orange, often with vague concentric bands of alternating shades of color; frequently fading in maturity and with direct sunlight. **Pore Surface:** Whitish; with 2–4 circular to angular pores per mm; tubes to 5 mm deep. **Stem:** More or less central; whitish; usually poorly defined. **Flesh:** Thick; soft and watery when young, becoming tough, eventually crumbling away; white. **Odor and Taste:** Not distinctive. **Spore Print:** White. **Microscopic Features:** Spores 4.5–5.5 × 3.5–4 µm; smooth; broadly ellipsoid to ovoid; inamyloid. Setae absent. Hyphal system dimitic. Clamp connections absent. **Comments:** Edible and good when young and fresh, but it must be thoroughly cooked. Compare with *Laetiporus sulphureus* (p. 252), which grows in shelving arrays on trees and logs above ground and has a yellow pore surface.

LAETIPORUS SULPHUREUS (BULLIARD) MURRILL

Ecology: Parasitic and saprobic on living and dead oaks (also sometimes on the wood of other hardwoods); causing a reddish-brown cubical heart rot, with thin areas of white mycelium visible in the cracks of the wood; annual; growing alone or, more typically, in large clusters on trees and logs above ground (not on the ground at the base of the tree trunk); summer and fall, rarely in winter and spring; widely distributed. **Fruiting Body:** Up to 60 cm across; usually consisting of several to many individual caps arranged in a shelving formation or, when on top of a log, forming a rosette. **Caps:** 5–30 cm across and up to 20 cm deep; up to 3 cm thick; fan-shaped to semicircular or irregular; more or less plano-convex; smooth to finely wrinkled; suede-like; bright yellow to bright orange when young, frequently fading in maturity and with direct sunlight. **Pore Surface:** Yellow; with 2–4 circular to angular pores per mm; tubes to 5 mm deep. **Stem:** Absent. **Flesh:** Thick; soft and watery when young, becoming tough, eventually crumbling away; white to pale yellow. **Odor and Taste:** Not distinctive. **Spore Print:** White. **Microscopic Features:** Spores 5.5–7 × 3.5–5 µm; smooth; ellipsoid to ovoid; inamyloid. Cystidia absent. Hyphal system dimitic. Clamp connections absent. **Comments:** Edible and good when young and fresh, but it must be thoroughly cooked. Sometimes called the "chicken of the woods." Compare with *Laetiporus cincinnatus* (p. 251).

Photo by Matt Kessler

LECCINELLUM ALBELLUM (PECK) BRESINSKY & MANF. BINDER

Ecology: Mycorrhizal with oaks—often with red oaks—and possibly also mycorrhizal with other hardwoods; frequently found in woods where oaks are mixed with pines; growing alone or gregariously; summer and fall; widely distributed, but more common below the Great Lakes. **Cap:** 2–7 cm across; convex, becoming broadly convex or flat; dry; bald or very finely hairy; whitish to pale grayish, pale pinkish, or pale yellowish; occasionally pitted with brownish to grayish veins; without an overhanging margin. **Pore Surface:** Depressed at the stem; whitish to grayish, becoming yellowish to olive buff; not bruising; with 1–2 round or angular pores per mm; tubes to 1 cm long. **Stem:** 4–9 cm long; 1–1.5 cm wide; at maturity more or less equal, or tapering to apex; whitish to pale olive or very pale gray; sometimes discoloring yellowish; finely scabrous with whitish to grayish or brownish scabers. **Flesh:** White or yellowish (especially in the stem); unchanging when sliced and exposed to air. **Odor and Taste:** Not distinctive. **Spore Print:** Olive brown. **Chemical Reactions:** Iron salts purplish gray on flesh. **Microscopic Features:** Spores subfusoid; inamyloid; yellowish in KOH; smooth; 10–24 × 4–6.5 µm. Pileipellis a trichoderm of chained elements, with the terminal elements subglobose or clavate. **Comments:** Compare with *Leccinum holopus* (below), which is associated with paper birch, has a different pileipellis, and often stains blue in the stem base.

LECCINUM HOLOPUS (ROSTKOVIUS) WATLING

Ecology: Mycorrhizal with paper birch; growing alone, scattered, or gregariously in wet, boggy areas; summer and fall; northern Midwest. **Cap:** 3–12 cm across; convex, becoming broadly convex or flat; tacky; bald or, when young, very finely hairy; whitish to pale yellowish or pale brownish; sometimes developing greenish to bluish hues with age; with a tiny (1 mm or less) overhanging margin. **Pore Surface:** Depressed at the stem; whitish, becoming pinkish to brownish; bruising yellowish to brownish; with 1–2 round or angular pores per mm; tubes to 2.5 cm long. **Stem:** 6–14 cm long; 1–2.5 cm wide; at maturity more or less equal, or slightly club-shaped; whitish; adorned with whitish scabers that usually darken to brown, grayish, or blackish. **Flesh:** White; unchanging when sliced and exposed to air, or changing to pinkish or reddish (eventually grayish); often blue in the base of the stem. **Odor and Taste:** Not distinctive. **Spore Print:** Cinnamon brown. **Chemical Reactions:** Ammonia pinkish on cap surface; negative on flesh. KOH negative on cap surface; negative to brownish on flesh. Iron salts negative on cap; negative to slightly olive on flesh. **Microscopic Features:** Spores fusoid; inamyloid; yellowish in KOH; smooth; 13–21 × 4–7 µm. Pileipellis a cutis. **Comments:** Edible. Compare with *Leccinellum albellum* (p. 252).

LECCINUM INSIGNE A. H. SMITH, THIERS, & WATLING

Ecology: Mycorrhizal with aspens, both big-toothed aspen and quaking aspen; growing alone, scattered, or gregariously; late spring, summer, and fall; northern Midwest. **Cap:** 4–15 cm across; convex, becoming broadly convex or flat; dry; finely hairy or nearly bald; reddish orange to orange, red, orangish brown, or reddish brown; with a substantial overhanging margin that splits into flaps. **Pore Surface:** Depressed at the stem; whitish, becoming yellowish to brownish or olive; bruising yellowish to grayish; with 1–2 round or angular pores per mm;

tubes to 2 cm long. **Stem:** 8–12 cm long; 1–2 cm wide; club-shaped; whitish; adorned with brownish scabers that darken to black. **Flesh:** White; changing slowly to purplish gray when sliced and exposed to air. **Odor and Taste:** Not distinctive. **Spore Print:** Yellowish brown. **Chemical Reactions:** Ammonia negative on cap surface; negative on flesh. KOH pale gray on cap surface and flesh. Iron salts negative on cap; bluish on flesh. **Microscopic Features:** Spores fusoid; inamyloid; yellowish in KOH; smooth; 13–18 × 4–5 µm. Pileipellis a cutis. **Comments:** Not recommended for the table; several red and orange *Leccinum* species are poisonous. Compare with *Leccinum vulpinum* (p. 255), which is associated with conifers and turns blue in the base of the stem.

LECCINUM RUGOSICEPS (PECK) SINGER

Ecology: Mycorrhizal with oaks; growing alone, scattered, or gregariously; summer and fall; widely distributed, but more common below the Great Lakes. **Cap:** 3–15 cm across; convex, becoming broadly convex or nearly flat; dry or slightly tacky; bald; frequently pitted and wrinkled when young, and prominently cracked when old; mustard yellow to orangish yellow when young, becoming brownish yellow or brown before fading to yellowish brown or tan; with a tiny (about 1 mm or less) overhanging margin. **Pore Surface:** Depressed at the stem; dull yellow to yellowish, becoming olive yellow or brownish; not bruising, or bruising brownish; with 1–2 round pores per mm; tubes to 2 cm long. **Stem:** 4–15 cm long; 1.5–3 cm wide; more or less equal; yellowish or whitish (but sometimes with reddish areas, especially in wet weather); adorned with yellowish to brown scabers. **Flesh:** White or yellowish; changing quickly to pinkish or reddish when sliced and exposed to air, then changing to grayish or blackish over the course of 20–60 minutes. **Odor and Taste:** Not distinctive. **Spore Print:** Brown to olive brown. **Chemical Reactions:** Ammonia reddish to negative on cap; yellowish to negative on flesh. KOH red on cap; yellowish to orangish on flesh. Iron salts gray on cap; greenish gray to olive on flesh. **Microscopic Features:** Spores subfusoid; inamyloid; yellowish in KOH; smooth; 10–21 × 3–6 µm. Pileipellis a trichoderm with swollen penultimate or antepenultimate elements. **Comments:** Edible and very good.

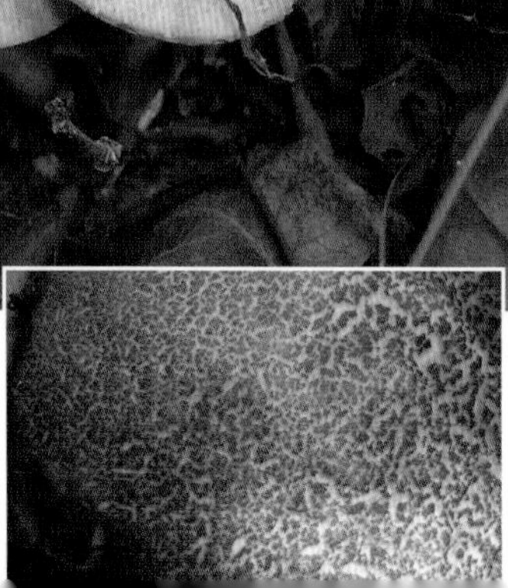

LECCINUM SUBGLABRIPES (PECK) SINGER

Ecology: Mycorrhizal with oaks, paper birch, and aspens, appearing in diverse ecosystems; growing alone, scattered, or gregariously; summer and fall; widely distributed. **Cap:** 3–15 cm across; convex, becoming broadly convex or nearly flat; dry or slightly tacky; bald; occasionally becoming pitted or corrugated-wrinkled; cinnamon brown to reddish brown or yellow brown; without an overhanging margin. **Pore Surface:** Depressed at the stem; yellow, becoming greenish yellow or olive; not bruising; with 1–3 round pores per mm; tubes to 1.5 cm long. **Stem:** 5–11 cm long; 1–2.5 cm wide; more or less equal; bright yellow at the apex; pale to bright yellow below; often becoming reddish-tinged in the middle or near the base; adorned with tiny, inconspicuous yellow scabers that often darken to red. **Flesh:** Yellow; soft; unchanging when sliced and exposed to air, or bluing faintly (especially over the tubes). **Odor and Taste:** Not distinctive. **Spore Print:** Olive. **Chemical Reactions:** Ammonia negative on cap; negative to bluish on flesh. KOH negative to grayish or reddish on cap; orangish on flesh. Iron salts negative on cap and flesh. **Microscopic Features:** Spores subfusoid; inamyloid; hyaline or greenish yellow in KOH; smooth; 10–20 × 3–5 µm. Pileipellis a trichoderm with swollen terminal elements. **Comments:** Also known as *Boletus subglabripes*. Edible but not very good. Compare with *Boletus longicurvipes* (p. 118).

LECCINUM VULPINUM WATLING

Ecology: Mycorrhizal with conifers; growing alone, scattered, or gregariously; summer and fall; widely distributed, but more common from the Great Lakes northward. **Cap:** 4–20 cm across; convex, becoming broadly convex or nearly flat; dry or slightly tacky; finely hairy; red to orange, brownish orange, or brownish red; with a substantial overhanging margin that splits into flaps. **Pore Surface:** Depressed at the stem; whitish, becoming grayish to brownish; bruising brownish to blackish; with 1–3 round pores per mm; tubes to 2 cm long. **Stem:** 7–20 cm long; 2–4 cm wide; more or less equal, or club-shaped; whitish, becoming grayish to brownish; adorned with brown scabers that darken to black. **Flesh:** White; changing to lilac gray when sliced and exposed to air; often blue to green in the stem base. **Odor and Taste:** Not distinctive. **Spore**

Print: Brown. **Chemical Reactions:** Ammonia negative on cap and flesh. KOH negative on cap and flesh. Iron salts negative on cap; blue on flesh. **Microscopic Features:** Spores subfusoid; inamyloid; yellow in KOH; smooth; 10–20 × 3–6 µm. Pileipellis a cutis. **Comments:** Not recommended for the table; several red and orange *Leccinum* species are poisonous. This is "*Leccinum aurantiacum*" in the sense of most North American authors. However, recent molecular studies (den Bakker and Noordeloos 2005) indicate that *Leccinum vulpinum* is probably a better name for our conifer-associated, red to orange species with black scabers. Compare with *Leccinum insigne* (p. 253).

LENTINELLUS MICHENERI (BERKELEY & CURTIS) PEGLER

Ecology: Saprobic; growing scattered or gregariously, usually in small clusters, on deadwood of hardwoods or conifers, or growing terrestrially in woody debris; summer and fall; widely distributed. **Cap:** 1–5 cm; convex when young, with a central depression; later broadly convex or nearly flat, with or without a deep central depression; moist; bald; pinkish brown or paler; changing color markedly as it dries out, often resulting in 2-toned caps; the margin not lined. **Gills:** Attached to the stem; nearly distant; with distinctively saw-toothed edges; whitish to pinkish brown; not bruising. **Stem:** 0.5–5 cm long; 1–3 mm thick; more or less equal; frequently grooved longitudinally; brown or reddish brown; sometimes off-center. **Flesh:** Pale brownish; insubstantial. **Odor and Taste:** Taste acrid or peppery (sometimes developing slowly); odor not distinctive. **Spore Print:** Creamy whitish. **Microscopic Features:** Spores 4–5 × 3–3.5 µm; ellipsoid; amyloid; very finely ornamented with warts and spines. Pleurocystidia fusiform. Gloeocystidia sometimes present. **Comments:** Also known as *Lentinellus omphalodes*. The saw-toothed gills, peppery taste, and the frequent "belly button" in the middle of the cap make good field characters.

LENTINELLUS URSINUS (FRIES) KÜHNER

Ecology: Saprobic; growing in groups or in shelf-like clusters on the deadwood of hardwoods (and, rarely, conifers); summer and fall; widely distributed. **Cap:** Up to 10 cm across; kidney-shaped to roughly semicircular; broadly convex, becoming flat or depressed; minutely hairy or velvety, at least over the inner third; brown, cinnamon brown, or pale; the margin inrolled. **Gills:** Close or nearly distant; with distinctively saw-toothed edges; whitish to pinkish. **Stem:** Absent. **Flesh:** Pale. **Odor and Taste:** Taste strongly acrid or peppery; odor not distinctive or a little fragrant. **Spore Print:** Creamy white. **Microscopic Features:** Spores 4–4.5 × 3–3.5 µm; ellipsoid; amyloid; very finely ornamented with warts and spines. Pleurocystidia rare; fusoid to sharply pointed. Gloeocystidia present; clavate. **Comments:** *Lentinellus vulpinus* is very similar but features a stubby lateral stem and a much paler, fuzzy cap surface.

LENZITES BETULINA (LINNAEUS) FRIES

Ecology: Saprobic on the deadwood of hardwoods and, occasionally, conifers; annual; growing alone or in overlapping clusters on logs and stumps; producing a white to straw-colored rot of the sapwood; summer and fall; widely distributed. **Cap:** Up to 10 cm across and 2 cm thick; semicircular, irregularly bracket-shaped, or kidney-shaped; flattened-convex; densely hairy, with concentric zones of texture; often radially bumpy or ridged; with zones of whitish, grayish, and brownish colors; flexible; without a stem; sometimes developing greenish colors in old age as a result of the growth of algae. **Gills:** Whitish; well spaced or fairly close; sharp; tough; up to 1 cm or more deep. **Stem:** Absent. **Flesh:** White; extremely tough and corky. **Chemical Reactions:** KOH negative on flesh. **Spore Print:** White. **Microscopic Features:** Spores 5–6 × 2–3 µm; smooth; cylindric; inamyloid. Cystidia absent. Hyphal system trimitic. **Comments:** Sometimes called the "gilled polypore." Compare with *Daedalea quercina* (p. 168), which has thick-walled, primarily maze-like pores/gills and turns black with KOH.

LEOTIA LUBRICA PERSOON

Ecology: Saprobic; growing gregariously under hardwoods or conifers, often in moss; late spring through fall; widely distributed. **Cap:** 1–4 cm; variable in shape but more or less convex; convoluted; with a smooth or slightly wrinkled surface; sticky or slimy when fresh, but sometimes drying out; the margin inrolled; buff, brownish yellow, or yellowish; underside smooth and pale. **Stem:** 2–8 cm long; up to 1 cm wide; bald or finely roughened; more or less equal; sticky or slimy when fresh; colored like the cap or paler; hollow or filled with gelatinous material. **Flesh:**

Gelatinous when fresh. **Microscopic Features:** Spores 16–25 × 4–6 µm; smooth; fusiform; often curved; becoming septate, with 5–7 septa at maturity. **Comments:** *Leotia viscosa* is similar but features a green cap and a bright yellow stem.

LEPIOTA ASPERA (PERSOON) QUÉLET

Ecology: Saprobic; growing alone or scattered, usually in hardwood leaf litter or near woody debris; occasionally growing from well-rotted wood; late summer and fall; widely distributed. **Cap:** 3–11 cm; convex, becoming broadly convex or nearly flat in age; dry; when young, densely covered with soft hairs that separate and become aggregated into small, sharp scales with maturity; orangish brown overall when young; when mature, with orangish-brown to dark brown scales over a whitish ground color that is exposed near the margin or nearly to the darker center. **Gills:** Free from the stem; white; close or crowded. **Stem:** 6–11 cm long; up to about 1.5 cm thick; more or less equal; dry; finely to densely hairy; with a ragged, flimsy, but fairly persistent ring that cannot be easily detached and often features brown scales (like those on the cap) on its underside. **Flesh:** White. **Odor and Taste:** Odor usually mild, but sometimes fragrant or pungent; taste not distinctive. **Spore Print:** White. **Chemical Reactions:** KOH negative on cap. **Microscopic Features:** Spores 6.5–11 × 2–3.5 µm; smooth; dextrinoid; long-ellipsoid to nearly fusoid. Cheilocystidia clavate, cylindric, or nearly round. Pleurocystidia absent. Pileipellis an interwoven cutis, with scattered erect chains of inflated cells (the squamules on the cap surface). **Comments:** Not recommended for the table. Also known as *Lepiota acutesquamosa.*

LEPIOTA CRISTATA (BOLTON) KUMMER

Ecology: Saprobic; growing scattered or gregariously, often in disturbed-ground areas (paths, ditches, lawns, and so on), but also on the forest floor; summer and fall; widely distributed. **Cap:** 1–5 cm; convex, becoming broadly convex to broadly bell-shaped or flat in age; dry; bald at first but soon becoming scaly, with pinkish to reddish-brown or brownish scales that are usually concentrically arranged; whitish, with the center typically remaining bald and darker. **Gills:** Free from the stem; white to buff; close. **Stem:** 2–8 cm long; 2–5 mm thick; more or less equal; bald; fragile; whitish, but often darker toward the base; with a fragile white ring (which may easily disappear) on the upper portion. **Flesh:** White; thin. **Odor and Taste:** Taste not distinctive; odor fragrant or strong and foul (occasionally not distinctive). **Chemical Reactions:** KOH negative on cap. **Spore Print:** White. **Microscopic Features:** Spores 5–8 × 3–5 µm; smooth; strongly to weakly dextrinoid; distinctively shaped like a wedge or a bullet. Cheilocystidia inflated-clavate. Pleurocystidia absent. Pileipellis hymeniform. **Comments:** Possibly poisonous. Compare with *Lepiota magnispora* (below).

LEPIOTA MAGNISPORA MURRILL

Ecology: Saprobic; growing scattered, gregariously, or in clusters in forest litter; found under hardwoods or conifers; summer and fall; widely distributed. **Cap:** 3–5 cm; convex to bell-shaped, becoming broadly convex, broadly bell-shaped, or nearly flat in age; dry; scaly; yellow to yellow brown or rusty brown with a darker, contrasting center. **Gills:** Free from the stem; white; close. **Stem:** 4–9 cm long; under 1 cm thick; more or less equal, with a slightly swollen base; hairy to shaggy; whitish to yellowish, or with scattered brownish scales; sometimes discoloring yellowish with age or on handling; with a sheathing ring or ring zone that sometimes disappears. **Flesh:** White. **Odor and Taste:** Not distinctive. **Chemical Reactions:** KOH negative on cap. **Spore Print:** White. **Microscopic Features:** Spores 15–21 × 4.5–6 µm; smooth; dextrinoid; fusiform, with a convex curve on the adaxial side; reminiscent of bolete spores. Cystidia absent. **Comments:** Poisonous. This mushroom is often featured in field guides as "*Lepiota clypeolaria*," but recent studies by Vellinga (2000, 2003) have uncovered several genetically distinct mushrooms in this group. Compare with *Lepiota cristata* (p. 258), which has a whitish cap with reddish-brown scales, a distinctive odor, and bullet-shaped spores.

LERATIOMYCES SQUAMOSUS VAR. THRAUSTUS (SCHULZER) BRIDGE & SPOONER

Ecology: Saprobic; growing alone or gregariously on woody debris in hardwood and conifer forests; summer and fall; widely distributed. **Cap:** 2.5–7 cm; convex, becoming broadly convex or broadly bell-shaped; slimy; reddish orange to brick red or orange; bald; when young adorned with white partial

veil remnants. **Gills:** Attached to the stem; close or nearly distant; pale at first, but later purplish gray to purple black; with whitish edges when mature. **Stem:** 6–12 cm long; up to 1 cm thick; dry; with a ring that is grooved on its upper surface and is usually arched gracefully downward and away from the stem; bald above the ring, densely scaly below; white at first, becoming brownish with maturity; base with white mycelial threads. **Flesh:** White, becoming brownish in the stem. **Odor and Taste:** Not distinctive. **Spore Print:** Dark purple brown to blackish. **Chemical Reactions:** KOH negative or slowly pinkish on cap. **Microscopic Features:** Spores 11–14 × 6–8.5 µm; smooth; ellipsoid; with an off-center pore. Pleurocystidia (chrysocystidia) absent. Cheilocystidia abundant; filamentous or subfusoid; often with subacute tips. Pileipellis a thin ixocutis of cylindric elements over a nearly cellular layer. **Comments:** Also known as *Stropharia squamosa* var. *thrausta*, *Stropharia thrausta*, and *Psilocybe thrausta*. Compare with species of *Pholiota* (pp. 308–12), which feature brown spore prints and usually grow in clusters on logs and stumps; also compare with *Limacella glioderma* (p. 265). This species is also illustrated on p. 401.

LEUCOAGARICUS AMERICANUS (PECK) VELLINGA

Ecology: Saprobic; growing alone, scattered, or gregariously in lawns and meadows, in sawdust piles or woodchips, near waste places, and on stumps, as well as in woods; late summer and fall; widely distributed. **Cap:** 3–15 cm, oval when young, becoming convex to broadly convex or flat in age; dry; bald at first; becoming scaly with reddish to reddish-brown scales; the center typically remaining bald in age; whitish but reddening with maturity or after being handled; the margin becoming lacerated and ragged in old age. **Gills:** Free from the stem; close; white when young; staining pinkish to reddish brown. **Stem:** 7–14 cm long; 0.5–2.5 cm thick; often distinctively swollen toward the base; bald; firm; white, but soon discoloring reddish to reddish brown; bruising fairly promptly yellow, then slowly reddish when rubbed; with a high, collar-like ring. **Flesh:** White throughout; bruising yellow to orange when young; in age drying reddish; thick. **Odor and Taste:** Not distinctive. **Spore Print:** White. **Microscopic Features:** Spores 8–14 × 5–10 µm; smooth; ellipsoid; dextrinoid; with a small pore. Cheilocystidia clavate or clavate with a long neck. Pleurocystidia absent. Pileipellis of long, upright, cylindric elements.

Comments: Edible. Compare with *Amanita rubescens* (p. 97), which bruises reddish without a yellow stage and is only found in woods. Also known as *Lepiota americana* and as *Macrolepiota americana.*

LEUCOAGARICUS NAUCINUS (FRIES) SINGER

Ecology: Saprobic; growing alone or gregariously in grassy areas or on disturbed ground (roadsides, cultivated areas, and so on); often in the vicinity of conifers; occasionally found in the woods; late summer through fall; widely distributed. **Cap:** 4–10 cm; convex or somewhat blocky when young ("lumpy-looking"), becoming broadly convex or nearly flat; dry; bald, or occasionally with a few tiny flakes or scales; white or grayish white (darker gray in some forms); often bruising yellowish; the margin not lined. **Gills:** Free from the stem; close; white, sometimes developing pinkish hues in age. **Stem:** 5–15 cm long; 0.5–1.5 cm thick; more or less equal, but frequently swollen at the base; dry; bald; often discoloring yellowish to brownish and/or bruising these shades; with a white ring on the upper stem that is fairly persistent but may fall away. **Flesh:** White; not changing on exposure to air. **Odor and Taste:** Odor not distinctive, or foul in some forms; taste not distinctive. **Spore Print:** White. **Microscopic Features:** Spores 7–9 × 5–6 µm; smooth; oval to ellipsoid; dextrinoid; with a small pore. Cheilocystidia variously shaped. **Comments:** Not recommended for the table; poisonous for some people. Compare with *Amanita bisporigera* (p. 89), which features a sac-like volva around the base of the stem.

LEUCOAGARICUS RUBROTINCTUS (PECK) SINGER

Photo by Melissa Bochte

Ecology: Saprobic; growing alone or scattered in woods (primarily in hardwood forests); sometimes in compost piles; summer and fall; widely distributed. **Cap:** 3–8 cm; at first egg-shaped and uniformly pinkish or orangish brown; becoming conical and eventually convex or nearly flat, with scattered pinkish to orangish-brown fibers over a white background; the center remaining distinctively darker; the margin not lined, but often splitting in age. **Gills:** Free from the stem; close; white; not bruising or staining. **Stem:** 4–16 cm long; 0.5–1 cm thick; more or less equal, but sometimes swollen at the base; the base often inserted fairly deeply in the ground; dry; bald or with tiny fibers; sometimes bruising or discoloring pale yellowish brown (but not dramatically, and not reddish),

especially in age; with a white ring on the upper stem that is fairly persistent but may fall away. **Flesh:** White; not changing on exposure to air. **Chemical Reactions:** KOH pale bluish green on cap. **Odor and Taste:** Not distinctive. **Spore Print:** White. **Microscopic Features:** Spores 6–10 × 4–6 µm; smooth; oval to ellipsoid; dextrinoid; with a small pore. Cheilocystidia variously shaped. **Comments:** Also known as *Lepiota rubrotincta*.

LEUCOCOPRINUS CEPISTIPES (SOWERBY) PATOUILLARD

Ecology: Saprobic; growing in groups or clusters in woodchips, cultivated soil, gardens, and so on (rarely in woods); summer; widely distributed. **Cap:** 2–8 cm, oval when young, becoming broadly conical or bell-shaped or nearly flat; dry; powdery with soft white granules; sometimes becoming scaly in age; white to pale pink, often with a darker yellowish or brownish center; the margin distinctly lined. **Gills:** Free from the stem; white; crowded. **Stem:** 4–14 cm long; 3–6 mm thick; more or less equal, but frequently swollen in places; bald or with white powder; often discoloring yellowish to brownish; with a white ring on the upper stem that is fairly persistent but easily removed. **Flesh:** White; very thin; sometimes bruising or discoloring yellowish to brownish. **Odor and Taste:** Odor fragrant, or not distinctive; taste not distinctive. **Chemical Reactions:** KOH negative on cap. **Spore Print:** White. **Microscopic Features:** Spores 6–11 × 5–8 µm; smooth; ellipsoid; dextrinoid; with a small pore; thick-walled. Cheilocystidia clavate to bottle-shaped (with a long neck). Pleurocystidia absent. **Comments:** Also known as *Lepiota cepistipes*.

LEUCOCOPRINUS FLAVESCENS (MORGAN) H. V. SMITH

Ecology: Saprobic; growing alone or scattered in the vicinity of black locust or honey locust trees (also reported from greenhouses); summer; distribution uncertain (see comments). **Cap:** 2–4 cm; egg-shaped when young, becoming bell-shaped to broadly convex or nearly flat at maturity; dry; grooved from the margin to the central "eye"; powdery or very finely scaly where grooved; bald in the center; light greenish yellow except for the brownish to tawny-brown center. **Gills:** Free from the stem; whitish to yellowish;

close or nearly distant. **Stem:** 3–8 cm long; only a few mm thick; more or less equal above, but with a swollen base; pale yellow; sometimes discoloring reddish brown; when fresh and young, covered with tiny powdery scales, but soon bald (especially after handling); with a yellowish ring on the upper stem that sometimes disappears. **Flesh:** Whitish to pale yellow; very thin. **Odor and Taste:** Not distinctive. **Chemical Reactions:** KOH negative on cap. **Spore Print:** White. **Microscopic Features:** Spores 5–7 × 3.5–5.5 µm; smooth; broadly ellipsoid to subglobose; dextrinoid; without a pore. Cheilocystidia clavate to fusoid-ventricose or bottle-shaped. Pleurocystidia absent. **Comments:** This species was originally described from Ohio under locust trees. It has since been reported from greenhouses in California and Massachusetts, and we report it here from Illinois woods. *Leucocoprinus birnbaumii* is a similar, brighter yellow species that often appears in the soil of potted plants.

LEUCOPAXILLUS ALBISSIMUS (PECK) SINGER

Ecology: Saprobic, decomposing the litter of conifers; growing scattered, gregariously, or in arcs or fairy rings; summer and fall; widely distributed. **Cap:** 3–20 cm; convex, with an inrolled margin when young, becoming broadly convex, flat, or shallowly depressed; dry; bald or very finely velvety (like kid leather); white, pinkish, buff, pale brownish, or pale tan; often darker with age and/or darker toward the center; the margin sometimes broadly lined at maturity. **Gills:** Attached to the stem or running down it; close; separable from the cap as a layer; whitish to dirty yellowish when mature; sometimes forking. **Stem:** 3–8 cm long; up to 3 cm thick; not infrequently slightly off-center; when young often slightly swollen near the base, but by maturity usually more or less equal; bald or very finely hairy, but not roughened-scaly; whitish; with prominent and copious basal mycelium. **Flesh:** White; thick; hard; not changing on exposure. **Odor and Taste:** Odor not distinctive or (more commonly) mealy to foul; taste mild, mealy, unpleasant, or bitter. **Spore Print:** White. **Chemical Reactions:** KOH negative to pale olive on cap. **Microscopic Features:** Spores 5–8 × 4.5–5 µm (including ornamentation); more or less ellipsoid; spiny with warts up to 0.5 µm; amyloid. Cheilocystidia scattered; long-cylindric. Pleurocystidia absent. **Comments:** Compare with *Leucopaxillus laterarius* (p. 264), which decomposes the litter of hardwoods and has smaller spores.

LEUCOPAXILLUS LATERARIUS (PECK) SINGER & A. H. SMITH

Ecology: Saprobic, decomposing the litter of hardwoods in oak and beech forests; growing scattered or gregariously; early summer through fall; widely distributed. **Cap:** 4–20 cm; convex, with an inrolled margin when young, becoming broadly convex or flat; dry; bald or very finely velvety (like kid leather), sometimes becoming patchy (but not truly scaly) over the center with age; white, pinkish, buff, or pale tan; the margin often broadly lined. **Gills:** Attached to the stem or running down it; crowded; separable from the cap as a layer; whitish to dirty yellowish when mature. **Stem:** 4–11 cm long; up to 2 cm thick at the apex; when young often slightly swollen near the base, but by maturity usually more or less equal; bald or very finely hairy; whitish; with prominent and copious basal mycelium (often found throughout the surrounding litter). **Flesh:** White; thick; hard; not changing on exposure. **Odor and Taste:** Odor mealy or foul (like coal tar or swamp gas); taste mild or bitter. **Spore Print:** White. **Chemical Reactions:** KOH pale olive on cap. **Microscopic Features:** Spores 3.5–5.5 × 3.5–5 µm (including ornamentation); short-ellipsoid or subglobose; spiny, with amyloid warts. Cheilocystidia absent or scattered. Pleurocystidia absent. **Comments:** Compare with *Leucopaxillus albissimus* (p. 263).

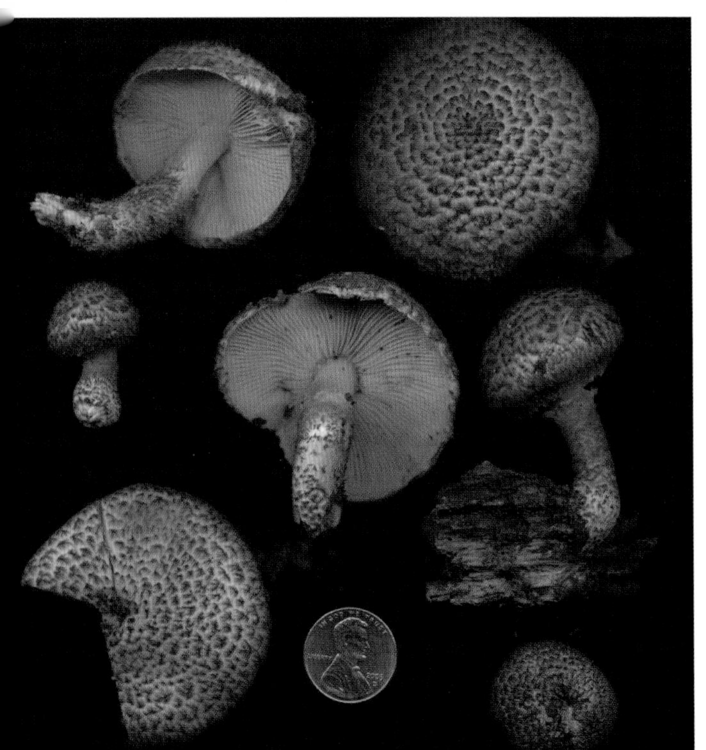

LEUCOPHOLIOTA DECOROSA (PECK) O. K. MILLER, T. J. VOLK, & BESSETTE

Ecology: Saprobic on the deadwood of hardwoods or conifers; growing alone, gregariously, or in clusters; late summer and fall; widely distributed, but more common in the eastern portions of the Midwest. **Cap:** 2.5–7 cm; round at first, becoming convex, broadly convex, or nearly flat; dry; covered with conspicuous brown to rusty-brown, pointed scales; the margin inrolled and hairy. **Gills:** Attached to the stem by a notch; close; white; at first covered by a partial veil of rusty-brown fibers. **Stem:** 2.5–8 cm long; up to 1.5 cm thick; dry; bald and white at the apex; sheathed below with rusty-brown scales and hairs; with a folded-over ring zone at the top of the sheath. **Flesh:** White; unchanging. **Odor and Taste:** Odor not distinctive; taste not distinctive, or bitter. **Chemical Reactions:** KOH negative to slowly pinkish on cap. **Spore Print:** White. **Microscopic Features:** Spores 5.5–6 × 3.5–4 µm; smooth; ellipsoid; amyloid. Cheilocystidia clavate to rostrate or fusiform. Pileipellis a trichoderm. Clamp connections present. **Comments:** Compare with *Pholiota squarrosoides* (p. 310), which is differently colored and has a brown spore print.

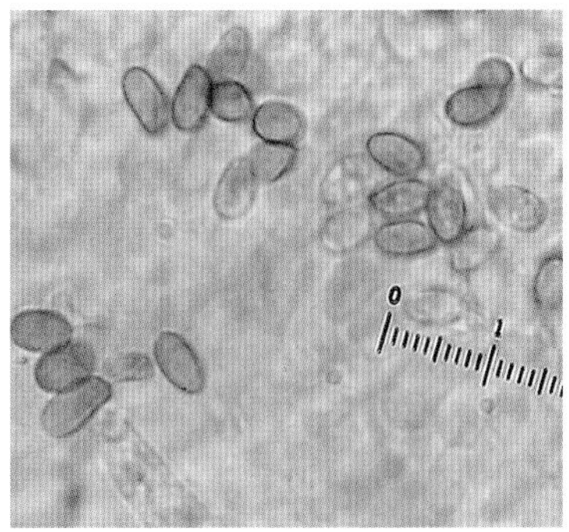

Spores

LIMACELLA GLIODERMA (FRIES) MAIRE

Ecology: Saprobic; growing alone or gregariously under hardwoods or conifers; summer and fall; widely distributed. **Cap:** 2.5–8 cm; convex, becoming flat, or developing a broad central bump; slimy when fresh and young, but often dry when collected; bald or finely granular; dark cinnamon to reddish brown, fading to pinkish tan. **Gills:** Free from the stem or attached by a tiny notch; close; whitish at first, becoming pinkish. **Stem:** 4–12 cm long; 0.5–1 cm thick; more or less equal; shaggy, with reddish-brown patches and scales in vaguely concentric patterns; sometimes with an ephemeral ring zone, but lacking a true ring; whitish under the fibers and scales. **Flesh:** Whitish, tinged pink. **Odor and Taste:** Mealy. **Chemical Reactions:** KOH olive gray on cap. **Spore Print:** White. **Microscopic Features:** Spores 3–5 µm; globose; smooth; inamyloid. Gill tissue divergent. **Comments:** Compare with *Leratiomyces squamosus* var. *thraustus* (p. 259), which features a purplish-black spore print, and with *Limacella glischra* (below).

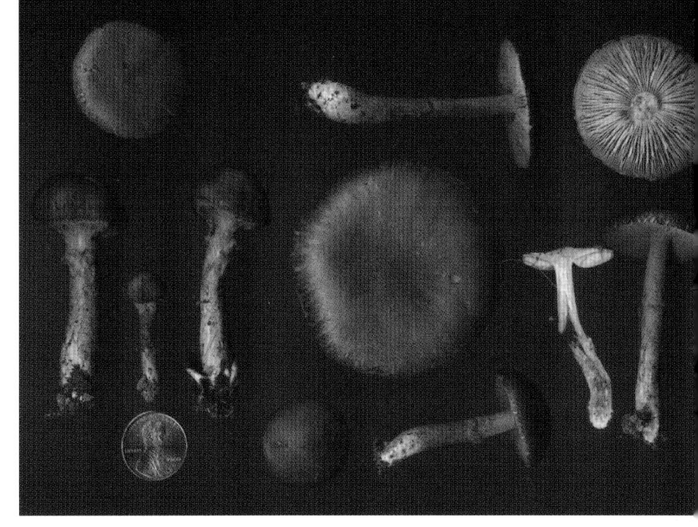

LIMACELLA GLISCHRA (MORGAN) MURRILL

Ecology: Saprobic; growing alone or scattered under hardwoods or conifers; summer and fall; widely distributed. **Cap:** 2–4 cm; convex or with a broad central bump; thickly slimy with reddish-brown slime when fresh; pale brownish to reddish brown beneath the slime; darker centrally. **Gills:** Free from the stem or attached by a tiny notch; close; white. **Stem:** 6–8 cm long; up to 1 cm thick; more or less equal; covered with reddish-brown slime; whitish beneath the slime; bald. **Flesh:** Whitish. **Odor and Taste:** Mealy. **Chemical Reactions:** KOH negative on cap. **Spore Print:**

White. **Microscopic Features:** Spores 3–4 µm; globose; smooth; inamyloid. Gill tissue divergent. **Comments:** Compare with *Limacella glioderma* (p. 265), which is less slimy and features a shaggy stem, as well as a cap that turns olive with KOH.

LYCOPERDON MARGINATUM VITTADINI

Ecology: Saprobic; growing alone, scattered, or gregariously in woods under hardwoods; summer and fall; widely distributed. **Fruiting Body:** More or less round, developing a flattened top and a pinched underside; 1–5 cm across; dry; covered with densely packed whitish warts about 2 mm high; with maturity breaking into patches and chunks that slough away as a layer; inner skin brownish and papery; with a white, fleshy interior at first; later with yellowish to olive granular flesh, and eventually filled with olive to brownish spore dust; small sterile base present, filled with whitish flesh. **Microscopic Features:** Spores 3.5–4.5 µm; globose; minutely spiny. Capillitial threads olive in KOH; 3–7 µm wide; thick-walled; flexuous. **Comments:** Compare with *Lycoperdon perlatum* (below) and with *Vascellum curtisii* (p. 387).

LYCOPERDON PERLATUM PERSOON

Ecology: Saprobic; growing alone, scattered, gregariously, or in clusters; usually found in woods under hardwoods or conifers, but also common along roadsides and in urban settings, decomposing the litter of trees; summer and fall; widely distributed and common. **Fruiting Body:** Shaped like an inverted pear, with a fairly prominent stem-like area and a roundish to flattened top; 2.5–7 cm wide; 3–7.5 cm high; dry; covered with whitish spines when young and fresh, but the spines usually fall away by maturity and leave scars on the surface; by maturity developing a central perforation through which spores are liberated by raindrops and wind currents; white, becoming discolored and eventually brownish; with a white, fleshy interior at first; later with yellowish to olive granular flesh, and eventually filled with brownish spore dust; sterile base prominent, filled with whitish flesh. **Microscopic Features:** Spores 3.5–4.5 µm; globose; minutely spiny. Capillitial threads olive in KOH; 3–7 µm wide; thick-walled; flexuous. **Comments:** Edible when the flesh is still white and firm. Compare with *Lycoperdon marginatum* (above), which has an outer skin that sloughs off in chunks as a layer, and with *Vascellum curtisii* (p. 387), which is round, grows in clusters in grass, and has a tiny sterile base.

Photo by Melissa Bochte

LYOPHYLLUM DECASTES (FRIES) SINGER

Ecology: Saprobic; usually growing in dense clusters in disturbed soil (roadbeds, paths, landscaping areas, and so on), but occasionally growing alone or scattered (and sometimes occurring in woods); summer and fall; widely distributed. **Cap:** 3–12 cm; convex, becoming broadly convex or flat; moist when fresh, but soon dry; bald; grayish brown to yellowish brown or brown (usually darker when young); often somewhat streaked in appearance; the margin inrolled at first, but later even, lobed, or upturned. **Gills:** Attached to the stem, sometimes by a notch, or beginning to run down it; close; white, sometimes yellowing somewhat with age. **Stem:** 5–10 cm long; up to 2 cm thick; bald; more or less equal; dry; whitish, sometimes becoming brownish toward the base. **Flesh:** White; firm; not changing on exposure. **Odor and Taste:** Taste pleasant and mild, or faintly radish-like; odor not distinctive, or somewhat fragrant. **Chemical Reactions:** KOH negative on cap. **Spore Print:** Pure white. **Microscopic Features:** Spores 4–6 µm; globose; smooth; inamyloid. Cystidia absent. Clamp connections present. **Comments:** Edible, but not recommended, because it is difficult to identify. Compare with species of *Leucopaxillus* (pp. 263–64), which feature gills that are separable as a layer, and with species of *Tricholoma* (pp. 375–81), which do not grow in clusters. Several poisonous species of *Clitocybe* (including some not featured in this book but present in the Midwest) are very similar and are best separated with microscopic analysis.

MACROCYSTIDIA CUCUMIS (PERSOON) JOSSERAND

Ecology: Saprobic; terrestrial; growing alone, gregariously, or in troops in woods, disturbed ground, grassy areas, gardens, and so on; summer and fall; widely distributed. **Cap:** 1–6 cm across; bell-shaped at first, becoming broadly bell-shaped, broadly convex, or nearly flat; bald, silky, or very finely velvety; dark reddish brown, often with a paler margin; fading with age. **Gills:** Attached to the stem (sometimes by a notch); close; whitish, becoming yellowish to pinkish yellow. **Stem:** Up to 8 cm long and 5 mm thick; more or less equal; dry; finely velvety; tough; colored like the cap, but paler above and darker below. **Flesh:** Insubstantial; brownish. **Odor and Taste:** Odor strong, reminiscent of fish or cucumbers; taste

Photo by Walt Sturgeon

mild or slightly fishy. **Spore Print:** Variable; whitish, pinkish, dirty yellowish, pale pinkish brown. **Chemical Reactions:** KOH dark olive, then gray on cap. **Microscopic Features:** Spores 7–9 × 3–4.5 µm; smooth; ellipsoid; inamyloid. Large, lanceolate cystidia (up to 90 µm long and over 20 µm wide) present on cap surface, gills, and stem surface. **Comments:** The fishy odor and overall appearance make good identifying features, but the impressive cystidia are definitive.

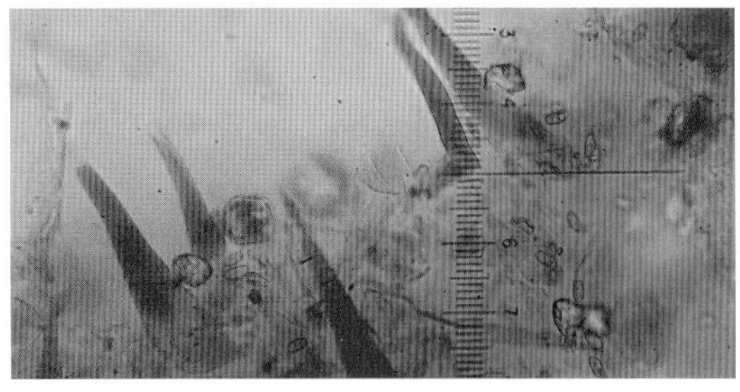

Cystidia

MACROLEPIOTA PROCERA (SCOPOLI) SINGER

Ecology: Saprobic; growing alone or scattered in woods or at the edges of woods, or in pastures, on trails, and in other disturbed-ground areas; late summer; widely distributed. **Cap:** 7–25 cm, oval when young, becoming convex to broadly convex in age, with a dark central bump; dry; at first bald and brownish, but soon becoming scaly, the scales brown, the surface below whitish and later grayish or brownish; often shaggy and ragged at maturity. **Gills:** Free from the stem; white when young, sometimes discoloring to pinkish or tan in maturity; close. **Stem:** 14–20 cm long; 0.5–1.5 cm thick; long and slender, with a slightly enlarged base; pale above the ring, covered below the ring with small brown scales that break up as the mushroom matures, creating zones or sometimes disappearing; with a double-edged ring that can be detached and moved freely up and down the stem. **Flesh:** White throughout; sometimes tinged reddish, but not staining reddish when exposed; soft. **Odor and Taste:** Not distinctive. **Chemical Reactions:** KOH negative to slowly pinkish on cap. **Spore Print:** White. **Microscopic Features:** Spores 12–18 × 8–12 µm; smooth; broadly ellipsoid; dextrinoid; with a small pore. Cheilocystidia clavate or cylindric. Pleurocystidia absent. **Comments:** Edible and very good when young and fresh. Often called the "parasol mushroom." Compare carefully with *Chlorophyllum molybdites* (p. 135), which grows only in grass and features a greenish spore print and greenish mature gills; also compare with *Chlorophyllum rhacodes* (p. 136), which is a stockier mushroom with a thicker stem and smaller spores.

Photo by Ron Kerner

Photo by Patrick Harvey

MARASMIUS CAPILLARIS MORGAN

Ecology: Saprobic on the fallen leaves of oaks and other hardwoods (rarely reported on conifer duff); growing alone or, more often, gregariously (many may be found on a single leaf); summer and fall; widely distributed. **Cap:** 2–15 mm across; convex, but soon with a central depression; pleated; bald or very finely velvety; dry; whitish or very pale grayish brown. **Gills:** Attached to a tiny "collar" that circles the stem; whitish; distant. **Stem:** Up to 60 mm long; <1 mm thick; equal; dry; shiny; wiry; pale above, dark brown to black below; inserted directly into the leaf. **Flesh:** Almost nonexistent. **Odor and Taste:** Taste not distinctive, or slightly bitter; odor not distinctive. **Spore Print:** White. **Microscopic Features:** Spores 7–11 × 3–5 µm; smooth; pip-shaped. Cystidia lacking on gills, but broom cells present. Pileipellis with broom cells. **Comments:** Compare with *Marasmius rotula* (p. 272), which is nearly identical but grows from wood rather than leaves; with *Tetrapyrgos nigripes* (p. 370); and with *Marasmius delectans* (p. 270).

MARASMIUS COHAERENS (PERSOON) COOKE & QUÉLET

Ecology: Saprobic on leaf litter and woody debris in hardwood forests; growing alone or, more typically, in clusters of 2 or 3; early summer through fall; widely distributed. **Cap:** 1–3.5 cm across; convex, becoming broadly convex; bald; the margin sometimes lined; yellowish brown to reddish brown, sometimes fading dramatically along the margin. **Gills:** Attached to the stem; distant or nearly so (but in one variety close or crowded); pale at first, becoming tan or even light brown; sometimes developing brown edges. **Stem:** 3–8 cm long; up to 3 mm thick; equal; dry; straight or slightly curved; whitish to yellowish brown at first, but soon darkening from the base up to dark brown or dark reddish brown; usually with copious, whitish basal mycelium. **Flesh:** Thin; insubstantial; pale. **Odor and Taste:** Taste mild, or with a slightly bitter or acidic aftertaste; odor mild, or pungent and unpleasant. **Chemical Reactions:** KOH pale olive on cap. **Spore Print:** White. **Microscopic Features:** Spores 7–10 × 3–5.5 µm; smooth; ellipsoid; inamyloid. Cystidia variously shaped, but often fusiform; thick-walled; dextrinoid. Broom cells present on gills and cap

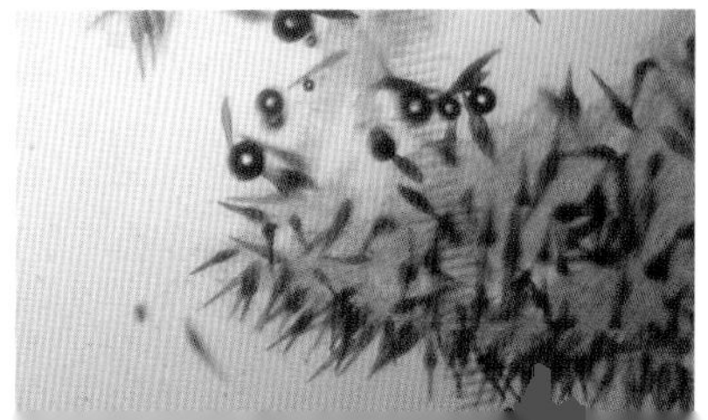

Cystidia

surface. **Comments:** Compare with *Marasmius sullivantii* (p. 274), which is bright orange to rusty orangish brown, and with *Rhizomarasmius pyrrhocephalus* (p. 335), which features a tough, hairy, elongated stem.

MARASMIUS DELECTANS MORGAN

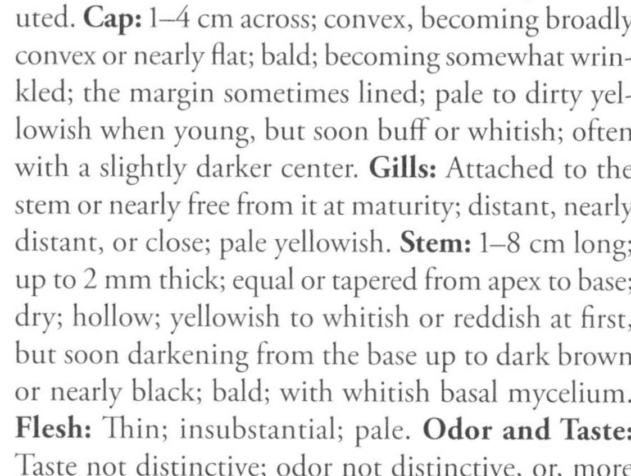

Ecology: Saprobic on leaf litter and woody debris in hardwood forests (especially oak woods); growing gregariously or in clusters; summer and fall; widely distributed. **Cap:** 1–4 cm across; convex, becoming broadly convex or nearly flat; bald; becoming somewhat wrinkled; the margin sometimes lined; pale to dirty yellowish when young, but soon buff or whitish; often with a slightly darker center. **Gills:** Attached to the stem or nearly free from it at maturity; distant, nearly distant, or close; pale yellowish. **Stem:** 1–8 cm long; up to 2 mm thick; equal or tapered from apex to base; dry; hollow; yellowish to whitish or reddish at first, but soon darkening from the base up to dark brown or nearly black; bald; with whitish basal mycelium. **Flesh:** Thin; insubstantial; pale. **Odor and Taste:** Taste not distinctive; odor not distinctive, or, more often, strong and foul. **Chemical Reactions:** KOH negative on cap. **Spore Print:** White. **Microscopic Features:** Spores 5.5–9 × 3–5 µm; smooth; ellipsoid; inamyloid. Cystidia variously shaped, but often fusiform; dextrinoid. Pileipellis with dextrinoid broom cells. **Comments:** Compare with *Marasmius capillaris* (p. 269) and *Maramius rotula* (p. 272), both of which have pleated caps and wiry stems, and with *Tetrapyrgos nigripes* (p. 370), which has a fuzzy black stem.

MARASMIUS FELIX MORGAN

Ecology: Saprobic on fallen leaves of sycamore trees (usually on leaves from the preceding year); growing alone or gregariously from petioles or major veins; summer, fall, and winter (during warm spells); probably to be expected throughout the midwestern range of the tree (south of the Great Lakes). **Cap:** 1.5–7 mm across; convex, becoming plano-convex; usually pleated by maturity; often somewhat wrinkled; dry; at first nearly white, becoming pinkish or pale pinkish brown with age. **Gills:** Attached to the stem, often by means of a collar that may or may not completely encircle the stem; distant; whitish or faintly pinkish. **Stem:** 10–85 mm long; <1 mm thick; equal; dry; wiry; sometimes slightly hairy; inserted directly into the leaf; translucent near apex, brownish below; occasionally branched. **Flesh:** Thin; insubstantial. **Odor and Taste:** Not distinctive. **Spore Print:** White. **Microscopic Features:** Spores 8–8.5 × 3–3.5 µm; smooth; subfusiform. Cystidia variously shaped; inamyloid. Pileipellis hymeniform; with pileocystidia. **Comments:** The overall appearance and the distinctive habitat on sycamore leaves make this mushroom fairly easy to recognize.

MARASMIUS NIGRODISCUS (PECK) HALLING

Ecology: Saprobic on litter under hardwoods or conifers; growing alone, scattered, or gregariously; summer and fall; widely distributed. **Cap:** 3–11 cm; convex, becoming plano-convex or nearly flat, usually with a broad central bump or nipple; dry; usually becoming somewhat wrinkled with maturity and developing fine lines along the margin; when young, pale brown, becoming creamy white or very pale brownish with a darker brown or reddish-brown center; in old age sometimes uniformly pale brownish or dirty cream. **Gills:** Attached to the stem; close; whitish, sometimes discoloring grayish. **Stem:** 5–10 cm long; about 1 cm thick; equal; dry; straight; whitish or very pale brownish; smooth or with shallow longitudinal grooves; basal mycelium white. **Flesh:** Whitish. **Odor and Taste:** Taste mild or slightly bitter; odor not distinctive or faintly of almonds. **Chemical Reactions:** KOH negative on cap. **Spore Print:** White. **Microscopic Features:** Spores 7–9 × 3–5 µm; smooth; more or less ellipsoid. Cystidia abundant on gill edges and faces. Pileipellis without broom cells. **Comments:** Compare with species of *Xerula* (pp. 394–95), which have long, underground taproots.

MARASMIUS OREADES (BOLTON) FRIES

Ecology: Saprobic on grass in lawns, meadows, and other grassy areas; growing gregariously in troops, arcs, or rings; summer and fall; widely distributed. **Cap:** 1–5 cm across; bell-shaped, with a somewhat inrolled margin at first, becoming broadly convex, with an even or uplifted margin, but often retaining a slight central bump; dry; bald; pale tan or buff—occasionally white, or reddish tan; often changing

color markedly as it dries out, resulting in 2-toned specimens; the margin sometimes faintly lined. **Gills:** Attached to the stem or free from it; distant or nearly so; white or pale tan. **Stem:** 2–8 cm long; 1.5–6 mm thick; equal; dry; tough and pliant; whitish or colored like the cap. **Flesh:** Tough; whitish. **Odor and Taste:** Not distinctive. **Spore Print:** White. **Microscopic Features:** Spores 7–10 × 4–6 µm; smooth; ellipsoid; inamyloid. Cystidia absent. Pileipellis hymeniform. **Comments:** Edible. Often called the "fairy ring mushroom," despite the fact that many other mushrooms grow in fairy rings. The bell-shaped caps, tough stems, well-spaced gills, and habitat in grass are good field characters.

MARASMIUS PULCHERRIPES PECK

Ecology: Saprobic on litter under hardwoods or conifers; growing gregariously; summer and fall; widely distributed. **Cap:** 0.5–2 cm; at first bell-shaped or convex, often with a central nipple; later broadly bell-shaped, convex, or nearly flat; pleated; bald or minutely roughened; dry; pink or pinkish brown (rarely brownish orange), fading with age, but retaining a darker center. **Gills:** Attached to the stem or free from it; rarely attached by means of a collar; distant or nearly so; white or pinkish. **Stem:** 2–6 cm long; <1 mm thick; equal; dry; wiry; often curved; pale pinkish at the extreme apex, darkening downward by degrees to a reddish-brown or black base; bald; basal mycelium white. **Flesh:** Thin; insubstantial. **Odor and Taste:** Taste mild or slightly bitter or radish-like; odor not distinctive. **Chemical Reactions:** KOH olive to negative on cap. **Spore Print:** White. **Microscopic Features:** Spores 11–15 × 3–4 µm; smooth; subfusoid. Cystidia present on gill faces; dextrinoid broom cells present on gill edges. Pileipellis with broom cells. **Comments:** *Marasmius siccus* (p. 273) is similar but orange. Also compare with *Mycena haematopus* (p. 284), which grows in clusters from decaying wood, has a soft stem, and exudes a purplish juice when sliced.

MARASMIUS ROTULA (SCOPOLI) FRIES

Ecology: Saprobic on sticks, logs, and woody debris in hardwood forests; growing alone, gregariously, or in clusters; spring through fall; widely distributed. **Cap:** 0.5–2 cm; convex, with a central depression; pleated; often appearing to have a flat top and squarish sides when viewed from the side; bald; dry; brownish in the depression, white elsewhere. **Gills:** Usually attached to a tiny collar that encircles the stem; distant; white to yellowish white. **Stem:** 1.5–8 cm long; 1–2 mm thick; equal; dry; shiny; wiry; pale at first, but soon dark brown to black except at the apex; base sometimes with stiff hairs. **Flesh:** Thin. **Odor and Taste:** Not distinctive. **Chemical Reactions:** KOH negative on cap. **Spore Print:** White or very pale yellowish. **Microscopic Features:** Spores 6.5–10 × 3–5 µm; smooth; ellipsoid. Cystidia absent on gill faces; inamyloid broom cells present on gill edges. Pileipellis with broom cells that feature very short projections. **Comments:** The squarish cap (when viewed from the side) and growth from wood (rather than leaves) help to characterize this species. Compare with *Marasmius capillaris* (p. 269), *Marasmius delectans* (p. 270), and *Tetrapyrgos nigripes* (p. 370).

Photo by Dan Molter

MARASMIUS SICCUS (SCHWEINITZ) FRIES

Ecology: Saprobic on leaf litter and woody debris in hardwood forests (but sometimes also found on the needle duff of white pine); growing gregariously; summer and fall; widely distributed. **Cap:** 0.5–3 cm; cushion-shaped or bell-shaped, with a central depression; conspicuously pleated; bald or minutely roughened; dry; orange when fresh, fading to pale orange. **Gills:** Attached to the stem or free from it; very distant; white to pale yellowish. **Stem:** 2.5–6.5 cm long; about 1 mm thick; equal; dry; wiry; whitish or yellowish above, brown toward the base; bald; basal mycelium white. **Flesh:** Thin; insubstantial. **Odor and Taste:** Taste mild or slightly bitter; odor not distinctive. **Spore Print:** White. **Microscopic Features:** Spores 16–23 × 3–4.5 µm; smooth; subfusiform. Cystidia with refractive contents present on gill faces; dextrinoid broom cells present on gill edges. Pileipellis with dextrinoid broom cells. **Comments:** Compare with *Marasmius pulcherripes* (p. 272).

Photo by Melissa Bochte

MARASMIUS STRICTIPES (PECK) SINGER

Ecology: Saprobic on leaf litter in hardwood forests; growing alone, gregariously, or occasionally in clusters; summer and fall; widely distributed. **Cap**: To 7 cm across; convex, becoming flat; bald; faintly lined at the margin; moist; dull yellow to orangish yellow. **Gills:** Attached to the stem or free from it; close or crowded; whitish, pale yellow, or orangish yellow. **Stem:** 3–9 cm long; up to 1 cm thick; equal; dry; straight; tough; bald, or sometimes with a faint bloom or dusting; with copious white basal mycelium; white or pale yellow. **Flesh:** Thin; insubstantial. **Odor and Taste:** Taste mild or slightly radish-like; odor not distinctive. **Chemical Reactions:** KOH negative on cap. **Spore Print:** White. **Microscopic Features:** Spores 6–10.5 × 3–4.5 µm; smooth; ellipsoid. Pleurocystidia absent; cheilocystidia present. Pileipellis hymeniform. **Comments:** Compare with *Gymnopus subsulphureus* (p. 191), which is slightly smaller, has crowded gills, and usually appears in late spring.

MARASMIUS SULLIVANTII MONTAGNE

Ecology: Saprobic on leaf litter and woody debris in hardwood forests; growing alone or gregariously; summer and fall; widely distributed. **Cap:** To 2.5 cm across; convex, becoming flat; not pleated; typically bald overall and faintly lined at the margin; dry; bright reddish orange or rust-colored. **Gills:** Attached to the stem or free from it; close; white, or with the edges faintly pinkish at first. **Stem:** 0.5–2.5 cm long; 1–1.5 mm thick; equal; dry; wiry; sometimes with a faint bloom or dusting at first, but soon bald; often with copious white basal mycelium; white or nearly clear at the apex, reddish to orangish in the midsection, reddish brown to black below. **Flesh:** Thin; insubstantial. **Odor and Taste:** Taste mild or slightly bitter; odor not distinctive. **Chemical Reactions:** KOH negative on cap. **Spore Print:** White. **Microscopic Features:** Spores 7–9 × 3–3.5 µm; smooth; ellipsoid. Cystidia versiform. Broom cells present in pileipellis. **Comments:** Compare with *Marasmius cohaerens* (p. 269) and *Rhizomarasmius pyrrhocephalus* (p. 335).

MEGACOLLYBIA RODMANI R. H. PETERSEN, K. W. HUGHES, & LICKEY

Ecology: Saprobic; growing alone or gregariously on rotting hardwood logs or from buried deadwood; May through July; widely distributed. **Cap:** 3–20 cm; convex when young, becoming broadly convex to flat or shallowly depressed in age; dry; brown to olive brown or pale grayish brown in form *rodmani*; gray brown to gray in form *murina*; radially streaked. **Gills:** Attached to the stem broadly or narrowly; close or nearly distant; whitish. **Stem:** 5–12 cm long and up to 1 cm wide in form *rodmani*; 5–9 cm long and up to 2.5 cm wide in form *murina*; finely silky; whitish; more or less equal above a slightly enlarged base, or tapering slightly to apex; base attached to copious and conspicuous rhizomorphs in form *murina*, or with inconspicuous or even absent rhizomorphs in form *rodmani*. **Flesh:** Whitish, not changing when sliced. **Odor and Taste:** Not distinctive. **Chemical Reactions:** KOH negative on cap of form *murina*. **Spore Print:** White. **Microscopic Features:** Spores 6–10 × 5–7.5 µm; smooth; ellipsoid; inamyloid. Cheilocystidia abundant; not projecting substantially in form *rodmani*; projecting in form *murina*. Pileipellis a cutis with clavate terminal elements. **Comments:** Previously known as *Megacollybia platyphylla* and *Tricholomopsis platyphylla*. Two forms of this species, f. *rodmani* and f. *murina*, exhibit minor differences and are separated in the description above. Compare with *Clitocybula lacerata* (p. 144), which is smaller and features distant, cross-veined gills.

MELANOLEUCA BREVIPES (BULLIARD) PATOUILLARD

Ecology: Saprobic; found in grassy areas and disturbed soil, often in urban areas; summer and fall; widely distributed. **Cap:** 2–8 cm across; broadly convex or flat, sometimes with a shallow central bump; bald; dry; dark gray to nearly black when young, becoming gray and eventually fading to dull brownish or paler. **Gills:** Attached to the stem, usually by a notch; fairly crowded; white. **Stem:** 1–3 cm long; up to 1 cm thick; firm; club-shaped when in the button stage, becoming equal, with a slightly swollen base; sometimes twisted; dry; whitish. **Flesh:** White in cap; white or brownish in the stem. **Odor and Taste:**

Not distinctive. **Spore Print:** White. **Microscopic Features:** Spores 6.5–9.5 × 5–6.5 µm; more or less ellipsoid; ornamented with amyloid warts. Pleurocystidia absent or rare. Cheilocystidia abundant; variously shaped; often capped with apical incrustations. **Comments:** The short stem, flat gray cap, and habitat in grass are good identification characters.

MELANOLEUCA MELALEUCA (PERSOON) MURRILL

Ecology: Saprobic; found in grassy areas and disturbed soil, often in urban areas; summer and fall; widely distributed. **Cap:** 2–3 cm across; convex, becoming flat, usually with a shallow central bump; bald; dry; the margin long remaining curved under; dark brown, fading to brownish. **Gills:** Attached to the stem, usually by a notch; crowded; white, developing slightly pinkish hues. **Stem:** 4–5 cm long; up to 4 mm thick; firm; more or less equal; dry; whitish to tan; bald, or with tiny whitish fibers. **Flesh:** White; thin. **Odor and Taste:** Odor not distinctive, or pungent; taste not distinctive. **Spore Print:** White. **Microscopic Features:** Spores 5.5–8 × 4.5–6 µm; more or less ellipsoid; ornamented with amyloid warts. Pleurocystidia and cheilocystidia absent. **Comments:** Compare with *Clitocybe eccentrica* (p. 141). Treatments of *Melanoleuca melaleuca* are inconsistent; we are following the contemporary European concept of the species, in which cystidia are lacking.

MERIPILUS SUMSTINEI (MURRILL) M. J. LARSEN & LOMBARD

Ecology: Parasitic on living oaks and other hardwoods, and saprobic on the deadwood of hardwoods; causing a white rot; growing in large clusters of rosettes near the bases of trees; often reappearing in the same place in subsequent years; summer and fall; widely distributed. **Fruiting Body:** Up to 30 cm across or more; composed of multiple caps sharing a branched, stem-like base. **Caps:** 5–20 cm across; fan-shaped; finely velvety or bald; whitish to yellowish, becoming brownish with age; often radially streaked and concentrically zoned; the margin thin, bruising and aging black. **Pore Surface:** Whitish, becoming dirty tan; bruising dark brown to black when fresh; with 6–8 round to angular pores per mm; tubes to 8 mm deep. **Stem:** Whitish, becoming brown to blackish with age; tough; short; often off-center. **Flesh:** Firm; white; somewhat stringy. **Odor and Taste:** Mild; pleasant. **Chemical Reactions:** KOH negative on flesh. **Spore Print:** White. **Microscopic Features:** Spores 5–5.5 × 4.5–5 µm; smooth; subglobose; inamyloid. Hyphal system monomitic. Clamp connections absent. **Comments:** Also known as *Meripilus giganteus*. Compare with *Grifola frondosa* (p. 185).

MICROSTOMA FLOCCOSUM (SCHWEINITZ) RAITVIR

Ecology: Saprobic on decaying hardwood sticks and logs (sometimes arising from buried wood and appearing terrestrial), early summer and summer; widely distributed. **Fruiting Body:** Goblet-shaped to cup-shaped; to about 1 cm across; inner surface bald, scarlet red; undersurface densely covered with white hairs; stem 3–5 cm long, 2–5 mm thick, whitish, hairy, often curving; flesh thin. **Microscopic Features:** Spores 20–35 × 15–17 µm; smooth; ellipsoid, with narrow ends. **Comments:** Compare with *Scutellinia scutellata* (p. 357), which is less deeply cup-shaped and features brown to black, rather than white, hairs.

MORCHELLA ANGUSTICEPS PECK

Ecology: Mycorrhizal; found under hardwoods, especially ashes and tulip trees; spring; widely distributed. **Cap:** 3–8 cm high; variable in shape, but usually somewhat elongated and pointed; pitted and ridged, with blunt-edged, finely velvety to bald ridges; pale when young (almost whitish when covered by leaves) and darkening with age until the ridges are black and the pits are pale yellowish brown to dark brown; attached to the stem with a slight overhang or rim; hollow. **Stem:** 2–8 cm long; 1–3 cm wide; whitish or pale tan; sometimes darkening to brown in age;

bald or mealy with flaky granules; equal or with an enlarged base; with age developing channels and folds, especially near the base; hollow. **Spore Print:** Creamy to yellowish or orangish. **Microscopic Features:** Spores 22–27 × 11–15 µm; smooth, ellipsoid; contents homogeneous. **Comments:** Edible and good. Compare with *Morchella septentrionalis* (p. 280), which has a strictly northern range and features smaller caps and smaller spores. *Morchella importuna*, which is similar but features strikingly regular, "laddered" pits and ridges and appears in woodchips, has been reported from the Midwest. Another black morel, *Morchella tomentosa*, has been reported in midwestern jack pine burn areas in the year following the fire; it features densely hairy, nearly black surfaces.

MORCHELLA DIMINUTIVA M. KUO, DEWSBURY, MONCALVO, & S. L. STEPHENSON

Ecology: Mycorrhizal; found under hardwoods, especially ashes, hickories, and tulip trees; spring; below the Great Lakes. **Cap:** 2–4 cm high; sharply to bluntly conic; pitted and ridged, with blunt-edged, bald ridges that sometimes erode with age and become sharp; pits and ridges vertically arranged; ridges pale when young, darkening slightly with age, but remaining yellowish to pale yellowish brown; pits brown or nearly black when young, becoming pale yellowish to pale yellowish brown; attached to the stem without a notable overhang or rim; hollow. **Stem:** 1–6 cm long; up to 1.5 cm wide; whitish or pale tan; bald; equal; hollow. **Spore Print:** Creamy to yellowish or orangish. **Microscopic Features:** Spores 20–24 × 11–16 µm; smooth, ellipsoid; contents homogeneous. **Comments:** Edible. Compare with *Morchella esculentoides* (below).

MORCHELLA ESCULENTOIDES M. KUO, DEWSBURY, MONCALVO, & S. L. STEPHENSON

Ecology: Mycorrhizal; found under hardwoods, especially ashes and recently dead elms; spring; widely distributed. **Cap:** 2–11 cm high; variable in shape but usually egg-shaped or cylindric, with a convex or bluntly conic apex; pitted and ridged, with blunt-edged, bald ridges that erode with age and become sharp; ridges pale when young, darkening slightly with age, but remaining yellowish to pale yellowish brown; pits randomly arranged, nearly black when young, becoming pale yellowish to pale yellowish brown; attached to the stem without a notable overhang or rim; hollow. **Stem:** 2–12 cm long; 1.5–8 cm wide; whitish or pale tan; sometimes darkening to brown in age; bald or mealy with flaky granules; equal, or with an enlarged base; with age developing channels and folds, especially near the base; in warm, wet weather sometimes becoming enormous and inflated; hollow. **Spore Print:** Creamy to yellowish or orangish. **Microscopic Features:** Spores 18–22 × 11–13 µm; smooth, ellipsoid; contents homogeneous. **Comments:** Edible and very good. Previously known as *Morchella esculenta*, which recent studies have determined to be strictly European. DNA reveals *Morchella cryptica*, which is macro- and microscopically indistinguishable, to be a distinct species; it should be expected throughout the Midwest, although it is not as common as *Morchella esculentoides*. Compare with *Morchella prava* (below), which features contorted pits and ridges, and with *Morchella diminutiva* (p. 278), which is smaller and pointier and features vertically elongated pits and ridges. *Morchella rufobrunnea*, which is similar but features surfaces that bruise red and appears in woodchips, has been reported from central Michigan in the fall.

MORCHELLA PRAVA
DEWSBURY, MONCALVO, J. D. MOORE, & M. KUO

Ecology: Mycorrhizal; found primarily under hardwoods, often in sandy soil near lakes and rivers; spring; possibly widely distributed, but more common in the northern Midwest. **Cap:** 5–10 cm high; variable in shape, but usually more or less egg-shaped or round, with a rounded apex; pitted and ridged, with blunt-edged, bald or finely velvety ridges that erode with age and become sharp; pits and ridges randomly arranged and irregular, often appearing contorted; ridges pale when young, darkening slightly with age, but remaining yellowish to pale yellowish brown; pits asymmetrical in shape, nearly black when young, often remaining dark throughout development, but sometimes becoming pale yellowish to pale yellowish brown; attached to the stem without a notable overhang or rim; hollow. **Stem:** 2.5–4 cm long; 1–3 cm wide; whitish or pale tan; sometimes darkening to reddish brown in age; bald; with an enlarged base; with age developing channels and folds, especially near the base; hollow. **Spore Print:** Creamy to yellowish or orangish. **Microscopic Features:** Spores 17–21 × 10–12 µm; smooth, ellipsoid; contents homogeneous. **Comments:** Edible and very good. Compare with *Morchella esculentoides* (p. 278).

MORCHELLA PUNCTIPES PECK

Ecology: Mycorrhizal; found under hardwoods; spring; widely distributed. **Cap:** 2–4.5 cm high; bluntly to sharply pointed; pitted and ridged, with blunt-edged, bald ridges; pale yellowish to brownish when young, and darkening with age until the ridges are black and the pits are pale yellowish brown to dark brown; attached in a skirt-like manner to the stem, roughly halfway from the apex, with a deep overhang or rim; hollow. **Stem:** 5–15 cm long; 1–4.5 cm wide; whitish or pale tan; finely mealy with flaky granules, or nearly bald; with an enlarged base; with age often developing ridges and folds near the base; in warm, wet weather sometimes becoming inflated; hollow. **Spore Print:** Creamy to yellowish or orangish. **Microscopic Features:** Spores 20–27 × 14–18 µm; smooth, ellipsoid; contents homogeneous. **Comments:** Edible. Also known as *Morchella semilibera*, which recent studies have shown to be strictly European. Compare with *Verpa bohemica* (p. 388), which has a cap that is completely free from the stem and sits like a thimble on the end of a pencil.

MORCHELLA SEPTENTRIONALIS M. KUO, J. D. MOORE, & ZORDANI

Ecology: Mycorrhizal; found under hardwoods, especially big-toothed aspen and ashes; usually growing near woody debris or growing directly from well-rotted wood; spring; found from roughly the 44th parallel northward. **Cap:** 3–4.5 cm high; bluntly to sharply pointed; pitted and ridged, with blunt-edged, finely velvety to bald ridges; pale when young (almost whitish when covered by leaves) and darkening with age until the ridges are black and the pits are pale yellowish brown to dark brown; attached to the stem with a slight overhang or rim; hollow. **Stem:** 2–3 cm long; 1–1.5 cm wide; whitish or pale tan; finely mealy with flaky granules; with an enlarged base; sometimes developing a few folds near the base; hollow. **Spore Print:** Creamy to yellowish or orangish. **Microscopic Features:** Spores 20–22 × 11–15 µm; smooth, ellipsoid; contents homogeneous. **Comments:** Edible and good. Compare with *Morchella angusticeps* (p. 277).

MORGANELLA PYRIFORMIS (SCHAEFFER) KREISEL & D. KRÜGER

Ecology: Saprobic on the deadwood of hardwoods or conifers; growing in dense clusters, or scattered; spring through fall; widely distributed and common. **Fruiting Body:** Shaped like an inverted pear, or more or less round; 1.5–5 cm wide; 2.5–5 cm high; dry; often covered with tiny white spines when young and fresh, but the spines usually disappear by maturity; typically with a pinched-off stem base and white rhizomorphs; by maturity developing a central perforation; whitish to yellowish brown; with a white, fleshy interior at first; later with yellowish to olive granular flesh and eventually filled with brownish spore dust. **Microscopic Features:** Spores 3.5–4.5 µm; globose; smooth; without a pedicel. Capillitial threads olive to brownish in KOH; 3–6 µm wide. **Comments:** Also known as *Lycoperdon pyriforme*. The habitat on wood and the abundant white rhizomorphs make this puffball easy to identify.

MUTINUS ELEGANS (MONTAGNE) E. FISCHER

Ecology: Saprobic; growing alone or gregariously in gardens, flowerbeds, meadows, lawns, woodchips, and cultivated areas (also occasionally appearing in woods); summer and fall; widely distributed and common. **Immature Fruiting Body:** Usually at least partially submerged in the ground; appearing like a whitish to pinkish or purplish "egg" up to 4 cm high; when sliced, revealing the stinkhorn-to-be encased in a gelatinous substance. **Mature Fruiting Body:** Cylindric; 4–17 cm high; 0.5–1.5 cm wide; gracefully tapered toward the apex; often slightly curved; orange or orangish red; sometimes with clinging whitish volval remnants; minutely pocked and pitted; with olive-brown to brown slime covering the upper portion, but usually not covering the extreme tip; the slime becoming foul and malodorous, and often quickly removed by insects; hollow; spongy; with a whitish, sac-like volva at the base. **Microscopic Features:** Spores 4–7 × 2–3 µm; ellipsoid or oblong; smooth. **Comments:** Compare with *Phallus rubicundus* (p. 304), which is very similar but has a structurally separate head.

MYCENA ATKINSONIANA A. H. SMITH

Ecology: Saprobic on fallen leaves of oaks and beech; growing scattered, gregariously, or in loose clusters; late summer and fall; widely distributed. **Cap:** Up to 3 cm across; convex to broadly conical, sometimes becoming bell-shaped; dry or slightly tacky; bald; reddish brown over the center, with golden to yellow shades developing elsewhere; the margin becoming lined with maturity; often with a thin maroon line at the outer edge. **Gills:** Narrowly attached to the stem; close; very pale yellow when young, becoming stained darker yellow with age; with maroon edges. **Stem:** 2–6 cm long; 2–3 mm thick; equal; hollow; distinctively adorned with tiny purplish-brown fibers (use a hand lens); reddish brown to brownish, fading to yellowish; exuding a yellow to orange or reddish-brown juice when sliced open; basal mycelium hairy and whitish, or when wet purplish brown. **Flesh:** Insubstantial; pallid or brownish; exuding a yellow to orange or reddish-brown juice when sliced. **Odor and Taste:** Not distinctive. **Chemical Reactions:** KOH on cap negative to yellow, erasing red pigments. **Spore Print:** White. **Microscopic Features:** Spores 7–9 × 3–6 µm; weakly to moderately amyloid; ellipsoid; smooth. Cheilocystidia abundant; fusiform. Pleurocystidia absent or rare; when present similar to cheilocystidia. **Comments:** *Mycena sanguinolenta* is similar but features pinkish to whitish gill faces and a stem that lacks purplish-brown fibers. Compare with *Mycena haematopus* (p. 284), which grows on wood and has gill edges colored like the gill faces.

Photo by Dan Molter

MYCENA CORTICOLA (PERSOON) GRAY

Ecology: Saprobic on the bark of standing or fallen trees, usually with moss present; frequently found on oaks but also on the bark of other hardwoods or conifers; growing scattered or densely gregariously; late summer and fall, but sometimes appearing in spring; widely distributed. **Cap:** Occasionally approaching 1 cm across, but usually 3–5 mm across; convex, becoming broadly convex; dry; becoming pleated; densely covered with tiny pale fibrils and granules (use a hand lens) that may begin to disappear with maturity; purple brown when young but soon fading to brown, orangish brown, or tan. **Gills:** Attached to the stem or beginning to run down it; distant; colored like the cap. **Stem:** Up to 1 cm long and under 1 mm thick; fragile; equal; covered with fibrils like those on the cap (densely so when young, creating a pale surface); colored like the cap. **Flesh:** Insubstantial. **Odor and Taste:** Not distinctive. **Spore Print:** White. **Microscopic Features:** Spores 9–11 µm; globose to subglobose; smooth; amyloid. Pleurocystidia absent. Cheilocystidia abundant; clavate; with tiny bumps or, frequently, with finger-like projections. Pileocystidia and caulocystidia irregular; densely covered with simple or branched nodules and projections. **Comments:** The habitat on bark, tiny size, and granulated, pleated cap are good field characters.

MYCENA EPIPTERYGIA VAR. LIGNICOLA A. H. SMITH

Cheilocystidia

Ecology: Saprobic on the barkless, mossy, well-decayed deadwood of conifers; growing gregariously; fall; apparently fairly widely distributed. **Cap:** Up to about 1.5 cm across; egg-shaped, becoming broadly conic to broadly bell-shaped; sticky when fresh; bald; yellow green to bright greenish yellow, fading to dull yellow; the margin sometimes faintly lined; cuticle fairly tough and elastic, peeling easily. **Gills:** Attached to the stem by a tooth; close or nearly distant; whitish to pale greenish yellow or yellow. **Stem:** 4–6 cm long; 1–1.5 mm thick; fragile; equal; bald; sticky; colored like the cap or paler. **Flesh:** Insubstantial; yellowish. **Odor and Taste:** Odor slightly to moderately mealy or slightly of iodine; taste similar. **Spore Print:** White. **Chemical Reactions:** KOH negative on cap. **Microscopic Features:** Spores 7–13 × 5–8 µm; weakly to moderately amyloid; ellipsoid; smooth. Cheilocystidia abundant; clavate to subglobose or occasionally saccate; covered with numerous rod-like projections. Pleurocystidia absent. Pileipellis an ixocutis. **Comments:** The habitat on the well-decayed wood of conifers and the sticky, yellow-green, conical cap are good field characters.

MYCENA GALERICULATA (SCOPOLI) S. F. GRAY

Ecology: Saprobic on well-decayed hardwood logs and stumps, and occasionally arising from subterranean wood, appearing terrestrial; causing a brownish rot of the heartwood; usually growing in loose or dense clusters, but occasionally growing alone or scattered; spring and fall; widely distributed. **Cap:** 1–6 cm; broadly conical, becoming broadly bell-shaped, and usually retaining a central bump; vaguely lined or grooved radially; bald; tacky; the margin at first even and somewhat inrolled, but

soon spreading, and, in age, often becoming somewhat tattered or splitting; brown to grayish brown or dirty tan, often with a darker brown center. **Gills:** Narrowly attached to the stem; distant or nearly so; with prominent cross-veins when mature; whitish, often becoming pink in age; not bruising or staining. **Stem:** 5–9 cm long above the substrate, but often rooting for several centimeters; 2–5 mm thick; equal; hollow; bald, or with a few tiny hairs; whitish above, tan to brownish downward. **Flesh:** Insubstantial; whitish to pale brownish. **Odor and Taste:** Odor not distinctive, or very slightly mealy. Taste slightly mealy. **Chemical Reactions:** KOH negative on cap. **Spore Print:** White. **Microscopic Features:** Spores 8–10 × 5.5–7 µm; amyloid; broadly ellipsoid; smooth. Pleurocystidia absent. Cheilocystidia abundant; of the broom cell type, with rod-like projections and nodes. Pileipellis elements diverticulate, with short nodes and rod-like projections. **Comments:** Compare with *Mycena inclinata* (p. 285), which features a toothed young cap margin, a stem that is yellow above and brown to reddish brown below, and a strongly mealy odor. Also compare with *Pluteus cervinus* (p. 316), which is usually larger and features close, free gills and a pink spore print.

MYCENA HAEMATOPUS

(PERSOON) KUMMER

Ecology: Saprobic on the deadwood of hardwoods (rarely reported on the wood of conifers), usually on logs that are well decayed and without bark; growing in dense clusters (but sometimes growing alone or scattered); causing a white rot; spring through fall; widely distributed and common. **Cap:** 1–4 cm across; oval, becoming broadly conic, broadly bell-shaped, or nearly convex; the margin often with a tiny sterile portion, becoming tattered with age; dry and dusted with fine powder when young, becoming bald and tacky; sometimes shallowly lined or grooved; dark brownish red to reddish brown at the center, lighter toward the margin; often fading to grayish pink or nearly whitish. **Gills:** Narrowly attached to the stem; close or nearly distant; whitish, becoming grayish to purplish; often stained reddish brown; edges colored like the faces. **Stem:** 4–8 cm long; 1–2 mm thick; equal; hollow; bald or with pale reddish hairs; brownish red to reddish brown or nearly purple; when fresh, exuding a purplish-red juice when crushed or broken. **Flesh:** Insubstantial; pallid or colored like the cap; exuding a purplish-red juice when crushed or cut. **Odor and Taste:** Odor not distinctive; taste mild or slightly bitter. **Spore Print:** White. **Microscopic Features:** Spores 8–11 × 5–7 µm; broadly ellipsoid; smooth; weakly amyloid. Cheilocystidia abundant; fusiform, with elongated, subacute apices. Pleurocystidia absent, scattered, or frequent; when present similar to cheilocystidia. Pileipellis a cutis, with the uppermost elements diverticulate. **Comments:** Compare with *Mycena atkinsoniana* (p. 282). *Mycena sanguinolenta* is very similar but grows from litter on the forest floor.

MYCENA INCLINATA (FRIES) QUÉLET

Ecology: Saprobic on the well-decayed wood of hardwoods; usually growing in dense clusters (but sometimes growing alone or scattered); spring and fall; widely distributed. **Cap:** 1–5 cm; broadly conical, becoming broadly bell-shaped and usually retaining a central bump; vaguely lined or grooved radially; bald; tacky; the margin usually featuring tiny, fringe-like "teeth" when young, and in age often becoming somewhat tattered or splitting; color variable (brown to yellowish brown, brownish or tan, but often developing yellow stains and areas); fading to dingy whitish with exposure to sunlight. **Gills:** Narrowly attached to the stem; close or nearly distant; sometimes with well-developed cross-veins when mature; whitish to pale grayish, sometimes becoming yellowish or pinkish in age; not bruising or staining. **Stem:** 5–10 cm long; 2–4 mm thick; equal; hollow; bald or with tiny hairs and flakes, especially when young; whitish near the apex, yellowish to yellow in the midsection, and brown to reddish brown below. **Flesh:** Insubstantial; pale. **Odor and Taste:** Odor mealy to foul; taste mealy. **Chemical Reactions:** KOH negative to brownish on cap. **Spore Print:** White. **Microscopic Features:** Spores 7–10 × 5–7 µm; amyloid; broadly ellipsoid; smooth. Pleurocystidia absent. Cheilocystidia abundant; of the broom cell type, with rod-like projections and nodes. Pileipellis elements diverticulate, with short nodes and rod-like projections. **Comments:** Compare with *Mycena galericulata* (p. 283).

MYCENA LEAIANA (BERKELEY) SACCARDO

Ecology: Saprobic on the deadwood of hardwoods; usually growing in tight, dense clusters, but sometimes found growing alone or scattered; late spring, summer, and fall; widely distributed. **Cap:** 1–4 cm; oval or bell-shaped when young, becoming broadly bell-shaped or convex; sticky to slimy when wet; bald; bright orange, fading to dull orange and, finally, almost whitish; occasionally developing olive-green stains when mature; the margin sometimes becoming lined. **Gills:** Attached to the stem; close or crowded; the edges bright orange, the faces orangish to creamy. **Stem:** 3–7 cm long; 2–4 mm thick; equal; hollow; bald; fairly tough and cartilaginous; sticky when wet; the base covered with orange to whitish powder or dust; orange or orangish yellow, but paler near the apex; sometimes exuding an orange juice when squeezed. **Flesh:** Insubstantial; pallid or orangish. **Odor and Taste:** Not distinctive, or slightly mealy. **Spore Print:** White. **Microscopic Features:** Spores 7–10 × 5–6 µm; ellipsoid; weakly to moderately amyloid, or nearly inamyloid when mature and separated from basidia. Cheilocystidia abundant; variable in shape, ranging from fusoid-ventricose to clavate or irregular, with 1 or more digitate projections. Pleurocystidia scattered to abundant; fusoid-ventricose to mucronate. Pileipellis an ixocutis. **Comments:** The bright orange colors, sticky surfaces, and contrasting gill edges are good field characters.

MYCENA LEPTOCEPHALA (PERSOON) GILLET

Ecology: Saprobic on the debris of conifers; growing scattered to gregariously on the ground; spring and fall; widely distributed. **Cap:** 1–4 cm; conical when young, becoming broadly conical, convex, or broadly bell-shaped; moist; with a whitish bloom when young, but soon bald; black or dark grayish brown when young, fading somewhat to grayish brown or gray with age; the margin faintly lined at first, later becoming more strongly lined. **Gills:** Attached to the stem by a tooth; nearly distant; whitish or pale grayish. **Stem:** 3–7 cm long; 1–3 mm thick; fragile; equal; hollow; with a whitish bloom at first, but soon bald; black to dark brown at first, becoming grayish or brownish; basal mycelium whitish. **Flesh:** Insubstantial; pallid or grayish. **Odor and Taste:** Odor strongly bleach-like; taste acidic and unpleasant. **Spore Print:** White. **Microscopic Features:** Spores 7–10 × 4–6 µm; weakly to moderately amyloid; ellipsoid; smooth. Cheilocystidia abundant; fusoid-ventricose, subcylindric, or clavate, without digitate projections. Pleurocystidia scattered or sometimes absent; similar to cheilocystidia. Pileipellis a cutis; uppermost elements digitate, with short rod-like projections. **Comments:** Compare with *Mycena semivestipes* (p. 289), which also smells like bleach but grows directly from the wood of hardwoods and features a convex cap and gills that run down the stem.

MYCENA LEPTOPHYLLA (PECK) SACCARDO

Ecology: Saprobic on terrestrial forest debris in hardwood forests (and occasionally reported in conifer forests), usually in the vicinity of rotting wood; usually growing gregariously, but sometimes found growing scattered or even alone; fall; widely distributed. **Cap:** Up to 2.5 cm across; conical to broadly conical or bell-shaped, often with a central nipple; moist when fresh; bald; dull orange, becoming orangish to yellowish over the center and whitish toward the margin; the margin lined. **Gills:** Attached to the stem by a tooth; close or nearly distant; whitish or pale pinkish to pale orangish. **Stem:** 3–7 cm long (above ground); 1–2 mm thick; fragile; equal; hollow; very finely silky, or bald; whitish to silvery grayish or very pale yellowish; basal mycelium hairy and white; often forming an underground taproot up to about 5 cm long. **Flesh:** Insubstantial; pallid or grayish. **Odor and Taste:** Odor not distinctive, or very faintly mealy; taste not distinctive. **Chemical Reactions:** KOH negative on cap. **Spore Print:** White. **Microscopic Features:** Spores 6.5–8 × 4.5–7 µm; inamyloid; mostly ovoid to subglobose, but occasionally broadly ellipsoid or nearly amygdaliform; smooth. Cheilocystidia fusoid-ventricose; only rarely branched. Pleurocystidia absent or very rare. Pileipellis a cutis, with the uppermost elements sparsely diverticulate. **Comments:** The habitat on hardwood debris, tiny size, bell-shaped to conic cap, orange to yellow colors, and taproot are good field characters. *Mycena adonis* is similar but features a scarlet cap and grows on debris of conifers.

MYCENA LUTEOPALLENS PECK

Ecology: Saprobic; growing from walnut and hickory shells, or from associated debris; occasionally found on the nut debris of other hardwoods, including black locust; typically growing gregariously in clusters of 2–4 but occasionally found growing alone; summer and fall; widely distributed. **Cap:** 8–15 mm across;

oval, becoming broadly bell-shaped or conic; the margin sometimes becoming wavy; bald; dry; sometimes shallowly lined or grooved; rich yellow to orange yellow when young; changing color markedly as it dries out; soon yellowish, whitish, or buff. **Gills:** Attached to the stem; nearly distant; pale to yellowish or tinged pinkish. **Stem:** 5–9 cm long; 1–2 mm thick; equal; hollow; bald or with tiny hairs; colored like the cap above, paler below. **Flesh:** Insubstantial; pallid or yellowish. **Odor and Taste:** Not distinctive. **Spore Print:** White. **Microscopic Features:** Spores 7–9 × 4–5.5 µm; ellipsoid; smooth; weakly to moderately amyloid when young; inamyloid when mature. Pleurocystidia and cheilocystidia abundant; fusoid-ventricose. **Comments:** Distinct by virtue of the habitat on nut debris and the colors.

MYCENA NIVEIPES (MURRILL) MURRILL

Ecology: Saprobic on the well-decayed, mossy deadwood (stumps and logs) of hardwoods (especially the wood of oaks, ashes, and maples); growing gregariously or in loose clusters; spring through fall; widely distributed. **Cap:** 1.5–7 cm; broadly conical, broadly bell-shaped, convex, or plano-convex; moist when fresh; bald; pale grayish to pale brownish when young, but soon white; sometimes with a slightly darker center; the margin faintly lined at first, later becoming more strongly lined and often splitting in age. **Gills:** Attached to the stem by a tooth; close or nearly distant; whitish or pale grayish (occasionally faintly pinkish). **Stem:** 4–10 cm long; 2–7 mm thick; fragile; equal; hollow; adorned with tiny whitish fibers at first, but often bald by maturity; silvery grayish at first, becoming whitish; sometimes discoloring a little brownish in the basal half with age or on handling; basal mycelium white. **Flesh:** Insubstantial; pallid or grayish. **Odor and Taste:** Odor usually strongly bleach-like but sometimes only weakly so, or not distinctive (especially in older specimens); taste acidic and unpleasant. **Spore Print:** White. **Chemical Reactions:** KOH negative on cap. **Microscopic Features:** Spores 8–11 × 5–7 µm; weakly to moderately amyloid; ellipsoid; smooth. Cheilocystidia abundant; fusoid-ventricose, without digitate projections. Pleurocystidia similar to cheilocystidia. Pileipellis a cutis. **Comments:** The large size (for the genus), pale grayish to white colors, and strong odor of bleach are good field characters.

Photo by Melissa Bochte

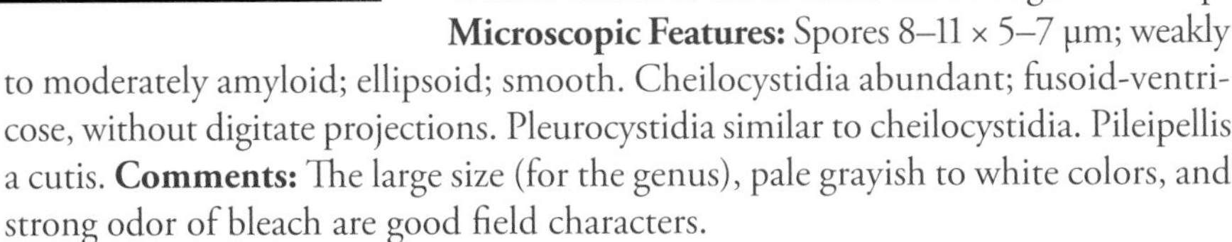

MYCENA PURA (PERSOON) KUMMER

Ecology: Saprobic on forest debris under hardwoods or conifers; growing alone, scattered, or gregariously; terrestrial; spring through fall; widely distributed. **Cap:** 2–6 cm; convex or bell-shaped, becoming flattened; the margin lined; bald; moist or dry; typically lilac to purple when young, but often fading or developing other shades (including whitish, yellowish, brownish, pinkish brown, or reddish). **Gills:** Attached to the stem by a tooth; close or nearly distant; whitish; developing cross-veins with maturity. **Stem:** 4–10 cm long; 2–6 mm thick; equal; hollow; bald or with tiny hairs; whitish or flushed with the cap color. **Flesh:** Insubstantial; watery grayish to whitish. **Odor and Taste:** Odor radish-like or sometimes not distinctive; taste strongly radish-like. **Chemical Reactions:** KOH negative on cap. **Spore Print:** White. **Microscopic Features:** Spores 6–10 × 3–4 µm; long-ellipsoid or nearly cylindric; faintly to moderately amyloid, or inamyloid when mature; smooth. Cheilocystidia and pleurocystidia rare to scattered or abundant; fusoid-ventricose, widely fusiform, or saccate. **Comments:** This species (or, more likely, species group) can be identified by the radish-like taste and the terrestrial habitat under conifers, but it is very variable in color; whitish, yellowish, pinkish, and even brownish forms are not infrequent.

MYCENA SEMIVESTIPES (PECK) A. H. SMITH

Ecology: Saprobic on the deadwood of hardwoods; causing a white rot; usually growing in dense clusters; fall and early winter (but occasionally found in summer and spring); widely distributed. **Cap:** 1–3.5 cm across; convex, becoming broadly convex or nearly flat; sticky when fresh; bald; dark brown or nearly black, fading to brown or grayish, but retaining a darker center; greasy when fresh; sometimes with reddish tones in wet weather; the margin lined. **Gills:** Broadly attached to the stem, beginning to run down the stem, or attached with a "tooth" that begins to run down the stem; close; white, or pinkish with age; sometimes developing reddish-brown spots. **Stem:** 2–6 cm long; 1–3 mm thick; fairly tough; equal; usually finely fuzzy near the base, at least when young; pale near the apex; brown to blackish near the base. **Flesh:** Insubstantial; pallid or brownish. **Odor and Taste:** Odor bleach-like, but sometimes indistinct in buttons. Taste unpleasant or slightly bitter. **Chemical Reactions:** KOH negative on cap. **Spore Print:** White. **Microscopic Features:** Spores 4–5 × 2.5–3 µm; weakly to moderately amyloid, or inamyloid when mature; ellipsoid; smooth. Pleurocystidia and cheilocystidia clavate, broadly fusoid-ventricose, saccate, or irregular; sometimes developing vague projections or lobes; inconspicuous. **Comments:** Compare with *Mycena leptocephala* (p. 286).

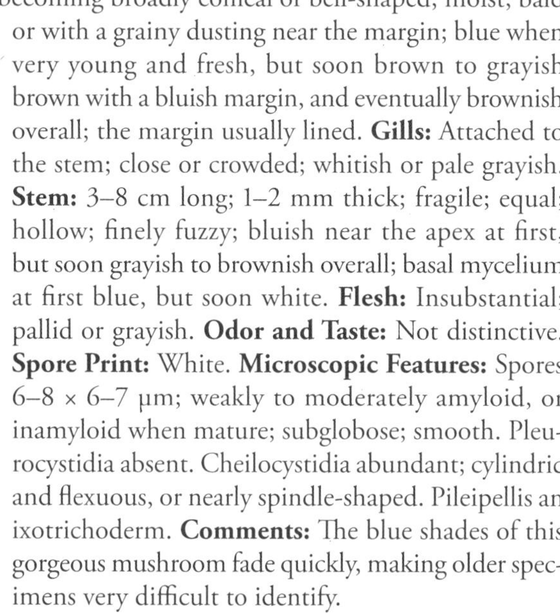

MYCENA SUBCAERULEA (PECK) SACCARDO

Ecology: Saprobic on the deadwood or woody debris of hardwoods, especially oaks; growing alone or scattered, often on or near stumps or fallen logs; apparently causing a brown rot; spring and again in fall; widely distributed. **Cap:** Up to 2 cm across; conical when young, becoming broadly conical or bell-shaped; moist; bald or with a grainy dusting near the margin; blue when very young and fresh, but soon brown to grayish brown with a bluish margin, and eventually brownish overall; the margin usually lined. **Gills:** Attached to the stem; close or crowded; whitish or pale grayish. **Stem:** 3–8 cm long; 1–2 mm thick; fragile; equal; hollow; finely fuzzy; bluish near the apex at first, but soon grayish to brownish overall; basal mycelium at first blue, but soon white. **Flesh:** Insubstantial; pallid or grayish. **Odor and Taste:** Not distinctive. **Spore Print:** White. **Microscopic Features:** Spores 6–8 × 6–7 µm; weakly to moderately amyloid, or inamyloid when mature; subglobose; smooth. Pleurocystidia absent. Cheilocystidia abundant; cylindric and flexuous, or nearly spindle-shaped. Pileipellis an ixotrichoderm. **Comments:** The blue shades of this gorgeous mushroom fade quickly, making older specimens very difficult to identify.

MYCENASTRUM CORIUM (GUERSENT) DESVAUX

Ecology: Saprobic; terrestrial; growing alone or gregariously in grassy areas, especially in manure-rich meadows and pastures, but also in lawns; summer and fall; widely distributed, but not common. **Fruiting Body:** Shaped more or less like a ball; up to 20 cm across; outer surface soft and whitish, breaking up irregularly with maturity to expose a tough brownish inner surface with skin about 2 mm thick; interior white and fleshy, becoming greenish yellow and eventually turning to dark olive-brown or purplish-brown spore dust; without a sterile base; without a stem. **Microscopic Features:** Spores 8–12 µm; globose; spiny, with spines up to 2 µm long; sometimes appearing

Spores and capillitial threads

nearly reticulate. Capillitial threads 10–30 µm wide; thick-walled; occasionally branched; bright olive yellow in KOH; with numerous spines and warts. **Comments:** The softball-sized fruiting body, the thick skin, and the lack of a sterile base are good characters for field identification, but the distinctive, spiny capillitial threads are definitive.

MYCORRHAPHIUM ADUSTUM (SCHWEINITZ) MASS GEESTERANUS

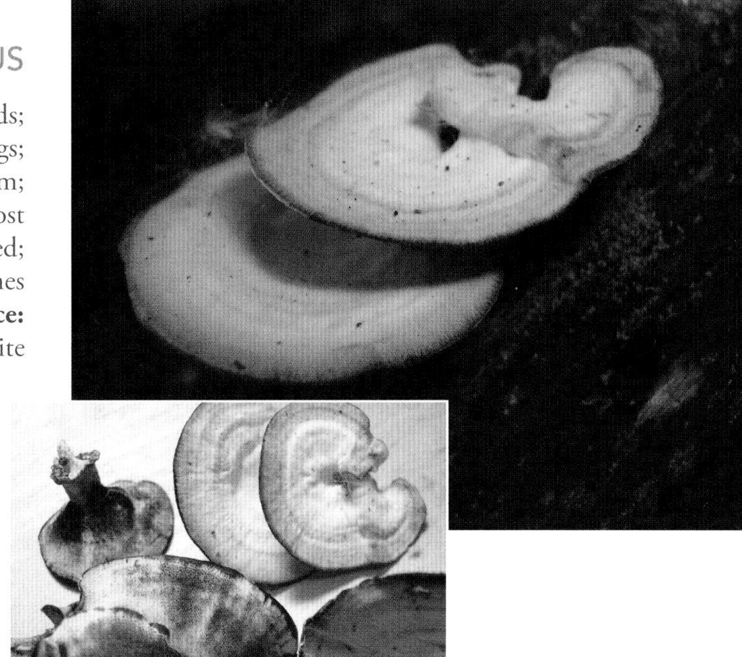

Ecology: Saprobic on the deadwood of hardwoods; growing alone or in clusters on sticks or small logs; summer and fall; widely distributed. **Cap:** 2–8 cm; flat to shallowly depressed; kidney-shaped or almost circular in outline; dry; bald, velvety, or roughened; white to tan, bruising grayish; with concentric zones of texture; the margin often black. **Undersurface:** Spines 1–3 mm long, often in fused groups; white at first, becoming pinkish to purplish, then dark brown and eventually black from the margin inward; bruising black. **Stem:** Often absent; when present 2–3 × 1–2 cm; central or lateral; whitish; velvety. **Flesh:** White; tough; unchanging when sliced. **Spore Print:** White. **Microscopic Features:** Spores 2.5–4 × 1–1.5 µm; smooth; cylindric. **Comments:** The blackening margin and spines, along with the habitat on wood, are good field characters.

NIDULARIA PULVINATA (SCHWEINITZ) FRIES

Ecology: Saprobic; growing scattered or gregariously on old deadwood (including driftwood); usually growing on the upper sides of logs; summer and fall; widely distributed. **Fruiting Body:** To about 1 cm across; shaped like a glob or a ball; outer surface at first shaggy, powdery, or velvety, becoming bald with age (but often appearing "lumpy" as a result of being pressed against the peridioles inside); brown to reddish brown or grayish brown, fading to nearly whitish; at maturity breaking up irregularly to expose an interior pile of peridioles. **Peridioles:** To 1 mm wide; irregularly shaped; silvery gray. **Microscopic Features:** Spores 6–10 × 4–7 µm; smooth; ellipsoid. **Comments:** Distinct among the bird's nest fungi in that it does not create a cup-like "nest."

OMPHALOTUS ILLUDENS (SCHWEINITZ) BRESINSKY & BESL

Photo by Brenda Nelson

Ecology: Saprobic; growing in large clusters on the stumps or buried roots of hardwoods (especially oaks); late summer and fall; widely distributed. **Cap:** 5–20 cm; convex, but soon flat, and eventually vase-shaped; the margin incurved; bald; bright orange. **Gills:** Running down the stem; crowded; bright orange. **Stem:** 5–20 cm long; 1–2 cm thick; tapering to base; solid; bright orange or darker below; bald. **Flesh:** Pale orange. **Odor:** Not distinctive, or sometimes disagreeable. **Spore Print:** White to cream or pale yellow. **Chemical Reactions:** KOH green on cap; ammonia greenish on cap. **Microscopic Features:** Spores 3.5–5 µm; round; inamyloid. **Comments:** Poisonous. Seemingly terrestrial when growing from buried roots. Sometimes called the "jack-o'-lantern mushroom" because the gills of fresh specimens glow in the dark. Chanterelles (pp. 131–34) feature false gills rather than true gills, do not grow in clusters on wood, are usually more yellow than orange, and do not turn greenish with ammonia. *Hygrophoropsis aurantiaca* (p. 215) features a soft, velvety cap and forked gills; it does not usually grow in clusters. Also compare with *Cortinarius hesleri* (p. 156).

Photo by Brenda Nelson

OTIDEA ONOTICA (PERSOON) FUCKEL

Ecology: Saprobic, growing terrestrially in woods under hardwoods or conifers; often clustered, but occasionally growing alone or scattered; summer and fall; widely distributed. **Fruiting Body:** Spoon-shaped, ear-shaped, or cup-like; often with a cleft down one side; up to 10 cm high and 6 cm across; inner surface yellowish to orangish, often with rose or pink areas; outer surface similarly colored, but lacking pink or rose shades, often finely fuzzy; stem if present whitish, small, and rudimentary; flesh pale yellowish; brittle. **Odor and Taste:** Not distinctive.

Microscopic Features: Spores 12–14 × 6–7 µm; smooth; ellipsoid; with 1 or 2 oil droplets. Paraphyses filiform; often with hooked or curved ends. **Comments:** Compare with *Aleuria aurantia* (p. 88).

PACHYELLA CLYPEATA (SCHWEINITZ) LE GAL

Ecology: Saprobic; growing alone or in small groups on rotting wood (primarily the wood of hardwoods) that is usually water-soaked; spring, summer, and fall; widely distributed. **Fruiting Body:** Occasionally to 8 cm across, but usually 2–4 cm across; cushion-shaped when young, but soon becoming saucer-shaped or shaped like a flattened cup; broadly attached to the wood so that only the edges can be lifted away from the substrate; upper surface sticky when fresh, medium to dark brown, sometimes with a hint of red or purple, bald, fading with age to tan; without a stem; flesh somewhat rubbery or gelatinous when fresh, sometimes becoming yellowish when torn. **Microscopic Features:** Asci with bluish tips in Melzer's reagent. Spores 18–25 × 13–16 µm; smooth; ellipsoid; usually with 2 oil droplets. Excipular surface with many thread-like elements embedded in a gel, creating a palisade. **Comments:** The flattened fruiting bodies attached broadly to the wood (which is usually soggy) are good field characters for the species group, but several similar species of *Pachyella* are virtually indistinguishable without microscopic examination.

PANAEOLUS FOENISECII (PERSOON) SCHRÖTER

Ecology: Saprobic; growing alone or gregariously on lawns, in meadows, and in other grassy areas; late spring, summer, and fall; very common; widely distributed. **Cap:** 1–3 cm; widely conical or bell-shaped, becoming convex or nearly flat; bald; dark brown to cinnamon brown, changing to light brown, tan, or buff, or with bands of these shades when in the process of drying out. **Gills:** Notched, attached to the stem, or pulling away from the stem; brown, becoming darker brown; sometimes with a mottled appearance; sometimes with pale edges; close. **Stem:** 4–8 cm long; 1.5–3 mm thick; more or less equal; sometimes with an enlarged base; bald; fragile; pale, becoming darker brown. **Flesh:** Thin; fragile. **Chemical Reactions:** KOH negative to grayish on cap. **Spore Print:** Dark brown to purple brown. **Microscopic Features:** Spores 12–17 × 7–11 µm; subfusoid to limoniform; rugose; dextrinoid; dark reddish brown in KOH. Cheilocystidia variously shaped (subfusoid to cylindric or

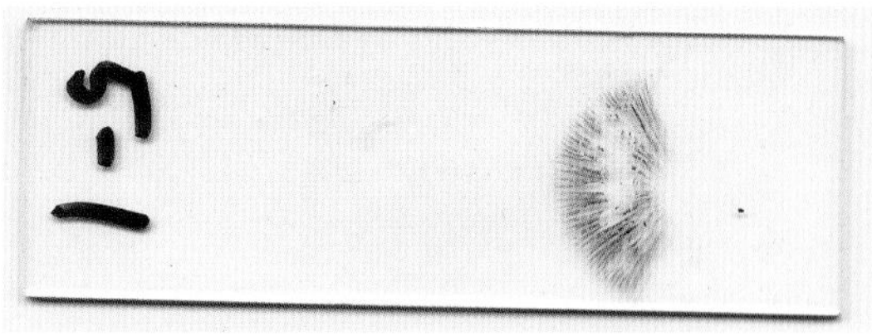

Spore print

subcapitate). Pleurocystidia absent, or scattered and scarcely projecting. Pileipellis hymeniform, with projecting pileocystidia. **Comments:** Also known as *Panaeolina foenisecii*, and sometimes given the common name of "lawnmower's mushroom." The small, 2-toned caps, along with the mottled gills and small size, are good field characters. Compare with *Agrocybe pediades* (p. 85), which has a yellowish-brown cap and a paler brown spore print.

PANAEOLUS PAPILIONACEUS (BULLIARD) QUÉLET

Ecology: Saprobic; growing alone to gregariously from the dung of horses or cows; spring, summer, and fall; widely distributed. **Cap:** 1–5 cm; obtusely conical to bell-shaped or nearly spherical when young, expanding to broadly bell-shaped with age; dry; bald to silky; often prominently cracked with age; sometimes developing a network of raised ridges; whitish, gray, brownish, brown, or reddish brown; the margin hung with white, tooth-like partial veil fragments, at least when young. **Gills:** Attached to the stem, or pulling away from it with maturity; close or crowded; grayish when young, but soon developing black areas and acquiring a mottled appearance; eventually black overall; with whitish edges. **Stem:** 4–16 cm long; up to 5 mm thick; more or less equal; finely hairy; often brittle; colored more or less like the cap, but paler at the apex, and darkening or turning reddish toward the base with maturity or on handling. **Flesh:** Insubstantial. **Spore Print:** Black or blackish. **Chemical Reactions:** KOH dull orangish on cap. **Microscopic Features:** Spores 11–18.5 × 7.5–12 µm; more or less ellipsoid, with a pore; smooth; dextrinoid. Pleurocystidia absent. Cheilocystidia abundant; subcylindric, often subcapitate or capitate. Pileipellis an epithelium, often featuring pileocystidia. **Comments:** Also known as *Panaeolus campanulatus* and *Panaeolus sphinctrinus*. *Panaeolus semiovatus* (see Kuo and Methven 2010) also grows on dung but is larger and features a ring on the stem, as well as a sticky cap that lacks teeth along the margin.

PANELLUS STIPTICUS (BULLIARD) KARSTEN

Ecology: Saprobic on the deadwood of hardwoods; usually growing in shelving clusters; spring through fall; widely distributed. **Cap:** 1–3 cm wide; convex, with an inrolled margin, becoming plano-convex, with the margin even or slightly curved under; semicircular to kidney-shaped or irregular in outline; dry; finely velvety to woolly; often becoming wrinkled and somewhat cracked or scaly in age; tan to pale yellowish brown, sometimes fading to off-white. **Gills:** Terminating abruptly at the stem; close; often forked; with cross-veins; pale yellowish brown. **Stem:** Up to about 10 × 5 mm; lateral or off-center; usually fuzzy-velvety with whitish, tan, or rusty-brown fuzz. **Flesh:** Whitish or pale brownish; tough. **Odor and Taste:** Odor not distinctive; taste usually bitter, but mild in some collections. **Spore Print:** White. **Chemical Reactions:** KOH gray to negative on cap. **Microscopic Features:** Spores 3–5 × 1–3 µm; ellipsoid; smooth; amyloid. Cheilocystidia prominent and abundant. Pileipellis a densely tangled cutis. Clamp connections present. **Comments:** Identifying features include the small size, the way the gills terminate in an abrupt line on the tiny, lateral stem, the woolly cap surface, and the bitter taste.

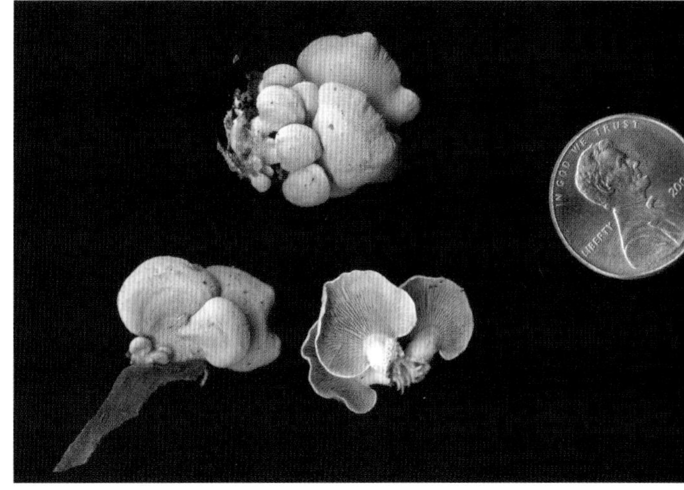

Photo by Lisa K. Suits

PANUS CONCHATUS (BULLIARD) FRIES

Ecology: Saprobic; growing alone or, more frequently, gregariously to clustered on hardwood sticks and logs; summer and fall; widely distributed. **Cap:** 5–15 cm wide; broadly convex at first, but soon with a central depression or vase-shaped; dry; bald or with minute hairs, but not prominently hairy; purplish to purplish brown when young, becoming reddish brown or tan in age, or fading to buff, but retaining a purplish margin; the colors often breaking up into patches with maturity; the margin inrolled. **Gills:** Running down the stem; close; often forking; purplish when fresh and young, later buff to pale brownish. **Stem:** 2–5 cm long; up to 3 cm wide; tough; usually off-center or lateral; dry; finely hairy when young; colored like the cap. **Flesh:** Whitish; very tough. **Odor and Taste:** Not distinctive. **Chemical Reactions:** KOH negative to yellowish on cap. **Spore Print:** White. **Microscopic Features:** Spores 5–7 × 2.5–3.5 µm; ellipsoid; smooth; inamyloid. Cheilocystidia and pleurocystidia ventricose or capitate. **Comments:** Also known as *Panus torulosus* and *Lentinus conchatus*. Compare with *Panus rudis* (p. 296), which features a densely hairy cap.

Photo by Lisa K. Suits

Photo by Walt Sturgeon

Photo by Martin Livezey

PANUS RUDIS FRIES

Ecology: Saprobic on the deadwood of recently fallen hardwoods; growing alone, gregariously, or in tight clusters; spring through fall; widely distributed. **Cap:** 2–10 cm wide; convex, with a tightly inrolled margin at first, becoming depressed or vase-shaped with an even margin; round in outline or irregular; densely hairy, with hairs 1–2 mm long; often purple at first, but soon fading to reddish brown, pinkish brown, orangish brown, or tan. **Gills:** Running down the stem; crowded; sometimes purplish when fresh and young, but soon whitish. **Stem:** 1–4 cm long; up to 1 cm wide; tough; often off-center or lateral; dry; densely hairy; colored like the cap or paler. **Flesh:** Whitish; tough. **Odor and Taste:** Odor not distinctive; taste mild or bitter. **Spore Print:** White. **Microscopic Features:** Spores 4.5–6.5 × 2.5–4 µm; ellipsoid; smooth; inamyloid. Pleurocystidia subclavate to subcylindric; with very thick walls, except at the apex. Clamp connections present. **Comments:** Also known as *Lentinus strigosus* and *Lentinus rudis*. Compare with *Panus conchatus* (p. 295).

PARAGYRODON SPHAEROSPORUS (PECK) SINGER

Ecology: Mycorrhizal with white oak, often in urban settings; growing gregariously; summer and fall; found from the Great Lakes region to Iowa and Kansas. **Cap:** 4–20 cm; convex, becoming broadly convex or flat; sticky or slimy; bald; yellowish at first, becoming brown; bruising dark brown; sometimes with partial veil remnants on the margin. **Pore Surface:** Attached to the stem or beginning to run down it; yellow, becoming brownish with age; bruising promptly and strongly brown; pores angular, about 1 per mm, not radially arranged; tubes about 1 cm deep. **Stem:** 4–10 cm long; 1–3 cm thick; more or less equal; bald near the apex; white to yellowish; bruising brown. **Partial Veil:** Whitish to yellowish; attached near the base of the stem, and eventually collapsing against it to form a sheathing ring. **Flesh:** White to yellowish; staining brown on exposure. **Odor and Taste:** Not distinctive. **Chemical Reactions:** On dried specimens we have

Photo by Carla Wick

received red to pinkish reactions from all surfaces with the application of KOH, negative reactions with ammonia, and grayish reactions with iron salts. **Spore Print:** Dark yellowish brown. **Microscopic Features:** Spores 6–9 × 6–8 µm; smooth; subglobose. Pleurocystidia fusoid-ventricose. **Comments:** The brown staining and sheathing ring near the base of the stem are distinctive. Compare with *Gyrodon merulioides* (p. 191).

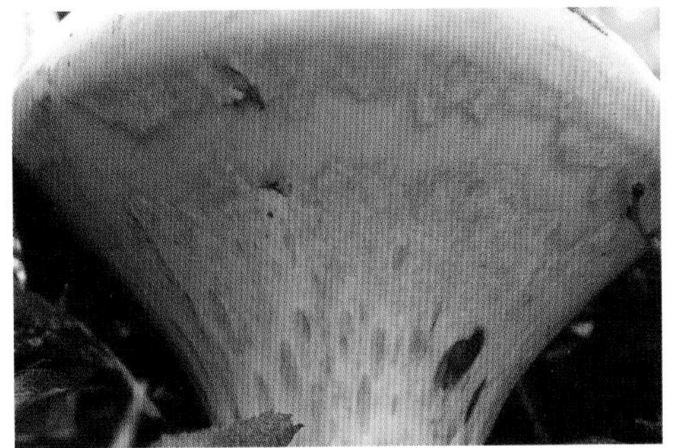

Photo by Carla Wick

PARASOLA AURICOMA
(PATOUILLARD) REDHEAD, VILGALYS, & HOPPLE

Ecology: Saprobic; growing scattered or gregariously on soil, in grass, or (more frequently) in woodchips; early summer, and sometimes again in fall; widely distributed. **Cap:** 10–60 mm across at maturity; egg-shaped at first, becoming convex or slightly conic, then nearly flat; bald to the naked eye, but finely hairy with a hand lens; becoming deeply grooved from the margin nearly to the center; orangish brown when young, becoming grayish in the grooves and eventually grayish overall, except for the center; without veil remnants. **Gills:** Free from the stem or nearly so; close or nearly distant; whitish at first, becoming dark gray and eventually black. **Stem:** 35–120 mm long; up to 3 mm thick; more or less equal; fragile; hollow; bald or very finely silky; whitish to yellowish; without a ring. **Flesh:** Insubstantial; whitish to grayish. **Odor and Taste:** Not distinctive. **Spore Print:** Blackish. **Microscopic Features:** Spores 10–16 × 6–9 µm; ellipsoid; with a prominent central pore; smooth. Cystidia cylindric, fusoid-ventricose, or utriform. Pileipellis hymeniform with scattered to abundant dark reddish-brown setae. **Comments:** Also known as *Coprinus auricomus*. Mature specimens that have lost their orangish-brown colors can be confused with *Parasola plicatilis* (p. 298).

PARASOLA CONOPILUS
(FRIES) ÖRSTADIUS & E. LARSSON

Ecology: Saprobic; growing scattered to gregariously or in loose clusters of 2–4 mushrooms (but not densely clustered) from the deadwood or litter of hardwoods, or rarely from dung; found in hardwood forests or more rarely in cultivated areas; spring and fall; widely distributed. **Cap:** 2–5 cm; broadly conical at first, often becoming broadly bell-shaped or nearly convex; bald; sometimes becoming

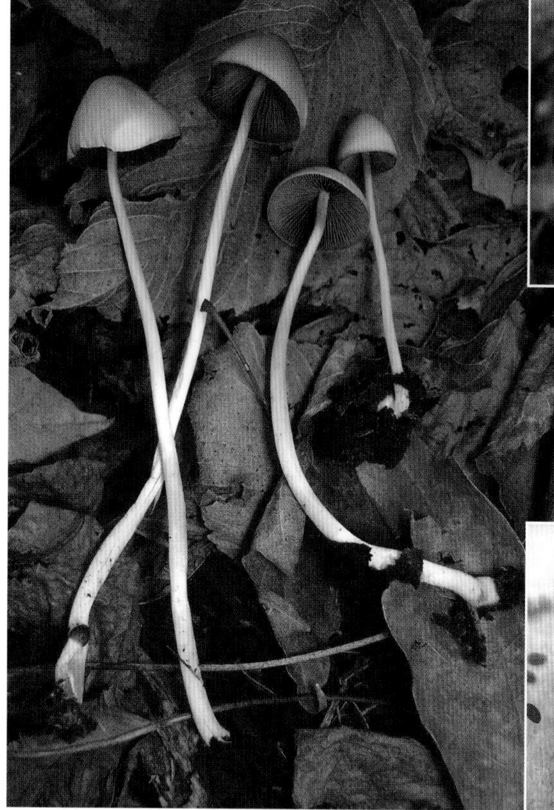

radially wrinkled; dull reddish brown, fading to buff; changing color markedly as it dries out; without veil remnants. **Gills:** Attached to the stem; close; brownish at first, becoming dark purplish brown to nearly black; with whitish edges. **Stem:** 6–19 cm long; up to 5 mm thick; equal; fragile; hollow; bald or very finely silky; white; without a ring. **Flesh:** Thin; fragile; watery brownish. **Odor and Taste:** Not distinctive. **Spore Print:** Black. **Microscopic Features:** Spores 14–19 × 7–8.5 µm; ellipsoid; with an eccentric pore; smooth. Pleurocystidia absent. Brachybasidioles present. Cheilocystidia fusoid-ventricose with a long neck. Pileipellis hymeniform with reddish-brown, aciculate, thick-walled setae. **Comments:** Difficult to identify without microscopic examination. *Psathyrella gracilis* is very similar but lacks setae in the pileipellis.

Setae

PARASOLA PLICATILIS
(CURTIS) REDHEAD, VILGALYS, & HOPPLE

Ecology: Saprobic; growing alone or scattered in grassy areas, usually in direct sunlight; summer and fall; widely distributed. **Cap:** 10–35 mm across at maturity; ovoid at first, becoming convex or bell-shaped, then flat; bald; deeply grooved from the margin nearly to the center; yellowish to orangish brown when young, becoming gray in the grooves and finally overall; without veil remnants. **Gills:** Free from the stem; close or nearly distant; whitish at first, becoming dark gray and eventually black. **Stem:** 3.5–10 cm long; up to 2 mm thick; equal above a slightly swollen base; fragile; hollow; bald or very finely silky; white; without a ring. **Flesh:** Insubstantial; whitish. **Odor and Taste:** Not distinctive. **Spore Print:** Black.

Microscopic Features: Spores 10–15 × 8–11 µm; angular-ovoid to limoniform or rarely subellipsoid; with a prominent, eccentric pore; smooth. Cystidia present; variously shaped. Pileipellis hymeniform. **Comments:** Also known as *Coprinus plicatilis*. Compare with *Parasola auricoma* (p. 297), which has a darker orange-brown cap when young and differs microscopically.

PAXILLUS INVOLUTUS (BATSCH) FRIES

Ecology: Mycorrhizal with a wide variety of hardwoods and conifers; found in woods and in urban settings; growing alone, scattered, or gregariously; summer and fall; widely distributed. **Cap:** 4–15 cm; convex to broadly convex, with a strongly inrolled, cottony margin; becoming plano-convex or centrally depressed; sticky or dry; bald or finely hairy; brown to yellow brown, olive brown, or grayish brown. **Gills:** Separable as a layer; running down the stem; close or crowded; often becoming convoluted or pore-like near the stem; yellowish to pale cinnamon or pale olive; bruising brown to reddish brown. **Stem:** 2–8 cm long; up to 2 cm thick; often tapered to base; dry; bald or finely hairy; colored like the cap or paler; bruising brownish to reddish brown. **Flesh:** Thick and firm; yellowish; discoloring brown when exposed. **Odor and Taste:** Taste acidic or not distinctive; odor not distinctive or somewhat fragrant. **Chemical Reactions:** KOH gray on cap. **Spore Print:** Purplish brown to yellow brown. **Microscopic Features:** Spores 6.5–10 × 5–7 µm; smooth; ellipsoid. Pleurocystidia and cheilocystidia more or less fusoid; with brown contents. Pileipellis a cutis. Clamp connections present. **Comments:** Poisonous. The brown-staining gills that are separable as a layer identify this species group handily.

PERENNIPORIA FRAXINOPHILA (PECK) RYVARDEN

Ecology: Parasitic on living ash trees; often appearing high on the tree; causing an extensive white heart rot; perennial; growing alone or gregariously; appearing year-round; widely distributed. **Cap:** Usually clearly defined, but sometimes merely a folded-over edge above a spreading pore surface; up to 40 cm across; convex to hoof-shaped; bald; brown to reddish brown, gray brown, or black; becoming cracked and furrowed; often hosting moss or algae; the margin thick, rounded, and whitish.

Pore Surface: Creamy white; not bruising appreciably; with 3–5 circular to angular pores per mm; annual tube layers to 5 mm thick. **Stem:** Absent. **Flesh:** Brownish to pale brown; corky to woody. **Odor:** Not distinctive. **Spore Print:** Presumably white, but not documented. **Microscopic Features:** Spores 6–9 × 5–6 µm; smooth; ellipsoid, with a severely truncated end; hyaline in KOH; in Melzer's sometimes dextrinoid; thick-walled. Cystidia and setae absent. Hyphal system dimitic. **Comments:** Compare to *Ganoderma applanatum* (p. 180), which has a brown-bruising pore surface and tends to attack deadwood (of many hardwoods and conifers, not just ashes) as a saprobe.

Asci and spores

PEZIZA BADIOCONFUSA KORF

Ecology: Mycorrhizal with conifers (especially white pine) or hardwoods; growing alone, gregariously, or in small clusters; often found near (or growing from) rotting wood in lignin-rich soil; late spring and early summer; widely distributed. **Fruiting Body:** Cup-shaped when young, but often flattening with age or becoming irregularly shaped; when clustered often becoming pinched and contorted; 3–15 cm across; upper surface bald, brown to reddish brown, purplish brown, or olive brown; undersurface roughened or finely mealy to granular, with tiny, reddish to orangish fibers, especially toward the margin; stem absent; attached to the substrate at a central location; flesh brownish and brittle. **Spore Print:** White. **Chemical Reactions:** KOH negative on all surfaces; Melzer's reagent blackish blue on upper surface of mature specimens. **Microscopic Features:** Spores 14–21 × 6.5–10.5 µm; at maturity finely roughened to warty; often developing smooth apical caps; fusoid to ellipsoid when immature, becoming ellipsoid. Asci with blue tips in Melzer's reagent. Paraphyses cylindric; with rounded, nonswollen tips. **Comments:** The fairly large size, late spring to early summer appearance, and colors make good field characters for this species, but microscopic analysis is probably essential for positive identification of most cup fungi.

PEZIZA DOMICILIANA COOKE

Ecology: Saprobic, growing alone or gregariously in indoor settings or outside in garages, concrete rubble, coal bins, sand, and so on; year-round; widely distributed. **Fruiting Body:** When young, circular in outline and cup-shaped, sometimes with a tiny stem; in age, flattening out to become irregularly saucer-shaped (but usually retaining a depressed center); 2–10 cm wide; upper surface at first whitish, darkening to yellowish brown or pale brown, smooth or wrinkled; undersurface paler brown or whitish, finely mealy; flesh pale, sometimes bruising slowly yellowish; often surrounded by whitish mycelium. **Microscopic Features:** Spores 11–15 × 6–10 µm; ellipsoid; smooth or slightly roughened at maturity; without oil droplets or with 2 small droplets. Asci with blue tips in Melzer's reagent. Paraphyses slender; septate; with slightly swollen tips. **Comments:** The rocky, man-made substrate preferred by this species makes it easy to identify. Although recent research (Tedersoo et al. 2006) suggests that some species of *Peziza* are mycorrhizal, this fungus clearly is not, given its habitat.

PEZIZA REPANDA PERSOON

Ecology: Saprobic on well-decayed logs, usually on the wood of hardwoods, but occasionally on woodchips or on the ground in soil that is rich with decayed wood; growing alone, gregariously, or clustered; typically found in colder weather (spring and fall), but sometimes appearing in summer; widely distributed. **Fruiting Body:** Initially cup-shaped and pale brown or whitish overall; in maturity flattened-irregular or bent backward; 6–12 cm across; the margin often splitting; upper surface brown and smooth, often "pinched" or somewhat wrinkled over the center; undersurface whitish and minutely fuzzy; attached to the substrate centrally, without a stem. Flesh brownish or pale; brittle. **Microscopic Features:** Spores 11–16 × 6–10 µm; smooth; ellipsoid; without oil droplets. Asci with blue tips in Melzer's reagent. **Comments:** The habitat on wood, along with the combination of a bald, brown upper surface with a whitish, fuzzy undersurface, will serve to identify this species in the field, but confirmation with microscopic analysis is probably essential for identification of most cup fungi. Although recent research (Tedersoo et al. 2006) suggests that some species of *Peziza* are mycorrhizal, this fungus is probably not, given its habitat.

PEZIZA SUCCOSA BERKELEY

Ecology: Mycorrhizal with hardwoods; growing alone, gregariously, or in small clusters on bare soil, often in damp areas; summer; widely distributed. **Fruiting Body:** Cup-shaped when young, and usually remaining so in maturity; when clustered becoming pinched and contorted; 2–5 cm across; upper surface bald, brown to grayish brown or olive brown; undersurface bald or finely granular, pale (often contrasting with the upper surface when fresh and young), sometimes stained yellow to greenish yellow; stem absent; attached to the substrate at a central location; flesh whitish to grayish, when squeezed exuding a juice that stains surfaces bright yellow to greenish yellow. **Spore Print:** White. **Microscopic Features:** Spores 16–22 × 8–12 µm; ellipsoid; at maturity warty; with 2 oil droplets. Asci with blue tips in Melzer's reagent. Paraphyses slightly clavate. **Comments:** Easily identified, when fresh, due to the yellow-staining juice.

PHAEOLUS SCHWEINITZII (FRIES) PATOUILLARD

Ecology: Parasitic on the roots and heartwood of living conifers (especially white pine) and saprobic on deadwood; appearing at the bases of tree trunks; causing a brown to reddish-brown cubical butt rot; annual; summer and fall; widely distributed. **Cap:** Usually with loosely arranged large lobes arising from a single stem-like structure that emerges from the ground, but occasionally in fused, shelving brackets attached to the base of the tree; up to 35 cm across; velvety to hairy when young, becoming bald in old age; roughening and developing more or less concentric grooves; bright yellow or orange at first, becoming brown to olive brown from the center to the margin with age; with concentric zones of color and texture; often when found more or less brown, with a yellow to olive margin. **Pore Surface:** Orange to bright yellow when young, becoming greenish yellow, then brownish, and eventually reddish brown; bruising promptly dark brown to black; with 1–2 angular, slot-like, or irregular pores per mm; tubes to 1.5 cm deep. **Stem:** Usually present as a more or less central structure up to about 6 cm long and 4 cm thick; brown and velvety below the pore surface. **Flesh:** Yellowish brown, becoming rusty brown; fairly soft when young, becoming stringy and leathery; often appearing zoned. **Odor:** Sweetly fragrant, or not distinctive. **Chemical Reactions:** KOH black on flesh and cap, often with a cherry-red intermediate stage (especially with younger specimens). **Spore Print:** Whitish to yellowish. **Microscopic Features:** Spores 6–9 × 2.5–5 µm; smooth; broadly ellipsoid; inamyloid; hyaline in KOH. Setae absent. Hyphal system monomitic. **Comments:** Distinguishing features include the orange to bright yellow young cap margin, the habitat near the bases of conifers, and the brown-bruising pore surface. Compare with *Phellinus gilvus* (p. 305).

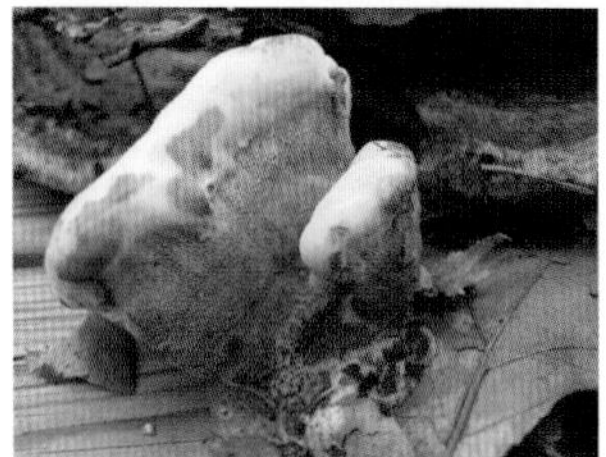

PHALLUS DUPLICATUS BOSC

Ecology: Saprobic; growing alone or gregariously in gardens, flowerbeds, meadows, lawns, woodchips, cultivated areas, and so on, also in hardwood forests; summer and fall; widely distributed, but more common below the Great Lakes. **Immature Fruiting Body:** Like a flesh-colored to whitish "egg" 4–7 cm high; when sliced, revealing the stinkhorn-to-be encased in a gelatinous substance. **Mature Fruiting Body:** Cylindric; 5–17 cm high; with a cap that is pitted and ridged by maturity, and covered with a malodorous, olive-brown spore slime that eventually wears off (or is carried away by flies), exposing a whitish to light brown surface; with a white stem that arises from a white to pinkish or purplish, sac-like volva; with a laced, white or sometimes pinkish "skirt" hanging 3–6 cm from the bottom edge of the cap (sometimes collapsing against the stem). **Microscopic Features:** Spores 3.5–4 × 1.5–2 µm; ellipsoid or flattened. **Comments:** The skirt, known as an indusium, develops slowly, lengthening downward from the bottom edge of the cap.

Photo by Walt Sturgeon

PHALLUS HADRIANI VENTENAT

Ecology: Saprobic; growing alone or gregariously in gardens, flowerbeds, meadows, lawns, woodchips, cultivated areas, and so on; summer and fall; widely distributed. **Immature Fruiting Body:** Like a purplish egg up to 6 cm across; usually at least partly submerged in the ground; when sliced, revealing the stinkhorn-to-be encased in a gelatinous substance. **Mature Fruiting Body:** Cylindric; to 25 cm high; with a 1.5–4 cm wide cap that is covered with olive-brown to dark brown spore slime; often developing a perforation at the tip; the cap surface pitted and ridged beneath the slime; sometimes with a whitish to purplish "skullcap" (a remnant of the volva); with a whitish hollow stem, 1.5–3 cm thick; the base enclosed in a purplish sac-like volva that is often at least partly submerged underground. **Microscopic Features:** Spores 3.5 × 1.5–2.5 µm ellipsoid or oblong; smooth. **Comments:** *Phallus impudicus* is identical but lacks purple shades on the egg and volva. Compare with *Phallus ravenelii* (below), which has a smooth (rather than pitted and ridged) cap surface.

PHALLUS RAVENELII BERKELEY & M. A. CURTIS

Ecology: Saprobic; growing alone or gregariously in gardens, flowerbeds, meadows, lawns, woodchips, sawdust piles, cultivated areas, and so on, also in woods; summer and fall; widely distributed. **Immature Fruiting Body:** Like a whitish to pinkish egg; when sliced, revealing the stinkhorn-to-be encased in a gelatinous substance. **Mature Fruiting Body:** Cylindric; to 20 cm high; with a 3–4.5 cm high

Photo by Andy Methven

cap that is smooth or slightly roughened, but not pitted and ridged, and covered with olive-brown to dark brown spore slime; developing a small hole with a white rim at the tip of the cap; with a whitish to yellowish or pinkish hollow stem, 1.5–3 cm thick; usually with a white or pink volva clinging to the stem and around the base; the base attached to whitish rhizomorphs. **Microscopic Features:** Spores 3–4.5 × 1–2 µm; ellipsoid; smooth. **Comments:** Compare with *Phallus hadriani* (p. 303).

PHALLUS RUBICUNDUS (BOSC, 1811) FRIES

Ecology: Saprobic; growing alone or gregariously in gardens, flowerbeds, meadows, lawns, woodchips, sawdust piles, cultivated areas (including soybean fields), and so on; spring through fall; widely distributed. **Immature Fruiting Body:** Like a whitish to pale brown egg; when sliced, revealing the stinkhorn-to-be encased in a gelatinous substance. **Mature Fruiting Body:** Cylindric; to about 20 cm high; with a 3–4.5 cm high fragile cap that is attached to the top of the stem (like a thimble atop a pencil) and is smooth or slightly roughened, but not pitted and ridged, and covered with olive-brown to dark brown spore slime; often developing a central apical perforation; stem reddish to orangish or pinkish, hollow, about 1.5 cm thick, and coarsely pocked with elongated potholes; with a whitish to pale brown volva clinging to the stem and around the base; with whitish rhizomorphs at the base. **Microscopic Features:** Spores long-ellipsoid; 3.5–5 × 1.5–2.5 µm; smooth. **Comments:** The separated, floppy cap structure is distinctive. Compare with *Mutinus elegans* (p. 281).

PHELLINUS GILVUS (SCHWEINITZ) PATOUILLARD

Ecology: Saprobic on the deadwood of hardwoods (especially oaks), causing a white rot of the sapwood; also apparently occasionally parasitic on the heartwood of living hardwoods; growing alone or in overlapping clusters; usually annual, but occasionally perennial; found year-round, but usually appearing in late spring, summer, and fall; widely distributed. **Cap:** Up to 15 cm across; more or less semicircular, irregularly bracket-shaped, or kidney-shaped; flattened-convex; rugged; sometimes somewhat velvety; the margin when growing velvety and mustard yellow to yellowish; elsewhere dark reddish brown or dark yellowish brown (eventually blackish). **Pore Surface:** Dark purplish brown to brown or reddish brown; pores minute (6–8 per mm); tubes 1–5 mm deep (for each layer, in perennial specimens). **Stem:** Absent. **Flesh:** Bright yellowish brown to orange brown; very tough. **Chemical Reactions:** KOH red, then black (or merely black) on all surfaces. **Microscopic Features:** Spores 4–5 × 3–3.5 µm; smooth; ellipsoid. Setae abundant; thick-walled; dark brown in KOH. Hyphal system dimitic. **Comments:** When actively growing, this fungus is easily recognized by the mustard-yellow margin and reddish-brown cap. Compare with *Phaeolus schweinitzii* (p. 302), which is usually larger, grows at the bases of conifers, and has a brown-bruising pore surface.

PHELLINUS ROBINIAE (MURRILL) A. AMES

Ecology: Parasitic on the heartwood of living black locust trees, and saprobic on the deadwood of black locust trees; causing a white rot; perennial; growing alone or gregariously; widely distributed where the host trees occur (below the Great Lakes). **Cap:** Up to 40 cm across; more or less semicircular, irregularly bracket-shaped, or kidney-shaped; flattened-convex, becoming convex, then more and more hoof-shaped with age; sometimes finely velvety, especially when young or along the margin; with age, becoming cracked and concentrically furrowed; brown to dark brown or black; often hosting algae and/or moss with age. **Pore Surface:** Brown; often appearing lighter or darker from different viewing angles; with 7–8 circular pores per mm; tube layers usually fairly clearly distinct, up to 9 mm deep. **Stem:** Absent. **Flesh:** Reddish brown to

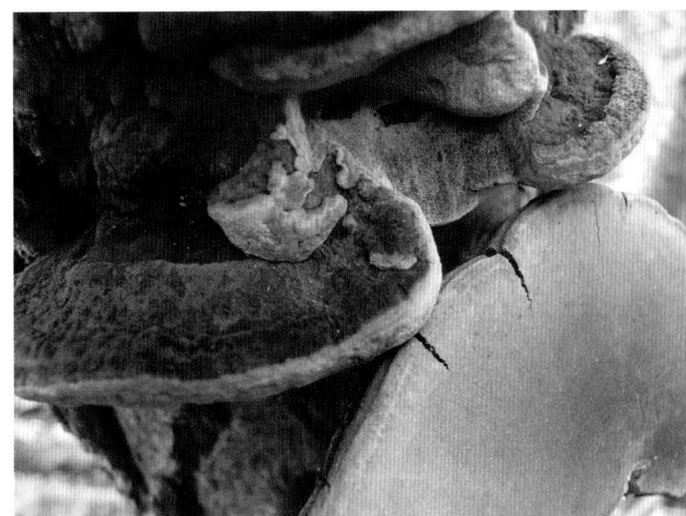

KOH on flesh and tubes

orange brown or yellow brown; woody. **Odor:** Fragrant when fresh. **Chemical Reactions:** KOH instantly black on flesh. **Microscopic Features:** Spores 5–6 × 4.5–5 µm; smooth; broadly ellipsoid to subglobose; reddish brown in KOH; inamyloid. Setae absent. Hyphal system dimitic. **Comments:** *Phellinus everhartii* is similar but grows on oaks.

PHELLODON ALBONIGER (PECK) BANKER

Photo by Noah Siegel

Ecology: Mycorrhizal with conifers (especially white pine and hemlock); sometimes reported under hardwoods; growing alone or gregariously; summer and fall; widely distributed, but more common in the northern Midwest. **Cap:** Single, or fused with other caps; 3–9 cm wide; convex, becoming plano-convex or nearly flat; velvety; whitish to pale gray, becoming gray with a whitish to bluish margin. **Undersurface:** Running down the stem; covered with crowded spines that are 2–4 mm long; whitish at first, becoming gray. **Stem:** 4–6.5 cm long; 1–4 cm thick at apex; extremely variable in shape; bald or finely velvety; colored like the cap. **Flesh:** 2-layered, with a whitish to pale grayish spongy upper layer and a hard black to bluish-black lower layer. **Odor and Taste:** Odor mild or, more commonly, fragrant (reminiscent of curry or maple syrup), becoming stronger when dried; taste mild. **Chemical Reactions:** KOH on flesh bluish to greenish, then brown to black. **Spore Print:** White. **Microscopic Features:** Spores 3.5–5 × 3–4.5 µm; globose to subglobose; echinulate, with spines about 0.5 µm long. Clamp connections absent. **Comments:** Compare with *Hydnellum caeruleum* (p. 208), which features an orangish stem, a mealy odor, and a brown spore print.

PHLEBIA INCARNATA (SCHWEINITZ) NAKASONE & BURDSALL

Photo by Lisa K. Suits

Ecology: Saprobic; growing in overlapping clusters on hardwood logs and stumps, particularly those of white oak, beech, maples, and paper birch; causing a white rot; annual; apparently associated with *Stereum ostrea* (p. 361), which is almost always found nearby; late spring, summer, and fall; widely distributed. **Cap:** 1.5–7 cm across; more or less semicircular, irregularly bracket-shaped, or kidney-shaped; flattened-convex; bald or finely hairy; bright coral pink, fading with age; the margin wavy, often white. **Undersurface:** Whitish to pinkish, becoming dirty white or tan; bald, but irregularly wrinkled, folded, or almost toothed; bruising mustard yellow on mature specimens. **Stem:** Absent. **Flesh:** White; soft at first, but soon fairly tough and leathery. **Chemical Reactions:** Cap surface and flesh yellowish green to olive yellow, then pale orange, with KOH. **Spore Print:** White. **Microscopic Features:** Spores 4–6 × 2–2.5 µm; smooth; ellipsoid; inamyloid. Clamp connections present. **Comments:** The pink color, habitat, and odd undersurface are good field characters.

Photo by Lisa K. Suits

PHLEBIA RADIATA FRIES

Ecology: Saprobic; spreading across logs and stumps of hardwoods or conifers; annual; causing a white rot; spring, summer, fall, and winter; widely distributed. **Fruiting Body:** 1–10 cm or more across; irregular in outline; up to about 3 mm thick; surface wrinkled, with the wrinkles and folds vaguely radiating from a more or less central point; orange to pink (more rarely tan with orangish edges, or purplish); occasionally developing a slightly folded-over, hairy edge. **Spore Print:** White. **Microscopic Features:** Spores 4–5.5 × 1.5–2 µm; smooth; allantoid; inamyloid. Cystidia cylindric to clavate. Clamp connections present. **Comments:** Compare with *Phlebia tremellosa* (below), which is more pale in color and develops more clearly defined individual fruiting bodies.

PHLEBIA TREMELLOSA (SCHRADER) NAKASONE & BURDSALL

Ecology: Saprobic; growing alone to gregariously, sometimes in overlapping clusters; found primarily on the deadwood of hardwoods, but also reported on conifer wood; causing a white rot; annual; late spring, summer, and fall; widely distributed. **Fruiting Body:** 3–10 cm across; irregularly shaped; spreading without a cap, except for a stubby upper edge; cap where developed woolly and whitish; without a stem; up to about 5 mm thick. **Surface:** Translucent; often somewhat gelatinous; orangish to pinkish, or orange to red when mature; elaborately wrinkled and pocketed, giving the illusion of being irregularly poroid. **Flesh:** Whitish; very thin. **Spore Print:** White. **Microscopic Features:** Spores 3.5–4.5 × 1–2 µm; smooth; sausage-shaped; inamyloid; with 2 oil droplets in KOH. Cystidia scattered; clavate; scarcely projecting; apices often encrusted. **Comments:** Compare with *Phlebia radiata* (p. 307).

PHOLIOTA LIMONELLA (PECK) SACCARDO

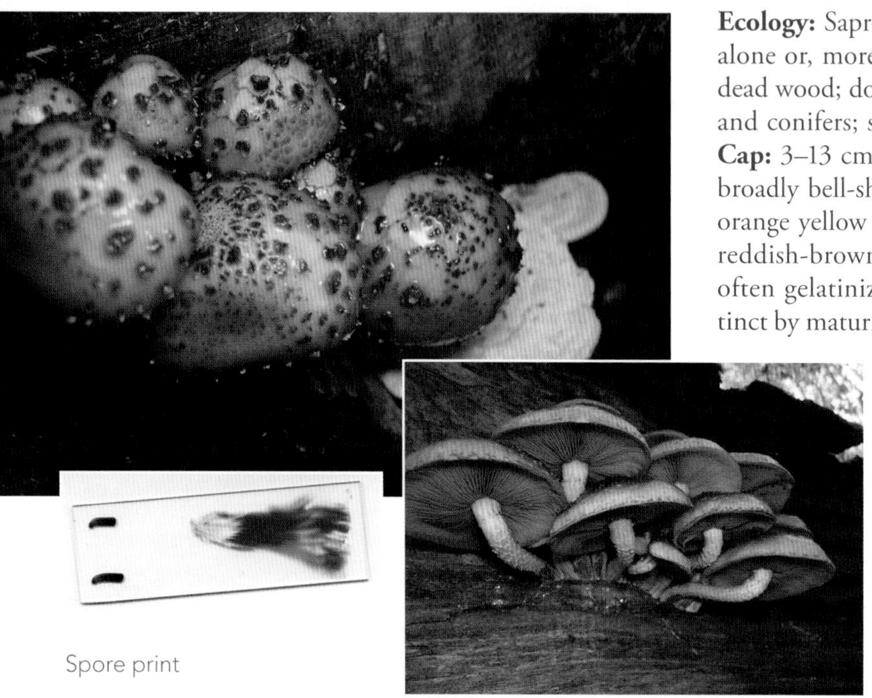

Spore print

Ecology: Saprobic and probably parasitic; growing alone or, more commonly, in clusters on living or dead wood; documented on a variety of hardwoods and conifers; summer and fall; widely distributed. **Cap:** 3–13 cm; convex, becoming broadly convex, broadly bell-shaped, or nearly flat; sticky or slimy; orange yellow to yellow; covered with brownish to reddish-brown scales that are soon scattered and often gelatinize, disappearing or becoming indistinct by maturity. **Gills:** Attached to the stem; close; whitish to yellowish when young, becoming rusty brown; at first covered by a whitish to yellowish cobwebby partial veil. **Stem:** 4–15 cm long; up to 2 cm thick; dry, or sticky near the base; silky near the apex; with a flimsy ring or ring zone (often indistinct); whitish to yellowish under reddish-brown to brownish or yellowish-brown scales that may be scattered or densely packed; base sometimes covered with whitish mycelium. **Flesh:** Yellow or whitish. **Odor and Taste:** Not distinctive. **Chemical Reactions:** KOH red to orangish on cap. **Spore Print:** Rusty brown to brown. **Microscopic Features:** Spores 6–9 × 4–5.5 µm; smooth; more or less ellipsoid; with an apical pore. Pleurocystidia clavate to clavate-mucronate; often with greenish-yellow contents (chrysocystidia). Pileipellis an ixocutis. Clamp connections present. **Comments:** The slimy yellow cap with reddish-brown scales and the dry, subscaly stem define this species group. Compare with *Pholiota squarrosoides* (p. 310), which has a thinly sticky cap that is whitish under the scales.

PHOLIOTA MUTABILIS (SCHAEFFER) KUMMER

Ecology: Saprobic; growing in clusters (rarely alone) on the deadwood of hardwoods or conifers; spring, summer, and fall; widely distributed. **Cap:** 2–16 cm; convex, becoming broadly convex or broadly bell-shaped; sticky or slimy when fresh; tawny to orangish brown, changing color markedly as it dries out and fading to yellowish (often passing through a 2-toned stage); the margin finely lined

when moist; bald, or with scattered whitish hairs when young. **Gills:** Attached to the stem or beginning to run down it; close or crowded; whitish to pale tan when young, becoming cinnamon brown; at first covered by a whitish to pale tan partial veil. **Stem:** 4–10 cm long; up to 1.5 cm thick; dry; silky near the apex; with a persistent (occasionally ephemeral) ring; whitish, becoming brown from the base up; covered with small whitish to brownish scales. **Flesh:** Whitish. **Odor and Taste:** Odor not distinctive, or fragrant; taste mild, or somewhat unpleasant. **Chemical Reactions:** KOH negative on cap. **Spore Print:** Cinnamon brown. **Microscopic Features:** Spores 5.5–7.5 × 4–5 µm; smooth; ellipsoid; with a well-developed apical pore. Pleurocystidia absent. Cheilocystidia subcylindric, subfusiform, or subcapitate; scattered; inconspicuous. Pileipellis a gelatinized layer in young, fresh specimens. Clamp connections present. **Comments:** Also known as *Kuehneromyces mutabilis*. The bald cap that changes color markedly as it dries out, the scaly stem, and the persistent ring make good field characters for this species. Compare with *Pholiota veris* (p. 311), which appears in spring and features a bald stem.

PHOLIOTA POLYCHROA (BERKELEY) A. H. SMITH & H. J. BRODIE

Ecology: Saprobic; growing alone or gregariously on the deadwood of hardwoods (rarely on conifer wood); summer and fall; widely distributed. **Cap:** 2–10 cm; convex, becoming broadly convex, broadly bell-shaped, or nearly flat; sticky or slimy; cuticle peeling with ease; variable in color, but usually mottled with shades of olive and pinkish purple (sometimes almost completely one or the other color) when young, developing yellowish to orangish areas with maturity; at first with scattered veil remnants, but usually soon bald overall; the margin usually hung with veil remnants. **Gills:** Attached to the stem, often by means of a notch; close or crowded; whitish to yellowish or slightly purplish when young, becoming grayish brown to purplish brown; at first covered by a partial veil. **Stem:** 2–6 cm long; up to 1 cm thick; dry, or sticky near the base; silky near the apex, but often covered with scales or veil patches below; with a flimsy ring or ring zone; usually yel-

Pleurocystidium

low to yellowish, but sometimes whitish, bluish, greenish, or brownish. **Flesh:** Whitish to yellow or greenish. **Odor and Taste:** Not distinctive. **Chemical Reactions:** KOH greenish yellow on cap; iron salts slowly deep green on cap. **Spore Print:** Brown to dark brown or slightly purplish brown. **Microscopic Features:** Spores 5.5–7.5 × 3.5–4.5 µm; smooth; ellipsoid; with a pore. Pleurocystidia fusoid-ventricose. Pileipellis an ixocutis. Clamp connections present. **Comments:** The colors are variable, but the overall appearance of this species (which may be a species group) is fairly distinct.

PHOLIOTA SQUARROSOIDES (PECK) SACCARDO

Ecology: Saprobic and possibly parasitic; growing in clusters (rarely alone or scattered) on the deadwood of hardwoods; summer and fall; widely distributed. **Cap:** 3–11 cm; convex, becoming broadly convex or broadly bell-shaped; usually sticky; whitish underneath conspicuous tawny scales. **Gills:** Attached to the stem or beginning to run down it; close or crowded; whitish, becoming rusty brown; at first covered by a partial veil. **Stem:** 4–10 cm long; up to 1.5 cm thick; dry; with an ephemeral ring or ring zone; whitish, sometimes becoming reddish brown near the base; covered with conspicuous tawny scales. **Flesh:** Whitish. **Odor and Taste:** Odor not distinctive, or somewhat fragrant; taste not distinctive. **Chemical Reactions:** KOH negative on cap. **Spore Print:** Cinnamon brown. **Microscopic Features:** Spores 4–6 × 2.5–3.5 µm; smooth; ellipsoid; lacking an apical pore. Pleurocystidia clavate to clavate-mucronate or fusoid-ventricose; lacking refractive contents in KOH. Cheilocystidia mucronate, fusoid-ventricose or clavate. Pileipellis partially gelatinized. Clamp connections present. **Comments:** *Pholiota squarrosa* is very similar but features a dry cap, gills that turn greenish before turning brown, an often garlicky odor, and different microscopic features. Compare with *Pholiota limonella* (p. 308) and with *Leucopholiota decorosa* (p. 264).

Photo by Dan Molter

PHOLIOTA TERRESTRIS OVERHOLTS

Ecology: Saprobic; growing in clusters on the ground, frequently in disturbed areas (roadbeds, pathsides, and so on); occasionally fruiting from wood; spring through fall; widely distributed. **Cap:** 2–8 cm; convex, becoming broadly convex, bell-shaped, or nearly flat; usually dry to the touch, but somewhat sticky in wet weather; with small brownish scales that may wear off in age; light brown, dark brown, yellowish brown, reddish brown, or grayish brown, often darker over the center; the margin usually finely hairy or scaly. **Gills:** Attached to the stem; crowded; pale at first, later becoming dirty yellowish and eventually cinnamon brown; at first covered by a whitish, hairy partial veil. **Stem:** 3–8 cm long; up to 1 cm thick; finely hairy and whitish or yellowish near the apex; sheathed below the apex with small brownish scales that terminate in a ring zone just below the cap; whitish or pale tan, becoming darker toward the base. **Flesh:** Whitish, pale yellowish, or brownish. **Odor and Taste:** Not distinctive. **Spore Print:** Brown. **Microscopic Features:** Spores 4.5–6.5 × 3.5–4.5 µm; smooth; ellipsoid; with a tiny apical pore. Pleurocystidia (chrysocystidia) variously shaped; scarcely projecting; with amorphous refractive contents in a KOH mount. Cheilocystidia numerous; variously shaped. Clamp connections present. **Comments:** The brown colors, small scales on the cap and stem, brown spore print, and growth pattern in clusters on the ground are good identification characters, but microscopic analysis may be needed to identify this species with certainty. Compare with *Stropharia kauffmanii* (p. 363), which is more robust and more prominently scaly and which features gills that become purplish gray to black, along with a purplish-gray to black spore print.

PHOLIOTA VERIS A. H. SMITH & HESLER

Ecology: Saprobic; growing alone, scattered, or in clusters on the well-decayed wood of hardwoods (especially oaks and beech); late spring; widely distributed. **Cap:** 2–6 cm; convex, becoming broadly convex, broadly bell-shaped, or nearly flat; moist at first; tan when young and fresh, fading markedly as it dries out, and eventually becoming buff-colored; bald overall, but often with tiny fibrils near the margin when young; the margin sometimes finely lined. **Gills:** Attached to the stem; close or crowded; whitish to pale tan when young, becoming cinnamon brown; at first covered by a partial veil. **Stem:** 4–9 cm long; up to 12 mm thick; dry; with an upward-flaring, whitish to pale tan ring that soon begins to collapse and develop a tawny-brown edge; pale tan; bald, or with inconspicuous fibrils just below the ring. **Flesh:** Pale brownish. **Odor and Taste:** Not distinctive. **Chemical Reactions:** KOH negative on cap. **Spore Print:** Cinnamon brown. **Microscopic Features:** Spores 5.5–7.5 × 4–5 µm; smooth; ellipsoid. Pleurocystidia and cheilocystidia fusoid-ventricose with a long neck. Pileipellis a partially gelatinized interwoven layer of cylindric hyphae. **Comments:** Also known as *Kuehneromyces rostratus*. The bald cap and the flaring ring that develops a tawny edge are good field characters. Compare with *Pholiota mutabilis* (p. 308).

Chemical reactions

PHYLLOPORUS RHODOXANTHUS (SCHWEINITZ) BRESÀDOLA

Ecology: Mycorrhizal with hardwoods, especially oaks and beech; growing alone, scattered, or gregariously; summer and fall; widely distributed. **Cap:** 2.5–8.5 cm; convex, becoming broadly convex to more or less flat; dry; very finely velvety, or nearly bald; sometimes beginning to crack in age; variable in color, ranging from red to reddish brown, or olive brown to brown. **Gills:** Running down the stem; close; yellow to golden yellow, dirtying with age; not bruising, but often developing reddish-brown spots with age; thick; sometimes forking; often with cross-veins. **Stem:** 2–9 cm long; 2–10 mm thick; more or less equal, or tapering to base; sometimes appearing ribbed near the apex at the termination points of the gills; yellowish, with reddish to brownish fibers; basal mycelium yellow. **Flesh:** White to pale yellow. **Odor and Taste:** Not distinctive. **Chemical Reactions:** Cap surface flashing blue with ammonia. **Spore Print:** Yellowish to dirty yellow. **Microscopic Features:** Spores 10–12 × 3.5–4.5 µm; smooth; subfusoid. **Comments:** Also known as *Phylloporus rhodoxanthus* ssp. *americanus*. This "gilled bolete" is quite variable in color; the crucial identifying features are the yellow basal mycelium, the nonbluing gills and flesh, and the ammonia reaction.

PHYLLOTOPSIS NIDULANS (PERSOON) SINGER

Ecology: Saprobic on the deadwood of hardwoods and conifers; growing alone or in overlapping clusters; fall; widely distributed. **Cap:** 2–8 cm across; more or less fan-shaped; flattened-convex; dry; prominently hairy; sometimes with a whitish coating at first, but soon bright orange, fading to yellowish orange; the margin inrolled when young. **Gills:** Close; bright to pale orange. **Stem:** Absent or poorly developed and lateral. **Flesh:** Pale orange; soft. **Odor and Taste:** Taste mild or foul; odor strong and foul (at least when fruiting on hardwoods), or mild. **Chemical Reactions:** KOH negative on cap. **Spore Print:** Very pale pink to pinkish brown. **Microscopic Features:** Spores 5–8 × 2–4 µm; smooth; inamyloid; long-ellipsoid. **Comments:** The densely hairy, stemless cap and bright orange colors are distinctive. Compare with *Crepidotus crocophyllus* (p. 164).

Spore print

PIPTOPORUS BETULINUS (BULLIARD) KARSTEN

Ecology: Saprobic on the deadwood of paper birch, and occasionally parasitic on living paper birch trees; causing a yellowish to brown cubical rot; annual, but found year-round; growing alone or gregariously; northern Midwest (where paper birch trees occur naturally). **Cap:** 5–25 cm; kidney-shaped in outline; broadly convex to more or less flat; growing shelf-like or hoof-like; dry; with a smooth or somewhat roughened "skin" that often peels away; whitish to pale brownish in age; the margin rolled over smoothly to form a wide rim around the pore surface. **Pore Surface:** Whitish, aging grayish brown; with 2–4 pores per mm; tubes to 1 cm long. **Stem:** Absent or rudimentary and stubby. **Flesh:** White; thick; corky. **Odor and Taste:** Taste slightly bitter; odor strong and pleasant. **Spore Print:** White. **Microscopic Features:** Spores: 3–6 × 1.5–2 µm; smooth; cylindric to long-ellipsoid. Cystidia and setae absent. Hyphal system dimitic to trimitic. **Comments:** Easily identified by the habitat on paper birch, the overall aspect, and the wide, smooth rim formed around the pore surface.

PLEUROTUS DRYINUS (PERSOON) KUMMER

Photo by Patrick Harvey

Photo by Patrick Harvey

Ecology: Saprobic; growing alone or in small clusters on dead and living wood of hardwoods (especially oaks and beech); summer and fall; widely distributed. **Cap:** 4–12 cm; convex, becoming broadly convex; circular in outline; finely hairy to cottony; whitish beneath the grayish to pale brownish hairs, often yellowing with age; the margin inrolled when young, with partial veil remnants. **Gills:** Running down the stem; close; whitish, yellowing with age. **Stem:** 4–10 cm long; up to 3.5 cm thick; tough; usually a little off-center; the lower portion covered with a densely fuzzy sheath that terminates in an ephemeral ring; surface above the ring smooth or with ridges resulting from the gills; whitish, yellowing with age. **Flesh:** Thick; tough; whitish. **Odor and Taste:** Odor not distinctive; taste mild. **Chemical Reactions:** KOH negative on cap. **Spore Print:** White. **Microscopic Features:** Spores 9–15 × 3.5–5 µm; smooth; ellipsoid; inamyloid. **Comments:** Compare with *Hypsizygus ulmarius* (p. 219). *Pleurotus levis* is a virtually indistinguishable biological species that can only be reliably separated with culturing in the laboratory.

PLEUROTUS OSTREATUS (JACQUIN) KUMMER

Ecology: Saprobic; growing in shelf-like clusters on dead logs and living trees (primarily hardwoods, but sometimes on conifers); causing a white rot; fall, winter, and early spring; common; widely distributed. **Cap:** 4–15 cm; convex, becoming flat or somewhat depressed; kidney-shaped to fan-shaped, or nearly circular if growing on the tops of logs; somewhat greasy when young and fresh; bald; pale brown to dark brown; the margin inrolled when young, later wavy, never lined. **Gills:** Running down the stem; close; whitish or with a gray tinge, sometimes yellowish in age. **Stem:** Usually rudimentary and lateral (or absent) when the mushroom is growing from the side of a log or tree, but when it grows on the tops of logs or branches or at an angle, it may develop a substantial, thick stem

that is dry and slightly hairy near the base. **Flesh:** Thick; white. **Odor and Taste:** Odor distinctive, but hard to describe (an "oyster mushroom" smell); taste mild. **Spore Print:** Whitish to grayish or lilac. **Microscopic Features:** Spores 8–10.5 × 3–3.5 µm; smooth; cylindric to narrowly kidney-shaped. **Comments:** Edible. Often called the "oyster mushroom." The gills are often filled with small black beetles. Compare with *Pleurotus pulmonarius* (below), which begins appearing in summer and features paler colors, a slightly lined cap margin, and a more developed stem. *Pleurotus populinus* grows on aspens in the northern Midwest and appears from spring through fall.

Spore print

PLEUROTUS PULMONARIUS (FRIES) QUÉLET

Ecology: Saprobic; growing in shelf-like clusters on dead and living wood of hardwoods; causing a white rot; beginning in summer, but continuing into fall and winter; widely distributed. **Cap:** 2–12 cm; convex, becoming flat or somewhat depressed; lung-shaped to semicircular, or nearly circular if growing on the tops of logs; somewhat greasy when young and fresh; bald; whitish to beige or pale tan, usually without dark brown colorations; the margin inrolled when young, later wavy and very finely lined. **Gills:** Running down the stem; close or nearly distant; whitish. **Stem:** Sometimes absent or rudimentary, but often present; 1–7 cm long and up to 1.5 cm thick; eccentric, lateral, or central. **Flesh:** Thick; white. **Odor and Taste:** Odor distinctive, but hard to describe (an "oyster mushroom" smell); taste mild. **Chemical Reactions:** KOH orangish on cap. **Spore Print:** Whitish, grayish, or lilac. **Microscopic Features:** Spores 7–10 × 2.5–5 µm; smooth; cylindric to long-ellipsoid. **Comments:** Edible. Compare with *Pleurotus ostreatus* (p. 314). *Pleurotus pulmonarius* is also illustrated on p. 8.

PLUTEUS AURANTIORUGOSUS (TROG) SACCARDO

Ecology: Saprobic on decaying hardwood logs and stumps; growing alone or in small groups; summer and fall; widely distributed, but not common. **Cap:** 2–5.5 cm; convex at first, becoming broadly convex or flat; dry or moist; bald or finely granular; the margin sometimes faintly lined at maturity; bright scarlet to orange when young, fading to bright yellow with age. **Gills:** Free from the stem; close; whitish, becoming pinkish; sometimes with yellowish edges. **Stem:** 3–6 cm long; to 1 cm

Photo by Lisa K. Suits

thick; equal; finely hairy; whitish to yellowish above; flushed with the cap color below; basal mycelium white or yellowish. **Flesh:** Whitish to yellowish; unchanging. **Odor and Taste:** Not distinctive. **Spore Print:** Pink. **Microscopic Features:** Spores 6–7 × 4.5–5 µm; ellipsoid; smooth. Pleurocystidia variously shaped; lacking antler-like projections. **Comments:** Easily identified by the colors, the free gills that become pinkish, the pink spore print, and the habitat on wood.

Photo by Melissa Bochte

Cystidia

Spore print

PLUTEUS CERVINUS (SCHAEFFER) KUMMER

Ecology: Saprobic on the deadwood of hardwoods and conifers; growing alone, scattered, or gregariously; spring through fall; common and widely distributed. **Cap:** 3–15 cm; convex at first, becoming broadly convex or nearly flat; pale to dark brown; bald and glossy, or streaked with fibers; slightly sticky when wet. **Gills:** Free from the stem; white, becoming pink and finally deep brownish pink; crowded or close. **Stem:** 5–13 cm long; 0.5–2.5 cm thick; more or less equal; sometimes enlarging slightly to base; white; sometimes streaked with brownish fibers. **Flesh:** Soft and white throughout; unchanging. **Odor and Taste:** Radish-like, or not distinctive. **Chemical Reactions:** KOH negative to pale orangish on cap. **Spore Print:** Pink to pinkish brown. **Microscopic Features:** Spores 5–8 × 4–6 µm; ellipsoid; smooth. Cystidia with thick walls and antler-like projections. Pileipellis elements without clamp connections. **Comments:** Also known as *Pluteus atricapillus*. Sometimes called the "deer mushroom," this common decomposer of fallen logs can be recognized by its brown cap, free gills that become pink, and pinkish-brown spore print. There may be several midwestern species in the *cervinus* group. Compare with *Pluteus petasatus* (p. 319), which has a white cap with brown scales over the center.

PLUTEUS CHRYSOPHLEBIUS (BERKELEY & M. A. CURTIS) SACCARDO

Ecology: Saprobic on decaying hardwood logs and stumps; growing alone or gregariously; summer and fall; widely distributed. **Cap:** 1–3 cm; convex at first, becoming broadly convex or flat (sometimes with a central bump); moist; bald; sometimes becoming finely veined over the center; the margin lined; bright yellow when young, dull yellow or brownish yellow in age. **Gills:** Free from the stem; close; whitish to pale yellowish, becoming pinkish. **Stem:** 3–6 cm long; 1–3 mm thick; equal; fragile; smooth; bright yellow; basal mycelium white. **Flesh:** Insubstantial; pale to yellowish. **Odor and Taste:** Not distinctive. **Spore Print:** Pink. **Microscopic Features:** Spores 5.5–7 × 4.5–6 µm; subglobose; smooth. Pleurocystidia mostly fusoid-ventricose; cheilocystidia similar, or clavate; lacking antler-like projections. Pileipellis hymeniform. **Comments:** Also known as *Pluteus admirabilis*. The combination of the small size, bright yellow colors, free gills that become pink, and habitat on wood is distinctive.

PLUTEUS FLAVOFULIGINEUS ATKINSON

Ecology: Saprobic on decaying hardwood logs and debris; causing a white rot; growing alone or scattered; late spring, early summer, and fall; widely distributed. **Cap:** 2–8 cm; convex or bell-shaped at first, becoming broadly convex or nearly flat; finely velvety, especially over the center; golden to dull or brownish yellow, with a brownish center. **Gills:** Free from the stem; close or crowded; whitish at first, becoming pink. **Stem:** 5–12 cm long; up to 1.5 cm thick; equal; bald or silky; variable in color, from white to yellowish or pinkish. **Flesh:** Thin; whitish; unchanging. **Odor and Taste:** Not distinctive. **Spore Print:** Pink. **Microscopic Features:** Spores 6–8 × 4.5–6.5 µm; broadly ellipsoid or subglobose; smooth. Cystidia fusoid-ventricose; lacking antler-like projections. **Comments:** Compare with *Xeromphalina tenuipes* (p. 393), which is more orange and features a velvety stem and a white spore print. Recent DNA analysis (Justo, Minnis, et al. 2011) suggests the possibility that *Pluteus flavofuligineus* is the same as the European species *Pluteus leoninus*.

PLUTEUS GRANULARIS PECK

Ecology: Saprobic on decaying wood of conifers or hardwoods; growing alone or scattered; summer and fall; widely distributed. **Cap:** 2–10 cm; convex at first, becoming broadly convex or flat; densely covered with dark brown granules over a pale brown undersurface; sometimes becoming wrinkled, veined, or nearly reticulate over the center; in age often becoming somewhat less granulated. **Gills:** Free from the stem; close or crowded; whitish at first, becoming pinkish; the edges colored like the faces. **Stem:** 3–8 cm long; up to 1 cm thick, but usually skinnier; more or less equal; whitish or pale brownish beneath darker brown granules arranged in stretched-out zones (especially near the base). **Flesh:** White; unchanging. **Odor and Taste:** Taste not distinctive, slightly radish-like, or slightly unpleasant; odor not distinctive. **Spore Print:** Pink. **Microscopic Features:** Spores 5–6.5 × 4–5 µm; broadly ellipsoid; smooth. Pleurocystidia fusoid-ventricose; lacking antler-like projections. **Comments:** The granulated brown cap, free gills that turn pink, habitat on wood, and pink spore print are good field characters.

PLUTEUS LONGISTRIATUS (PECK) PECK

Ecology: Saprobic on decaying hardwood logs and debris; growing alone or gregariously; summer and fall; widely distributed. **Cap:** 1–3 cm; convex at first, becoming broadly convex, sometimes with a central depression or a central bump; fragile; gray to grayish brown; with cracks and fissures extending from the margin almost to the center; with whitish flesh revealed in the cracks; sometimes minutely granular or hairy, especially over the center. **Gills:** Free from the stem; close; whitish at first, becoming pinkish; soft and collapsing. **Stem:** 2–5 cm long; up to 3 mm thick; equal; whitish, with grayish fibers. **Flesh:** Insubstantial; pale; unchanging. **Odor and Taste:** Not distinctive. **Spore Print:** Pink. **Microscopic Features:** Spores 6–7.5 × 5–5.5 µm; broadly ellipsoid; smooth. Pleurocystidia lacking antler-like projections. **Comments:** The small size, grayish-brown cap that is lined and grooved from the center to the margin, and pink mature gills are good field characters for this species group.

PLUTEUS MAMMILLATUS (LONGYEAR) MINNIS, SUNDBERG, & METHVEN

Ecology: Saprobic on the decaying wood of hardwoods; growing alone or gregariously; summer and fall; distribution uncertain (originally recorded from Michigan, but rarely reported since, except in southeastern Missouri, where it is common in the Mingo National Wildlife Refuge). **Cap:** 1–7 cm; conical at first, becoming broadly bell-shaped, broadly convex, or nearly flat; dry; finely silky; medium to bright yellow, fading on exposure; the margin slightly lined. **Gills:** Free from the stem; close; whitish at first, becoming pink at maturity. **Stem:** 1–8 cm long; up to 1.5 cm thick; equal or tapering upward; solid; bald or finely silky; whitish to pale yellowish; with a fragile white ring on the lower half. **Flesh:** Insubstantial; white; unchanging. **Odor and Taste:** Not distinctive. **Spore Print:** Pink. **Microscopic Features:** Spores 5–7 µm; subglobose; smooth. Cystidia fusoid-ventricose or broadly clavate; lacking antler-like projections. **Comments:** Also known as *Chamaeota sphaerospora*. This *Pluteus* is easily distinguished from others on the basis of the ring on the stem.

PLUTEUS PETASATUS (FRIES) GILLET

Ecology: Saprobic on the wood of hardwoods, but frequently found in wood mulch, sawdust piles, woodchips, and the like, or on buried wood, appearing terrestrial; growing alone or in clusters; summer and fall; common and widely distributed. **Cap:** 4–15 cm; convex at first, becoming broadly convex to nearly flat; dry; whitish with a brown, hairy to scaly center. **Gills:** Free from the stem; crowded; white and remaining so for quite a while, then finally pink. **Stem:** 4–10 cm long; 0.5–3 cm thick; more or less equal, or swollen in the middle in more robust specimens; sometimes with a slightly enlarged base; white, discoloring below; sometimes streaked with brownish fibers. **Flesh:** Firm and white throughout; unchanging. **Odor and Taste:** Not distinctive, or somewhat radish-like. **Chemical Reactions:** KOH negative on cap. **Spore Print:** Pink. **Microscopic Features:** Spores 5–9.5 × 3.5–5 µm; ellipsoid; smooth. Pleurocystidia with thick walls; fusiform; only occasionally with antler-like projections. **Comments:** Compare with *Pluteus cervinus* (p. 316).

PLUTEUS ROMELLII (BRITZELMAYR) SACCARDO

Ecology: Saprobic on decaying hardwood logs and debris; growing alone or gregariously; summer and fall; widely distributed. **Cap:** 1–5 cm; convex at first, becoming broadly convex or nearly flat, often with a central bump; olive brown to brown (often olive brown in the center and paler brown elsewhere); somewhat wrinkled, especially over the center; not slimy or sticky, but with a greasy or almost waxy texture when fresh; the margin finely lined. **Gills:** Free from the stem; almost distant; whitish at first, becoming yellowish and finally pinkish as the spores mature. **Stem:** 2–3 cm long; up to 3 mm thick; equal; bald or finely hairy; bright yellow to greenish yellow (often brighter toward the base). **Flesh:** Insubstantial; pale; unchanging. **Odor and Taste:** Not distinctive. **Spore Print:** Pink. **Microscopic Features:** Spores 6–7 × 5–6 µm; broadly ellipsoid to subglobose; smooth. Pleurocystidia variously shaped; lacking antler-like projections. Pileipellis hymeniform. **Comments:** Also known as *Pluteus lutescens*. The brown cap, yellow stem, and free pink gills at maturity are good field characters.

Photo by Dan Molter

PLUTEUS THOMSONII (BERKELEY & BROOME) DENNIS

Ecology: Saprobic on decaying hardwood logs and debris; growing alone or gregariously; summer and fall; widely distributed. **Cap:** 1–3.5 cm; convex at first, becoming broadly convex with a central bump; blackish brown, fading to dull brown; bald; with a slightly to prominently wrinkled or veined (sometimes nearly reticulate) center. **Gills:** Free from the stem; close or nearly distant; whitish or grayish at first, becoming pinkish. **Stem:** 2–4.5 cm long; 1.5–6 mm thick; equal; bald or silky; whitish. **Flesh:** Insubstantial; pale; unchanging. **Odor and Taste:** Not distinctive, or slightly radish-like to bleach-like. **Spore Print:** Pink. **Microscopic Features:** Spores 6–8 × 5.5–6 µm; ellipsoid; smooth. Cystidia rostrate, with short to long apical projections. Pileipellis hymeniform, with some cystidium-like projections. **Comments:** When prominently veined and picturesque this species is easily identified, but microscopic analysis may be required when the veins are poorly developed. Spores of this species are illustrated on p. 18.

PODOSCYPHA ACULEATA (BERKELEY & M. A. CURTIS) BOIDIN

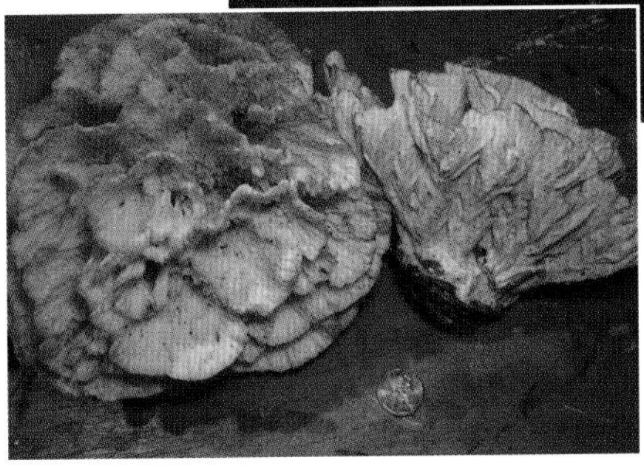

Photo by Robert Johnson and Matthew Johnson

Ecology: Saprobic; growing alone or scattered on the ground under hardwoods; fall; in the Midwest known from southern Missouri and southern Indiana. **Fruiting Body:** Up to 10 cm across and 13 cm high; composed of tightly packed branches, which arise from a common base, forming a rosette; branches wide and flattened, whitish to creamy, becoming grayish to pinkish or faintly brownish in old age; upper surfaces rugged; margins fringed; undersurface rugged, yellowish to cream; flesh thin, tough and leathery. **Spore Print:** Undocumented; probably white. **Microscopic Features:** Spores 4.5–7 × 4–5 µm; smooth; ellipsoid to ovate; inamyloid. Gloeocystidia present. Hyphal structure dimitic. Clamp connections present. **Comments:** This is a rare fungus, often mistaken for a species of *Cotylidia* or *Sparassis*. Its range is uncertain; outside of the Midwest it is known from South Carolina and Brazil.

POLYPORUS ALVEOLARIS (DE CANDOLLE) BONDARTSEV & SINGER

Ecology: Saprobic on decaying sticks and logs (occasionally on living branches) of hardwoods; causing a white rot; growing alone or gregariously; spring to fall; widely distributed. **Cap:** 1–10 cm broad; variable in shape, but generally semicircular or kidney-shaped; orange; fading with age; scaly, becoming more bald. **Pore Surface:** Running down the stem; whitish to yellowish white; pores diamond-shaped or hexagonal, radially arranged. **Stem:** Typically lateral and stubby, but occasionally centrally located and more substantial (in which case the cap is round, rather than kidney-shaped). **Flesh:** To 2 mm thick; white.

Spore Print: White. **Microscopic Features:** Spores 9–11 × 3–3.5 µm; smooth; cylindric. Cystidia and setae absent. Hyphal system dimitic to trimitic. **Comments:** Also known as *Favolus alveolaris* and *Polyporus mori*. Very common in late spring, and easily recognized by the orange color and the hexagonal pores. The species is very tough, and faded, months-old specimens are often encountered in late summer and fall.

POLYPORUS ARCULARIUS (BATSCH) FRIES

Ecology: Saprobic on the deadwood of hardwoods; causing a white rot; growing alone or in small groups; occasionally arising from buried wood and appearing terrestrial; spring; widely distributed. **Cap:** 1–8 cm; convex to shallowly vase-shaped; dry; bald or finely scaly; brown to golden brown, the colors frequently breaking up into rough concentric zones; the margin fringed with tiny hairs (use a hand lens). **Pore Surface:** White, sometimes running down the stem; 0.5–2 pores per mm; hexagonal or angular. **Stem:** Central or slightly off-center; 2–6 cm long; 1.5–4 mm wide; equal; dry; brown to yellowish brown; bald or slightly scaly; the base sometimes with tiny hairs; tough. **Flesh:** White; thin; tough. **Spore Print:** White. **Microscopic Features:** Spores 7–9 × 2.5–3 µm; smooth; cylindric. Cystidia and setae absent. Hyphal system dimitic. **Comments:** The overall aspect, the appearance in spring, and the hairy cap margin are good field characters.

POLYPORUS BADIUS (PERSOON) SCHWEINITZ

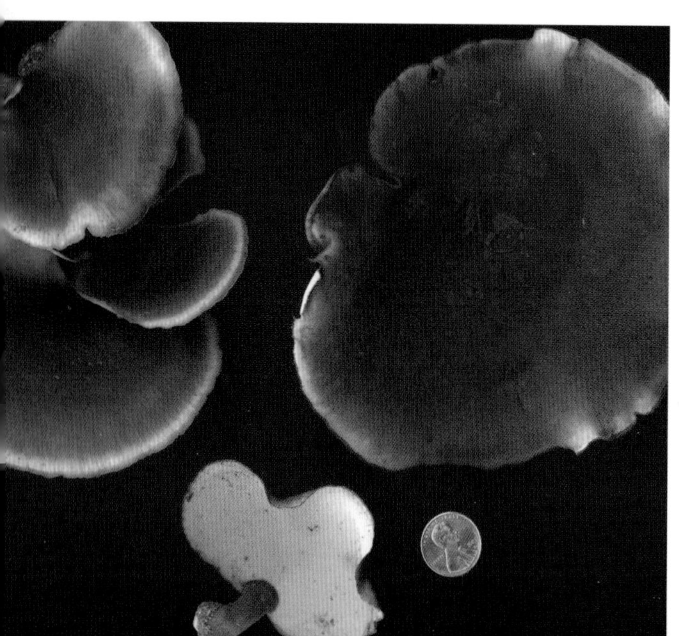

Ecology: Saprobic on decaying hardwood and conifer wood; causing a white rot; growing alone or in small groups; spring, or fall and winter; widely distributed. **Cap:** 4–20 cm; broadly convex to shallowly vase-shaped; round in outline, kidney-shaped, or lobed; dry; bald; dark reddish brown to dark brown, often paler toward the margin (rarely pale overall, with a reddish-brown center). **Pore Surface:** White, becoming dingy in age; often running down the stem; pores circular and very tiny (4–6 per mm), not easily separable from cap. **Stem:** Central or off-center to lateral; 1–6 cm long; 0.5–1.5 cm wide; equal; dry;

pale at the apex, but soon black nearly overall; tough. **Flesh:** White; thin; very tough. **Spore Print:** White. **Microscopic Features:** Spores 5–10 × 3–4 µm; smooth; cylindric to ellipsoid. Cystidia and setae absent. Hyphal system dimitic. **Comments:** The color of the cap is quite variable, perhaps because the mushrooms are tough and survive for a long time. Compare with *Polyporus varius* (p. 324), which is much smaller and has a cinnamon to tan cap.

POLYPORUS RADICATUS SCHWEINITZ

Photo by Dan Molter

Photo by Dan Molter

Ecology: Saprobic on the roots of dead hardwoods (or the dead roots of living hardwoods); causing a white rot; growing alone or scattered; summer through fall; widely distributed, but more common below the Great Lakes. **Cap:** 3.5–10 cm; broadly convex to flat or shallowly sunken; round in outline; dry; velvety or roughened; yellowish brown to reddish brown. **Pore Surface:** White or in age dingy yellowish; running down the stem; 2–3 angular pores per mm; tubes 1–5 mm long. **Stem:** More or less central; 6–15 cm long; 0.5–2.5 cm wide; equal, or enlarged toward base; dry; dirty yellowish above ground; with a 6–13 cm black taproot extending underground. **Flesh:** White; tough. **Spore Print:** White. **Microscopic Features:** Spores 12–15 × 6–8 µm; smooth; ellipsoid. Cystidia and setae absent. Hyphal system dimitic. **Comments:** The distinguishing feature of this terrestrial polypore (the long, rooting stem) is likely to be snapped off when the mushroom is picked.

POLYPORUS SQUAMOSUS (HUDSON) FRIES

Ecology: Saprobic on decaying hardwood logs and stumps and parasitic on living hardwoods (especially silver maple and box elder); causing a white heart rot; annual; growing alone or in clusters of 2 or 3; typically found in spring, but also sometimes found in summer and fall; widely distributed. **Cap:** 5–30 cm across; up to 4 cm thick; variable in shape, but generally fan-shaped or almost funnel-shaped; dry; pale tan to creamy yellowish (often darkening in age), with an overlay of darker, brownish scales that are vaguely radially arranged. **Pore Surface:** Whitish to cream; not bruising or discoloring; pores large, angular, and frequently irregular. **Stem:** Lateral; tough; blackening as the mushroom matures, at least toward the base. **Flesh:** Thick; soft when young, but soon corky and tough, especially toward the stem; white. **Odor and Taste:** Mealy. **Spore Print:** White. **Microscopic Features:** Spores 10–16 × 4–6 µm; smooth; broadly ellipsoid to oblong. Cystidia and setae absent. Hyphal system dimitic. **Comments:** The large size, scaly cap, mealy odor, and blackening stem are good field characters.

POLYPORUS UMBELLATUS (PERSOON) FRIES

Ecology: Saprobic or parasitic on the roots and wood of hardwoods; causing a white rot; fruiting at the bases of trees; often reappearing in the same place in subsequent years; summer and fall; rare, but widely distributed. **Fruiting Body:** 30–50 cm across or more; composed of multiple caps atop discrete stems that fuse into a large stem structure. **Caps:** 1–4 cm across; more or less circular; pale smoky brown or whitish; often becoming finely scaly. **Pore Surface:** White; running down the stems; with 1–3 angular pores per mm; tubes to 2 mm deep. **Stem:** White; irregular; central to the caps; fusing into 1 or more larger structures; arising from an underground knot of tissue. **Flesh:** Firm; white. **Odor and Taste:** Not distinctive. **Spore Print:** White. **Microscopic Features:** Spores 7.5–10 × 3–4 µm; smooth; cylindric; inamyloid. Cystidia and setae absent. Hyphal system dimitic. **Comments:** Compare with *Grifola frondosa* (p. 185).

POLYPORUS VARIUS (PERSOON) FRIES

Ecology: Saprobic on decaying hardwood sticks and small logs (rarely on conifer debris); causing a white rot; growing scattered or alone; summer and fall; widely distributed. **Cap:** 2–10 cm; broadly convex to flat; round in outline, or kidney-shaped; dry; bald or finely hairy; sometimes radially lined; tan, cinnamon tan, or paler; the margin frequently wavy. **Pore Surface:** White when young, becoming dingy brownish in age; running down the stem; 4–6 angular pores per mm; tubes to 3 mm deep. **Stem:** Central or off-center to lateral; 0.5–7 cm long; 2–10 mm wide; equal; often curving; dry; bald or finely velvety; pale tan at the apex, but black below (at least at the base, and usually for half or more of the stem's height); tough. **Flesh:** Whitish to dingy brownish or cinnamon; thin; very tough. **Spore Print:** White. **Microscopic Features:** Spores 7–10 × 2–3.5 µm; smooth; cylindric to allantoid. Cystidia and setae absent. Hyphal system dimitic. **Comments:** Also known as *Polyporus elegans*. Compare with *Polyporus badius* (p. 322).

PORODAEDALEA PINI (BROTERO) MURRILL

Ecology: Parasitic on the heartwood of living conifers; also saprobic on the deadwood of conifers; very rarely reported on hardwoods; causing a white pocket rot; growing alone, gregariously, or in shelving clusters; widely distributed. **Cap:** Occasionally absent, but usually present as a turned-over upper edge or, more commonly, as a well-developed structure; up to about 25 cm across; vaguely kidney-shaped to semicircular or irregular; convex, becoming hoof-shaped; hairy toward the margin or overall; becoming furrowed and rough; usually zoned; reddish brown to gray brown, dark brown, or black. **Pore Surface:** Brownish yellow to yellow brown; with 1–4 angular to nearly slot-like pores per mm; tube layers up to 6 mm deep. **Stem:** Absent. **Flesh:** Reddish brown to yellow brown; corky to woody. **Chemical Reactions:** KOH black on flesh. **Microscopic Features:** Spores 4.5–7 × 3.5–5 µm; smooth; broadly ellipsoid; inamyloid. Setae abundant; thick-walled; dark brown in KOH. Hyphal system dimitic. **Comments:** Also known as *Phellinus pini*.

PORONIDULUS CONCHIFER (SCHWEINITZ) MURRILL

Ecology: Saprobic on the deadwood of hardwoods (primarily elms); annual; causing a white rot; growing in clusters on branches, logs, and stumps; spring through fall; widely distributed. **Fruiting Body:** At first cup-like; developing a cap as an extension of the cup. **Cups:** Saucer-shaped to cup-shaped; to about 15 mm wide; upper surface white to brown, usually with zones of color, bald; undersurface white; with a tiny

Photo by Ron Kerner

stem-like structure. **Cap:** Up to 5 cm across and 3 cm deep; semicircular, irregularly bracket-shaped, or kidney-shaped; occasionally fusing laterally with other caps; bald; radially furrowed and wrinkled; whitish to pale brownish; with concentric zones of color. **Pore Surface:** Whitish, becoming a little yellowish with age; with 2–4 circular to angular pores per mm; tubes to 2 mm deep. **Flesh:** White; fairly tough. **Odor and Taste:** Not distinctive. **Chemical Reactions:** KOH on flesh negative to yellowish. **Spore Print:** White. **Microscopic Features:** Spores 5–7 × 1.5–2 µm; smooth; cylindric; inamyloid. Cystidia absent. Hyphal system trimitic. Asexual spores that are produced by cups are rod-shaped; 3–8 × 3 µm. **Comments:** The unusual combination of fruiting body forms is distinctive, but when this polypore is found without the immature, cup-like forms present, it can be difficult to identify.

PSATHYRELLA BIPELLIS (QUÉLET) A. H. SMITH

Ecology: Saprobic; growing scattered to gregariously or in small clusters in woods or in urban areas (in gardens, brush piles, woodchips, and so on); spring and summer; widely distributed. **Cap:** 1–5 cm; convex, broadly conical, or nearly flat; bald; sometimes becoming wrinkled or nearly reticulate; the margin finely lined; dark purple to purple red when young and fresh, fading to purplish, pinkish, or reddish brown; changing color markedly as it dries out; when young, with wisps of veil tissue along the margin. **Gills:** Attached to the stem; close or nearly distant; purplish at first, becoming dark purplish brown to dark gray; with whitish edges. **Stem:** 4.5–10 cm long; up to 5 mm thick; equal; fragile; pinkish to purplish in the upper half, and whitish elsewhere; bald or very finely silky; without a ring. **Flesh:** Thin; fragile; purplish in the cap. **Odor and Taste:** Not distinctive. **Chemical Reactions:** KOH instantly dark gray on cap. **Spore Print:** Purplish brown

Spore print

to purplish black. **Microscopic Features:** Spores 12–15 × 6–8 µm; ellipsoid; with a pore; smooth; dark brown in KOH. Pleurocystidia utriform or fusoid-ventricose; with slightly thickened (to about 1 µm) walls. Cheilocystidia subfusiform to subutriform or clavate; walls thin or slightly thickened. Pileipellis hymeniform. **Comments:** Macroscopic identification features include the purple to pinkish-brown colors, the wispy veil tissue on the young cap margin, and the pinkish to purplish flush on the upper stem. However, microscopic analysis may be required to identify this species with certainty.

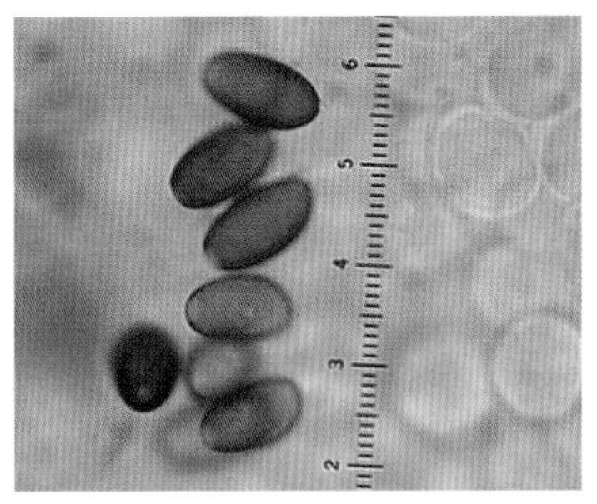

Spores

PSATHYRELLA CANDOLLEANA (FRIES) MAIRE

Ecology: Saprobic; growing alone or gregariously in lawns, pastures, and cultivated areas, also in woods; typically near recently dead hardwood trees, their roots, stumps, and so on; usually appearing in spring and early summer, but sometimes appearing in fall; widely distributed and common. **Cap:** 3–11 cm; rounded-conical or convex when young, expanding to broadly convex, broadly bell-shaped, or nearly flat; bald; often developing shallow radial wrinkles; dry; honey yellow when young, changing color markedly to pale brownish or nearly white as it dries out; the young margin adorned with partial veil remnants; mature margin often splitting radially in places. **Gills:** Attached to the stem or nearly free from it; whitish at first, becoming grayish and finally dark brown; close or crowded. **Stem:** 4–13 cm long; 3–8 mm thick; equal; fragile; white; hollowing; bald or slightly lined and/or silky; almost always lacking a ring, but sometimes with loosely clinging partial veil remnants in a ring-like zone. **Flesh:** Very thin; fragile; brownish to whitish. **Odor and Taste:** Not distinctive. **Chemical Reactions:** KOH pinkish (sometimes fleetingly) to lilac gray or brownish gray on cap. **Spore Print:** Dark purplish brown. **Microscopic Features:** Spores 6.5–9.5 × 4–5 µm; ellipsoid with a truncated end; smooth; dark brown in KOH. Pleurocystidia absent. Cheilocystidia abundant; hyaline in KOH; thin-walled; subcylindric to subutriform, clavate, subclavate, or saccate. Pileipellis hymeniform. **Comments:** *Psathyrella incerta* is very similar but has a clear yellow cap when young and smaller spores.

PSATHYRELLA DELINEATA (PECK) A. H. SMITH

Ecology: Saprobic on the deadwood of hardwoods; growing alone, scattered, gregariously, or in clusters; summer and fall; widely distributed. **Cap:** 3–10 cm; more or less convex at first, expanding to broadly convex or flat; usually finely corrugated and wrinkled, especially in mature caps; sometimes covered with fine fibers

when young; dark reddish brown to brown, fading to brownish or tan; the margin typically with whitish partial veil remnants. **Gills:** Attached to the stem; close; pale brownish at first, becoming dark brown. **Stem:** 6–10 cm long; 0.5–1.5 cm thick; more or less equal; whitish; hollowing; bald or finely silky; almost always lacking a true ring, but sometimes with loosely clinging partial veil remnants; basal mycelium white and copious. **Flesh:** Thin; fragile; watery brownish to whitish. **Odor and Taste:** Not distinctive. **Chemical Reactions:** KOH negative to grayish on cap. **Spore Print:** Purplish brown to purplish black. **Microscopic Features:** Spores 6.5–9 × 4.5–5.5 µm; ellipsoid; smooth; with an inconspicuous pore, but not substantially truncated; brown in KOH. Pleurocystidia and cheilocystidia thin-walled; mucronate to subclavate or subfusiform, with prominent, finger-like mucros. Pileipellis hymeniform. **Comments:** Compare with *Cortinarius corrugatus* (p. 154).

PSATHYRELLA PSEUDOVERNALIS A. H. SMITH

Ecology: Saprobic; growing scattered to gregariously or in small clusters in hardwood forests, often near woody debris; spring; widely distributed. **Cap:** 2–4.5 cm; convex, broadly conical, broadly bell-shaped, or nearly flat at maturity; bald; the margin finely lined; medium yellow brown, fading markedly as it dries out to brownish buff; when young with wisps of veil tissue, especially along the margin. **Gills:** Attached to the stem; close or nearly distant; whitish to pale brownish at first, becoming dark brown. **Stem:** 3–10 cm long; up to 5 mm thick; equal; fragile; white, but often discoloring dirty yellowish to brownish in the middle with maturity; bald or very finely silky; without a ring. **Flesh:** Thin; fragile; brownish. **Odor and Taste:** Not distinctive. **Chemical Reactions:** KOH on cap surface at first negative, but turning purplish after 60–90 seconds. **Spore Print:** Dark brown to nearly black. **Microscopic Features:** Spores 7.5–9.5 × 4–5.5 µm; ellipsoid; with a pore; smooth; dark brown in KOH. Pleurocystidia fusoid-ventricose; thin-walled. Cheilocystidia subfusiform; infrequent; thin-walled. Pileipellis hymeniform. **Comments:** Also known as *Psathyrella vernalis.* This species is often encountered by morel hunters. *Psathyrella spadiceogrisea* is nearly identical but features utriform cystidia.

PSEUDOCOLUS FUSIFORMIS (E. FISCHER) LLOYD

Ecology: Saprobic; growing alone or in groups at the borders of woods, or in parks and gardens; summer and fall; possibly widely distributed, but more common below the Great Lakes. **Immature Fruiting Body:** Like a whitish to brownish egg 1–2 cm across; when sliced, revealing the stinkhorn-to-be encased in a gelatinous substance. **Mature Fruiting Body:** 2.5–7 cm high; with 3 (sometimes 4 or 5) individual arms that arise from a central stem; arms roughened, fused at the tips (occasionally separating), whitish below and yellow to orange above; stem 2–4.5 cm long, 1.5–3 cm thick, roughened, spongy, hollow; volva grayish brown to grayish or whitish, roughened above, wrinkled and tough; inner sides of arms covered with malodorous olive-brown spore slime. **Microscopic Features:** Spores 4.5–5.5 × 2–2.5 µm; ellipsoid to ovoid; smooth. **Comments:** *Clathrus columnatus* (see Kuo and Methven 2010) is similar but lacks a central stem structure; when lifted carefully away from the volva, its arms are separate. Although it is primarily subtropical and tropical, we have seen it in an Illinois landscape setting.

Photo by Ron Kerner

PSEUDOHYDNUM GELATINOSUM (SCOPOLI) KARSTEN

Ecology: Saprobic on the wood or woody debris of conifers; sometimes growing from standing trees; growing alone, scattered, or gregariously; late summer and fall; widely distributed, but more common where conifers occur naturally. **Cap:** 1–7 cm across; tongue-shaped or kidney-shaped; broadly convex or flat; gelatinous, but not slimy to the touch; bald or finely fuzzy; translucent white to grayish, brown, or fairly dark brown; the margin tucked under when young. **Undersurface:** Running down the stem; composed of spines 1–3 mm long; translucent white or pale grayish; sometimes faintly bluish. **Stem:** To 6 cm long; either lateral and stubby (when specimens are growing from the sides of logs) or well developed and vertical (when specimens are growing from the tops of logs or from terrestrial woody debris); gelatinous; bald; colored like the cap or paler. **Flesh:** Translucent; gelatinous. **Spore Print:** White. **Microscopic Features:** Spores 4.5–8 µm; globose; smooth. Basidia longitudinally septate. **Comments:** The combination of a toothed undersurface and gelatinous consistency is distinctive.

PULVEROBOLETUS RAVENELII (BERKELEY & M. A. CURTIS) MURRILL

Ecology: Mycorrhizal, primarily with conifers (especially pines, hemlock, and spruces) but also with hardwoods (including oaks and rhododendrons); growing alone, scattered, or in small clusters; summer and fall; widely distributed. **Cap:** 2–12 cm; convex to broadly convex or nearly flat in age; at first covered with bright yellow veil material, but soon brick red to orangish, reddish, or reddish brown centrally and yellow along the edge; dry or a little sticky after the yellow veil has disappeared; bald; the edge often with veil remnants. **Pore Surface:** At first covered with a bright yellow veil; whitish at first, becoming yellow to yellowish brown or olive; bruising greenish blue; pores round or angular, 1–3 per mm; tubes to 1 cm deep. **Stem:** To 15 cm long and 2 cm thick; equal or tapering to the base; yellow or whitish; sometimes with a flimsy ring; basal mycelium whitish or yellowish. **Flesh:** Whitish or pale yellow throughout; usually bluing faintly in the cap when sliced, and pinkish in the stem. **Odor and Taste:** Taste not distinctive, or slightly acrid; odor not distinctive. **Chemical Reactions:** Ammonia brownish on cap; negative on flesh. KOH orange on cap; orange on flesh. Iron salts negative on cap; orangish on flesh. **Spore Print:** Olive. **Microscopic Features:** Spores 9–12.5 × 4.5–6.5 µm; smooth; long-ellipsoid. **Comments:** The bright yellow veil and the blue bruising make good field characters for this species.

PYCNOPORUS CINNABARINUS (JACQUIN) KARSTEN

Ecology: Saprobic on the deadwood of hardwoods (usually with bark still adnate) and rarely on the wood of conifers; causing a white rot; annual; spring through fall; widely distributed. **Fruiting Body:** Semicircular to kidney-shaped; plano-convex; 2–13 cm across; up to 2 cm thick; upper surface finely hairy to suede-like, becoming roughened or nearly bald (but often pocked in age), bright reddish orange to dull orangish; undersurface bright reddish orange, with 2–4 round to angular (or sometimes slot-like) pores per mm, occasionally extending onto the substrate below the cap; tubes to 5 mm deep; stem absent; flesh tough, reddish to pale orange. **Odor and Taste:** Odor fragrant or not distinctive; taste not distinctive. **Chemical Reactions:** Cap surface purplish to reddish, then gray to black with KOH; pore surface olive green with KOH; flesh slowly reddish to blackish or in older specimens yellowish with KOH. **Spore Print:** White. **Microscopic Features:** Spores 5–8 × 2.5–3 µm; smooth; cylindric or long-ellipsoid; inamyloid. Cystidia and setae absent. Hyphal system trimitic. **Comments:** Easily recognized in the field by its orange colors, this species is avidly sought out by those who use mushrooms as a source of dye.

KOH on cap and pore surface

RAMARIA BOTRYTIS (PERSOON) RICKEN

Ecology: Mycorrhizal; growing alone, scattered, or in groups under hardwoods or conifers; summer and fall; widely distributed. **Fruiting Body:** 7–20 cm high; 6–30 cm wide; stocky; repeatedly short-branched. **Branches:** Densely packed; basal branches thick, smooth, and whitish; terminal branches crowded, short, and pink to purplish or red; tips cauliflower-like, especially when young. **Base:** 3–4 cm long; to 6 cm wide; whitish, developing yellowish or brownish colors. **Flesh:** Whitish; firm. **Odor and Taste:** Odor not distinctive; taste mild or bitter. **Spore Print:** Yellowish. **Chemical Reactions:** Iron salts green on branches. **Microscopic Features:** Spores 11–20 × 4–6 µm (usually about 14–16 × 5 µm); subfusoid to stretched-ellipsoid; finely stippled; by maturity the ornamentation aggregated into very faint lines, creating a twisted-striate effect; cyanophilic. Clamp connections present. **Comments:** The stocky stature, pink colors, and short, cauliflower-like branches are good field characters.

Photo by Andy Methven

RAMARIA FENNICA (KARSTEN) RICKEN

Ecology: Mycorrhizal with hardwoods; growing alone, scattered, or gregariously; summer and fall; widely distributed. **Fruiting Body:** 5–12 cm high; 7–8 cm wide; base well developed; branching repeatedly. **Branches:** Vertically oriented and elongated;

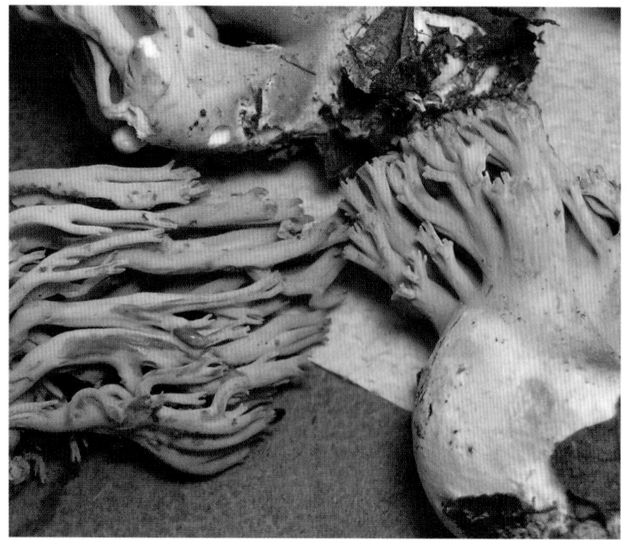

smooth; purplish below; olive yellow to yellow or smoky yellowish above, becoming grayish to orangish or brownish as the spores mature; tips concolorous. **Base:** Usually well developed; to 5 cm wide; white below; lilac to purple above. **Flesh:** Whitish, often with watery areas; firm. **Odor and Taste:** Odor not distinctive; taste usually bitter, or reminiscent of sauerkraut. **Spore Print:** Yellowish to orangish. **Chemical Reactions:** Iron salts green on branches; KOH red on branches. **Microscopic Features:** Spores 8.5–12 × 3.5–5.5 µm; subfusoid to stretched-ellipsoid; roughened. Clamp connections present. **Comments:** Distinguishing features for this species group (the "real" *Ramaria fennica* may be strictly European) include the purple to lilac shades on the lower branches, the bitter taste, and microscopic features.

RAMARIA FORMOSA (PERSOON) QUÉLET

Ecology: Mycorrhizal with hardwoods (occasionally with conifers); growing alone, scattered, or gregariously; summer and fall; widely distributed. **Fruiting Body:** 7–20 cm high; 3–15 cm wide. **Branches:** Vertically oriented; smooth or wrinkled; coral pink when young and fresh, becoming pinkish, then orangish to yellowish tan with age; tips clear yellow, becoming orangish to yellowish tan. **Base:** Variable; sometimes insubstantial, but usually well developed beneath main branches, which are separated so that at maturity the coral appears to be a cluster of smaller corals; whitish below, pink above. **Flesh:** Whitish to pinkish; soft; chalk-like in the base when dried. **Odor and Taste:** Odor not distinctive; taste bitter. **Spore Print:** Yellowish to orangish. **Chemical Reactions:** Iron salts green on branches. **Microscopic Features:** Spores variable in size, but often 8–13 × 3–6 µm; subfusoid to stretched-ellipsoid; roughened; cyanophilic. Clamp connections present. **Comments:** The pink branches that contrast with the yellow tips when the mushroom is young, the soft, fleshy base, and microscopic features define this species. At maturity the species is uniformly orangish tan, like many other species of *Ramaria*.

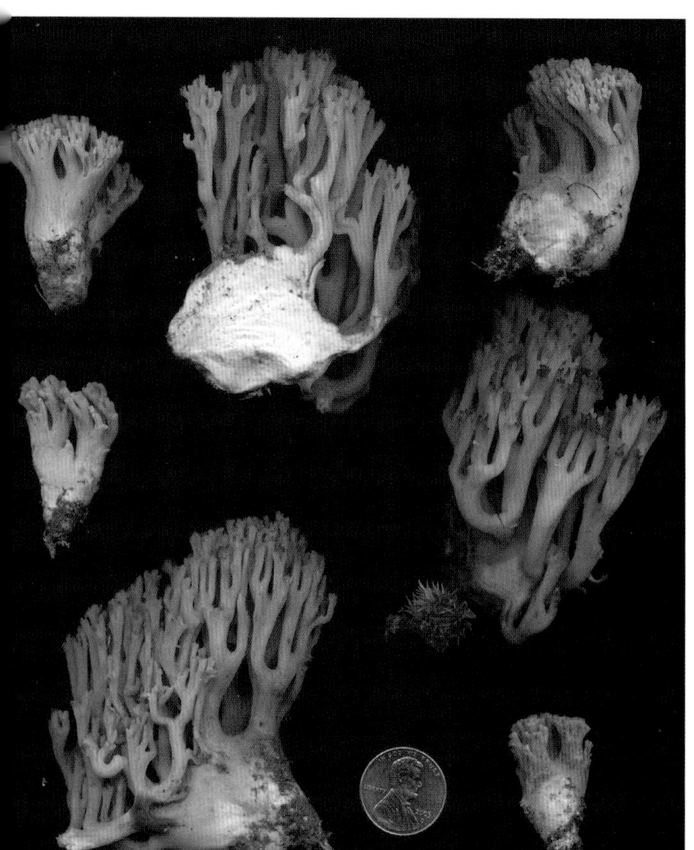

RAMARIA STRICTA (PERSOON) QUÉLET

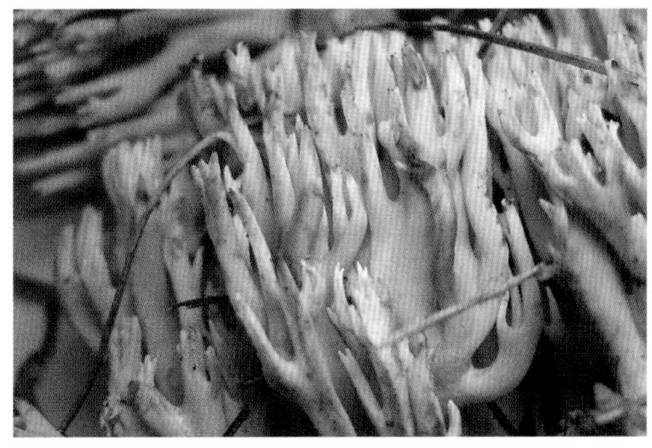

Ecology: Uncertain; while most ramarias are thought to be mycorrhizal, the wood-inhabiting species might be mycorrhizal or saprobic; growing from the dead (but sometimes buried) wood of conifers (and sometimes hardwoods); appearing alone, scattered, or gregariously; early summer through fall; widely distributed. **Fruiting Body:** 4–14 cm high; 4–10 cm wide; base well developed or nearly absent; branching repeatedly. **Branches:** Vertically oriented and elongated; often flattened; smooth; yellowish buff, becoming orangish buff as the spores mature; bruising and discoloring purplish brown; tips yellow when fresh and young. **Base:** Nearly absent, or fairly well developed; to 2 cm wide; white below; colored like the branches above; attached to numerous white rhizomorphs. **Flesh:** Whitish; fairly tough. **Odor and Taste:** Odor not distinctive, or sweet and fragrant; taste bitter. **Spore Print:** Rusty yellowish. **Chemical Reactions:** Iron salts green on branches. **Microscopic Features:** Spores 7.5–10.5 × 3.5–5 µm; stretched-ellipsoid; roughened; cyanophilic. Clamp conncctions present. **Comments:** The habitat on wood, vertically elongated branches, and purplish-brown bruising are good field characters.

RAMARIOPSIS KUNZEI (FRIES) CORNER

Ecology: Probably saprobic; growing terrestrially or rarely from well-decayed wood; growing scattered or gregariously in woods; summer and fall; widely distributed. **Fruiting Body:** 2–12 cm high; up to 10 cm wide; repeatedly branched. **Branches:** 1–5 mm thick; smooth; white, often developing dirty pinkish hues with age; tips bluntly pointed, white. **Base:** When present, 0.5–3 cm long; to about 1 cm wide; whitish, sometimes becoming pinkish or yellowish; finely fuzzy. **Flesh:** Whitish; brittle and fragile, or in some collections fairly pliable. **Odor and Taste:** Not distinctive. **Spore Print:** White. **Chemical Reactions:** Iron salts negative on branches. **Microscopic Features:** Spores 3–5 × 3–4.5 µm; globose, subglobose, or broadly ellipsoid; minutely spiny. Clamp connections present. **Comments:** Compare with *Clavulina cristata* (p. 139), which has distinctively "cristate" branch tips, and with *Tremellodendron pallidum* (p. 374).

RESUPINATUS ALBONIGER (PATOUILLARD) SINGER

Ecology: Saprobic; growing alone or gregariously on the recently dead wood of hardwoods; summer and fall (or over winter during warm spells); widely distributed. **Cap:** 2–10 mm across; saucer-shaped and attached from a more or less central point when growing on the undersides of logs, otherwise semicircular to fan-shaped and attached from a lateral point; bald, but sometimes with fine grayish fuzz in places; flat black to dark gray brown. **Gills:** Radiating from the point of attachment; close or nearly distant; black to dark blackish brown; sometimes with whitish edges. **Stem:** Absent. **Flesh:** Blackish; insubstantial. **Odor and Taste:** Odor not distinctive; taste mild. **Chemical Reactions:** KOH negative on cap. **Spore Print:** White. **Microscopic Features:** Spores 5.5–8 × 2.5–4 µm; long-ellipsoid to nearly allantoid; smooth; inamyloid. Cheilocystidia fusoid to broadly fusoid, lecythiform, or clavate; often featuring irregular knobs and projections. Pleurocystidia absent. Pileipellis a poorly defined cutis of dark brown encrusted elements with knobs and projections.

RETIBOLETUS GRISEUS (FROST) BINDER & BRESINSKY

Ecology: Mycorrhizal with oaks and other hardwoods; growing alone, scattered, or gregariously; early summer through fall; widely distributed. **Cap:** 5–14 cm; convex, becoming broadly convex or nearly flat; dry; with tiny, appressed, grayish fibers over a pale to gray or brownish-gray base color; darkening with age and sometimes on handling. **Pore Surface:** Whitish to dirty gray; not bruising, or bruising brown or darker gray; tubes to 2 cm deep. **Stem:** 4–14.5 cm long; 1–3.5 cm thick; more or less equal; frequently (but not always) curved near the base; whitish, staining yellow from the base upward with age; prominently and widely reticulate (usually over the whole stem) with a yellowish reticulum that becomes brownish or blackish in age or when handled; solid. **Flesh:** White, not staining, or staining dingy red or brownish when sliced. **Odor and Taste:** Not distinctive. **Chemical Reactions:** Ammonia negative on cap; negative to pale pinkish-gray on flesh. KOH negative to olive on cap; negative to pinkish or orangish on flesh. Iron salts negative on cap; negative to bluish gray on flesh. **Spore Print:** Pinkish brown to olive brown. **Microscopic Features:** Spores 9–13 × 3–5 µm; smooth; subfusoid.

Comments: Also known as *Boletus griseus.* This is one of the most common boletes in the Midwest's oak-hickory forests, easily recognized by the gray to grayish-brown cap and the widely reticulate stem that yellows from the bottom up.

RETIBOLETUS ORNATIPES (PECK) BINDER & BRESINSKY

Photo by Melissa Bochte

Ecology: Mycorrhizal with hardwoods, especially oaks; growing alone, scattered, or gregariously; often growing in moss; summer and fall; widely distributed. **Cap:** 4–16 cm; convex, becoming broadly convex or nearly flat in age; dry; bald or felty, sometimes nearly velvety; variable in color, ranging from yellow to pale gray to yellow brown or olive brown; frequently yellow along the margin. **Pore Surface:** Bright yellow, becoming olive yellow with age; not bruising, or bruising brighter yellow or orangish (rarely brownish); with 2–3 round pores per mm; tubes to 15 mm deep. **Stem:** 6–15 cm long; 1–2.5 cm thick; more or less equal, sometimes tapered toward the top or the bottom; prominently and coarsely reticulate, with a yellow reticulum that becomes brownish with age or on handling; bright yellow, discoloring brownish in age; bruising orangish yellow; solid; basal mycelium yellow. **Flesh:** Yellow (light yellow, becoming golden yellow when cut), not staining blue on exposure. **Odor and Taste:** Odor not distinctive; taste mild or somewhat bitter. **Chemical Reactions:** Ammonia orangish to pale brown on cap; negative to pale brown on flesh. KOH dark reddish brown on cap; orangish on flesh. Iron salts negative on cap; negative to whitish on flesh. **Spore Print:** Olive brown. **Microscopic Features:** Spores 9–14 × 3–4 µm; smooth; subfusoid. **Comments:** Also known as *Boletus ornatipes.*

RHIZOMARASMIUS PYRRHOCEPHALUS (BERKELEY) R. H. PETERSEN

Ecology: Saprobic on leaf litter and woody debris in hardwood forests (especially oak-hickory woods); growing alone or gregariously; spring, summer, and fall; widely distributed. **Cap:** Up to 2.5 cm across; convex, becoming broadly convex or nearly flat; smooth or finely wrinkled; the margin often slightly lined; orange to yellowish orange, darkening with age to brownish orange or nearly brown. **Gills:** Attached to the stem; close or nearly distant; whitish, becoming dingy or yellowish; sometimes developing brownish spots or discolorations. **Stem:** 3–10 cm long; up to

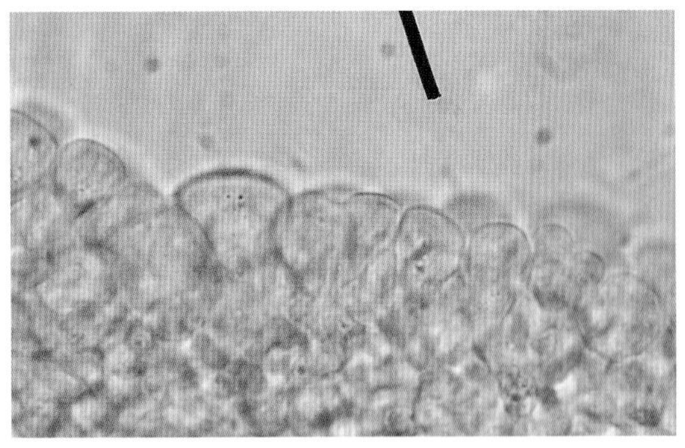

Pileipellis

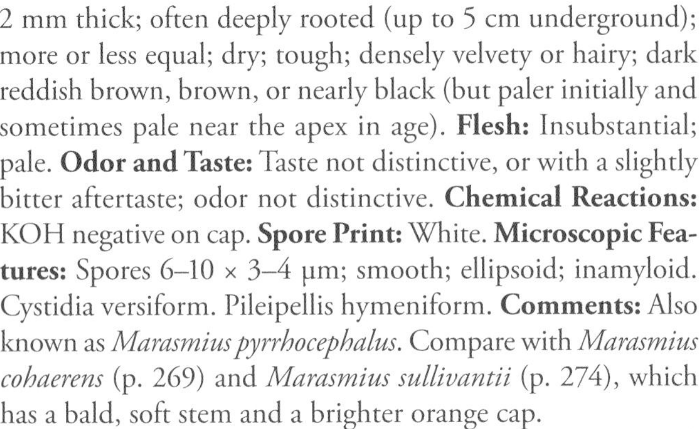

2 mm thick; often deeply rooted (up to 5 cm underground); more or less equal; dry; tough; densely velvety or hairy; dark reddish brown, brown, or nearly black (but paler initially and sometimes pale near the apex in age). **Flesh:** Insubstantial; pale. **Odor and Taste:** Taste not distinctive, or with a slightly bitter aftertaste; odor not distinctive. **Chemical Reactions:** KOH negative on cap. **Spore Print:** White. **Microscopic Features:** Spores 6–10 × 3–4 µm; smooth; ellipsoid; inamyloid. Cystidia versiform. Pileipellis hymeniform. **Comments:** Also known as *Marasmius pyrrhocephalus*. Compare with *Marasmius cohaerens* (p. 269) and *Marasmius sullivantii* (p. 274), which has a bald, soft stem and a brighter orange cap.

Spores

RHODOCOLLYBIA BUTYRACEA (BULLIARD) LENNOX

Ecology: Saprobic; decomposing the litter of conifers, especially pines; late summer and fall; widely distributed. **Cap:** 2–10 cm across; convex, becoming broadly convex or nearly flat; moist when fresh; bald; reddish brown, fading to cinnamon. **Gills:** Narrowly attached to the stem or nearly free from it; close or crowded; whitish, sometimes developing pinkish tones with age; often developing finely jagged edges. **Stem:** Up to 10 cm long and 1 cm thick; usually slightly to moderately club-shaped; moist or dry; bald; whitish to buff above; colored like the cap below; becoming hollow. **Flesh:** Whitish. **Odor and Taste:** Not distinctive. **Spore Print:** Pale yellowish, pale pinkish, or merely white. **Microscopic Features:** Spores smooth; 6–10.5 × 3.5–5 µm; ellipsoid; at least a few (often many) dextrinoid. Pleurocystidia absent. Cheilocystidia variously shaped (often diverticulate or lobed). Pileipellis a cutis. **Comments:** Also known as *Collybia butyracea*. Compare with *Gymnopus dryophilus* (p. 189).

RHODOCOLLYBIA MACULATA (ALBERTINI & SCHWEINITZ) SINGER

Ecology: Saprobic; decomposing the deadwood or litter of conifers; late spring, summer, and fall; widely distributed. **Cap:** 4–12 cm across; convex, becoming broadly convex or nearly flat; dry or slightly moist; bald; whitish to pinkish buff, developing cinnamon to rusty spots with age. **Gills:** Attached to the stem;

Photo by Noah Siegel

crowded; whitish to creamy; often developing rusty spots with age. **Stem:** Up to 15 cm long and 2 cm thick; equal, often with a rooting portion; bald or very finely hairy; whitish; developing cinnamon to rusty spots with age. **Flesh:** Whitish. **Odor and Taste:** Odor not distinctive, or fragrant; taste slightly to moderately bitter. **Spore Print:** Pale pinkish (requires a very thick print and good light to distinguish from whitish). **Chemical Reactions:** KOH negative on cap. **Microscopic Features:** Spores 4–6 µm; subglobose; smooth; at least a few (often many) dextrinoid. Pleurocystidia absent. Cheilocystidia variously shaped (often diverticulate or lobed). Pileipellis a cutis. **Comments:** Also known as *Collybia maculata*. Compare with *Clitocybe subconnexa* (p. 143), which does not develop reddish spots. A variety of *Rhodocollybia maculata* with a yellowish cap, gills, and stem, along with ellipsoid spores, is sometimes called var. *scorzonerea*.

RHODOCYBE MUNDULA (LASCH) SINGER

Ecology: Saprobic; growing scattered or gregariously under hardwoods or conifers; summer and fall; widely distributed. **Cap:** 3–7 cm; convex, with an inrolled margin, becoming flat or centrally depressed, with a wavy margin; dry; bald or very finely suede-like; whitish to grayish or brownish; developing distinctive, more or less concentric cracks with maturity. **Gills:** Running down the stem; close or crowded; often forked; whitish at first, then brownish or pinkish. **Stem:** 3–7 cm long; up to about 1.5 cm thick; equal, or tapering to base; bald; dry; colored like the cap; discoloring brownish basally. **Flesh:** White; not discoloring when sliced. **Odor and Taste:** Odor mealy; taste mealy and quite bitter. **Chemical Reactions:** KOH on all surfaces red to brownish red. **Spore Print:** Pale pink. **Microscopic Features:** Spores 4–6 × 3.5–5 µm; subglobose to ellipsoid; tuberculate. Cystidia absent. Pileipellis a cutis with encrusted elements. **Comments:** Hallmarks include the gills that run down the stem, the pale pink spore print, the distinctively cracked cap, and the KOH reaction.

RHODOTUS PALMATUS (BULLIARD) MAIRE

Photo by Andy Methven

Ecology: Saprobic; growing alone, scattered, or (more commonly) in troops on the wet, well-decayed wood of hardwoods; late spring through fall; widely distributed. **Cap:** 2–9 cm; convex, with an incurved margin when young, becoming broadly convex or flat; slimy and gelatinous; becoming conspicuously

netted with whitish ridges and veins, or sometimes without veins and ridges; salmon to pinkish orange. **Gills:** Attached to the stem; close; whitish when young, becoming pink to salmon from spores. **Stem:** 1.5–5 cm long; up to 1 cm thick; pinkish; slightly hairy; often a little off-center; tough. **Flesh:** Pinkish; rubbery. **Odor and Taste:** Not distinctive. **Chemical Reactions:** All surfaces instantly dark green with iron salts; negative with KOH. **Spore Print:** Pinkish. **Microscopic Features:** Spores 6–9 × 6–7.5 µm; subglobose; finely warty; inamyloid. Pleurocystidia absent. Cheilocystidia fusiform to lageniform. Pileipellis hymeniform. **Comments:** Unmistakable when fresh and photogenic, but also often found looking rather drab.

Photo by Melissa Bochte

RICKENELLA FIBULA (BULLIARD) RAITHELHUBER

Ecology: Saprobic; growing alone, scattered, or gregariously in moss beds; early summer through early winter; widely distributed. **Cap:** Up to 1.5 cm across, but usually smaller; convex, becoming broadly convex or somewhat centrally depressed; tacky; bald; the margin lined, inrolled at first, and usually remaining so; orange or yellowish orange when fresh, often fading to buff. **Gills:** Running down the stem; close or nearly distant; sometimes with cross-veins; whitish or creamy. **Stem:** Up to 5 cm long and almost 2 mm thick; more or less equal; dry; very finely hairy; colored like the cap. **Flesh:** Insubstantial; pale. **Odor and Taste:** Not distinctive. **Chemical Reactions:** KOH negative on cap. **Spore Print:** White. **Microscopic Features:** Spores 4–6 × 2–2.5 µm; smooth; ellipsoid; inamyloid. Cystidia present on gills, cap, and stem apex; cylindric or subfusiform. **Comments:** The very tiny size, orange colors, gills that run down the stem, and habitat in moss are good field characters. Compare with *Xeromphalina campanella* (p. 393), which is a little larger and usually grows in large troops on deadwood.

RUSSULA AERUGINEA FRIES

Ecology: Mycorrhizal with hardwoods or conifers; growing alone, scattered, or gregariously; summer and fall; widely distributed. **Cap:** 5–9 cm; convex when young, becoming broadly convex to flat with a shallow depression; dry or slightly moist; bald, or minutely velvety over the center; grayish green to yellowish green; the margin often lined by maturity; the skin peeling about halfway to the center. **Gills:** Attached or running slightly down the stem; close; often forking near the stem; creamy to pale yellow; sometimes becoming spotted brownish in places. **Stem:** 4–6 cm long; 1–2 cm thick; whitish; dry; bald; discoloring brownish in places, especially near the base. **Flesh:** White; brittle; not changing when sliced. **Odor and Taste:** Not distinctive. **Chemical Reactions:** KOH orange on cap. Iron salts on flesh and stem surface slowly pink. **Spore Print:** Creamy to pale yellow. **Microscopic Features:** Spores 6–8.5 × 5–7 µm; ellipsoid; with isolated warts up to 0.8 µm high; connectors scattered, usually not forming a reticulum. Pileipellis with a turf-like upper layer of septate elements with inflated and barrel-shaped subterminal cells, with clavate, cylindric, or elongated and tapered terminal cells; pileocystidia clavate to fusiform. **Comments:** Compare with *Russula virescens* (p. 351), which has a quilted cap, and with *Russula variata* (p. 349), which has *repeatedly* forked gills and a cap that is usually mottled with purple shades and is only rarely green overall.

RUSSULA BALLOUII PECK

Ecology: Mycorrhizal with oaks; growing scattered or gregariously; summer, fall, and early winter; widely distributed, but apparently less common in northern areas. **Cap:** 3–9.5 cm; convex when young, later flat or broadly convex, with a central depression; dry; densely covered with pigment patches that break up as the mushroom matures; brownish yellow to rusty, orangish brown; the margin not lined; the skin not peeling easily. **Gills:** Attached to the stem or beginning to run down it; crowded or close; whitish to creamy; not bruising, but sometimes yellowish brown where damaged by insects. **Stem:** 3–6.5 cm long; 1–2 cm thick; more or less equal; dry; textured and colored like the cap. **Flesh:** White; unchanging when sliced. **Odor and Taste:** Odor not distinctive, or reminiscent of dough; taste acrid. **Chemical Reactions:** Iron salts negative to pale pink on stem. KOH red to brownish red on cap. **Spore Print:** Whitish or creamy. **Microscopic Features:** Spores 7–9 × 5.5–7.5 µm; ellipsoid to ovoid; warts 0.2–1 µm high; connectors forming a partial reticulum. Pileipellis a cutis with areas of reddish brown, poorly defined encrusted elements; pileocystidia cylindric to subclavate, 0–2 septate. **Comments:** Compare with *Russula compacta* (p. 340).

RUSSULA CESSANS PEARSON

Ecology: Mycorrhizal with white pine and possibly other pines; growing gregariously; October and November; widely distributed. **Cap:** 3–8 cm; convex, becoming broadly convex to flat; dry; bald; crimson to purplish red, frequently with a darker center; the margin even or becoming slightly lined at maturity; the skin peeling fairly easily. **Gills:** Attached to the stem; close; pale yellow; unchanging. **Stem:** 3–5 cm long; up to 2 cm thick; usually slightly swollen toward the base; bald; white; not bruising. **Flesh:** White; unchanging on exposure. **Odor and Taste:** Not distinctive. **Spore Print:** Yellow. **Chemical Reactions:** KOH yellow on cap; iron salts negative to pinkish on stem. **Microscopic Features:** Spores 8–9 × 7–8 µm; broadly ellipsoid or subglobose; with warts projecting to about 1 µm; connecting lines present, often forming a partial reticulum. Pileipellis a cutis embedded in a gelatinous matrix; pileocystidia cylindric to clavate; 0–3 septate. **Comments:** The mushroom featured here is "*Russula cessans*" in the sense of North American authors, as opposed to the more variably colored species often described by European authors.

RUSSULA COMPACTA FROST

Ecology: Mycorrhizal with hardwoods, and with conifers in northern areas; growing scattered or gregariously; summer and fall; widely distributed. **Cap:** 3–18 cm; convex when young, becoming flat or broadly convex; often with a slightly sunken center; sticky when fresh; bald; the skin peeling about halfway to the center; white to whitish or orangish yellow when young, but soon discoloring dirty yellowish to reddish brown, and in age appearing completely tawny brown; bruising reddish brown; the margin not lined. **Gills:** Attached to the stem; crowded, close, or almost distant; white to cream, eventually yellowish cream; bruising and discoloring reddish brown. **Stem:** 3–10 cm long; 1–3.5 cm thick; sturdy; more or less equal; dry; bald; whitish, but soon flushed reddish brown; bruising reddish brown. **Flesh:** White; discoloring yellowish to yellowish brown or reddish brown on exposure; thick. **Odor and Taste:** Odor foul and somewhat fishy, the pungency increasing as the mushroom ages; odor of dried specimens strongly unpleasant; taste mild or slightly acrid. **Chemical Reactions:**

KOH green to olive on cap. Iron salts grayish green on stem and flesh. **Spore Print:** White. **Microscopic Features:** Spores 7–10 × 6–8.5 µm; ellipsoid; ornamented with low warts extending to about 0.5 µm high; with scattered connectors that sometimes form a partial, broken reticulum. Pileipellis a cutis; pileocystidia absent. **Comments:** Compare with *Russula ballouii* (p. 339), which does not stain and bruise reddish brown, does not smell unpleasant, and turns olive with KOH. Also compare with *Lactarius allardii* (p. 230).

RUSSULA CRUSTOSA PECK

Ecology: Mycorrhizal with oaks and perhaps with other hardwoods; growing alone, scattered, or gregariously; summer; widely distributed. **Cap:** 5–10 cm; round to convex when young, becoming broadly convex to flat or uplifted, with a shallow depression; dry; soon cracking up into clearly defined patches that have fairly abrupt edges; buff, yellowish brown, or faintly olive; the margin lined at maturity; the skin peeling about halfway to the center. **Gills:** Attached to the stem; close or crowded; some forking; white to creamy. **Stem:** 3.5–9 cm long; 1.5–3 cm thick; white; dry; bald. **Flesh:** White; brittle; thick. **Odor and Taste:** Not distinctive. **Chemical Reactions:** KOH negative on cap. Iron salts negative or pink (sometimes slowly and/or faintly) on stem. **Spore Print:** White to creamy. **Microscopic Features:** Spores 6–9 × 5.5–7 µm; ellipsoid to nearly round; warts extending to about 0.5 µm high; connectors scattered and rare, usually not forming a reticulum. Pileipellis a cutis beneath a trichodermial layer (the patches) of erect, chained elements, with the terminal cell featuring a blunt to somewhat elongated projection with a rounded (only rarely subacute) apex; pileocystidia very long. **Comments:** Compare with *Russula virescens* (p. 351).

RUSSULA DENSIFOLIA GILLET

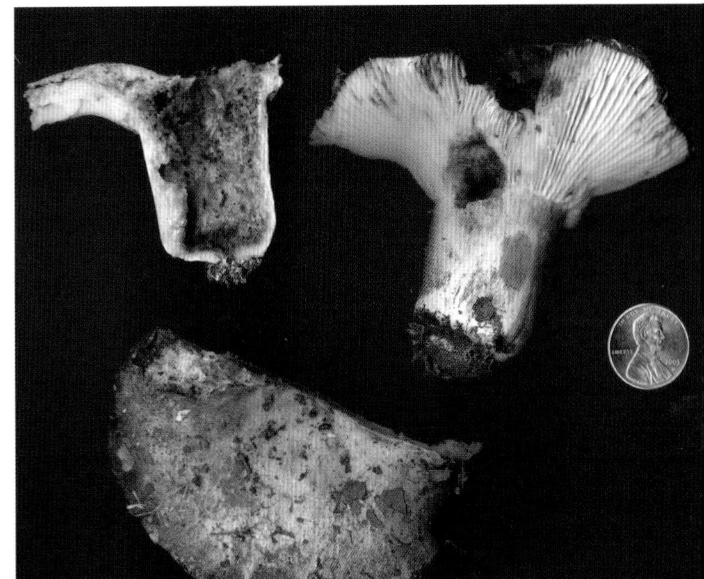

Ecology: Mycorrhizal with hardwoods or conifers; growing alone, scattered, gregariously, or in dense troops; summer and fall; widely distributed. **Cap:** 4–15 cm; broadly convex when young, later flat with a central depression, or shallowly vase-shaped; sticky at first or when wet; bald, or finely felty to the touch; initially white, but soon discoloring to brownish, ashy gray, brown, or blackish; bruising slowly reddish, then blackish; the margin initially somewhat inrolled, not lined or lined faintly and widely; the skin peeling easily about halfway to the center. **Gills:** Attached or running very slightly down the stem; narrow; close or crowded (rarely nearly distant); white to cream, eventually yellowish; bruising slowly reddish, then blackish. **Stem:** 1.5–9 cm long; 1–3.5 cm thick; white, but soon darkening like the cap; bruising reddish, then blackish over the course of as much as half an hour; bald or finely felty. **Flesh:** White; hard; bruising promptly or slowly reddish on exposure, then blackish over the course of as much as half an hour. **Odor and Taste:** Odor not distinctive; taste mild or slowly slightly to very acrid. **Chemical Reactions:** KOH negative on cap. Iron salts negative on stem. **Spore Print:** White. **Microscopic Features:** Spores 7–11 × 6–8.5 µm; ellipsoid to subglobose; with warts to 0.7 µm high; connectors usually forming a partial or complete reticulum. Pileipellis up to 500 µm thick; occasionally disposed as a single, cutis-like layer, but more commonly 2-layered, with the lower level densely interwoven and cutis-like, and the upper level composed of fairly erect elements embedded in a gelatinous matrix; pileocystidia absent. **Comments:** *Russula dissimulans* is very similar and also widely distributed in the Midwest; it has more widely spaced gills, a waxy-feeling cap surface, and, under the microscope, a single-layered pileipellis. Both of these species can serve as hosts for *Asterophora lycoperdoides* (p. 104).

RUSSULA EARLEI PECK

Ecology: Mycorrhizal with hardwoods (especially oaks); growing alone, scattered, or gregariously; summer and fall; widely distributed. **Cap:** 3–11 cm; convex, becoming broadly convex to nearly flat; sticky when wet; finely rugged, with a waxy-granular feel; the surface often cracking with age; straw yellow to dirty orangish yellow; the margin not lined, or faintly lined at maturity; the skin tightly adnate, not peeling easily. **Gills:** Attached to the stem or beginning to run down it; distant; whitish to creamy, becoming dull yellow; often with a water-soaked appearance; sometimes spotting and discoloring reddish brown. **Stem:** 2.5–7 cm long; 0.5–2.5 cm thick; whitish to dull yellow; dry, but with a waxy feel and a water-soaked appearance; sometimes discoloring reddish brown near the base; bald; basal mycelium white. **Flesh:** White to yellowish. **Odor and Taste:** Odor not distinctive; taste mild, or slightly bitter or acrid. **Spore Print:** White. **Chemical Reactions:** KOH dull red to reddish brown on cap; iron salts negative to pinkish on stem. **Microscopic Features:** Spores 3.5–6.5 × 5.5–7 µm; broadly ellipsoid; warts mostly isolated, extending to about 0.5 µm high; connectors scattered, not forming a reticulum. Pileipellis a partially gelatinized cutis, hyaline to brownish in KOH, with cylindric-irregular terminal cells that feature rounded to squarish apices; pileocystidia absent. **Comments:** Easily recognized by the waxy yellowish cap and stem and the distant gills.

RUSSULA FLAVISICCANS BILLS

Ecology: Mycorrhizal with oaks and perhaps with other hardwoods in oak-hickory forests; growing alone, scattered, or gregariously; summer and fall; widely distributed. **Cap:** 2–11 cm; convex when young, becoming broadly convex to flat, sometimes with a shallow depression; dry; very finely velvety, or nearly bald; sometimes developing cracks with maturity; pinkish red to pink when fresh, but often fading to orangish or yellowish pink; sometimes mottled with yellowish or creamy areas; the margin usually not lined at maturity; the skin peeling with difficulty, usually only near the margin. **Gills:** Attached to the stem or running slightly down it; close or crowded; white when young, but creamy or pale yellowish with maturity; often discoloring and staining brownish. **Stem:** 2–6 cm long; 1–3.5 cm thick; white (rarely with a flush of pink); staining and discoloring brownish; dry; bald. **Flesh:** White; unchanging when sliced. **Odor and Taste:** Odor not distinctive; taste bitter or disagreeable. **Spore Print:** Creamy. **Dried Specimens:** Gills, stem, and flesh turning dull, dirty yellowish; cap surface retaining dull pink colors, but showing yellowed flesh in the cracks. **Chemical Reactions:** KOH pink to red on cap; iron salts negative to pinkish or pink on stem. **Microscopic Features:** Spores 7–9 × 6.5–8.5 µm; nearly round; with low warts up to 0.5 µm high; connectors a partial to complete reticulum. Pileipellis a cutis beneath a trichoderm with multiseptate hyphal ends, with barrel-shaped subterminal cells beneath a fusiform to aciculate terminal cell; pileocystidia cylindric to clavate. **Comments:** The Latin name of this species means "drying yellow," and drying the mushrooms makes identification easier. Compare with *Russula pulchra* (p. 346), which has a similar cap surface.

Dried specimens

RUSSULA FRAGRANTISSIMA ROMAGNESI

Ecology: Mycorrhizal with hardwoods or conifers; growing alone, scattered, or gregariously; summer and fall; widely distributed. **Cap:** 7.5–20 cm; convex or cushion-shaped when young, becoming broadly convex to flat, with or without a shallow depression; sticky when wet and fresh; dull yellow to yellowish or brownish yellow; the margin lined at maturity; the skin peeling easily at the margin, sometimes beyond halfway to the center. **Gills:** Attached to the stem;

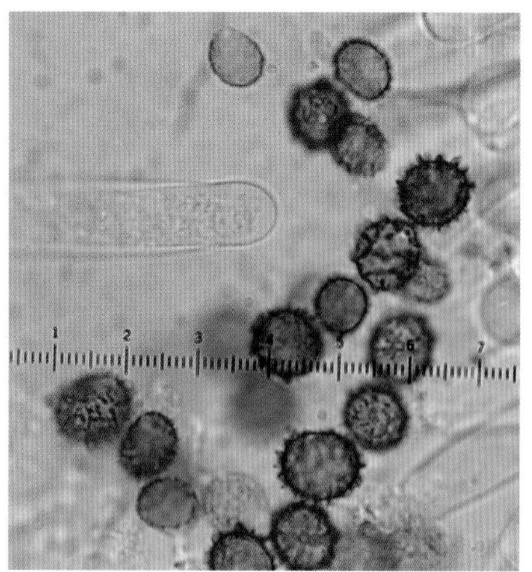

Spore print

close or nearly distant; sometimes forked near the stem; whitish to creamy; often discoloring yellowish brown to brownish, but not bruising. **Stem:** 7–15 cm long; 1.5–6 cm thick; white, discoloring brownish to yellowish or reddish near the base; dry; often becoming cavernous; bald. **Flesh:** White; unchanging when sliced. **Odor and Taste:** Odor strong and fragrant, reminiscent of maraschino cherries, almonds, or benzaldehyde, with a foul component that begins to take over, especially in age; taste mild to moderately acrid. **Chemical Reactions:** KOH negative to pinkish on cap; iron salts negative to pinkish on stem. **Spore Print:** Creamy. **Microscopic Features:** Spores 6–9 × 6–8 µm; broadly ellipsoid or subglobose; with warts and ridges up to 1 µm high, sometimes with connecting lines that may form a partial or nearly complete reticulum. Pileipellis a cutis embedded in a gelatinous matrix; pileocystidia clavate to fusiform. **Comments:** Other russulas with a similar odor and stature include *Russula mutabilis* (p. 345), which is more orange; *Russula ventricosipes* (p. 349), which grows in sand and has a reddish stem; and 2 species best separated with microscopic features: *Russula foetentula*, which has spores with isolated warts and lacks pileocystidia, and *Russula laurocerasi*, which has spores with strikingly large ornamentation extending up to 2.5 µm or more.

RUSSULA MARIAE PECK

Ecology: Mycorrhizal with hardwoods, especially oaks; growing scattered to gregariously; common and frequently encountered; late spring to fall; widely distributed. **Cap:** 2–10 cm; convex when young, becoming broadly convex to flat, with a shallow depression; dry; when fresh with a whitish bloom or dusting; purple to purplish red, or reddish, pinkish, or even olive, yellow, or brown, sometimes mottled with several of these shades; the margin usually lined by maturity; the skin peeling fairly easily, usually more than halfway to the center. **Gills:** Attached to the stem or beginning to run down it; close or crowded; sometimes forking; white at first, but soon cream-colored to pale yellow; occasionally with pinkish edges from contact with the stem in the button stage. **Stem:** 2–6 cm long; 0.5–2 cm thick; usually flushed pink or purplish; dry; bald, but feeling greasy or sticky to the touch. **Flesh:** White; unchanging when sliced. **Odor and Taste:** Odor oily; taste mild, slightly acrid, or oily and unpleasant. **Chemical Reactions:** KOH orange on cap. Iron salts negative on stem. **Spore Print:** Creamy to pale yellow. **Microscopic Features:** Spores 6.5–8.5 × 5.5–8 µm; usually globose or subglobose; warts and ridges up to 1.2 µm high; connectors usually forming a partial to complete reticulum. Pileipellis a cutis underneath a turf-like layer; the uppermost hyphae septate, with the

Pileipellis elements

subterminal cells barrel-shaped and the terminal cell clavate, cylindric, or (more commonly) elongated-fusiform; clearly differentiated pileocystidia (aside from the fusiform hyphal ends) absent. **Comments:** The purple cap with the velvety white bloom and the pinkish to purplish stem are good field characters.

RUSSULA MUTABILIS MURRILL

Ecology: Mycorrhizal with oaks; growing alone, scattered, or gregariously; summer and fall; widely distributed. **Cap:** 4–8 cm; convex, becoming broadly convex to flat, with a shallow depression; sticky when wet and fresh; brownish orange to orangish brown; sometimes bruising slowly deep red; when young, covered with fine yellow powder, especially near the margin; the margin lined; the skin peeling away easily at the margin, about halfway to the center. **Gills:** Attached or beginning to run down the stem; close or nearly distant; sometimes forked near the stem; creamy; often spotting or discoloring reddish brown to brownish. **Stem:** 2–6 cm long; 1–3 cm thick; whitish above, becoming bright yellow to orangish yellow below; bruising deep red, especially near the base; dry; bald. **Flesh:** Whitish. **Odor and Taste:** Odor weakly to moderately or strongly foul, reminiscent of maraschino cherries, almonds, or benzaldehyde; taste slowly but strongly acrid. **Chemical Reactions:** KOH deep red on cap and stem. **Spore Print:** Creamy. **Microscopic Features:** Spores 6–9 × 5–7 µm; broadly ellipsoid; with warts up to 1.5 µm high, connecting lines scattered and infrequent. Pileocystidia absent. **Comments:** Compare with *Russula fragrantissima* (p. 343).

RUSSULA PECTINATOIDES PECK

Ecology: Mycorrhizal with hardwoods or conifers; growing alone, scattered, or gregariously; summer and fall; widely distributed. **Cap:** 2.5–8 cm; convex, becoming broadly convex to flat, with a shallow depression; sticky when wet and fresh, but typically dry when found; pale yellowish brown to brownish yellow overall; the margin lined and pimply for 1–2 cm, often with tiny spots of pink or cinnamon interspersed with the lines; the skin peeling away easily, usually at least halfway to the center. **Gills:** Attached or pulling away from the stem; close or nearly distant; buff or yellowish; sometimes spotting or discoloring brownish. **Stem:** 1.5–7 cm long; 0.5–2 cm thick; whitish, discoloring yellowish to brownish or reddish brown; often becoming cavernous; bald. **Flesh:** White; unchanging when sliced. **Odor and Taste:** Odor weakly to moderately reminiscent of maraschino cherries, almonds, or benzaldehyde, with a waxy or spermatic component; taste mild or oily, sometimes a little acrid. **Chemical Reactions:** KOH negative to very pale magenta on cap; iron salts negative on stem. **Spore Print:** Creamy. **Microscopic Features:** Spores 5.5–9 × 4.5–6 µm; broadly ellipsoid; with warts up to 1 µm high, and sparse to nearly absent connectors. Pileipellis an interwoven cutis of mostly hyaline elements, embedded in a gelatinous matrix; pileocystidia absent. **Comments:** Compare with *Russula pulverulenta* (p. 347).

RUSSULA PULCHRA BURLINGHAM

Ecology: Mycorrhizal with oaks, beech, and other hardwoods; growing alone, scattered, or gregariously; summer and fall; widely distributed. **Cap:** 5–10 cm; convex when young, becoming broadly convex to flat, sometimes with a shallow depression; sticky when fresh or wet, but usually dry when collected; very finely velvety, or nearly bald; often developing cracks with maturity; scarlet to pinkish red when fresh, but often fading to orangish red or peach red; the margin usually lined at maturity; the skin peeling with difficulty, usually only near the margin. **Gills:** Attached to the stem or running slightly down it; nearly distant; white when young, but creamy with maturity. **Stem:** 3–7 cm long; 1–2 cm thick; white, often with a flush of pink; dry; bald. **Flesh:** White; unchanging when sliced. **Odor and Taste:** Not distinctive. **Spore Print:** Creamy. **Chemical Reactions:** KOH yellow on cap. **Microscopic Features:** Spores 6.5–9 × 5.5–7.5 µm; broadly ellipsoid; with warts up to 1.5 µm high; connectors scattered and infrequent, or sometimes frequent, creating reticulated areas. Pileipellis a cutis of pinkish to hyaline elements beneath trichodermial areas with multiseptate, barrel-shaped, subterminal cells beneath an obovoid to subfusiform terminal cell; pileocystidia absent. **Comments:** Compare with *Russula flavisiccans* (p. 343), which has a bitter to unpleasant taste, a stem that is never flushed with pink, different microscopic features, and surfaces that often become brownish when handled. Additionally, its flesh, stem, and gills become yellow when dried.

Pileipellis elements

RUSSULA PULVERULENTA PECK

Ecology: Mycorrhizal with hardwoods or conifers; sometimes found in urban settings; usually growing alone or scattered; summer and fall; widely distributed. **Cap:** 3.5–8 cm; convex, with an inrolled margin when young, becoming broadly convex to flat with a shallow depression, with a more or less straight margin that is prominently grooved and pimply; dry or slightly moist; when young covered by a dense layer of orange-yellow to yellow material, which eventually breaks up to form loose patches that often wear off with age; dark grayish brown to yellowish brown; the skin peeling away easily at the margin, sometimes about halfway to the center. **Gills:** Attached to the stem; close or almost distant; not generally forking, or occasionally forking near the stem; white; sometimes discoloring brownish to yellowish in age. **Stem:** 3.5–5 cm long; 1–2 cm thick; when young, white, overlaid with yellow granules; later whitish toward the top and yellowish below; sometimes discoloring yellowish brown with age; dry; often becoming cavernous; bald. **Flesh:** White to pale yellowish; unchanging when sliced; olive to olive brown around worm holes. **Odor and Taste:** Odor sweet and fragrant, or slightly foul, or in some specimens absent; taste slightly to moderately acrid. **Chemical Reactions:** KOH orange to orangish or negative on cap; iron salts negative on stem. **Spore Print:** Creamy. **Microscopic Features:** Spores 6–8 × 5–7 µm; with warts 0.4–1.2 µm high; broadly ellipsoid or subglobose; connecting lines scattered, occasionally forming a partial reticulum. Pileocystidia absent. Floccose patches on cap and stem composed of warty, septate hyphae that are yellow in a water mount. **Comments:** Compare with *Russula pectinatoides* (p. 345), which lacks the felty yellow covering.

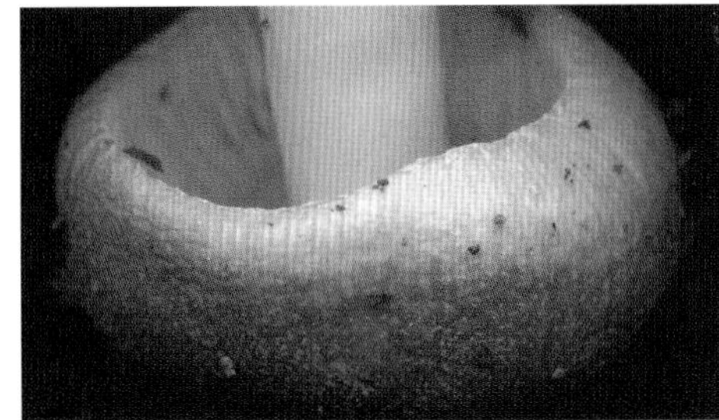

RUSSULA TENUICEPS KAUFFMAN

Ecology: Mycorrhizal with oaks, especially northern red oak, and perhaps with other hardwoods; growing alone, scattered, or gregariously; summer and fall; widely distributed. **Cap:** 7–12 cm; convex when young, becoming broadly convex to flat, sometimes with a shallow depression; sticky when fresh or wet; bald; bright red, but sometimes fading in age; the margin lined at maturity; the skin peeling fairly easily, often over halfway to the center; fragile and easily crumbling apart. **Gills:** Attached to the stem or running slightly down it; close or crowded; white when young, but dull yellow with maturity. **Stem:** 5–9 cm long; 2–2.5 cm thick; fragile and soon hollowing; flushed red over a white base color; dry; bald. **Flesh:** Ex-

tremely fragile and brittle; white; unchanging when sliced. **Odor and Taste:** Odor not distinctive; taste strongly acrid (sometimes slowly so). **Spore Print:** Yellowish to orangish yellow. **Chemical Reactions:** KOH negative to yellowish or orangish on cap; iron salts negative to slowly pinkish on stem. **Microscopic Features:** Spores 6–9 × 5–7 µm; with warts 0.5–1 µm high; connectors scattered, or occasionally forming a partial reticulum. Pileipellis a cutis of hyaline elements embedded in a gelatinous matrix; pileocystidia cylindric to subclavate or sometimes subfusoid to subcapitate. **Comments:** *Russula tenuiceps* is so fragile that handling it casually usually results in a crumbled mess; the stem becomes hollow and brittle within a few hours of maturity, and the cap quickly falls apart. *Russula sanguinea* is very similar in appearance but is associated with conifers and is not notably fragile.

RUSSULA UNCIALIS PECK

Ecology: Mycorrhizal with hardwoods, especially oaks and hickories; growing alone or gregariously; often in grassy areas, and frequently found in lawns; summer and fall; widely distributed. **Cap:** 2–6 cm; convex, becoming broadly convex to flat, with a shallow depression; rather thin and fragile; sticky when wet and fresh, but soon dry; bald or finely dusted; dull pinkish red to blood red or rose red; evenly colored, but often with a slightly darker center; the margin becoming lined at maturity; the skin peeling fairly easily, often more than halfway to the center. **Gills:** Attached to the stem; close; a few forked near the stem; white; unchanging. **Stem:** 1–5 cm long; up to 1 cm thick; more or less equal; bald; white, often flushed with the cap color. **Flesh:** White; unchanging on exposure. **Odor and Taste:** Not distinctive. **Spore Print:** White. **Chemical Reactions:** KOH negative to yellowish or yellow on cap; iron salts negative on stem. **Microscopic Features:** Spores 7–9 × 5.5–7 µm; broadly ellipsoid; with warts projecting under 1 µm; connecting lines scattered and sparse, not forming a reticulum. Pileipellis a hyaline cutis with hyphal ends rounded to subacute or elongated-fusoid; pileocystidia absent. **Comments:** The Latin species name refers to the small size of this mushroom, which is usually about 1–2 inches across.

RUSSULA VARIATA BANNING

Ecology: Mycorrhizal with hardwoods, especially oaks; growing alone or gregariously; summer and fall; widely distributed. **Cap:** 5–15 cm; round to convex when young, becoming broadly convex to flat or shallowly depressed; dry or slightly moist; fairly smooth, or sometimes becoming cracked with age; green to olive green or purplish, or with these and other shades mottled; the margin sometimes slightly lined in older specimens; the skin peeling fairly easily, sometimes halfway to the center. **Gills:** Attached to the stem or beginning to run down it; close or crowded; forking frequently and conspicuously; white; occasionally spotting slightly brownish in age, but not bruising; when young, soft, greasy, and flexible. **Stem:** 3–10 cm long; 1–3 cm thick; white, occasionally discoloring brownish in places, but not actually bruising; brittle; dry; often becoming cavernous; bald. **Flesh:** White; brittle; thick. **Odor and Taste:** Odor not distinctive; taste mild, or, more frequently, slowly moderately acrid (at least the gills), becoming mild with age. **Chemical Reactions:** KOH negative to orangish on cap; iron salts negative on flesh and stem. **Spore Print:** White. **Microscopic Features:** Spores 7–11.5 × 6–8 µm; with fairly isolated warts 0.3–1 µm high; connectors present, but not forming a reticulum. Pileipellis a cutis beneath a turf-like upper level of elements with variously shaped, slender tips; clearly defined pileocystidia absent. **Comments:** The color of the cap is highly variable but usually involves a mixture of purples and greens. The frequently forking white gills are the best diagnostic field character. *Russula cyanoxantha* is very similar but has gills that do not fork (or fork only near the stem) and a wrinkled-veined cap surface.

RUSSULA VENTRICOSIPES PECK

Ecology: Mycorrhizal with conifers and perhaps with hardwoods; growing alone or gregariously in sand dunes along the Great Lakes; summer and fall. **Cap:** 4.5–13 cm; convex, with a tucked-under margin when young, becoming broadly convex to flat, with a shallow depression; sticky when wet and fresh (with sand "glued" to the surface), but soon dry; covered with a felty, pinkish to orangish layer when young, but soon becoming bald overall, or remaining felty along the margin; yellowish brown, sometimes with orangish shades; the margin lined at maturity; the skin peeling away easily from the margin, sometimes beyond halfway to the center. **Gills:** Attached or pulling away

from the stem; close; sometimes forked near the stem; yellowish white, developing orangish or reddish edges; often spotting or discoloring yellowish brown to brownish. **Stem:** 2–10 cm long; 1.5–5 cm thick; often swollen in the middle; stuffed and thick; white underneath a layer of reddish to brownish-red scurf that begins at the base and may extend nearly to the apex. **Flesh:** Whitish; becoming slowly pale yellowish on exposure or with age. **Odor and Taste:** Odor weakly to moderately reminiscent of maraschino cherries, almonds, or benzaldehyde; taste acrid. **Chemical Reactions:** KOH negative on cap. **Spore Print:** Creamy. **Microscopic Features:** Spores 7–10 × 4.5–6 µm; broadly ellipsoid; with very tiny warts projecting less than 0.5 µm (appearing nearly smooth, even with oil immersion); connecting lines rare and scattered. Pileipellis an interwoven cutis; clearly defined pileocystidia absent. **Comments:** Easily identified due to its habitat, red stem, and odor.

RUSSULA VINACEA BURLINGHAM

Spore print

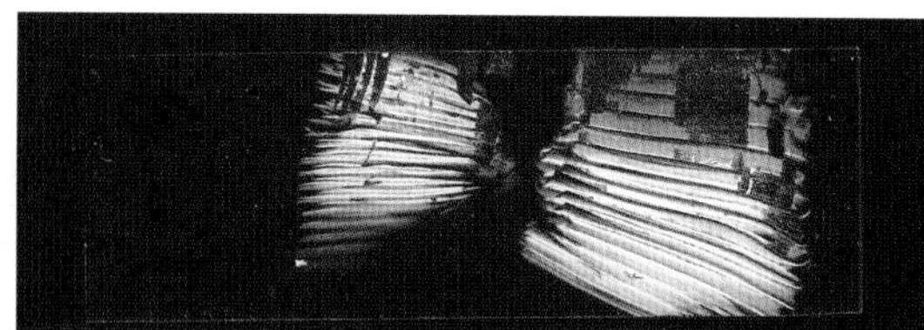

Ecology: Mycorrhizal with oaks and other hardwoods; growing alone, scattered, or gregariously; spring and early summer; distribution uncertain. **Cap:** 4–12 cm; convex when young, becoming broadly convex to flat, with a shallow depression; dry or slightly moist; bald; red to purplish red, often becoming streaked or mottled with yellowish to creamy areas; the margin often lined by maturity; the skin peeling about halfway to the center. **Gills:** Attached to the stem; close; white to creamy. **Stem:** 3.5–8 cm long; 1–3 cm thick; dry; bald; white; sometimes bruising brownish; with age discoloring grayish to gray. **Flesh:** White; brittle; not changing when sliced. **Odor and Taste:** Odor not distinctive; taste mild or very slightly acrid. **Chemical Reactions:** KOH negative to pale orange on cap. Iron salts pink on flesh and stem. **Spore Print:** White. **Microscopic Features:** Spores 7–10 × 6–7 µm; ellipsoid; with isolated warts up to 1 µm high; connectors scattered and infrequent. Pileipellis a cutis with scattered encrusted primordial hyphae. **Comments:** This species is a regular late spring mushroom in our area (central Illinois), characterized by its colors, graying stem surface, mild taste, white spore print, iron salts reaction, and microscopic features. It may well be an officially undescribed species, though we are provisionally applying the North American name *Russula vinacea* to it. The names *Russula krombholzii* and *R. atropurpurea* are also sometimes used to describe similar mushrooms; the taxonomy of this species group requires further research.

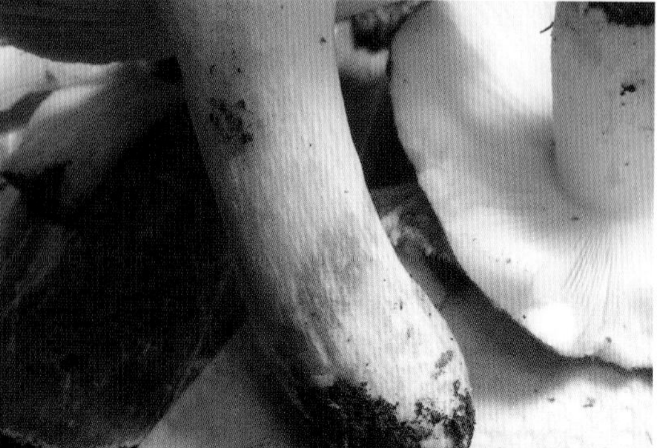

Iron salts on stem

RUSSULA VIRESCENS (SCHAEFFER) FRIES

Ecology: Mycorrhizal with hardwoods (but rarely found under conifers with no hardwoods nearby); growing alone or gregariously; summer and fall; widely distributed. **Cap:** 5–15 cm; round to convex when young, becoming broadly convex to flat to uplifted, with a shallow depression; dry; finely velvety; the surface soon cracking into a distinctive mosaic of small, crustose patches; green to yellowish green; the margin not lined to very slightly lined; the skin peeling about halfway to the center. **Gills:** Attached to the stem or nearly free from it at maturity; close or crowded; white to cream. **Stem:** 3–9 cm long; 2–4 cm thick; brittle; dry; bald; white; discoloring brownish with age. **Flesh:** White; brittle; thick; not changing when sliced. **Odor and Taste:** Not distinctive. **Spore Print:** White. **Microscopic Features:** Spores 6–9 × 5.5–7 µm; ellipsoid to subglobose; warts extending to 0.5 µm high; connectors variable (nearly absent, scattered, or creating partially reticulated areas). Pileipellis a cutis overlaid with epithelium-like areas (the crustose patches) composed of elements of chained cells diminishing in width from base to tip; terminal cell with an elongated and tapered apical projection; pileocystidia cylindric, with capitate apices. **Comments:** "*Russula virescens*" has been determined (Buyck, Mitchell, and Parrent 2006) to be a cluster of phylogenetic species, several of which may be indistinguishable, although one segregated species that occurs in the Midwest, *Russula parvovirescens*, can be identified on the basis of its blue-green color, slightly smaller stature, larger crustose patches, and different pileipellis (see Kuo and Methven 2010).

RUSSULA XERAMPELINA (SCHAEFFER) FRIES

Ecology: Mycorrhizal with conifers or hardwoods; early summer through late fall; widely distributed. **Cap:** 4–30 cm; convex, becoming broadly convex, flat, or shallowly depressed; sticky when fresh, or dry; bald or finely velvety, especially when young; the margin not lined, or lined only faintly; colors ranging from reds to purples (see comments). **Gills:** Attached to the stem or beginning to run down it, but often becoming separated from it with age; close; white to creamy at first, becoming creamy to yellowish or orangish yellow by maturity; often bruising and discoloring yellowish brown to brown. **Stem:** 3–12 cm long; 1–4 cm thick; more or less equal; dry; bald; white, or flushed with reddish to purplish shades;

Iron salts on stem

Spore print

bruising slowly yellowish, then brown. **Flesh:** White; discoloring slowly yellowish brown to brownish or brown when sliced. **Odor and Taste:** Odor fish-like or shrimp-like, especially in age or when dried; taste mild. **Chemical Reactions:** Iron salts green to gray green or olive on stem and flesh. **Spore Print:** Creamy, yellowish, or orangish yellow. **Microscopic Features:** Spores broadly ellipsoid; with fairly isolated warts that extend 0.5–1.5 µm high; connectors absent to scattered. Pileocystidia present. **Comments:** "*Russula xerampelina*" is a collective species that is poorly documented in North America. The most common midwestern versions we are familiar with (illustrated) are associated with oaks: a purplish spring and early summer species, and a bright red summer species.

SARCODON SCABROSUS (FRIES) KARSTEN

Ecology: Mycorrhizal with conifers and hardwoods; growing alone or gregariously; summer; widely distributed. **Cap:** 3–10 cm wide; convex to broadly convex, with a central depression; dry; when young, appressed-hairy to nearly scaly; with maturity, developing well-defined scales with darkened tips; reddish brown to purplish brown; the margin often inrolled. **Undersurface:** Running down the stem; covered with crowded spines or teeth that are 2–8 mm long; spines pale brown with whitish tips at first, becoming darker brown overall with age. **Stem:** 4–10 cm long; 1–2.5 cm thick; often tapered to the base, which frequently extends into the ground like a root; dry; fairly bald, except where punctuated by aborted spines; pale or brownish; base with prominent white to pink mycelium over a greenish to bluish or black ground color. **Flesh:** Whitish to pinkish; gray to black or greenish in stem base; soft. **Odor and Taste:** Taste bitter (sometimes developing slowly); odor mealy, or not distinctive. **Chemical Reactions:** Flesh and cap surface at first green with KOH, then resolving to gray. **Spore Print:** Brown. **Microscopic Features:** Spores 5–7.5 µm; irregularly globose to subglobose; nodulose. Clamp connections absent. **Comments:** Defining macroscopic features for this species group include the scaly reddish-brown cap, the greenish to bluish stem base, and the bitter taste. *Sarcodon fennicus*, in the sense of some authors, is another name for this mushroom.

SARCOSCYPHA AUSTRIACA (O. BECK EX SACCARDO) BOUDIER

Ecology: Saprobic on decaying hardwood sticks and logs (but sometimes the wood is buried, and the mushrooms appear terrestrial); spring; widely distributed. **Fruiting Body:** Cup-shaped to disc-shaped or irregular; 2–7 cm across; upper surface bright red, fading with age, bald, often becoming wrinkled with maturity (especially near the center); undersurface whitish to pinkish or orangish, downy; stem absent or rudimentary, colored like and continuous with the undersurface; flesh thin, whitish; odor not distinctive. **Microscopic Features:** Spores 25–37 × 9.5–15 µm; ellipsoid to nearly football-shaped, with rounded or, frequently, flattened ends; smooth; typically with many small (<3 µm) oil droplets; when fresh and viewed in a water mount, sometimes appearing partially sheathed at the ends (with "polar caps"). Excipular surface with abundant hairs that are elaborately curved, twisted, and intertwined. **Comments:** *Sarcoscypha dudleyi* is identical to the naked eye but features fully sheathed spores with 2 large oil droplets and rounded ends, as well as short, straight excipular hairs. Compare with *Sarcoscypha occidentalis* (below), which is smaller, begins to appear in early summer, and features a stem.

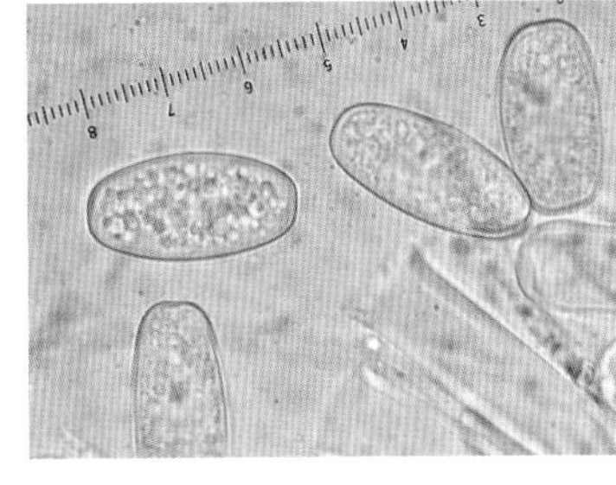

Spores

SARCOSCYPHA OCCIDENTALIS (SCHWEINITZ) SACCARDO

Ecology: Saprobic on decaying hardwood sticks and logs (sometimes on buried sticks, appearing terrestrial, and, rarely, on leaf litter); early summer through fall; widely distributed. **Fruiting Body:** Cup-shaped to saucer-shaped; minute to 2 cm across (rarely up to 4 or 5 cm across); upper surface scarlet red, fading with age, bald; undersurface whitish (but the red color of the upper surface often shows through), bald; stem 1–3 cm, colored like and continuous with the undersurface, base with hairy white mycelium; flesh thin. **Microscopic Features:** Spores 18–22 × 10–12 µm; ellipsoid; smooth; with 2 or more oil droplets; not sheathed; ellipsoid; hyaline. Paraphyses filiform; with orangish contents in KOH. **Comments:** Compare with *Sarcoscypha austriaca* (above).

Photo by Lisa K. Suits

SCHIZOPHYLLUM COMMUNE FRIES

Ecology: Saprobic on the deadwood of hardwoods, or occasionally parasitic on living hardwood trees; growing alone or, more frequently, gregariously to clustered; spring through fall; widely distributed. **Cap:** 1–5 cm wide; fan-shaped when attached to the side of the log; irregular to shell-shaped when attached above or below; finely hairy; dry; white to grayish or tan. **Undersurface:** Composed of gill-like folds that are distinctively split down the middle; whitish to grayish. **Stem:** Absent. **Flesh:** Thin; tough and leathery; whitish. **Spore Print:** White. **Microscopic Features:** Spores 3–4 × 1–1.5 µm (sometimes reported as somewhat larger); cylindric to ellipsoid; smooth. Cystidia absent. Pileipellis a cutis. Clamp connections present. **Comments:** This widely distributed and common fungus is easily recognized by its distinctively "split" gills.

Photo by Lisa K. Suits

KOH on surface

SCLERODERMA AREOLATUM EHRENBERG

Ecology: Mycorrhizal with hardwoods and conifers in moist, shady woods, but also possibly saprobic, since it is also found in open areas, gardens, and so on; growing gregariously or clustered (rarely alone); summer and fall; widely distributed. **Fruiting Body:** 1–5 cm across; round, or shaped like an inverted pear; the surface bald and bruising reddish when young, becoming scaly (especially near the apex) and by maturity acquiring a "leopard-skin" appearance, with small brownish scales over a yellowish base color; rind 1 mm thick or less; without a stem, or occasionally with a poorly defined pseudostem; with white rhizomorphs attached to the base. **Odor:** Sweetish or not distinctive. **Spore Mass:** Whitish and fleshy at first, but soon hard and dark purplish or olive brown; eventually powdery. **Chemical Reactions:** Surface instantly yellowish brown or dark red with KOH. **Microscopic Features:** Spores 11–15 µm; globose; densely spiny, but not reticulate; with spines up to 2 µm long. **Comments:** The small, leopard-skin scales on mature fruiting bodies are distinctive.

SCLERODERMA BOVISTA FRIES

Ecology: Probably saprobic, but possibly mycorrhizal with hardwoods; growing alone, scattered, or gregariously in open areas; usually in grass, but sometimes in disturbed ground (ditches, pathsides, and so on); fall; widely distributed. **Fruiting Body:** 2–5 cm across; round or nearly round; occasionally with a small, pinched-looking pseudobase; surface bald or very finely scaly; developing small pinkish cracks with age; dirty whitish to pale tan; bruising purplish red or pinkish when rubbed; rind about 1 mm thick, whitish, but turning pinkish or purplish when sliced; odor not distinctive. **Spore Mass:** Black and hard, with scattered whitish threads; eventually powdery. **Chemical Reactions:** KOH instantly red on fresh surface; reddish brown or yellowish brown on dried surface. **Microscopic Features:** Spores 8–15 µm (including ornamentation); globose; densely spiny, with spines up to 2 µm long; partially reticulate. **Comments:** The relatively small size, bald and reddish-bruising surface, and red KOH reaction make good field characters.

SCLERODERMA CITRINUM PERSOON

Ecology: Mycorrhizal with hardwoods or conifers; often found in mossy areas (occasionally on well-rotted wood); growing alone, scattered, or gregariously; summer and fall; widely distributed. **Fruiting Body:** 2–10 cm across; round or somewhat flattened; the surface hard and scaly, with prominent and well-spaced individual scales, yellowish to yellow brown, often becoming cracked; rind 2–6 mm thick, whitish when sliced, but often blushing pinkish; sometimes pinched at the base, where mycelial strands are attached. **Spore Mass:** Thick and white at first; becoming purple to purple black from the center outward; eventually blackish to brownish and pow-

Photo by Dan Molter

Photo by Dan Molter

dery. **Chemical Reactions:** Surface dark reddish with KOH. **Microscopic Features:** Spores 8–13 µm; globose; prominently reticulate. **Comments:** The yellowish colors, fairly large size, and well-spaced individual scales are good field characters. This species is occasionally parasitized by *Boletus parasiticus* (p. 120).

SCLERODERMA POLYRHIZUM (GMELIN) PERSOON

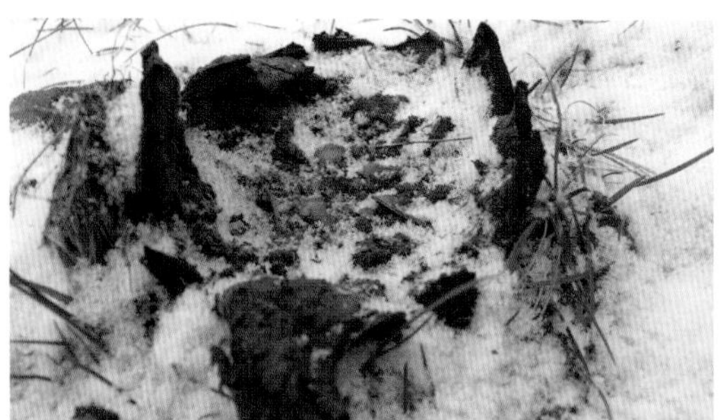

Ecology: Probably saprobic, but possibly mycorrhizal; growing alone, scattered, or gregariously in grass and in disturbed ground, often in urban settings; summer, fall, and early winter; widely distributed. **Fruiting Body:** 8–13 cm across before splitting and spreading; round or nearly round; very tough; partially submerged in the ground; surface when young fairly smooth, often covered with whitish down, with age becoming pocked, pitted, or minutely scaly in places, and usually covered with adhering soil and debris; often bruising reddish or yellowish when rubbed; with maturity splitting near the top and peeling back in irregular rays to expose the spore mass; rind to 5 mm thick or more, whitish, but blushing pink when sliced; sometimes with white rhizomorphs attached to the base; odor not distinctive. **Spore Mass:** Black to purplish black and hard, becoming dark brown and powdery; with whitish to pale yellowish threads interspersed. **Chemical Reactions:** Fresh surface negative or slightly yellowish with KOH. **Microscopic Features:** Spores 7–10 µm; globose; with very tiny spines (mostly under 0.5 µm); partially but not completely reticulate. **Comments:** Also known as *Scleroderma geaster* and *Scleroderma polyrhizon*. Common on lawns, this fungus is easily identified by its large size, its purplish-black spore mass, and the way the rind splits and peels backward in irregular rays.

SCLERODERMA SEPTENTRIONALE JEPPSON

Ecology: Perhaps mycorrhizal with hardwoods and/or conifers, but possibly saprobic, since it is usually found far from trees; growing scattered or gregariously in sand or sand dunes; summer and fall; northern Midwest. **Fruiting Body:** 2.5–6 cm across; with a more or less round structure sitting atop a well-defined "stem" measuring 5–10 cm long and composed of bundled whitish rhizomorphs that extend into the sand; surface yellowish and often mottled, bald, or with small and irregular scales that tend to be concentrated near the top; bruising dark reddish; rind 1–3 mm thick; developing irregular tears and holes at maturity. **Spore Mass:** Fleshy and white at first, becoming purplish brown, then black and powdery. **Chemical Reactions:** KOH on surface dark reddish brown. **Microscopic Features:** Spores 8–16 µm; globose; densely spiny and reticulate, with spines 2–4 µm (or more) long. **Comments:** The habitat in sand and the distinctive stem structure formed by aggregated rhizomorphs are good field characters.

SCUTELLINIA SCUTELLATA (LINNAEUS) LAMBOTTE

Ecology: Saprobic on wet, rotting wood, or on damp soil near rotting wood; growing gregariously or in clusters; spring through fall; widely distributed. **Fruiting Body:** Cup-shaped to broadly cup-shaped, up to 1.5 cm across; upper surface scarlet red to bright orange, bald; undersurface brownish or pale orangish, covered with tiny dark hairs; the margin with longer eyelash-like dark hairs; without a stem; flesh thin and insubstantial. **Microscopic Features:** Spores 17–23 × 10.5–14 µm; ellipsoid; smooth when immature, and remaining so for a long time, but in maturity sculpted with warts and ribs extending to about 1 µm high; with several oil droplets. Paraphyses with swollen tips. Marginal hairs brownish in KOH; thick-walled; septate; with branched bases. **Comments:** Tiny and often overlooked, but gorgeous and distinctive. Sometimes called the "eyelash fungus." Several similar species differ primarily on microscopic features.

SIMOCYBE CENTUNCULUS (FRIES) KARSTEN

Ecology: Saprobic on the deadwood of hardwoods; often found on stumps, but also on fallen logs; summer and fall (but occasionally seen in late spring or in winter during warm spells); widely distributed. **Cap:** 1–2.5 cm; convex, becoming flat; dry; finely velvety or powdery, becoming bald; olive to olive brown, fading markedly as it dries out; usually with a dark

Photo by Dan Molter

Photo by Dan Molter

center and a paler marginal area by maturity; finely lined. **Gills:** Attached to the stem; close; whitish or pale brownish, becoming brown to olive brown; with whitish, frayed-looking edges. **Stem:** 1–3 cm long; under 5 mm thick; equal; bald, but adorned with tiny white flakes near the apex; colored like the cap; hollow; with whitish basal mycelium. **Flesh:** Insubstantial. **Odor and Taste:** Odor not distinctive, or slightly unpleasant to spermatic. **Spore Print:** Brown. **Chemical Reactions:** KOH red to brownish red on cap. **Microscopic Features:** Spores 6–8 × 4–5 µm; smooth; mostly kidney-shaped, but a fair number deviating to subglobose, sublacrymoid, or subellipsoid; inamyloid. Pleurocystidia absent. Cheilocystidia cylindric to clavate. Pileipellis hymeniform with cystidium-like elements. **Comments:** The growth habit on wood, the finely lined olive-brown cap with a darker center, the gills with whitish edges, and the tiny white flakes at the apex of the stem characterize this species in the field.

SPARASSIS SPATHULATA (SCHWEINITZ) FRIES

Photo by Dan Molter

Photo by Ron Kerner

Ecology: Pathogenic and saprobic; growing from the roots or bases of trees; found primarily under hardwoods, especially oaks, but occasionally reported under conifers; annual, but often recurring yearly in the same location; causing a brown rot or a butt rot; summer and fall; widely distributed. **Fruiting Body:** 10–40 cm broad; composed of tightly packed branches, which arise from a common base; branches long and flattened, whitish to yellowish or tan, with fairly conspicuous zones of color. **Spore Print:** Whitish. **Microscopic Features:** Spores 6–8 × 5–6 µm; smooth; broadly ellipsoid; inamyloid. Clamp connections absent. **Comments:** Edible and good. Sometimes called the "cauliflower mushroom." Specimens with azonate, short branches that arise from multiple, large basal branches are often labeled "*Sparassis crispa*," but whether or not that European species name can be accurately applied to North American collections is debated.

SPATHULARIOPSIS VELUTIPES (COOKE & FARLOW) MAAS GEESTERANUS

Photo by Andy Methven

Ecology: Saprobic; growing gregariously or in clusters on the decaying wood of conifers, or on the ground on conifer debris; summer and fall; widely distributed, but more common where conifers grow naturally. **Fruiting Body:** More or less spatula-shaped, with a flattened apical portion at the top of a stem; the flattened portion usually running down the stem on either side of it, up to 5 cm across, yellowish or cream-colored, slightly wrinkled; when young with a veil-like covering (almost never actually seen by collectors); stem up to 6 cm long and 1 cm thick, brownish, velvety or fuzzy, with orangish basal mycelium; flesh insubstantial, whitish; odor not distinctive. **Microscopic Features:** Spores 33–43 × 1.5–3 µm; needle-shaped; smooth; often septate. **Comments:** *Spathularia flavida* is very similar but yellow overall; its stem is not fuzzy and lacks the orangish basal mycelium.

SPONGIPELLIS PACHYODON (PERSOON) KOTLABA & POUZAR

Ecology: Parasitic on oaks and other hardwoods; causing a white heart rot; annual; growing gregariously or in shelving or fused clusters; summer and fall; widely distributed. **Fruiting Body:** Variable, sometimes merely a spreading pore surface, sometimes with a folded-over edge of a cap, sometimes with poorly to well-developed caps. **Cap:** When present, up to about 5 cm across; plano-convex to flat; very finely velvety, becoming bald; white to dull yellowish; sometimes finely radially grooved. **Pore Surface:** Creamy white to dull yellowish; not bruising appreciably; composed of flattened, tooth-like spines and irregular, angular pores; spines to about 1 cm long. **Stem:** Absent. **Flesh:** Whitish; soft above and tougher below. **Odor:** Not distinctive. **Spore Print:** Not documented; presumably white. **Microscopic Features:** Spores 5–6.5 µm; smooth; globose; inamyloid; thick-walled. Cystidia absent. Hyphal system monomitic; clamp connections present. **Comments:** Readily distinguished by the shelving growth habit and the flattened, tooth-like spines.

Photo by Ron Kerner

STECCHERINUM OCHRACEUM (PERSOON) GRAY

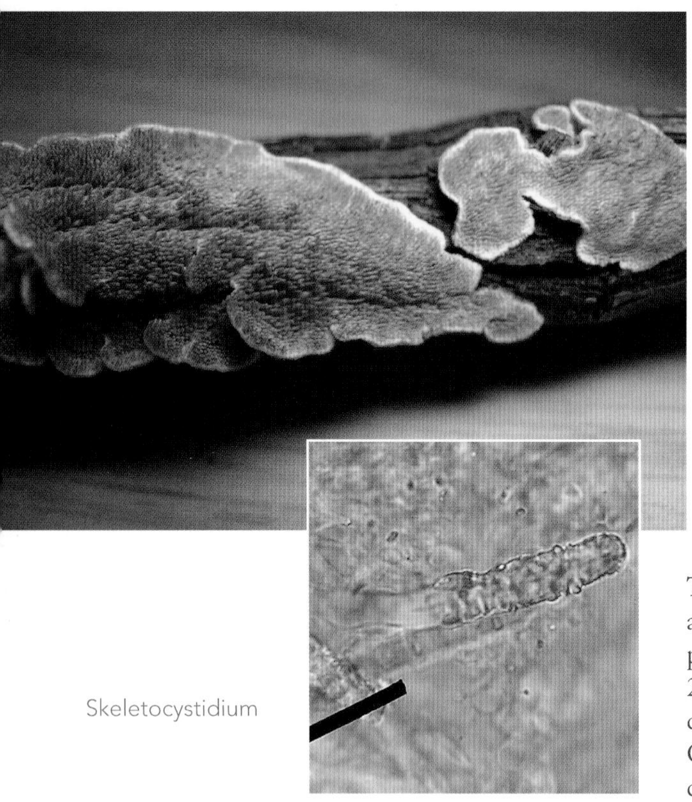

Skeletocystidium

Ecology: Saprobic on the deadwood of hardwoods and, rarely, conifers; growing alone or gregariously on sticks, logs, or stumps; causing a white rot; late spring through fall; widely distributed. **Fruiting Body:** Variable; usually a patch of densely packed spines up to about 3 cm across, with folded-over edges (especially when growing on logs and sticks), but sometimes with a well-defined cap and even, at times, a stem (especially when growing on stumps). **Upper Surface:** When present, grooved and hairy to velvety; with more or less concentric zones of color and texture; grayish to brownish or whitish; margin white, scalloped. **Undersurface:** Composed of densely packed spines up to 3 mm long; orange, fading to yellowish or brownish when old. **Stem:** When present, up to 8 mm long and 2 mm wide; colored like the upper surface. **Flesh:** Tough; leathery; whitish. **Odor and Taste:** Not distinctive. **Chemical Reactions:** KOH negative on all surfaces. **Spore Print:** Undocumented, but probably white. **Microscopic Features:** Spores 3.5–5 × 2–2.5 µm; smooth; ellipsoid; inamyloid. Skeletocystidia cylindric to subfusiform; thick-walled; usually encrusted. Context hyphal structure dimitic. **Comments:** The orange colors and tiny spines make this fungus easy to recognize.

STEREUM COMPLICATUM (FRIES) FRIES

Ecology: Saprobic on the deadwood of hardwoods, especially oaks; growing densely gregariously, often from gaps in the decaying bark; causing a white rot of the heartwood; often serving as a host to algae; sometimes parasitized by jelly fungi; especially common in spring, but also appearing in summer, fall, and winter; widely distributed. **Fruiting Body:** Individually up to about 2 cm across, but usually fused together; fan-shaped, semicircular, irregular, or not infrequently lacking a cap structure or with only a folded-over edge; densely velvety, hairy, or with appressed hairs, but sometimes nearly bald in age; with concentric zones of color and texture; colors ranging from tan to orange brown, pinkish, or cinnamon; laterally attached, without a stem. **Undersurface:** Bald; orange. **Flesh:** Insubstantial; tough. **Chemical Reactions:** KOH red (or at first red, then black)

on upper surface. **Spore Print:** White; difficult to obtain. **Microscopic Features:** Spores 5–7.5 × 2–3 µm; smooth; cylindric; amyloid. **Comments:** Frequently encountered by morel hunters, this crust fungus is very bright orange when fresh. *Stereum gausapatum* is very similar but exudes a red juice when scratched.

STEREUM OSTREA (BLUME & NEES) FRIES

Ecology: Saprobic on the deadwood of hardwoods; growing densely gregariously, often from gaps in the bark of recently fallen trees; causing a white rot of the heartwood; often serving as a host to algae; sometimes parasitized by jelly fungi; sometimes associated with *Phlebia incarnata* (p. 306); spring, summer, fall, and winter; widely distributed and common. **Cap:** 1–7 cm across; frequently shaped like a funnel that has been sliced down one side, but also often fan-shaped, semicircular, or irregularly kidney-shaped; not usually fusing with other caps; densely velvety or hairy at first, but often bald by maturity; with concentric zones of red, orange, yellowish, brown, and buff shades (sometimes developing greenish shades in old age as a result of algae); without a stem. **Undersurface:** Bald; whitish to grayish or pale reddish brown. **Flesh:** Insubstantial; tough. **Chemical Reactions:** KOH red (or at first red, then black) on all surfaces. **Spore Print:** White; difficult to obtain. **Microscopic Features:** Spores 5.5–7.5 × 2–3 µm; smooth; cylindric; amyloid. **Comments:** One of the most common and frequently encountered fungi in the Midwest. The bald, hard underside of this crust fungus separates it readily from *Trametes versicolor* (p. 371) and other species of *Trametes* that feature pore surfaces.

STROBILOMYCES FLOCCOPUS (VAHL) KARSTEN

Photo by Melissa Bochte

Ecology: Mycorrhizal with hardwoods, especially oaks; common; summer and fall; widely distributed. **Cap:** 3–15 cm; convex, becoming broadly convex in age; dry; covered with coarse, black, woolly scales over a whitish to grayish base color; the margin frequently hung with veil remnants. **Pore Surface:** Whitish, soon becoming gray, and finally turning black; bruising reddish, then black; pores angular; tubes to 1.5 cm deep; at first covered by a whitish

to grayish partial veil. **Stem:** 4–12 cm long; 1–2.5 cm thick; more or less equal; grayish to blackish; shaggy; sometimes reticulate above; sometimes with an ephemeral ring or ring zone; solid. **Flesh:** Whitish throughout, turning pinkish to red when exposed, then blackening over the course of as much as an hour. **Odor and Taste:** Not distinctive. **Chemical Reactions:** Ammonia brown to brownish black on flesh; KOH brown to black on flesh; iron salts black on flesh. **Spore Print:** Blackish brown to black. **Microscopic Features:** Spores 9.5–15 × 8.5–12 µm; globose to subellipsoid; widely reticulate and spiny. **Comments:** Sometimes called the "old man of the woods," this unmistakable bolete is very common in the Midwest's oak-hickory forests. A recent study (Petersen et al. 2012) has determined that North American *Strobilomyces* species are phylogenetically distinct from European species. Thus, since the species name *floccopus* represents a European mushroom, the names of our North American species are likely to change.

STROPHARIA CORONILLA (BULLIARD) QUÉLET

Chrysocystidia

Ecology: Saprobic; growing alone or gregariously on lawns, in pastures, and in other grassy places; summer and fall; widely distributed. **Cap:** 2–6 cm; convex, becoming broadly convex to flat; sticky when fresh; golden brown to yellowish, often fading to buff or creamy white; bald. **Gills:** Attached to the stem; close; pale at first, becoming purplish gray to purple black. **Stem:** 2–5 cm long; 3–6 mm thick; dry; bald below, but cottony above the ring; with a persistent ring that is usually grooved on its upper surface and typically collects purplish-gray spores; base sometimes with white rhizomorphs. **Flesh:** White throughout; soft. **Odor and Taste:** Not distinctive. **Chemical Reactions:** KOH slowly reddish on cap. **Spore Print:** Dark purple brown to blackish. **Microscopic Features:** Spores 7–11 × 4–5.5 µm; smooth; ellipsoid. Chrysocystidia present. **Comments:** Compare with *Agrocybe molesta* (p. 85).

STROPHARIA HARDII ATKINSON

Ecology: Saprobic; growing alone or gregariously on woody debris in hardwood forests (but also occasionally reported on woodchips); summer and fall; widely distributed. **Cap:** 4–10 cm; convex, becoming broadly convex or flat; sticky at first, but soon dry; dirty yellow to brownish yellow; bald or with inconspicuous dark brownish tiny scales. **Gills:** Attached to the stem; close; pale at first, becoming grayish or purplish brown, or merely dark brown. **Stem:** 5–9 cm long; up to 1.5 cm thick; dry; with a ring; bald or finely hairy, but not conspicuously shaggy or scaly; white; base attached to white rhizomorphs. **Flesh:** White; unchanging on exposure. **Odor and Taste:** Not distinctive, or unpleasant and somewhat mealy. **Spore Print:** Purple brown. **Microscopic Features:** Spores 5–9 × 3–5 µm; smooth; ellipsoid. Chrysocystidia present. **Comments:** Compare with *Agrocybe praecox* (p. 86).

STROPHARIA KAUFFMANII A. H. SMITH

Ecology: Saprobic; growing alone, scattered, or gregariously on litter and woody debris in hardwood and conifer forests; summer and fall; northern Midwest. **Cap:** 5–15 cm; convex, becoming broadly convex or flat; dry; yellow to brownish yellowish; covered with innate, fibrillose scales; the margin sometimes adorned with veil remnants. **Gills:** Attached to the stem, often by a notch; close or crowded; pale at first, later purplish gray to purple black. **Stem:** 6–10 cm long; up to 3 cm thick; equal, or with a slightly swollen base; dry; with a fragile whitish ring or ring zone; prominently scaly, at least when young; base with rhizomorphs. **Flesh:** White. **Odor and Taste:** Odor slightly fragrant or slightly foul; taste mild or slightly foul. **Chemical Reactions:** KOH pinkish orange on cap. **Spore Print:** Dark purple brown to black. **Microscopic Features:** Spores 6–7 × 4–4.5 µm; smooth; ellipsoid. Chrysocystidia present. **Comments:** Compare with *Pholiota terrestris* (p. 311).

Chrysocystidia

STROPHARIA RUGOSOANNULATA FARLOW EX MURRILL

Ecology: Saprobic, growing scattered or gregariously (sometimes in clusters) on woodchips, in gardens, and in other cultivated areas; spring through fall; widely distributed. **Cap:** 4–15 cm; convex or broadly bell-shaped at first, becoming broadly convex to flat; sticky when fresh, but often dry when collected; bald; wine red to reddish brown, fading to tan or paler, or in one form whitish throughout development; sometimes developing cracks in old age; the margin sometimes with veil remnants. **Gills:** Attached to the stem; whitish to pale gray at first, becoming purplish gray to purple black; close. **Stem:** 7–15 cm long; 1–3 cm thick; dry; equal, or with an enlarged base; bald or finely hairy; white, discoloring yellowish to brownish in age; with a thick ring that is finely grooved on its upper surface (and often blackened by spores) and radially split on its underside; base with white rhizomorphs. **Flesh:** Substantial and white throughout; firm. **Odor and Taste:** Not distinctive, or, in the white form, unpleasant and creosote-like. **Chemical Reactions:** KOH olive green on cap of red form; yellow on cap of white form. **Spore Print:** Dark purple brown to blackish. **Microscopic Features:** Spores 10–14 × 6–9 µm; smooth; broadly ellipsoid. Chrysocystidia present. **Comments:** The wine-capped form is edible and good. Edibility is not reliably documented, however, for the white form of this species (which has an unpleasant odor anyway). The white form should be compared with *Agaricus arvensis* (p. 81) and *Agaricus xanthodermus* (p. 84), which have brown mature gills and spore prints.

SUILLUS AMERICANUS (PECK) SNELL

Ecology: Mycorrhizal with white pine in both natural and artificial settings; typically growing gregariously; summer and fall; widely distributed. **Cap:** 3–10 cm; convex, with an inrolled margin when young, but soon broadly convex to wavy and irregular; with white to yellowish brown veil tissue hanging from the margin; slimy; bright to dingy yellow; developing reddish to reddish-brown patches and markings. **Pore Surface:** Yellow, becoming darker with age; bruising reddish brown; pores angular and vaguely radially arranged, 1–2 mm across; tubes 7–10 mm deep. **Stem:** 3–10 cm long; up to about 1 cm thick; frequently crooked or bent; with reddish-brown glandular dots; occasionally with a ring or ring zone, but often bare; frequently bruising reddish brown; tough. **Flesh:** Yellow throughout; staining purplish brown. **Odor and Taste:** Not distinctive. **Chemical Reactions:** Ammonia red on cap and flesh. KOH black on cap and flesh. Iron salts negative to grayish or pale olive on cap and flesh. **Spore Print:** Cinnamon to brown. **Microscopic Features:** Spores 8–12 × 3–4 µm; smooth; fusoid. **Comments:** Easily recognized by the stickiness, the yellow colors that develop reddish-brown discolorations, the glandular dots, and the habitat under white pine.

SUILLUS CAVIPES (OPATOWSKI) A. H. SMITH & THIERS

Ecology: Mycorrhizal with tamarack; growing alone or gregariously; fall; northern Midwest. **Cap:** 3–10 cm; convex, becoming broadly convex or flat, or sometimes with a broad central bump; dry; densely hairy with whitish to brownish hairs; yellowish brown, reddish brown, or brown; often with white veil remnants on the margin. **Pore Surface:** Yellow or greenish yellow; not bruising; pores angular and radially arranged, about 1 mm across; tubes to 5 mm deep. **Stem:** 4–9 cm long; 0.5–1.5 cm thick; sometimes somewhat bulbous; yellow and bald toward the apex, brownish and hairy below; sometimes with a fragile ring; becoming hollow in the base. **Flesh:** White to yellowish; not staining on exposure. **Odor and Taste:** Not distinctive. **Chemical Reactions:** Ammonia red on cap; sea green on flesh. KOH blackish red on cap; negative or yellowish on flesh. Iron salts negative on cap and flesh. **Spore Print:** Olive brown to brown. **Microscopic Features:** Spores 7–10 × 3.5–4 µm; smooth; subfusoid. **Comments:** Edible and good.

SUILLUS GRANULATUS (LINNAEUS) ROUSSEL

Photo by Noah Siegel

Ecology: Mycorrhizal with various pines in natural and artificial settings; often appearing in plantations of white pine; growing alone or gregariously; summer and fall (often among the first species of *Suillus* to appear); widely distributed. **Cap:** 5–15 cm; convex, becoming broadly convex; sticky or slimy; bald; variable in color, but typically buff, yellowish, or pale cinnamon at first, becoming darker cinnamon brown or orangish brown, often with the color breaking up in maturity to form a patchwork pattern; without veil remnants. **Pore Surface:** Whitish at first, but soon yellowish; often with droplets of cloudy liquid when young; not bruising, or bruising and spotting cinnamon to brownish; pores about 1 mm wide at maturity; tubes about 1 cm deep. **Stem:** 4–8 cm long; 1–2 cm thick; equal, or with a tapering base; with tiny tan or brownish glandular dots on the upper half; without a ring; white, often developing yellow shades near the apex or overall. **Flesh:** White at first, but soon pale yellow; not staining on exposure. **Odor and Taste:** Not distinctive. **Chemical Reactions:** Ammonia pale gray to negative on cap; pale gray on flesh; dull salmon to rusty orange on pore surface. KOH flashing blue, then black to gray on cap; pink, becoming grayish on flesh; dull salmon to rusty orange on pore surface. Iron salts gray to olive on cap; pale green to blue on flesh; olive on pore surface. **Spore Print:** Cinnamon brown to brown. **Microscopic Features:** Spores 7–9 × 2.5–3.5 µm; smooth; subfusoid. **Comments:** The ringless stem with small glandular dots, the dull yellow pore surface, and the brown to reddish-brown cap that develops a mottled appearance are good field characters. Edible, but insipid and sticky.

SUILLUS INTERMEDIUS (A. H. SMITH & THIERS) A. H. SMITH & THIERS

Ecology: Mycorrhizal with pines; growing alone, scattered, or gregariously; summer and fall; widely distributed, but more common in the northern Midwest. **Cap:** 3–17 cm; convex, becoming more or less flat; bald; slimy; yellowish, darkening somewhat with age; often with yellowish partial veil remnants on the margin. **Pore Surface:** Pale yellow when young, darker yellow at maturity; not bruising, or bruising slowly brownish; 2–3 angular pores per mm; tubes to 6 mm deep. **Stem:** 4–10 cm long; up to 12 mm thick; more or less equal; fairly tough; yellowish below brownish glandular dots that blacken with maturity; usually blackening on handling; when young, with a thin, bracelet-like, gelatinous ring that dries out and

flattens against the stem surface with maturity. **Flesh:** Whitish to yellowish in the cap; pale salmon orange in the stem; not staining on exposure. **Odor and Taste:** Odor not distinctive; taste of the slime on the cap acidic or mild. **Chemical Reactions:** Ammonia negative to grayish on cap; reddish to bright pink on flesh. KOH blue green on cap; bluish to gray on flesh. Iron salts negative on cap; orangish to negative on flesh. **Spore Print:** Cinnamon brown. **Microscopic Features:** Spores 8–11 × 3.5–5 µm; smooth; subfusoid. **Comments:** Also known as *Suillus acidus* var. *intermedius*. The thin, gelatinous ring and the blackening stem are good field characters. Compare with *Suillus salmonicolor* (p. 369), which has a much thicker, slimy ring.

SUILLUS LUTEUS (LINNAEUS) ROUSSEL

Ecology: Mycorrhizal with various conifers; growing gregariously; late summer and fall, or in winter during warm spells; widely distributed. **Cap:** 5–12 cm; convex when young, becoming broadly convex to flat; bald; slimy; shiny when dry; veil tissue often hanging from the margin; dark brown to dark reddish brown to yellow brown; fading with age. **Pore Surface:** Covered with a whitish veil when young; whitish to pale yellow, becoming yellow to olive yellow with age; not bruising; pores under 1 mm across; tubes 4–15 mm deep. **Stem:** 3–8 cm long; 1–2.5 cm thick; equal; with glandular dots above the ring; whitish overall, but yellowish toward apex; discoloring brown to purplish brown near the base in age; with a flaring white ring that develops purple shades on the underside and is often somewhat gelatinous in humid or wet weather. **Flesh:** White to pale yellow; not staining on exposure. **Odor and Taste:** Not distinctive. **Chemical Reactions:** Ammonia pinkish to negative on cap; pinkish on flesh; pinkish red on pore surface. KOH dark gray on cap; pinkish, then pale bluish on flesh; dark brown on pore surface. Iron salts dark olive on cap; bluish on flesh; brown on pore surface. **Spore Print:** Brown. **Microscopic Features:** Spores 7–9 × 2.5–3 µm; smooth; subfusoid. **Comments:** Edible. Sometimes called the "slippery jack." The slimy dark brown cap, glandular dots, and prominent ring with a purplish edge are good field characters.

SUILLUS PICTUS (PECK) KUNTZE

Ecology: Mycorrhizal with white pine; growing alone or gregariously; late summer and fall; northern Midwest, and in southern Indiana and southern Ohio. **Cap:** 3–12 cm; convex, with an inrolled margin when young, but soon broadly convex to flat; covered with large pinkish to brick-rose scales; whitish veil tissue often hanging from the margin; dry; fading with age. **Pore Surface:** Covered with a whitish veil when young; yellow, becoming darker with age; sometimes running slightly down the stem; often bruising reddish or brownish; pores small to large, 0.5–5 mm across, vaguely radially arranged; tubes 4–8 mm deep. **Stem:** 4–12 cm long; 1–2.5 cm thick; equal or sometimes wider in the base; without glandular dots, but shaggy to scaly below the whitish to grayish ring; not bruising. **Flesh:** Yellow throughout; sometimes staining slightly reddish. **Odor and Taste:** Not distinctive. **Chemical Reactions:** Ammonia black on cap; olive to blackish on flesh. KOH black on cap; olive to brown on flesh. Iron salts black on flesh. **Spore Print:** Brown. **Microscopic Features:** Spores 8–12 × 3.5–5 µm; smooth; subfusoid. **Comments:** Also known as *Suillus spraguei*.

SUILLUS PUNCTIPES (PECK) SINGER

Ecology: Mycorrhizal with conifers, especially white pine; growing alone or gregariously; summer and fall; widely distributed. **Cap:** 3–10 cm; convex, becoming broadly convex; slimy; when very young, with a thin tomentum, but soon bald; yellow to yellow brown. **Pore Surface:** Brown to pale brown at first, becoming yellowish or olive; not bruising; with about 2 round or angular pores per mm; tubes under 1 cm deep. **Stem:** 4–9 cm long; 1–1.5 cm thick; equal, or with a slightly swollen base; densely covered with glandular dots that are pale brown at first and become darker with age; whitish to yellowish under the glandular dots; without a ring. **Flesh:** Whitish or pale yellow overall, but often orangish or reddish in the stem base; not staining on exposure. **Odor and Taste:** Taste mild; odor strong and fragrant, or not distinctive. **Chemical Reactions:** Ammonia negative on cap and flesh. KOH purple on cap and flesh. Iron salts negative on cap; negative to grayish blue

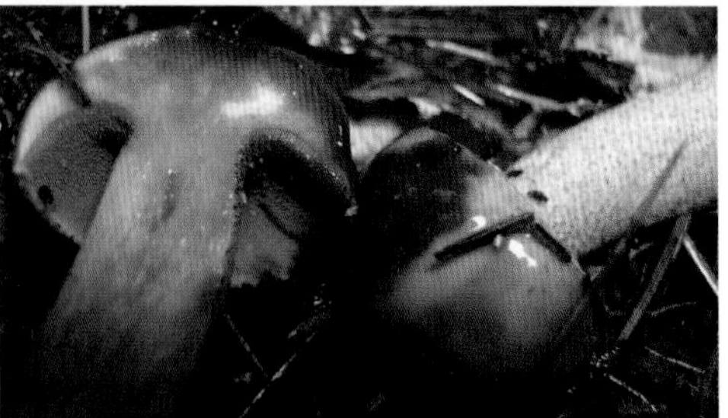

KOH on cap and flesh

on flesh. **Spore Print:** Brown. **Microscopic Features:** Spores 7.5–10 × 3–3.5 µm; smooth; subfusoid. **Comments:** The brown young pore surface, slimy yellow-brown cap, and dense covering of glandular dots on the stem are good field characters.

SUILLUS SALMONICOLOR (FROST) HALLING

Ecology: Mycorrhizal with pines, especially jack pine and pitch pine; growing alone or gregariously; late summer and fall; northern Midwest and Ohio. **Cap:** 3–10 cm; convex, becoming broadly convex or flat; slimy; bald; orangish, dirty yellowish, brownish, olive brown, or cinnamon. **Pore Surface:** At first covered with a thick, orangish to grayish partial veil that is baggy and rubbery, with a white roll of tissue on the lower edge; yellow to orangish, becoming brownish with age; not bruising; 1–2 round or angular pores per mm; tubes to about 1 cm deep. **Stem:** 3–10 cm long; up to 1.5 cm thick; equal, or with a slightly enlarged base; covered with glandular dots that are pale reddish brown at first and become darker with age; whitish to yellowish or orangish; with a gelatinous ring. **Flesh:** Orangish to yellowish, often salmon orange in the stem base; not staining on exposure. **Odor and Taste:** Not distinctive. **Chemical Reactions:** Ammonia purplish on cap and flesh. KOH purple on cap and flesh. Iron salts negative on cap and flesh. **Spore Print:** Cinnamon brown or brown. **Microscopic Features:** Spores 7–10 × 3–3.5 µm; smooth; subfusoid. **Comments:** Compare with *Suillus intermedius* (p. 366).

TAPINELLA ATROTOMENTOSA (BATSCH) ŠUTARA

Photo by Ron Kerner

Ecology: Saprobic; growing alone, gregariously, or in clusters on conifer stumps or the wood of living conifers; summer and fall; northern Midwest and Ohio. **Cap:** 4–15 cm; convex, becoming flat or vase-shaped; dry; velvety or finely hairy; yellow brown to reddish brown, becoming dark brown in age; the margin inrolled at first. **Gills:** Running down the stem; close or crowded; whitish to tan or yellowish tan; frequently forked, or with cross-veins near the stem; separable as a layer. **Stem:** 2–12 cm long; 1–3 cm thick; frequently off-central or even lateral; thick and sturdy; pale and bald near the apex, but brown to blackish brown and velvety below. **Flesh:** Thick and firm; whitish to yellowish. **Odor and Taste:** Not

distinctive. **Chemical Reactions:** KOH black on cap. **Spore Print:** Yellowish to brownish. **Microscopic Features:** Spores 5–6.5 × 3–4.5 µm; smooth; ellipsoid; dextrinoid. **Comments:** Also known as *Paxillus atrotomentosus*. The distinctively velvety cap and stem, separable gills running down the stem, and habitat on conifer wood are good field characters.

TETRAPYRGOS NIGRIPES (FRIES) E. HORAK

Ecology: Saprobic on leaf litter and woody debris in hardwood forests; growing alone or gregariously; summer and fall; widely distributed. **Cap:** To 2 cm across; convex, becoming flat; bald or finely dusted; wrinkled; white. **Gills:** Attached to the stem or beginning to run down it; distant or nearly so; with cross-veins; white; sometimes bruising reddish in places. **Stem:** 2–5 cm long; less than 2 mm thick; equal; dry; straight; inserted directly into the substrate; tough; whitish when young, but soon black; covered with tiny white hairs. **Flesh:** Thin; rubbery. **Odor and Taste:** Not distinctive. **Spore Print:** White. **Microscopic Features:** Spores 8–9 µm; smooth; triangular or jack-shaped. **Comments:** Also known as *Marasmiellus nigripes*. Compare with *Marasmius rotula* (p. 272) and *Marasmius capillaris* (p. 269), which have pleated caps and bald, wiry stems, and with *Marasmius delectans* (p. 270).

TRAMETES ELEGANS (SPRENGEL) FRIES

Ecology: Saprobic on the deadwood of hardwoods; annual or occasionally perennial; causing a white rot of the sapwood; growing alone or gregariously on logs and stumps; spring through fall; widely distributed, but more common below the Great Lakes. **Cap:** Up to 35 cm across and 3 cm thick; semicircular, irregularly bracket-shaped, or kidney-shaped; flattened-convex; lumpy near the point of attachment, smoother toward the thin margin; often with concentric zones of texture; whitish to buff; sometimes becoming darker with age, especially near the point of attachment or along the margin. **Pore Surface:** Whitish; variable, ranging from poroid, with round to angular pores (1–2 per

Photo by Martin Livezey

mm), to maze-like, with slots up to 2 mm wide, to gill-like, or not infrequently with all 3 of these conditions present; tubes or slots up to 6 mm deep; not bruising, or bruising yellowish in some collections. **Stem:** Usually absent, but occasionally present as a stubby lateral structure. **Flesh:** Whitish; tough and corky. **Chemical Reactions:** KOH yellow on flesh. **Spore Print:** White. **Microscopic Features:** Spores 5–7 × 2–3 µm; smooth; cylindric to long-ellipsoid. Cystidia and setae absent. Hyphal system trimitic. **Comments:** Also known as *Lenzites elegans*. Compare with *Daedaleopsis confragosa* (p. 168).

TRAMETES PUBESCENS (SCHUMACHER) PILÁT

Ecology: Saprobic on the deadwood of hardwoods (rarely reported on conifer wood); annual; causing a white rot; growing in clusters on logs and stumps; summer and fall; widely distributed. **Cap:** Up to 8 cm across; semicircular, irregularly bracket-shaped, or kidney-shaped; sometimes fusing laterally with other caps; velvety to finely velvety, sometimes becoming nearly bald with age; often finely, radially lined and furrowed, especially on the margin; cream-colored; sometimes with faint textural zones, but without contrasting zones of color. **Pore Surface:** Creamy, becoming yellowish with age; with 3–5 angular pores per mm; tubes to 6 mm deep. **Flesh:** Insubstantial; whitish; tough and corky. **Odor and Taste:** Not distinctive. **Chemical Reactions:** KOH on flesh yellow. **Spore Print:** White. **Microscopic Features:** Spores 5–7 × 1.5–2 µm; smooth; cylindric; inamyloid. Cystidia and setae absent. Hyphal system trimitic. **Comments:** The yellowing pore surface with 3–5 pores per mm and the cream-colored velvety cap that lacks strongly contrasting zones are good field characters.

TRAMETES VERSICOLOR (LINNAEUS) LLOYD

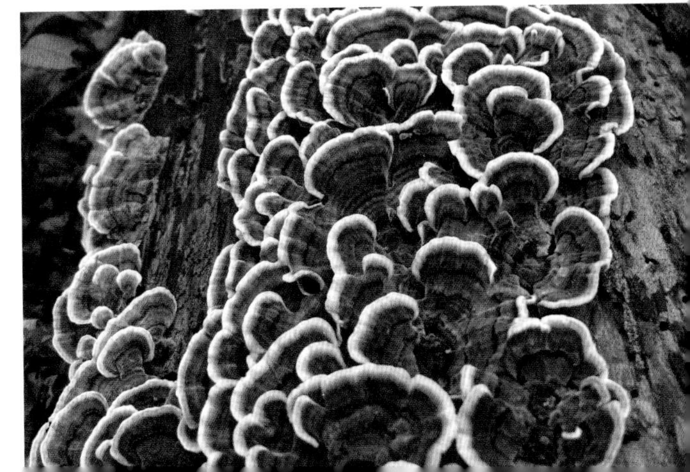

Ecology: Saprobic on the deadwood of hardwoods, or rarely on the wood of conifers; annual; causing a white rot of the sapwood; growing in dense, overlapping clusters or rosettes on logs and stumps; spring, summer, and fall; widely distributed and common. **Cap:** Up to 10 cm across; only a few mm thick; flexible when fresh; circular, semicircular, bracket-shaped,

Photo by Lisa K. Suits

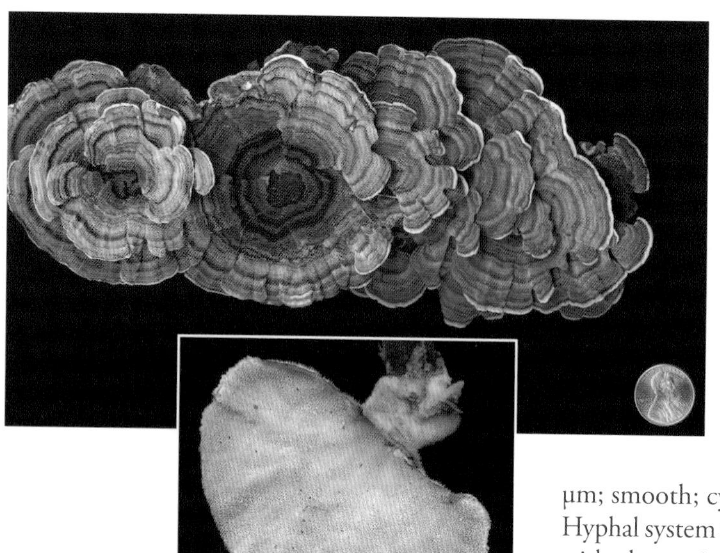

or kidney-shaped; often fused with other caps; densely hairy or velvety, often with alternating zones of texture; with concentric zones of white, brown, cinnamon, and reddish brown (but highly variable in color, and sometimes with other shades, including blue, green, and orange). **Pore Surface:** Whitish to pale grayish; not bruising; with 4 or more pores per mm; tubes up to 3 mm deep. **Flesh:** Insubstantial; whitish; tough and leathery. **Odor and Taste:** Not distinctive. **Chemical Reactions:** KOH negative to yellowish on flesh. **Spore Print:** Whitish. **Microscopic Features:** Spores 5–6 × 1.5–2 µm; smooth; cylindric; inamyloid. Cystidia and setae absent. Hyphal system trimitic. **Comments:** The tiny pores, fuzzy caps with alternating zones of colors, and flexible fruiting bodies characterize this very variable species. Compare with *Stereum ostrea* (p. 361).

TRAMETES VILLOSA (SWARTZ) KRIESEL

Ecology: Saprobic on the deadwood of hardwoods and conifers (especially red cedar); annual; causing a white rot; growing in clusters on logs and stumps; summer and fall; below the Great Lakes. **Cap:** Up to 7 cm across and 3 mm thick; semicircular, irregularly bracket-shaped, or kidney-shaped; often fused laterally with other caps; very densely hairy; with concentric zones of texture; zones with whitish and grayish shades. **Pore Surface:** Whitish, becoming a little brownish with age; with 1–3 angular pores per mm; pores becoming elongated with maturity and often approaching a tooth-like condition; tubes to 1 mm deep. **Flesh:** Insubstantial; whitish; tough and corky. **Odor and Taste:** Not distinctive. **Spore Print:** White. **Microscopic Features:** Spores 5.5–8.5 × 2.5–3.5 µm; smooth; cylindric. Cystidia and setae absent. Hyphal system trimitic. **Comments:** The grayish colors, fuzzy cap, pore surface with 1–3 pores per mm, and tendency for the pores to become irregular and nearly tooth-like with age are good field characters. *Trametes hirsuta* is similar but has smaller pores that do not become tooth-like.

TREMELLA FOLIACEA PERSOON

Ecology: Possibly parasitic on the mycelium or fruiting bodies of crust fungi, and/or possibly saprobic on the decaying wood of hardwoods (especially oaks); summer and fall; widely distributed. **Fruiting Body:** Firm and gelatinous; 3–12 cm across; composed of many leaf-like lobes; brown to reddish brown; blackening with age or when dried out; surfaces bald; without a stem. **Microscopic Features:** Spores 8–13 × 7–9 µm; ovoid; smooth. Basidia 4-spored; becoming longitudinally septate (cruciate) with maturity. Clamp connections present. **Comments:** The large fruiting body composed of many leaf-like lobes is distinctive. Compare with *Auricularia auricula* (p. 105).

TREMELLA FUCIFORMIS BERKELEY

Ecology: Possibly parasitic on the mycelium of *Hypoxylon archeri* (an ascomycete that forms small carbon-like balls on deadwood), or potentially saprobic on the deadwood of hardwoods and involved in an undetermined symbiosis with the *Hypoxylon*; growing alone or gregariously with *Hypoxylon* fruiting bodies frequently nearby; summer and fall; primarily tropical and subtropical in distribution, but recorded from Missouri, Indiana, and Kansas. **Fruiting Body:** Gelatinous, but fairly firm; composed of graceful lobes; translucent; whitish; up to about 7 cm across and 4 cm high; surface bald and shiny. **Microscopic Features:** Spores 7–14 × 5–8.5 µm; ovoid; smooth. Basidia 4-spored; becoming longitudinally septate (cruciate) with maturity. Clamp connections present. **Comments:** The graceful lobes and translucent large fruiting bodies characterize this species. Compare with *Ductifera pululahuana* (p. 170), which is more glob-like, usually less translucent, and differs microscopically.

TREMELLA MESENTERICA RETZIUS

Ecology: Parasitic on the mycelium of species of *Peniophora* (resupinate crust fungi); found on the decaying sticks and logs of oaks and other hardwoods, usually when bark is still attached; growing in amorphous clusters; spring, summer, fall, and during winter warm spells; widely distributed. **Fruiting Body:** Gelatinous; when young and fresh, composed of

Photo by Andy Methven

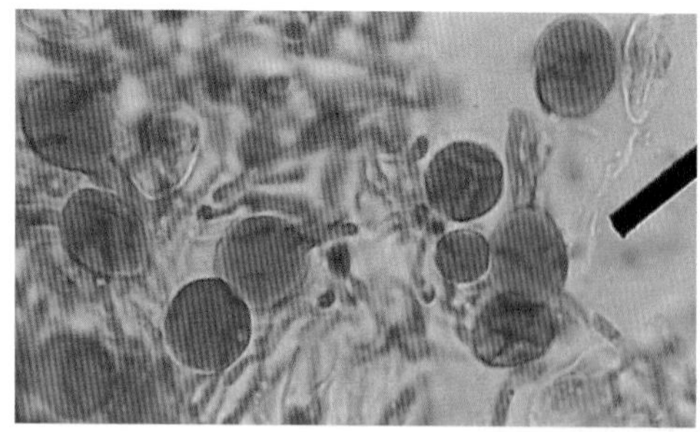
Basidia

lobes or brain-like sections, but rather formless in age or in wet weather; up to about 5 cm across; orange to yellow, fading when mature or when wet; without a stem; sometimes becoming tough and crust-like when dried out. **Microscopic Features:** Spores 10–15.5 × 7–12 µm; ellipsoid to oval; smooth. Basidia 4-sterigmate; longitudinally septate. **Comments:** Several species of jelly fungi are very similar; microscopic analysis may be required to identify this species with confidence.

TREMELLA RETICULATA (BERKELEY) FARLOW

Ecology: Probably mycorrhizal; growing terrestrially (often near stumps) or on well-rotted wood in hardwood forests (especially under oaks); summer and fall; widely distributed. **Fruiting Body:** Gelatinous, but fairly firm; when young and fresh, composed of flattened lobes or sections arising from a more or less central area; with age the lobes developing into hollow, finger-like branches; up to 8 cm high and 15 cm across; with a bald surface; white, becoming creamy or slightly brownish with age. **Spore Print:** White. **Microscopic Features:** Spores 9–11 × 5–7 µm; more or less ellipsoid; smooth. Basidia 4-spored; becoming longitudinally septate (cruciate) with maturity. **Comments:** Also known as *Sebacina sparassoidea*.

Photo by Ron Kerner

TREMELLODENDRON PALLIDUM BURT

Ecology: Probably mycorrhizal; growing alone or gregariously on the ground under hardwoods; spring through late fall; widely distributed. **Fruiting Body:** A mass of flattened and fused branches; up to 12 cm high and 15 cm across; white, but often developing sordid colors in age, or greenish hues from algae; flesh very tough and cartilaginous. **Spore Print:** White. **Microscopic Features:** Spores 7–12.5 × 4–6 µm; allantoid; smooth. Basidia longitudinally septate; ovoid. **Comments:** This coral mushroom is closely related to the jelly fungi, despite its tough consistency. Compare with *Clavulina cristata* (p. 139) and *Ramariopsis kunzei* (p. 333), which are not tough and cartilaginous.

TRICHAPTUM BIFORME (FRIES) RYVARDEN

Photo by Melissa Bochte

Ecology: Saprobic; growing in overlapping clusters on hardwood logs and stumps; causing a straw-colored sapwood rot in standing trees; late spring, summer, and fall; widely distributed. **Cap:** Up to 6 cm across and 3 mm thick; more or less semicircular, irregularly bracket-shaped, or kidney-shaped; flattened-convex; hairy, finely hairy or bald; with zones of whitish to grayish-white colors; the margin sometimes purple to pale lilac. **Pore Surface:** Purple to lilac, with the strongest shades near the margin; fading to buff or brownish in age; with 3–5 angular pores per mm; usually eroding and developing spines or teeth with maturity (sometimes when old appearing more like a toothed mushroom than a polypore); not bruising. **Stem:** Absent. **Flesh:** Whitish; tough and leathery. **Chemical Reactions:** KOH negative to pale yellowish on flesh and cap. **Spore Print:** White. **Microscopic Features:** Spores 6–8 × 2–2.5 µm; smooth; cylindric to slightly allantoid; inamyloid. Cystidia abundant; more or less fusoid; apically encrusted. Hyphal system dimitic. **Comments:** Easily recognized when fresh and still purple on the pore surface, but rather nondescript when faded.

TRICHOLOMA AURANTIUM (SCHAEFFER) RICKEN

Ecology: Mycorrhizal with conifers; growing scattered or gregariously, sometimes in clusters; summer and fall; widely distributed. **Cap:** 3–9 cm; broadly convex or nearly flat; slimy or sticky when fresh; orange to dull reddish orange, bruising dark red; bald, or with scattered, appressed fibers and scales; the margin initially inrolled. **Gills:** Attached to the stem, often by means of a notch; close; whitish, developing brown to reddish-brown discolorations. **Stem:** 4–8 cm long; 1–2 cm thick; more or less equal, or tapering to the base; covered with dense orangish scales that terminate in a line near the apex; white above the line; often hollowing. **Flesh:** White; not changing on exposure. **Odor and Taste:** Mealy. **Chemical Reactions:** KOH red on cap. **Spore Print:** White. **Microscopic Features:** Spores 5–6 × 3–4 µm; smooth; ellipsoid; inamyloid. Clamp connections absent. **Comments:** The dense orange scales that terminate in a line near the stem apex are distinctive.

TRICHOLOMA CALIGATUM (VIVIANI) RICKEN

Ecology: Mycorrhizal with hardwoods, especially oaks; growing scattered or gregariously, sometimes in clusters; late summer and fall; widely distributed. **Cap:** 4–12 cm; broadly convex or nearly flat; dry; white, overlaid with prominent tan to dark brown fibers and scales. **Gills:** Attached to the stem; close; white, developing brown stains and spots with age. **Stem:** 4–9 cm long; 1–3 cm thick; more or less equal; white above the ring, covered with brown fibers and scales below; dry; partial veil white and tissue-like, collapsing to form a prominent ring with a white upper edge and a brownish lower edge. **Flesh:** White; not changing on exposure. **Odor and Taste:** Taste usually bitter; odor mealy, unpleasant, or not distinctive. **Chemical Reactions:** KOH negative on cap. **Spore Print:** White. **Microscopic Features:** Spores 5–8 × 4.5–5 µm; smooth; ellipsoid; inamyloid. Clamp connections absent. **Comments:** Also known as *Armillaria caligata*. Compare with the matsutake, *Tricholoma magnivelare* (p. 377), which has a pleasantly spicy odor and taste and grows under conifers. *Tricholoma caligatum* is also illustrated on the back cover.

Photo by Ron Kerner

TRICHOLOMA EQUESTRE (LINNAEUS) KUMMER

Ecology: Mycorrhizal with pines; growing scattered or gregariously; fall; widely distributed. **Cap:** 3–12 cm; broadly convex or nearly flat; sticky when fresh, but often dry when collected; bright yellow when young and fresh, often with an olive-brown or brownish center; becoming yellow brown by maturity; bald, or with a few appressed fibers over the center (but not prominently overlaid with blackish radiating fibers); the margin initially rolled under. **Gills:** Attached to the stem, often by means of a notch; close; pale to bright yellow. **Stem:** 2–10 cm long; up to 2 cm thick; more or less equal, or with an enlarged base; bald or very finely hairy; pale yellow or whitish near the apex, yellow below; often discoloring yellow brown, especially near the base. **Flesh:** White to very pale yellow near the cap surface; not changing on exposure. **Odor and Taste:** Mealy, or not distinctive. **Spore Print:** White. **Chemical Reactions:** KOH reddish or negative on cap. **Microscopic Features:** Spores 5–8.5 × 3–6 µm;

smooth; ellipsoid; inamyloid. Clamp connections absent. **Comments:** Also known as *Tricholoma flavovirens*. Possibly poisonous; the European version of this species has been documented to be seriously toxic. The growth under pines, the bright yellow cap that becomes brownish with age, and the yellow gills are good field characters. Compare with *Tricholoma sejunctum* (p. 379), which has a greenish-yellow cap that is prominently overlaid with blackish fibers.

TRICHOLOMA FULVUM
(FRIES) BIGEARD & H. GUILLEMIN

Ecology: Mycorrhizal with various hardwoods; often found in moss; growing alone, scattered, or gregariously; summer and fall; widely distributed. **Cap:** 3–10.5 cm; convex, becoming broadly convex to nearly flat when mature; sticky when fresh, but soon dry; bald, or with appressed fibers over the center; yellow brown to reddish brown; often paler toward the margin; sometimes becoming minutely pitted with age. **Gills:** Attached to the stem by a notch; close; pale yellow; sometimes discoloring and spotting reddish brown. **Stem:** 2–7 cm long; 0.5–1.5 cm thick; more or less equal, or somewhat swollen below; finely silky; at first creamy to yellowish; developing reddish-brown to brown colors, except at the apex. **Flesh:** Whitish to pale yellow; not changing on exposure. **Odor and Taste:** Mealy. **Spore Print:** White. **Chemical Reactions:** KOH reddish brown to brownish red on cap. **Microscopic Features:** Spores 5.5–7 × 4–6 µm; smooth; ellipsoid; inamyloid. Clamp connections absent. **Comments:** The midwestern representative from this species group may not be the same as the European version.

TRICHOLOMA MAGNIVELARE
(PECK) REDHEAD

Ecology: Mycorrhizal with jack pine; growing scattered or gregariously; summer and fall; northern Midwest. **Cap:** 5–20 cm; convex, becoming broadly convex or nearly flat; dry, or a little sticky; white at first; soon with brownish discolorations and pressed-down fibers; the margin rolled under when young. **Gills:** Attached to the stem, sometimes by means of a notch; crowded; white, developing brown or reddish-brown stains and spots with age. **Stem:** 4–15 cm long; up to 5 cm thick; more or less equal, or with a slightly tapered base; white above the ring, colored

Photo by Noah Siegel

like the cap below; partial veil white and thick, collapsing to form a sheath around the lower stem and a prominent flaring ring at the top edge of the sheath. **Flesh:** White; firm; not changing on exposure. **Odor and Taste:** Taste pleasant and spicy; odor strong, fragrant, and distinctive, somewhat reminiscent of cinnamon. **Spore Print:** White. **Microscopic Features:** Spores 5–7 × 4–6 µm; smooth; ellipsoid; inamyloid. Clamp connections absent. **Comments:** Edible and popular; often called the "matsutake." Also known as *Armillaria ponderosa*. Compare with *Tricholoma caligatum* (p. 376). *Catathelasma ventricosum* is somewhat similar but features a rooting stem with a double ring, an indistinct odor, and amyloid spores; it grows under various conifers and is not limited to jack pine.

TRICHOLOMA ODORUM PECK

Ecology: Mycorrhizal with hardwoods in oak-hickory or beech-maple forests; usually growing gregariously, sometimes in loose clusters; late summer and fall; widely distributed. **Cap:** 2–9 cm; broadly convex or nearly flat, often with a shallow central bump; dry; bald or very finely velvety; pale yellowish or pale greenish when young, but usually becoming pale tan or buff fairly quickly. **Gills:** Attached to the stem, often by means of a notch; close; yellow to pale yellow when young, often fading to buff by maturity (but occasionally demonstrating a pinkish cast); not bruising or discoloring. **Stem:** 3–11 cm long; up to 1.5 cm thick; more or less equal; light greenish or light yellowish when young, usually remaining at least slightly yellowish into maturity; sometimes discoloring brownish. **Flesh:** Pale yellowish to whitish; not changing on exposure. **Odor and Taste:** Taste mealy; odor strong and foul, reminiscent of coal tar or swamp gas. **Spore Print:** White. **Chemical Reactions:** KOH negative or pinkish on cap. **Microscopic Features:** Spores 9.5–11.5 × 5–7 µm; smooth; amygdaliform; inamyloid. Clamp connections present. **Comments:** The strong, unpleasant odor and fading shades of yellow are good field characters. *Tricholoma sulphurescens* is similar and also smells foul; it bruises and stains yellow, however, while the yellow shades in *Tricholoma odorum* are innate.

TRICHOLOMA PESSUNDATUM (FRIES) QUÉLET

Ecology: Mycorrhizal with various hardwoods and conifers; growing alone, scattered, or gregariously; summer and fall; widely distributed. **Cap:** 2.5–10 cm; convex, becoming broadly convex, broadly bell-shaped, or nearly flat; sticky when fresh, but soon dry; bald or very finely hairy; brown to reddish brown over the center, and paler (often yellowish brown) toward the margin, or eventually more or less reddish brown overall. **Gills:** Attached to the stem by a notch; close; whitish when young, developing brown to yellowish-brown or reddish-brown spots and discolorations and eventually becoming reddish brown overall. **Stem:** 2–7 cm long; 0.5–2 cm thick; more or less equal; finely silky; whitish, discoloring brown to brownish or reddish brown from the base upward. **Flesh:** Whitish; not changing on exposure. **Odor and Taste:** Mealy. **Spore Print:** White. **Chemical Reactions:** KOH reddish brown, orangish brown, or negative on cap. **Microscopic Features:** Spores 5–8 × 3–5 µm; smooth; ellipsoid; inamyloid. Clamp connections absent. **Comments:** Members of this species group feature brown to reddish-brown sticky caps, whitish gills that develop brown to reddish-brown spots and discolorations, and a mealy odor.

TRICHOLOMA SEJUNCTUM (SOWERBY) QUÉLET

Ecology: Mycorrhizal with hardwoods or conifers; growing scattered or gregariously; late summer and fall; widely distributed. **Cap:** 5–7.5 cm; broadly convex, flat, or with a central knob; sticky or dry; yellowish to yellowish olive; with dark, radiating, appressed fibers (especially over the center); the margin often somewhat inrolled when young. **Gills:** Attached to the stem by a notch; close; white, developing yellow tinges near the cap margin in age. **Stem:** 5–10 cm long; 1–2 cm thick; equal; bald; dry; whitish or with yellow tinges. **Flesh:** White; not changing on exposure. **Odor and Taste:** Mealy. **Chemical Reactions:** KOH negative on cap. **Spore Print:** White. **Microscopic Features:** Spores 5–7.5 × 4–6 µm; smooth; ellipsoid to oval; inamyloid. Clamp connections absent. **Comments:** Possibly poisonous. Compare with *Tricholoma equestre* (p. 376).

TRICHOLOMA SQUARRULOSUM BRESÀDOLA

Ecology: Mycorrhizal with various hardwoods; growing alone, scattered, or gregariously; fall; Great Lakes region. **Cap:** 2–10 cm; broadly convex to nearly flat when mature; dry; grayish underneath a dense covering of dark gray to nearly black fibrils and scales; the margin inrolled and hairy when young. **Gills:** Attached to the

stem by a notch; close; whitish to dull grayish, often becoming flushed with pink; not infrequently discoloring gray on the edges. **Stem:** 4–8 cm long; 0.5–1.5 cm thick; more or less equal, or somewhat swollen below; with gray to nearly black fibrils and scales over a grayish to whitish ground color; dry. **Flesh:** Pale grayish; not changing on exposure. **Odor and Taste:** Mealy to disagreeably mealy. **Spore Print:** White. **Chemical Reactions:** KOH negative on cap. **Microscopic Features:** Spores 6–7 × 3.5–5 µm; smooth; ellipsoid; inamyloid. Clamp connections absent. **Comments:** The gray fibrils and scales on both the cap and the stem, along with the mealy odor and the habitat under hardwoods, are good field characters.

TRICHOLOMA SUBRESPLENDENS (MURRILL) MURRILL

Ecology: Mycorrhizal with hardwoods in oak-hickory and beech-maple forests, or under paper birch; growing scattered or gregariously, sometimes in clusters; late summer and fall; widely distributed. **Cap:** 3–11 cm; broadly convex, flat, or with a central knob; sticky when fresh and young, but soon dry; white, often with tan shades over the center or elsewhere; bald or with minute, appressed hairs (especially over the center); sometimes bruising and discoloring bluish. **Gills:** Attached to the stem by a notch; close; white. **Stem:** 4–11 cm long; 1–2.5 cm thick; equal or somewhat swollen below; with silky appressed fibers; dry; white; sometimes bruising or discoloring bluish, especially near the base. **Flesh:** White; not changing on exposure. **Odor and Taste:** Mealy, or not distinctive. **Spore Print:** White. **Chemical Reactions:** KOH negative on cap. **Microscopic Features:** Spores 5–7 × 4–5 µm; smooth; ellipsoid; inamyloid. Clamp connections present at the bases of basidia and basidioles. **Comments:** The white colors and the faint blue staining on the cap and stem characterize this species. Compare with *Hygrophorus sordidus* (p. 216).

TRICHOLOMA VENENATUM ATKINSON

Ecology: Mycorrhizal with hardwoods in oak-hickory and beech-maple forests; growing scattered or gregariously, sometimes in clusters; usually fruiting in summer and fall, but sometimes collected in late spring or early summer; widely distributed. **Cap:** 2.5–7 cm; broadly convex, flat, or broadly bell-shaped; dry; white, overlaid with appressed tan to brown fibrils and scales, which radiate from the center; white on the margin. **Gills:** Attached to the stem by a notch; close; white; not discoloring. **Stem:** 3–6 cm long; 1–2 cm thick; equal or somewhat swollen below; silky; dry; white to buff, becoming dingy with age. **Flesh:** White; not changing on exposure. **Odor and Taste:** Mealy. **Spore Print:** White. **Microscopic Features:** Spores 7.5–8.5 × 5–7 µm; smooth; ellipsoid; inamyloid. Clamp connections present. **Comments:** Possibly poisonous. The brownish fibers radiating over the whitish cap and the mealy odor characterize this species.

TRICHOLOMOPSIS RUTILANS (SCHAEFFER) SINGER

Ecology: Saprobic on the deadwood of conifers; occasionally found in woodchips, sawdust, and lignin-rich soil; growing alone, scattered, or in small troops; summer and fall; widely distributed. **Cap:** 3–12 cm; convex, with an incurved margin, becoming broadly convex, broadly bell-shaped, or nearly flat; dry; densely covered with red to purplish-red or brick-red fibrils; with maturity the fibrils aggregating into small scales, and the yellow ground color beneath showing through. **Gills:** Attached to the stem; close or crowded; yellow. **Stem:** 4–12 cm long; up to 2 cm thick; yellow, covered with red fibrils like those on the cap, but often more sparsely, especially in age; with a bald yellow zone at the extreme apex. **Flesh:** Yellow to pale yellow. **Odor and Taste:** Odor fragrant or not distinctive; taste mild or slightly radish-like. **Chemical Reactions:**

KOH red on cap. **Spore Print:** White. **Microscopic Features:** Spores 5–7 × 3–5 µm; smooth; broadly ellipsoid; inamyloid. Pleurocystidia and cheilocystidia present. Pileipellis a cutis. **Comments:** The fibrillose red to purple-red cap, the yellow gills, and the habitat on conifer wood distinguish this species.

Spore print

TYLOPILUS ALBOATER (SCHWEINITZ) MURRILL

Ecology: Mycorrhizal with hardwoods (especially oaks); growing alone or scattered; summer and fall; widely distributed. **Cap:** 3–15 cm; convex, becoming broadly convex or flat; dry; finely velvety; sometimes with a white dusting when young; black or dark grayish brown; often darkening on handling. **Pore Surface:** Whitish becoming pinkish; bruising red, then brown to black; pores angular, 2 per mm; tubes to 1 cm deep. **Stem:** 4–10 cm long; 2–4 cm thick; more or less equal, or enlarging toward base; colored like the cap or paler; sometimes with a white dusting; bald; not reticulate, or merely finely so near the apex; darkening on handling. **Flesh:** Thick and white; discoloring pinkish on exposure to air, then turning slowly grayish; black in the stem base. **Odor and Taste:** Not distinctive. **Chemical Reactions:** Ammonia negative on cap and flesh. KOH red to black on cap; negative to dark pink on flesh. Iron salts bluish green on cap; blue to blue green on flesh. **Spore Print:** Pink. **Microscopic Features:** Spores 7–11 × 3.5–5 µm; fusiform to subfusiform; smooth. Pileipellis a cutis. **Comments:** Edible. Compare with *Tylopilus sordidus* (p. 385), which stains blue and has a brownish pore surface when mature.

TYLOPILUS BALLOUII (PECK) SINGER

Ecology: Mycorrhizal with hardwoods, especially oaks and beech; growing alone, scattered, or gregariously; summer and fall; primarily distributed below the Great Lakes. **Cap:** 5–12 cm; convex, becoming broadly convex or nearly flat in age; dry; bald or finely velvety; bright reddish orange when young, soon fading to reddish brown, cinnamon brown, or tan. **Pore**

Photo by Martin Livezey

Surface: Creamy whitish; bruising brown; eventually brownish; pores circular, 1–2 per mm; tubes to 1 cm deep. **Stem:** 2.5–12 cm long; up to 2.5 cm thick; equal or with a swollen base; dry; smooth or finely reticulate near the apex; orangish when young, but soon pale orange, yellowish, or whitish. **Flesh:** White; soft; unchanging when sliced. **Odor and Taste:** Taste mild or slightly bitter; odor not distinctive. **Spore Print:** Pale brown to reddish brown or purplish brown. **Microscopic Features:** Spores 8–10 × 4–5 µm; ovoid to ellipsoid; smooth. Pileipellis a cutis or ixocutis. **Comments:** The orange cap and brown-bruising pore surface are good field characters.

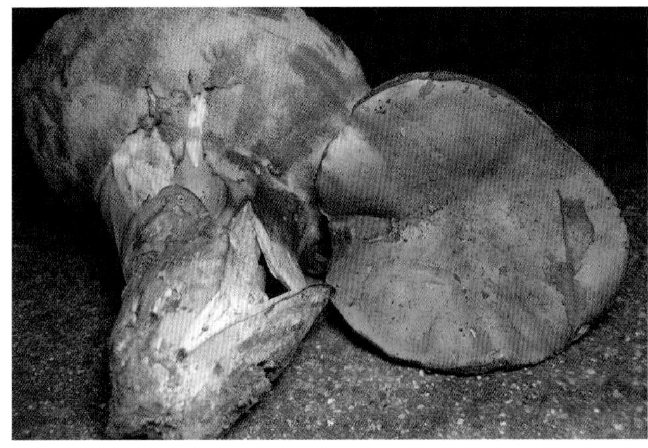

TYLOPILUS FELLEUS (BULLIARD) KARSTEN

Ecology: Mycorrhizal with conifers and, infrequently, with hardwoods; growing alone or scattered; summer and fall; widely distributed, but more common where conifers occur naturally. **Cap:** 5–30 cm; convex to broadly convex or nearly flat in age; dry; bald, unpolished; sometimes becoming cracked; brown to tan, usually with cinnamon shades, becoming paler in age. **Pore Surface:** Whitish, becoming pinkish to pink; sometimes bruising brownish; pores circular, 1–2 per mm; tubes to 2 cm deep. **Stem:** 4–20 cm long; 1–3 cm thick; club-shaped and bulbous; pale above, colored like the cap downward, or brown overall; strongly reticulate, at least over upper third; sometimes with olive stains in age. **Flesh:** Thick and white; unchanging or staining pinkish. **Odor and Taste:** Taste very bitter; odor not distinctive. **Chemical Reactions:** Ammonia negative to pale orange on cap; negative on flesh. KOH reddish orange on cap; yellow on flesh. Iron salts negative on cap; pale gray on flesh. **Spore Print:** Pink to pinkish tan. **Microscopic Features:** Spores 11–17 × 3–5 µm; fusiform to subfusiform; smooth. Pileipellis a cutis. **Comments:** The bitter taste, strongly reticulate stem, and pinkish mature pore surface are good field characters.

TYLOPILUS INDECISUS (PECK) MURRILL

Ecology: Mycorrhizal with hardwoods (especially oaks); growing alone, scattered, or gregariously; summer and fall; widely distributed. **Cap:** 5–17 cm; convex to broadly convex or nearly flat in age; dry; bald or finely felty; brown to tan, usually with cinnamon shades. **Pore Surface:** White, becoming pinkish, and eventually nearly brownish; bruising brown; pores angular, 2 per mm; tubes to 12 mm deep. **Stem:**

4–10 cm long; 1–3 cm thick; more or less equal; whitish when young; bruising and discoloring brownish; bald; sometimes very finely reticulate near the apex. **Flesh:** Thick and white; staining pinkish to brownish on exposure. **Odor and Taste:** Not distinctive. **Chemical Reactions:** Ammonia negative to reddish or yellowish on cap; negative on flesh. KOH black on cap; negative to pale orangish on flesh. Iron salts dark gray on cap; negative to greenish or bluish on flesh. **Spore Print:** Flesh-colored to pinkish brown. **Microscopic Features:** Spores 10–15 × 3–5 µm; smooth; fusiform to subfusiform. Pileipellis a cutis. **Comments:** Field characters include the pinkish mature pore surface, which bruises brown, the mild taste, and the nonreticulate stem that does not develop olive shades. Compare with *Tylopilus rubrobrunneus* (p. 385), which is bitter and features a longer, club-shaped stem that discolors olive with age.

TYLOPILUS PLUMBEOVIOLACEUS (SNELL & E. A. DICK) SNELL & E. A. DICK

Ecology: Mycorrhizal with hardwoods (especially oaks); growing scattered or gregariously; summer and fall; widely distributed. **Cap:** 4–15 cm; convex, becoming broadly convex or nearly flat in age; dry; bald or finely velvety when young; sometimes dusted with whitish powder; dark purple or purple brown when young, becoming brown, purplish gray, brown, cinnamon, or tan. **Pore Surface:** Whitish, becoming pinkish; not bruising; pores circular, 1–2 per mm; tubes to 2 cm deep. **Stem:** 8–12 cm long; 1–2 cm thick; more or less equal, or enlarging toward base; purple when young (sometimes somewhat mottled, with whitish areas), fading to purplish gray or purplish brown (but hints of purple usually remain as the mushroom develops); sometimes bruising or staining olive; bald; sometimes very finely reticulate near the apex. **Flesh:** White; unchanging when sliced. **Odor and Taste:** Taste very bitter; odor not distinctive. **Chemical Reactions:** KOH orange on cap. Iron salts pink on flesh. **Spore Print:** Pinkish brown. **Microscopic Features:** Spores 10–13 × 3–4 µm; fusiform to subfusiform; smooth. Pileipellis a cutis. **Comments:** Compare with *Tylopilus rubrobrunneus* (p. 385), which never features purple colors on the stem.

Photo by Walt Sturgeon

TYLOPILUS RUBROBRUNNEUS MAZZER & A. H. SMITH

Ecology: Mycorrhizal with hardwoods (especially oaks and beech), but also reported in mixed woods and under hemlock; growing alone, scattered, or gregariously; summer and fall; widely distributed. **Cap:** 8–30 cm; convex, becoming broadly convex or nearly flat in age; dry; bald or finely felty; sometimes becoming cracked; the margin inrolled at first; dark purple or purple brown when young, quickly becoming purplish brown, brown, cinnamon, or tan. **Pore Surface:** Whitish at first, becoming pinkish and finally dingy brown; bruising brownish; pores circular, 1–2 per mm; tubes to 20 mm deep. **Stem:** 6–20 cm long; 1–5 cm thick; more or less equal when young, but usually enlarging toward the base with maturity; whitish to brownish or purplish; typically developing olive-brown stains or bruising this color; bald; sometimes very finely reticulate near the apex. **Flesh:** Thick and white; sometimes discoloring olive around worm holes. **Odor and Taste:** Taste very bitter; odor not distinctive. **Chemical Reactions:** Ammonia negative to yellowish on cap; negative on flesh. KOH rusty orange to orangish on cap; negative on flesh. Iron salts negative on cap; negative to pinkish on flesh. **Spore Print:** Dull pinkish to reddish brown. **Microscopic Features:** Spores 10–14 × 3–4.5 µm; nearly oblong, or fusoid; smooth. Pileipellis of mostly erect, cylindric elements with rounded or subclavate apices. **Comments:** This is one of the most common summer boletes in the Midwest's oak-hickory forests. Field characters include the bitter taste, purple and then brown cap, brown-staining pore surface, and large stem that develops olive stains. Compare with *Tylopilus indecisus* (p. 383), *Tylopilus plumbeoviolaceus* (p. 384), and *Xanthoconium purpureum* (p. 391).

TYLOPILUS SORDIDUS (FROST) A. H. SMITH & THIERS

Ecology: Mycorrhizal with hardwoods and conifers; growing alone or scattered; often found in disturbed-ground settings like roadsides, ditches, and so on; summer and fall; widely distributed. **Cap:** 2–5 cm; convex, becoming broadly convex or nearly flat in age; dry; finely velvety when young, typically cracking and splitting with maturity, exposing whit-

ish flesh that may stain pinkish or bluish; dark brown to grayish, often with bluish tints by maturity, at least near the margin. **Pore Surface:** Whitish to yellowish at first, becoming brown to reddish brown; bruising blue, then reddish brown; pores circular, 1–2 per mm; tubes to 1 cm deep. **Stem:** 4–8 cm long; up to 1 cm thick; more or less equal; colored like the cap; not reticulate. **Flesh:** White; staining pinkish to red and/or blue when sliced. **Odor and Taste:** Taste mild; odor not distinctive, or slightly bleach-like. **Chemical Reactions:** Ammonia dark purple or black on cap (sometimes after a red stage); bluish, then yellowish to orangish on flesh. KOH red to pinkish or negative on cap; orangish on flesh. Iron salts negative on cap; bluish to greenish or negative on flesh. **Spore Print:** Brown to reddish brown or purplish brown. **Microscopic Features:** Spores 10–17 × 4–8 µm; subfusoid to ellipsoid; smooth. Pileipellis a cutis with occasional cystidioid elements. **Comments:** The grayish-brown cap, whitish and then brownish pore surface, and blue staining are good field characters. Compare with *Tylopilus alboater* (p. 382).

Photo by Dan Molter

TYROMYCES CHIONEUS (FRIES) KARSTEN

Ecology: Saprobic on the deadwood of hardwoods; causing a white rot; annual; growing alone or with 2 or 3 other fruiting bodies; summer and fall; widely distributed. **Cap:** Up to 12 cm across; convex; semicircular to kidney-shaped; very finely velvety at first, becoming bald and, in old age, developing a crusty surface that becomes wrinkled or shriveled; white to off-white or, in age, yellowish to brownish; soft. **Pore Surface:** White, becoming yellowish in old age or when dried out; not bruising appreciably; with 3–5 circular to angular pores per mm; tubes to 8 mm deep. **Stem:** Absent. **Flesh:** White; soft and watery when fresh. **Odor and Taste:** Odor fragrant when fresh; taste not distinctive, or slightly bitter. **Chemical Reactions:** KOH negative on cap and flesh. **Spore Print:** White. **Microscopic Features:** Spores 4–5 × 1.5–2 µm; smooth; cylindric to slightly allantoid. Cystidia and setae absent, but fusoid cystidioles present. Hyphal system dimitic. **Comments:** The whitish to pale brownish cap, fragrant odor, and soft flesh are good field characters for this species.

URNULA CRATERIUM (SCHWEINITZ) FRIES

Ecology: Saprobic on sticks and small logs (often buried) of hardwoods; growing alone, scattered, or in dense clusters; spring; widely distributed. **Fruiting Body:** 2–15 cm; shaped like a deep cup or an urn; the opening narrow at first, but soon expanding; the margin becoming torn and folded back; in age often splitting and breaking apart; dark brown on the outside (becoming darker with age), with blackish areas; usually black on the inner surface; outer surface rough and gritty when young, becoming bald; stem to 2.5 cm long, colored like the fruiting body and continuous with it, tough, black toward the base; flesh somewhat tough and leathery. **Microscopic Features:** Spores 24–36 × 10–15 µm; smooth, ellipsoid to subfusoid. **Comments:** Sometimes called the "devil's urn." This distinctive fungus is often encountered by morel hunters.

VASCELLUM CURTISII (BERKELEY) KREISEL

Ecology: Saprobic; growing alone, scattered, gregariously, or (usually) in small clusters; in grass, often in disturbed-ground areas like ditches; late summer and fall; widely distributed. **Fruiting Body:** Shaped like a small ball, 1–2 cm across, but frequently misshapen as a result of clustered growth; densely spiny when young; spines up to 5 mm long, often joined at their tips, and easily rubbing off; in maturity often fairly smooth, with a powdery coating; white, becoming pale brown; developing a small hole at the top; with a tiny sterile base, or appearing merely pinched together at the bottom; with a white, fleshy interior at first; later with yellowish to olive granular flesh, and eventually filled with brownish or purplish-brown spore dust. **Microscopic Features:** Spores 3–3.5 µm; globose; minutely spiny. Capillitial threads 3–7 µm wide; branching; both thin-walled elements and thick-walled elements present. **Comments:** Also known as *Lycoperdon curtisii*. Compare with *Lycoperdon marginatum* (p. 266), which is larger, grows in woods, and features shorter spines and an outer skin that sloughs away in chunks.

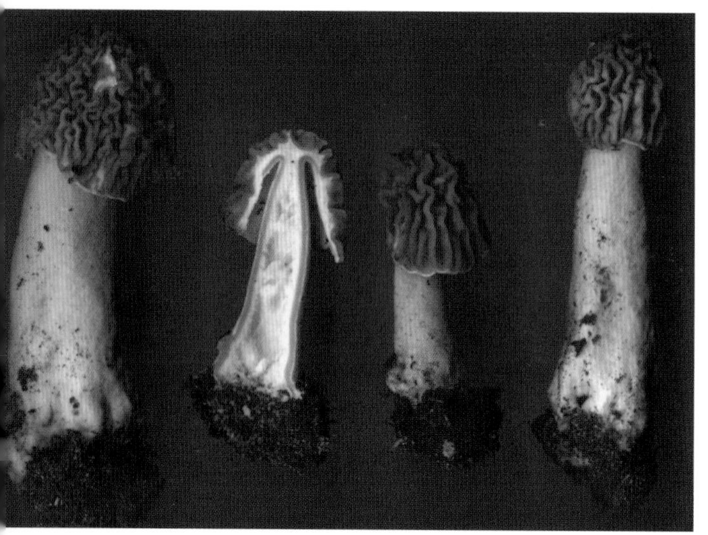

VERPA BOHEMICA (KROMBHOLZ) SCHRÖTER

Ecology: Potentially mycorrhizal and/or saprobic; found under hardwoods (and sometimes under conifers); early spring; northern Midwest. **Cap:** Attached only at the stem's apex; 1–5 cm; nearly conical or irregularly bell-shaped; deeply wrinkled longitudinally; occasionally appearing pitted; tan to brown to dark yellow brown. **Undersurface:** Whitish to brownish. **Stem:** 6–15 cm long; 0.5–3 cm thick; more or less equal; sometimes tapered upward or downward; creamy white, sometimes tinged with brown shades, frequently with darker granules forming belts of color. **Flesh:** Nearly nonexistent, or sometimes loosely stuffed; with wispy, cotton-candy-like fibers in the stem. **Odor and Taste:** Not distinctive. **Microscopic Features:** Spores 45–87 × 15–22 µm; smooth; elongated-ellipsoid; sometimes slightly curved; without oil droplets. Asci 2-spored. **Comments:** Mildly poisonous to some people. Compare with *Morchella punctipes* (p. 280).

VERPA CONICA (O. F. MÜLLER) SWARTZ

Ecology: Potentially mycorrhizal and/or saprobic; found under hardwoods in spring; widely distributed. **Cap:** Attached only at the stem's apex; 1.5–4 cm; convex or, more frequently, thimble-shaped; typically with a slightly outcurved margin when mature; tan to brown to dark brown; bald; tacky when wet; typically smooth or very slightly wrinkled at maturity, but sometimes broadly lumpy, wrinkled, or very finely ridged. **Undersurface:** Tan to brown to dark brown. **Stem:** 2.5–11 cm long; 0.5–1.5 cm thick; more or less equal; sometimes tapered toward the base; creamy white, sometimes tinged with brown shades. **Flesh:** Nearly nonexistent, or sometimes loosely stuffed; with wispy, cotton-candy-like fibers in the stem. **Odor and Taste:** Not distinctive. **Microscopic Features:** Spores 17–26 × 11–15 µm; smooth; ellipsoid; without oil droplets. Asci 8-spored. **Comments:** Not recommended for the table. The relatively smooth cap surface readily separates this species.

Photo by Dan Molter

VOLVARIELLA BOMBYCINA (SCHAEFFER) SINGER

Photo by Noah Siegel

Ecology: Saprobic on the wood of diverse hardwoods, either on dead trees or from the wounds of living trees; growing alone or gregariously; late spring, summer, and fall; widely distributed. **Cap:** 5–20 cm; oval at first, becoming bell-shaped to broadly convex or nearly flat; whitish or tinged yellowish to brownish in age; the margin not lined; dry; covered with silky hairs. **Gills:** Free from the stem; whitish, becoming pink; crowded. **Stem:** 6–20 cm long; 1–2 cm thick; more or less equal, but usually tapering somewhat to apex; dry; white; bald; without a ring; the base encased in a thick, white to yellowish or brown, sac-like volva. **Flesh:** White; unchanging. **Odor and Taste:** Not distinctive. **Chemical Reactions:** KOH negative on cap. **Spore Print:** Pink. **Microscopic Features:** Spores 6.5–10.5 × 4.5–7 µm; ellipsoid; smooth. Cystidia present; variously shaped. Pileipellis a cutis. **Comments:** The habitat on wood and the silky whitish to pale brownish cap identify this species. Compare with *Volvariella taylori* (p. 390) and *Volvariella volvacea* (p. 390).

VOLVARIELLA PUSILLA (PERSOON) SINGER

Ecology: Saprobic; growing alone or gregariously; usually found in gardens, lawns, woodchips, and so on, but also sometimes found in woods, at least in areas of disturbed ground (pathsides and so on); summer and fall; widely distributed. **Cap:** Up to 3.5 cm; oval at first, becoming convex to broadly convex or nearly flat; white, but sometimes very slightly darker over the center; the margin lined; slightly sticky when fresh, but soon dry. **Gills:** Free from the stem; whitish, becoming pink; close or nearly distant. **Stem:** 1–5 cm long; 1–3 mm thick; more or less equal; dry; white; bald; without a ring; the base encased in a thick, white to grayish, sac-like volva, which may be buried. **Flesh:** Thin; white; unchanging. **Odor and Taste:** Not distinctive. **Chemical Reactions:** KOH negative on cap. **Spore Print:** Pink. **Microscopic Features:** Spores 5.5–8 × 4–6 µm; ellipsoid; smooth. Pleurocystidia and cheilocystidia mostly fusoid-ventricose. Pileipellis a cutis. **Comments:** If the volva is missed, this species might be confused with *Conocybe apala* (p. 147), which has a pointed cap and brown, rather than pink, mature gills.

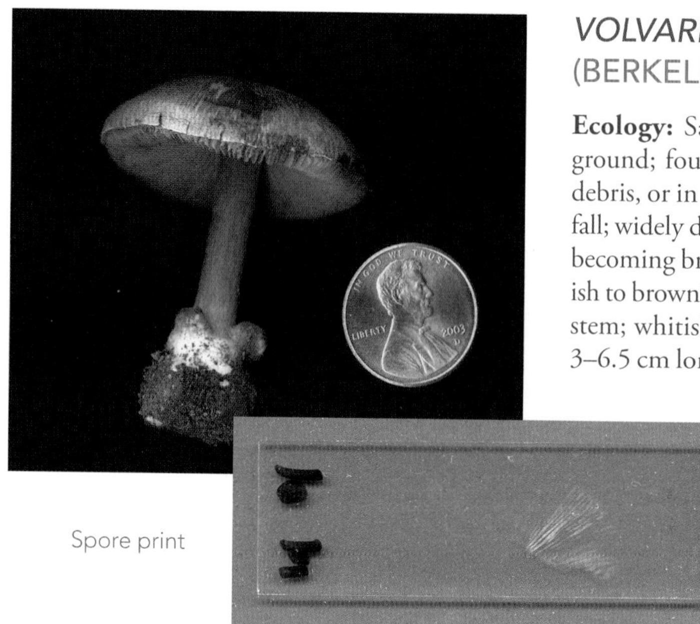

Spore print

VOLVARIELLA TAYLORI (BERKELEY & BROOME) SINGER

Ecology: Saprobic; growing alone or gregariously on the ground; found in woods, often near brush piles and woody debris, or in urban areas in grassy waste places; spring through fall; widely distributed. **Cap:** 2–6 cm; convex or broadly conic, becoming broadly convex to nearly flat; dry; finely hairy; grayish to brownish gray; the margin not lined. **Gills:** Free from the stem; whitish, becoming pink; close or nearly distant. **Stem:** 3–6.5 cm long; 3–7 mm thick; tapering gradually to the apex, with a slightly swollen base; dry; whitish or grayish; bald or, at the apex, finely hairy; the base encased in a thick, gray to brownish, sac-like volva. **Flesh:** White. **Odor and Taste:** Not distinctive, or radish-like. **Spore Print:** Pink. **Microscopic Features:** Spores 5.5–9 × 4–6 µm; ellipsoid; smooth. Pleurocystidia and cheilocystidia mostly fusoid-ventricose. Pileipellis a cutis. **Comments:** Compare with *Volvariella bombycina* (p. 389), which grows from wood and has a white to very pale brownish cap.

VOLVARIELLA VOLVACEA (BULLIARD) SINGER

Ecology: Saprobic; growing gregariously or in clusters; found in woodchips, greenhouses, gardens, compost piles, and similar locations; spring through fall (or over winter in greenhouses); widely distributed in introduced settings. **Cap:** 5–16 cm; egg-shaped when young, expanding to convex or broadly conic, becoming broadly convex or nearly flat; dry; radially streaked with hairs; gray to brownish gray or grayish brown or nearly black when young, with a paler marginal area; soft; the margin not lined, but often splitting with age. **Gills:** Free from the stem; white, becoming pink; close or nearly crowded. **Stem:** 4–14 cm long; up to 2 cm thick; tapering gradually to apex, with a swollen base; dry; whitish or brownish; silky; the base encased in a thick, sac-like volva that is brownish gray to nearly black above and whitish below. **Flesh:** White. **Odor and Taste:** Not distinctive. **Chemical Reactions:** KOH negative on cap. **Spore Print:** Pink. **Microscopic Features:** Spores

7–10.5 × 4.5–7 µm; more or less ellipsoid, or somewhat ovoid; smooth; inamyloid. Pleurocystidia and cheilocystidia variously shaped, but mostly fusoid-ventricose. Pileipellis a cutis. **Comments:** Edible; we have not tried it. This is a robust and distinctive *Volvariella* found in woodchips and other introduced settings.

VOLVOPLUTEUS GLOIOCEPHALUS (DE CANDOLLE) JUSTO

Ecology: Saprobic; growing alone or gregariously in gardens, lawns, woodchips, fields, and so on, but also found in woods; late spring to fall; widely distributed, but rare. **Cap:** 5–15 cm; oval at first, becoming convex to broadly convex or bell-shaped (occasionally nearly flat); bald; sticky when fresh; shiny when dry; white to grayish (sometimes whitish, but darker toward the center); the margin not lined. **Gills:** Free from the stem; whitish, becoming pink; close or crowded. **Stem:** 5–20 cm long; 1–2.5 cm thick; more or less equal; sometimes tapering slightly to top; dry; white; bald; without a ring; the base encased in a thick, white to grayish, sac-like volva that may be prominent or not and that may be buried. **Flesh:** Soft; white; unchanging. **Odor and Taste:** Not distinctive, or unpleasant. **Chemical Reactions:** KOH negative on cap. **Spore Print:** Pink to brownish pink. **Microscopic Features:** Spores 11.5–21 × 7–12.6 µm; ellipsoid; smooth. Pleuro- and cheilocystidia variously shaped (including fusoid, fusoid-ventricose, lanceolate, and clavate). Pileipellis an ixocutis. **Comments:** Also known as *Volvariella gloiocephala* and *Volvariella speciosa*, but recent DNA studies (Justo, Minnis, et al. 2011) support placing this species in a separate genus. Compare with *Amanita bisporigera* (p. 89), which features a ring and has a white spore print and white mature gills.

XANTHOCONIUM PURPUREUM SNELL & DICK

Ecology: Mycorrhizal with oaks; growing alone, scattered, or gregariously; early summer through fall; widely distributed. **Cap:** 3–7 cm, convex, becoming broadly convex; dry; bald or very minutely velvety; purplish red to maroon or reddish brown, fading to tan. **Pore Surface:** Whitish, becoming yellowish brown; not bruising, or bruising vaguely brownish; pores circular; tubes to 15 mm deep. **Stem:** 5–8 cm long; 0.5–1.5 cm thick; more or less equal; bald; not reticulate; pale at apex, streaked with the cap color below. **Flesh:**

Whitish; unchanging. **Odor and Taste:** Not distinctive in most specimens; odor often becoming foul (like bad meat) as the spores mature. **Chemical Reactions:** Ammonia sea green on cap, resolving to purplish; negative on flesh. KOH negative on cap and flesh. Iron salts negative on cap and flesh. **Spore Print:** Bright yellow brown. **Microscopic Features:** Spores 9–13 × 3–4 µm; smooth; subfusoid. Pileipellis hymeniform. **Comments:** The purplish-red to reddish-brown colors, absence of staining reactions, nonreticulate stem, yellow-brown spore print, and ammonia reaction are good identification characters. *Xanthoconium affine* (also known as *Boletus affinis*) is similar but brown; its cap does not turn green with ammonia. Compare with *Xanthoconium separans* (below), which has a cap that soon turns yellowish brown, a wrinkled to reticulate stem, and surfaces that turn green with KOH (as well as ammonia), and with *Tylopilus rubrobrunneus* (p. 385), which has a pinkish pore surface and bitter taste.

Photo by Dan Molter

XANTHOCONIUM SEPARANS (PECK) HALLING & BOTH

Ecology: Mycorrhizal with hardwoods (especially oaks); growing alone, scattered, or gregariously; summer and fall; widely distributed. **Cap:** 5–20 cm; convex, becoming broadly convex; dry; usually somewhat wrinkled; the margin often with a very small projecting sterile portion; color variable, but typically lilac brown or liver red when young, becoming yellowish brown in age. **Pore Surface:** White when young, becoming yellowish and finally brownish; not bruising; pores appearing "stuffed" when young; at maturity with 1–2 circular pores per mm; tubes to 3 cm deep. **Stem:** 6–15 cm long; 1–3 cm thick; more or less equal, or tapering somewhat to apex; solid; bald; usually wrinkled, and sometimes reticulate; pale at apex, but flushed with the color of the young cap below. **Flesh:** White; unchanging. **Odor and Taste:** Not distinctive. **Chemical Reactions:** Ammonia green on young, liver-hued caps; pinkish to red on older, yellow-brown caps; green on stem; pinkish to purplish or negative on flesh. KOH flashing green on cap; negative to grayish or pinkish on flesh. Iron salts gray on cap; negative to grayish on flesh. **Spore Print:** Brownish to pale reddish brown or yellowish brown. **Microscopic Features:** Spores 12–16 × 3.5–5 µm; smooth; subfusiform. Pileipellis hymeniform. **Comments:** Edible and very good when fresh and young. Compare with *Xanthoconium purpureum* (p. 391).

Photo by Lisa K. Suits

Ammonia on stem

XEROMPHALINA CAMPANELLA (BATSCH) MAIRE

Ecology: Saprobic on the deadwood of conifers; usually growing in dense clusters on stumps and logs, but occasionally growing alone or gregariously; spring through fall; widely distributed. **Cap:** 0.5–2.5 cm across; convex, becoming broadly convex, with a central depression and an arched margin; bald; dry; widely lined on the margin when wet; brownish yellow, rusty, yellowish, or orange; usually darker toward the center; fading. **Gills:** Running down the stem; fairly distant; usually with many cross-veins; pale yellow or orangish. **Stem:** 1–5 cm long; 1–3 mm thick; more or less equal; yellowish above, darker below; bald above, finely hairy at the base; rather wiry and tough; often curved. **Flesh:** Insubstantial. **Odor and Taste:** Not distinctive. **Spore Print:** White. **Microscopic Features:** Spores 5–8 × 3–4 µm; smooth; ellipsoid; weakly amyloid. Pleurocystidia and cheilocystidia fusiform. Caulocystidia clavate to fusiform. **Comments:** *Xeromphalina kauffmanii* is nearly identical but grows on the deadwood of hardwoods and has smaller spores. Compare with *Rickenella fibula* (p. 338).

XEROMPHALINA TENUIPES (SCHWEINITZ) A. H. SMITH

Photo by Melissa Bochte

Ecology: Saprobic on the deadwood and litter of hardwoods; growing alone, scattered, or gregariously either directly from wood or terrestrially in the vicinity of deadwood; spring and early summer; widely distributed. **Cap:** 2–7 cm across; convex, becoming broadly convex; very finely velvety or nearly bald; dry; widely lined on the margin when wet; orangish brown to brownish orange, with a slightly darker center. **Gills:** Broadly attached to the stem; close or nearly distant; whitish to yellowish; often forked. **Stem:** 5–8 cm long; 2–8 mm thick; more or less equal; brownish orange to orangish brown; prominently velvety-hairy; rather tough; sometimes rooting. **Flesh:** Brownish; unchanging. **Odor and Taste:** Odor not distinctive; taste not distinctive, or slightly bitter. **Chemical Reactions:** KOH dark

reddish brown on cap. **Spore Print:** White. **Microscopic Features:** Spores 6.5–8 × 3–4.5 µm; smooth; ellipsoid; weakly amyloid. Pleurocystidia clavate to fusiform. Cheilocystidia irregular; often contorted. Caulocystidia cylindric; thick-walled. **Comments:** The habitat (on deadwood or scattered around it), fuzzy stem, and overall aspect are good field characters. Compare with *Flammulina velutipes* (p. 177).

XERULA FURFURACEA
(PECK) REDHEAD, GINNS, & SHOEMAKER

Ecology: Saprobic on decaying debris of hardwoods, but not typically growing on logs or stumps unless they are well decomposed; usually terrestrial; spring through fall; widely distributed. **Cap:** 2–12 cm; convex to bell-shaped when young, becoming broadly convex to flat in age and typically retaining a central bump; smooth or, more often, wrinkled and puckered over the center; bald; greasy in normal weather conditions; dark brown to grayish brown or yellow brown, but not infrequently fading to brownish or buff; the margin incurved when young, sometimes uplifted in maturity, not lined. **Gills:** Attached to the stem or notched; close or nearly distant; whitish; thick; yellowish to brownish after being dried for the herbarium. **Stem:** 7–15 cm long above ground; 0.5–1.5 cm thick; tapering to the apex; usually finely hairy; white near the apex, but colored like the cap below; with maturity, the brown areas often stretch into snakeskin or chevron patterns; rather stiff; with a long, tapered taproot extending underground; the taproot sometimes bruising rusty brown. **Flesh:** Whitish; unchanging. **Odor and Taste:** Not distinctive. **Chemical Reactions:** KOH negative on cap. **Spore Print:** White. **Microscopic Features:** Spores 14–17 × 9.5–12 µm; smooth; inamyloid; ellipsoid to broadly ovoid. Cheilocystidia narrowly fusoid to fusoid-ventricose. Pleurocystidia fat-cylindric; thin-walled. Pileipellis hymeniform, with thin-walled pileocystidia. **Comments**: The long, underground root is a good feature for recognizing the genus. However, several species of *Xerula* are very similar and best differentiated with a microscope. Compare with *Xerula megalospora* (p. 395), which is generally smaller, has bright orange gills when dried, and has different microscopic features.

XERULA MEGALOSPORA (CLEMENTS) REDHEAD, GINNS, & SHOEMAKER

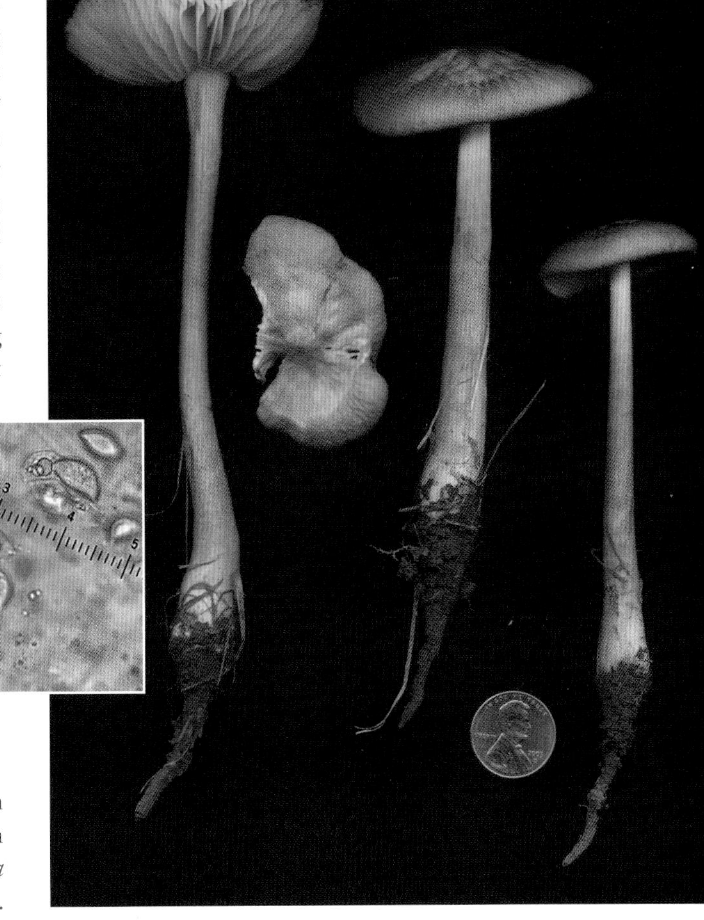

Ecology: Saprobic on decaying debris and roots of hardwoods, but not typically growing on logs or stumps unless they are well decomposed; usually terrestrial; spring through fall; widely distributed. **Cap:** 2–8 cm; convex or broadly conical when young, becoming broadly convex to flat in age; fairly smooth, or wrinkled in a zone around the center; bald; greasy in normal weather conditions; pale grayish brown to buff or nearly white; the margin often uplifted in maturity. **Gills:** Attached to the stem or notched; distant or nearly so; whitish; thick; bright orange after being dried. **Stem:** 6–13 cm long above ground; up to about 1 cm thick; tapering to the apex; bald; white; with a long, tapered taproot extending underground; the taproot sometimes bruising rusty brown. **Flesh:** Whitish; unchanging. **Odor and Taste:** Odor not distinctive, or reminiscent of carrots; taste not distinctive. **Chemical Reactions:** KOH negative on cap. **Spore Print:** White. **Microscopic Features:** Spores 18–23 × 10–14 µm; finely pitted; inamyloid; prominently limoniform to amygdaliform. Cheilocystidia usually conspicuously capitate. Pleurocystidia cylindric; thin-walled. Pileipellis hymeniform, with thin-walled pileocystidia. **Comments:** Compare with *Xerula furfuracea* (p. 394). A dried specimen of *Xerula megalospora*, featuring orange gills, is illustrated on p. 13.

Spores

XYLARIA LONGIPES NITSCHKE

Ecology: Saprobic on decaying hardwood logs and sticks (especially the debris of beech and maples), growing alone or gregariously, directly from the wood; causing a soft rot; spring through fall; widely distributed. **Fruiting Body:** 2–8 cm tall; up to 2 cm across; tough; shaped more or less like a club; with a rounded tip; grayish to brownish when young, becoming black with maturity; surface becoming finely, distinctively cracked and scaly in a mosaic pattern with maturity; stem usually proportionally long, but sometimes short or nearly absent.

Microscopic Features: Spores 13–15 × 5–7 µm; smooth; fusiform; with a spiral germ slit that runs the length of the spore. **Comments:** Compare with *Xylaria polymorpha* (below).

Photo by Charya Peou

XYLARIA POLYMORPHA (PERSOON) GREVILLE

Ecology: Saprobic on decaying hardwood stumps and logs, usually at or near the base of the stump; sometimes appearing terrestrial, but actually attached to buried wood; growing alone or, more commonly, in clusters; causing a soft rot of the wood; appearing in spring and not decaying until late summer or fall. **Fruiting Body:** 3–10 cm tall; up to 2.5 cm across; tough; shaped more or less like a club or a finger, but occasionally flattened; usually with a rounded tip; in spring coated with a pale to bluish or purplish dust of conidia (asexual spores), except at the whitish tip, but as the season progresses, becoming blackish with a pale tip and, eventually, black overall; surface becoming minutely pimpled and wrinkled with maturity. **Flesh:** Whitish; very tough. **Microscopic Features:** Spores 20–31 × 5–10 µm; smooth; widely fusiform; with straight germ slits extending half to two-thirds of the spore's length. **Comments:** Sometimes called "dead man's fingers." Compare with *Xylaria longipes* (p. 395), which often features a distinct stem, has a surface that develops a mosaic pattern of fine cracks, and differs microscopically.

6 THE EVOLUTIONARY PICTURE

By the time the manuscript we're writing right now is sent to the printer, some of the information included in the tables below will have changed—and by the time you are reading this, even more changes may have occurred. The DNA revolution in mycology (see chapter 1) has only just begun, and we have little doubt that in future years the names and taxonomic arrangements presented here may appear just as quaint as names like "*Collybia dryophila*" and "*Boletus scaber*" appear to today's readers. But if theories and assumptions weren't constantly revised on the basis of new data, mycology would be a tradition rather than a science; learning different names and discovering different relationships is inherent in the scientific process.

The tables below include only the genera represented in this book; dozens (even hundreds) of mushroom genera are missing. The information is culled from *Ainsworth & Bisby's Dictionary of the Fungi* (2008 edition; see Kirk et al. 2008), along with data from several publications that have appeared since, and information from Index Fungorum (www.indexfungorum.org) and MycoBank (www.mycobank.org).

Phylum: Ascomycota
- Subphylum: Pezizomycotina
  - Class: Leotiomyces
    - Order: Helotiales
      - Family: Helotiaceae
        - Genera: *Bisporella*
    - Order: Leotiales
      - Family: Leotiaceae
        - Genera: *Leotia*
    - Order: Rhytismatales
      - Family: Cudoniaceae
        - Genera: *Spathulariopsis*
  - Class: Pezizomycetes
    - Order: Pezizales
      - Family: Discinaceae
        - Genera: *Gyromitra*
      - Family: Helvellaceae
        - Genera: *Helvella*
      - Family: Morchellaceae
        - Genera: *Disciotis*, *Morchella*, *Verpa*
      - Family: Pezizaceae
        - Genera: *Pachyella*, *Peziza*
      - Family: Pyrenemataceae

Genera: *Aleuria, Humaria, Otidea, Scutellinia*

Family: Sarcoscyphaceae

Genera: *Microstoma, Sarcoscypha*

Family: Sarcosomataceae

Genera: *Galiella, Urnula*

Class: Sordariomycetes

Genera: *Camarops, Cordyceps, Elaphocordyceps, Hypomyces, Xylaria*

Phylum: Basidiomycota

Subphylum: Agaricomycotina

Class: Dacrymycetes

Order: Dacrymycetales

Family: Dacrymycetaceae

Genera: *Calocera*

Class: Tremellomycetes

Order: Tremellales

Family: Tremellaceae

Genera: *Tremella*

Class: Agaricomycetes

Order: Agaricales

Family: Agaricaceae

Genera: *Agaricus, Calvatia, Chlorophyllum, Coprinus, Crucibulum, Cyathus, Cystodermella, Lepiota, Leucoagaricus, Leucocoprinus, Lycoperdon, Macrolepiota, Morganella, Mycenastrum, Nidularia, Vascellum*

Family: Amanitaceae

Genera: *Amanita, Limacella*

Family: Bolbitiaceae

Genera: *Bolbitius, Conocybe*

Family Clavariaceae

Genera: *Clavaria, Clavulinopsis, Ramariopsis*

Family: Cortinariaceae

Genera: *Cortinarius*

Family: Entolomataceae

Genera: *Clitopilus, Entoloma, Rhodocybe*

Family: Fistulinaceae

Genera: *Fistulina*

Family: Hydnangiaceae

Genera: *Laccaria*

Family: Hygrophoraceae

Genera: *Ampulloclitocybe, Hygrocybe, Hygrophorus*

Family: Inocybaceae

Genera: *Crepidotus, Flammulaster, Inocybe, Simocybe*

Family: Lyophyllaceae

Genera: *Asterophora, Calocybe, Hypsizygus, Lyophyllum*

Family: Marasmiaceae

Genera: *Connopus, Clitocybula, Crinipellis, Gerronema, Gymnopus, Macrocystidia, Tetrapyrgos, Marasmius, Megacollybia, Omphalotus, Rhizomarasmius, Rhodocollybia*

Family: Mycenaceae

Genera: *Mycena, Panellus, Xeromphalina*

Family: Physalacriaceae

Genera: *Armillaria, Flammulina, Rhizomarasmius, Rhodotus, Xerula*

Family: Pleurotaceae

Genera: *Hohenbuehelia, Pleurotus*

Family: Pluteaceae

Genera: *Pluteus, Volvariella, Volvopluteus*

Family: Psathyrellaceae

Genera: *Coprinellus, Coprinopsis, Lacrymaria, Parasola, Psathyrella*

Family: Schizophyllaceae

Genera: *Schizophyllum*

Family: Strophariaceae

Genera: *Agrocybe, Galerina, Hebeloma, Hypholoma, Leratiomyces, Pholiota*

Family: Tapinellaceae

Genera: *Tapinella*

Family: Tricholomataceae

Genera: *Arrhenia, Callistosporium, Clitocybe, Collybia, Infundibulicybe, Leucopaxillus, Leucopholiota, Melanoleuca, Resupinatus, Tricholoma*

Family: Uncertain

Genera: *Gymnopilus, Panaeolus, Phyllotopsis, Rickenella, Tricholomopsis*

Order: Auriculariales

Family: Auriculariaceae

Genera: *Auricularia, Exidia*

Family: Uncertain

Genera: *Ductifera, Pseudohydnum*

Order: Boletales

Family: Boletaceae

Genera: *Austroboletus, Boletellus, Boletus, Chalciporus, Heimioporus, Leccinum, Phylloporus, Pulveroboletus, Retiboletus, Strobilomyces, Tylopilus, Xanthoconium*

Family: Calosomataceae

Genera: *Calostoma*

Family: Gomphidiaceae

Genera: *Chroogomphus*

Family: Gyroporaceae

Genera: *Gyroporus*

Family: Hygrophoropsidaceae

Genera: *Hygrophoropsis*

Family: Paxillaceae

Genera: *Gyrodon, Paragyrodon, Paxillus*

Family: Sclerodermataceae

Genera: *Scleroderma*

Family: Suillaceae

Genera: *Suillus*

Order: Cantharellales

Family: Cantharellaceae

Genera: *Cantharellus, Craterellus*

Family: Clavulinaceae

Genera: *Clavulina*

Family: Hydnaceae

Genera: *Hydnum*

Order: Geastrales

Family: Geastraceae

Genera: *Geastrum*

Order: Gomphales

Family: Clavariadelphaceae

Genera: *Clavariadelphus*

Family: Gomphaceae

Genera: *Gomphus, Ramaria*

Order: Hymenochaetales

Family: Hymenochaetaceae

Genera: *Coltricia, Inonotus, Phellinus, Porodaedalea*

Order: Phallales

Family: Phallaceae

Genera: *Mutinus, Phallus, Pseudocolus*

Order: Polyporales

Family: Fomitopsidaceae

Genera: *Daedalea, Fomitopsis, Ischnoderma, Laetiporus, Phaeolus, Piptoporus*

Family: Ganodermataceae
Genera: *Ganoderma*
Family: Meripilaceae
Genera: *Abortiporus*, *Grifola*, *Meripilus*
Family: Meruliaceae
Genera: *Bjerkandera*, *Gloeoporus*, *Mycorrhaphium*, *Phlebia*, *Podoscypha*, *Steccherinum*
Family: Phanerochaetaceae
Genera: *Climacodon*
Family: Polyporaceae
Genera: *Cerrena*, *Daedaleopsis*, *Fomes*, *Hapalopilus*, *Lenzites*, *Panus*, *Perenniporia*, *Polyporus*, *Poronidulus*, *Pycnoporus*, *Spongipellis*, *Trametes*, *Trichaptum*, *Tyromyces*
Family: Sparassidaceae
Genera: *Sparassis*

Order: Russulales
Family: Albatrellaceae
Genera: *Albatrellus*
Family: Auriscalpiaceae
Genera: *Artomyces*, *Auriscalpium*, *Lentinellus*
Family: Bondarzewiaceae
Genera: *Bondarzewia*
Family: Hericiaceae
Genera: *Hericium*
Family: Russulaceae
Genera: *Lactarius*, *Russula*
Family: Stereaceae
Genera: *Stereum*
Order: Sebacinales
Family: Sebacinaceae
Genera: *Tremellodendron*
Order: Thelephorales
Family: Bankeraceae
Genera: *Hydnellum*, *Phellodon*, *Sarcodon*

BIBLIOGRAPHY AND WORKS CITED

BIBLIOGRAPHY

Arora, D. 1986. *Mushrooms demystified: A comprehensive guide to the fleshy fungi.* Berkeley: Ten Speed Press.

Barron, G. 1999. *Mushrooms of northeast North America.* Edmonton, AB: Lone Pine Publishing.

Binion, D. E., H. H. Burdsall Jr., S. L. Stephenson, O. K. Miller Jr., W. C. Roody, and L. N. Vasilyeva. 2008. *Macrofungi associated with oaks of eastern North America.* Morgantown: West Virginia University Press.

Graham, V. O. 1944. *Mushrooms of the Great Lakes region.* Chicago: Chicago Academy of Sciences.

Horn, B., R. Kay, and D. Abel. 1993. *A guide to Kansas mushrooms.* Lawrence: University Press of Kansas.

Huffman, D. M., L. H. Tiffany, G. Knaphus, and R. A. Healy. 2008. *Mushrooms and other fungi of the mid-continental United States.* Iowa City: University of Iowa Press.

Kauffman, C. H. (1918) 1971. *The gilled mushrooms (Agaricaceae) of Michigan and the Great Lakes region.* Vols. 1 and 2. Reprint, New York: Dover.

Kuo, M. 2007. *100 edible mushrooms.* Ann Arbor: University of Michigan Press.

———. *MushroomExpert.Com.* www.mushroomexpert.com.

Kuo, M., and A. Methven. 2010. *100 cool mushrooms.* Ann Arbor: University of Michigan Press.

Largent, D. L. 1973. *How to identify mushrooms to genus I: Macroscopic features.* Eureka, CA: Mad River Press.

Largent, D. L., D. Johnson, and R. Watling. 1973. *How to identify mushrooms to genus III: Microscopic features.* Eureka, CA: Mad River Press.

Largent, D. L., and H. D. Thiers. 1973. *How to identify mushrooms to genus II: Field identification of genera.* Eureka, CA: Mad River Press.

Lincoff, G. H. 1992. *The Audubon Society field guide to North American mushrooms.* New York: Knopf.

McFarland, J., and G. M. Mueller. 2009. *Edible wild mushrooms of Illinois and surrounding states.* Urbana: University of Illinois Press.

McKnight, K. H., and V. B. McKnight. 1987. *Mushrooms.* Peterson Field Guides. New York: Houghton Mifflin.

McNeil, R. 2006. *Le grand livre des champignons du Québec et de l'est du Canada.* Waterloo: Éditions Michel Quintin.

Money, N. P. 2002. *Mr. Bloomfield's orchard: The mysterious world of mushrooms, molds, and mycologists.* New York: Oxford University Press.

———. 2005. "Why picking wild mushrooms may be bad behaviour." *Mycological Research* 109:131–35.

———. 2011. *Mushroom.* New York: Oxford University Press.

Mushroom Observer. www.mushroomobserver.org.

Peattie, D. C. 1991. *A natural history of trees of eastern and central North America*. New York: Houghton Mifflin.

Phillips, R. 2005. *Mushrooms and other fungi of North America*. Boston: Firefly Books.

———. *Roger's Mushrooms*. www.rogersmushrooms.com.

Preston, R. J. 1989. *North American trees exclusive of Mexico and tropical Florida*. Ames: Iowa State University Press.

Roody, W. C. 2003. *Mushrooms of West Virginia and the central Appalachians*. Lexington: University Press of Kentucky.

Smith, A. H., H. V. Smith, and N. S. Weber. 1979. *How to know the gilled mushrooms*. Dubuque: Wm. C. Brown.

———. 1981. *How to know the non-gilled mushrooms*. Dubuque: Wm. C. Brown.

Stone, M. 2010. *Missouri's wild mushrooms*. Jefferson City: Missouri Department of Conservation.

Volk, T. *Tom Volk's fungi*. www.tomvolkfungi.net.

WORKS CITED

Buyck, B., D. Mitchell, and J. Parrent. 2006. "*Russula parvovirescens* sp. nov., a common but ignored species in the eastern United States." *Mycologia* 98:612–15.

Czederpiltz, D. L. L., T. J. Volk, and H. H. Burdsall Jr. 2001. "Field observations and inoculation experiments to determine the nature of the carpophoroids associated with *Entoloma abortivum* and *Armillaria*." *Mycologia* 93:841–51.

Dahlman, M., E. Danell, and J. W. Spatafora. 2000. "Molecular systematics of *Craterellus*: Cladistic analysis of nuclear LSU rDNA sequence data." *Mycological Research* 104:388–94.

den Bakker, H. C., and M. E. Noordeloos. 2005. "A revision of European species of *Leccinum* Gray and notes on extralimital species." *Persoonia* 18:511–87.

Flynn, T., and O. K. Miller Jr. 1990. "Biosystematics of *Agrocybe molesta* and sibling species allied to *Agrocybe praecox* in North America and Europe." *Mycological Research* 94:1103–10.

Guzmán-Dávalos, L., G. M. Mueller, J. Cifuentes, A. N. Miller, and A. Santerre. 2003. "Traditional infrageneric classification of *Gymnopilus* is not supported by ribosomal DNA sequence data." *Mycologia* 95:1204–14.

Hallen, H., R. Watling, and G. Adams. 2003. "Taxonomy and toxicity of *Conocybe lactea* and related species." *Mycological Research* 107:969–79.

Halling, R. E., M. Nuhn, T. Osmundson, N. Fechner, J. M. Trappe, K. Soytong, D. Arora, D. S. Hibbett, and M. Binder. 2012. "Affinities of the *Boletus chromapes* group to *Royoungia* and the description of two new genera, *Harrya* and *Australopilus*." *Australian Systematic Botany* 25:418–31.

Hesler, L. R., and A. H. Smith. 1979. *North American species of Lactarius*. Ann Arbor: University of Michigan Press.

Hughes, K. W., D. A. Mather, and R. H. Petersen. 2010. "A new genus to accommodate *Gymnopus acervatus* (Agaricales)." *Mycologia* 102:1463–78.

Justo, A., A. M. Minnis, S. Ghignone, N. Menolli Jr., M. Capelari, O. Rodriguez, E. Malysheva, M. Contu, and A. Vizzini. 2011. "Species recognition in *Pluteus* and *Volvopluteus* (Pluteaceae, Agaricales): Morphology, geography and phylogeny." *Mycological Progress* 10:453–79.

Justo, A., A. Vizzini, A. M. Minnis, N. Menolli Jr., M. Capelari, O. Rodriguez, E. Malysheva, M. Contu, S. Ghignone, and D. S. Hibbett. 2011. "Phylogeny of the *Pluteaceae* (*Agaricales, Basidiomycota*): Taxonomy and character evolution." *Fungal Biology* 115:1–20.

Kauffman, C. H. (1918) 1971. *The gilled mushrooms (Agaricaceae) of Michigan and the Great Lakes region*. Vols. 1 and 2. Reprint, New York: Dover.

———. 1924. "Inocybe." *North American Flora* 10:227–60.

Kirk, P. M., P. F. Cannon, D. W. Minter, and J. A. Stalpers, eds. 2008. *Ainsworth and Bisby's dictionary of the fungi*. Wallingford, UK: CAB International.

Kuo, M., and A. Methven 2010. *100 cool mushrooms*. Ann Arbor: University of Michigan Press.

Matheny, P. B., E. A. Austin, J. M. Birkebak, and A. D. Wolfenbarger. 2010. "*Craterellus fallax*, a black trumpet mushroom from eastern North America with a broad host range." *Mycorrhiza* 20:569–75.

McFarland, J., and G. M. Mueller. 2009. *Edible wild mushrooms of Illinois and surrounding states*. Urbana: University of Illinois Press.

Miller, O. K., Jr. 2003. "The Gomphidiaceae revisited: A worldwide perspective." *Mycologia* 95:176–83.

National Science Foundation. 2012. Award Abstract

#1206115. Digitization TCN: Collaborative: The Macrofungi Collection Consortium: Unlocking a biodiversity resource for understanding biotic interactions, nutrient cycling and human affairs. www.nsf.gov/awardsearch/showAward.do?AwardNumber=1206115.

Padamsee, M., P. B. Matheny, B. T. M. Dentinger, and D. J. McLaughlin. 2008. "The mushroom family Psathyrellaceae: Evidence for large-scale polyphyly of the genus *Psathyrella*." *Molecular Phylogenetics and Evolution* 46:415–29.

Petersen, R. H., K. W. Hughes, S. Adamčik, Z. Tkalčec, and A. Mešić. 2012. "Typification of three European species epithets attributable to *Strobilomyces* (Boletales)." *Czech Mycology* 64:141–63.

Redhead, S. A., F. Lutzoni, J.-M. Moncalvo, and R. Vilgalys. 2002. "Phylogeny of agarics: Partial systematics solutions for core omphalinoid genera in the Agaricales (Euagarics)." *Mycotaxon* 83:19–57.

Stubbe, D., J. Nuytinck, and A. Verbeken. 2010. "Critical assessment of the *Lactarius gerardii* species complex (Russulales)." *Fungal Biology* 114:271–83.

Tedersoo, L., K. Hansen, B. A. Perry, and R. Kjoller. 2006. "Molecular and morphological diversity of pezizalean ectomycorrhiza." *New Phytologist* 170:581–96.

Tulloss, R. E., and J. E. Lindgren. 1994. "*Amanita novinupta*—a rubescent, white species from the western United States and southwestern Canada." *Mycotaxon* 51:179–90.

Vellinga, E. C. 2000. "Notes on *Lepiota* and *Leucoagaricus*. Type studies on *Lepiota magnispora*, *Lepiota barsii*, and *Agaricus americanus*." *Mycotaxon* 76:429–38.

———. 2003. "Type studies in Agaricaceae—*Chlorophyllum rachodes* and allies." *Mycotaxon* 85:259–70.

Wolfe, B. E., M. Kuo, and A. Pringle. 2012. "*Amanita thiersii* is a saprotrophic fungus expanding its range in the United States." *Mycologia* 104:22–33.

GLOSSARY AND INDEX

Note: Boldface references indicate the start of full mushroom descriptions; italicized references indicate illustrations; capitals are used to distinguish glossary items.

ZONATE: With concentric zones of color and/or texture; see the cap of *Lenzites betulina* on p. 257.

MICHAEL KUO is an English instructor at Eastern Illinois University and the principal developer of MushroomExpert.com. He is the author of *100 Edible Mushrooms* and *Morels*.

ANDREW S. METHVEN is a professor of mycology at Eastern Illinois University. He is the author of *Agaricales of California*, Volume 10: Lactarius and *The Genus* Clavariadelphus *in North America*.

The authors previously collaborated on *100 Cool Mushrooms*.

The University of Illinois Press
is a founding member of the
Association of American University Presses.

Designed by Dustin Hubbart
Composed in Adobe Garamond Pro
with Frontage display
by Jim Proefrock
at the University of Illinois Press
Manufactured by Versa Press, Inc.

University of Illinois Press
1325 South Oak Street
Champaign, IL 61820-6903
www.press.uillinois.edu